1945

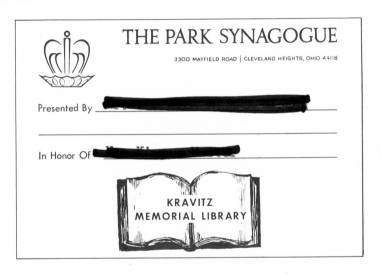

Beauty in Holiness

STUDIES IN JEWISH CUSTOMS
AND CEREMONIAL ART

Beauty in Holiness

STUDIES IN JEWISH CUSTOMS
AND CEREMONIAL ART

Edited by

JOSEPH GUTMANN

KTAV PUBLISHING HOUSE INC.

SBN 87068-012-9

Manufactured in the United States of America
Library of Congress Catalog Card Number 70-106999

TABLE OF CONTENTS

SABBATH

HANUKKAH

WEDDING

CUSTOMS AND CEREMONIES

INTRODUCTION

It is not much of an exaggeration to say that the scientific study of Jewish ceremonial art and Jewish customs and ceremonies does not antedate the closing years of the nineteenth century. Only then were Jewish Museums established in such cities as Vienna, Hamburg, and Frankfurt, their founding a response to the ethnographic museums set up during the second half of the 1800's to collect and study the art of primitive and exotic peoples. Rabbi Max Grunwald helped establish the Hamburg Jewish Museum and, from 1898, edited the *Mitteilungen der Gesellschaft für jüdische Volkskunde,* a magazine devoted to the scientific exploration of Jewish ceremonies and folkways. Heinrich Frauberger helped establish the Frankfurt Jewish Museum and, from 1900, edited the *Mittheilungen der Gesellschaft zur Erforschung jüdischer Kunstdenkmäler,* a publication devoted primarily to the scientific study of Jewish art. Ironically enough it was a Gentile who first awakened the interest of the Jews in their own artistic heritage. The pioneer in the study of Jewish ceremonial art was the editor of the Frankfurt *Mitteilungen,* the German Catholic, Heinrich Frauberger, Director of the Industrial Arts and Crafts Museum in Düsseldorf, Germany. Frauberger's interest in Jewish ceremonial art and the establishment of the Frankfurt society came about in a very curious way. In 1895, an architect sought his advice about a design for a grilled enclosure for a Jewish grave, but Frauberger found he could be of little help in suggesting appropriate Jewish symbols because there were neither studies nor resource people available on the subject. This incident led Frauberger to begin collecting Jewish ceremonial objects and, in 1897, to help establish the first society in Frankfurt am Main dedicated to preserving, studying and researching these art objects.

The studies initiated by Frauberger and his circle were continued in this country by such diligent and devoted students as the late Franz Landsberger and Guido Schoenberger, and in Israel by the late Mordechai Narkiss. The studies on Jewish ceremonies, first undertaken by Max Grunwald and his colleagues, were splendidly continued by such enterprising scholars as the late Jacob Z. Lauterbach, the late Samuel Krauss, and Solomon B. Freehof.

The two fields—Jewish ceremonial art and Jewish customs—have attracted no surfeit of scholars, since the halakhically minded have frequently regarded *minhagim,* or Jewish customs, as diversions fit at best for women, but certainly not worthy of serious study. Similarly, aesthetics and art have not been valued highly and have been categorized by trained halakhists (legalists) as something outside the realm of Judaism. Unfortunately these prejudices still linger on even in so-called enlightened Jewish circles. Nonetheless, as the present volume attests, some progress has been made, and it has been possible to collect these twenty-one basic essays which answer in authoritative fashion a good many of the questions scholars and laymen ask about Jewish customs and ceremonial art.

What do the ensuing studies reveal?

1. They show Judaism as a dynamic religion whose ceremonies and art forms reveal constant innovation and change as Judaism encountered new civilizations and cultures in the course of its long history.

2. They refract not the unity in art forms, customs and ceremonies so frequently stressed in popular textbooks, but rather a rich diversity of expression varying from country to country and from century to century.

3. They demonstrate that sensitive religious leaders in different countries and periods often introduced new cus-

toms and art forms, or tried to modify or to adapt old ceremonies and art forms to fit new conditions. Then, too, there were objectionable customs which, despite efforts to abolish them, continued to flourish in Judaism.

The involvement of Jews in the Roman, Christian and Islamic civilizations, for instance, demanded constant and major changes in ceremonies and their art forms. Thus the *huppah* used by Jews in the Roman period was not the same in form or meaning as the *huppah* familiar to Jews in Catholic medieval Europe, although the identical name, *huppah,* is maintained; the same might be said for the *havdalah* ceremony whose art forms and meanings in pagan Rome varied considerably from what later developed in the context of Christian Europe. The Jewish experience in medieval Christian Europe engendered within Judaism the mourner's Kaddish, Yahrzeit and Bar Mitzvah. Such beloved and hallowed practices were unknown in earlier generations.

This constant encounter with new cultures and civilizations brought about a rich diversity in Judaism—a diversity that sometimes proved divisive. Jacob ben Asher's *Turim,* written in fourteenth-century Spain, for example, were unacceptable to the Sefardim because the Ashkenazi author included, and often favored, Ashkenazic practice. Joseph Caro's *Shulhan Arukh,* in turn, was not universally acceptable because its Sefardi compiler neglected Ashkenazic *minhagim.* Moses Isserles, an Ashkenazi from Poland, was criticized because he overlooked German *minhag* in his commentary to the *Shulhan Arukh.* The great diversity existing in Judaism at all times is nowhere better highlighted than by the instructive retort of Isaac de Pinto, a Sefardi who observed in his *Critical Reflections* of 1762:

Mr. Voltaire cannot be ignorant of the scrupulous exactness of the Portuguese and Spanish Jews not to intermix in marriage alliance, or any other way with the Jews of other nations. He has been in Holland and knows that they have separate synagogues, and that, although they profess the same religion and the same articles of faith, yet their ceremonies have often no resemblance. The manners of the Portuguese Jews are also very different from those of the rest; the former have no beards nor any thing peculiar in their dress. The rich among them vie with the other nations of Europe in refinement, elegance and show, and differ from them in worship only. Their variance with their other brethren is at such a height, that if a Portuguese Jew in England or Holland married a German Jewess, he would of course lose all his prerogatives, be no longer reckoned a member of their synagogue, forfeit all civil and ecclesiastical preferments, be absolutely divorced from the body of the nation, and not even be buried with his Portuguese brethren. (H. J. Zimmels, *Ashkenazim and Sephardim,* London, 1958, pp. 61–62).

Religious leaders, ever sensitive and responsive to new needs, probably introduced a practice like the *havdalah* ceremony in the Talmudic period; they sanctioned such popular medieval superstitions as the breaking of the glass at weddings by linking it to the destruction of the Temple in Jerusalem, and they changed and adapted such customs as the *huppah* in the medieval period. In some cases—the placing of the Decalogue in the synagogue is a prime example—rabbinic censure did not prevail, and popular fancy managed to win out.

It is hoped that the studies brought together in this volume, will encourage further scientific research in a fascinating new field in order to unravel how the dynamic and unique involvement of Judaism produced constant novelty and change in its customs, ceremonies and art forms. These essays should lead to greater understanding, to the relinquishing of the common clichés and pious guesses, and their replacement with accurate knowledge.

I

All too often discussions of Jewish ceremonial art or of Jewish art in general dismiss any active Jewish interest or participation in the arts by citing the so-called Second Commandment in Exodus 20:4–5: "You shall not make yourself a sculptured image, or any likeness of what is in the heavens above or on the earth below, or in the waters under the earth. You shall not bow down to them or serve them." Rarely is it pointed out that the very same book of the Bible depicts Bezalel as filled with "the spirit of God, with wisdom, intelligence and knowledge in every craft: to devise artistic designs, to work in gold, silver and copper, to cut stones for setting and to carve wood—to work in every craft" (Exodus 31:3–5).

Nowhere in surviving ancient annals is an artist-craftsman so splendidly endowed with diverse talents as Bezalel, or presented as so intimately involved with the sacred duty of fashioning and decorating a sanctuary for his God. Jewish tradition embroidered the high esteem in which the Bible cast this artist-craftsman by claiming that although Moses excelled most men in every endeavor, he was inferior to Bezalel in the realm of art. "Twice he [Moses] ascended Mount Sinai," according to the Midrash, "to receive instructions from God, and twice he forgot the instructions on his descent. The third time, God took a menorah of fire and showed him every detail of it. And yet Moses found it hard to form a clear conception of the menorah. Finally God told him 'Go to Bezalel, he will make it.' When Bezalel had no difficulty in executing it, Moses cried out in amazement: 'To me it was shown many times by the Holy One, blessed be He, yet I found it hard to grasp, but you without seeing it, could fashion it with your intelligence. Surely you must have been standing in the shadow of God (*b'zel-el*), while the Holy One was showing me its construction (*Numbers Rabbah* 15.9). My essay on the "Second Commandment and the Image in Judaism" tries to point out that, contrary to accepted opin-

ion, the attitude of Jews toward the Second Commandment
and art throughout their long history reflects neither dog-
matic pious adherence to law nor inherent forces of attrac-
tion and revulsion, but rather varying and changing Jewish
needs that are largely determined by the specific social
structure of which Jews were a part at any given moment
of their history. The artistic needs of a tribal leader, like
Abraham, living in a semi-nomadic society, completely
differed from those of a monarch like Solomon living in a
sedentary, agricultural society. It is only to be expected,
therefore, that their attitudes towards art and their use
of art should differ, as is amply underscored in the Bible.
Similarly, as will be shown, the attitudes of Jews towards
art and their involvement with and production of art in a
Christian environment differ substantially from those of
Jews in an Islamic milieu. The differences cannot be explained by invoking traditional Jewish strictures on art,
but rather by examining the differing needs for art dictated
by the dominant prevailing cultures in which Jews resided.
    Mark Wischnitzer in his "Notes to a History of the Jew-
ish Guilds"—which should be read along with his fine *A
History of Jewish Crafts and Guilds* (New York, 1965)—
clearly reveals the role that Jews played as artisans in a
variety of different civilizations, cultures and countries from
the biblical period to the end of the eighteenth century.
Particularly fascinating are the accounts dealing with Jewish craftsmen in medieval Sicily and Spain. The role of the
Jewish craftsmen in fifteenth-century Sicily was extremely
vital, so much so that Christian officials feared that, owing
to the lack of Christian craftsmen, the expulsion of the Jews
at the end of the fifteenth century would raise prices. The
master-carpenter Joseph Caschisi so distinguished himself
in the construction of the royal palace that he was appointed warden of the Jewish carpenter's guild in Palermo.
Jewish craftsmen in medieval Spain were so active and numerous that many streets in the Jewish quarters of leading
cities were named after the type of craftsmen who resided
there. So widespread was the role of Jewish craftsmanship

that the bull of Pope Benedict XIII in 1415, for example, found it necessary to decree that Jews in Spain were not allowed to "fashion or repair a cross, chalice, or sacred vessel."

Whereas the interests of the Church and the Christian guild system in medieval Western Europe generally forced Jews to become moneylenders and petty traders, the situation was quite different in Eastern Europe. Here the struggle of king and nobles and the absence of a native middle class, especially in Poland, led to the encouragement and promotion of Jewish craftsmanship and the formation of Jewish guilds. Thus, while Jewish ceremonial objects in many Western European countries had to be commissioned from leading Christian craftsmen, they were often fashioned by the Jews themselves in Eastern Europe. The problems that a Jewish journeyman in Eastern Europe had to face in the Jewish and non-Jewish guilds, his arduous training and difficult working conditions, are beautifully captured in the article on "Jewish Artisans and Guilds in Former Poland" by a martyred young Polish Jewish historian. It is part of a larger work plucked from the fires of the Holocaust.

No monopolistic guilds, hereditary aristocracy or privileged church became rooted in the United States to abrogate or deny the Jew the possibility of exercising his talents as a craftsman. Consequently, it is not surprising to find that one of the most noted silversmiths of early America was a Jew, Myer Myers (1723–1795). His reputation and distinction were such that in 1786 he was elected Chairman of the New York Gold- and Silversmith Society. His large oeuvre, discussed by Jeannette W. Rosenbaum in *Myer Myers, Goldsmith* (Philadelphia, 1954), includes his elegant *rimmonim* made for the leading Sefardic congregations in Newport, New York and Philadelphia. Guido Schoenberger in "The Ritual Silver made by Myer Myers," ably analyzes the influence English *rimmonim* exerted on Myers' delicate and original creations.

Alfred Werner in "Modern Ritual Art" briefly discusses

a new and fascinating development in Jewish ceremonial art. Leading American artists such as Ibram Lassaw, Herbert Ferber, Seymour Lipton, and Ludwig Wolpert are now being engaged to fashion objects which often employ traditional Jewish symbols, but endeavor to express them in exciting and daring new forms.

II

Hiddur Mitzvah is a rabbinic concept which demands that all ceremonial objects used for the performance of religious duties in the home or synagogue be aesthetically pleasing.

As the Torah or pentateuchal scroll is the center of Jewish worship, much attention has been lavished on its adornment. "Origin of European Torah Decorations," "A German Torah Ornamentation," by Franz Landsberger, and my "Torah Ornaments, Priestly Vestments and the King James Bible" discuss the origin and development of different types of Torah adornments. These articles demonstrate that the Torah scroll itself is an adaptation, for Jewish purposes, of the ancient Hellenistic book form. Like the Hellenistic scroll, the Torah scroll was furnished with rods or rollers and was often placed in a protective case (*tik*), or covered with expensive scroll coverings or wrappings, called *mappot,* or *mitpahot* in the Talmudic period. No objects have survived from this early period, while literary and artistic evidence allows for no definite conclusions. Maimonides and certain Cairo Genizah fragments do speak of *rimmonim* for the Torah, and it is likely that in the Islamic environment, the Torah headpieces originally had the shape of pomegranates (*rimmonim*), although the earliest surviving *rimmonim* from fifteenth-century Sicily already reveal the now customary tower-shape form for the *rimmonim*. In Christian countries in the Middle Ages the headpieces were often called apples (*tapuhim*), probably because they were nonremovable spherical knobs placed at the ends of the Torah rods or staves. As Jewish tradition likened the Torah to a bride and princess, so the scroll was regally adorned. Among the regal adornments which developed first in Islamic communities along with the *rimmonim* was the Torah crown (first called *atarah* and later *keter torah*) placed over the Torah staves. The Torah shield arose in fifteenth-century Europe out of purely practical needs. It became customary in Ashkenazic synagogues, which had many Torah scrolls, to place on the scroll cover a plain metal plate (called *pah*, and later an ornamental shield called *tas*) to indicate the festive occasion for which the scroll was to be used. Pointers (*yadim*) to prevent the reader from touching the sacred text of the Torah while reading, were not known prior to the sixteenth century, and also probably arose out of practical needs. It is rather amusing and even ironic that the current designation of the Torah shield as *hoshen* or "breastplate" and its association with the *hoshen* worn by the priest Aaron (Exodus 28:4) do not stem from rabbinic tradition which refers to the Torah shield as *tas*. The erroneous attribution of a priestly character to the *tas* is due solely to a mistranslation of *hoshen* as "breastplate" in the King James Bible; the mistranslation was subsequently accepted in Jewish circles.

Many of the Torah ornaments discussed by Landsberger were fashioned by outstanding Christian silversmiths, such as Georg Zeiller and Jeremias Zobel. The tower-shape form of the Torah headpieces, as is pointed out, was often inspired by the spires and turrets of local churches; crowns were modeled after crowns for the Madonna and for royalty, while the Torah shield was patterned after plaques with chains fashioned for special occasions of the Christian crafts-and marksmen guilds.

The Torah when not in use is housed in a decorated ark usually placed on the eastern wall of the synagogue. A textile adornment or curtain which covers the front of the ark doors is now found in most Ashkenazic congregations. In Sefardic congregations the custom was to place the curtain behind the ark doors. Franz Landsberger's "Old-Time Torah-Curtains" traces the development of this custom. He points out that in the early synagogue a curtain did not hang before the ark, but most likely was placed in front of the Torah niche or before the apse in which the Torah ark stood, as can still be seen in depictions of surviving early synagogue mosaic floors. The evidence from antiquity and the Middle Ages, however, is very scant on this subject. Only from the fifteenth century do we have both artistic evidence, as in an illustration of a 1459 German *mahzor* showing a Torah curtain before the ark, and literary evidence of the same period that it was common practice to hang curtains in front of the ark in Ashkenazic synagogues. Maharil (*Sefer Maharil, Hilkhot Shavuot*) mentions that "they spread the curtain for the coming Holiday before the ark (*aron ha-kodesh*) at the outgoing of the Sabbath," and Israel Isserlein (*Terumat ha-Deshen* No. 68) also cites the practice of some communities of spreading a white curtain in front of the Torah ark prior to the *Neilah* service on Yom Kippur. The oldest surviving Torah ark curtain, dated 1592, was executed in Prague and is displayed in Prague's State Jewish Museum (See Otto Muneles, ed., *Prague Ghetto in the Renaissance Period,* Prague, 1965, figs. 56–57, p. 108). The curtain, cited by Landsberger on p. 368 and illustrated by fig. 4 as coming from fifteenth-century Italy, however, probably stems from the late seventeenth century. (Cf. *Treasures of a London Temple,* London, 1951, p. 53, n. 66.)

Some magnificent embroidered Torah ark curtains coming from eighteenth-century Bavaria are analyzed by Landsberger. They are the handiwork of two gifted professional Jewish embroiderers, Elkanah Naumburg of Fürth and Jakob Koppel Gans of Hochstadt.

III

To claim, with Asher Ginzberg (Ahad ha-Am), that "far more than Israel has kept the Sabbath, it is the Sabbath that has kept Israel," is, perhaps, not an overstatement. One of the most important duties of the Jewish woman has been to welcome the "Queen Sabbath" by the kindling of lights. In antiquity, as is pointed out in Landsberger's "The Origin of the Ritual Implements for the Sabbath," these lights were kindled in clay oil lamps. In the Middle Ages, two distinct lamps developed—the hanging oil-burning Sabbath lamp, known as *Judenstern*, and the standing candelabrum. The hanging lamp was usually made of brass (although wealthy families had elaborate ones of silver) with a heavy shaft and hooks; the oil lamps had burners and channels leading to a drip bowl. As these lamps could be lowered by means of a saw-tooth attachment, they gave rise to the popular saying "Lamp' herunter, Sorg' hinauf—lamp down worry up." In Eastern Europe, especially Poland, a brass candelabrum, with three to five sockets for wax candles, often topped by a Polish eagle and adorned with lions and stags, was employed. Although we have become accustomed to two lights on Sabbath eve, this is not required by Jewish law. Seven lights, for instance, representing the seven days of the week, or ten for the Ten Commandments, have also been used.

No other Jewish ceremonial object so fired the artist's imagination or spawned such a variety of forms as did the spice box used during the *havdalah* ceremony at the outgoing of the Sabbath. It is mentioned for the first time by Israel Isserlein of the fifteenth century, who writes that his *hadas* [the early name for the spice box] was made of silver. (Cf. the fine Hebrew study by Mordechai Narkiss, "The Origin of the Spice Box known as the 'Hadass,' " *Eretz-Israel*, VI [1960], 189–98). From the sixteenth century on, Christian goldsmiths produced the familiar tower-shape with turrets for spice boxes. Some of the early spice boxes are still extant. These tower-shaped receptacles are in form not unlike Christian monstrance and reliquary containers which may have served as their models. In Eastern Europe, spice towers with intricate filigree work were popular, as well as containers in the shape of fruits and flowers. Sometimes, as Landsberger shows, fascinating spice boxes were created which ingeniously combined the spice box with a candleholder, or sometimes the spice container or a socket for the braided *havdalah* candle were attached to the lid of a *kiddush* cup.

"The Origin and Development of two Sabbath Ceremonies" by Lauterbach, and Finesinger's "The Custom of Looking at the Fingernails at the Outgoing of the Sabbath" shed much light on the origin and development of the *havdalah* ceremony in which the spice box is used. Lauterbach tries to unravel, layer by layer, the complex development of the *havdalah* ceremony and points out that this ceremony was unknown in the Bible and was only introduced by the rabbis. It grew out of the common Roman meal customs which usually began and ended with a wine libation to the gods. Spices (called *mugmar* in the Talmud) heated on a bed of hot coals (*gimur*) were often brought in at the conclusion of the Roman meal to aid in the digestive process and to purify the air. It must be realized that *havdalah* was originally recited only over a cup of wine at the end of the Sabbath meal. In the early Talmudic period spices were not an obligatory part of the *havdalah* ceremony. By the Geonic period, the *havdalah* ceremony had taken more concrete shape. It was now completely separate from the meal and instead of spices over hot coals, the myrtle twig (*hadas*) had come into general use. It also became customary at this period to look at the fingernails during the *havdalah* ceremony. This practice, which has become traditional, was originally a means of divination, for by looking at the reflection of light in the shiny surface of the nail while reciting "who createst the lights of fire" one hoped to discover favorable omens for the ensuing week. The myrtle (*hadas*), according to mystic belief, became in Christian Europe the vehicle by means of which the additional soul, with which every Israelite is endowed on the Sabbath, enters and leaves his nostrils. Some rabbis, such as Ephraim of twelfth-century Regensburg, objected to the use of the myrtle, and kept different kinds of spices (*besamin*) in a glass container during the *havdalah* ceremony. This practice had become standard, as we indicated, in Ashkenazic communities by the fifteenth century. Instead of the glass container, a spice box was now in use, but it was still called *hadas*—an allusion to the earlier practice of the myrtle twig.

IV

Hanukkah, because of its competition with Christmas in the present-day West, has assumed an importance in Jewish life far beyond what the rabbis of the Talmudic period would have envisaged. They wanted, if anything, to play down and perhaps even erase the memory of the glorious Hasmonean victory over the Syrians and the rededication of the Temple in Jerusalem in 165 B.C.E., as recorded in the apocryphal Book of Maccabees, and so they devoted exactly one paragraph to the Hanukkah holiday (*Babylonian Talmud, Shabbat* 21b). Instead of recounting the military triumph and its jingoistic celebration, they tried to transform the holiday by explaining it in terms of a divine miracle: "On the 25th day of Kislev the days of Hanukkah, which are eight, [on which] a lamentation for the dead and fasting are forbidden. For when the Greeks entered the Temple, they defiled all the oils therein, and when the Hasmonean dynasty prevailed against and defeated them, they made search and found only one cruse of oil which lay with the seal of the High Priest [hence untouched and undefiled], but which contained sufficient oil for one day's lighting only; yet a miracle was wrought therein and they lit [the lamp] therewith for eight days. The following year these [days] were appointed a Festival." In commemoration of this miracle, the Hanukkah lights are kindled for eight days—one on the first night and one more on each subsequent night than on the preceding night. A ninth servant light (*shammash*), often placed above the other lights, is used to kindle them.

In Landsberger's "Old Hanukkah Lamps" we learn that the earliest Hanukkah lamps in the Talmudic period were probably clay oil lamps with wicks. In the later Middle Ages, a metal bench-type oil lamp with a triangular back developed. This lamp was at first hung on the left doorpost of the house opposite to the *mezuzah*. In different countries, many variations of this basic type occur, both in decoration, metal and form employed. Eastern Europe preferred silver filigree lamps with animal and bird forms. In Italy there emerged a bronze bench-type lamp which was frequently topped with the figure of Judith brandishing a sword and holding the head of Holofernes, for this heroic maiden had become linked with Hanukkah in medieval Jewish folklore. Along with the development of the bench-type Hanukkah lamp, there arose in the Middle Ages the custom of placing a large standing Hanukkah lamp in the synagogue. This lamp was intended for wayfarers so that when all were assembled "the miracle might be spread and proclaimed." Only from the sixteenth century on, did the nine-branched lamps begin to resemble in shape the seven-branched Temple menorah. Some splendid examples have survived and are illustrated in the Landsberger article (cf. also Mordechai Narkiss' Hebrew monograph, *The Hanukkah Lamp,* Jerusalem, 1939. The Hanukkah lamp from Italy, which Landsberger dates fifteenth century, p. 365, fig. 13 was probably made much later).

V

No Jewish ceremony echoes more with what the prophet Jeremiah called "the voice of mirth and the voice of gladness" than the Jewish wedding. From ancient times until today no expense has been spared for its artistic embellishment, as is made amply clear in my "Wedding Customs and Ceremonies in Art." Already in the Talmud, we read of the bridal pavilion of "crimson silk embroidered with gold" set up in the groom's house. In this bridal pavilion, the original *huppah,* the marriage would be privately consummated. The use of a bridal pavilion or chamber among Jews was of course paralleled by Roman marriage customs. The *huppah* used by Jews in the Talmudic period is entirely different from the *huppah* used by Jews in medieval Christian Europe. Under Christian influence, not only were the *erusin* (betrothal) and *nissuin* (nuptial) ceremonies combined—in Talmudic times they had been two separate ceremonies held a year apart—but the *huppah* itself was now reduced to a *tallit* (prayer shawl) or *sudar* (cloth) spread over the bridal couple. The use of the *tallit* or *sudar* was symbolic of the husband spreading his loving protection over his wife in the newly established household. The *huppah*, originally a bridal chamber and then a symbolic protective covering, underwent yet another change. In the sixteenth century, when the wedding was shifted to the courtyard of the synagogue, the *huppah* became the now customary portable canopy, held aloft by four boys. The cloth of the new *huppah* often had Hebrew inscriptions, and its color was frequently blue with depictions of sun, moon and stars—a symbolic omen, since it was hoped that the children of the bridal couple would be as numerous as the stars in heaven. One name, *huppah*, with three distinct forms and meanings clearly spells out Judaism's unique and fascinating involvement with different cultures, which constantly engendered and demanded dynamic new interpretations and changes within Judaism.

Equally as interesting as the origin and development of the *huppah* is the origin and use of the glass at weddings. This custom arose, as is indicated in Lauterbach's "The Ceremony of Breaking a Glass at Weddings," in medieval Europe and is not mentioned in literary sources prior to the twelfth century. (Lauterbach's attempt to link this custom with Talmudic sources is not convincing. The story in *Berakhot* 30b-31a, where a glass is broken in anger by the rabbis attending the overly hilarious festivities, does not refer to the cup of benediction to be shattered by the bridegroom, nor is the act of throwing an intricate part of the wedding ceremony itself, as medieval custom prescribed.) In the Middle Ages, it became standard Ashkenazic practice, especially in Germany, to throw one of the glasses used for the benedictions, often still filled with wine, against a so-called "*huppah* stone" frequently affixed to the north wall of the synagogue building. The stone sometimes had a carved octagonal or hexagonal star on it and the initial Hebrew letters of Jeremiah 7:34—"the voice of mirth and the voice of gladness, the voice of the bridegroom and the voice of the bride." The glass was thrown at the north side of the synagogue wall, since it was a popular belief that demons resided in that region. The wine within the glass was intended as a bribe for the demons. The shattering glass would not only hurt them but frighten them away so that they could do the bridal couple no harm. In the fifteenth century, the rabbis tried to sanction this superstitious custom by claiming that the breaking of the glass was a symbolic reminder of the destruction of the Temple in Jerusalem. Among the Sefardim of Holland, on the other hand, the glass was not shattered against a *"huppah* stone" as was Ashkenazic custom, but was broken instead upon a decorated silver platter placed on the floor. For the Sefardim the breaking of the glass symbolically denoted the fragility of life and the fact that amidst joy there can be sorrow.

The *ketubah* described in Landsberger's "Illuminated Marriage Contracts" (see also David Davidovitch, *The Ketuba, Jewish Marriage Contracts through the Ages* [Tel Aviv, 1968]), used to be one of the most distinctive art objects associated with the Jewish wedding. The *ketubah* itself was instituted by the rabbis of the Talmudic period as a legal document which stipulated the bridegroom's personal and financial obligations to his bride after marriage or in case of death or divorce. Gradually, the *ketubah,* with its rich ornamentation, became a work of art—so much so that in some eighteenth-century Italian Jewish communities the communal authorities thought it necessary to limit the sum to be expended on the preparation of the marriage contract. Prior to the seventeenth century, we have only isolated examples of ornamented *ketubot.* Public reading of the *ketubah* during the wedding ceremony in the sixteenth century no doubt invited lavish ornamentation, especially in Italy, where some of the finest examples have survived.

Every Italian Jewish community had its distinct variants: in Rome, for instance, it was customary to use pagan personifications in the margins and to artistically trim the bottom edge of the *ketubah*; in other communities, it was common to decorate the top of the *ketubah* with a biblical scene alluding to the groom's or the bride's name. Many wealthy Italian Jewish families insisted on having their distinct family badges prominently displayed on the *ketubah*. Special verses, such as "He who finds a wife finds good" (Proverbs 18:22), or "Your wife shall be like a fruitful vine within your house" (Psalms 128:3), were placed within the decorative architectural portals drawn on the *ketubah*. In a few cases we even have the names of Jewish artists, such as Yehuda Frances and Shalom Italia, who were commissioned to decorate the *ketubah*, just as in our day the late Ben Shahn was commissioned to do a modern *ketubah*.

VI

"How Traditional are our Traditions?" is a question that has, of course, already been posed by many of the preceding articles. Jews who today would not think of setting foot in a synagogue which fails to display the *ner tamid,* or the Tablets of the Ten Commandments may be astonished to learn that these common synagogal features are actually of very recent origin. No eternal light burned in the early or medieval synagogue; it was probably not introduced before the seventeenth century and only in the Italian synagogue. Extant eternal lights from eighteenth-century European synagogues betray their origin, since they closely resemble those hung in neighboring churches. Eternal lights, to be sure, burned in the medieval church where they symbolized the corporeal presence of Christ.

The placing of the Decalogue on walls, a standard practice in some sixteenth-century churches, was again unknown in the medieval synagogue. The rabbis had removed the Decalogue from the daily liturgy in the Talmudic period because of the sectarians (*Berakhot* 12a), and later rabbis strictly forbade the use of the Decalogue in the liturgy and as decoration. Despite the rabbis, this Christian practice has become standard in most synagogues.

The hat on - hat off controversy is still a very heated issue, and Jews accustomed to worshipping with bare heads are often castigated as nonbelievers and followers of gentile practices. Not a few contemporary synagogues have split over the issue of whether a head covering is necessary or not. It may come as a surprise to some readers to discover that there is no law in the Bible or Talmud prescribing the covering of the head for men performing a religious ceremony or participating in a religious service. "The Jewish Rite of Covering the Head" by Samuel Krauss clearly documents the fact that the wearing of the hat is simply a custom. Although it was generally accepted by Jews living in medieval Muslim countries—since Muslims also pray with their heads covered—it was not universally accepted by orthodox medieval Jewish communities living in Christian countries. In thirteenth-century France, for instance, our sources reveal, traditional Jews still prayed bareheaded.

"The Origin of the Decorated Mezuzah" like the origin of the head covering is a greatly misunderstood subject. It is not clear from available evidence whether the verses of Deuteronomy were, in ancient times, written directly on the doorposts (*mezuzah* means doorpost), or whether a roll was placed in a special cavity in the doorpost. Josephus in his *Antiquities* (Book IV, Chapter VIII.13) writes that the Jews "are also to inscribe the principal blessings they have received from God upon their doors." The custom of enclosing the parchment scroll within a metal or wooden container and affixing it to the right-hand doorpost of every Jewish home dates from the Middle Ages. The *mezuzah* was to serve as a reminder of God and his commandments as well as a safeguard against evil spirits. The oldest illustration of a *mezuzah* is found in the late fifteenth-century Rothschild Manuscript No. 24 (illustrated on p. 201, fig. 170, *From the Beginning, Archaeology and Art in the Israel Museum,* Jerusalem, 1968). The practice of placing the parchment scroll in such a manner that the reverse side reveals the word *Shaddai* (Almighty), visible through an opening in the outside container, is already attested to in such sixteenth-century sources as Rabbi Joseph Yuspa Hahn of Frankfurt am Main (*Sefer Yosif Ometz*, No. 480). Rabbi Hahn mentions placing a miniature door on the *mezuzah*, as seen in later surviving examples illustrated in Landsberger's article, to enable anyone entering or leaving the house to lift the door leaves and kiss the word *Shaddai* with his fingers. The door covering, of course, was also intended to shield the Name of God from any profanation through unnecessary exposure. In the illustration of the aforementioned *mezuzah* from fifteenth-century Italy, the *mezuzah* holds a vertical position as recommended in the *Shulhan Arukh*. Some rabbis preferred a horizontal position, and current prevailing practice compromises on a sloping position (Isserles to *Shulhan Arukh* 289.6).

How many Jews would associate such hallowed Jewish customs as the mourner's Kaddish, *Yahrzeit* and the Bar Mitzvah with Catholicism? Yet, truth being so often stranger than fiction, as Freehof's "Ceremonial Creativity among the Ashkenazim" splendidly reveals, these practices arose in medieval Christian Europe and were not known in earlier times. The text of the Kaddish is indeed found in the Talmud, but it has no association whatsoever with the dead and appears solely as a doxology—a prayer praising and exalting God. Only in the thirteenth century, do we read in rabbinic sources from Ashkenazic Europe that the orphan should recite the Kaddish for the benefit of his father's soul. Undoubtedly it was under the impact of the Requiem Mass that the now accepted practice of the orphan's Kaddish came into being. The very word *Yahrzeit* (the time of the year) is German, not Hebrew, and appears in rabbinic sources, as Solomon Freehof points out, only in the fifteenth century.

Bar Mitzvah, too, is unknown in the Bible or Talmud and like the mourner's Kaddish, makes its appearance in Christian Europe in the thirteenth century. Among the

Sefardic Jews of Spain, as Freehof shows, mourner's Kaddish and Bar Mitzvah were not practiced. In fact, the whole notion of the living helping the dead through the Kaddish prayer was a repugnant idea to the philosophically minded Sefardim. Abraham ben Hiyya of medieval Barcelona wrote: "Anyone who believes that after his death he can be benefited by the actions of his sons and their prayers for him, is harboring false ideas [i.e., self-delusion]; for we do not find in the Torah any citation from which we can derive that any action of the living in this world can benefit the dead." The Sefardim had their own unique customs and ceremonies, as we can glean from Freehof's "Home Rituals and the Spanish Synagogue," which were distinctive, and often at variance with those practiced by the Ashkenazim.

VII

The Jewish participation in the arts, the ceremonial art and the customs associated with them, which are discussed in detail in the ensuing articles, testify to the rich and vibrant diversity of Judaism. Not only did the forms and meanings of the objects and their ceremonies change from country to country and century to century, but the customs and the objects themselves differ widely. Rather than diminishing Judaism, these customs and their expression in art reveal the dynamic flexibility and adaptability of Judaism, which constantly introduced new ceremonies and objects to meet specific needs growing out of the dominant cultural environment. Yet for all their diversity, the customs and their art objects testify to an essential unity—the striving of the Jews at all times to fulfill their obligation to God in the "beauty of holiness."

JOSEPH GUTMANN
Professor of Art History
Wayne State University
Detroit, Michigan

ART-ARTISANS

THE "SECOND COMMANDMENT" AND THE IMAGE IN JUDAISM

JOSEPH GUTMANN

Hebrew Union College - Jewish Institute of Religion, Cincinnati

THE term "art" — pictorial or visual — when applied to Judaism, tends to evoke an array of negations. Some critics, claiming that a literal interpretation of the Second Commandment was always the rule in Jewish life, have virtually discounted the possibility of visual art among the Jews. The Second Commandment, they have insisted, was designed to accentuate the spirituality of God in contrast, for example, to the Greek worship of beautiful form. The Jew, it has been argued, was concerned with the "beauty of holiness"; the Greek, with the "holiness of beauty." Other writers have attributed the Jew's supposed iconoclasm, his rejection of visual art, to an inherent conservatism calculated to preserve Jewish identity in a variety of places and circumstances. Still others have explained the anti-iconic Second Commandment, and the abstinence from painting assumed to have been enjoined 'by that Commandment, on the grounds — extraordinary grounds, to be sure — of an allegedly defective sense of color on the part of the Jews. The Jew, it has been said, is more an "aural" than a "visual" being; his feelings relate more to time than to space, and his primary concern is with God's word, not God's picture. We are asked to believe, therefore, that the Jew, though excelling in the splendor and rapture of the word, was denied a talent for the visual.[1]

How is one to account for the common misunderstanding about the Jew vis-à-vis the visual arts? The misunderstanding has arisen largely because writers on the subject have quoted indiscriminately from literary sources such as the Bible, Josephus, and Philo, to bolster their preconceived notions, while they have neglected to consider that these sources derive from diverse social contexts and from different epochs. In ignoring key factors like time and social milieu, scholars have virtually hypothesized an identity between the semi-nomadic Jew's view of art and the views of Jews, such as King Solomon or Joseph Caro, with sharply contrasting attitudes. A more adequate understanding of the complex problem of art and its role in Jewish

[1] Cf. H. Howarth, "Jewish Art and the Fear of the Image," *Commentary*, IX, No. 2 (February, 1950), 142–50.

Reprinted from *Hebrew Union College Annual,* Vol. XXXII, 1961.

life is afforded through an examination of certain key statements in
the Bible and in later works. Through such an examination the scholar
will be enabled to grasp the intricate relationship between these
statements and the particular social and cultural contexts which gave
rise to them.

A.   *The Implication of the Second Commandment in Biblical Times.*

The earliest pronouncement about art seems to be the so-called
Second Commandment in Exod. 20:4. Only the phrase, "You shall
not make yourself a graven image," has been associated by many
Bible scholars with the desert experience; the rest of the Commandment may be a much later addition.[2] In attempting an evaluation of
this commandment, one does well to bear in mind the direct inter-
connection that inevitably exists between man's way of life and his
ideas about God. Man, that is to say, characteristically invests the
divine with powers and attributes relevant to his own particular
environment and way of life.

Yahweh, the God of the Hebrews in the wilderness, was regarded
much as a tribal leader who had an intimate relationship with the
tribes. He accompanied the tribes to give them protection and His
home was wherever the tribes happened to be. In speaking or writing
about Him, the nomad conceived of Him in human terms. (Exod.
33:23: "I will take away My hand, and you shall see My back; but
My face shall not be seen"; Exod. 24:11: "He did not lay His hand";
Exod. 24:10: "there was under His feet.") Yet His only visible feature
was the cloud in which He enwrapped Himself during the desert
wanderings. (Exod. 33:9: "when Moses entered the Tent, the pillar
of cloud descended, and stood at the door of the Tent; and [the Lord]
spoke with Moses"; Num. 12:5: "And the Lord came down in a pillar
of cloud, and stood at the door of the Tent.") God was believed to
travel with the tribes, and His presence was associated with the holy
Ark and the Tent. These cult objects, the Ark and the Tent, can be
definitely attributed to a desert experience, and are in perfect consonance with the practices of certain primitive nomads, ancient as
well as modern.[3]

---

[2] Cf. S. R. Driver, *An Introduction to the Literature of the Old Testament* (New
York, 1956), pp. 34 ff. and M. Noth, *Das zweite Buch Mose, Exodus* (Göttingen,
1959), pp. 130–31.

[3] On the many difficult problems relating to the Ark and the Tent, cf. E. L.
Ehrlich, *Kultsymbolik im Alten Testament und im nachbiblischen Judentum* (Stuttgart,
1959), pp. 22–24. Cf. also J. Morgenstern, *The Ark, the Ephod, and the "Tent of
Meeting"* (Cincinnati, 1945), and K. H. Bernhardt, *Gott und Bild* (Berlin, 1956),
pp. 134 ff.

That God's presence was intricately bound up with the Ark, a notion surviving even into a later epoch when the transition from a nomadic to a sedentary state had already been accomplished, is discernible in the account of the battle against the Philistines at Eben Ezer. When the Ark was brought into the camp, the author of I Sam. 4:7 ff. tells us, "the Philistines were afraid, for they said: 'God has come into the camp.'" Indeed, with the capture of the Ark, God exiled Himself among the Philistine captors and wrought great havoc in their midst (I Sam. 5:2 ff.). Again, we read in II Sam. 6:6 ff. that Uzzah touched the Ark and was killed.

The proscription against making graven images, as it is set down in the Second Commandment, must therefore be understood within the context of a semi-nomadic experience, an experience whose forms persisted even into the subsequent sedentary milieu. God, though conceived of and comprehended in human terms, remained invisible within the cloud, and thus could not be depicted visually in physical terms. The purpose of the law forbidding images seems to have been to assure loyalty to the invisible Yahweh and to keep the nomads from creating idols or adopting the idols of the many sedentary cultures with which they came in contact during their desert sojourn. Eventually, of course, when the Israelites themselves had passed beyond nomadism, their contact with the surrounding sedentary cultures did lead them to adopt a number of idolatrous practices characteristic of a sedentary way of life.

The erection of the Solomonic Temple marked the consolidation of a new phase in Jewish history, a phase radically different from the semi-nomadic era of the Tent. Yahweh was now no longer the wandering God, the tribal chieftain of a semi-nomadic people. He was identified with the land and the monarch. He was the God of a unified people and, as such, needed to be placed within a permanent abode, a beautiful structure like that of the king, who enjoyed a permanent capital resplendent with luxurious palaces. Emulating other oriental rulers, Solomon adapted the palaces and Temple buildings of neighboring monarchs and introduced an elaborate priestly ritual for the Temple of Yahweh.

Were the Second Commandment in its entirety to be taken literally, the construction of Solomon's Temple, with its graven images, such as the cherubim and the twelve oxen which supported the molten sea, would obviously have been a direct violation and transgression. Yet no censure was invoked by the biblical writers.

Although Yahweh probably remained the unseen God of the desert experience, as well as the chief God, other gods, introduced through Solomon's numerous commercial and diplomatic alliances with foreign countries, were not successfully prevented from invading the country, as is evident from I Kings 11. Again it should be noted that later writers censured Solomon, not for transgressing the Second Commandment, but only for the henotheism which flourished during his reign (I Kings 11:4 ff. and I Kings 14:8 ff.).

The invisible God of the wilderness tribal experience, the God who had travelled within a cloud, was now gloriously enshrined within a permanent sanctuary (I Kings 8). Two specially designed cherubim were fashioned to guard His desert Ark. Although we cannot be certain that the concept, יֹשֵׁב הַכְּרֻבִים (who sits upon the cherubim), stems from the time of Solomon's Temple, it seems reasonable to assume that the cherubim served in the capacity of a throne for the invisible God, just as the visible gods of the Orient, the gods of the Canaanites, the Hittites, and the Arameans, were represented as either seated or standing upon similar animal thrones.[4]

While the cherubim were appropriate enough for Solomon's Temple, their presence in the desert Tent seems anachronistic with the desert experience. So late an account as II Sam. 6:2 ff., speaks of David's returning only the Ark, and I Kings 8:1 ff., speaks of Solomon's bringing only the Ark to the Temple. No mention is made in either account of the cherubim, or the elaborate "lampstand of pure gold" fashioned by Bezalel (Exod. 37:17 ff.), or of any of the other costly materials which according to Exodus were in the Tent. Many Bible scholars have concluded, therefore, that these appurtenances to the Tent did not exist in the desert, but were inserted into the account at a later time by the final redactors.[5]

---

[4] As confirmed by W. F. Albright, *From the Stone Age to Christianity* (Baltimore, 1942), pp. 202–3, 229–30. If the cherubim had been intrinsic features of the Tent, why should it have been necessary to fashion them again for the Temple? Cf. the similarity in language between Exod. 37:7 ff. and I Kings 6:23 ff. and 8:7 ff. Cf. now M. Haran, "The Ark and the Cherubim, Their Symbolic Significance in Biblical Ritual," *Israel Exploration Journal*, IX, No. 1 (1959), 30–38 and IX, No. 2 (1959), 89–94, for an exhaustive treatment of the problem. Haran believes that the cherubim served as a throne for Yahweh. Cf. also H. Schäfer and W. Andrae, *Die Kunst des Alten Orients* (Berlin, 1925), pp. 588–89, for depictions of Hittite gods, standing or sitting on the backs of animals, and F. P. Bargebuhr, "The Alhambra Palace of the Eleventh Century," *Journal of the Warburg and Courtauld Institutes*, XIX, Nos. 3–4 (1956), 213, and 249, n. 66.

[5] Driver, *op. cit.*, pp. 31 ff. assigns this section to the Priestly Code. Cf. also Noth, *op. cit.*, pp. 220 ff. It is most likely, however, that the tradition of Bezalel was known to the priestly writers and was not invented by them. They probably utilized and embroidered it in order to show that the appurtenances of the Temple were already found in the Tent of the desert. By thus making the Tent a movable Temple, the Zadokite priests hoped to establish a claim of an unbroken tradition as

Likewise the costly materials, not to mention the skills in weaving, embossing, and the like, which were necessary to produce the appurtenances described in Exodus are, of course, completely out of keeping with a semi-nomadic existence. It is inconceivable that a semi-nomadic tribal group would possess such costly materials; it is equally unlikely that such a group would have the surplus necessary to purchase such valuable goods, much less the wherewithal to train and develop such highly skilled artists in its midst. There is little reason to doubt, therefore, that the Pentateuchal description of the elaborate appurtenances and decorations of the Tent was inserted during a much later period, probably in an attempt to give Mosaic sanction to the elaborate Temple cult as well as to glorify the already venerated past. It is a fact that archeological investigation of the pottery and ceramics of the monarchical period has shown them to be much cruder than their Canaanite counterparts, a crudeness which testifies eloquently to the lack of native skills available for Solomon's project. For this very reason we find in I Kings 7:13 ff. that the king had to import Hiram of Tyre to fashion the two pillars of bronze, the molten sea supported by twelve oxen, the stands of bronze, and the like, for his Temple.

It is entirely understandable that a nation so underdeveloped artistically, yet surrounded by such advanced cultures as Egypt and Mesopotamia with their splendid artistic traditions, would attempt to read into its history and Sacred Scripture a tradition of artistic accomplishment which would place it on a footing at least as high as that of its more sophisticated neighbors. Surely, the God of Israel could not have endowed the newly formed nation with less talent than any other nation; to have done so would have been to admit its backwardness, and hence the inferiority of its God. Then, too, although graven images had been forbidden in the desert experience, the changed conditions of life under the monarchy now made it necessary to find a way to invest such images with religious sanction.

By contrast, it is particularly instructive in this regard to read the biblical descriptions of Hiram and Bezalel. I Kings 7:14 characterizes Hiram, a court artist of wealthy, highly cultured Phoenicia, as "filled with wisdom, intelligence and knowledge, to work any work in bronze,"[6] whereas Exod. 31:3 ff. says of Bezalel, a mere desert artist,

---

hereditary functionaries of the cult from the time of the Tent in the desert, and to justify therewith the artistic appurtenances of the Temple.

[6] Cf. II Chron. 2:13, a much later version of the construction of the Temple, a version which attributes to Hiram a range of talents which seems to place him on the same universal artistic plane as Bezalel — "skilled to work in gold, silver, bronze,

that God Himself "filled him with the spirit of God, in wisdom, intelligence and knowledge and all craftsmanship, to devise artistic designs, to work in gold, silver, and bronze, in cutting stones for setting, and in carving wood, to work in every craft." Hiram, a Phoenician court artist, is described as having received no direct inspiration from God and as having been skilled only in the working of bronze, whereas for Bezalel, the Jewish desert artist, the claim is made not only that he received his inspiration directly from God, but that he was endowed with skills surpassing those of even the greatest artists in the ancient Near East. What nation could boast of an artistic tradition equal to this?[7]

Thus it becomes clear that the projection of an artistic tradition back into the desert experience served to overcome two inherent difficulties. On the one hand it allowed the new nation to boast of a worthy artistic heritage, and on the other hand it prepared the way for the making of graven images which would otherwise have been considered a transgression of sacred law.

As was pointed out earlier in these pages, attitudes toward art within a society generally express the needs of such a society, or, at least, the needs of certain elements within it. Any statement in reference to Jewish art can be evaluated adequately only by taking this important factor into consideration. A clear demonstration of this principle is provided in I Kings 12:28, where we read that Jeroboam, the new king of the Northern Kingdom of Israel, met the threat to his power and prestige by discouraging his subjects from worshipping in the Temple at Jerusalem, capital of the Southern Kingdom of Judah. Jeroboam, we are told, "made two calves of gold" and represented them to his people as "your gods, O Israel, who brought you up out of the land of Egypt." To be sure, the account

---

iron, stone, and wood, and in purple, blue, fine linen, and in crimson, and to grave all types of engraving and devise any artistic design that may be assigned to him." It should be noted, however, that Hiram's skills were not held to be derived from or inspired by God and that he was merely requested to add his skills to those already existent among the Jewish craftsmen in Judah — "to be with the wise craftsmen who are with me (i. e., Solomon) in Judah and in Jerusalem, whom David my father provided." (II Chron. 2:6). Cf. K. Galling, *Die Bücher der Chronik, Esra, Nehemia* (Göttingen, 1954), p. 83, for such variations of the name Hiram as חוּרָם אָבִי in II Chron. 2:12; חוּרָם in II Chron. 4:11; and חוּרָם אָבִיו in II Chron. 4:16.

[7] The story of Bezalel, the craftsman inspired by God, seems to follow the epic pattern. Thus in the related Canaanite myths, it is a divine craftsman who builds the house for Baal. Cf. J. B. Pritchard, *Ancient Near Eastern Texts Relating to the Old Testament* (Princeton, 1950), p. 133, and S. R. Driver, *Canaanite Myths and Legends* (Edinburgh, 1956), pp. 10 ff. I am indebted to Dr. Harry M. Orlinsky for calling this fact to my attention. On the name Bezalel, cf. Noth, *op. cit.*, pp. 196–97.

in I Kings censures Jeroboam, but one may well wonder whether the redactors of the Bible, who were Southern Judeans, censured Jeroboam because he transgressed the Second Commandment or because they were determined to defend the Jerusalem Temple and its cult against all rivals.

A further demonstration that attitudes toward art reflect the needs of certain elements in a society, is supplied by such prophets as Amos and Hosea. The pronouncements of these prophets who lived during the time of the kings have often been invoked as examples of how scrupulously the Second Commandment, with all its ramifications, was observed and enforced. Those who cite prophetic statements in this connection entirely overlook the fact — a fact that these prophets themselves certainly did not overlook — that the establishment of a flourishing monarchical structure in Palestine endangered the semi-nomadic way of life which had never disappeared and which these prophets equated with loyalty to Yahweh. These prophets who spoke out so vehemently against idol worship, (Hos. 8:4, 13:2) and against objects of art, (Amos 3:15; 6:4) were moved, not so much by a revulsion against art or by a desire to enforce the Second Commandment, as by a pressing need to preserve the semi-nomadic way of life. The importation of foreign cults, which had resulted from the commercial interests of the kings, the elaborate Temple ritual and the maintenance of a privileged priesthood, the luxurious life at court and the comforts and pleasures of the wealthy landowners, all threatened to undermine the influence and heritage of the semi-nomad. These prophets, who spoke for the uprooted, the impoverished and the unprivileged elements in the society, tried to prevent the destruction of a social structure which they venerated as divinely ordained. They blamed the evils within Jewish society — evils which were particularly noticeable during times of stress — on the extravagances of the monarchy, the priesthood, and the wealthy landowners. Furthermore, since these institutions and classes had not existed during the desert experience, the prophetic pronouncements could idealize the wilderness wanderings; they could imply that abolition of these new institutions and their extravagances would insure the welfare of the unprivileged classes. The exhortations of these prophets and their zealous desire to guard the purity of the original Yahweh cult must be understood and evaluated in this light.

Of particular importance to a study of the problem of art in biblical times are the statements about art which are linked up with the Deuteronomic reform. These statements are, in essence, nothing more than insertions into, and amplifications of the Second Commandment in the Book of Exodus; the same is true of the very severe strictures against idols in the Book of Deuteronomy itself. Stemming from the reign of the seventh century Judean king, Josiah, these utterances have often been cited as reflective of the Jewish historic experience and the Jewish attitude towards art, not only under the regime of King Josiah, but throughout all of the Jewish history which preceded his reign. Yet the severely anti-iconic strictures characteristic of Josiah's reign had little genuine association with the scrupulous observance of the Second Commandment. Already, even before Josiah's time, idols and "high places" devoted to Yahweh or Baal, or to both, were not only profuse, but, in fact, as indicated in II Kings 23:4 ff., had become accepted practice. Josiah, however, apparently at the insistence of the Jerusalem priesthood, on whom he may have depended for support and who no doubt lost prestige — and tithes — when many sacrifices were diverted to the numerous "high places," insisted on the centrality of worship. To accomplish this end, an unwavering affirmation of Yahweh's exclusiveness and the centrality of the Yahweh cult was necessary; all attempts to decentralize the cult and to worship other gods had, of course, to be eliminated. Viewed against the historic background, then, the severity of Josiah's iconoclastic strictures bear little relation to the Second Commandment, particularly since there is no evidence in II Kings 23 that he removed any of the elaborate graven images from the period of Solomon, such as the cherubim, from the Temple at Jerusalem. Josiah's denunciations of idolatry were primarily measures designed to strengthen the monarchy and its priestly allies.

B. *The Implication of the Second Commandment in the Late Hellenistic and Early Roman Periods.*

The rise of Hellenism following the conquest of Palestine and the Near Eastern world by Alexander brought in its wake momentous and drastic changes for Judaism. It marked the gradual introduction of the polis (i. e., the Greek-type city) into a society that had remained essentially agricultural. This, in turn, called forth new artisan, shopkeeper, and merchant classes, classes which ultimately came to exercise rather complete control over the older agricultural classes. The emergence of these new classes posed a number of new problems. The Pentateuchal laws, which were made for a society that was largely agricultural and featured, as such, sacrificial offerings to a central cult in order to insure the sufficiency of the crops, had little meaning for the new classes which had been elevated into domination of Jewish life. Since no provision was made in the Pentateuch for these classes they felt their share in the agriculturally oriented Jewish religion to be highly attenuated, for they were unable to offer either their merchandise or their handicrafts to the Temple as sacrifices.

The discontents arising in Jewish life as a result of the encounter with Hellenism involved more than the complaints of an urban populace fettered with a cult that was intrinsically rural. There were intellectual consequences as well. While the Jewish merchant and craftsmen found fault with the non-urban character of the religion, Jewish thinkers, particularly those living in a Greco-Roman environment outside of Palestine, who sought to remain loyal to Judaism, found fault with Judaism's non-philosophical character. Jewish intellectuals attracted to Hellenistic philosophy measured their tradition against the heritage of Plato and Aristotle, and found Judaism wanting.

The ideas of the Pentateuch, founded as they were on revelation and divine authority, came to be regarded by many as incompatible with the systems expounded by Hellenistic thinkers. To remedy this in the realm of historiography, Josephus sought to refashion the annals of the Jews in imitation of the works of Greek historians such as Thucydides and Polybius. In the realm of philosophy, Philo attempted to allegorize the Pentateuch and sought thereby to reconcile it with Platonic thought.

Josephus, the celebrated Jewish historian who lived during the first century C. E., attempted to use Greek historiography as a model for his own recapitulations of Jewish history. A striking feature of Josephus' work is that, unlike the Bible, it is virtually devoid of appeals to divine authority, to divine intercession in, or divine direction of, history. His work appeals, rather, to reason, to the objective viewing of facts, to their essential truth and consistency. Yet, in presenting history in this objective fashion, Josephus' task was complicated by the Jewish revolt against Rome and by the ultimate defeat of the Jews, in which he had been personally involved. Josephus had been in command of the army in Galilee before his surrender to the Romans. Taken to Rome as a privileged captive, Josephus had settled down at the Flavian court to write his volumes on Jewish history and tradition — *The Jewish War*, *The Antiquities of the Jews*, and *Against Apion*. He also wrote an autobiographical work. He attempted, in these books, to portray Jewish history as longer, more reliable, and more factual than Greek history or, for that matter, than the history of any other people. The Torah he described as a constitution similar to the legal systems with which the Greeks and Romans were familiar;

Moses he presented as a lawgiver, the Jewish counterpart to Solon. In all this, of course, Josephus felt himself compelled to adopt a highly apologetic tone; the nature of his task demanded it, for he had set out, on the one hand, to rationalize and justify to his Jewish compatriots his betrayal of their cause and, on the other hand, to defend and win sympathy for Judaism in a Greco-Roman world hostile to the Jews.

Committed to writing history in the manner of the Greek and Roman historians, Josephus sought to render his presentation as consistent and as objective as possible. Yet, since he was determined to excuse certain of his own actions as well as those of his fellow Jews which might give offense to his Roman patrons, he was equally committed to writing an *apologia*.

The predicament in which Josephus found himself — the dilemma of the factual as against the apologetic — is nowhere more obvious than in his remarks regarding art. The demands of his *apologia* led him to circumvent the implications of the facts he was presenting. Hence, for example, in recounting Jewish demonstrations against Roman images and military standards, Josephus found it necessary to ascribe them to a Jewish insistence on the strict observance of the anti-iconic Second Commandment rather than to a Jewish hatred of Rome's oppressive rule. As he states it:

> Furthermore our Lawgiver forbade the making of images, not as if prophetically indicating that the power of the Romans was not to be honored, but as though scorning a matter that was useful neither to God nor man. (*Against Apion*, II, 6).

Of interest in this connection is Josephus' treatment of the episode in which, during the last days of Herod, the leaders of the revolutionary party incited their followers to tear down the golden eagle — symbolic of Rome — which had been set up by Herod over the great gate of the Temple. Josephus excused this act of insurrection on the grounds that Herod had violated the Second Commandment in erecting the eagle; the insurrectionists had been justified in destroying the eagle because in so doing they had sought to uphold the law, not to evince hatred of Rome. Nevertheless, it is evident from Josephus' account that the ruling authorities among the Jews had sided with Herod in condemning the culprits to death, for in *Antiquities*, XVII, 6, 3-4, he relates that Herod "summoned the leaders of the Jews" who "said that these deeds had been done without their knowledge, and that it seemed to them that these deeds should not be exempt from punishment." Josephus' demurral notwithstanding, the religious authorities had obviously seen no infringement of the law in Herod's erection of the eagle, which "he had dedicated" (to the Temple). Since the eagle was not an image intended for idolatrous purposes the king undoubtedly had the sanction of the important religious authorities from the very beginning (*Antiquities*, XVII, 6, 2, and *Wars*, I, 33, 2-3).

Again, in recounting how under the hated procurators riots broke out in reaction to the appearance in Jerusalem of a military detachment with its standards on which the image of the Roman Emperor appeared. Josephus disposed of the incident by observing that "our law forbids us to make images." (*Antiquities*, XVIII, 3, 1, and *Wars*, II, 9, 2.)[8]

His insistence that acts of rebellion against Rome were to be attributed to a zealous upholding of religious law forced Josephus, for the sake of consistency, to condemn King Solomon himself; the graven images of the Temple, Josephus claimed, had made Solomon guilty of violating the Second Commandment. Although the biblical account itself had never seen fit to censure King Solomon on such grounds, Josephus declared, in *Antiquities* VIII, 7, 5 that

> as he (Solomon) advanced in age, and his reason became in time too feeble to recollect the customs of his own country . . . . . he sinned, and went astray in the observance of the laws, namely when he made the images of the bronze bulls that supported the molten sea, and the images of the lions around his own throne, for it was impious to make them.[9]

Yet, despite his valiant attempts at consistency, Josephus was compelled on occasion to allow certain facts concerning art to stand without censure or the claim of violation of the Second Commandment. These instances invariably involved royal Jewish personages who either had presented gifts of art to the Romans or had imitated Roman artistic practices. Consequently, while, on the one hand, he criticized Herod for violating the law of the land in erecting the eagle

---

[8] This study is not intended to be an exhaustive treatment of all Jewish sources bearing on art in the Hellenistic and Roman periods. For other sources in Josephus bearing on this subject and for different interpretations of sources cited, cf. R. Meyer, "Die Figurendarstellung in der Kunst des späthellenistischen Judentums," *Judaica*, V, No. 1 (March, 1949), 1-12 and C. Roth, "An Ordinance Against Images in Jerusalem, A. D. 66," *Harvard Theological Review*, XLIX, No. 1 (July, 1956), 169-77.

[9] Though Josephus condemns Solomon for such non-Pentateuchal additions to the Temple as the molten sea, he accepts without censure the cherubim in Solomon's Temple, which were also graven images. Since the cherubim were included in the Pentateuch, Josephus, who was a priest in the Temple of Jerusalem, had obviously accepted them without question. He describes them in the section dealing with the Tent in the desert as follows: "in form unlike anything that man has seen, though Moses said that he saw them carved on the throne of God." (*Antiquities*, III, 6, 5).

over the Temple (*Antiquities*, XVII, 6, 2, and *Wars*, I, 33, 2–3), he reported without censure, on the other hand, that Herod's palace in Jerusalem had been decorated with figures (*Wars*, V, 4, 4).[10] Similarly, the pictures of her children sent by Alexandra, daughter of Hyrcanus II, to Antony (*Antiquities*, XV, 2, 6), were neither censured nor condemned as violations of tradition. Nor did Josephus see fit to criticize the popular Jewish king, Herod Agrippa I, who had had statues of his daughters made (*Antiquities*, XIX, 9, 1).

Had Josephus, in these latter instances, insisted on the strict observance of the Second Commandment, his criticism would have been interpreted by the Romans as a direct insult to their friendship and ties with Jewish royalty. Where, however, insurrections and riots were concerned, had he not ascribed them to zeal for the Second Commandment, they would have been viewed by the Roman reader as overtly anti-Roman acts of hostility on the part of the Jews. In either case, Josephus, caught on the horns of a dilemma, had no choice but to resolve the issues without antagonizing his Roman patrons.

An examination of Philo's attitude towards the visual arts is particularly helpful in leading us to determine the extent to which he superimposed Platonic thought patterns on the existent biblical thought patterns. In *On the Giants*, XIII, 59, he offered it as his opinion that

> [Moses] banished from his own commonwealth painting and sculpture, with all their high repute and charm of artistry, because their crafts belie the nature of truth and work deception and illusions through the eyes to souls that are ready to be seduced.[11]

In *The Decalogue*, XIV, 66–67, Philo denounced those who

> filled the habitable world with images and wooden figures and the other works of human hands fashioned by the craftsmanship of painting and sculpture, arts which have wrought great mischief in the life of mankind. For these idolators cut away the most excellent support of the soul, the rightful conception of the Ever-living God.[12]

[10] Yet the palace of Herod Antipas in Tiberias (*Life*, 12), which had figures of living creatures, he urged to have destroyed, despite the protestations of the local authorities. He counselled in this manner on the pretext that he was ordered to do so and that the figures were a violation of Jewish law. This action of Josephus was motivated no doubt to prove to the Jews of Galilee that he sided with the radical elements in Judea and upheld their cause against Rome and its friends.

[11] *Philo*, with an English translation by F. H. Colson and G. H. Whitaker (London and New York, 1929), II, p. 475.

[12] *Philo*, with an English translation by F. H. Colson (Cambridge, Mass. and

These sentiments appear to agree with the anti-iconic attitude found in a number of biblical passages. In fact, however, they differ radically from those of the Bible. What Philo has done is to echo the Platonic concept that certain arts — the "amusement" and "imitative" arts — should be banned from the ideal state, since they are deceptive and arouse passions which the reasonable faculty is unable to control.[13] The biblical antagonism to art had been called forth primarily by the desire to avoid an idolatry which might endanger the purity of the Yahweh cult. Philo's strictures bore little relation to the Temple cult, which in its own day was known far and wide for its artistically wrought appurtenances, but were expressed in terms of how one might best attain the goals established by a philosophic system.

Two hundred years later some of the early Church Fathers, in their fight against paganism and its cult of images, were confronted with a similar problem of reconciling Platonic tradition with naïve, revelationary texts (the Old and New Testaments), and came to similar conclusions about the visual arts. Clement of Alexandria declared, for example, that

> Moses, much earlier, made an express and public Law against the making of any carved or molten or moulded or painted image and representation, in order that we might not direct our attention to sensible objects, but might proceed to that which is perceptible to the mind.[14]

Again the stress is placed on the idea that the representation of objects is unworthy, because it is deceptive and misleading to the earnest seeker of philosophic truth.

London, 1937), VII, pp. 39–41. For other passages in Philo bearing on this subject, cf. E. R. Goodenough, *By Light, Light* (New Heaven, 1935), pp. 256–59. Cf. also H. A. Wolfson, *Philo — Foundations of Religious Philosophy in Judaism, Christianity and Islam* (Cambridge, 1948), I, pp. 29–30.

[13] The prevalent conception that Plato banished the artist (or poet) from his ideal commonwealth is largely a misunderstanding of passages in *The Republic*. Plato wished to banish only "amusement" art because he felt that it provoked childish passions and emotions which had no useful purpose in the ideal republic where law and reason should rule. Philo, for his own purposes, may have preferred to interpret Plato as desirous of banning the artist from his ideal republic. Cf. R. G. Collingwood, *The Principles of Art* (New York, 1958), pp. 47 ff. and 98 ff., and G. M. A. Grube, *Plato's Thought* (Boston, 1958), pp. 179 ff. I am indebted to Rabbi Jack Bemporad for these references.

[14] *Stromata*, V, 5 (Migne, *Patrologia Graeca*, IX, 50). Cf. E. Bevan, *Holy Images* (London, 1939), pp. 107 and 84 ff. for the attitude of the early Church towards art. Cf. also J. Kollwitz, "Zur Frühgeschichte der Bilderverehrung," and H. F. von Campenhausen, "Die Bilderfrage als theologisches Problem der alten Kirche," in *Das Gottesbild im Abendland* (Witten und Berlin, 1959), pp. 57–108.

Clearly, the statements of Philo cannot be used to establish an antagonism toward images on the part of Judaism; nor do they indicate a strict enforcement of the Second Commandment during the Hellenistic period.

Similarly, were one to take literally the statements made by some of the early Church Fathers with regard to artistic expression, they would lead one to believe that pictorial art in the early Church was virtually non-existent. What, however, of the elaborately painted catacombs and the sculptured sarcophagi of the patristic age? Scholars who have appealed to Philo or certain early Church Fathers to establish a thesis of Jewish or early Christian iconoclasm have simply overlooked the fact that, in their attitudes toward art, Philo and his patristic successors voiced the philosophic sentiments and aspirations of highly select groups. These utterances cannot constitute evidence to support a contention that the Second Commandment was observed, nor can they serve to explain the existing practices of the masses in general.

It is evident, therefore, that sources like Josephus and Philo cannot be cited in support of any thesis which would affirm the ubiquitous observance of the Second Commandment.

The conclusion to which one is inevitably drawn from an examination of the surviving material, both literary and archeological, from the Biblical and Hellenistic-Roman periods, is that a rigidly and uniformly anti-iconic attitude on the part of the Jews remains as much a myth as the Procrustean bed on which Jewish art history has so often been made to lie.

NOTES TO A HISTORY OF THE JEWISH GUILDS

MARK WISCHNITZER, Yeshiva University

GUILDS of artisans, merchants, priests, scribes and persons of other professional groups already existed in ancient times. Guilds were formed for the mutual economic, social and cultural benefit of their members. The nucleus of the guild was the working family. The heads of the artisan families taught their sons the skills they had acquired from their ancestors. Later, families practicing the same craft joined together in clans, thus preparing the ground for the emergence of the guild. Herbert Spencer put it this way : « The branching of the family through generations into a number of kindred families carrying on the same occupation produced the germ of the guild. » [1]

Now already in antiquity the family of the artisan included apprentices not related to him; the youngsters were initiated into their trade by the heads of the artisan families, and became part of the household. The institution of apprenticeship existed as early as the reign of the Babylonian king Hammurabi (about 1728-1686 B.C.E.). [2] In Hammurabi's time there were Babylonian guilds of weavers, carpenters, goldsmiths and barbers. [3] They clustered together in separate city quarters.

---

[1] Spencer, Herbert, *Principles of Sociology*, p. 491. Quoted by Lambert, J. M., *Two Thousand Years of Guild Life*, Hull, 1891, p. 13.

[2] Finegan, J., *Light from the Ancient Past*, Princeton, 1946, p. 47 and n. 6.

[3] Mendelsohn, I., « Guilds in Babylonia and Assyria, » in *Journal of the American Oriental Society*, No. 60 (1940), pp. 68-72; *idem*, « Guilds in Ancient Palestine, » in *Bulletin of the American Schools of Oriental Research*, No. 80 (December, 1940), p. 17.

Reprinted from *Hebrew Union College Annual,*
Vol. XXIII, Part II, 1950-1951.

The Assyrian and Babylonian guilds served as patterns for the artisans' associations of ancient Israel, which sprang up long before the Hellenistic epoch, when Jewish guilds are believed to have originated. [4]

Ancient Palestine

In biblical times a craftsman would attach the designation of his craft, prefixed by *ben* (son, actually member), to his name. Thus *Hanania ben Harakkahim* (Neh. 3:8) was a member of the association of perfumers. *Uzziel ben Harhaia ben Hazorfim* and *Malkiah ben Zorfi(m)* (Neh. 3:8,31) were members of the guild of goldsmiths. *Mishpaha* (family), when used in connection with crafts, meant the guild of the specific craft. Thus, there occur in biblical sources *mishpahot* (guilds) of the weavers and the scribes. This is in line with our general notion of artisans' families as the nuclei of the guilds. The « house » (*Bait*) of Ashbea (I Chron. 4:21) represented a clan of families carrying on the weaver's trade. The guilds of ancient Judah clustered, like those of Babylonia, in separate streets, city quarters, fields, or valleys. There were a bakers' street, and a potters' street in Jerusalem, a fullers' field near the city, a goldsmiths' quarter in Jerusalem, a valley of woodworkers in the territory of the tribe of Benjamin. The head of the guild was sometimes called « ab » or « father » of the guild. I Chron. 4:14 refers to « Joab, father of the Craftsmen's Valley (*Ge Harashim*). » [5]

Arts and crafts developed greatly in the period of the Second Commonwealth, particularly under the rule of the Hasmoneans and Herod. Jerusalem, with a population of 100,000 before the destruction of the Temple, in 70 C.E.,

---

[4] *Idem, Guilds in Ancient Palestine*, p. 17.

[5] For archaeological data on Jewish industries in ancient Palestine, see Albright, W. F., « The Excavations of Tell Beit Mirsim in Palestine, » in *The Annual of American Schools of Oriental Research*, 17 (1936/37); Glueck, Nelson, *The Other Side of the Jordan*, New Haven, 1941.

possessed a whole array of districts, streets and markets occupied by guilds of blacksmiths, goldsmiths, tanners, dyers, cheese-makers and others. The weavers of Jerusalem had their own synagogue and burial place. Lydda, Sepphoris and Tiberias had also weavers' synagogues. [6]

When the artisan walked through the city or went to a nearby village he was recognized by the badge he wore. The tailor carried a needle stuck in the front of his dress, the wool carder a woolen thread; the dyer carried several threads dyed in different colors from which customers could select the shades they desired; the carpenter displayed a sort of measuring rule; the weaver wore a small distaff beneath the ear; the scribe carried a pen. [7] « Every artisan, » said the tanna Elieser ben Azariah, « boasts of his trade, carrying his badge in the street. » [8]

The tendency of workers of a trade to come together in a separate street or quarter grew in the course of time, becoming particularly marked at the close of the Second Commonwealth and later on in Palestine as well as in Babylonia, Egypt and other countries of the Diaspora. Sticking together, the group could « keep an eye on one's fellow and watch prices. » The mistrust the artisan harbored toward his fellow-worker is mentioned in the Mishnah. [9] However, an awareness of common interest also grew. There was the constant threat of competition from craftsmen coming from the outside to sell

---

[6] Bell. V, 81; Jeremias, Joachim, *Jerusalem zur Zeit Jesu*, Part I : *Die Wirtschaftlichen Verhältnisse*, Leipzig, 1923, pp. 4 and 5; Büchler, Adolph, *Economic Conditions of Judaea after the Destruction of the Second Temple*, London, 1912, passim; Krauss, S., *Synagogale Altertümer*, Berlin-Vienna, 1922, pp. 201 and 206.

[7] Louis, S., « Handicrafts and Artisans Mentioned in Talmudical Writings, » in *Transactions of the Society of Biblical Archaeology*, London, vol. VIII (1885), pp. 398-411. Also Krauss, S., *Talmudische Archaeologie*, Leipzig, 1910-12, vol. II, pp. 257 ff.

[8] *Abbot de Rabbi Nathan*, 23 a, ed. S. Schechter, New York, 1945.

[9] *Massechtoth Kallah*, ed. Michael Higger, New York, 1936, p. 326.

their products on market days, who would attempt to set up workshops and acquire permanent residence. To protect themselves against intruders the artisans of a locality joined hands to form a guild. According to Tosephta Baba Meziah (XI, 16), the residents of an alley were entitled « to prevent anyone in their midst from bringing in a tailor, a tanner, or any other artisan. » [10] Such concerted pressure implies a great deal of solidarity within the group.

In the absence of such guild statutes for this early period as are available for later centuries, one has to piece together the scattered references in the Mishnaic and Talmudic literature to get a picture of the practices and policies of the guilds. Thus we learn from Tosephta Baba Meziah (XI, 24) that all the wool weavers and dyers together were permitted to by up whatever goods came to town. [11] The monopolizing of the market was justified when done by the collectivity. A somewhat conjectural passage in the Tosephta Baba Meziah (XI, 25) is understood by the author to refer to a bakers' strike. The word « *regiah* » — generally taken to mean « combination » (« bakers are allowed to form a combination ») — is translated by Isidore Epstein as « stoppage of work. » [12]

Regulations were binding on the members of a guild; but if a rabbi of distinction saw fit to alter one or another regulation his decision was valid. [13] It should be kept in mind that many of the rabbis who worked on the compilation of the Mishnah and the Palestinian and Babylonian Talmud were artisans themselves, which accounts for their interest in the guilds and their authority among the working people.

To refer once more to Tosephta Baba Meziah, a significant passage (XI, 25-26) deals with the insurance of guild members

10 Mendelsohn, *Guilds in Ancient Palestine,* p. 19.

11 *Ibidem,* p. 19.

12 Epstein, Isidore, *Social Legislation in the Talmud,* published by *Tnuath Torah ve Avodah,* London, n. d. p. 11.

13 BT Baba Bathra, 9 a.

against losses of tools or animals. « The mariners, » it is said
there, « are entitled to stipulate that one who lost his ship
should be provided with another. If the loss was caused
by his own fault, they would not have to provide him with
another ship; but if there was no negligence (on his part), he
was to be provided with another ship. » The same provision
was adopted by the ass-drivers' guild. If an ass was lost and it
had been proved that no negligence on the part of the driver
was involved, the guild replaced the animal. Apparently the
guilds possessed funds to compensate their members for
losses sustained by the latter.

The guilds furthered the training of apprentices and saw
to it that members taught their sons their skills. The rabbis
keenly supported these policies which aimed at the preservation
of a healthy artisanship. Of the numerous references of the
rabbis to this matter, it will suffice to quote the following
maxim : « A father who fails to teach his son a trade virtually
teaches him robbery. » [14] Midrashic literature is especially rich
in records concerning vocational training of the youth. The
rabbinic academies variously took up the matter. In the academy
of Usha, Galilee, the tanna Juda ben Ilai, himself a cooper
(who is incidentally known to have lectured sitting on his cask),
staunchly advocated vocational training. [15] Choice of trades and
directions to be given to fathers were eagerly discussed. [16]

The guild was headed by the « rabban, » or « rosh. » The
guild member or master was sometimes called « rav » and his
apprentice « talmid, » but the usual designation for apprentice

[14] BT Kidd. 29 a.

[15] Krauss, *Talmudische Archaeologie*, vol. II, pp. 256-257.

[16] See Büchler, Adolph, *The Political and Social Leaders of the
Jewish Community in Sepphoris in the Second and Third Centuries*,
London, 1909, pp. 72 ff.; also Friedlaender, M. H., *Die Arbeit nach der
Bibel, dem Talmud und den Aussprüchen der Weisen in Israel*, Pisek,
1890, p. 14, n. 5.

was « shulayu. » The terms of the apprenticeship were agreed
upon between the master and the parents of the youth. [17]

In the period following the Bar Kochba rebellion (135 C.E.)
until the Arab invasion (634), arts and crafts prospered.
The total population of Palestine at the time of the invasion
had reached about four million. There was a wide market for
local industries and imported goods. Various localities were
reputed for their specialties. Tiberias, Usha, Sepphoris and
Giscalah excelled in the manufacture of linen, coarse and fine
cloth, silk and mats. All along the Mediterranean coast down
to the Negev, people were engaged in purple dyeing. [18]

Sassanian Persia

The old Babylonian community of Jewish exiles in Persia,
under Sassanian rule, numbered two to three million. The
Babylonian Talmud mentions as Jewish trades metal, stone
and woodwork, carpet weaving, textile industries, washing and
dyeing of cloth, pearl perforation, tailoring, leather work,
pottery, embroidery, food and beverage production, extractive
industries, shipping and the building trade. [19] One should
remember that King Nebuchadnezzar deported in 598 B.C.E.
one thousand metal workers to Babylonia (II Kings, 24:16).
Jewish trades, therefore, had an old tradition in the country.

[17] Krauss, *op. cit.*, vol. II, pp. 256 and 258.

[18] Büchler, *Economic Conditions of Judaea*, p. 18; Avi-Jonah, Michael,
« Ha-Mischar ve Hatassiyah be Erez Israel be Tekufah ha Romaith-ha
Bizantinith, » in *Safrah le Yediath Erez Israel*, Jerusalem, 1937, pp.
96-98; idem, *Bimei Roma Uvisantion*, Jerusalem, 1946, pp. 6 and 7.

[19] See Gezow, N. S., *Al Naharot Babel*, Warsaw, 1888; Krauss,
Talmudische Archaeologie, vol. I-III, passim; Obermeyer, Jacob, *Die
Landschaft Babylonien im Zeitalter des Talmuds und des Gaonats*, Leip-
zig, 1929, pp. 170 ff., 194 ff., 239, 294, 299, 304, 334; Heichelheim,
Fritz M., « Roman Syria, » in *Ancient Rome*, ed. Tenney Frank,
Baltimore, 1938, vol. IV, pp. 189-98; *idem*, Wirtschaftsgeschichte des
*Altertums vom Palaeolithikum bis zur Völkerwanderung der Germanen,
Slaven und Araber*, Leiden, 1938, vol. I, pp. 820, 822.

It should further be remembered that Babylonian craft guilds, going back as far as the time of King Hammurabi, were time-honored institutions. The Babylonian Talmud gives us a lively picture of the bazars of Nehardea with their butchers' stands and tanners' and shoemakers' shops, [20] and makes us familiar with the linen-producing centers of Borsippa and Pumbedita. Pum Nehara, a locality exclusively populated by Jews, was famous for its cloth; Sura manufactured ropes; Rodia specialized in sacks. There is the interesting case of the wool weavers in Pum Nehara who made a complaint against outside wool dealers. Rabbi Kahana, the local judge, settled the matter. [21] A decision of rabbi Samuel, famous amora of the third century, refers to the fringes on Persian breeches familiar to us from Sassanian art (BT Baba Meziah, 60 b). It is interesting to learn that the Jewish garment industry produced this highly valued article of Persian wearing apparel. There is abundant reference in Talmudical sources to sack-makers, basket-makers and boat-haulers and their associations. [22]

Very much as in Palestine, the Jewish guilds in Persia had to fight outside competitors. There too they were supported in their policy by the rabbis. (Whether the Babylonian guilds, like many Polish guilds in later periods, had their own rabbis, is not known). The amora Huna ben Joshua (second half of the fourth century), in a decision recalling the one found in Tosephta Baba Meziah (XI, 16), approved of the right of the residents of a town to keep out people from other places (BT Baba Bathra 21 b). However, there were apparently limits to the jurisdiction of the guild. If the applicant paid the government poll tax (*Kraga*) in that city, he was not to be denied residence. L. Rabinowitz suggests that the case may have

[20] See Funk. S., *Die Juden in Babylonien,* 200-500, Berlin, 1902, vols. I and II, passim.

[21] Obermeyer, *op. cit.,* p. 194.

[22] See BT Ketuboth 67 a; Baba Bathra 22 a. About boat-haulers, cf. M. Judilowitz, « Ha Ir Sura, » in *Sinai,* I, No. 2, (1937), pp. 173-4.

involved moving from one place to another within the same taxation district. [23] However this may be, the Jewish guild tried to regulate the influx of workers and watched over the living standard of its members. The same monopolistic tendencies were to be observed among non-Jewish merchants and artisans in the late antiquity and Middle Ages. We have them in Byzantium and also in the early guilds in Pisa and Ravenna. [24] Fritz M. Heichelheim, in his *Wirtschaftsgeschichte des Altertums,* [25] goes so far as to trace the monopolistic policies of the non-Jewish guilds in the early Middle Ages back to the Sassanian Empire of the beginning of the fifth century, and specifically to the practice of the Jewish artisans' associations as illustrated by the decision of Huna ben Joshua. In view of the scarcity of the sources the question must remain open. This much can be said, that the Jewish guilds which begin to emerge in the Middle Ages in Europe, were most probably patterned upon those in the Eastern diaspora.

Egypt in the Roman Era

Egypt ranks next as far as Jewish population numbers are concerned. Philo listed four Jewish occupational groups in Alexandria : artisans, farmers, shippers and merchants. [26] The artisans were organized in guilds. There were the goldsmiths', silversmiths', coppersmiths', blacksmiths', and weavers' guilds. The tanna rabbi Judah (second century C.E.) noted, on his visit to Alexandria, that the five guilds had their own separate

---

[23] Cf. Rabinowitz, L., « The Talmudic Basis of the Herem Hayyishub, » in *Jewish Quarterly Review,* NS XXVIII, pp. 217-25; idem, *The Herem Hayyishub,* London, 1945, pp. 27 ff.

[24] Cf. Mickwitz, Gunnar, *Die Kartellfunktionen der Zünfte und ihre Bedeutung bei der Entstehung des Zunftwesens,* Helsingfors, 1936, pp. 186-88.

[25] Vol. II, pp. 1218-19, n. 2. Cf. Rabinowitz, *Herem,* pp. 140-41.

[26] *In Flaccum,* VIII.

seats in the great synagogue-basilica. [27] If an artisan was in need he could turn to his group in the synagogue to receive assistance « for himself and his family. » [28] Social service, as in the general guilds, was an important function of the Jewish guilds in Alexandria. Just what their economic functions and policies were is not known, nor do we know very much about their legal status and constitution. The guild of Jewish sailors (*navicularii*) in Alexandria was organized as a corporation under Roman law. [29] It is noteworthy that, in the Roman period, Jewish artisans in Egypt also joined general trade corporations. They did not participate, however, in the pagan religious ceremonies. [30] Similar cases were to be found in Christian Europe in much later times, as, for instance, in Grodno, Lithuania, in the seventeenth century. The Jewish tailors, furriers and cap-makers of that city affiliated with the Christian guild of tailors, furriers and cap-makers were excused from attending the celebration of Christian festivals. [31]

Byzantium

In the Byzantine Empire, in the Balkans and the East Mediterranean islands, the Jews were engaged in weaving, dyeing, cloth-making, tanning, furriers' work and other trades. [32] There seem to have existed no Jewish guilds in those areas

[27] See Tosephta Sukkah, IV, 6; BT Sukkah 51 b and other Talmudical sources quoted by Tcherikover, A., *Ha Yehudim be Mizraim be Tekufah ha Helenistith ha Romith le-Or ha Pappirologiah*, Jerusalem, 1945, p. 78. Also Gordon, H. L., « The Basilica and the Stoa in Early Rabbinical Literature, » *The Art Bulletin*, Vol. XIII, No. 3 (1931), p. 11.

[28] Gordon, *loc. cit.*, p. 11.

[29] Juster, Jean, *Les Juifs dans l'Empire Romain*, Paris, 1914, vol. I, p. 486, n. 2 and II, pp. 264-255.

[30] *Ibid.*, vol. I, pp. 486-87.

[31] See my article, « Remeslenniki, » in *Evreiskaia Enciclopedia*, St. Petersburg, vol. XIII.

[32] Starr, Joshua, *The Jews in the Byzantine Empire, 641-1204*, Athens, 1939, *passim*.

before the twelfth century, nor did Jews find admittance
to the Christian Byzantine guilds. In the neighboring Moslem
countries, however, Jews did have access to guilds. [33] The
hostile attitude toward Jews of guilds in the Byzantine lands
may be accounted for to some extent by the fact that the guilds
were controlled by the government, which in the early Middle
Ages discriminated against Jews. The situation changed for
the better under Manuel I of the Comnenian dynasty, which
on the whole adopted a more liberal policy toward aliens. [34]
An interesting fact will illustrate the new attitude. In 1147,
King Roger II of Sicily invaded the Peloponnese and Ionian
Isles and carried away a number of Jewish silk garment
workers to Sicily, where they built up a silk industry. [35]
Apparently under the impact of this loss Manuel I granted
Jews, about a year later, « official tolerance » for the establishment of a guild, and liberal by-laws of a special kind which were
incorporated in the old law book of Leo VI. [36]

Benjamin of Tudela in the account of his travels (about
1170) has much to say about Jewish tanners in Pera, a district
of Constantinople, and the garments of gold, silver, and purple
manufactured by Jews in Pera, Thessalonica and Thebes. He
does not mention guilds, however. [37] In the beginning of the
fourteenth century, there existed a combined guild of Jewish
tanners and furriers in Pera, and we learn that the hides they
worked were imported from the Crimea.

Southern Europe

While Jewish trades were virtually suppressed in medieval Central Europe owing to the restrictive measures of the

[33] Lopez, Robert S., « Silk Industry in the Byzantine Empire, » in
Speculum, vol. XX, No. 1 (1945), pp. 23-24.

[34] *Ibid.,* p. 24.

[35] Starr, *op. cit.,* p. 223.

[36] Lopez, *op. cit.,* p. 24.

[37] *Masaot R. Benjamin,* ed. L. Gruenhut and M. N. Adler, p. 21

Christian craft guilds, they were allowed to flourish in Spain, Southern France, Sardinia and Sicily. The whole economic stratification of the Jewish people in these countries was different from that obtaining in the North. In addition to handicrafts, Jews were engaged in farming, not being confined to commerce and money-lending only. One of the factors responsible for the more balanced character of the Jewish economy in Southern Europe was the fact that the Jews were not the only non-Christians there. Moslems had also to be reckoned with. The notion that Jews ought to be shut out from the economic system of the Christian world had not yet dawned upon the leading minds of Southern Europe. As late as 1451, we meet with a Joseph Caschisi, master carpenter in the royal palace. He was appointed by the viceroy as warden of the Jewish carpenters' guild in Palermo. The Jewish guild was then an officially recognized body. [39]

Spain in the Later Middle Ages

Much light has lately been shed on Jewish artisanship in Medieval Spain. Old records, taken out of dusty archives, show the names of thousands of men who once were clothiers, milliners, weavers, dyers, tailors, curriers, leather workers, shoemakers, basket-makers, rope-makers, saddlers, armorers, steel- and ironworkers, braziers, cutlers, tin- and copper, gold- and silversmiths, potters, bridle-makers, carpenters, and sailors. [40]

---

[38] Starr, Joshua, *Romania, The Jewries of the Levant after the Fourth Crusade*, Paris, 1949, pp. 28 ff.

[39] *Codice Diplomatico dei Giudei di Sicilia*, ed. Bart. and Giuseppi Lagumina, vol. I, 1884, p. 505. Cf. Roth, Cecil, *The History of the Jews in Italy*, Philadelphia, 1946, pp. 229, 271 ff., for particulars about handicrafts practiced by the Jews of Sicily.

[40] The list of trades is given in the Ordinance of King John (Juan) II of Castile concerning Jews and Moors, dated April 6, 1443, published in English translation by E. H. Lindo, *The History of the Jews of Spain*

James W. Thompson notes that « the most skilled workmen in Spain had not been Christians, but rather Moors and Jews, » which makes him think that « in skilled industry as in skilled agriculture, the expulsion of the Jews and the Moors was detrimental.» [41] He points out that in Catalonia, in the latter half of the fifteenth century, « there were fulling mills, tanneries, forges, iron works, etc., and artisans of gold and silver work, and pottery. These crafts were mainly exploited by Jews and *Mudéjares.* » [42] Julius Klein, in his study on medieval Spanish guilds, likewise stresses the part the Jews and Moors played in the production process. [43] Yzhak (Fritz) Bear's publications on the history of the Jews in medieval Christian Spain and Abraham A. Neuman's *The Jews in Spain* abound in source material concerning the Jewish contribution to the industrial life of that country. [44]

What was the attitude of the Christian guilds in Spain toward the Jews? Klein's suggestion that previous to the reign of Ferdinand of Aragon and Isabella of Castile, Jews were « permitted to enter the guilds, » [45] is not corroborated by documentary evidence. The Christian guilds were always barred to Jews. What Ferdinand and Isabella did was to introduce the racial motive as the ultimate justification of the anti-Jewish policy. An apprentice had under the new law to submit his baptismal certificate and full proof of « *limpiezza de*

and Portugal, London, 1848, pp. 221-6; also Neuman, Abraham A., *The Jews in Spain,* Philadelphia, 1944, vol. I, pp. 185-190.

[41] James W. Thompson, *Economic and Social History of Europe in the Later Middle Ages* (1300-1530), New York, 1931, p. 347.

[42] *Ibid.,* pp. 360-1.

[43] Klein, Julius, « Medieval Spanish Guilds, » in *Facts and Factors in Economic History,* Cambridge, 1932, p. 184.

[44] Baer, *Die Juden im Christlichen Spanien,* Berlin, 1929 and 1936, vols. I and II. *Idem, Toledoth ha Yehudim be Sfarad ha Nozrith,* Tel Aviv, 1905, vol. I and II. On trades see particularly I, pp. 138, 286 and 336-7. Neuman, *op. cit.,* vol. I, ch. IX.

[45] Klein, *op. cit.* p. 184.

sangre,» or purity of blood, to be admitted to a Christian guild (1474). [46]

In the fourteenth century, the Crown did not yet share the anti-Jewish attitude of the Christian guilds. Jewish craft guilds sprang up [47] with the knowledge and support of the Crown. Thus in 1336 Pedro IV of Aragon granted recognition to the newly founded Jewish guild of shoemakers of Saragossa. [48]

The statutes of the shoemakers guild of Saragossa, the only ones so far published, offer invaluable insight into the duties and functions of the membership. Sick care was an important concern. The guild wardens were bound to visit their sick twice a week, on Mondays and Thursdays. Members who had become destitute owing to illness were to receive two dineros daily from the guild treasury. On Saturdays it was the duty of every member to visit the ailing. In case of death the whole membership remained with the body till the burial and conducted religious services in the house of the deceased. The guild took part in the family events of the members, weddings, *brith milah,* etc. The clause providing for exclusion from the brotherhood for the duration of one month as punishment for personal offenses bespeaks the high sense of honor of the Spanish Jews. [49]

Since the statutes contained no regulations regarding working conditions, standardization of products, control of output and other matters of guild life, we must assume that this Saragossa guild was of the type of a Spanish *cofradia,* representing an early stage of the craft guild. [50] However it would be erroneous to think that economic matters were of no concern

[46] *Ibid.,* 184.
[47] Cf. Neuman, *op. cit.* I, p. 182.
[48] Klein, *op. cit.,* p. 179, n. 3.
[49] The Saragossa statutes were published by D. Manuel de Bofarull y de Sartorio, *Gremios y Cofradias de la antigua Corona de Aragón,* Barcelona, vol. I (1876), 131-133.
[50] Klein, *op. cit.,* p. 173.

to the Spanish artisan fraternities, or, for that matter, to the Jewish shoemakers' guild of Saragossa.

There existed a number of Jewish guilds in Spain. Some of them were quite prosperous. The Jewish turners of Saragossa possessed their own synagogue.[51] The tailors of Perpignan ran their own hospital. The weavers of Calatayud supported their own Beth-ha-Midrash.[52]

The rabbinical responsa reflect the contemporary attitude toward the guilds. The well-known Rabbi Solomon ben Abraham Adret of Barcelona (1235-1310), giving his opinion on the status of the guilds of butchers, dyers and sailors (probably in Barcelona), says : « If these guilds pass an ordinance regarding their trade, it is as binding upon the individuals of the trade as are the laws of the Torah; for every trade organization is a city unto itself and does not require the consent of the outer community for its enactments... The members of a guild are as autonomous in their own affairs as are the citizens of the city. And so each group is permitted to conduct its affairs and to prescribe fines and punishments which are not in the laws of the Torah... This is the practice in all the holy congregations and no one has questioned its legality. »[53] The rabbi expresses here his complete approval of the broad jurisdiction of the guilds, which he supports by quoting the pertinent views of the Tosephta and Talmud.

Rabbi Adret's decision shows that the guilds enjoyed an autonomous status within the kehillah or community, much to the concern perhaps of some other elements. It may be noted that in Poland and Lithuania the situation was very similar. Moreover, Christian guilds likewise were autonomous bodies within the municipalities. To be sure, it took time before the guilds acquired this status. The Christian guilds bitterly fought

[51] Baer, *Toledoth*, etc. vol. I, p. 286.
[52] Bergman, Yehuda, *Ha Tzedakah be Israel Toldothea u Mosdoteha,* Jerusalem, 1944, pp. 73, 74 and 154.
[53] Quoted by Neuman, *op. cit.*, vol. I, p. 183.

the tutelage of the town councils ruled by the patriciate, whereas the Jewish guilds fought the interference of the Kahal, which of course never possessed the vast powers of the Christian town councils. Being responsible to the Crown for the collection of Jewish taxes, the Kahal in Eastern Europe had to keep an eye on the guilds and watch their earnings. It may be noted that in Poland, in the 16th and 17th centuries, the Kahal had frequently taken the initiative in establishing guilds. In the course of time, however, the antagonism grew and the struggle of the guilds with the Kahals became intense, particularly in the 19th century. [54]

Bohemia and Moravia in the Early Modern Period

The 16th century was marked by momentous shifts in the occupational structure of the Jewries of Eastern Europe. Commercial and moneylending pursuits did not provide a sufficiently broad economic basis for the growing Jewish populations in Bohemia, Moravia and Poland, and there emerged in the 16th century a Jewish artisanship in these countries. [55] According to Z. Winter, an authority on Czech economic history, « in the 16th century in Prague there were to be found Jewish masters in a number of crafts... Jews were also penetrating into trades in the province. In the city of Nachod there were Jewish glaziers, basket-makers, bridle-makers and cutlers. » [56] In 1509, Jewish swordmakers are recorded in Prague. [57] The numerous references to tailors and butchers in the archival

---

[54] See my article « Remeslenniki, » in *Evreiskaia Enciklopedia*, St. Petersburg, vol. XIII.

[55] See my article « Evrei-remeslenniki i cechovaya organizacya ich, » (Jewish Artisans and Their Guild Organization) in *Istoria Evreiskago Naroda*, Moscow, 1914, vol. XI, pp. 286-7. For Bohemia, see Winter, Z., *Dějiny Řemesel a Obchodu v Cechách v XIV a XV stoleti*, Prague, 1906, p. 410.

[56] Winter, *Řemeslnictvo a živnosti XVI veku v Cechách* (1526-1620), Prague, 1909, p. 13.

[57] Winter, *Dějiny*, etc. p. 410.

files of that period are less surprising as Bohemian Jews were already working in these trades in the Middle Ages, though almost exclusively for Jewish customers. However, in the period under consideration, Jewish tailors and butchers attempted to secure a clientel among non-Jews despite stern opposition from the Gentile tailors' and butchers' guilds. In addition, Jews began to practice a great number of other trades. One may mention here gold- and silversmiths, some of whom found favor with Emperor Rudolf II (1576-1612), as well as musical instrument makers, furriers, pewterers, embroiderers in silk and pearls, glove makers, upholsterers, cartwrights, dice-makers and shoemakers. [58]

The Christian guilds waged war against Jewish artisans and non-organized labor in general. The grievances which the Prague guilds submitted to the authorities usually concerned the allegedly inferior quality of Jewish work and the employment of Christian journeymen. The Jewish masters were called intruders and « bunglers. » The struggle grew sharper as time went on, its target being in the 17th century the newly founded Jewish guilds. [59]

The best known Jewish guilds in Prague were those of the butchers, tailors, embroiderers, shoemakers and goldsmiths. [60] Southeast, in Moravia, we have tailors' guilds (Nikolsburg and Ungarisch-Brod). [61] These guilds were of course in a better position to defend Jewish labor and negotiate with the Christian guilds and town councils. The Jewish guilds

---

[58] See Jakobovits, Tobias, « Die jüdischen Zünfte in Prag, » in *Jahrbuch der Gesellschaft für Geschichte der Juden in der Čechoslovakischen Republik*, Prague, vol. VIII. (1936) pp. 47-145.

[59] *Ibid.*, pp. 72-3.

[60] *Ibid.*, pp. 74 ff. and 98 ff.

[61] The Czech names of these cities are Mikulov and Uhersky Brod. Heilig, B., « Die Vorläufer der mährischen Konfektionsindustrie, » in *Jahrbuch, etc.* vòl. III, (1931), pp. 307-448, and Bretholz, B., « Die Judengemeinde von Ungarisch-Brod etc., » in *Jahrbuch*, vol. IV, (1932), pp. 107-181.

were recognized by the government and by the lords of the cities and hamlets where Jews resided. [62] They possessed, as a rule, their own banner which used to be displayed during festivals and carried in processions on special occasions. [63] Some guilds had their emblems, such as the boot of the shoemakers and the axe of the butchers.

The guild statutes were drafted after the pattern of non-Jewish guilds and were sometimes imposed by the authorities. However, specifically Jewish needs were taken into consideration. The guild ordinances fixed the status of masters and journeymen, terms of apprenticeship, standards for products, size of output, and mode of election of the wardens. Membership dues and penalties were clearly defined. An important item was the protection of the members against interference from outside and unfair competition. The guild maintained various services which cared for the spiritual and physical welfare of its members. Sick care, provision for orphans and widows, religious education, belonged in the sphere of the guild.

The statutes of the Prague shoemakers' guild may be cited here as an illustration. It was forbidden to guild members to take away customers from each other, or to belittle one another's goods to customers. Guild members were prohibited from selling their products in more than one shop. Candidates for the rank of master had to testify before the guild wardens that they were natives of Prague. The document admitting to the rank of master had to be signed by all wardens. Bachelors could not become masters. An applicant had to declare his

[62] Heilig, *op. cit., passim.*

[63] Volavkova, Hana, *The Synagogue Treasures of Bohemia and Moravia*, Prague, 1949. On p. 23, there is a reproduction of a drawing representing the procession of the Jewish guilds of embroiderers and tailors, with their banners, in Prague, in 1741. On the processions of the Prague Jewish guilds, cf. Jakobovits, *op. cit.*, pp. 92 and 133.

intention actually to practice the trade. The fee for the conferring of mastership was three gulden, two for the wardens and one for the guild treasury. A newly married master was allowed to employ one journeyman in his shop but no apprentices. After the first year he was entitled to employ an apprentice, whom he was obliged to train. Work had to be stopped on Friday afternoon and on the eve of festivals, in summer at 3 P.M., in winter at 1 P.M. This rule applied to masters, journeymen and apprentices alike. Infractions were penalized. Most interesting is the provision according to which all shoemakers were required to attend on Saturdays a course in Jewish law given by a specially engaged scholar; absentees had to provide half a pound of candles for the school for poor children (*Armen-Kinder-Studier-Haus*). The guild wardens held office monthly, in turn, reporting on financial matters and guild policies to their successors. [64]

The tailors' guild of Ungarisch-Brod strictly forbade individuals to accept orders from the lord of the town or from the army unless all members were to benefit. Offenders against this rule were fined three gulden, half the amount to be paid to the city and half to the guild. It was up to the synagogue beadle to see to it that no outside tailor got customers in the city. The fine was as much as three Reichsthaler. [65]

Very similar regulations obtained in the Jewish guilds of the 17th and 18th centuries in Poland and Lithuania. [66]

---

[64] Jakobovits, who published the full text of the statutes in the German original, *op. cit.*, pp. 143-5, assumed that they were drafted in the 1730's.

[65] The Ungarisch-Brod statutes were published in the German original by Bretholz, *op. cit.*, pp. 161-2. No year is given, but they may be dated in the 17th century.

[66] See my essay « Die jüdische Zunftverfassung in Polen und Litauen im 17. und 18. Jahrhundert, » in *Vierteljahrschrift für Sozial- und Wirtschaftsgeschichte*, Stuttgart, 1928, pp. 433-451.

Concluding Remarks

In summing up, we may note that since ancient times Jewish society has shown a high regard for manual labor. Jewish spiritual leaders, many of whom earned their living by the work of their hands, defended the interests of artisans.

It has been found that what Thompson once termed « the medieval tendency toward association, » had its roots in remote antiquity; the original Jewish guilds, too, were associations of particular kinds of artisans.

The relations of non-Jewish labor with Jewish workmen took various forms. In Roman Egypt, though Jews joined pagan guilds, as a rule, they possessed their own craft guilds, which were not infrequently patterned after similar non-Jewish organizations. A non-Jewish influence on the structure and practices of Jewish guilds could already be noted in ancient Babylonia. The history of Jewish guilds in the medieval and early modern period offers many striking instances of outside influence. However, there were important features of the guilds which derived from Jewish law and custom.

A study of the evolution of the Jewish guild within the context of the general guild system is the subject of a book now being prepared by the writer. In these notes it was only possible to touch upon some aspects of the Jewish guild.

JEWISH ARTISANS AND GUILDS IN FORMER POLAND, 16th-18th CENTURIES

BY MOSES KREMER

Editor's Note: The publication of this manuscript, found in the recovered part of the Vilna Yivo Archives, expresses the sense of obligation felt by the editors toward its author, the martyred Jewish historian, Dr. Moses Kremer.

Moses Kremer was born in 1914 in the Galician city of Jaroslaw, the son of a well-to-do family of timber merchants. In the early 1930's, after graduation from the secondary school in his home city, he went to Warsaw, where he matriculated at the Institute for Jewish Studies and at the Division of Humanities of the University of Warsaw. Kremer completed the work for his master's degree under the direction of Professor Meyer Balaban in 1935. Two years later he received his doctorate at the University of Warsaw. His master's thesis was entitled "Jews in Przemysl at the End of the 17th and the Beginning of the 18th Centuries" (Polish, about 300 pages). This work was preserved in the archives of the University, and is now to be found in the collections of the Jewish Historical Institute in Poland.*

Dr. Moses Kremer's field of specialization was Jewish handicraft in Poland, which was the subject of his doctoral dissertation. Sections of the dissertation appeared in Hebrew as "A Study of Handicrafts and Artisans' Guilds among the Jews of Poland in the 15th-18th Centuries," *Zion* (Jerusalem, 1937) p. 294-325. In this study the author presents a synthetic survey of the central problems of handicraft among Jews in former Poland. Other sections were published in Yididsh in "Jewish Artisans in the Christian Guilds in Former Poland," *Bleter far geshikhte*, vol. ii (Warsaw, 1938) p. 3-22.

The present article is the third fragment of Moses Kremer's work to appear in print. These three articles, however, constitute but a part of a study of great scope. In his introduction to the *Zion* article, Dr. Kremer wrote that he considered it "as an introduction to a far more extensive work, covering the following topics: 1. The dynamic aspects—the conditions of development of Jewish handicrafts in the struggle against the municipal guilds; 2. The structural aspects—the role of handicrafts in Jewish life in general and the question of organization of Jewish artisans in

*Biuletyn Żydowskiego Instytutu Historycznego w Warszawie, 9-10, p. 20.

Reprinted from *YIVO Annual of Jewish Social Science,*
Vol. XI, 1956-1957.

particular; and 3. An attempt at a statistical analysis of the significance of Jewish handicrafts in Poland."

Clearly, Dr. Kremer was engaged in the creation of a grand, synthetic work encompassing all aspects of the history of Jewish handicrafts in Poland. To the great loss of Jewish-Polish historiography, this significant achievement, already complete in manuscript, suffered the fate of its author. All that remains of this work, the fruits of years of intensive research, is found in the three fragments: the aforementioned two published articles, and the present paper. In addition to a thorough utilization of the comprehensive general and Jewish literature on the subject of handicraft in Poland, Dr. Kremer also used as source material 13 minute-books of Jewish artisan guilds, the greatest part of which is no longer extant, and a vast number of original documents located in many central and local archives in Poland.

Thanks to his general and Jewish scholarship, and his training in scientific methodology, Dr. Kremer was well-qualified to become the historian of Jewish crafts in Poland. Young and industrious, much could be expected from this scholar. Fate, however, decreed otherwise. In 1937 Moses Kremer settled in Palestine. In the summer of 1939, he and his wife, Teophila Mahler of Cracow (she, too, was a graduate of the Institute for Jewish Studies and of the University of Warsaw) returned to Poland on a visit to his parents. Before they could leave the country, the war engulfed them. For some time (presumably 1939-1942) they lived in Lvov. The manner and time of their death is not known.

The study which Dr. Kremer submitted to Yivo in Vilna consisted of an introduction and four chapters. Unfortunately, the first chapter, on apprentices, was not recovered (except the notes). Hence the present article contains the introduction and the chapters Journeymen; Non-Jewish Journeymen in Jewish Shops; Journeymen's Associations.

INTRODUCTION

There is no synthetic work on the economic history of the Jews in former Poland in general or on the history of Jewish handicrafts there in particular. Various studies, specially monographs on communities and guilds,[1] contain important data and sometimes even entire chapters on the subject. Polish historiography, too, lacks a synthetic work in this field.[2]

[1] We have in mind primarily the well-known monographs on the history of the Jews in Poland, such as the studies of Friedman on the Jews in Lodz, of Wurm on the Jews in Brody, of Sosis and Margolis on the Jews in Russia, and others. The monographs on the various cities published recently are referred to in the appropriate footnotes.

[2] The popular work of Rutkowski, *Zarys gospodarczy dziejów Polski*, 1923, is essentially a textbook. It was recently republished in two volumes under the title *Historia gospodarcza Polski*, Poznań, 1950.

The same may be said of Szelęgowski, *Rozwój ekonomiczny i społeczny w*

The studies of Jewish handicraft and guilds may be divided in two groups: 1. unpublished dissertations, occasionally containing unknown archival materials, but at times based entirely on published materials:[3] 2. published but little known materials, mainly excerpts of minute-books of artisans' guilds.[4]

The common shortcoming of practically all works in the second group is their failure to take into consideration important data found in the minute-books, stressing only the statutes. The latter do not always constitute the most important part of the minute-books. As a rule they are repeated year after year in these sources and reflect but poorly the development of handicraft and the true internal conditions of the artisans' guilds. It is precisely from the scattered data in the minute-books that we can learn about the workshop production, the tendencies in the guilds, their influence in the Jewish and general Polish economy and the like. Needless to say that caution must be exercised in the use of these data, taking into consideration authorship and the degree of dependence of the guild in question upon the Jewish community administration. Due regard must also be paid to those data that shed light on the mode of life and to the artisan folklore.

The second significant shortcoming of these studies is their lack of a broad basis of analysis—many phenomena can be understood only in the light of a thorough acquaintance with the problems of the general guilds in the cities. In the general literature on the Polish economy, particularly among the monographs on the cities and guilds, written in recent years, there are several very important and basic studies.[5] But even these do not contain a synthetic study,

---

Polsce. The most important works of recent years are devoted to individual problems such as Rybarski, R., *Handel Poznania* (1930); Koczy, *Handel i polityka handlowa* (1928-1929); Tarnowski, *Działalność gospodarcza Jana Zamojskiego* (1935).

A number of significant dissertations appeared in *Roczniki dla dziejów społeczno-gospodarczych* (18 volumes).

[3] Detailed bibliographical notes may be found in the studies of Mark Wischnitzer on the Jewish guilds in Poland. Perla Kramer published a study in *Miesięcznik Żydowski*, Sept.-Oct., 1932, utilizing the minute-book of the Bilgoraj artisans' guild. Bella Mandelsberg wrote about Lublin and Rebecca Notik, about Lithuania. Several studies on the 19th century appeared. These were written by P. Kon, Rombach and Hendel (further details may be found in my article in *Zion*, II, 3-4, 5697).

[4] In addition to the generally known studies, there appeared in recent years E. Ringelblum's work on the tailors' guild in Plock, Heilperin's on Luboml, Bialystok and Tykoczyn, the statute of the guild in Czortkow and others.

[5] Some of them will be mentioned later on.

determining the influences at work on the city guilds in various parts of Poland. The rich literature on the city guilds in Europe advances certain general theories about the rise of the guilds, compulsory guild membership of artisans, guild autonomy and others that have to be applied also to the Jewish guilds. On the other hand it must be borne in mind that the rise of the Jewish guilds and their development in the 17th and 18th centuries was something of an anomaly in general economic history. Many a historian of economic development, particularly Sombart, would have formulated his view of the structure of Jewry differently had he been acquainted with the constitution of Polish Jewry in former years and the activities of the Jewish guilds.

If there are lacunae and gaps in the study of Jewish handicrafts and guilds, it can be safely stated that we know practically nothing with regard to journeymen and apprentices in Jewish workshops. In this article we wish to shed light on this problem to the extent of the availability of materials.

The chronological limits of our study coincide with the end of the 18th and the beginning of the 19th centuries. Concurrently with the general political changes in the country there also occurred modifications in the state of Jewish handicraft, in the production and in the organization of the guilds in the three parts of Poland. Most of the facts under consideration in our study apply to the 17th and 18th centuries, and in the first instance to the callings that were most widespread among Jews and organized in guilds, that is tailors, jewelers, butchers, barbers, bakers and the like.

This work is constructed in the following order: first we discuss the apprentices, then the journeymen and their course from the moment they entered the workshop to the time they became master workmen and we conclude with the problem of Jewish apprentices' associations, touching but briefly on the subject of non-Jewish journeymen in Jewish workshops and vice versa. For technical reasons we omitted two important chapters: 1. the problem of Jewish journeymen regulated on the basis of agreements between the city guilds and Jewish artisans, on which there is quite interesting archival material; 2. an attempt at a statistic of Jewish journeymen in the 18th century.

The most important source is the minute-books, both those that have been published and those that we use for the first time. In the case of published material we merely refer to the source. In the case of unpublished materials we deem it necessary to cite the passage that bears on the subject. We cite thereby the outstanding examples and precise details only in those instances where they have general significance and lead to unequivocal conclusions. Wherever possible only the text is cited without interpretations.

Undoubtedly there are many gaps in the picture. It must be borne in mind that the minute-books deal essentially only with the master workman and his interests. But it is patent that the influences affecting the Jewish guilds in general also affected the journeymen. Also regional differences must be taken into consideration, particularly those between Crown Poland, Lithuania and White Russia.

To complete the picture we adduce some data from the guild in Piatra Neamt, Romania. The data on the journeymen in Bohemia and Moravia (Prague and Nikolsburg) are included in the chapter about the agreements with the city guilds.

We have not utilized the responsa and moralistic literature of the 18th century as well as the not inconsiderable folkloristic material. We admit that this constitutes one of the shortcomings of our study—although it is quite conceivable that these sources would not have yielded much information.

Journeymen

The minute-books of the Jewish artisans' guilds contain more information on journeymen[6] than on apprentices. The status of the journeymen demanded a precise definition of their rights and obligations. Nevertheless, here too as well as in the entire complex of problems of Jewish handicraft and guilds in Poland there are many questions to which there are no answers. At its best only conjectures may be ventured on the basis of conditions in contemporary non-Jewish guilds.

The transition from apprentice to journeyman was apparently effected without any particular formalities. Upon the completion of the specified term of apprenticeship the apprentice became a journey-

---

[6] In the materials utilized by us they are referred to as *poel, tovarish, gezel.* The designation *tovarish* occurs not only in the guilds of Lithuania and White Russia (e.g. Keidan), but even in Kurnik, in Western Poland.

In the city guilds they are called *Geselle, czeladnik, robieniec, towarzysz, socius, Knecht.* Occasionally, according to their occupation, e.g. *krawczyk* (little tailor), *stolarczyk* (little carpenter).

man. He was not always at liberty, however, to choose his own master workman. His former master had priority to his services. There is no indication of a special ceremony upon passing from one category to the other, as was the custom in the city guilds. It is possible that the new journeyman had to give a dinner and was called up to the Torah reading at the Sabbath services in the conventicle of the guild. It is certain, however, that on this occasion as well as at the time of the transition to master workman the custom of the city guilds of conferring a ridiculous nickname on the candidate, which usually stuck for the rest of his life, was utterly unknown among the Jews.[7]

As a rule anyone who had completed his apprenticeship could submit his indentures and become a journeyman. There were guilds, however, whose wardens or a special committee of master workmen had the right to reject the candidate journeyman as detrimental to the prestige of the guild.[8]

As in the case of the apprentices, not every master workman had the right to employ a journeyman. Moreover, even in those guilds in which the master workman had the right to employ an apprentice immediately following his admission, he generally had no right to engage a journeyman. In some guilds the master workman obtained this right after his marriage or one year after his admission to the guild. In some instances he had to wait as many as ten years,[9] although as a rule the period was only three years.[10] This was in con-

---

[7] This was known as *cognomen in propina* (drinking name), in Polish, *przeszynek, przemianek, otrzęsiny.* Although the statutes prohibited vulgar nicknames, we find such names as *pierdziwól* (wind breaker), *mokrowstal* (wetpants), *moczygęba* (guzzler), cf. Ptaśnik, P., *Miasta i mieszczaństwo w dawnej Polsce,* 1934, p. 142.

In the 18th century this practice was little known.

[8] Statutes of Keidan: "For instance, that it is not in keeping with the dignity of the guild" (Wischnitzer, M., in *Bleter far yidisher demografye, statistik un ekonomik,* no. 5).

[9] According to the Keidan statutes, § 47.

[10] On the Luboml guild, see Heilperin, L., in *Yediot haarkhiyon vehamuzeon shel tenuat haavoda,* ii, 1935; on Czortkow, *Yubileum-bukh fun 40yoriker eksistents funem tshortkever shapiro-fareyn in nyu-york* (Czortkow statutes, § 17); on Plock, Ringelblum, E., "Pinkes fun der khevre khayotim in plotsk," *Ekonomishe shriftn,* ii, 1930; on Lissa, Lewin, L., *Geschichte der Juden in Lissa.* The Kurnik statutes of 1754 state: "One full year after his marriage he may employ a journeyman . . . prior to that he may not employ a journeyman, but he may take in an apprentice to teach him the tailor's trade . . ." Similarly the Drohobycz statutes (1801, § 1) read: "And he is strictly forbidden to employ a journeyman, and even after his marriage he shall not employ a journeyman." The Sokolow statutes state: "Also the hatmakers are not permitted to employ a journeyman within that

sonance with the general system of gradually obtaining full membership rights. Here, too, exceptions were made for sons and relatives of old members and upon payment of a given sum for this privilege, when the guild was in financial straits. The master workman could temporarily forfeit the right to employ a journeyman for failure to live up to one of the regulations of the guild or for lack of professional competence.[11]

Practically all Jewish guilds had regulations limiting the number of journeymen in one establishment to one, two and rarely three.[12] In some guilds the number depended upon the taxes and other payments that the master workman paid to the Jewish community and the guild.[13] Occasionally guild members of long standing and guild wardens had the right to employ a larger number of journeymen and apprentices in compensation for the time devoted to guild affairs.[14]

Indentures. Practically all statutes insisted that indentures must be concluded in the presence of guild authorities (the wardens and

time, immediately after their marriage . . ." (1731, § 8). A later regulation of Sokolow reads: "Tailors are strictly forbidden from employing a journeyman up to three years after their marriage . . . but because of the difficult times we have come to modify this restriction in such manner as to permit them the employment of a journeyman on condition that they pay annually 10 zlotys to the trustee of the guild for a period of three years [after their marriage]. Thereafter they are exempt from such payments" (p. 9).

[11] According to the statutes of the mixed guild in Kutno, § 14.

[12] In Płock (§ 5) and Keidan (§ 45) only one journeyman was permitted. Similarly in Przemysl (Schorr, M., *Żydzi w Przemyślu do końca XVIII w.*, 1903, Mat. X).

In the busy season, the Kutno guild permitted the employment of a second journeyman, a married man. In the furriers guild of Lvov the wardens complained that the foreman gave permission to some master workmen to employ two journeymen. In Czortkow the employment of two journeymen was permitted (statutes of 1732, § 7).

[13] In Przemysl the master workmen paying high taxes were permitted to employ three journeymen (Schorr, *op. cit.*, Mat. X, 1714). In Lutsk the master workmen paying 150 zlotys annually in taxes were entitled to employ two journeymen. Those paying higher taxes, three journeymen (§ 21). Normally this was the maximum number of journeymen employed.

[14] Practically all city guilds extended this privilege to the guild wardens until the Commission on Good Order (*bonis ordinis*) put a stop to it. In the city guilds the regulations governing the number of journeymen to be employed were more lenient. As a rule a master workman had two journeymen and one or two apprentices, cf. Rodkiewiczówna, *Cech introligatorów w Wilnie*, 1929, p. 35.

Some Warsaw guilds permitted the employment of five and even eight apprentices, cf. Wojciechowska, *Cech krawiecki Starej Warszawy w XVIII w.*, 1931, p. 80.

In the 16th century several Cracow guilds had no restrictions whatsoever on the number of employees, see Stesłowicz, "Cechy krakowskie w okresie powstania i wzrostu," *Kwartalnik historyczny*, 1892, p. 325.

the guild rabbi or a special "committee of eight"[15]) and entered in the minute-book. Occasionally they specified that all stipulations be fully enumerated in the indentures to avoid ambiguities and ultimate conflicts.[16] There were instances where the indentures were signed also by an outside witness,[17] and in case of a conflict between the master workman and a journeyman, the guild was guided by the stipulations in the indentures as recorded in the minute-book.[18] A contract concluded outside the framework of the guild was invalid. Thus the guilds attempted to control the shops, the wages of the journeymen and the like. There was generally a fee for entering the indentures in the minute-book (which went to the guild rabbi), paid either by the master workman or the journeyman.[19] Occasionally concessions were made or limitations imposed. Concessions were generally made for sons and sons-in-law of members. On the whole, however, they had fewer privileges than their colleagues in the city guilds (the so-called *mastki, masełki*). There are few regulations extant granting privileges to this group of journeymen. Theory and practice, however, did not coincide in this respect. The privileges they enjoyed were mainly with reference to their term of service and guild fees. Nor were they included in the number of employees limited by regulation.[20] In the Kurnik guild instances were recorded where only the oldest son of the master workman enjoyed these privileges. The others were ordinary journeymen.[21]

Limitations were generally imposed on non-resident journeymen.

[15] The statutes of Keidan, § 23; Lissa, § 20. The Drohobycz statutes repeat several times that the employer is not permitted "to keep an employee without indentures signed in the presence of the guild rabbi . . . violations will be punishable with a fine of half a thaler for the synagogue and half a thaler for the guild rabbi.

[16] The statutes of Lutsk, § 20; the statutes of the mixed guild in Kutno, § 22; for the Posen guilds see Feilchenfeld, W., "Eine Innungsordenung für die jüdischen Handwerker zu Posen," *Zeitschrift der historischen Gesellschaft für die Provinz Posen*, 1895, X (§ 29).

[17] Feilchenfeld, *op. cit.*, § 29.

[18] The statutes of Lutsk, § 27; Krasinski, "Mipinkse lutsk," *Measef* I, 1902.

[19] In the Posen guilds the fee was 15 groshn for the guild preacher (§ 13); in Kurnik it was generally five groshn for the scribe; in Kutno it was a copper groshn (§ 29). The Jaroslaw minute-book reads: "If an apprentice wants to learn tailoring or wants to become a journeyman for a master tailor, he has to be registered in our book. The fee for such registration shall be no more than four Polish zlotys (§ 14). In the city guilds the registration fee at the end of the 18th century was fixed by the Commission on Good Order at two groshn (Morawski, *Monografia Wrocławka*, 1933, p. 138).

[20] The statutes of Keidan, § 18.

[21] The minute-book of Kurnik, fo. 56, 1789.

They were forbidden by regulation to take up work so long as there were local journeymen without employment. Their stay in one community was limited to three years.[22] In some places this was even further restricted to two years and their masters had to pay a specified sum to the guild.[23]

The above regulations derive from two neighboring cities (Lissa and Posen) and no general conclusion may be drawn from them. Nevertheless a certain degree of xenophobia in most guilds cannot be denied. On the other hand there were instances where non-resident journeymen were employed under more favorable terms than the local ones, notably in Kurnik, which had a number of regulations against non-resident journeymen.[24] It may be assumed that these were traveling journeymen, although no regulation of a Jewish guild speaks of a compulsory traveling period, as was the case in the city guilds, where a traveling period was one of the most important requisites for becoming a master workman, particularly in the 16th and 17th centuries. There are indications, however, that the custom— not the requirement—prevailed in many places.[25] It is difficult to determine whether these travels were motivated by a desire to acquire specialized training in various cities, the lack of work in a given place or the difference in wages. It seems that the Jewish guilds generally assumed a negative attitude to the non-resident journeymen. They had to fulfill all the obligations imposed upon them by the regulations under penalty of expulsion from the city. It is quite conceivable that in this respect the interests of the master workmen clashed with those of the rest of the community. It was to the advantage of the master workmen to have a large number of journeymen in the city, affording a better selection. This fact undoubtedly had its effect on wages. The community, on the other

---

[22] Feilchenfeld, *op. cit.*, § 10.

[23] In Lissa, both the out-of-town journeyman and his employer paid two florins to the guild (Lewin, *op. cit.*, § 19).

[24] In the years 1770-85, the Kurnik guild had many journeymen from Swarzedz, Kobylin, Posen, Krotoszyn and other towns and townships.

[25] Thus we find in a decree to the Jewish guild in Berdichev, of 1732, which ordered the wandering tailor and furrier journeymen to register in the guild (Archiv Yugo-Zapadnoi Rosii).

The Jewish tailors' guild in Lvov complained to the office of the under-voyevoda about the wandering journeymen who upon arrival in town failed to register in the guild and in addition worked for non-Jewish employers in contravention of the regulations. See Pazdro, *Organizacja i praktyka żydowskich sądów podwojewodzińskich*, 1903, Mat. 15, 1765.

hand, representing some of its members who wanted their sons to become journeymen, had to see to it that non-residents should not flood the town and jeopardize the opportunities of local aspirants to these jobs. These were the arguments advanced by the representative of the owner of Lissa. In a regulation of 1786 the Kurnik community chided the wardens for employing non-resident journeymen to the detriment of the guild as a whole. Mention should be made here of the fact that compulsory traveling was gradually abolished in the city guilds beginning with the 18th century. Moreover, some guilds were altogether opposed to compulsory traveling.[26]

The rights and obligations of the master workman in respect to the journeyman were those of an employer. Occasionally, special rights were granted him, such as the privilege of ceding the journeyman, with his consent, to another master.[27] (In some guilds this practice was forbidden.[28]) In the minute-book of Kurnik are recorded several indentures permitting the master workman to discharge the journeyman at the end of six months.[29] The journeyman could also be employed outside the shop, working in the villages and helping in the sale of the finished goods, to the extent that this was permitted in the regulations.[30] In addition to the wage stipulated in the indentures, the master workman occasionally had to provide the journeyman with board and lodging. Some indentures specify decent clothing and laundry.[31] In most guilds the master workman had to pay a specified sum for each journeyman he employed.[32] This

---

[26] Pęckowski, *Dzieje m. Rzeszowa do końca XVIII w.*, 1913, p. 255.

[27] The statutes of Keidan, § 7.

[28] The Przemysl guild, Schorr, *op. cit.*, Mat. xv, 1729.

[29] Minute-book of Kurnik, mainly for the years 1770-1785.

[30] Cf. notes 67, 68, 69 and others.

[31] Cf. Wetstein, "Kadmoniyot mipinksaot yeshanim," *Ozar hasafrut*, IV, 1892, p. 636, a contract with a hatmaker for the year 1721.

[32] In Tyszowce the payment was six groshn a week. "Journeymen working for master workmen have to pay six groshn a week to the guild treasury. This sum must be paid in by the employer. Journeymen working privately have to pay the amount fixed by the guild . . ." (Statutes, § 26, pp. 16a, 63a). The decisions of the Jaroslaw guild (end of the 18th cent.) on this question read: "A journeyman employed by a master workman must also pay two kreuzer a week . . ." "Every one has obligated himself to pay eight kreuzer in Viennese currency monthly for himself and 10 kreuzer in Viennese currency for each journeyman . . . The tailors have flourished . . . with regard to the new enactment, which the journeymen have confirmed by their signature, that every journeyman working for a master workman is obligated to pay two kreuzer a week or eight kreuzer a month to the collector of this fund, without delay, it has been resolved that in case of failure to pay on the part of the journeyman his master is obligated to pay for him month after month and the journeyman will be fined the fine of him who separates from the

payment did not exempt the journeyman from his own fees to the guild.

The journeyman was in duty bound to work diligently and honestly. Some indentures specify the minimum daily production of the journeyman.[33] He was not allowed to take on outside work. Normally, he was not permitted to leave his master prior to the expiration of his term, particularly before the holidays. The insistence upon exclusive work for the master occasionally went to such extent that the journeyman had to promise not to help his father, an artisan, upon coming home in the evening.[34] In several guilds, in addition to board and lodging the journeyman was also entitled to tips. For various important reasons he could leave his master before the expiration of his term. In such a case, however, he had to submit his reasons to the guild administration and abide by its decision.[35] Besides, there were all sorts of individual stipulations. An out-of-town journeyman, for example, stipulated that he should be free for several days to visit the graves of his parents.[36] There was also a category of journeymen that were employed on a "partnership" basis and received one-half or one-third of the profits from certain types of work.[37]

---

community . . . In witness thereof the journeymen have affixed their signatures . . ."

In another regulation from about the same period we read: ". . . According to the statutes of the founding of the guild, as explained in paragraph 16, every journeyman employed by a master workman must pay two kreuzer a week. Otherwise the master must pay this sum for him. The master has the right to deduct this sum from the weekly wage of the journeyman" (regulation of 1824).

The mixed guild of Kutno had a regulation requiring the master to pay four szelag a week and the journeyman—two (§30).

The Sokolow minute-book (1770, p. 9) reads: ". . . We have come to add to the former regulations . . . that each master workman may employ a journeyman only on condition that he pay into the hands of the trustee of the guild ten zlotys per year . . . for a period of three years, according to the regulation . . ."

[33] In a contract with a Cracow hatmaker (1723) the journeyman is required to produce three hats a day, and on Friday—two (Wetstein, *op. cit.*, p. 629).

[34] *Ibid.*, p. 323, a contract with a buttonmaker in 1654.

[35] The Kurnik statutes read: ". . . And if the journeyman has any claims on his employer he must present them to the officers and wardens of the tailors' guild . . ." (§6, p. 8a).

In the minute-book of Tyszowce there is a resolution to protect the rights of the journeyman: "At the time of the election it was unanimosuly resolved that the wardens and the trustee shall bring all pressure to bear on an employer who fails to pay the journeyman's wages . . . Similarly, the employer must pay the fees due to the guild . . ." (1720, p. 7a).

[36] The Kurnik statutes read: ". . . He is obligated to permit the journeyman to visit the graves of his parents eight days after the Feast of Pentecost." (p. 38). The journeyman in question came from Kobylin).

[37] The Płock statutes, §7; statutes of the Cracow barbers' guild of 1640 (Wetstein, *op. cit.*, p. 604).

The journeymen did not participate in the administration or official life of the guild. It is possible that they were permitted to be present at the elections, but had no vote. In general, the term "journeymen's rights" was interpreted to mean membership in the guild without political or professional rights. Occasionally a master workman would be penalized for some "infraction." He would then be deprived temporarily of his previous rights and given journeymen's rights.[38]

The minute-books contain regulations governing initiation fees of journeymen. These fees were determined by their wages. If the journeyman was paid per piece, the fee was a certain percentage of his earnings, generally from one to three groshn per zloty (30 groshn).[39] Otherwise, he made weekly, monthly or annual payments. Some guilds had a fixed fee, similar to that of the master workmen. In others the guild administration determined individually the size of the fees. In some guilds the journeymen's fees had to be paid by their employers.

The minimum period of indentures was an important measure in the attempts to eliminate or at least to reduce the inner conflicts among the master workmen in the guild. Practically all guilds prohibited the employment of journeymen for a short period or for piecework. In some guilds the minimum period was three months or the

---

[38] The minute-book of Luboml records a case of a master workman who competed unfairly with his fellow. His punishment was ". . . suspension from the guild for a period of two years, during which time he was reduced to the status of a journeyman." (p. 7; end of the 18th century).

[39] The Kurnik statutes prescribe: "The journeyman has to pay to the guild one groshn for every zloty earned" (§6, p. 8a).

The minute-book of Czortkow records the payment of one groshn per zloty (regulations of 1732, §8). Later on the payment was raised to two groshn (regulations of 1791, §19); in Keidan—3 groshn (§23). In Luboml a journeyman had to pay annually two zlotys (Heilperin, *op. cit.*, regulations of 1720, §10). In Miedzyrzec—2 zlotys (". . . a journeyman gainfully employed by a master workman for a period of one year must pay into the guild treasury one zloty on every *Hol hamoed* [twice a year]. These dues must be withheld by the employer. If the employer paid out the wage in full and the journeyman fails to pay his dues, these shall be collected from the employer" (§20).

In Lissa the payment was half a groshn weekly (§9), on the Jaroslaw guild see n. 32.

There are data indicating that journeymen, like their masters, had to pay Jewish communal taxes according to their earnings. A regulation governing the payment of the meat-tax in Minsk, in 1750, states: "The journeymen have to contribute two groshn from every zloty earned . . . young men earning up to 20 zlotys a year are exempt from these contributions; those earning over 20 zlotys have to contribute. Maidservants are exempt from payment, regardless of earning . . ." (Levitats, "Der pinkes fun dubner kohol," *Historishe shriftn,* Yivo, II, p. 100).

work season;[40] in others, half a year and in still others at least a year.[41] Under exceptional circumstances even a long-term contract could be invalidated by either of the parties.[42] The regulations generally provide severe penalties for employing a journeyman for a day, a week or even a month, let alone for piecework.[43] There were also exceptions. The Lutsk guild permitted the employment for a short period of master workmen who had to work as journeymen for others.[44] In Drohobycz, on the other hand, the ban on short-term employment applied only to orders of Jewish customers and not to those of the gentry.[45] There were also isolated cases where the master was given special permission to employ a journeyman for the pre-holiday period only, on condition that he dismiss him soon thereafter.[46]

There is no mention in the literature of any definite period of journeymanship. The indentures speak generally of a term of from one to two years. After this period the journeyman could apply for permission to become a master workman, having also fulfilled all the other requisites. He also had the privilege of journeymen on the

[40] In the Lutsk guild (§21), Czortkow (Regulations, 1721, §21), Przemysl Schorr, *op. cit.*, Mat. XVIII, 1843); in the minute-book of Kurnik there are many contracts reading "for the summer season."

[41] For at least half a year: in Lissa (§6), Plock (§27); for a minimum of a year: in Jaroslaw. (We cite here the regulation of 1796 in full because it also touches upon other details that we discuss: ". . . Today we met with the consent of the trustees and we resolved to erect a fence in defense of the guild—and whoso breaketh through a fence, a serpent shall bite him—namely that no employer shall engage a journeyman by the piece under the penalty of excommunication, for therefrom arise controversies to the great detriment of the association. A journeyman must be engaged for a whole year. If the master workman has engaged a journeyman, he cannot engage another one without the consent of the wardens . . .") The minute-book of Drohobycz reads: ". . . No tailor shall employ a journeyman by the week, but engage him for a year by means of a contract signed in the presence of the rabbi . . ." (Regulations of 1801, §2).

[42] Minute-book of Kurnik, pp. 51-55.

[43] In the Czortkow regulations the prohibition is formulated exactly as in the Jaroslaw regulations: "A tailor shall not employ a journeyman by the day, week or month, but for at least a quarter. Similarly, he is forbidden to employ a journeyman for piecework" (regulations of 1781, §7). The same holds true in the Przemysl guild (Schorr, *op. cit.*, Mat. X and XVIII).

[44] The Lutsk statutes, §21.

[45] The minute-book of Drohobycz reads: "The regulation prohibiting employment of a journeyman by the week governs only those working on orders for Jews. Those working on orders for the gentry may engage a journeyman by the week, but must pay the guild dues" (regulation of 1801, §6).

[46] In the Przemysl guild a master workman received permission in an exceptional case to employ a journeyman for a period of six weeks only prior to the holidays. "Thereafter he is no exception, and cannot be employed for a period of less than three months . . ." (Schorr, *op. cit.*, Mat. XVIII).

eve of marriage, namely to do piecework or daywork[47] for a period
of four weeks or more. (Marriage was frequently the most important factor in gaining the status of master workman.)

We have no information on the length of the working day of
the journeyman. In one of the Cracow indentures of the second half
of the 17th century the journeyman's working day was defined thus:
wintertime the whole day and five hours after sunset, and summertime—to the time of the return of the residents from the city to the
Jewish residential district (Kazimierz). He was also obligated to
work overtime in case of need, but for this work he had to be paid
extra. On Friday he worked only till 2 o'clock in the afternoon in
the wintertime and till four o'clock summertime. He could sleep
home.[48]

Apparently there were no significant differences in conditions
between the Jewish and the city guilds. In the latter the working
day was 15 to 17 hours, beginning 5 o'clock in the morning summertime and 6 o'clock wintertime. It ended at 9 o'clock in the evening.
On Saturdays work stopped at 5 o'clock in the afternoon.[49] There
were, however, significant differences between the various occupations. In addition, the Jewish journeymen were exempt from work
on those days in which the masters were not allowed to work, such
as the eve of a holiday, Hol Hamoed (the four intermediate days
of Passover and the Feast of Tabernacles), occasionally the forenoon of the New Moon, Saturday night and similar half-holidays.

It is quite conceivable that also the Jewish journeymen made
their own "rest days" very much like their non-Jewish colleagues
had their "blue Monday," which was bitterly fought by the guilds.[50]

[47] Cf. the Posen guild (Feilchenfeld, p. 8); Jaroslaw statutes, §10; the Kurnik minute-book reads: ". . . A journeyman may engage in tailoring for himself
only four weeks before his wedding, either in our community or in the surrounding villages. And he is obliged to come to the guild and purchase right of residence . . ." (statute of 1764, p. 8a). The same enactment is also found in the
statutes of the Gniezno guild (Posen Archive, Generalia A VIII, §2).

[48] Cf. Wetstein, op. cit., p. 623.

[49] Groszkowski, Monografia cechu mosiężników i browarników m. Warszawy,
1922, p. 20; Bogusławska, Historia cechu szmuklerzy w XVII-XVIII w., w Warszawie, 1929, p. 26; Pazdro, Uczniowie i towarzysze cechów krakowskich w połowie
XV—połowy XVII w., 1900.
In the Cracow city guilds journeymen received on the average five groshn a
day and maintenance. See Piekosinski, Prawa, przywileje i statuty m. Krakowa, p.
1302.

[50] The penalty was prohibition of work for a week or more (cf. Morawski,
op. cit., p. 149; Ptaśnik, op. cit., p. 141 ff.).
Similar conditions obtained in many Western European guilds, particularly in

The custom of going to bathe may have prevailed in the Jewish guilds as in those of the non-Jews.[51]

Wages. In this instance, too, there were differences between the various guilds. Generally wages were paid once a year, twice a year, quarterly or weekly.[52] The individual differences in wages were considerable. In the 17th and in the beginning of the 18th centuries wages in the Cracow guilds fluctuated between 17 and 40 zlotys a year. Occasionally there was a weekly supplement of six groshn (which amounted to 10 zlotys a year). There are also on record wages of 70 zlotys a year, that is 42 groshn a week.[53] At about the same time the Lutsk guild fixed wages at 40 zlotys a year.[54] In the second half of the 18th century wages in Kurnik range between 18 and 50 zlotys, averaging from 20 to 30 zlotys a year.[55] In Lissa the journeymen were paid by the piece—15 groshn.[56] There was extra pay for overtime, and occasionally the journeymen were paid "for hooks and buttons."[57] Although there are no data in the minute-

---

Germany. Cf. Otto, Eduard, *Das deutsche Handwerk in seiner kulturgeschichtlichen Entwicklung,* Leipzig, 1900, p. 88; Schantz, Georg, *Zur Geschichte der deutschen Gesellenverbände aus der Zeit des 14-17 Jahrhunderts,* Leipzig, 1877.

[51] Herbst, *Toruńskie cechy rzemieślnicze,* p. 49.
Particular attention was paid to washing the head. In the city guild of Lowicz washing was compulsory every day (Arch. gł. akt dawnych, ks. sk. oddz. 91).
In Cracow the journeymen had to bathe every two weeks (Pazdro, *Uczniowie . . .*).

[52] The journeymen in the Kurnik guild were paid annually. Similarly in Cracow (Wetstein, *op. cit.,* pp. 623 and 629). In Lutsk they were paid quarterly (§27). In Lissa—by the piece (§17). Both here and in the city guilds the term "weekly wage" meant a rate of the annual wage and not weekly payments.

[53] Wetstein, *op. cit.,* pp. 623 ff.

[54] The statutes of the Lutsk guild, §28. Margolis, in his *Geshikhte fun yidn in rusland,* Vol. I, 1930 (Mat. 100, p. 374) cites from the Lutsk minute-book of 1736-37 an indenture of a journeyman furrier, who was paid 28 zlotys for half a year and maintenance. If his employer wanted to retain him for the second half of the year he had to pay 33 zlotys. The employer, however, had priority on his services.

[55] The wages were apparently the same as in the city guilds, or even higher. As stated in n. 49, wages in the Cracow city guild were five groshn a day, which amounts to 26 zlotys half a year. In the indenture cited in n. 54 the Jewish journeyman was paid 28 and 33 zlotys. In the 17th and 18th centuries the journeymen in the Rzeszow city guilds received on the average 24 zlotys a year and maintenance (Pęckowski, *op. cit.,* p. 253); in the Wloclawek city guilds the journeymen received in addition to maintenance and laundry one grosh a week and two groshn for repairing old things. (Morawski, *op. cit.,* p. 147).

[56] Lewin, *op. cit.,* §17.

[57] ". . . And the journeyman has the right to sell laces, hooks and buttons . . . Laces, hooks and buttons belong to the journeyman" (Minute-book of Kurnik).

books on tips, there is no doubt that this practice also took root in Jewish life. On the whole, in the 18th century wages ranged between 20 and 50 zlotys a year. It must be borne in mind, however, that there were differences between occupations, personal qualifications and undoubtedly there also must have been regional differences. In the minute-books there are indications that there were some highly qualified journeymen, whom the masters attempted to lure by promises of higher wages. This led to conflicts in the guilds. To obviate such conflicts some guilds fixed maximum wages for journeymen and penalized "overpayment." The guilds demanded that all the sums paid out to the journeymen be entered in the minute-book.[58] We have previously mentioned partnerships between journeymen and master workmen. It is quite possible that certain trades, say barbers, worked on a percentage system of earnings.[59] Very characteristic are several indentures drawn up between fathers and sons, in which the son was paid a fixed salary.[60]

Other aspects, such as board, lodging, clothing and laundry, were also stipulated in the indentures. Occasionally the journeymen received full maintenance.[61]

Another important question: Did the system of free choice of journeymen and masters prevail in the Jewish guilds? Did the guild assign journeymen to the master workmen or group the latter in a certain order and accordingly assign journeymen to them? On the basis of the many regulations it is almost certain that in contrast to the city-guilds a system of free or practically free choice prevailed in the Jewish guilds.[62]

[58] Lutsk minute-book §28.

[59] This was the practice in the city guilds, where the journeyman received 50% of the earnings in mid-week and 10% on Sunday, cf. Orlamowski, *Dzieje pszemyskich cechów rzemieślniczych w dawnej Polsce*, 1931, p. 38.
In other guilds the employer and the journeymen were partners to certain earnings. Cf. Giedroyć, *Ustawy cechów cyrulskich w dawnej Polsce*, 1897, p. 7.

[60] The minute-book of Kurnik reads: ". . . A journeyman employed by his father is not permitted to work for himself, but must work for his father both in the villages and in the townships. Neither is he permitted to engage in brokerage. The journeyman must pay half a zloty to the guild weekly . . ." (§58, 1790).

[61] In contrast to many city guilds, where the journeymen worked without maintenance and dined in the "journeymen's commons" (Piekosinski, *op. cit.*, p. 1302). In the city guilds the journeymen were paid only for the first day of a holiday (Pazdro, *Uczniowie* . . .).

[62] In some city guilds, in which there was a scarcity in journeymen, particularly wandering journeymen, the problem was regulated thus: the master workmen who were looking for journeymen were listed on a board and assigned journeymen in the order of their application (Groszkowski, *op. cit.*, p. 22).

Prohibition of Private Work. Such prohibition was stressed in practically all regulations. The journeymen could work only for their masters. The guild regulations were formulated in such a way that they confined the work of the journeyman to his master's shop. The large number of resolutions on this subject indicates the gravity of this problem in guild life. The main argument against separate work on the part of the journeyman—as well as against all "botchers," that is people who did not qualify for membership in the guild, in general—was the deprivation of the livelihood of the masters, who paid taxes to the community and dues to the guild. Thus one regulation states:

> . . . These are the young journeymen who work privately and thus deprive the master workmen, who have dependents and bear the burden of various taxations, of their livelihood. These young journeymen are a stumblingblock to all classes and groups in our community.[63]

Similarly another source complains:

> . . . This has reference to the cries and groans of some of the artisans, men with dependents, who are destitute and penniless and out of work because of the journeymen who usurp their places. These journeymen work for lower wages thereby degrading the craft, and causing the poor masters to be swollen from starvation. Therefore we strictly forbid the journeymen to engage in any manner of private work before their marriage, even to the stitching of one stitch. They must take employment with one of the masters of the guild . . .[64]

The prohibition extended to every type of work, regardless of quantity or whether the order was placed by "Poles" or "Jews." It was binding out of town as well as in town, within the jurisdiction of the guild.[65] The guilds fought bitterly the out-of-town journey-

---

[63] The statutes of Lutsk, §5.

[64] Przemysl, Schorr, *op. cit.,* x, p. 268. Similarly the minute-book of Tyszowce states: ". . . As explained in paragraph 26, that the journeymen who work privately must make weekly payments according to the decision of the guild . . . but now we have come to the realization that this leads to a jeopardy of our livelihood therefore we have resolved unanimously to forbid all journeymen to work before their marriage. To confirm this resolution we have affixed our signatures . . ." (regulation of 1816, §60a). In the same manner is formulated the prohibition in the Posen guilds (Feilchenfeld, §7) and in several others.

[65] In the minute-book of Kurnik there is a regulation of 1784 that reads: "Although we have recently warned that we cannot exist unless [all fulfill] all the regulations of the journeymen tailors recorded in this minute-book in the most effective manner, nevertheless these regulations are ignored and there is no hour without its evil and no minute without its calamity. Therefore we have unanimously adopted the following resolution: If any journeyman tailor works privately

men who took private work without qualifying for membership in the guild. They were even forbidden to work at the fairs that were held in distant places, so long as they were unmarried and had not joined the guild.[66] The prohibition included commercial transactions on behalf of the master and brokerage.[67] Some guilds went so far as to forbid the master to utilize the journeyman in any manner whatsoever outside the workshop in order to obviate all possibility of unfair competition between masters. Others forbad the masters to send their journeymen to the villages and estates to solicit orders for them.[68] A few guilds allowed the journeyman to remain in the village to finish the work left uncompleted by his master.[69] Generally, only a guild member of long standing had the right to take a journeyman along with him to the village.[70] Exceptions were made

---

in the villages of our district or another district, he must pay every week 24 groshn to the guild up to four weeks before his marriage. No journeyman in our community is allowed to take up private work, but in conjunction with a master workman. And if a journeyman is caught working privately either in the villages or in the townships he shall be fined five marks for the synagogue and five for the authorities . . . Today there came to us the journeyman . . . and took upon himself all the above conditions, barring none . . ." (1784, p. 46a).

The minute-book of Jaroslaw contains several such regulations. One, of the 19th century, a pledge on the part of the journeymen, reads: "We, the association of journeymen tailors, have obligated ourselves under severe penalty to refrain . . . from private tailoring even to the extent of one stitch . . . but all work must be done for the master workman, who is a member of the guild. In case a journeyman will fail to comply with this resolution and will work at tailoring privately . . . then the guild masters have a right to deal with him as they please, that is to confiscate his garments for the benefit of the guild, or impose a monetary fine upon him. We have also fully authorized the guild masters to exert all kinds of pressure upon a recalcitrant journeyman, in case of litigation . . ." (1832).

The Gniezno statutes subjected to the same limitations also out-of-town journeymen (§3). Similarly the Luboml guild (Heilperin, *op. cit.,* regulations of 1757, §2, ". . . to do work . . . either for a non-Jew or a Jew . . .").

[66] Wetstein, *op. cit.,* p. 619, about a dispute with a Lithuanian fur dyer in Cracow in 1650.

[67] Wetstein, F. W., *Dvarim atikim,* 1900, p. 7, about journeymen butchers.

[68] In the Płock statutes, §20; the Sokolow minute-book states: "If a master has a great deal of work . . . he cannot employ a journeyman off the street, that is one who has no master, but must engage an artisan or journeyman employed by a master workman who is a guild member. Also this regulation was unanimously accepted: The tailors may go to the villages with their journeymen, apprentices, or sons. The journeyman is not permitted to go to the villages by himself. A tailor may go to the villages in partnership with another tailor" (Statutes, § 9); the Drohobycz guild ruled that ". . . the journeymen may not go to work in the villages unless in the company of their masters. Violators of this regulation may be enjoined from pursuing their work at the discretion of the master tailors . . ." (1801, §3).

[69] Płock statutes, §20.

[70] The Sokolow statutes read: "A tailor may take his journeyman with him to the village only three years after his marriage . . ." (§8).

for masters who made a special payment to the guild. There are also regulations unconditionally forbidding the master to take a journeyman along with him to the village, fairs or markets.[71] Occasionally, the journeyman stipulated in the indentures that he could not be compelled to go to the fairs.[72] Some regulations even forbad the journeyman to accept an order from a customer in the name of his master.[73] As a rule these prohibitions were aimed at the sons of the masters, even when they worked for their fathers.[74] Sanctions were in the form of monetary fines, confiscation of goods, or in case of a repeated offense—expulsion from the city.[75] Journeymen on the eve of marriage, that is several weeks before their wedding, were exempt from these prohibitions.[76] In addition, the journeymen were subject to all the prohibitions that applied to the master workmen, such as the regulations governing internal competition, unfairly taking away customers, and the like.[77]

The regulations governing these matters, as recorded in the minute-books, are as strict as those of the city guilds, sometimes even stricter.[78] The reasons for this phenomenon must be sought in the general structure of the Jewish guilds and in their processes of development. Many regulations deal with the prohibition to take away journeymen from their masters. This is forbidden both "by means

---

[71] Kutno guild (§20). The Przemysl guild decreed that "a master worker is absolutely forbidden to give garments to his journeyman for peddling in the market or in the streets . . ." (Schorr, *op. cit.*, Mat. vi, 1690). Similarly the Kurnik guild declared: "No apprentice, journeyman tailor or wife of a master tailor has a right to go on market day to the market . . ." (p. 14a). In those guilds in which the master workmen were not allowed to work for Polish customers the journeyman was likewise forbidden to work for them, e.g. the Luboml guild, which stated explicitly: ". . . Master tailors who do Polish work are not allowed to work for Jewish customers. Similarly, one may not employ a journeyman to work for Polish customers, even if he works out of town at a distance of two miles from the city." (Heilperin, *op. cit.* regulations of 1757, §1).

[72] Wetstein, "Kadmoniyot . . .," p. 629.

[73] The Czortkow statutes read: ". . . The journeyman is not allowed to go in the name of the master to accept new work. The master workman must go there himself . . ." (statutes of 1781, §7).

[74] Kurnik minute-book, p. 58.

[75] Schorr, *op. cit.*, Mat. VI, ". . . To take away that garment from the journeyman and give it to the poor . . ." In the Posen guild the fine for the first offense was 10 thaler and for the second offense banishment from the city (§7).

[76] Cf. n. 47.

[77] Cf. Pazdro, *Organizacja . . .*, Mat. 45, where the assistant voyevoda issued regulations governing competition in the barbers' guild, which were also obligatory upon the wives, children and journeymen of the master workmen.

[78] Strictly forbidden was working without guild permission after work hours and working for a tip.

of words or by means of money."[79] To obviate such possibilities, some guilds fixed maximal wages for journeymen.[80] A master exceeding this maximum was subject to a monetary fine and had to discharge the journeyman involved.[81] At any rate, the Jewish guilds combatted this evil no less vigorously than the city guilds.[82]

Only the guild or one of its duly constituted bodies had the right to arbitrate conflicts between master and journeyman. In Posen such conflicts were under the jurisdiction of the guild rabbi and four wardens. In cases involving a sum not exceeding 10 zlotys and the penalty was no higher than 10 ducats the decision of the guild was final. In other cases each of the sides had the right to appeal to the city administration.[83]

One of the statutes stated that so long as the guild court had not settled a given dispute the journeyman was deprived of his rights and could not work for another master without the consent of the wardens.[84] Occasionally a decision of the guild defended the rights of the journeymen and threatened sanctions against the masters for failing to pay the journeymen their wages.[85] There were also complaints of masters accusing the journeymen of theft, assault on the master or his wife, and similar offenses.[86] No general conclusion, however, can be drawn from these few data, since the minute-books generally

[79] Statutes of the Cracow barbers, Wetstein, "Kadmoniyot . . .," p. 604. Similarly the Jaroslaw statutes read: ". . . No member of one guild may induce a journeyman to leave his master—particularly during the season may no member take away another member's journeyman . . ." (§8). Also the Miedzyrzec statutes declare: "No master may induce his colleague's journeyman to come to work for him. Even if the journeyman left his employer on his own account, another master workman may not employ him during the period of his indenture." (§17).

[80] Lutsk statutes, §28.

[81] The Kutno guild provided a fine of six grzywnias for inducing a journeyman to leave his master (§24). In the Lvov Jewish guild there was a case of a goldsmith who sued a colleague for taking away his journeyman unfairly. The defendant was fined 50 zlotys and was forced to discharge the journeyman (Pazdro, *Organizacja* . . ., Mat. 57).

[82] In the city guilds the fine for this was generally 16 or 32 pounds of wax, cf. Veigt, *Cech grzebieniarzy*, p. 15.

[83] Feilchenfeld, *op. cit.*, §3.

[84] Plock statutes, §36; Kurnik statutes, §6; the Sokolow minute-book reads: "In case a journeyman or an apprentice was engaged for a period of a year or more, and in the course of that period a conflict arose between the employer and the employee and the latter wanted to quit his employer, no other member of the guild is permitted to engage that employee without the consent of the wardens of the guild . . ." (regulations of 1757, §3, p. 11a).

[85] In the Tyszowce statutes, p. 7a, quoted in n. 35.

[86] Pazdro, *Organizacja* . . ., pp. 66 and 121. In one instance the journeyman was punished by imprisonment, flogging and pillory.

record only the grievances of the master. Significant are the entries about journeymen leaving their masters before the expiration of their term.

The journeyman could quit his master at the end of the stipulated term or illegally, through measures adopted by one of the sides.

Practically all statutes state that the disaffected had the right to present their grievances before the guild tribunal. If their grievances were deemed justified, they were permitted to quit their master and take on work elsewhere.[87] If their grievances were deemed unfounded, they were compelled to return to their master under threat of sanctions. One of the statutes specified the penalty as banishment from the city.[88] Even in those instances where they were permitted to remain in the city they were denied the privilege of work over a given period, even without pay. One decision permits a journeyman to take work with another master, after he had been refused by his former master as a result of a dispute.[89] On the whole, the journeyman was forgiven his offense against the master if he repented and went back to work within the year.[90] Some guilds required the journeyman to give four weeks notice of quitting.[91] In case of quitting before the specified term, the journeyman was deprived of his rights, generally for a period of one month, in which he was not permitted to work.[92] Masters employing such a journeyman had to pay a heavy monetary fine. To obviate the excuse of ignorance of the circumstances under which the journeyman had quit his former master,

[87] Wetstein, "Kadmoniyot . . .," p. 629.

[88] The minute-book of Kurnik states: ". . . Then he cannot work for another tailor in our community and his employer does not have to pay him anything for the time that he had worked for him . . ." (statutes §6, p. 13a). The Tyszowce statutes read: ". . . It is strictly forbidden to employ a journeyman who left his employer. If said journeyman after leaving his master has been elsewhere for a whole year he may be employed" (§31, p. 60). Similar enactments are found in other statutes and regulations.

[89] Kurnik minute-book of 1778, p. 38a, although the decision of the community was "that the journeyman Zechariah . . . of Grudziadz has no right to take up paid or gratuitous employment in our community, any master tailor employing him will be fined 10 mark for the court and 10 mark for the guild . . ."

[90] The Drohobycz statutes declare: "A journeyman who left his master must not be employed by any other tailor. This enactment is calculated to compel him to return to his master" (§8). The Kutno statutes imposed a fine of four grzywnias on a master workman who employed a journeyman prior to the completion of his term with his former employer (§23).

[91] The Czortkow statutes of 1781 read: "If a journeyman wants to quit his master he has to give him four weeks notice . . ." (§8).

[92] The Czortkow statutes read: ". . . At any rate he must be deprived of employment for a period of four weeks" (§21).

some guilds required the approval of the latter prior to the signing of the new indentures.[93] Another statute required the master's consultation with the former master prior to engaging a new journeyman.[94] Generally, however, a certificate from the former master was deemed sufficient.

The problem of wages for the journeyman quitting before the expiration of his term was solved variously in different guilds. According to the regulations in the Kurnik minute-book, the master need not pay him anything.[95] In some instances the matter was settled thus: If the master discharged him prior to the expiration of his term he had to pay him for the period of his work, if on the other hand the journeyman broke the contract he was paid only one-third or one-fourth of the wages that were due to him.[96] The conditions are clearly stipulated in the Plock tailors' guild:

> A master and a journeyman have entered into a contract and the journeyman has quit under pretext of being oppressed or subject to abuse by the master. If the pretext is substantiated, and the journeyman has quit summertime, the master has to pay him for the entire summer pro rata. If he has quit wintertime, he has to pay him for the number of weeks he worked double pro rata and the journeyman may take work with another master. (All this provided the master has continued to mistreat the journeyman despite court warnings.) But if the master claims that the journeyman does not discharge his duties faithfully or is guilty of any other delinquency and these claims are substantiated, the master pays him summertime for each week of work one-third pro rata and wintertime one-half pro rata. The journeyman in this case is not allowed to take on work with any master in our community for the entire duration of his former indentures. (All this provided he has been given proper warning.)

[93] The Kutno statutes, see n. 90.

The statutes of the Piatra Neamt (Romania) guild contain the following paragraph: "No member of the guild may engage a journeyman or apprentice until he has completed his year with his former employer. If anyone engages a journeyman without a release from his employer—although he has not directly induced him to leave—he will be fined 12 thaler for the guild and 60 zlotys for the chief of police. The journeyman cannot take employment with another employer under promise of higher wages, until two days after the completion of the year of his service. Failure to comply with this regulation will be punished" (§41).

[94] The Luboml minute-book reads: "...He may not engage a journeyman under contract with another employer till the employer and the employee have appeared before the guild and have submitted their grievances" (Heilperin, *op. cit.*, regulations of 1797).

[95] See above no. 69.

[96] A contract of the year 1788, p. 30.

When a contract terminated normally, the journeyman had the right to enter into a new contract with the same or another master, or begin work independently, provided he met all the requisites for this condition.

We do not know if there were two categories of journeymen in the Jewish guilds as was the case in the city guilds, which had ordinary journeymen (*robieńcy*) and specially qualified journeymen (*towarzysze*).[97] All we know is that there existed a category of journeymen who but a short while ago had been apprentices and another one the members of which had been active as journeymen for a number of years and therefore entitled to take steps to become masters. In the Polish text of the Kurnik minute-book a member of the latter group is referred to as *kawaler-młodzian*.[98] There might have been also other categories among the journeymen.

The minute-books contain no data on the private life of the journeymen nor regulations governing their morals. To begin with, the minute-books contain only materials about the master workmen and their organization. Data on journeymen are cited only insofar as they are related to the master. Secondly, the minute-books generally contain little information on the workaday life of the guild. It is significant that the minute-books do not contain regulations governing conduct, which abound to a large measure in the statutes of the city guilds.[99]

Some general regulations governing Jewish journeymen could be gleaned from trades that were not even organized in guilds. Cracow indentures of the first half of the 17th century forbad a journeyman printer to work privately in the city. He was not allowed to work for a Cracow printer even after he had quit his former

---

[97] Erecinski, Tadeusz, *Prawo przemysłowe Poznania w XVIII w.*, 1934; Chmielewski, *Cech ślusarski i puszkarski w Warszawie w XVIII w.*, 1927.

According to him *towarzysze* were those who passed a test and paid in a certain sum to the guild treasury.

There were journeymen called *cytownicy* (from the middle High German *zit*). According to Chmielewski (pp. 28 ff.) they had worked in the province for a number of years and then came to Warsaw for a brief period. According to Pazdro, these were journeymen that took up specialized training at their own expense.

[98] In the Polish translation of the statutes (§2, p. 6).

[99] Among others there are regulations against card and dice playing, sleeping in bed with shoes on or "other forms of uncleanness." Cf. Korotyński, *Z życia cechowego*, pp. 225-235.

Several monographs on the guilds discuss the regulations against sleeping with a fellow "with braids," consorting with women of ill repute and similar regulations.

master. He was also obligated to teach the trade—for a stipulated remuneration—to an apprentice in the printery.[100]

In some trades, for example among apothecaries, the journeyman who was occasionally brought from a foreign country was also bound to impart to his employer the secrets of the trade as practiced in the country of his origin.[101]

There are no exact data available on the age of the journeymen; generally they were unmarried.[102] Noteworthy are several details not mentioned in the minute-books that loomed larger in the regulations of the city guilds. It is quite possible that the same situation obtained in the Jewish guilds. Considerable attention was paid not only to the appearance of the master but also of the journeyman, particularly in the street or in guild quarters.[103] On the other hand, an attempt was made to distinguish between the master and the journeyman in the manner of dress. Non-Jewish journeymen, for instance, were not permitted to wear certain sashes or shoes. This led to considerable bickering. Such enactments were reflections of the sumptuary laws (leges sumptuaria) imposed by the nobility on the burghers and the Jews. They found expression also in the Regulations of the Province of Lithuania. Taking into consideration the well-known struggles between householders and artisans about the right to wear shtrayml, 'fur caps,' and similar attire[104] and that in

[100] Bałaban, M., Dzieje Żydów w Krakowie i na Kazimierzu, I, 1913, p. 431.

[101] Wetstein, "Kadmoniyot . . .," p. 624, a contract with a young man of Florence obligating him to teach his employer, an apothecary, all the secrets of alchemy.

[102] Many city guilds refused to admit married journeymen (cf. Herbst, op. cit., p. 28). They were called wozowcy, 'wagoners,' because they came with their wives and belongings loaded on wagons. See Chotkowski, Rzemiosła i cechy krakowskie XV w., p. 63.

[103] One city guild passed a resolution that a journeyman who came barefoot or improperly dressed to the butcher shop would be given as many lashes as there were steps between his house and the shop (Pęckowski, op. cit., p. 238); elsewhere he was fined for this half a groshn (Arch. Gł. Ks. Sk. Oddz. 91, ks. 25 (33), no. 8). Cf. also Bulinski, Sandomierz, that the journeyman is forbidden to go barefoot or without a strap. In the Kurnik minute-book: "Whereas there came before us Jonah, the journeyman, without upper garment, wearing only a waistcoat, which is improper, therefore, we, the heads of the community. with the consent of the majority of guild members, have imposed a fine of three zlotys upon said journeyman (resolution of 1814, on the last page of the minute-book).

To make it impossible for journeymen to steal material they were frequently compelled to wear coats and hats made of one piece (Chotkowski, op. cit., p. 74). In some guilds this applied to the master workmen and their wives in order to discourage them from the practice of appropriating remnants of the customer's cloth. See Warschauer, A., Die mittelalterische Gesellschaft für die Provinz Posen, p. 460.

[104] This is the famous conflict of Keidan in the 19th century, cited by Wischnitzer in his studies on the Jewish guilds in Poland. See also Historishe shriftn,

several places the guild masters were distinguished in their Sabbath wear from the non-guild members,[105] it may be safely assumed that the Jewish masters imposed restrictions on their journeymen similar to those of their non-Jewish colleagues. It is quite possible that smoking was forbidden during working hours and that there were other limitations similar to those of the city guilds.[106]

Some statutes of the city guilds granted the journeymen the right to quit their master if the latter committed a shameful deed, such as theft, or even if he killed a dog. At times the journeymen exploited this right to blackmail their masters, demanding *milczkowe* (hush money).[107] Such instances occurred mainly in the earlier period, up to the 18th century. It is quite possible that similar conditions may have obtained in the Jewish shops.

NON-JEWISH JOURNEYMEN IN JEWISH SHOPS

The problem of non-Jewish employees and particularly journeymen who worked for Jews was discussed at practically all synods, in the deliberations of the regional Sejms, and in the Sejm, and referred to in city ordinances, guild statutes and similar enactments.[108] These discussions were motivated both by religious and economic reasons.[109] We shall confine ourselves solely to the problem as it affected non-Jewish journeymen in Jewish guilds.

The city guilds assumed a negative attitude toward all forms of co-operation with the "disturbers," hence also toward non-Jewish

---

Yivo, Vol. II, p. 590, and the jubilee volume of the Keidan *landsmanshaft* in Brooklyn (1930), p. 38.

[105] Perla Kramer, *op. cit.*, p. 27, tells that the masters of the Bilgoraj guild forbad non-members to come to the synagogue on the Sabbath in a summer garment (*letnik*), which could be worn only by guild masters.

In one of the Posen city guilds a conflict between masters and journeymen raged for years over the right of the latter to wear a strap of the same width as that of the masters. See Zalecki, August, *Cech krawiecki*, p. 22.

In Cracow, on the other hand, the journeymen were not permitted to wear shoes, but wooden-soled sandals. See Daszyńska-Golińska, *Miasta i cechy w dawnej Polsce,* 1906, p. 88.

[106] Cf. Pęckowski, *op. cit.,* p. 255.

[107] Cf. Orłamowski, *op. cit.,* p. 39.

[108] Gumplowicz, *Prawodawstwo polskie względem Żydów,* 1864 (on the resolution of the Kalisz synod of 1420, §8); *Volumina Legum,* V (resolution of 1690, §15); Kraszewski, Józef Ignacy, *Wilno,* 1840, p. 172 (decree of the Vilna City Council of 1767 and others).

[109] Thus a decree of 1665 issued by King Jan Kazimierz to the Vilna voyevoda prohibited Jews under the threat of heavy fines from employing non-Jewish journeymen. The decree referred to earlier decrees and enactments pointing out that the Jews deprived the non-Jews of their livelihood. See Codex diplomaticus Vilnaensis, Bibl. Ord. Krasinskich.

journeymen who worked for Jewish masters, and imposed heavy fines upon them. Whereas non-Jewish journeymen who worked for non-guild masters could later on under certain conditions be admitted to the guild, those who worked for Jews were as a rule permanently barred from it.[110]

The decrees and regulations were of little avail. The struggle between the Jewish artisans and the non-Jewish guilds continued. Occasionally these limitations were also imposed on other national groups, such as the Tatars in Lithuania.[111]

The problem continued to be raised in all the complaints of the guilds to the review commissions up to the end of the 18th century and even beyond this period. Its importance for the development of Jewish handicraft is patent in the emphasis in many complaints of the fact that these non-Jewish journeymen taught Jews new handicrafts.[112]

Occasionally an agreement would be reached in this respect, as indicated by the well-known pact between the Jewish and city guilds in Grodno. According to this pact, Jewish masters were permitted to employ non-Jewish apprentices and journeymen who were registered in the city guilds and paid dues. The apprentices were subsequently certified and given the same rights as those trained by non-Jewish masters.[113] In those places where Jewish artisans were admitted to the city guilds there was no prohibition against the employment of non-Jewish artisans and journeymen by Jewish masters.[114]

---

[110] See Erecinski, *op. cit.*, p. 199.

[111] Akty Vilenskoi Arkheograficheskoi Komissii, VII, 160, 11, 1712.

[112] Bałaban, M., *Żydzi lwowscy na przełomie 16go i 17go wieku*, Mat. 75, y. 1627.

The complaints are leveled mainly at the Jewish tailors who paid high wages to non-Jewish journeymen. See Slaski, *Cech złotniczy w Warszawie*; Bałaban, M., *Dzieje Żydów a Krakowie, i.*, pp. 311, 314, 325 sq.

The style of the complaints to the Complaint Commission is practically the same everywhere. The emphasis is on the harm to non-Jewish employers resulting from the employment of non-Jewish journeymen by Jewish employers, e.g. in the Przemysl furriers' guild, 1663-1864, see Arch. Gł. Akt Dawn, Lustr. ks. 50, p. 25; Arch. Skarb. Invent. P. I. p. 105.

In 1604 the furriers' guild in Cracow complained that in a raid on the Jewish section they found not only a considerable Jewish fur trade, but many non-Jewish journeymen working for Jewish masters. Similarly in the year 1688 (Arch. m. Krakowa, Dep. 549).

[113] Cf. Wischnitzer's article in: *Istoria evreiskogo naroda* XI, 1914; *Regesty i nadpisi*, 1385.

[114] Included herein are such cities as Zloczow, Zborow, Rzeszow, Wegrow and others. Cf. my article in *Zion*, II, no. 3-4, 1937, pp. 308 ff.

What tempted the non-Jewish journeyman to accept work with a Jewish master in spite of all the difficulties put in his way? In the first place the higher wages paid by Jewish masters to non-Jewish journeymen, a fact frequently protested by the guilds. Some non-Jewish journeymen and even master workmen tended altogether to ignore guild regulations. Others, such as children of peasants or of illegitimate birth, could not gain admittance to the guilds. Occasionally, non-Jewish journeymen simply could not find work with non-Jewish masters.[115]

The Jewish masters, on the other hand, employed non-Jewish journeymen for different reasons. There was a dearth of Jewish qualified journeymen, particularly in the 16th and 17th centuries. Some handicrafts were at that time practically or completely unknown to Jews. With the aid of the journeymen and non-guild masters they could acquire and become adept in these skills. Possibly, they also had non-Jewish customers and because of them had to employ non-Jewish journeymen. The non-Jewish journeymen working for Jewish masters were of course subject to the general regulations governing private work, unfair competition, and the like. But they were undoubtedly exempt from paying dues to the Jewish guild. On the whole, they had more freedom working for Jewish masters than for non-Jewish ones.

This much is almost certain. Later on, in the 18th century, when there was no lack of qualified Jewish journeymen and the necessity of learning a new skill from a non-Jewish journeyman declined, employment of non-Jewish journeymen and apprentices fell off sharply. At that time it came to be taken for granted that Jewish guilds would employ only Jewish journeymen, although only one minute-book has a special paragraph strictly forbidding the employment of non-Jewish journeymen.[116]

Far less frequent was the employment of Jewish journeymen by non-Jewish masters. In the few rare instances where Jewish journeymen were employed by non-Jewish masters, it was generally in such

[115] In the documents of the furriers' guild in Cracow there is a petition, dated 1604, of a group of non-Jewish furriers and journeymen for permission to take employment with Jews. Otherwise, they state, they face starvation.

[116] The minute-book of Drohobycz, statute of 1801: "No tailor shall employ a non-Jewish journeyman. Offenders are liable to a fine of 15 zlotys for the purchase of candles for the synagogue and 15 zlotys to the guild (§9). The Jewish guild was also otherwise engaged in a bitter struggle with the city guild.

trades in which the city guilds had no special skills.[117] There are also data indicating that the Jewish guilds had a negative attitude toward Jewish journeymen who worked for non-Jewish masters.[118] The statutes of many city guilds decree that a master employing a Jewish journeyman loses the right of work in his trade.[119]

JOURNEYMEN'S ASSOCIATIONS

Essentially this problem is no part of our subject, since we have confined this study to the end of the 18th century and the data on this subject are from the first half of the 19th century. But we have also utilized later data concerning other aspects of our study, primarily those in which a difference of several decades is of no great consequence. The lack of data on journeymen's associations in the 18th century is no proof that they were not in existence then.

There was a time in Europe when there was no distinct journeymen's class at all. The guilds of the feudal period had three classes: apprentice, journeyman and master workman. Each shop employed only two or three people. The term of employment was from three to seven years. To obviate "pirating" of journeymen on the part of the employers, maximum wages were fixed. The working day was from 14 to 16 hours. This was of no great significance to the journeyman so long as he knew that ultimately he too would become a master workman. When, however, the guilds began to restrict admittance and strove gradually altogether to deny admittance save to relatives of master workmen, there emerged a distinct journeymen's class. According to Ashley, England had a journeymen's class as far

---

[117] We hear of the indispensability of Jewish silversmiths in Lvov. See Charewiczowa, *Lwowskie organizacje zawodowe za czasów Polski przedrozbiorowej*, 1929, p. 27.

Similarly at the time of the expulsion of the Jews from Warsaw toward the end of the 18th century at the request of the city guild an exception was made for three silversmiths and five seal engravers who were the only ones of these callings. See Marcinkowski, *Cech jubilerów, złotników i grawerów w Warszawie* (Prace dyplomowe W.S.H. rkp. 379), 1929, p. 36; Zaleski, *Konfraternia kupiecka Starej Warszawy*, p. 74.

The glovers' guild in Torun brought in two Jewish embroiderers from Lissa, well known in their field (Herbst, *op. cit.*, p. 72). In addition there were such craftsmen as bookbinders, art workers, furriers and lacemakers.

[118] A complaint by the Jewish tailors' guild to the voyevoda against an out-of-town journeyman states that not only had he failed to register in the guild but had also taken employment with non-Jewish masters, which is contrary to the regulations.

[119] Pazdro, *Uczniowie* . . .; *Organizacja* . . . Mat. 55, 1765; Piekoszyński, *op. cit.*, Vol. VIII, XII, 1715, §8.

back as the 14th century. In the 15th and 16th centuries here were uprisings of journeymen practically all over Western Europe. They threatened to leave town if their demands were not granted (*dem meister den hammer legen*). A similar process took place at the time of the rise of the guilds. At first, the journeymen's associations had a purely religious-philanthropic character. In time, they began to voice economic demands. A sense of solidarity, similar to that which came into being among masters in certain trades, also developed among the journeymen. In their struggle with the guilds, the journeymen's associations aroused also the opposition of the municipal and government organs, particularly when the last began regulating guild affairs (17th and 18th centuries). The subsequent development, such as the rise of the home workers class and others belongs to the history of the labor movement.[120]

In Poland, where all economic developments were somewhat late, social conflicts also came late. Only in the 16th century began the "uprisings" and strikes. Journeymen's associations were organized whose function was the protection of the health of their members. They also served as a kind of burial association. In this instance the master workmen admitted the representatives of the journeymen to the guild administration.[121]

If we assume that the Jewish guilds were largely founded on the same principles as the city guilds and were to a certain extent influenced by them, the question arises: were there Jewish journeymen's associations? When did the relationship between master and journeyman crystallize as that of employer and employee, that is when did the "patriarchal" relationship end? The manifesto of the journeymen in the Sokolow association indicates that a relationship of employer and employee set in toward the end of the 18th century. Exclusive tendencies appeared in some Jewish guilds in the 18th century, but not to the same extent as in the city guilds. There are no data on "uprisings" of journeymen in the Jewish guilds of that period. It is quite conceivable that such incidents were deliberately omitted from the minute-books. On the other hand, it is also possible

---

[120] On the problem of associations of journeymen see Kulischer, *Allgemeine Wirtschaftsgeschichte*, II, pp. 146 ff.; *Handwörterbuch der Staatswissenschaft*, VI; Schantz, *Geschichte der deutschen Gesellenverbände*, 1896; Ashley, *Englische Wirtschaftsgeschichte*, 1896.

[121] Pazdro, *Uczniowie . . .*

On the conditions in the Polish journeymen associations see the aforementioned works of Erecinski, Orłamowski, Chotkowski, Ptaśnik, and others.

that in the Jewish guilds the opportunities of a journeymen's uprising were less because the journeyman could more easily become a master workman and perhaps his condition on the whole was better than that of his non-Jewish colleague. We must also take into consideration the fact that just as the Polish journeymen's associations were some two hundred years behind those of Western Europe, the Jewish associations were behind the Polish. Since most of the Jewish guilds had come into being in the 17th and 18th centuries, the Jewish journeymen's associations had their rise toward the end of the 18th and the beginning of the 19th centuries. Here the general character and the specific functions of the Jewish guild, the general conditions of Jewish life and similar factors were decisive. Nonetheless, the possibility of "uprisings" of Jewish journeymen in the 18th century cannot be excluded, hence the possibility of the existence of separate organizations is quite likely.

There are some data on Jewish journeymen's associations from the 19th century. Mention is made of a journeymen's association in the Bialystok minute-book, without further details.[122] The Minsk community minute-book contains an entry of 1841 stating that the journeymen having quarrelled with their masters wish to establish their own organization and synagogue. The community administration, however, undoubtedly under the inspiration of the master workmen's guild, strongly opposed this move and refused permission.[123] Only one minute-book of a journeymen's association has been found. It is that of the "Holy Association of Journeymen Tailors, known as Tailors of the Second Category,"[124] established in Jaroslaw in 1832. The first pages of the minute-book state:

> These are the words of the men that came to the Holy Association, recorded in this minute-book:

---

[122] See Heilperin, *Zion*, 1937, no. 1. The founding act makes mention of the fact that a journeymen's guild had been in existence before. There is also reference to a conflict between the master workmen and the journeymen on account of a Scroll of the Torah donated by the latter. The Scroll of the Torah was finally given back to them on condition that they should refrain from establishing a guild (*ibid.*, p. 84).

[123] Brafman, J. A., *Kniga kagala*, ii, p. 1046.

[124] The title-page reads: "Minute-book of the Holy Association of Journeymen tailors, known as tailors of the second category, the men that have recently come into the covenant of the Lord and have taken sweet counsel together to found an association like all the holy associations of Israel to gather on the Sabbaths and festivals and to read in the book of the Law of the Lord according to the regulations. In the year of which the chronogram is "Thou shalt gather the scattered" (1832).

We, holy association of journeymen tailors, known as tailors of
the second category, have organized recently into one band to fulfill the word of God and His teachings. For until now we have not
merited to bestir our hearts to return to God and to His holy teachings. But this is the day we looked for; we have found, we have
seen it—to do all that is upright and good in the eyes of God. We
assembled together and resolved to pursue the knowledge of God,
to read on the Sabbaths and festivals in the book of the Laws of
God distinctly and with the proper intonation at the time when
the Scrolls of the Law of the other holy associations in this city
are taken out [from the ark]. Now we have seen that we have not
fulfilled the obligation of reading in the Law of God, for the regulations require that every person be called up to the Torah at
least once a month, but this has been impossible because of the
large number of people, may the Lord increase them a thousand-
fold. And last year we saw that the Lord was displeased with the
House of Israel and His hand was upon us. Death came up into
our windows and a fire was kindled against Jacob. Anger went up
against Israel, the remnant of Israel was wholly consumed and the
upright were cut off [the cholera of 1832-33]. Therefore we said:
Let us search and try our ways, and return to the Lord. For if we
hold our peace . . . punishment, God forbid, will overtake us. And
wherefore are we to be kept back from the rest of our brethren the
sons of Israel, who are assembled together to hear the reading of
the Law of God? Therefore it has occurred to us to band together
in this holy association, for we have seen that the Lord delights in
us to preserve us alive, as it is at this day. We have done this so
that every one of us may be called up to the Torah at least once
a month. And because of the merit of the Torah that shields and
saves, may God save the remnant from all evil, may God deal kindly with us and no longer chastise us and gather. . . . Therefore we
present our supplication before the glory of Israel, the leaders of
the congregation, the dignitaries and princes of our community,
the leaders of this holy community together with the just court
of this community to endorse the establishment of this holy association with their signatures so as to constitute a corner-stone and
a peg in a sure place. . . . We also have taken upon ourselves to
contribute one half of the weekly collection to the fund for visiting the sick. Also all fines levied by the heads of the congregation
shall go to the same fund. And may God be with us that we grow
and prosper. Amen.

The minute-book contains no regulations. A few details may be
gathered from fragmentary notations. Also non-artisans figure in the
pages of the minute-book, but only as honorary members. There
are only a few regulations about payment of dues and becoming
conduct. Married journeymen were also included in the association.

Full membership status was only gained after participation in the annual elections.[125] Every member was obligated to participate in the study circles that met on Saturdays and sometimes also during the week. There is a note to the effect that some members withdrew from the association because they could not attend the study circle. Like in the master workmen's guild, the administration consisted of three to six wardens, representatives, auditors and others. For a certain period they maintained their own preacher. Several years later a split took place in the association. The property of the association was divided between the two groups. After that a reconciliation was effected and bothe groups obtained the right to conduct their services in the main synagogue on certain Sabbaths.

The association was established with the consent of the rabbi and the master workmen's guild. The agreement was entered in the minute-book of the master workmen thus:

Agreement of the Holy Association of the Tailors of the Second Category:

1. Every member is obligated to pay weekly dues as is the custom in other associations. The money in the treasury shall be divided thus: one half to the first association, the older, and the other half to the second association called journeymen.

2. Second, at each election there shall be elected two wardens from the first association. Their consent must be secured for the withdrawal of money from the treasury or for launching any enterprise.

3. Third, the money collected from the members of the association shall remain during the entire month in the hands of the monthly warden. Thereafter the warden must turn over the money to the trustee.

The above excerpts clearly indicate the fact that this was a journeymen's association. It is quite conceivable that behind the religious motives advanced by the organization were also economic-professional interests.

[125] The admission of a new member was generally recorded thus: ". . . There came before us . . . of his own free will to be like one of us with reference to religious matters, weekly dues, the reading of the Torah and all the needs of the association in being called upon to contribute to a worthy cause. He shall have a vote, God willing, on Hol Hamoed Passover 5592. Prior to his vote he shall deport himself according to the regulations—and meet all the obligations."

The minute-book of the journeymen's association was bound together with the minute-bok of the masters' guild. First comes the minute-book of the journeymen's association. The leaves of the minute-book are bound in disorderly fashion. The tailors' guild dates probably from 1738. In one place there is a German entry: "Buch der jüd. Schneider bei der Judgengemeinde in Jaroslau, verfolgt in Jahre 5498 nach Erschaffung der Welt."

THE RITUAL SILVER MADE BY MYER MYERS*

By Guido Schoenberger

Each discussion on works of art for ritual use has three main aspects: first, the strictly historical question of the time of origin of the master and workshop; secondly, the artistic aspect of form and style; and thirdly, the aspect of their ritualistic significance which may be merely practical, highly symbolic, or both.

All three aspects are, of course, intrinsically connected. Yet, in this paper on the ritual silver made by Myer Myers, we intend to concentrate mainly on the artistic aspect and the symbolic significance. This is all the more justified since we are looking forward to the publication of a monograph on the life and work of the New York silversmith, Myer Myers, by Mrs. Robert Rosenbaum of Philadelphia, in which all the historical questions will be discussed, and which will include a catalogue of his works. Furthermore, it is most fortunate that the exhibition in the Museum of Fine Arts of Boston, so beautifully and expertly arranged by Mrs. Kathryn Buhler, offered us an opportunity to study some of the pieces that Myer Myers made for the synagogues of this country.

It is quite unusual to find an eighteenth century Jewish silversmith except in Eastern Europe and Asia Minor or North Africa. In Western Europe, the Jews were normally excluded from the craftsmen's guilds and Christian masters worked for the Jewish communities. Yet, Myer Myers, who was born in New York in 1723, was a devoted and honored member of Congregation Shearith Israel, the Spanish-Portuguese Synagogue of New York. He became freeman of New York City in 1746, and served as President of New York's Gold and Silversmiths' Society for some time around the period of the Revolution and later in 1786. He died in New York in 1795.[1] One may assume that he did quite a number of Jewish ritual pieces. Nevertheless, only a few of them which can definitely

---

* Paper read at the Fifty-first Annual Meeting of the American Jewish Historical Society at the Boston Public Library, Boston, Massachusetts on February 14, 1953. (Dr. Schoenberger is associated with the Jewish Museum, New York, and with the Institute of Fine Arts, New York University.)

[1] David de Sola Pool, *Portraits Etched in Stone* (New York, 1952), pp. 280, 300. See also Caroline Cohen, *Records of the Myers Hays and Mordecai Families from 1707 to 1913* (Washington, s. a.). Francis Hill Bigelow, *Historic Silver of the Colonies* (New York, 1948), p. 427, figures 313–314.

Reprinted from *Publication of the American Jewish Historical Society*, Vol. XLIII, 1953.

be attributed to Myers are preserved; just a small number of silver ornaments for Torah scrolls, namely, five pairs of silver Torah head-pieces, or bells, or *rimonim*, as we call them. Besides, there is a circumcision shield and probe which was formerly owned by Moses Seixas and is now in the Collection of Captain N. Taylor Phillips at the American Jewish Historical Society.

It is an important fact that the text of the Torah Scroll was, and is, never allowed to be illustrated with any kind of representation or ornament. On the other hand, in order to emphasize the importance of the Torah Scroll, beautiful exterior Torah ornaments were permitted and developed in the course of time which served both practical and symbolical purposes. The Scroll is protected from the outside and at the same time decorated by a mantle, beneath which the two parts of the Scroll on the two rollers are kept together by an often beautifully embroidered band, the Torah-wrapper; a silver staff is provided with a hand at its end; this is the pointer or *yad* (hand) which is used to follow the lines when reading since the text is considered so sacred that it may not be touched by one's own hand. On top of the two wooden rollers are found a pair of silver head-pieces, which we mentioned above, and of which fortunately some made by Myer Myers are still preserved.

Before we discuss these, we would like to mention briefly what we know about the history and significance of this ornament. Most likely it originated not as a moveable ornament which can be taken off the upper wooden end of the rollers, but as an ornament of the wooden roller itself, carved, gilded, or covered by a fixed silver-gilt mount. We know this type from medieval book illustrations.[2] In silver, sometimes also carved in ivory, it is still found today in many cases.

Preference, however, is given to the moveable head-pieces. Figure 1 shows an example from Persia which is actually rather late eighteenth century (or even nineteenth) but preserves the simple spherical form which is found in many earlier examples. This and the chased floral decoration of body and shaft point to the original symbolism of these ornaments which we know first from a very distinguished twelfth century source, namely, from Maimonides who in the *Mishneh Torah* states: "Silver and golden *rimonim* made to beautify the scroll of the Torah." He goes on to say that they are sacred objects and that one is allowed to sell them only in order to

---

[2] See Maḥzor, Budapest, Akademie der Wissenschaften. King Solomon's throne to the left shows a Torah scroll in a niche with gilded spherical knobs on the upper end of the Torah rollers which apparently represent such a fixed metal mount.

buy a Torah-Scroll or a Pentateuch.[3] We mention this passage not only because it may account for the disappearance of many of the older head-pieces, but also because it proves clearly that Maimonides speaks of the removable form. The name *rimonim* means "pomegranates," and it is most clearly indicative of the symbolism of these ornaments. The pomegranate, because of its great number of seeds, is a widespread symbol of fruitfulness and occurs in the rich floral ornaments on the top of the two famous columns which stood, according to the description in *I Kings* 7:15–18, in front of the Temple of Solomon. In these columns is embedded, on the basis of a still older phallic symbolism, one of the most widespread Mesopotamian and Palestinian symbols, the "Tree of Life," which is in Judaism, and its very positive approach to life, of paramount importance. In our case this is borne out by the fact that the two rollers of the Torah are called *Eẓ Ḥayyim* which means the "Tree of Life." This name is of course *pars pro toto*, signifying actually that the Torah is the Tree of Life. Thus it is easy to understand that the two ornaments, the two *rimonim*, or pomegranates, are the fruits of the Tree of Life.

In addition to this line of symbolism comes another which explains why the great majority of *rimonim* have one or two rows of bells hanging down. There are several instances which link the garments and ornaments of the Torah with the garments of the High Priest as they are described in *Exodus* 28. One instance is that, according to *Exodus* 28:34, the lower seam of the High Priest's skirt was beset with an alternating sequence of pomegranates and golden bells:

> And it shall be upon Aaron when he ministers, and his sound shall be heard when he goes into the Holy Place before the Lord and when he comes out, lest he die.

Here the old basic protective significance of the bells is still expressed to chase away evil influences when the High Priest functions in the Holy Place. Transferred to the Torah ornaments, the bells of the *rimonim* indicate by their sound the solemn moment of the service when the Torah is taken out and put back into the Torah-Ark. One should assume that the form of these Persian *rimonim*, which in a general stylized way, spherical with florals and fruits ornament, recalls the form of the pomegranates, was used more or less exclusively everywhere. This also is the case in the Orient where the

---

[3] רמוני כסף וזהב וכיוצא בהן שעושין לספר תורה לנוי תשמישי קדושה הן ואסור להוציאן לחול
אלא אם כן מכר אותן לקנות בדמיהן ספר תורה או חומש. Maimonides, *Mishneh Torah*, Book II [*Sefer 'Ahabah*], *Hilkot Sefer Torah* 10:4. We wish to thank Dr. Franz Landsberger for this reference.

form was used throughout the centuries with many slight, but never basic, variations.

Yet, on the other hand, it is a fact that in Europe, at least since the later Middle Ages, another form developed, not on the basis of a fruit form, but on the basis of a tower form. Cecil Roth tells us about a pair of *rimonim* which are now in the treasury of the Cathedral of Palma de Mallorca. They are in the form of a tower. Roth thinks that they are from the fifteenth century, and that they might come from Camerota in Sicily where there once was a Jewish community which was despoiled in 1492.[4] A similar form apparently has survived and is found in the late sixteenth and the seventeenth centuries in Italy as well as in Holland, used by the Sephardic and Ashkenazic congregations. Figure 2 is a Dutch example of the seventeenth century owned by the Jewish Museum of New York, in the form of a four-tiered turret of hexagonal form with six open arches in which bells are hanging, surmounted by a crown at the very top. The general stylistic appearance rather resembles a baroque church tower, and it can be said that artistically these turrets are harmonious and solemn finials for the Torah Scroll. Yet, the significance of this form is not easy to explain specifically. One may quote the famous *Psalm* 18:3:

> The Lord is my rock and my fortress — In Him I take refuge; my shield and my horn of salvation, my "high tower."

This of course could be a noble explanation for these crowning ornaments on the Holy Scriptures; yet as far as we know, there is no written source which connects such a verse from the Psalms with these Torah ornaments.

There is also the possibility of an influence from another form of ornament surmounting the Torah Scroll: a single crown, namely, which is called the "crown of the Torah" and occurs also since the Middle Ages. Such a crown with outspoken architectural form is described in a source from Arles in France of the year 1439.[5] The influence of the single crown on the two head-pieces might also be seen in the crown-finials which these most frequently show.

---

[4] See also A. G. Grimwade, *Treasures of a London Temple* (London, 1951), p. 11. It is also mentioned by M. Narkiss in his book on the Hanukkah Lamp (Jerusalem, 1939). They are reproduced in Moïse Schwab "Rapport sur les Inscriptions hébraïques de l'Espagne," *Nouvelles Archives et Missions Scientifiques*, vol. XIV (1907), pp. 174, 176, and figure 22 in appendix.

[5] See Georges Stenne, *Collection de M. Strauss* (Paris, 1878), p. viii; Stephen S. Kayser, "A Polish Torah Crown," *Hebrew Union College Annual*, vol. XXIII, part II (Cincinnati, 1950–1951), p. 494.

FIG. 1

FIG. 2

FIG. 3

RIMONIM

FIG. 4a   FIG. 4b   FIG. 4c

FIG. 5   FIG. 6

RIMONIM

71

Fig. 8

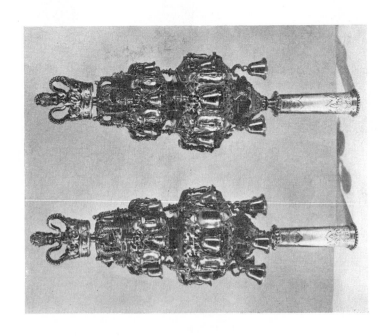

Fig. 7

FIG. 9

RIMON

73

It has to be mentioned that the floral, or fruit-ornaments, are not omitted in the turret form. They are used, and often abundantly, especially in Italy but also in Central Europe, as an enrichment of the basic architectural form [see Fig. 2]. This indicates that even in the West the *rimonim* (pomegranate) symbolism was never completely forgotten.

And it comes to life again vigorously in the eighteenth century if only in the general way of flower and fruit motives. If we turn to the works of Myer Myers, first showing a pair of his *rimonim* [Fig. 3] made *circa* 1770 for the new Synagogue at Newport (built in 1759), we see that the architectural form has disappeared. In 1769, new Torah Scrolls were presented to the Synagogue, and for these the bells were probably made. The build-up on slender cylindrical shafts in three tiers is the only feature still recalling the architectonic elevation. But these three tiers consist of three bulbous knobs connected by receding, rather slender, neck-pieces, the knob in the middle being the largest. The bells no longer hang in window-like openings but on S or C-shaped brackets attached to the knobs. On top is a well-proportioned crown with high staves and pineapple finials. The upper knob has a chased decoration of hanging leaves, the lower one an abstract ornament of a sling or arch motive. The center knob is delicately decorated with *ajouré* and chased work in a rich pattern of flowers and foliage. What is most interesting for us is the revival of the old "Tree of Life" iconography in a modified formal way.

Where does this come from? We can consider influences from Holland as well as from England. The ties of the American Sephardic congregations were especially strong with London. Fortunately the ritual silver of the Bevis Marks Synagogue of London, and other London synagogues has been well described by A. G. Grimwade and by Cecil Roth.[6]

A row of three single Torah head-pieces from the Bevis Marks Synagogue proves that around 1700 the turret form still prevailed [Fig. 4]. The furthest one on the left is an Amsterdam piece of 1696. The two right ones are not a pair, but one is of Amsterdam, 1692, and the other almost exactly copied by a London master in 1712.

But then the interesting change takes place: Master Gabriel Sleath of London in 1718 made a pair of head-pieces of which we see one [Fig. 5] in three-tiered form, each section pierced and chased

---

[6] A. G. Grimwade, see *supra*, note 4; Cecil Roth, "The Jewish Museum [of London]," *The Connoisseur* ([London] Sept., 1933), pp. 3 ff.

with panels of flowers and foliage, with scroll brackets for the bells, surmounted by a crown with foliage finials. We can acknowledge that this compares well with the Myer Myers *rimonim*. The difference is that the English master made the lowest knob the largest, the next two receding gradually. Thus the form is still somewhat nearer to the architectural tiers of the turrets, and, on the other hand, by piercing all three tiers in floral patterns, gives more emphasis to the pomegranate iconography proper. Around 1720, apparently, this change back to the old iconography took place in London where this form with slight variations became a standard pattern in the eighteenth century. The one which we see was originally made for the Sephardic Congregation at Barbados in the West Indies. Since Rabbi [Isidore S.] Meyer told us that the Jewish connections between Barbados and New York were very close, this is another way in which the new-old form might have come to the knowledge of an American silversmith by way of drawings or description. However, the actual source is London in any case.

It is difficult to say how the change came to pass. It surely cannot be explained by mere stylistic reasons. The tower-form could have been developed just as well in the eighteenth century style, and in fact sometimes was. But this is a deliberate change in iconography, surely not invented by the Christian master, but most probably done according to the wishes of the Jewish customers, primarily the Sephardic Congregation of London. If one compares a pair of head-pieces [Fig. 6] made in Persia in the eighteenth century, in three open tiers, but also pierced in floral patterns, one may ask if the change came perhaps through influences from the Sephardic Congregations of the Near East where the pomegranate, better, the Tree of Life iconography had never disappeared. Grimwade, in discussing the aforementioned London piece and finding no real parallel in other English silver work, also senses "the general effect of Oriental riches."

As for Myer Myers, he was influenced from London directly or indirectly, which is surely the most natural thing geographically and historically. This can be seen also in other instances. One of these is especially interesting, because it connects the earliest Jewish silversmith in London with the earliest Jewish silversmith in America. The Torah head-pieces which are now in the Jewish Museum of London [Fig. 7] were done by Abraham d'Oliviera, the Jewish silversmith who was most probably a member of the Bevis Marks Congregation. Done in 1724, they combine the bulbous knobs with pierced foliage ornaments with obvious remnants of the older Dutch-English architectural form, with at least part of the bells

76   RITUAL SILVER MADE BY MYER MYERS

hanging down in window-like openings. What forms an actu
bridge to Myer Myers' work are the top crowns with the characteristically high-swung staves which are found to be exactly the same
on the beautiful pieces by Myer Myers which are now the proud
possession of the Spanish-Portuguese Synagogue of New York
[Fig. 8]. They are similar to the pair from Newport [Fig. 3]. The
right top crown is not preserved in its original state, but on the left,
one sees the same high curved staves. Their date, *circa* 1770, is like
that of the Newport pair. That both the Newport pair and the New
York pair are relatively late followers of the English models is
shown especially by the decoration of the lower knob where the
foliage is replaced by the abstract arched ornament of Louis XVI
character.

Thus, the establishment of an outspoken Myer Myers' type makes
it easy to reject as genuine, pieces which sometimes turn up and
which in some way or other bear a spurious Myer Myers' mark. In
spite of a general similarity, one will find, if one compares carefully,
that the proportions, the floral motives, the form of the crown, the
form of the brackets for the bells, the form of the shafts are different.
These differences reveal that they are pieces of the second half of
the nineteenth century, of Eastern European origin. The forms
came to Poland perhaps from the Near East directly, perhaps also
through Western European works of the eighteenth century, like
the London examples. But, it is also not excluded that such pieces
were made in more recent times in the United States after nineteenth
century Polish models.

Myer Myers' genuine work is not without variations. In 1781,
during the Revolutionary War and the English occupation of New
York, Myer Myers moved temporarily to Philadelphia and became
a member of the Congregation Mikveh Israel.[7] From that time this
Congregation has two pairs of *rimonim*. Thanks to Mrs. Robert
Rosenbaum we can mention these here. She will publish them in her
book on Myer Myers, but she has kindly granted us permission to
discuss them here.[8]

One pair, having the Myers' master mark, is basically different
from the ones of New York and of Newport. Yet the form of the
bell brackets in the shape of two C's facing different directions
connects it stylistically with the other pairs. However, there is no
floral decoration and the fruit symbolism appears — if at all — in a

---

[7] See Samuel Oppenheim, "The Jews and Masonry in the United States before 1810,"
Publications of the American Jewish Historical Society, no. 19 (1910), p. 30.

[8] They are reproduced for the first time in Jacob R. Marcus, *Early American Jewry,
1655–1790* (Philadelphia, 1953), vol. II, p. 165.

very generalized way only in the pear-shaped body. Otherwise, it is a kind of general baroque form of Western Europe especially shown by the lower spiral part, lacking the trends of Oriental *rimonim* which the other Myer Myers form has. They may be compared without pretention of a too close connection to a pair of German *rimonim* of the Jewish Museum in New York made in Nuernberg about 1750, which have a more complicated profile, yet are also partially spiral-twisted, and exclude also the floral decoration as well as any nearer affinity to the architectural form.[9] The date of the Myer Myers pair should also be around 1750.

However, there is no doubt that the form which we have discussed first is the Myer Myers form par excellence. The pair in Figure 9, also of Newport, shows this form with one difference, namely that the decoration of all three tiers is engraved and that also the center tier is not done in *ajouré* work. One also clearly finds here the characteristic form of the top-crown with the high curved staves.

Another pair which Myers also gave to the Congregation Mikveh Israel of Philadelphia shows perhaps the finest and iconographically the most consequential development of his main type. The three tiers are the same as in the first Newport pair and especially in the New York pair. As there, the center-tier is very delicately done in pierced and chased work. The details show the same fruit and flower motives which appear also in the New York pair between the foliage, and are again of course most intrinsically connected with the general idea of the Tree of Life symbolism. To strengthen this idea, the master even discarded in this case the top motif in the form of a crown, and changed it to a leaf-finial, approaching just by this change, still more, the basic Oriental origin of this iconography.

To sum up, we had to emphasize many facts which are characteristic in this complex, and which add up to an evaluation of these few rare pieces of ritual silver of Myer Myers which have fortunately been preserved:

(1) The development of an Eastern and a Western Iconography of the Torah headpieces, both of a deeply symbolical meaning: in the East, the Tree of Life with its fruit; in the West, the towers, perhaps a symbol of the towering might and protection of God.

(2) Christian masters working in the West exclusively and emphasizing, perhaps overemphasizing a little in the course of time, the bell-tower form.

---

[9] Jewish Museum, New York, F3043.

(3) A change of this Western iconography by stronger influences from the East which never loses its sacred fascination, giving to the Tree of Life motif a new Western European expression.

(4) This change carried through *circa* 1720 by Christian masters in London according to the wishes of the Jewish customers.[10]

(5) And finally the adoption of this new form by Jewish masters in England and America where the Jews were no longer excluded from the craftsmen's work.

These forms have come about through long and complicated ways. They are the long and complicated ways of Jewish history.

ILLUSTRATIONS

Fig. 1. Persia, 18th–19th Century. Courtesy of the Jewish Museum, New York, F3225 (photograph by Frank Darmstaedter).

Fig. 2. Amsterdam, 17th Century. Courtesy of the Jewish Museum, New York, F3281 (photograph by Frank Darmstaedter).

Fig. 3. Myer Myers, New York, *circa* 1770. Courtesy of the Touro Synagogue, Newport, Rhode Island (photograph by Museum of Fine Arts, Boston, Mass.).

Fig. 4. a. Amsterdam, 1696. b. Samuel Wastell, London, 1712. c. Amsterdam, 1692. Courtesy of Bevis Marks Synagogue, London (photograph by Vallentine, Mitchell and Co., London).

Fig. 5. Gabriel Sleath, London, 1718. Courtesy of Bevis Marks Synagogue, London (photograph by Vallentine, Mitchell and Co., London).

Fig. 6. Persia, 18th Century. Courtesy of the Jewish Museum, New York, F3141 (photograph by Frank Darmstaedter).

Fig. 7. Abraham d'Oliviera, London, 1724. Courtesy of the Jewish Museum, London (photograph by London Jewish Museum).

Fig. 8. Myer Myers, New York, *circa* 1770. Courtesy of Congregation Shearith Israel, New York (photograph by Frank Darmstaedter).

Fig. 9. Myer Myers, New York, *circa* 1770. Courtesy of the Touro Synagogue, Newport, Rhode Island (photograph by Museum of Fine Arts, Boston, Mass.).

---

[10] Shortly after the Boston meeting of the American Jewish Historical Society, Dr. Harry G. Friedman acquired for the Jewish Museum of New York one of a pair of *rimonim*, made in London, 1809–1810, by Master John Robins [F3443] which discards the three-tier form for one bulbous knob only, thus being quite similar to the Persian *rimonim* [Fig. 1], but at the same time retaining the open work with flowers of the English and American three-tier type.

MODERN RITUAL ART

ALFRED WERNER

It is common belief that Jews, thanks to the commandment prohibiting "graven images," have taken little interest in ritual art. True, the harrassed ghetto Jew, knowing that tomorrow might bring renewed persecution and flight, developed over the course of centuries indifference and even a callousness toward esthetics. The feeling for beauty, suppressed, often died for lack of nourishment.

But it would be an error to believe that the pre-Emancipation Jew was by nature unconcerned about the look and form of objects used within the framework of his religious service. Maimonides, we are told, closed his eyes while praying lest he be distracted by the decorative tapestries, but he did not scorn the objects themselves. Some rabbis opposed stained glass windows, others tolerated them. Nor can one judge by the surviving objects alone. For tragic historic reasons, little of medieval Jewish art survived; most ritual art extant is no more than 200 or 250 years old.

It is therefore necessary to consult Hebrew literature to learn about Jewish attitudes toward art in the synagogue. The Talmud, for instance, explains the Biblical words, "This is my God and I will adorn Him," with the following admonition:

> Make a beautiful *sukkah* in His honor, a beautiful *lulav,* a beautiful *shofar,* beautiful *tzitzit* and a beautiful Scroll of the Law and write it with fine ink, a fine reed . . . and wrap it about with beautiful silks.

A similar attitude is found in the exhortation of the 14th-century Spanish Jewish philosopher, Profiat Duran:

> The House of Learning should be beautiful and pleasing in structure. This increases the desire for learning, and strengthens the memory because the viewing of pleasing forms and beautiful reliefs and drawings rejoices the heart and strengthens the mind.

The modern Jew is bound to agree. In America, in particular, he does not display the negative attitude toward the beautiful that was forced

Reprinted from *Jewish Heritage,* Fall, 1961.

upon his European grandfather by poverty, persecution and, in part, by lack of esthetic training. The truth is that in Jewish life there were periods of esthetic heights, and periods of decline.

In the comparative safety and security of the 18th century Jewish ritual art reached a peak. All over Europe, Jews developed an affinity for the Baroque which brought "the heavens down into the terrestrial orbit in manifestations of glory and splendor" (Stephen S. Kayser). The Baroque, exuberant and sometimes flamboyant, was in essence very appealing to the Jew. It was also during the Baroque era (and that of its successor, the Rococo) that anti-Jewish discrimination began to abate.

Some of the silver pieces from that period may seem to us over-decorated, but the majority are acceptable even to present-day standards of taste. Most were the work of gentiles, since Jews were not allowed to join the guilds of gold- and silversmiths and were kept in ignorance of methods of treating precious metals. Since the gentile craftsman was often instructed by the Jewish purchaser in minute detail, the resulting works were a fine example of Jewish art.

Instruction in some cases dealt exclusively with requirements of piety (the work must not be done on the Sabbath or High Holidays) rather than with esthetic matters. Often, too, pieces made for the synagogue greatly resembled items produced for the church or for the secular pleasures of gentile burghers and noblemen. In any event, these pieces— carefully wrought silver repoussé work, elaborately brocaded textiles, glass vessels with minutely drawn illustrations—reveal that the pre-Emancipation Jew had eyes for beauty.

If the sculpture of Bernini or Goujon was unknown to him, he looked with satisfaction at the silver in his *shul*: the elaborately decorated Torah breastplate, often studded with semiprecious stones (for the tribes of Israel); the Torah pointer, sometimes shaped like a fish out of which stretches a hand holding another hand (as the Torah is likened to water, the element of the fish); the spice box, with turrets and pennants; the wine cup decorated with every kind of image; and, of course, the lamps for various festivals.

With the French Revolution came great changes in social conditions and the habits of millions, including that of the Jewish minority. Modern industrialism drove the formerly independent craftsman into the factory; his small workshop and handtools could not compete with the powerful machine that quickly turned out cheap products and yielded its owner immediate financial returns.

Ecclesiastic art of all denominations sank to a low level in the period between the Napoleonic wars and World War I. Little of significance and value in Jewish ceremonial art has come to us from this period. While the Emancipation made it possible for many Jews to study arts and crafts at the finest academies and schools, those who manufactured ceremonial objects failed to infuse new ideas into their work. They imitated patterns and designs of the Baroque or Rococo era, which were no more appropriate to the age of the railroad than were the curled peruke or the satin breeches of Louis XIV. "As the breath of the craftsman, so the shape of the vessel," is an old Jewish adage.

Congregations, proud of their wealth and prestige, commissioned silversmiths to furnish their altars with pompously over-decorated ritual objects. The 19th-century Jew frequently considered only the richness of material and ornament when he presented a Torah or menorah to his temple. The notion was that simplicity was synonymous with poverty—so vulgar excesses were all too frequent.

The earliest attempts to produce Jewish ritual art in keeping with the modern spirit were made by young men and women who had studied at the Bauhaus Academy and other progressive schools of Germany. Both the founder of the Bauhaus in Dessau, Walter Gropius, and the founder of Jerusalem's Bezalel Academy, Boris Schatz, agreed (without ever having met) that arts and crafts had badly deteriorated.

Schatz blamed everything on the machine, which he envisaged as the devil incarnate. He forbade its use, ordering the Bezalel artisans to employ the simplest tools. Gropius, on the other hand, urged his students to exploit power-driven devices to save work and conserve energy (an approach introduced into Bezalel only after Schatz's death). Notable among these Bauhaus-inspired German Jewish pioneers in ritual art are Ludwig Wolpert, who now conducts a workshop for silversmiths at New York's Jewish Museum, and D. H. Gumbel, who is active in Israel.

In the United States, modern ritual art is on the upswing; congregation leadership has passed from a generation with little interest in the newer forms of esthetic expression to one with an acquired taste for the simple and the refined. Gradually, art forms—good and bad—are being used that mirror the spiritual and physical predilections of educated Jews in mid-20th century America. If the glass used for scotch and soda at social gatherings is an elegant product of unobtrusive 20th-century craftsmanship, why should the Kiddush cup be an overdecorated imitation of an 18th-century piece?

This new emphasis is seen in the work of Wolpert and Gumbel, and in that of the many younger artist-craftsmen who exhibited at the Jewish Museum's "Contemporary Ceremonial and Synagogue Art" shows in 1958, and again last spring.

These artists avoid, as far as possible, ornate showpieces, elaborately ornamented, which are the mannerisms of Baroque tradition. Their works stress simplicity, without coldness. There is a healthy balance between form, material and costs of production. While the bleakness characteristic of earlier pioneering functionalism has passed, ornament is still used rather sparingly, and the obvious symbols—the *Magen David* and the Tablets of the Law—have almost disappeared, or are used in an abstract, sophisticated manner.

To these craftsmen quality is not inextricably bound up with luxury; clarity, order, harmony, functional integrity are preferred.

First among modern masters is the late Eric Mendelsohn, the eminent architect. When he needed ceremonial objects, such as seven-branched candelabra, he often designed them himself to fit into the quiet grandeur of the synagogue interior; he did not, of course, execute these objects, but gave his sketches to craftsmen who translated them into metal.

The famed silversmith, Ilya Schor, who died in New York last spring, was closer to the traditional than to the modern approach. He loved detail, adorning the pieces he made both for congregations and individuals with all sorts of figurative decor. But he was modern in the simplification of his figures, in "distortions" for the sake of emotional emphasis and drama, in composition that sees the highest goal in superb design.

Schor's most celebrated pieces are the Torah Crown he created for Milwaukee's Emanu-El B'nai Jeshurun Synagogue, and the silver doors to the Ark at Temple Israel in Great Neck, New York (this is composed of thirty-six panels wrought in silver, eighteen on each side, depicting Biblical episodes).

The art of Ludwig Wolpert—encompassing Torah ornaments, eternal lights, candle holders, Sabbath and seder plates, *etrog* boxes, *menorot* and *mezuzot*—is more austere. In the catalogue for his one-man show at the Jewish Museum, Wolpert's guiding principles were outlined:

> His main esthetic objective is to adjust the simplicity of form to the nature of the special kind of metal used. . . . This aim of pure form as an organic creation, based on the inherent quality of the material, is supplemented by the ornamental use of the Hebrew letter.

Indeed, the Hebrew script, in a terse and often archaic form, is frequently the only ornament Wolpert permits himself to use. Typical in this respect is the copper and silver Torah case, designed by him and presented in 1948 to President Harry Truman on behalf of Chaim Weizmann. The twenty-five-inch high cylinder consists of a simple crown and a band, on which are engraved the lines from the 19th Psalm: "The statutes of the Lord are right, rejoicing the heart. . . ."

Several other masters in the United States produced works to delight the mind and senses. A silver Eternal Light fashioned by Mitzi Solomon Cunliffe has a definitely modern look, though it is based on the oil lamps of antiquity. It was commissioned by the architect Percival Goodman, who prefers oil lamps or wax candles to electricity in ritual fixtures.

Excellent work has also been done by Herbert Ferber, who became famous through the extraordinary "Burning Bush" sculpture he made for a façade of the B'nai Israel synagogue in Millburn, New Jersey. For the Temple of Aaron Congregation in St. Paul, Minnesota, he created a large menorah, simple, yet original. Seymour Lipton's menorah for Temple Israel in Tulsa, Oklahoma, departs greatly from the conventional type that repeats, with slight variations, its prototype on the triumphal arch in Rome. Lipton's free-standing menorah has a gradually tapering, hollow base. His Eternal Light, in the same temple, is composed of a number of sharply angular wings, held together by a winged crown.

Ibram Lassaw's Eternal Light for the St. Paul congregation is in the form of a metal cage. Most interesting is the Eternal Light which Arnold Bergier fashioned for the Baltimore Hebrew Congregation: two winged cherubim, semi-abstract in form, float in space; from the junction of their draped outstretched arms springs a jet of flame which is reflected in the oval, concave form of their faces. This work, in steel and bronze, is poetically free, yet retains all the characteristics of a *Ner Tamid.*

Among several excellent textile designers, Amalia Rothschild is particularly noteworthy. She is responsible for the tapestry for the Ark in the Baltimore Hebrew Congregation. The four needle-point panels represent, symbolically, themes from the Bible. There is enough unrest, enough color contrast to keep the eye occupied, yet the over-all composition is strong and holds together the component parts.

It is difficult to sum up in a few sentences the esthetic philosophy of this new art applied to Judaism. The modern designer knows that the cultured Jew of today does not require every pictorial idea to be spelled out in obvious graphic language. The artist-craftsman is aware that abstract art can and does produce an austere and sacred atmosphere.

An ever-increasing number of master-craftsmen, both Jews and Christians, who enthusiastically execute works for Jewish religious purposes, have learned to maintain a healthy balance between the free flow of imagination and the restraint necessary for the object's quick identification and untrammeled usefulness. They discuss their sketches with the rabbi, with the building committee, and there is a constant exchange of suggestions and ideas.

In the past, Torah curtains were usually heavy with embroidered decoration, often commemorating the donor in elaborate script. Modern weavers, however, generally avoid pearls, precious brocade, gold and silver threads, and attempt to please the onlooker by subtle color combinations, unobtrusive reference to Biblical events, and textural variations.

Modern Jewish ritual art has come a long way in the United States during the past fifteen years. Mistakes have been made and there is much that is not good. On the whole, however, the prospect for the future is bright. More and more Jewish leaders—rabbis and laymen—are taking an interest in the arts. And, like Dickens' Barkas, the artists "are willing."

TORAH DECORATIONS

THE ORIGIN OF EUROPEAN TORAH DECORATIONS

FRANZ LANDSBERGER

Hebrew Union College-Jewish Institute of Religion, Cincinnati

THE scroll of the Torah, dressed in a mantle and adorned with headpieces, breastplate, and pointer, in the manner prevalent in European synagogues, has gotten to be, for Jewish worshippers, such matter of course as to create the impression that the Torah has always presented this appearance. Such, however, is not the case. That set-up of the scroll was achieved only after centuries of development. It is the purpose of this article to trace that development so far as at present ascertainable.

ANTIQUITY

The beginnings go back to times and places in which Judaism was under Hellenistic influence, that is to say, the first centuries of the Christian era and the centuries immediately preceding. At that time, the effort originated to write the Torah on a single scroll. In the representations of the Torah on Roman-Jewish gilt-glasses, the Torah is pictured as distributed over several scrolls laid on a pile and lying in the Holy Ark (illustration on next page). With privately owned Torahs, that continued for a long time. By contrast, it became customary and, in the fourth century, mandatory for the Torah of the synagogue to be inscribed on one scroll only.[1]

With the enforcement of that practice, our present subject is vitally linked. The length of the scroll had to be increased; the smaller format would have made it too thick and too clumsy. Naturally this heightened stateliness of the scroll spurred the wish to enhance the stateliness of its total appearance.

---

[1] So Rabbah (died about 330) and Rab Joseph (died 333) in Git. 60a.

Reprinted from *Hebrew Union College Annual,* Vol. XXIV, 1952-1953.

TORAH SHRINE FROM THE BOTTOM OF A JEWISH GILT GLASS.
Last in Berlin, Kaiser Friedrich Museum. Enlarged.

It was a mode of the heathen world to equip scrolls with an inner rod. The rod would be removed before reading and restored after reading.[2] The purpose of this rod was to prevent the squeezing and mutilating of the scrolls as they lay piled on one another or as they underwent use. Such a rod came to be inserted also in the scroll of the Torah. In the above representation of a Torah chest, we can recognize the rod by the recurrent black spots. The Greek word for the rod was ὀμφαλός; the Latin was umbilicus, "navel." We shall presently learn the origin of these terms. The Jews chose a more elegant word עמוד, "pillar," probably alluding to the pillars in front of the Solomonic Temple.

When several scrolls made up the Torah, one rod sufficed

[2] A rod fastened to the scroll is mentioned only by Hero of Alexandria, the mathematician, in his work on the automatic theatre. The shaping of the book in antiquity is dealt with in Theodor Birt, Die Buchrolle in der Kunst, Leipzig, 1907, and Wilhelm Schubert, Das Buch bei den Griechen und Roemern, 2nd revised edition, Berlin, 1921. For the Jewish Book compare Ludwig Blau, Studien zum althebraeischen Buchwesen, Budapest, 1902.

for each. But when the Torah comprised one scroll only, it became advisable to use not one rod but two and to stitch the rods to the parchment. This brought advantages both religious and esthetic; religious because, by means of the rods, the scroll could be lifted from its chest, placed on a table and unrolled, the parchment remaining untouched. The great reverence accorded the Torah gave rise to the rule which forbade putting upon it one's hand. The Talmud cautions: "Whoso touches a naked Torah will lie naked when buried" (Sab. 14a). The esthetic advantage lay in the fact that, as permanent parts of the scroll, the rods invited ornamentation. Eliezer b. R. Zadok, who lived before the destruction of the Second Temple, characterizes such a scroll by observing: "Other kinds of scrolls are rolled from end to end but, supplied with a "pillar" [עָמוּד] at each side, the scroll of the Law is rolled toward the middle. The scribes in Jerusalem were wont to fashion their scrolls in this way" (Baba Batra 14a).

That last sentence would lead us to ask whether the scroll with two rods may not have been a Jewish invention. In my opinion, it was not. We are informed that scrolls with two rods — probably detachable rods — were known among the Romans. That was during the reign of Emperor Domitian (81–96 of our era), hence almost contemporaneous with the mention of such scrolls in the Talmud.[3] Considering how superior the material resources of the Romans were to those of the Jews, the Jews must have been the copiers. To be sure, the use of this technique among the Romans was but casual while, in connection with the Torah among the Jews, it became the prevalent mode and the start of an artistic unfolding.

As already stated, the Greek and Roman names for the rod signified "navel." The surmise is correct that the expression refers to the knob at the upper end. That knob was also adopted by the Jews. On a Chinese Torah scroll, pictured in an old drawing, the knob is discernible (see illustration on next page).[4]

[3] Cf. Dziatzko, article "Buch," in Pauly-Wissowa, *Real-Encyclopaedie der klassischen Altertumswissenschaft*, Neue Bearbeitung, 5. Halbband, Stuttgart, 1897, col. 956.
[4] Cf. W. Ch. White, *Chinese Jews*, I, Toronto, 1942, p. 8.

READING THE TORAH IN THE SYNAGOGUE OF KAI-FUNG-FOO, CHINA.
Drawing from 1722 in Paris, Ste. Geneviève, Jesuit Archives.
Notice that the scroll, probably containing only part of
the Torah, has only one rod with its knob.

The Greek satirist, Lucian, (second century of our era), reports that wealthy book lovers would possess rods made of gold.[5] Could the Jews have adopted that custom also; not, of course, for their secular scrolls but, as a token of homage, for the Torah scrolls? If such be the case, we would have here the inception of an adornment first noticeable in later centuries. We refer to the Torah-rods with headpieces of gold or silver.

Heathen antiquity bestowed on its book-scrolls such care as to keep them in casings of substantial materials like metal or wood, yet not excluding cloth. The Jews, solicitous about the

[5] *De mercede conductis* 41; *Adversus indoctum* 7; quoted from Dziatzko, l. c., col. 957.

protection of their sacred books, took over this practice also. The solid containers in which the Jews kept their scrolls impart to oriental scrolls a peculiar appearance. But, upon this, we may not dwell, because our subject is Torah ornamentation in Europe. We are concerned here solely with textile wrappings which, originating in antiquity, became current in Europe during the Middle Ages and in modern times. The Greeks called their scroll-wrappings φαινόλης. The Romans called them *paenula*. Both words signify a thick outer garment or cloak. The Jews gave their scroll coverings the name מטפחת with reference to a certain shawl-like garment (Isa. 3.22, Ruth 3.15). There occurs, in addition, the word מפה, a term borrowed from the Latin where it means a handkerchief or napkin or table-cloth. This is the wrapping to which allusion is made in the Talmudic admonition: "Have a beautiful scroll of the Law prepared, copied by an able scribe, with fine ink and fine calamus; and wrap it in beautiful silk" (Sab. 133b). This passage calls for beauty of material. From another passage, we learn of scroll covers richly adorned. A discussion of clean and unclean (Kelim XXVIII, 4), dating from the first century of our era, lets scroll covers figure in the following discussion:[6] "Scroll-wrappers, whether figures are portrayed on them or not, are susceptible to uncleanness. So the school of Shammai. And the school of Hillel say: If figures are on them they are not susceptible to uncleanness [since the embroidery proves that the wrappers were for ornament only and not for use]; if figures are not portrayed on them they are susceptible. Rabban Gamaliel says: In either case they are not susceptible to uncleanness." It is not entirely clear what is meant by those "figures," מצויירות. Perhaps we should understand embroideries which, in order to avoid representation of the human form, consisted of abstract or floral figurations.

We discover from another Talmudic discussion of clean and unclean that the Torah cover might receive still further ornamentation; to it might be stitched bells. The Talmudic passage reads: "Bells for a mortar, a cradle, a scroll-cover or a child's cloak are, if they have a clapper, unclean; without a clapper,

[6] I follow Herbert Danby's translation of the Mishnah, Oxford, 1933, p. 646.

they are clean" (Sab. 58b). Bells were thus by no means restricted to covers of scrolls; they were fastened also to mortars, to children's cloaks, and to cradles; to the last named probably for the purpose of lulling the child to sleep with the tinkling. For our present study, it is significant that, with these bells, a motif begins which was later to play a prominent part in scroll decoration. Only, the bells were attached not so much to the scroll-covers as to the metallic accessories.

Since we possess no surviving sample, we have only our imagination with which to picture how the Torah of late antiquity must have looked. Inscribed on one large scroll, edged with two rods, possibly of gold in some cases, their knobs protruding above the scroll, the scroll was wrapped in some rare material, ornamented with embroideries and hung with bells. Thus did Hellenic delight in the beautiful, spreading to the Jews, endow the scroll of the Torah with an attractive exterior.

THE MIDDLE AGES

The inclination to adorn the Torah, together with the ability to adorn, was bequeathed by the Jews of antiquity to the Jews of the Middle Ages. As we survey Jewish artistic talent of that period, we always meet the goldsmith. The Jewish goldsmith found royal favor at the court of King John of England (1167–1216). In fifteenth century Spain, he served not only his co-religionists but even Christian churches and monasteries.[7] That goldsmiths of such talent should have longed to enhance the glamor of the Torah need not surprise us. As nothing from that period has survived, our reliance must rest on written accounts supplemented, in rare instances, by illustrations from illuminated manuscripts.

A twelfth century source apprises us that the Torah-rods were ornamented with headpieces. This does not denote that headpieces existed no earlier. We have already surmised that these headpieces developed from the *umbilici*, the knobs which

---

[7] Cf. my articles "The Jewish Artist before the Time of Emancipation," and "New Studies in Early Jewish Artists," in the *Hebrew Union College Annual*, XVI, 1941, pp. 342 ff., 347 and XVIII, 1944, p. 289.

the book-rods carried at their upper ends. If these rods were of gold, we are all the more justified in regarding the headpieces as their sequel. This supposition is strengthened by the fact that the hollow metallic headpiece ends in a small globe; hence the term *Rimmonim*, "pomegranates." In Samaritan (Fig. 1) and in Sephardic headpieces, that spherical form has persisted.

To the Jew, the designation *Rimmonim* sounded familiar. It reminded him of the pomegranates surmounting, with other motifs, the columns fronting the Temple of Solomon (I Kings 17.18). Yet, in their origin and shape, these headpieces derived not from any biblical reminiscence but from the terminating knobs or, if the scroll was large, from the terminating spheres, and from the fact that those spherical endings invited metallic reproduction. If we credit this derivation, the *Rimmonim* may well have existed centuries before their first mention.

These headpieces are a topic of none less than Maimonides who, coming from Spain where the Jews rivalled the Moham- medans in technical ability, writes in his *Mishneh Torah*: "The silver and golden *Rimmonim* made to beautify a scroll of the Torah are sacred objects. It is forbidden to take them out of the ark for any profane purpose except one sells them in order to buy a Torah or a Pentateuch" (*Sefer Torah*, X, 4).

From the thirteenth century, some evidence has reached us concerning metallic headpieces in Germany. A responsum of R. Meir of Rothenburg (ca. 1220–1293)[8] discusses the following case: A has assigned to B some gold to make into golden caps [צפוי זהב] for the end-points of the Torah rods. B accepts the com- mission. But when the completed product reaches A, A discovers that, for the gold entrusted, B has substituted silver. The word *Rimmon* is not used here. We merely assume that the German headpiece possessed the same form as the Spanish, and that the *Rimmonim* entered Germany from Spain.

The Middle Ages produced yet another ornament for the Torah-rods, namely, the crown. In Jewish antiquity, "crown" was a familiar metaphor for Torah. In the Sayings of the Fathers (IV, 17), the crown of the Torah is enumerated along with the

[8] Cf. Responsa of Maharam (Meir of Rothenburg), ed. Prag 1608, No. 879 (Fol. 85b).

crown of the kingship and the crown of the priesthood as inferior to the grandest crown of all, the crown of a good name. It has been supposed[9] that this saying has in mind a literal crown, like the crown of a king or the crown-like diadem of the High Priest or like the golden crown or the wreath bestowed as a crown upon some citizen as a token of distinction.[10] Against this assumption, stands the fact that, throughout ancient Jewish literature, a literal crown is mentioned nowhere in connection with the Law. In fact, the word for "crown" in the Sayings of the Fathers is כתר while, in medieval sources, the word is עטרה. Soon we shall see why.

The first notice of such a Torah crown brings us approximately to the year 1000, and that is earlier than the first mention of the *Rimmonim*. Still it were rash to conclude that the Torah crown antedated the *Rimmonim*. We have already noted that time of mention does not indicate time of origin. The earliest notice of a Torah crown occurs in an opinion of Hai ben Sherira (939–1038) Gaon of Pumbeditha, Babylonia. The opinion is transmitted by Isaac ben Judah ibn Ghayyat, a Spanish Jew of the 11th century.[11] The passage reads:

> It was furthermore asked of him [Hai Gaon] whether the use of women's jewelry in the following customs was permissible or not. They make a crown [עטרה] for the Torah, of gold, or of silver, or of myrtle, or of women's jewelry, such as ear-rings, rings and the like, hanging such jewelry on to this crown, and then they place the crown on the Torah scroll when it is in the Torah-case [תיק], or they place it on top of its case, on the day of Simḥath Torah.
>
> He [Hai Gaon] answered: Whether one or the other, it is permitted to place them on the Torah scroll. And as for the suspicion [that this ought to be prohibited] because they [i. e. the jewelry] will thus acquire holiness, this suspicion does not apply, for they were not specially pre-

---

[9] Cf. *The Jewish Encyclopedia*, IV, New York and London, 1903, article by I. D. Eisenstein "Crown," p. 372.

[10] Apropos the citizen's crown cf. S. Krauss, *Synagogale Altertuemer*, Berlin and Wien, 1932, p. 163. — Highly instructive is also the article "Kranz und Krone" published by Leopold Loew in 1867. Reprinted in *Gesammelte Schriften von Leopold Loew*, III, Szegedin, 1893, pp. 407 ff.

[11] In the work *Sha'are Simḥah*, ed. Fuerth, 1862, pp. 117 f. For the translation of this as well as of the following citation, I am indebted to the kind assistance of Rabbi Jacob Petuchowski.

pared, but are a temporary measure, having been placed there with the knowledge of [the ceremony's] short duration. Therefore there is nothing to be said against it, for such "preparation" is not a real matter. And as to placing it on the head of the reader, which might have been thought to be forbidden because of the prohibition to wear a woman's garment, this prohibition does not apply, for this is not the way a woman wears her jewelry. And there is nothing to be said against it, except that it is not proper to place this on the head of human beings. But if those who follow the custom consider it as proper in their own eyes, they may continue doing so, and nothing is to be said against it. But the Gaon said that it is forbidden to put the crown, which one places on the Torah scroll on Simḥath Torah on the head of the bridegroom [of the Law], for "in holy matters we ascend but do not descend."

From this opinion, we learn that this crown does not, like the *Rimmonim*, belong to the scroll's fixed ornamentation. Rather was it placed in position on the day of the Rejoicing of the Law, a festival which originated centuries after the destruction of the Second Temple. "Bridegroom-of-the-Law" is the one who is called up to read the last section of the pericope. The crown originated in that nomenclature. Just as, in the Book of Canticles (3.11), Solomon wears a crown on his wedding day — where also the word is עטרה — so is a crown appropriate for the bridegroom-of-the-Law. The bride — by which is meant the Torah — also receives a crown. Hai Gaon raises no objection to the crown of the Torah or to the crown of the bridegroom-of-the-Law. What he objects to is placing the crown on the Torah first and then upon the bridegroom-of-the-Law.

A second mention of this custom appears in a thirteenth century work called *Ha-Manhig*,[12] begun in the year 1204. The author is Abraham ben Nathan Hajarchi of Lunel, afterward of Toledo, Spain. He writes:

> The Crown [עטרה] of the kind that is customary on Simḥath Torah, which they surround with the veil of women, stitching and weaving its circumference, and placing upon it all manner of ornaments and gold, and the ear-rings of women, and their rings, and the jewelry that they wear, the putting of the crown on the Torah and on the heads of the readers at the time of reading, although there is no holiness whatever in this jewelry even if they have been prepared for this . . . . [quotes talmudic discussion about holiness] at any rate we have to fear disgrace on account

12 Ed. Goldberg, Berlin, 1855, No. 59, p. 72.

of the law that a man must not wear women's clothes. For they beautify themselves with the jewelry of women, moreover with jewelry with which the women might have adorned themselves at the time of their ritual impurity. It is not right to put this on the Torah, and it is a disgrace and a shameful thing to place it back afterwards on the women; for 'in holy matters we ascend but do not descend.' Moreover, through this they come to a desecration of the holy day, for they weave and sew and pluck grass with aroma, in order to place it upon it [the Torah] and upon themselves. In this connection I quote Scriptures: 'For thus saith the Lord: the mitre shall be removed, and the crown taken off' [Ezek. 21.31]. The mitre has departed from the head of the High Priest and the crown from the head of every man. And praise be to God, I have abolished [this custom] in one congregation where I spent the Festival [of Sukkoth] in the year 1204,[13] and I have prevailed upon them to make a silver crown. And thus they did, and also a Mikvah. May God remember this to me for good!

Likewise Rabbi Abraham ben Nathan does not protest against the crown that figures on the feast of the Rejoicing of the Law. He himself encourages the preparation of such crowns. What he remonstrates against is the added feminine attire and finery; and also the transfer of the crown from the Torah to the head of the reader.

We hear of a Torah crown in Arles, Provence, in the fifteenth century. The information comes from a contract, dated 1439,[14] in which the Jewish community orders, from a Christian goldsmith, a six-cornered crown which is to resemble a city wall with portals and with towers. The goldsmith is, in addition, obligated to provide some further embellishment for a crown already in existence. This indicates the presence of a Torah crown in Arles prior to 1439. The employment of a Christian goldsmith must, at that period, still have been rare. It may nevertheless have happened that, in small communities, Jewish goldsmiths were few or entirely lacking. The Jewish goldsmith was excluded from the Christian guild.

In Sicily, which contained, in the fifteenth century, a large Jewish population including many artisans, conditions in this

---

[13] Not 1104 as the printed book states incorrectly.

[14] Printed in French translation in the *Collection de Mr. Strauss*, Poissy, 1878, pp. VIII ff. Unfortunately the book fails to state where the contract is being preserved.

regard may have been more favorable. The Jewish traveler, Obadiah of Bertinoro visiting, in the year 1488, the city of Palermo, is amazed at the size of the synagogue and the magnificence of the religious equipment. He mentions many scrolls of the Torah "with their cases, their crowns, their head ornaments [ראשי] and, at the ends of their circular rods, their *Rimmonim* of silver and of precious stones."[15]

Finally we infer the existence of a Torah crown from a document of the year 1517[16] now preserved in the state museum of Brünn, Czechoslovakia. The document tells how the Arabic governor Amrad Bey had looted the synagogue at Hebron. A crown and two *Rimmonim* which it was possible to rescue, were brought to Beyrouth and afterward to Corfu. The Torah crown must accordingly have been known in Palestine.

We are uninformed whether the crowns here mentioned were used only on days of the Rejoicing of the Law or whether they graced the Torah likewise on the High Holy Days or even permanently. In Italy, these crowns were, we know not from what period, pulled over the Torah in such wise as to become an ornamental supplementation of the *Rimmonim*.

Regarding the structure of these medieval crowns our knowledge is but scant. The Haggadah of Sarajevo, a Spanish manuscript of the early fourteenth century, contains an illustration of a Torah Ark (Fig. 2). The ark holds three scrolls arrayed in colored mantles. One can easily recognize, on the middle scroll, in addition to the head-pieces that come to a point, a flat crown.[17] Considering that this page stands in a Haggadah, that incidence of a crown has nothing to do with the day of the Rejoicing of the Law. The Torah crown, ordered at Arles in the

---

[15] The Hebrew account is printed in *Jahrbuch fuer die Geschichte der Juden und des Judentums*, Leipzig, 1863, pp. 195 ff., with German translation. An English translation is provided in the *Publications of the Society of Hebrew Literature*, I, London, 1872, pp. 113 ff.

[16] Cf. the periodical *Ben Chananja*, IV, 1861, pp. 378 ff.

[17] Still more distinctly in the colored reproduction of this page by Mueller-Schlosser, *Die Haggadah von Sarajevo*, Wien, 1898, Fol. 34. Head-pieces that come to a point, minus the crown, are discernable in another Spanish Haggadah of the fourteenth century, to be found now in the British Museum, Add. 14761. Reproduction in *Encyclopaedia Judaica*, II, col. 377/378.

fifteenth century, must have exhibited a more elaborate structure. It may well be surmised that the path of development ran from the simple circlet to more and more complicated formations.

MODERN TIMES

The addition of the *Rimmonim* and the crown concludes the medieval contribution, but the ornamenting of the Torah did not yet cease. Still to be considered are the breastplate and the pointer, added in modern times.

It is well known that two or even three scrolls are used on certain Sabbaths and holidays. The wish arose to provide certain marks by which these scrolls could be distinguished from one another. It appeared advisable to construct certain plaques with changeable inserts, on which were engraved the names of the holidays. Although such plaques might have been devised at any epoch, they appear neither in antiquity nor in the Middle Ages. The earliest date for such a breastplate — so-called in commemoration of the breastplate worn by the High Priest — happens to be the years before 1612. This is the date of the Torah plaque dedicated to the young Sephardic community of Amsterdam, Holland (Fig. 3). Written accounts carry us back a few decades earlier. For these accounts, we are indebted to Humanism which had its rise in the fifteenth century, awakening interest not only in classical antiquity but also in the language, the history, and the customs of the Jews. Using the new device of the printed book, Humanism sought to impart some knowledge of Judaism to the Christian world. There appeared at Augsburg in 1530 a German book, *Der Gantz juedisch Glaub* (*The Entire Jewish Faith*). The author was Anthonius Margaritha, an Israelite who, after going over to Christianity, treated his former religion with a combination of knowledge and of contempt. By no means a pleasant chap, this Margaritha! His work nevertheless ranks high as a source of information on the Jewish ritual of his country and his age. Thus, in Chapter Si, occurs the observation that, "over the Torah robe hangs a silver *blech* [metal plaque] by a silver chain and, on that plaque is indicated when those books are to be used, there being a different book for the Sabbath. On some of these plaques stands *Keser Torah* כתר תורה 'Crown of the Law'; on another, *Kodesh Ladonai*, קדש ליהוה 'Holiness unto the Lord.' " This latter inscription alludes to the plate on the mitre of Aaron, engraved with the same words (Exod. 28.36–38).

As with the Maimonidean reference to the *Rimmonim*, so here also, the date of mention need not coincide with the date of origin, particularly since Margaritha does not speak of the practice as a recent innovation. Meanwhile, we find in a German Machsor of 1459, the picture of a Torah ark with three Torah scrolls on none of which this plaque appears.[18] We do well to set the origin of the breastplate not too long before 1530; in all events, not before 1459.

Since its first mention occurs in connection with the Jews of Germany, I venture the surmise that Germany was the country in which the breastplate originated. It is most likely that the Jews of Holland, while still at the beginning of their Dutch sojourn, often sought counsel of their Ashkenazic brethren. There may have found its way into Holland a breastplate of German model or even of German make. Later, with the arrival of Sephardic Rabbis, the breastplate vanishes from the Sephardic milieu.

A further indication that the breastplate originated in Germany is the fact that it fits so readily into the German scheme. In the craft and marksman guilds, such plaques, hanging from chains, were a familiar motif. At guild collations, they appear as embellishments of bowls, and at guild funerals, as adornments of bier and bier-cloth. The makers of breastplates may have had such guild plaques as models,[19] particularly since Christian artisans were the makers both of the Jewish and of the non-Jewish appurtenances. Goldsmiths who were Jewish had, by that time, disappeared from Germany.

[18] Munich, State and University Library, Cod. hebr. 3, Machsor vol. I, fol. 48a. A reproduction in my article "Old Time Torah-Curtains," *Hebrew Union College Annual*, XIX, 1946, Ill. 3.

[19] Cf. R. Hallo, "Juedische Kultaltertuemer aus Edelmetall . . ." in *Notizblatt der Gesellschaft zur Erforschung juedischer Kunstdenkmaeler*, No. 23, 1929, p. 13 f. Compare further the article of Hans Wenzel "Bahrschild" in *Reallexikon der Deutschen Kunstgeschichte*, I, Stuttgart, 1937, col. 1385 f.

Some of these Christian masters are named in the "Probier-meisterbuch," listing the works of the goldsmiths in Frankfurt a. M., after having checked the percentage of pure silver in every piece. This book, kept in the municipal archives of Frankfurt, covers the years 1512–1576. Hermann Gundersheimer and Guido Schoenberger have separated the items referring to Jews.[20] Such notices as bear upon the existence of breastplates, I choose from this compilation:

"1545 (p. 104). Master Rudolf Kolb, a *Judentafel* [a Jews' plaque], weighs 1½ mark."

As the compilers suggest, a breastplate must be intended here because hardly anything else could have been meant by a Jewish plaque.

"1552 (p. 133). Master Carl Sand, two Jews' *Zehngebot*, weigh 20 lot."

The compilers understand, by *Zehngebot* [Decalogue], also a breastplate, such breastplates being sometimes ornamented with the two tablets. Breastplates of that kind do indeed exist. Still it would seem, by analogy with the Dutch piece of ca. 1612 (Fig. 3), that the sixteenth century breastplates were much simpler. Following, in their proportions, the width of their changeable inserts, such breastplates would hardly have had room for two vertical tablets. Add to this the fact that, in the German language of that time, *Zehngebot* signified a Pentateuch — putting the most important part, namely, the Decalogue, for the whole. If the list speaks of two decalogues, some kind of an ornamental pair must be the reference, and that could be nothing except *Rimmonim*, capping the two rods of the Torah scroll.

"1563 (p. 189) Master Heinrich Heidelberger, two silver *Deckel* [lids] over the Jews' *Zehngebot*. Weigh 1 mark 12 lot."

Here also, the compilers interpret the *Zehngebot* [Decalogue] as breastplate. A breastplate, however, needs no silver lid.

---

[20] Cf. Hermann Gundersheimer and Guido Schoenberger, "Frankfurter Chanukkahleuchter aus Silber und Zinn," in *Notizblatt der Gesellschaft zur Erforschung juedischer Kunstdenkmaeler*, No. 34, 1937.

No, here also "Decalogue" means Torah scroll, and the two covering lids are *Rimmonim* such as cap the ends of both Torah rods.

"1576 (p. 279), Master Jost Koch, a large silver *blech* made for a Jew. Weighs 16 lot."

As with Margaritha, the word *blech* is used here for "breastplate." This time I agree with the compilers. The word does refer to a breastplate.

To sum up: Though the list begins with 1512, the breastplate is referred to for the first time in 1545; a date but little later than that of the book by Margaritha. Breastplates began, at this period, to be ordered from Christian goldsmiths, though not in any large number.

We come upon such a *blech* again about the year 1600. Such an object is among the pieces disposed of in the will of Mordecai Meisel (1528–1601), the wealthy head of the Jewish community in Prague.[21] Evidently, the usage penetrated to Bohemia. Further south it did not go. In Italy, as we have seen, the Torah mantle was adorned by a crown, which left, for the breastplate, no room.

The last of our decorative pieces is the pointer. Heathen antiquity knows nothing of such a contrivance; one pointed the lines with one's fingers. As regards the Jews, we recall once more the caution: "Whoso touches a naked Torah will lie naked when buried." At any period, the use of a pointer would have been furthered by such a prohibition, and yet, strange to say, such a pointer is mentioned in no source, ancient or medieval, nor is it pictured in any illuminated manuscript.

Seeking the earliest incidence of the device, I turned to that outstanding authority on Islam, Prof. L. A. Mayer of Jerusalem. I thought that, perhaps in Islam, the use of a pointer may have some parallel. Mayer's answer was: "The Sheika use no pointer. The Koran lies open before them but, as a rule, they rely on their memory. The Koran is not read; it is recited."

[21] Cf. *Monatsschrift fuer Geschichte und Wissenschaft des Judentums,* Neue Folge, I, 1893, p. 140.

Once more, as in the case of the breastplate, I consulted the book by Margaritha, *The Entire Jewish Faith*, published in 1530. Here I found this passage: "When they read the Decalogue, they place, on each side, a silk cloth so as not to touch the scroll with the bare hand." Nowhere is there mention of a pointer. The pieces of cloth at the two sides of the scroll must have served instead. The reader, placing his hands on the cloth and bending down, would not need to touch the "naked Torah."

Once more I examined the list of the Frankfurt goldsmiths and noted the following lines:

"1568 (p. 233) Master Cunrat Schenk, two *beschleg* [platings] over two *Juden staff* [Jews' sticks], weigh 2½ mark."

The compilers are inclined to spot a pointer in the "*Juden staff*." But a pointer is not plated; it is of metal entirely. Meanwhile, the two rods on which the Torah was rolled were sometimes capped by *Rimmonim* which were not always removable. To me it seems that the passage refers to the two *Rimmonim* covering two ends of the rods.

Inasmuch as the only notice that could be construed as referring to a pointer is this statement in the Frankfurt goldsmith book, we continue uninformed as to the earliest appearance of that object.

To our aid comes a pointer made by a silversmith in Nuremberg in the year 1570. The pointer was formerly in the Museum of Arts and Crafts at Hamburg.[22] I say "formerly," for when I wrote to the Museum, seeking an illustration to place before my readers, I learnt that, during the Hitler years, the pointer had been hidden away and that it has not yet reappeared. Since the Margaritha book of 1530 and the Frankfurt list of goldsmiths which runs to the year 1576 mention no pointer, the year 1570 would have to be the approximate *terminus a quo*. Here also, as in the case of the breastplate, we have to surmise German origin.

[22] Cf. Fuehrer durch das Hamburgische Museum fuer Kunst und Gewerbe IX: *Deutsches Kunstgewerbe der Barockzeit*, Hamburg, 1925, p. 19. Quoted from the *Notizblatt der Gesellschaft zur Erforschung juedischer Kunstdenkmaeler*, No. 19, 1928, p. 10.

Considering the scarcity of the data available for the solving of this question, it might be permissible to pursue the inquiry about the pointer a little further. An Englishman named Philip Skippon who, in the year 1663, visited the Sephardic synagogue in Amsterdam, gives the following report in his *An Account of a Journey made Through Part of the Low Countries, Germany, Italy, France*.[23] Apropos the pointer, he remarks: "The Rabbi, while he was reading, had a little silver rod in his hand." Like that of the breastplate, the use of the pointer may have spread from Germany to the Portuguese-Dutch immigrants. Unlike the breastplate, however, the pointer persisted in the Sephardic environment.

In England, the pointer appears in 1662, brought there doubtless by Sephardic Jews coming from Holland. John Greenhalgh who, in that year, visited the Sephardic synagogue in London, gives, in a letter,[24] a vivid account of his impressions. The pointer is mentioned in that letter: "Then the priest laid the Law upon the altar and took in his hand a small silver cane or quill with the sharp end thereof pointing at the lines of the Law as he read; for the greater reverence it was half a yard long."

While the Dutch account says nothing about the pointer's shape, the English account mentions its length and its sharp end. We of today are accustomed to a pointer terminating in a hand with the index finger outstretched. But Greenhalgh obviously refers to a stick ending in a point. Both forms were probably extant (Fig. 4). From Italy comes mention of yet a third form, a pointer with an end resembling "not so much a hand as a palm branch."[25]

With the emergence of the pointer in the sixteenth century, the process of Torah decoration concludes, after one and a half thousand years. From the seventeenth century down to our own time, the devices named have grown more and more elaborate.

---

[23] Cf. A. Cohen, *An Anglo-Jewish Scrapbook*, London, 1943, p. 247.

[24] The letter is reproduced by Cecil Roth, *Anglo-Jewish Letters*, London, 1938, p. 62.

[25] Cf. H. Frauberger, "*Ueber alte Kultusgegenstaende in Synagoge und Haus*," 1903, p. 3.

But the number of them is not increasing; aside from the fact that, due to its limited size, the Torah is hardly accessible to further ornamentation.

This investigation shows that the decorative elements of the Torah scroll are not to be explained entirely in terms of Jewish origin. Like Jewish art in general, so also the adornment of the scroll can be understood only in the light of the relationship between the Jews and the surrounding world. Credit is due the Jewish people for having always worked over independently the influences pouring in upon them. In this way, they so unified the Torah scroll and its adornment as to vouchsafe, to the worshipper, both religious edification and esthetic satisfaction.

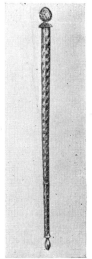

1) SAMARITAN TORAH SCROLL AND CASE WITH THREE *Rimmonim*.
2) HOLY ARK WITH THREE TORAH SCROLLS.
   Detail of a page in the Haggadah of Sarajevo, 14th Century Spanish manuscript.
3) BREASTPLATE DONATED, BEFORE 1612, TO THE PORTUGUESE COMMUNITY IN AMSTERDAM, HOLLAND, BY JACOB TIRADO.
   Taken from H. K. Brugmans and H. Frank: "Geschiedenis der Joden in Nederland," I, Amsterdam, 1940, facing p. 208.
4) POINTER FROM MOROCCO, ENDING IN AN OVALSHAPED KNOB.
   New York, The Jewish Museum.

A GERMAN TORAH ORNAMENTATION

FRANZ LANDSBERGER

Hebrew Union College - Jewish Institute of Religion, Cincinnati

WHEN, in the year 1923, the Hebrew Union College acquired, from Berlin, the Sally Kirschstein collection, the College came into possession of an ornamental breastplate and two ornamental headpieces (*Rimmonim*), such as serve to decorate a scroll of the Pentateuch. Judging from their style and their material, all of these objects must have belonged together (Illust. 1). Ordinarily such a set contains also a pointer, and a pointer was found (Illust. 3). At first the yellowish color of these four pieces led me to suppose that they were of brass. Closer scrutiny showed them to be of silver overlaid with gold.

An oval plaque screwed to the breastplate carries a Hebrew inscription reading in translation: "The possession of Asher ben Naphtali Niedermeier of טאלמעסינגען, the first of Sivan 618 by the small reckoning" (the Gregorian year 1858). טאלמעסינגען is doubtless the present Thalmaessing. This is the name of a village in the district of Hippoltstein; also a village, in the district of Regensburg, both in Bavaria. To find out anything about Asher Niedermeier was impossible. He must have been a man of wealth; otherwise he could not have acquired such costly objects. And wealthy villagers were not unusual, particularly in Bavaria. For centuries the Jews were forbidden to reside in the Bavarian cities. Jews were "Country Jews" (*Landjuden*), living in the villages. But, conducting business in the cities which they were allowed to enter by day, Jews often amassed means.

The year 1858 might be regarded as the year in which those pieces were made. Yet their style induces us to surmise an earlier date. I removed the oval plaque, hoping to find an older inscription beneath it. But such was not there. However, a careful inspection of the breastplate and the headpieces revealed silver markings,[1] recogniz-

---

[1] The pointer lacks those markings, probably because there was no way of applying a stamp to its round shaft. However, the chain of the pointer resembles the chain of the breastplate in all respects.

Reprinted from *Hebrew Union College Annual*, Vol. XXIX, 1958.

able as the hallmark, the name of the place, and the maker's mark, that is, the artist's initials. The hallmark pictures a monk with outstretched arms, the "Munich Childlet," so-called, such as was commonly stamped on silver pieces made in that city. To the left of the monk stands a figure 2; to his right, a figure 8. Combining these with the style of the pieces, we arrive at the conjecture that the pieces were produced in the year 1828.

The maker's mark displays a G next to a Z on a rectangular field which has all of its four corners blunted. To anyone informed about goldsmithery, these letters are familiar. In the Damenstift church of Munich, they appear on two embossed figures representing Saint Joseph and John the Baptist. They appear, likewise in Munich, on a monstrance in the church of Saint Peter — that is, not on the original work but on various renovations. What was the full name of G. Z.? Research as to Bavarian goldsmiths[2] has divulged a Georg Zeiller, the son of a farmer in Hohenlegehofen. Zeiller had studied silvercraft under a master, Spiegelberger, in Landshut. In Munich, Zeiller was himself ordained master about the year 1780. Zeiller could be traced in Munich up to the year 1803. After that, all vestiges of him were lost. In all likelihood it was this Georg Zeiller who created those pieces for the Munich churches. It is equally probable that our Torah decorations were his product. With these suppositions, the life and the work of Georg Zeiller extend in two directions. Ordained master in 1780, he was still living in 1828, producing, in his later years, the pieces which we have mentioned; while this same artist, working for the Catholic churches, rendered service also for the Jews at least in this one instance.

This need occasion no surprise. In Western Europe, the Jews had, long before, lost the skills at goldsmithery for which they had once been famed. Even had they possessed the talent, they would have been debarred from membership in the Christian guilds and from the right to sell their output to the Gentiles.[3]

The employment of Christian artists by Jews did not signify that the artists were free to do as they pleased. The artists were, in one particular, unhindered: their works could adhere to the style

---

[2] Cf. Max Frankenburger, *Die Alt-Muenchner Goldschmiede und ihre Kunst*, Munich 1912, pp. 201, 241, 422 f. 486. Concurring is Marc Rosenberg, *Der Goldschmiede Merkzeichen*, third edition, Vol. II, Frankfurt am Main, 1923, No. 3576.

[3] For example, it was that way, in the eighteenth century, with the Bavarian Jew, Abraham Uhlfelder, the grandfather of Friedrich Julius Stahl. Cf. Gerhard Masur, *Friedrich Julius Stahl*, Berlin 1930, p. 20, note 1.

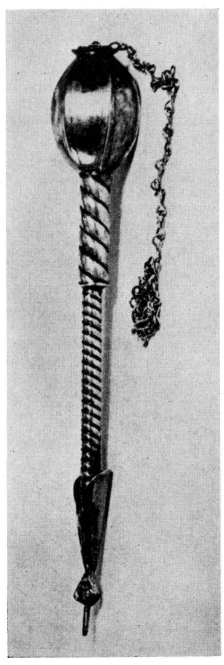

2. POINTER IN ROCOCO STYLE,
Collection of the HUC-JIR in Cincinnati.

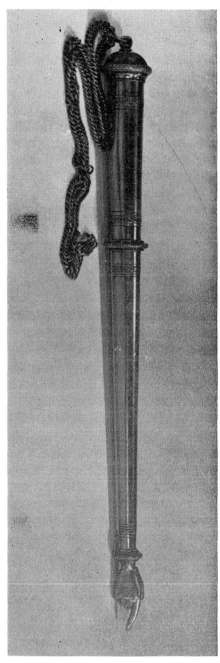

3. POINTER IN NEO-CLASSICAL STYLE,
Belonging to the Torah Decoration of Ill. 1;
Collection of the HUC-JIR in Cincinnati.

of their country and their age. But the Jewish patron demanded more. The art objects which he ordered had to comport with the tenets of his faith, particularly when those objects were of religious import.

Take, for example, the pointer. There was a predilection for shaping the pointer like a scepter, thus fulfilling a two-fold purpose. The pointer functioned as an outstretched finger to guide the reading of the text. It also satisfied the religious longing for a scepter to express the Torah's royal exaltedness. About the middle of the eighteenth century, the style of such a pointer assumed the elegance of rococo. Our example in illustration 2 shows an oval ball from which there emerges a spirally twisted staff ending in a hand with a gauntlet, the gauntlet betokening the attire of a cavalier. But, toward the end of the eighteenth century, tastes underwent a change. Such was the influence of antiquity as to instil a preference for magnitude and simplicity. Hence, in our Munich example (Illust. 3), the absence of the ball, of the spiral, and of the gauntlet and, instead of these, a smooth tapering staff, the plainness of which is interrupted only by a few rings.[4]

More complex must be our suppositions about the headpieces, the *Rimmonim* (pomegranates). At first the headpieces were spherical. Like the tinkling bells by which they are often accompanied, we can interpret the pomegranates as symbols derived from the bells and the pomegranates in the garb of the ancient high priest. Both of these, especially the bells, were supposedly imbued with the power to repel demons.[5] Exodus 28.35 reads: "And it shall be upon Aaron to minister; and the sound thereof shall be heard when he goeth unto the holy place before the Lord, and when he cometh out, that he die not." In the synagogue, the "holy place" became the holy ark out of which the scroll of the Pentateuch would be lifted and to which, after the reading, the scroll would be restored.

While these forms persisted in the orient, the pomegranates were, in the occident, repeatedly supplanted by "towers." Christian gold-smiths evidently associated bells with the tower of a church.[6] The

---

[4] A Bavarian pointer, similarly inornate, is to be found in the Jewish Museum of New York. Illustration in Kayser-Schoenberger, *Jewish Ceremonial Art*, Philadelphia 1955, pl. XXII, No. 64.

[5] Cf. James George Frazer, "The Golden Bells," in his *Folklore in the Old Testament*, New York, 1923, pp. 417 ff.

[6] The oldest extant tower-shaped Torah headpieces, usually dated as originating in the fifteenth century, are those kept in the treasury of the cathedral at Palma in Mallorca.

4. 18th Century Rimmonim Fashioned by Jeremias Zobel
in Frankfort on the Main.
Collection of the HUC-JIR in Cincinnati.

shape of the towers changed from country to country and from
age to age. Again we take an example from the eighteenth century
(Illust. 4). Here the towers consist of two polygonal stories with bells
filling the insides. The towers culminate in the curve of a crown
likewise supplied with a bell. Jewish art of that time indulged itself
such playfulness.

Our Munich headpieces, by contrast, exhibit simplicity and
magnitude (Illust. 1). From a massive shaft, there arises, in the
classical manner, a single — hence a much higher — story (Illust. 1),
the artist taking his hint perhaps from the old Munich town hall

(Illust. 5). But the artist changed the pillars into columns. Following antique models, the story, its roof consisting of palm branches, ascends like a circular temple. A crown here also caps the whole.

5. OLD MUNICH TOWNHALL.
Notice the Helmet of the Tower (Spire)
with its Open Gallery.

Finally the breastplate. I take this opportunity to rectify a view which I expressed on a previous occasion,[7] namely, that the breastplate, introduced by the Ashkenazic Jews, first appeared about the year 1530. From a communication of Dr. M. Narkiss, now deceased, I learn that the breastplate was known as far back as the late Middle Ages. It is mentioned in a rabbinic pronouncement of Israel ben Pethahiah Isserlein who lived in Austria ca. 1390–1460.[8] The passage, in free translation and abbreviation, reads: "To me it looks like a lowering of its sanctity if a rod, from which ark curtains are suspended, is converted into plates for scrolls of the Pentateuch — those plates that indicate the occasions on which the scrolls are to be used. Such plates are purely a matter of expediency. They are nothing but

[7] Cf. "The Origin of European Torah Decorations," *HUCA*, XXIV, 1952/53, p. 145.

[8] Cf. his book, *Terumat Hadeshen*, Part II, par. 225.

markers for preventing errors with regard to which scroll is to be read from at a given time. Those plates serve neither the purpose of beautifying the scroll nor that of chastely covering the scroll."[9]

Accordingly such breastplates must have existed in the fifteenth century, perhaps earlier. We gather from this source that the breastplate served predominantly a practical purpose. Our view that the *artistically ornamented* breastplate is a product of modern times is thus justified with some qualification.

The artistry was at first ornamental on the whole. For example, a breastplate of the early seventeenth century, prepared for the new immigrants at Amsterdam, is adorned almost entirely by tendrils. Its one and only symbol is a crown of the Torah.[10] But gradually the breastplate gathered more and more Jewish motifs, even while the Christian goldsmith clung to the style of his time and his land. A breastplate dating from the middle of the eighteenth century (Illust. 6) shows, on its bottom, three heads of lions, bells dangling from their mouths. This repeats the motif of the demon-repelling sounds. As regards the two unicorns — unicorns figure not seldom in Jewish art[11] — we promptly recall Psalm 92.11, "But my horn hast Thou exalted like the horn of the wild-ox," quoted in the prayers for the Sabbath. The crown here is again the crown of the Torah. The rampant lions at the side allude to Genesis 49.9, "Judah is a lion's whelp." The double-headed eagle on top brings us into the secular, the breastplate having been designed in Nuremberg, a free city; hence the eagle with two heads.

The style of the breastplate is rococo with all its charm. The contour seems to fluctuate. Flowerets lie strewn over the intervening spaces. Semi-precious stones, green and red, put additional touches of color upon the silver surface.

How different is the style of the breastplate from Munich (Illust. 7)! Like the Nuremberg breastplate, the Munich breastplate has three pendant bells. Also common to the two, the symbols and ornaments are not embossed on the plaque but, separately cast, are screwed on. Their contrast lies in the fact that, at the borders of the Munich breastplate, two columns arise, tall and fluted. These bring to mind the columns of the Solomonic Temple, while the flaming braziers over

---

[9] An allusion to the Talmudic adage, "Whoso touches an unclad Torah will lie unclad in his grave" (Sabbath 14a).

[10] For an illustration of this piece, see my book *A History of Jewish Art*, Cincinnati, 1946, p. 23.

[11] Cf. Rachel Wischnitzer, "The Unicorn in Christian and Jewish Art," in the periodical, *Historia Judaica*, XIII, 1951, pp. 141 ff.

6. Breastshield in Rococo Style, Nuremberg,
Germany, 1752.
Collection of the HUC-JIR in Cincinnati.

the capitals recall the burnt offerings in the Temple court. In artistic
terminology, these columns exemplify the undeviating straight line,
so different from the restless contour of the breastplate in rococo.
The lions of Judah, greatly enlarged, lie there powerful in repose. The
two tables of the Decalogue, enfolded in branches but themselves
rigidly straight, hang hoisted above the small removable plates which
indicate the days on which the particular scroll was to be utilized.[12]

[12] Our breastplate still possesses only one of these removable plates, the one
inscribed פסח.

7. Breastplate from our German Torah Ornamentation Ill. 1.

Far toward the top shines a crown comparable to that on the breast-plate from Nuremberg.

A classical majesty emanates from all these objects and forms. Only the pointed arches, intersecting one another over the tables of the Decalogue, embody the Gothic style. And these are not the only instances in which this period looks back to the Christian Gothic and, at the same time, to heathen antiquity.[13]

Another distinguishing feature of our Torah ornamentation is its costliness. We have referred to the silver plaque with its golden overlay. The original silver remains in the removable plates and in the two tables of the Decalogue, but not elsewhere. To these two colors, other colors are added, enriching the color scheme. Around the small removable plate are set rubies, while another row of those precious stones adorns the fillet of the upper crown. Tiny diamonds gleam between the projections of this crown. The points of these projections are studded with pearls.

This lavishness raises the question: What synagogue was it that could have housed such magnificence? Inasmuch as the artificer lived in Munich, we think of Munich from the outset. But what was Jewish existence like in that city? From Munich the Jews had, for centuries, been excluded. A small Jewish community, founded there at the end of the seventeenth century, was soon driven out.[14] Not until the eighteenth century did some Jews again venture, under humiliating conditions, to make Munich their home. Building a synagogue was forbidden; for prayer assemblies, the Jews had to content themselves with a humble room. Only in the wealth of some individuals among them did the Jews find compensation for the paucity of their numbers and their liberties. It was, accordingly, a great event when, in the early nineteenth century, their privileges expanding with emancipation, permission was granted to build a synagogue. Bavaria, perpetually short of money, needed Jews to prop its wobbling finances. It became possible to engage, for the new structure, a noted Christian architect; like goldsmithery, architecture had ceased to be cultivated by the German Jews for centuries. The edifice reared by this Christian architect — his name was Jean-Baptiste Metivier — succumbed to

[13] The railings of the *Rimmon* towers are also shaped Gothic. More on the subject of the classic and the Gothic in the style of this period will be found in my book, *Die Kunst der Goethe-Zeit, Kunst und Kunstanschauung von 1750–1830*, Leipzig, 1931, *passim*.

[14] A sample of this era, a silver Elijah-cup, the work of the Christian goldsmith, Johann Michael Ernst, dated 1680, is in the possession of the well known art collector, Dr. Heinrich Feuchtwanger, formerly of Munich, now of Jerusalem

fire in 1887. But reproductions enable us to conjure up a picture. A medal, cast for the dedication, has preserved the appearance of the exterior.[15] According to this medal, the structure extended breadth-wise, less like a synagogue than like a palace of the Renaissance.

The interior, according to its likeness preserved in a drawing (Illust. 8), must have been of striking grandeur. Beneath a wide barrel vault, extends a broad nave, the balconies for the women resting upon its columns. One misses the *Bimah*, the reading desk which, in those days, usually stood in the center of the auditorium. Possibly this reading desk was, in the course of time, removed so as to supply more room for the growing congregation and also to lead the gaze toward the great alcove containing the Torah, and toward the lectern in front of the alcove. From this lectern resounded the sermons which, delivered in German, so that all might understand, occupied since the nineteenth century, more and more of a place in the service.

The aforementioned medal carries a German inscription which, translated, reads: "Built during the glorious reign of His Highness, Max Joseph I, now deceased. Dedicated on the eve of Passover, 5586 — April 21, 1826[16] — in the presence of King Ludwig I of Bavaria and of Queen Therese. Long may God preserve them!" In other words, the construction of the synagogue proceeded during two reigns. Building was begun at the time of Max Joseph I who was a friend of the Jews and who donated to the synagogue four of its columns.[17] Max Joseph, dying October 12, 1825, was succeeded by the art loving King Ludwig I. Ludwig also was favorably disposed toward the Jews, as becomes manifest by his presence at the dedication.

The edifice was consecrated in 1826. Our Torah ornaments are dated 1828. All of which strengthens the surmise that the synagogue for which these ornaments were prepared was the synagogue at Munich. Of course, the synagogue must already have had a scroll of the Pentateuch in 1826. The memorable dedication may, nevertheless,

[15] An illustration is to be found in the periodical, *Das Bayerland*, XXXVII, No. 20, Munich 1926.

[16] An error underlies the assertion of Salomon Taussig, *Geschichte der Juden in Bayern*, Munich, 1874, p. 70, that the synagogue was dedicated in 1827. For references to the literature on the Bavarian Jews of this period, I am indebted to Dr. Selma Stern-Taeubler of Cincinnati.

[17] Mentioned in the dedication sermon preached by Rabbi Hirsch Aub of Munich and printed as a pamphlet, Munich 1826, p. 8.

have prompted the wealthy congregation or one of its members to provide an additional scroll for use on special occasions.

In support of this surmise, we add two further surmises. The crown, adorned with pearls, rubies, and diamonds — was it meant purely as a crown of the Torah and not also as an allusion to the crown of Bavaria? In 1806 Max Joseph I had elevated his duchy into a kingdom. It could well have been expected that Ludwig I, his successor, would delight in beholding a magnificent crown amid the ornamentation of the synagogal breastplate. Similarly the two lions may have carried not only a Jewish significance, but also a Bavarian significance — above all, a significance for Munich. Munich, founded by Henry, the Lion (1129–1195), proudly displayed a lion on its coat of arms.

Finally the two lovely branches, one of palm and one of oak. There can be no doubt that this combination also was symbolic. The palm represents Judaism; the oak, Germanism. These two branches looped together implied: "We regard ourselves both as Jews and as Germans; and we yearn to have ourselves thus regarded by the Christians." Sentiments like that flourished particularly among the Jews of Munich. Not altogether lacking was the bent for Reform which permeated Jewish life at that time. Indicative of this was the preaching of sermons in German, remote though the Jews of Munich may have been from the more thoroughgoing Reform movements such as stirred, at that time, in Seesen, in Berlin, and in Hamburg. In Munich the prime striving was to adjust Judaism to the state,[18] sacrificing life itself, if need be. Thus we gain an understanding of those sacred appurtenances only when we connect them with their time and their place of origin.

A single question remains. How did those Torah decorations, fashioned in 1828, come thirty years later, into the private possession of that Asher ben Naphtali Niedermeier who has confided to us his name and the year of his acquisition? We can attempt only a conjecture. This we base upon the difficulty which must have been encountered whenever those ornaments were put to use. The cast adornments make the breastplate weigh five pounds. The two Torah headpieces weigh 6.4 pounds. Adding to this the poundage of the scroll itself, we get a weight well-nigh too heavy to hold, by all means too heavy to carry in procession as required by the ritual of *Simḥat*

---

[18] This is the view of Gerhard Masur in his excellent book about the convert, Friedrich Julius Stahl, the founder of the Conservative Party in Germany, Berlin, 1930, p. 23.

8. The Old Munich Synagogue, Succumbed to Fire in 1887.
Watercolor Painting by Ferdinand Petzl. Private Possession.

Torah. As a consequence, the Torah decoration may, despite all good intentions, have had to be laid aside and may eventually have been sold or presented to someone of means who, treasuring it for its notable history, would preserve it in his domicile. From the hands of this owner, these ornaments may have gotten into the hands of Sally Kirschstein, finally to reach the Hebrew Union College as parts of his collection. Here, though withdrawn from all religious use, these ornaments offer proof of the care which the Jews bestowed upon the beautification of their ritual objects.

TORAH ORNAMENTS, PRIESTLY VESTMENTS, AND THE KING JAMES BIBLE

JOSEPH GUTMANN

It is customary to read in many religious textbooks that silver adornments for the Torah scroll, like the Torah shield and headpieces, are analogous to the adornments worn by the High Priest. Such an assumption implies a long, hallowed and unbroken tradition for the use of these objects in the Jerusalem Temple and later in the synagogue. The Torah shield is usually called *hoshen* to correspond to the "breastpiece" (Exod. 28.4), or, less frequently, *tzitz,* "the frontlet" of pure gold (Exod. 28.36), both worn by the priest. The Torah headpieces (*rimmonim*) are derived from the "golden bell and pomegranate (רמון) all around the hem of the [High Priest's] robe" (Exod. 28.34).

How did the association of Torah ornaments with the High Priestly vestments come about, since neither this association nor the words *hoshen* or *tzitz* are found for the Torah shield in rabbinic literature? Moreover, the words חושן משפט. (Exod. 28.15) denote an oracular pouch, worn by the High Priest, which was made of cloth and not of metal, as is the case with the Torah shield.

The entry of the word breastplate into the English language and the subsequent Jewish designation of the Torah shield as a breastplate are due to the King James Bible translation of 1611. The word *hoshen* is here rendered as breastplate, and hence the assumed association probably arose between the High Priestly vestments and the Torah decorations. Such common ornamentation as the twelve tribal stones (Exod. 28.15 ff.), so frequently found in contemporary synagogue Torah shields in imitation of those on the *hoshen,* is therefore totally unwarranted, as no link seems to exist between the Torah shield and the priestly *hoshen.*[1]

What then was the origin of the Torah shields is found in a responsum of Israel ben Pethahiah Isserlein who lived in 15th-century Austria. He mentions the practice of converting Torah ark curtain rods into metal plates (פחים), which indicate the festive occasion for which the Torah scrolls were to be used (*Terumat ha-Deshen,* Part II, Par. 225). Hence, the Torah shields arose out of practical needs.[2] Elaborate and ornate Torah shields probably began to be fashioned from the 16th century on,

Reprinted from *Central Conference of American Rabbis Journal,* January, 1969.

although the earliest surviving one comes from early 17th-century Holland. Anthonius Margaritha in his *Der Gantz Jüdisch Glaub,* published in Augsburg in 1530, calls the Torah shield *ein silberins blech* (a silver plate).[3] Apparently, no special name had yet been attached to the Torah shield. Only in the 18th century does the name טס appear as the designation for the Torah shield—a term that has no association with the High Priestly vestments. The word *tas* itself is engraved on a Torah shield dating from 1780,[4] and Elazar Fleckeles from Prague, in a responsum of about 1809, also calls Torah shields טסים (*Teshuvah Me-Ahavah,* II, 232).[5]

Rimmonim are referred to as decoration for the Torah by Maimonides (*Yad, Hilkhot Sefer Torah* X.4) and in Cairo Genizah fragments.[6] The earliest surviving *rimmonim,* kept in the Cathedral Treasury of Palma de Majorca, may come from 15th-century Camarata, Sicily. These *rimmonim* are in the now familiar tower-shaped form.[7] Although the accepted name for Torah headpieces in Islamic communities was *rimmonim,* they were also called צפויי זהב (Responsa of Maharam, ed. Prag, 1608, No. 879) and תפוחים (Jacob ben Asher, *Tur, Yoreh Deah* 282) in medieval European Christian communities.[8] These golden ornaments or apples were apparently simply spherical knobs placed at the ends of the Torah staves, as can be seen in medieval Hebrew miniatures.

Crowns for the Torah are already referred to in Gaonic sources of the 10th century, which speak of the עטרה for Torah scrolls on *Simhat Torah;*[9] Cairo Genizah fragments also mention silver Torah crowns.[10] Nowhere, however, to my knowledge, is a link made in rabbinic literature between the High Priestly vestments and either the *rimmonim* or the crown.

Likewise, the *yad* has no connection with any High Priestly adornments. It does not seem to have come into being prior to the 16th century, for Anthonius Margaritha in 1530 still states: "When they read the Decalogue (i.e., the Torah), they place, on each side, a silk cloth so as not to touch the scroll with the bare hand.[11] Moses Isserles (*Orah Hayyim* 154.6) cites for the first time the practice of making עצים (wooden pointers) from Torah ark curtain rods to guide in the reading of the Torah.[12] Pointers in the shape of a hand are known from the late 16th century on and are referred to in a 1581 archival source from Prague.[13] The shape of the pointer probably led to the accepted term *yad.*

Thus we see that silver Torah objects used in contemporary synagogues, such as the *rimmonim* and crowns, are only mentioned in rabbinic literature from the 10th century on, while Torah shields and pointers do not seem to make their appearance until about the 16th century. However, the association of these objects with the High Priestly vestments, although widely accepted, has no foundation in rabbinic sources.

NOTES

[1] G. Schoenberger, "Der Frankfurter Goldschmied Johann Matthias Sandrart," *Schriften des Historischen Museums Frankfurt am Main,* XII (1966), 144-45, 169. Most Jewish translations, such as Isaac Leeser's (London, 1823) and that of the Jewish Publication Society (Philadelphia, 1917), accepted the King James rendering of *hoshen* as breastplate.

[2] F. Landsberger, "A German Torah Ornamentation," *Hebrew Union College Annual,* XXIX (1959), 322-23.

[3] F. Landsberger, "The Origin of European Torah Decorations," *Hebrew Union College Annual,* XXIV (1952-53), 144 ff., fig. 3.

[4] S. Kayser, *Jewish Ceremonial Art* (Philadelphia, 1959), p. 62, No. 49.

[5] S. B. Freehof, unpublished responsa on "Torah Decorations," which the author graciously put at my disposal. [See now S. B. Freehof, *Current Reform Responsa* (Cincinnati, 1969), pp. 18-21.]

[6] S. D. Goitein, "The Synagogue Building and its Furnishings According to the Records of the Cairo Genizah," *Eretz Israel,* VII (1964), 95.

[7] J. Gutmann, *Jewish Ceremonial Art* (New York, 1964), p. 16, fig. 1.

[8] Cf. Freehof, *op. cit.,* and Landsberger, *op. cit.,* pp. 139 ff.

[9] Landsberger, *ibid.,* pp. 140 ff.

[10] Goitein, *op. cit.,* pp. 94-95. Medieval rabbinic sources generally refer to the Torah crown as *atarah.* The term *keter torah.* appears underneath the Torah crown, embroidered on the 1592 Bohemian Torah ark curtain, now in the State Jewish Museum of Prague. Cf. O. Muneles, ed., *Prague Ghetto in the Renaissance Period* (Prague, 1965), Figs. 56-57.

[11] Landsberger, *op. cit.,* p. 148.

[12] Freehof, *op. cit.*

[13] J. Hrásky, "La corporation juive d'orfèvrerie à Prague," *Judaica Bohemiae,* II/1 (1966), 21.

OLD-TIME TORAH-CURTAINS

Apropos a New Acquisition of the Jewish Museum in New York

FRANZ LANDSBERGER, Hebrew Union College, Cincinnati

A NUMBER of years ago, an art dealer of New York City sent me a photograph showing the toppiece of a curtain such as hangs before an Ark of the Law (fig. 10). Embroidered on this toppiece was a double eagle which led the dealer to suppose that the piece was of Russian origin. Taking as numbers the letters נ and ש which appear, each in one of the margins alongside of a bird, the dealer concluded that the toppiece must have been produced about the year 1559–1560.

Neither inference seemed to me cogent. It is true, the double eagle stands on the Russian coat-of-arms. But it also stands on that of the Holy Roman Empire and, after the dissolution of the Holy Roman Empire (1806), on the coat-of-arms of Austria. Dots on Hebrew letters, while commonly indicating numbers, can likewise signify abbreviations of words. In any case, the number of the year could hardly have been meant here, since the toppiece betrays, by its Baroque style, not 16th century but 17th or 18th century production. Especial evidence of this are the five scallops alternating with pendant tassels. Bernini employed this form, in bronze, using it in 1633 on his huge canopy in St. Peter's at Rome. Since that time, this mode turns up recurrently on lambrequins of the 17th and, above all, of the 18th century.

When, a number of years later, I paid one of my visits to the Jewish Museum in New York, Prof. Alexander Marx showed me, among his new acquisitions, a superb ark-curtain (fig. 10), the gift of Dr. H. G. Friedman, the well known collector of Jewish ritual objects. Obtaining a photograph of this curtain,

Reprinted from *Hebrew Union College Annual*, Vol. XIX, 1945-1946.

I held this photograph and that of the toppiece alongside of one another. I then began to supect that the two belonged together. The material, in both cases, was red brocade. On both was embroidered the double eagle with the unusual *motif* of two fishes on its breast. The two embroidered crowns were of identical structure. Both stretches of cloth were of the same width. A toppiece must, of course, cover a curtain's uppermost reaches if it is to conceal the unsightly ropes by means of which the curtain is manipulated.

Later I learned that the toppiece, too, had ended up in the Jewish Museum of New York, donated by the same collector though acquired at a different time and from a different source. Here, likewise, it had been recognized that the two pieces belong together, and thus a new light was shed upon the toppiece. Also the curtain was supplied with numerals which, when added, yielded the date 1772–73. This date comports with the stylistic peculiarities, for the curtain was certainly a product of Baroque art which may well have been created in the 18th century. Even the names of the donors were found to be listed on the curtain, a certain Jakob Kitzingen — after the Bavarian town Kitzingen — and his wife Hendel Ulma who came from Pfersee, Bavaria. Finally the artist had embroidered his own name and place of origin on the curtain: Jakob Koppel Gans from הוכשתת, the town of Höchstädt, or Höchstadt, referring either to the town of this name on the Danube or the one on the Aisch, both in Bavaria.

The curtain and its toppiece, therefore, stemmed from 18th century Bavaria. Attractive for their beauty alone, the two pieces gained additional importance in the light of this conclusion. As is well known, the synagogues of Germany were burnt in November 1938 by infamous Nazi hordes and together with the buildings, ritual objects of great worth were destroyed. In this case, a valuable piece of synagogal equipment had in some unknown manner escaped destruction and had found a secure haven in America. This alone would have sufficed to justify closer consideration of that object. Further appeal was lent to such an undertaking by the fact that the curtain is no singular, isolated phenomenon but belongs to an entire group whose quality surpasses all curtains of its time. It is particularly gratifying that these textiles were created by Jews themselves, a practice not at all prevalent in the Germany of the 18th century. At that time, all houses of worship and all silver decorations for synagogues and homes in Germany were made by Christians — *for* Jews, but not *by* Jews. The reason for this is that the strictly enforced laws of the guilds had excluded the Jews from many artistic endeavors. The Jewish embroiderer, on the other hand, occupied his rightful place in the large communities, like the Jewish scribe who frequently adorned his Haggadoth, his scrolls of the Book of Esther and his marriage-contracts with rich decorations, and also like the Jewish seal-engraver who tended to treat his products artistically.[1] It was Jews who created the Torah-curtains, the mantles around the Torah-scrolls, the covers for the Torah-tables and the cantor's desk. This, naturally, makes these textiles exceedingly valuable to us.

What finally induced me to write this article was the conspicuous lack of literature upon this subject.[2] I was led to trace the origin and development of the Torah-curtain, as far as this is at all possible at this time and from this locality. Moreover I welcome the chance to assign to the New York curtain its true place in history.[3]

[1] About the influence and importance of the Jewish embroiderer for his co-religionists as well as for gentiles, see my articles: "The Jewish Artist before the Period of Emancipation," *HUCA*, XVI, 1941, pp. 399 f. and "New Studies in Early Jewish Artists," *ib*. XVIII, 1944, pp. 299 f.

[2] See Heinrich Frauberger, "Ueber alte Kultusgegenstaende in Synagoge und Haus," *Mitteilungen der Gesellschaft zur Erforschung juedischer Kunstdenkmaeler*, III/IV, Frankfurt a/M, 1903, pp. 13–17; Ida Posen, "Die Mainzer Torah-Vorhaenge," *Notizblaetter der Gesellschaft zur Erforschung juedischer Kunstdenkmaeler*, No. 29; Elisabeth Moses, "Juedische Kult- und Kunstdenkmaeler in den Rheinlanden," in the Collection: *Aus der Geschichte der Juden im Rheinland*, Duesseldorf, 1931, pp. 138–144; in addition the pertinent articles in the Jewish encyclopedias.

[3] Again my colleagues at the Hebrew Union College have given me all the information I requested. I mention, with special gratitude, Samuel Atlas, Alexander Guttmann, Moses Marx, Isaiah Sonne, Max Vogelstein, Michael Wilensky. My gratitude also goes out to Dr. Aron Freimann, New York, Dr. Selma Taeubler, Cincinnati, O., and Dr. Wolfgang Stechow at Oberlin College, Oberlin, O.

I. Antiquity

The Bible, in its description of the Tent of Meeting and of Solomon's Temple, mentions a curtain which separated the main hall from the Holy of Holies (Ex.26.31–33, 36.35–36, II Chron. 3.14). Behind the curtain stood the holiest of the cult objects, the Ark, above which God would reveal Himself between golden cherubim.

Cherubim were also embroidered on the curtains which were wrought of the costliest materials known to the art of the Orient.

When the synagogue arose alongside of the Temple — we know not when — it contained neither Holy of Holies nor Ark, and consequently no protecting curtain. The Torah, written on one or several scrolls, had at first no fixed depository but was brought in for the reading and removed after the service.[4] Probably a low box, round or square, served for its transportation, a box similar to the one used for such purposes by pagans. On the wall paintings of the synagogue of Dura Europos, dating from the third century of our era, can be seen a man in erect position, wearing Ẓiẓit on his garment and hence an Israelite (fig. 1). He spreads out a scroll before his breast, while a round box stands alongside, undoubtedly a box such as that in which the scrolls were kept. The box is covered with a red cloth, probably because the writings which it contains are holy. Also the biblical Ark was covered with a cloth during transportation. (Num. 4.6).[5]

This interpretation is based on the assumption that the male figure really holds a Torah. It could be objected that, in seizing the scroll with his hands, he acts contrary to the statement: "One who holds a Scroll of the Law naked will be buried naked" (Sab. 14 a and elsewhere). But Rabbi Jochanan bar Nappaḥa who

---

[4] Cf. Samuel Krauss, *Synagogale Altertuemer*, Berlin-Vienna, 1922, p. 371; E. L. Sukenik, *Ancient Synagogues in Palestine and Greece*, London, 1934, p. 52.

[5] Cf. Mesnil du Buisson, *Les peintures de la synagogue de Doura-Europos*, Rome, 1939, p. 94.

uttered these words lived as late as the third century, so that the viewpoint represented by him may not have been generally accepted at that time.

A fact definitely in favor of the assumption that the scroll does represent the Torah is the circumstance that the male figure — together with three others — stands above a niche in which the scrolls are contained. A scroll painted in this location can hardly be anything but a Torah-scroll and the man who holds it must stand in close relation to it. For this reason, the male figure is to be interpreted either as Moses by whom the Torah was put into writing or as Ezra who read it to the people and proclaimed it the official legislative code of the community. Most recently it has been suggested that, in this figure, we recognize Samuel.[6] In that case, the scroll would contain the regulations for the newly established kingdom. But since the Bible states explicitly that Samuel recited these regulations orally to the people and wrote them down later not in order to read them but rather to lay them "before the Lord" (I Sam. 10.25), the interpretation of the figure as Samuel has little in its favor.

On the other hand, when it is assumed that the portable container for the Torah-scroll was covered with a piece of cloth, a statement in the Talmud becomes intelligible which, in my opinion, has until now been explained incorrectly. The problem is being discussed what to do with ritual objects that are no longer usable. "Our rabbis taught: accessories of religious observances [when worn out] are to be thrown away; accessories of holiness are to be stored away" (Meg. 26b). Rabba adds: "At first I used to think that the cover (פרסא) is an accessory of an accessory. When, however, I observed that it is folded over and a scroll placed on it"— apparently due to the great dignity of the Torah — "I came to the conclusion that it is itself an accessory of holiness." The commentators assume that this statement refers to the curtain of the Torah-shrine. But how

[6] Rahel Wischnitzer-Bernstein, "The Samuel Cycle in the Wall Decoration of the Synagogue of Dura-Europos," *Proceedings of the American Academy for Jewish Research*, XI, 1941, pp. 85 ff.

is one to imagine that such a curtain would be taken off at every reading in order to deposit the Torah on it? On the other hand, no trouble would be entailed in putting the loose cover of the scroll-box on the table the moment that the scroll was taken out of the box.

There may have been a time when no textiles were used in the synagogue in connection with the Torah except the one which covered the box and which was, when needed, spread under the scroll. In Dura Europos, however, i. e. in the third century of our era, we come upon a cover which corresponds to the Torah-cover in the sense later adopted, that is, a hanging cloth. As already stated, a niche in the synagogue served to contain the Torah-scrolls (fig. 2). It has been assumed that this niche held a permanent Torah-shrine which was subsequently lost.[7] It is more likely that a Torah-box stood in the niche not permanently but merely for the duration of the services,[8] because, in the first place, the niche is not very large, and, in the second, it is decorated, and that would be superfluous if the niche were constantly filled. These decorations would serve a purpose if a low box were placed in the niche for short periods. The rounded rear wall of the niche would provide an excellent receptacle for the round form of the box.

There are traces, in this niche, indicating that a curtain hung in front of it.[9] Such curtains may have become customary when the portable Torah-container was supplanted by a permanent Torah-shrine and when this shrine was placed in an apse, that is, a semicircular or rectangular chamber pushed back into the rear wall. The fragmentary remains of synagogues with such apses date only from periods more recent than the fourth century of the Christian Era. For instance, in front of the apse in the synagogue at Beth Alpha (6th century), there have been found two round holes. These holes may have been

[7] Mesnil du Buisson, l. c., p. 10.

[8] Cf. E. L. Sukenik, *The Ancient Synagogue of El- Hammeh*, Jerusalem, 1935, p. 74.

[9] Mesnil du Buisson, l. c., p. 10, note 1: "On a revelé seulement les traces des cordes qui servaient à suspendre un rideau."

fastenings for posts, and curtains may have hung between those posts.[10]

It must be remembered that these curtains were not as yet integral parts of the Torah-shrine, as were those with which we shall deal later. They hung rather in front of the niche or apse in which the Torah-scrolls were temporarily or permanently kept. They hung as the curtain hung in the Tent of Meeting and before the Holy of Holies in the Temple, of which they surely constitute a reminiscence. For that reason the curtain was called *Paroket*, the same designation which had been given to the curtains in the old sanctuaries (Ex. 26.3, II Chron. 3.14). By analogy, the chamber hidden by the curtain should have been called *Debir*, like the Holy of Holies in the Temple. Though, for easily understood reasons, that name was not employed, it is nonetheless significant that the niche was called *Hekal*, the name of the main hall of the Temple which lay immediately in front of the Holy of Holies.

Here, too, a regulation becomes comprehensible which is recorded in the Talmud several times, that is, in the Palestinian Talmud.[11] The question is raised what to do on certain holidays when several diversely located passages were to be read while only one Torah-scroll was at hand. In such a case, declared R. Jose (probably Jose ben Zebida who lived in Palestine in the 4th

[10] Cf. E. L. Sukenik, *The Ancient Synagogue of Beth Alpha*, Jerusalem and London, 1932, p. 13. Sukenik (pp. 20 f.) thinks he has discovered such poles in front of a Torah-shrine also on a gilt-glass found in a Jewish catacomb. The glass is today in the Vatican. The curtain itself, he maintains, has been omitted in order not to disturb the view of the shrine. This is incorrect. We have here not a shrine but rather the Temple, and the two pillars are Yachin and Boaz which stood in front of the Solomonic sanctuary. Sukenik believes them to be more "like wooden poles than columns." But already Perrot and Chipiez, *History of Art in Sardinia, Judaea, Syria and Asia Minor*, II, London-New York, 1890, p. 23, correctly noted their bronze color in harmony with the Biblical report that they were molten. Jewish art of the Middle Ages, moreover, uses the representation of these two columns in connection with the Temple, *e. g.* in the Egyptian Pentateuch of 930 in the Public Library of Leningrad. Reproduction in D. Guenzburg and W. V. Stassoff, *L'Ornament Hebreu*, Berlin 1905, pl. III.

[11] J. Meg. IV, 5; J. Yoma, VII, 1; J. Sot., VII, 6; J. Sopherim, XI, 3; — It was already noticed by S. Krauss, *Synagogale Altertuemer*, l. c., p. 380.

century), the synagogue beadle should go behind the curtain to roll the parchment to the second or third passage; evidently because it would be unbecoming to do so in sight of the worshiping congregation. It is difficult to imagine how someone could step behind a curtain which was affixed to the Torah-shrine. Such would be possible, on the other hand, if the curtain hung before a niche or an apse.

The recollection awakened, by this curtain, of the corresponding curtain in the old Tent of Meeting and in the Temple was intensified by adjacent paintings which represented or, at least, pointed to the biblical sanctuaries. An example of such decoration has been preserved in the synagogue of Dura Europos (fig. 2). Above the niche we see the seven-branched candelabrum, the Temple itself,[12] and finally the sacrifice of Isaac on Mount Moriah, the latter, no doubt, because it, too, stands in some relation to the Temple. "Solomon began to build the house of the Lord at Jerusalem on Mount Moriah" is the phrase in II Chron. 3.1.

We should like to know the looks of such a curtain which hung before the container of the Torah. No such curtain has, however, been preserved. A curtain of this type is believed to be pictured on a panel (here reproduced) of the floor mosaic

PANEL FROM THE MOSAIC FLOOR IN BETH ALPHA

[12] Joseph C. Sloane, "The Torah Shrine in the Ashburnham Pentateuch," *Jewish Quarterly Review*, N. S., XXV, 1934/35, p. 3, identifies this building as a Torah-shrine, interpreting the flanking columns as supports for the missing curtain. Highly improbable!

in the synagogue of Beth Alpha. The hypothesis has been advanced that this picture represents the interior of a synagogue with its Torah-shrine; in front of which there is tucked a white curtain in which rows of colored flowers have been embroidered.[13] I doubt the correctness of this interpretation. The central object is more likely the Ark of the Covenant. If it were a Torah-shrine, there would not be an obstructing pillar right in the center where the doors of the shrine would come together. The two lions are the cherubim which, in the Solomonic Temple, stood in front of the Ark; here they have been moved to the sides because the artist of this late period transposes every depth into the perspective of a two dimensional area. The birds, too, are cherubim. Apparently those cherubim on the cover of the Ark were at times regarded as birds. At least Philo, in his Life of Moses (III, 8), thus construes them. Furthermore, what sense would there be in painting the picture of a synagogue within a real synagogue? It would, on the other hand, be very meaningful to place in the synagogue a reminder of the Temple whose reconstruction in the days of the Kingdom of God was looked forward to with such longing. For that reason, the wall of the synagogue, toward which the face of the worshipper was turned, lay in the direction of Jerusalem. For that reason, too, stone lions were placed in some synagogues, similar to the ones on the mosaic of Beth Alpha, as reminders of the cherubim in the Temple. For that reason, finally, synagogues were provided with seven-branched candelabra. A Greek inscription which has been preserved in the synagogue of Sideh in Pamphylia testifies explicitly to the presence of such candelabra.[14] In Beth Alpha, just as in Dura Europos, the representation of the Temple is supplemented by that of the sacrifice of Isaac. The story of the sacrifice has here been characteristically moved to the beginning of the mosaic while the Temple appears at its end, close to the wall which faces Jerusalem.

In view of these considerations, the curtain of Beth Alpha cannot figure in our investigation. It is not the curtain of a

---

[13] E. L. Sukenik, *The Ancient Synagogue of Beth Alpha, l. c.* p. 34.
[14] Cf. S. Krauss, *Synagogale Altertuemer, l. c.* p. 236.

synagogue but of the Temple. With the latter it has only one element in common: it is not attached to an object; rather it shuts off a separate room.

It is conceivable that these synagogal curtains were brought to a high degree of excellence. For the ancient synagogue was deeply influenced by Hellenism with which it shared the joy that was felt in the attractive formation of each and every detail. Upon the curtain a great deal of care may, accordingly, have been lavished.

The appearance of those ancient Torah-arks is known from pictures only. The best of these — like the one shown here in an enlarged reproduction — are to be found on gilt-glass cups, which are so called because of bottoms with gold drawings.

TORAH SHRINE FROM BOTTOM OF A JEWISH GILT GLASS
Enlarged. Berlin, Museum.

On these pictures, an ark is to be seen with both doors open. The interior is furnished with shelves on which the scrolls are placed horizontally. In front of the door no curtain is visible, which is another proof that the curtain fastened external to the shrine was not yet the custom. On the other hand, a few of these representations — for example, the one here reproduced — reveal, upon closer examination, a curtain *behind* the doors. The curtain is pulled aside in such a way that only two small

1. MOSES OR EZRA
From Dura-Europos

2. TORAH NICHE
From Dura-Europos

3. GERMAN MAḤSOR, 1459
Munich, State Library

4. (above) TORAH CURTAIN
Padua, Synagogue

5. (right) TORAH CURTAIN
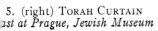 at Prague, Jewish Museum

135

6. (above) Torah Curtain
Last at Prague, Jewish Museum

7. (right) Embroidered Torah Curtain

8. (above) ELKONE NAUMBURG: TORAH CURTAIN
   From the Hambro Synagogue in London

9. (right) JACOB KOPPEL GANS: TORAH CURTAIN
   Last at Synagogue of Krumbach

137

138

10. Jacob Koppel Gans: Torah Curtain with Toppiece
New York, Jewish Museum

triangles can be discerned. The curtain may have served practical purposes, like the entire ark which was originally a useful piece of furniture. In this respect, the ark is comparable to the cupboards of Hellenistic times in which scrolls and the like were kept. Since the scrolls in our ark carry no covers, double protection may well have been essential — namely the ark itself plus the curtain. But sacramental considerations may also have played a part. The curtain may have betokened reverence for the scrolls of the Law. Be that as it may, the ancient synagogue shows here, in connection with the Torah, another kind of curtain, a curtain which does not appear in front of the doors, but which becomes visible only after the doors are opened.

II. THE MIDDLE AGES

It is exceedingly difficult to form a clear picture of Torah-curtains in the Middle Ages. From this period, as little has been preserved as from the period of antiquity. Eagerly one seeks pictures of the synagogues of that time in the hope of gaining some information. A few pictures can be found in that branch of the arts which the Middle Ages brought to florescence, that is, in illuminated manuscripts. The famous Haggadah of Sarajevo, a Spanish manuscript of the 14th century, vouchsafes us, on one of its pages, a glimpse into a synagogal service. The double doors of the Torah-shrine are open. Inside, three Torah-scrolls, no longer in horizontal but rather in vertical positions, are visible, dressed in beautiful mantles and crowned with golden *Rimmonim*. A Torah-curtain is not to be seen. Was there one?[15]

Among illuminated Italian books, we possess a manuscript of Jacob Asher's *'Arba' Turim*, written in 1436 in Mantua, (Rome, Library of the Vatican, Cod. Ross. 555). One of its pages likewise offers an insight into the service of a synagogue.[16]

---

[15] Colored reproductions in Heinrich Mueller and Julius von Schlosser, *Die Haggadah von Serajevo*, Vienna, 1898.

[16] Only the rear wall of the room is here decorated with curtains. Reproductions in the Hungarian work by E. Munkacsi, *Illuminated Manuscripts in Italian Libraries*, Budapest, n. d., fig. 22; from it, *Juedisches Lexikon*, V, pl. 152.

One sees a beautifully carved Torah-shrine in Gothic style with doors open. But here also no curtain is visible.

Closed Torah-shrines are represented also in Italian manuscripts; in the *Yad Haḥazaḳah* of Maimonides which, when last heard of, was part of a private collection in Frankfort (early 15th century),[17] and in the *Book of Rituals* of the University Library at Princeton, N. J. (late 15th century).[18] Here also no trace of a curtain can be discovered.

The only curtain which I could find was in a German *Maḥzor* written in 1459 and preserved in the Munich Staatsbibliothek (fig. 3).[19] Both doors of a Torah-shrine are open. Behind one of the wings, a half-concealed curtain can be seen. As in the gilt glass picture previously shown, the curtain is attached to the ark. But while, in the former case, the curtain becomes visible only after the doors were opened, here the curtain hangs in front of the door. What we have here is apparently the historical continuation of the curtain which, in antiquity, closed off the *Hekal*. This room was often omitted in the Middle Ages. When money or space was insufficient, that room could be discarded by placing the Torah-shrine directly before the wall. Hence the custom of hanging the curtain from the top of the chest itself.

This type of curtain may have arisen in the small German communities which underwent constant persecution in the Middle Ages, and may then have been brought to other countries by emigrants. This type characterizes the Ashkenazic synagogue.

At the same time, the other type — the curtain visible only when the doors were opened — has not disappeared. Though no specimens of that type have been preserved from the Middle Ages, not even in pictures, there are, at least, some modern examples. These can be found in Italy and in synagogues of the Sephardic ritual. These curtains have been assumed to be "a

[17] Cf. Heinrich Frauberger, *Verzierte hebraeische Schrift und juedischer Buchschmuck*, Frankfurt a/M, 1909, fig. 6.

[18] Cf. Erwin Panofsky in the *Journal of the Walters Art Gallery*, Iv, 1941, pp. 27 ff.: "Giotto and Maimonides in Avignon," reproductions facing pp. 27 and 33.

[19] The reproduction according to Richard Krautheimer, *Synagogen des Mittelalters*, Berlin 1927, fig. 28.

relic of the times when such receptacles had to be concealed from the offices of the Inquisition."[20] To me it seems more probable that such curtains continue the tradition of just the type of curtain which we have already discovered in the pictures on some of the Jewish gilt glasses.

It appears that the Sephardic Jews did not consistently adhere to this custom in the centuries subsequent to the Middle Ages. The Spanish born Joseph ben Ephraim Caro, author of the *Shulḥan 'Aruk*, speaks of a curtain in front of, not behind, the doors of the Torah-shrine (*'Oraḥ Ḥayyim* 154,3). In a description of the Sephardic service held in 17th century England, we hear likewise that the priest "drew the curtain, and opening the double door of it, the Law appeared."[21] Lastly, the fact is striking that the most important Sephardic synagogue in Holland, dedicated in Amsterdam in the year 1675, has no Torah-curtain whatsoever.[22] When the many doors of the broad ark are opened, the magnificent mantles in which the scrolls are wrapped become visible; but there is no curtain, either outside or inside. Apparently the utilization of a curtain was not considered obligatory among Sephardic Jews, and here we recall that the synagogue of the Sarajevo *Haggadah* also showed no curtain.

The Talmud once interprets the verse "This is my God and I will glorify Him" (Ex. 15.2) in the following manner: "Make a beautiful *Sukkah* in His honor, a beautiful *Lulab*, a beautiful *Shofar*, beautiful *Ẓiẓit*, and a beautiful scroll of the Law, and write it with fine ink, a fine reed, and a skilled penman, and wrap it about with beautiful silks!" (Sab. 133b). A Torah-curtain is not mentioned here. This admonition undoubtedly

[20] So Joseph Jacobs and Lucien Wolf, *Catalogue of the Anglo-Jewish Historical Exhibition*, London 1887, London, 1888, p. 85.

[21] John Greenhalgh in a letter from London to the Rev. Thomas Crompton in the year 1662, reprinted in the *Anglo-Jewish Letters*, ed. Cecil Roth, London, 1938, pp. 59 ff.

[22] Reproductions in B. Picart, *Cérémonies et coutumes réligiéuses de tous les peuples du monde*, vol. I, Amsterdam, 1723, facing p. 125, — Also the Italian rabbi Leon de Modena (1571–1648) in his *Riti Ebraici*, Part I, Chapter 10, in connection with the description of a synagogue, mentions no Torah curtain.

exerted a certain influence on mediaeval Jewry which considered the Talmud the norm of Jewish ritual. Inasmuch as there was a specific exhortation to provide a beautiful Torah-mantle but not any exhortation concerning a curtain, the curtain may often have been omitted and the dress of the scroll deemed sufficient.

If we consider as typical the only Torah-curtain of the Middle Ages which we could show pictorially, we must draw the conclusion that the standard mediaeval curtain was extremely simple. It consisted of a hanging piece of cloth without toppiece, even when it hung exterior to the door. This conclusion must, however, be held with strong reservations owing to the meagerness of our information.

III. THE MODERN ERA

The enthusiasm for beauty which marked the Renaissance and the striving for splendor which characterized the following period of Baroque exerted a decisive influence on Jewish art. Frequently Christians served as architects and decorators of synagogues and thus transferred to the Jewish houses of worship the style to which they were accustomed in their churches. Though the Christian Church never erected shrines for its Holy Scriptures, the altar and altar-pictures which stood in their place were not without their effect. The Torah-shrine was now often flanked by magnificent pillars resembling those of the altar pictures, and the beauty of the paintings found its counterpart in the beauty of the Torah-curtain. Thus, not for ritual but rather for esthetic reasons, was greater emphasis placed on the Torah-curtain in modern times.

The material itself is selected with great care. Sometimes it is silk, sometimes velvet; but rarely are curtains made of wool or camel-hair. Often different kinds of cloth are combined so as to produce the effect of greater variety by means of the change of material. For the central rectangle, called the mirror, velvet would, for instance, be used, while the surrounding strips would be made of silk or vice versa.

The cloth is richly embroidered and, in order to increase the effect of magnificence and pomp, gold and silver threads are liberally applied. At times details are cut in leather, buttressed by some soft material. This would naturally increase the cost of such a curtain, but there were enough donors who could afford the prices. Sometimes these donors were organizations such as societies for sick relief or for burials. More often individuals would donate gifts on the occasion of special joy or in memory of deceased kin. These gifts show the prompting not only of religion but also of the desire for conspicuousness. The latter is one of the characteristics which distinguish modern times from the Middle Ages with their lowliness, a trend which no doubt also developed to some extent among the Jews. Accordingly the donor often wishes to have his name embroidered upon the curtain, thus securing for himself a lasting memorial. Frequently he adds the name of his wife, thus betokening the warmth of Jewish family life.

The question whether the name of the artist may also be noted requires differing answers. An embroiderer of the 17th century in the Moravian community of Prossnitz, who donated a curtain and placed his name on it, was forced by the enraged elders, with the support of Rabbi Krochmal, chief rabbi of the province, to eliminate the name.[23] On the other hand, in 1630, a woman by the name of Rachel née Olivetti who embroidered a curtain for the Levantine synagogue in Ancona, Italy, informs us to that effect in a Hebrew inscription. This woman was the wife of the donor, Juda Leon Montefiore.[24]

In the 18th century, especially in Bavaria, the embroiderers often state their identity. We have noticed that the curtain of the Jewish Museum in New York bears the signature of the artist. After all, the artist too may have been engulfed in the period's ambition for fame, or sometimes the donor may have desired to endow the curtain with greater value by indicating that it is the work of a recognized embroiderer.

Now that the giving of Torah-curtains becomes one of the

[23] See S. Krochmal, *Semah Sedek*, No. 50, according to S. W. Baron, *The Jewish Community, Its History and Structure to the American Revolution*, III, Philadelphia, 1942, p. 147, note 17.

[24] Cf. Lucien Wolf, "Anglo-Jewish Coats of Arms," *Transactions, The Jewish Historical Society of England*, Session 1894/95, p. 112.

most favored forms of donation, the number of such curtains naturally increases, and synagogues exist which own not one but numerous specimens. Their multiplicity leads to a differentiation in usage. Simple curtains decorate the ark on week-days, richer ones on Sabbaths and New Moons, while the richest are put up for the High Holy Days. The various colors are, on the New Year's Day and on the Day of Atonement, replaced by white to accord with the solemn and awe-filled mood of these occasions. On the Day of the Destruction of the Temple, black curtains sometimes appear, or the ark is left naked in order to symbolize Jerusalem robbed of its treasures. Special curtains are at times brought out on days of circumcisions and of marriages.

From now on we can trace the development of the Torah-curtains more closely, because specimens are available, at first a few, but more of them when we come to examples of the 17th and 18th centuries. How many may have succumbed to the brutal Nazi spirit of destruction and to the desolation wrought by war can at this time not be conjectured.

From the motherland of the Renaissance, Italy, we possess a curtain of knotted wool which, to conclude from its style, comes from the late 15th century. It hangs today in the synagogue of Padua (fig. 4). Its main motif is a portal whose arch rests on two fluted pilasters. The Hebrew words of the Psalm "This is the gate of the Lord; the righteous shall enter into it" (Ps. 118.20), running across the curtain above the portal, clarify its symbolic meaning. A fountain under the gate is probably also to be understood symbolically as the fountain of life, the fountain of the Law.[25] Affixed around the portal are wide stripes which produce the effect of a frame around a painting. All this imparts to the curtain an atmosphere of calm and harmony in tune with the taste of the Renaissance.

It is well known that the forms of the Renaissance traversed the Alps in the 16th century and reached not only Christians but also Jews in Northern Europe. Prague, one of the most flourishing Ashkenazic communities of that period, gave these southern forms a particularly hearty welcome. These forms are

[25] So Irmgard Schueler in Rahel Wischnitzer-Bernstein's book *Symbole und Gestalten der juedischen Kunst*, Berlin-Schoeneberg, 1935, p. 60.

found in book-decorations; the first Ashkenazic printing press of Hebrew books having stood in Prague. They are found on tomb-stones and even in private buildings. No wonder then that this style also appears on Torah-curtains. Proof of that is the curtain which was donated by Jacob ben Abraham Bassevi (c. 1570–1639) and his wife Hendel, daughter of Abraham Geronim (fig. 5). Bassevi is the famous financier and court-Jew who was the first Bohemian Jew, in fact the first Jew, to be elevated to the nobility (1622). It can hardly be a coincidence that it is just in this year, 1622/23, that the curtain was donated. Bassevi may have wanted to demonstrate that his worldly honors did not cause him to neglect his duties toward the community. Here, too, classical architecture — but removed from the centerpiece to the borders — lends the main motifs for the curtain. Two flat pilasters rise from high bases. Because, as so often in the North, the love of ornament obscures the tectonic clarity, the architectural structure of the curtain is not quite so distinct as on the curtain from Italy.

A third curtain, also fabricated in Prague in the 17th century, cannot be dated exactly (fig. 6). The inscription merely reveals that Loeb ben Gerson Karpeles had it restored in 1696 after it escaped the great fire which raged through the Ghetto in 1689. It must therefore have been made before 1689. From its style we can conclude that it must have been fashioned later than the Bassevi curtain of 1622/23. Here, too, columns appear on the edges, but they seem more luxurious because of the vines which climb around them. The vine is a favorite metaphor of Jewish literature. The prophets compare Israel to a vine (Hos. 10.1); the Talmud uses it as a simile of the world, the Torah, and Jerusalem (Hul. 92a). How well the last of these comparisons apply to a curtain which is suspended in the direction of Jerusalem and which protects the Torah!

Unfortunately we cannot here describe the Torah-curtains which belonged to the synagogues of Vienna. The Jews were expelled from the Austrian capital in 1670. But it is characteristic of the love for beauty among these Jews that they bought the best obtainable synagogue equipment, before they left the city, and carried it with them on their wanderings:

candlesticks, Torah-scrolls with their rich silver adornments and, what interests us most in this context, Torah-curtains.[26] Wherever Viennese Jews came, to Poland, Moravia, Bohemia, Brandenburg, Bavaria, they must have exerted a vitalizing influence by means of the treasures which they brought along.

Concluding from those pieces which have been preserved, Torah-curtains reached a peak of artistic perfection during the first decades of the 18th century, just when the style of the Baroque lost some of its initial heaviness and gained greater lightness and elegance, foreshadowing the Rococo. No wonder that this peak was attained in the Ashkenazic countries where, as we learned, the curtains were suspended in front of the doors and thus at all times visible to everyone entering the synagogue. In this manner they gained an importance which the Sephardic curtains, hidden behind the doors, did not achieve. What is more, those curtains which hung in front of the doors offered an additional opportunity for decoration in the form of the toppiece which the interior curtains lacked. Just at that time this toppiece is adorned by great numbers of motifs, thus giving the initially festal curtain a brilliant termination.

It is impossible to describe the multiplicity of curtain types which now arise. Too much has been lost and too little is accessible even in reproductions to justify such an endeavor. We can examine, with a degree of thoroughness, only one area, that of Bavaria, to illustrate the beauty of 18th century Ashkenazic curtains.

Also to Bavaria, Austrian émigrés had come, usually the richest in that group. Ancient communities existed here which just then were growing and flourishing and which offered economic opportunities promising also to newcomers.

The electors of Bavaria were among the most pomp loving German princes of the late 17th and early 18th century, and accordingly inclined toward the practice of employing Jews to procure the money necessary for such luxuries. What is more, the Bavarian sovereigns at that time engaged in a number of expensive military ventures. Maximilian II Emmanuel (1679–

---

[26] Cf. David Kaufmann, *Die letzte (sic!) Vertreibung der Juden aus Wieu und Niederoesterreich*, Budapest, 1889, p. 150.

1726) made war on the Turks and fought in the War of the Spanish Succession alongside of France. His son and successor, Charles Albert (1726–1745), disputed the validity of the Pragmatic Sanction which insured the throne for Maria Theresia after the death of the Austrian emperor Charles IV, and had himself crowned emperor in 1742. That, however, proved a short lived dream, for soon Austrian troops victoriously invaded Bavaria.

For these enterprises, too, Jews were employed. No public institutions existed at that time to supply the army with all its needs, horses, fodder, food, etc. Consequently one turned to the Jews who, thanks to their numerous connections and their organizational talents, were able to provide these things in the shortest possible time. As a consequence, Bavaria soon had a number of wealthy Jews who could well afford to donate adornments to their houses of worship.

As we have already stated, when silver implements were to be donated, one turned to Christian artists, but for the creation of Torah-curtains Jewish artists abounded, some of whom, especially in Bavaria, were men of high standing.

Three names are known to us today. One is that of Gerson Mayer whose work of embroidery was so highly esteemed that even the Church made use of it. In the Cathedral of Bamberg, the tombstones of Emperor Henry and his wife the Empress Kunigunde had been erected in Gothic times as one of his chief works by the sculptor Tilman Riemenschneider. In 1738, this grave was to receive a new cover whose central adornment was to consist of a coat of arms. Since a competent Christian embroiderer could apparently not be found, the work was given to Gerson Mayer who accomplished the costly project.[27] Though that cover is not preserved, and though no other artistic productions of his have to this day come to light, it may be assumed that Mayer supported himself by fabricating Torah-curtains and other synagogal textiles.

More information is available about the second Bavarian embroiderer, Elkone of Naumburg. Elkone was born in Gross-

[27] Franz Landsberger, "New Studies in Early Jewish Artists," *HUCA* XVIII, 1944, p. 300.

Glogau, also known simply as Glogau, an old community in Silesia which then belonged to Austria. Therefore the city of Naumburg from which he derived his name may be assumed to be not the one in Saxonia, famous for its old cathedral, but to be either the Naumburg on the river Queis or the one on the river Bober, both of them small towns in Silesia. His father had brought him to Fuerth, Bavaria, the old community which enjoyed great prosperity in the early 18th century, some of whose members owned superb houses on the market-place and in the most beautiful streets of the city, as reported by a contemporaneous Christian observer.[28] This observer adds the antisemitic remark: "A haughty people which so clothes itself in gold, velvet and silk that even its own leaders had to set a limit how far anyone could go according to class and sex." These *Takkanot* of the year 1728 are preserved. Our observer quotes them in German translation but forgets to add that such sumptuary laws were also quite common among Christians.

Here in Fuerth, Elkone's father became a cantor, a profession into which his son followed him.[29] In his case musical talents were combined with a gift for art. We find Elkone's name on two magnificent Torah-curtains of the years 1713/14 and 1723/24. We may thus estimate that Elkone was born in the second half of the 17th century and was active in the first half of the 18th.[30] Neither the year of his birth nor the year of his death is recorded.

In order to gain an impression of Elkone's art, let us consider a curtain which he fashioned for the community of Kriegshaber near Augsburg. Upon the dissolution of the community of Kriegshaber, this curtain, together with two others, was given to the community of Augsburg (fig. 7). There it was probably burnt or stolen during the Nazi outrages. But at least the last rabbi of Augsburg, Dr. Ernest I. Jacob, now in Springfield, Missouri, took care to have these pieces photographed and to

---

[28] Andreae Wuerfel, *Historische Nachrichten von der Judengemeinde in der Hofmarkt Fuerth*, Frankfurt and Prague, 1754, pp. 6 ff.

[29] Also his descendants were cantors. One of them was Samuel Naumbourg (1817–1880), the well known liturgical composer.

[30] Already in 1713 the cantor Elkone is mentioned as assisting a woman in her endeavor to obtain a bill of divorce. Cf. J. J. Schudt, *Juedische Merckwuerdigkeiten*, 4th part, 2, Frankfurt and Leipzig, 1717, p. 218.

describe them in a memorandum of which he is the author. Mr. Ernst Mayer of Hayward, Calif., a friend of Dr. Jacob, was kind enough to provide me with descriptions and pictures.

According to the inscription on the top of the curtain, it was donated by Judah Loeb, son of the late president and director of the Jewish regional district, Simon Ulma, and by his wife Guendele, daughter of the president of the Jewish regional district, Isashar Beer. A second inscription, placed at the bottom, is taken from the Book of Deuteronomy (33.7), "Hear, O Lord, the voice of Judah," and alludes, of course, to the name of the donor. Simultaneously dots over some of the letters indicate the year of its manufacture: 1723/24.[31] Beneath it the artist identifies himself: "Work of my hands with the help of God, Elkone, cantor in Fuerth."

The mirror of the curtain consists of green velvet on which are embroidered rhombs filled with flowers and fruit. In the borders of red velvet, two columns stand on high bases formed according to the technique of application just mentioned. Winding around these columns are vines pleasantly surrounded by their leaves, blossoms, and grapes. Such columns, covered with vines, appear already on a curtain from Prague of the 17th century (fig. 6), and we may assume that this custom came to Bavaria from Prague if not from Vienna. While, in Prague, the columns are straight, here they wind spirally so that the outlines resemble the curves of a wavy line.

What these columns represent leaves no doubt: they are the columns which stood in front of the Solomonic Temple in Jerusalem. Since the curtain was suspended on the east side of the synagogue where the eyes of the worshipper turned toward Jerusalem, this allusion to the lost Temple was quite apt. We discovered similar mementoes over the Torah-niche of Dura Europos. We can but marvel at the tenacity with which Judaism adhered to the memories of the lost Temple and to the hope for its reconstruction.

But why do the columns on our curtain have this strange spiral form? This is commonly explained as the effect of the style

[31] Dr. Jacob, in his memorandum, arrives at the number 1729. But the ה in the Divine Name must not be read as a numeral.

SPIRAL COLUMN FROM ST. PETER'S IN ROME

of the age, Baroque which, in these twisted columns, manifested its love of movement. Actually, however, their origin lies further back, in some ancient columns which are preserved in St. Peter's at Rome. The best known of these columns stands there in the Capella della Pietà. It, as well as the other columns, is reputed to have come from Solomon's Temple. Yet one glance at our reproduction of it suffices to brand this opinion as legend. Such rich forms, developed out of Greek columns, belong to the last period of Hellenism. Probably they did not arise before the 4th century of our era. But such precise knowledge was made possible only by 19th century research. Formerly it was deemed certain that these columns had adorned the Solomonic Temple. They were accordingly regarded with the highest reverence. Again and again we find imitations of them in real or painted columns from the Middle Ages down to the 17th and 18th centuries when their popularity reached its peak.

It remains to be asked how the knowledge of them, at first restricted to Christian circles, filtered through to the Jews? The Jews, though in outward matters rigidly segregated from Christians, came in constant contact with Christians and may therefore easily have heard that columns of Solomon's Temple still existed in Rome's foremost church. When Michelangelo's statue of Moses for the tomb of Pope Julius II was erected in St. Pietro in Vincoli, the Jews followed the event with deep interest. Vasari, the well known writer on art, in his biography of Michelangelo, reports: "Well may the Hebrews continue to go there as they do every Sabbath, both men and women like flocks of starlings, to visit and adore the statue; for they will be adoring a thing not human but divine."[32] Thus individual Jews may have entered St. Peter's in order to view the famous columns or, at the least, they may have heard about them.

The first trace of any knowledge of the columns among Jews is revealed in books printed in Hebrew in 16th century Italy. It is well known that the printed Hebrew book in the 15th century did not yet possess a title-page. The first title-page appears in the 16th century. In the beginning these title-pages were ornamented with initials and decorative border-lines, but later a portal becomes a favorite motif. The entrance of the book is likened to the entrace of a house. At first the columns of the portal are straight, but already in the middle of the 16th century spiral columns are to be found on prints of Mantua.[33] Soon such columns, acquiring great popularity, get to be utilized in other countries likewise. Thus they appear in the 17th century in Holland, then the main market for Hebrew books; for example in the work *Hesed l'Abraham* which was issued in 1685 by Immanuel Athias in Amsterdam. From there the motif wandered to Germany. I deliberately offer as an example the title-page of a German *Maḥzor* which was printed first in 1690 and then in 1708 in Bavaria. This is the very same Bavaria in which was created the curtain of Elkone Naumburg. The influence upon the Torah-curtains shows itself not only in the columns but also in the flower vases which, with their curved handles, rest upon the columns.

On our curtain, two rampant lions are to be seen between these two vases, turning toward a crown adorned with semi-precious stones. According to the inscription, this is the crown of the Torah, after the well known metaphor in the Sayings of the Fathers (4.17). Usually these two lions which occur so frequently in Jewish art are interpreted as symbols of Judaism. "Judah is a lion's whelp," says the Blessing of Jacob. In my opinion it would be more correct to regard these lions as cheru-

---

[32] Vasari, *Lives of the most Eminent Painters, Sculptors and Architects*, translated by Gaston du C. de Vere, London; 1912–1915, IX, p. 24.

[33] Cf. I. Sonne, "Druckwesen," in *Encyclopaedia Judaica*, VI, col. 55 ff.

MAHSOR, PRINTED 1708–09 IN SULZBACH, BAVARIA

bim, successors of the lion-cherubim which used to flank the Ark or the Torah-chest in the art of antiquity. The crown would then be a substitute for the Torah which the cherubim are adoring.

This crown of the Torah appears once more on the toppiece, this time at the extreme right edge, followed by two further crowns. According to the same statement in the Sayings of the Fathers, these are the crowns of the priesthood and of the kingship. In this sequence — for, in Jewish art, pictures also are read from right to left — these crowns are enumerated in the Sayings of the Fathers.

The common name for this top-piece is *Kapporet*. This is also the name by which the cover-plate of the Ark was designated. The name must have stimulated the artist's imagination for, on that toppiece, we find all the paraphernalia which were kept in the Tent of Meeting. Reading from right to left, we notice the Ark itself and the Tablets of the Law which, though they actually rested inside of the Ark, are here placed above it. The laver of brass which stood between the Ark and the altar is followed by the seven-branched candelabrum which, due to its symmetrical structure, serves well as centerpiece. Then we perceive the altar of burnt-offerings, recognizable by its lattice-work,. and finally the table with the shew-bread.

At the extreme top, the *Kapporet* bears the line: "I have set the Lord always before me" (Ps. 16.8) and "Know before whom thou art standing" (Ber. 28b). These words are evidently directed to the cantor who, in the ancient synagogue, had his lectern next to the steps which led up to the Torah-shrine. From that position the words were easily legible. In the eighteenth century, the custom arose of inscribing these words on a special tablet, the *Shiviti*-table, placed over the cantor's desk.

Let us finally mention that Elkone Naumburg, apart from his work on the Torah-curtain, embroidered a Torah-mantle for the same synagogue. A developed taste would have both pieces in the same style. For that reason, the spiral columns, the rampant lions, and the crown of the Torah occur also on the mantle. Beneath the crown, the date 1723–24 appears — the same as on the curtain.

From the community of Kriegshaber, a second curtain came to Augsburg. This curtain, though unsigned, bears all the characteristics of Elkone Naumburg's art. Not only are the same motifs used, but these appear also with the same finesse which we noticed previously on the signed curtain. The *Kapporet* is even more richly decorated: not five, but seven scallops hang down from it and, to the above mentioned objects embroidered on it, are added the Tent of Meeting and the censer.[34] The curtain was donated by Abraham, son of the president and the director of the Jewish regional district, Elia Ansbach, and by his wife, Pesle, daughter of the late Judah Loeb. The dotted letters, according to the memorandum of Dr. Jacobs, indicate

[34] This Torah-curtain is reproduced in *Juedisches Lexikon*, IV, pl. 134; also in Theo Harburger, "K'le Kodesh und Parochoth im bayerischen Synagogenbesitz," in *Bayerisch-Israelitische Gemeindezeitung*, 1929, p. 121. There, likewise, a reproduction of the above mentioned Torah mantle of Elkone Naumburg.

the year 1731. Due to the extreme diminuitiveness of the picture, I was unable to verify this observation.

A third curtain of Elkone Naumburg's, this time supplied with his name, was once to be found in the Jewish School in Hildesheim, Prussia.[35] According to the inscription, the curtain was donated in the year 1714 by Joseph Oppenheim and his wife, Toelze. Joseph was the only son of David Oppenheim, the famous Rabbi and bibliophile. His wife was the daughter of Samson Wertheimer, the incalculably rich court Jew of Vienna, one of the few permitted to continue residence in the Austrian capital after the expulsion of 1670. The combined wealth of the two donors permitted them to turn to an eminent artist who indeed did his best to merit his reputation. The mirror is of green velvet; the rest, of the same material in red. Otherwise the same motifs return which we have already discovered on the curtains from Augsburg: the columns, the crowns, the cherubim, and, on the *Kapporet*, the implements of the Tent of Meeting. Here, too, the embroiderer supplied, in addition to the curtain, a Torah-mantle which was later cut in two, and also a cover for the reading desk, all of them in a form resembling that of the curtain.

We hear of a fourth curtain of Elkone Naumburg only from an old report. The curtain itself, for which I searched while still in Germany, seems to have been lost. Andreae Wuerfel, in the previously mentioned book about the Jewish community of Fuerth, which appeared in the year 1751, mentions the oldest local synagogue (p. 26), its curtain, and its *Kapporet*, and then adds the words: "The Cantor Elkone created both pieces for the Jewish community of Amsterdam. But because they turned out to be too sumptuous, they were returned by the community of Amsterdam. Later they were bought for 1200 Gulden by the Gumberts in Fuerth, and then generously donated to the old

---

[35] The instructor, Oskar Stern in Hildesheim, owned a photograph of the curtain and sent a copy for me to the Jewish Museum in Berlin. The Museum, with its great photographic treasures, was pillaged by the Nazis. Mr. Stern seems to have been one of the victims. — Compare also Leopold Loewenstein, "Zur Geschichte der Juden in Fuerth," in the *Jahrbuch der Juedisch-Literarischen Gesellschaft*, VIII, Frankfurt a/M, 1911, p. 155.

main synagogue." The Dutch employers were certainly not Sephardim but rather Ashkenazim. The evidence lies in the fact that the curtain possesses a toppiece. Some among these Ashkenazim could match their wealth with that of the Sephardim; for example, a few members of the widely branched family Gumbert, also known as Gumpert or Gomperz, who went to Holland.[36] It is not impossible that these may have donated the curtain and that when it was rejected by the directorate of the community, the Gumberts may have turned to their relatives in Fuerth and induced them to buy the curtain.

It is quite characteristic that the curtain was rejected in Amsterdam because of its costliness. The Jews, living here in an environment dominated by a Calvinist population, may have been impressed by the simplicity of the Calvinistic services. In Bavaria, on the other hand, the Jews had ample opportunity to observe the pomp and magnificence of the Catholic church and may have desired to imitate that splendor.

If I do not err, a second commission came to Elkone from a foreign country, this time, from England. Here too, Ashkenazic, not Sephardic, circles ordered the curtain. In the year 1726, the so-called Hambro synagogue was erected in London, named after its founder, the Ashkenazi Mordecai B. Moses, called Hambro because he came from Hamburg. Today the synagogue no longer exists and the curtain has disappeared.[37] The curtain was displayed at the Anglo-Jewish historical exhibition which took place in London in 1887, and the richly illustrated catalogue contains a tablet from which our reproduction has been taken (fig. 8). The donor, whose name is embroidered on the curtain, was a member of the widely branched Ashkenazic family Margolioth, specifically, Isaak Margolioth from Bunzlau, probably the Bunzlau in Bohemia, and his wife, Gittele, the daughter of Ephraim, from רוזין בירג. The year of the donation is 1726–27. Thus the curtain was donated on the occasion of the synagogue's dedication. The name of the artist is not indicated, but the style

---

[36] Cf. David Kaufmann and Max Freudenthal, *Die Familie Gomperz,* Frankfurt a/M, 1907, p. 266.

[37] Kindly communicated by Dr. Cecil Roth, Oxford, England.

of the curtain resembles in detail the one we have observed in other creations of Naumburg. It suffices to compare it with the Augsburg curtain (fig. 7) in order to notice the likeness. Since the London curtain is somewhat broader, the artist has placed between the columns and the mirror the motif of two vertical stripés. But even these stripes recur in the oeuvre of Naumburg. They are to be found in the second Augsburg curtain which we could with certainty ascribe to this artist. In view of all this, we are justified in assuming that Elkone Naumburg was the leading embroiderer of Torah-curtains in 18th century Germany.

Finally, we come to the third embroiderer of Bavaria whose name has been preserved, the fashioner of the curtain in the Jewish Museum of New York. The exact name is Jakob Koppel Gans, son of Judah Loeb, from Höchstädt or Höchstadt in Bavaria. The facts of this man's life are unknown to us. All that we do know is that he was active from 1726/27 and possibly until 1772/73, judging from the dates with which the curtains are inscribed. To the latter date we shall come back presently.

On a curtain which he worked for the synagogue in Krumbach, Bavaria, Gans calls himself an embroiderer in gold, *Goldsticker*, and the same is meant, of course, on the New York curtain, by the abbreviation for *Goldsticker* ז״ש, which follows his name. Gans is thus professionally what Naumburg was avocationally, a *Goldsticker*, as that craft was called in Germany, because he knew the art of using thin threads of gold and silver to enhance the splendor of his workmanship.

One certain product of his hands is the curtain just mentioned, the curtain in Krumbach. That curtain surely does not exist any more today, but I can at least offer a reproduction (fig. 9) which was first published in my *Einfuehrung in die juedische Kunst* (Berlin, 1935). According to the inscriptions which Theo Harburger extracted from the original,[38] the donor is a certain Loeb, son of the congregational president, Abraham, from Kriegshaber. We have heard of this place already in connection with two curtains which Naumburg had embroidered for that small but wealthy community. Hendel, daughter of Nathan

---

[38] In the previously quoted article K'le Kodesch and Parochoth, p. 121.

Segal, is named as Loeb's wife. The dotted letters are computed by Harburger as 1727, and though my own calculation yields the date 1733 to 1734, I must give credence to Harburger's decision.

From the point of view of style, this curtain is closely related to the one made by Elkone Naumburg. Here too the mirror is treated in a purely ornamental manner. It also is flanked by spiral columns entwined with vines. Here too the *Kapporet* has five scallops which are filled with ritual objects from the Tent of Meeting. Finally, here too, the curtain is topped by three crowns and inscribed with the previously quoted Hebrew verses.

With this close relationship the question arises: Did Elkone Naumburg precede Jakob Koppel Gans, or was Gans influenced by Naumburg? To me it appears more probable that Naumburg had the more creative part in that relationship; first, because Naumburg was the older — his activity began in 1714, that of Gans in 1726/27 — and secondly, because the quality of his products is superior to that of Gans, and may, for that very reason, have invited imitation. Compare the Augsburg curtain of Naumburg (fig. 7) with the Krumbach curtain of Gans (fig. 9). In Gans' curtain the mirror is divided into 24 rhombs, in Naumburg's it is divided into 32; each one of them treated much more delicately. It appears possible that Gans may first have worked in Naumburg's workshop in Fuerth and only later settled in Höchstädt, or Höchstadt, as an independent artist.

A second curtain created by Gans is identified, in the afore-mentioned article by Harburger, among those to be found in Ichenhausen, a town not far from Augsburg. The donor was Abraham, son of the president of the Congregation of Kriegs-haber, Josle, and his wife, Blümle, daughter of Moses, the president of the Congregation in Öttingen, Bavaria. The date of the year is to be read either 1730 or 1737.

The third curtain by Gans, apparently the only one pre-served, is the one which is now in the Jewish Museum in New York (note figure 10). Its general structure is the same as that of the others: again the spiral column entwined with vines, again the flower vases above the capitals, again the crown of the Torah, and, in the *Kapporet*, the three crowns respectively of the Torah, of the priesthood, and of the kingship, and again the ritual objects belonging with the Tent of Meeting.

In addition, however, there are discernible some variations from the norm. The first consists in the fact that not lions but griffins flank the crown of the Torah. Above we have voiced the assumption that the lions at the sides of the crown are not to be interpreted as symbols of Judah but rather as cherubim. The same should be said of the griffins, those legendary birds shaped in the rear like lions. These are frequently used in Jewish art, probably under the supposition that the word "griffin," γρύψ in Greek, is related linguistically to the Hebrew word *Kerub*.

On the toppiece, at the sides of the crown, two birds with lifted wings appear. These also may be cherubim. We have recalled that Philo, in his description of the cover of the Ark, characterized the cherubim as birds. And we have further seen that ancient art at times represented the cherubim on the Ark as birds: such at least is the case with the floor mosaic in Beth Alpha (p. 360). But because Philo's writings, composed entirely in Greek, were read very rarely by Jews, the representation of the cherubim as birds was abandoned in later centuries. This does not preclude that occasionally representations of birds may have appeared anew, perhaps through the medium of Christian scholars who had mastered Greek. Since the days of Humanism, when the Christian world began to study Judaism with renewed vigor, a lively exchange of ideas had taken place between scholars of both religions. Notable in this connection is what Johannes Buxtorf the Elder (1564 to 1629), the great Christian Hebraist, had to say in his *Synagoga Judaica* about the Torah-curtain of the Jews: "They like to have birds embroidered upon them, because birds hovered over the Ark of the Covenant in the Old Testament."[39] Here we find Philo's view re-echoed.

In the introduction to our essay, we pointed out that next to these birds are to be found the letters ש and כ falsely identified as numerals. In reality these letters are abbreviations of Hebrew

---

[39] I am quoting in accordance with the German edition of the *Synagoga Judaica*, Basle, 1643, p. 309.

words and should be read שני כרובים.[40] That such cherubim appeared on the toppiece is surely related to the fact that it was called *Kapporet*, like the cover on the Ark.[41]

It is a further peculiarity of the New York curtain that the mirror is filled not with ornaments but with a seven-branched candelabrum in magnificent gold embroidery. It must have been well known, in those times, that the Talmud prohibited the erection of a seven-branched candelabrum in the Synagogue (R. H. 24a) in order to avoid duplicating the revered implements of the Temple. Hence the alternative of representing the candelabrum pictorially. Indeed, since the Middle Ages, the candelabrum, together with other appurtenances of the Tent of Meeting and of the Temple, frequently appears in Pentateuchs and in Pentateuchal commentaries. In this tradition, the Menorah likewise appears on our curtain. It figures here not merely as a decorative object, but also as a starting point for all of the pertinent information available at that time. The Bible (Ex. 25.31) and the Talmud (Men. 28b) distinguished three adornments on this candelabrum: the flowers, the knobs, and the cups. The flowers, according to the Talmud, resemble the blossoms on the capitals of architectural columns and therefore appear on the curtain like the capitals of Ionic columns. The knobs are supposed to be reminiscent of Cretan apples from which they receive their spheric form. The cups have, according to the Bible, the form of almonds; while, according to the Talmud, they are comparable to Alexandrian cups. In outline, our embroiderer has reproduced the form of the almond, but simultaneously he represents a cup which, like many old cups, is supplied with a cover.

It is not by chance that even the flames over the seven lamps are so drawn that the one in the middle rises vertically while

[40] I had inquired of Professor Alexander Marx in New York regarding the significance of the two letters, but hardly had I sent the letter off when the thought occurred to me that ש כ might indicate "Two Cherubim." I was all the more delighted when Prof. Marx replied that Professor Ginzberg whom he had consulted had suggested the same interpretation.

[41] Also the Augsburg curtain of Elkone Naumburg (fig. 7) bears over the embroidered Ark on the toppiece the cherubim in the form of birds.

the ones on the side lean toward it. In his Commentary to the Pentateuch (Ex. 25.37), Rashi, with Talmudic support, (Men. 98b) says concerning these flames: "As for the six lamps atop the six branches that extend from the sides of the middle shaft, turn the mouths of those lamps toward the middle lamp so that, facing the mouth of the middle lamp, they may throw their light toward the middle shaft, the main part of the candelabrum." Here, as in the case of the cherub bird, one gains the impression that a man of great Jewish knowledge must have assisted the embroiderer.

Two doves perch on the richly decorated base of the candelabrum, olive leaves in their beaks. The significance of these doves can be gleaned from the Talmudic statement: "The assembly of Israel is like a dove, as it is written: 'Ye are as the wings of a dove covered with silver' " (San. 95a).

Naturally the two double eagles on the curtain and the toppiece are also not to be considered mere ornaments. They likewise have their special significance. But what significance? According to the inscription which has been placed over the mirror, the donors of this curtain were Jakob Kitzingen — Kitzingen is a town in Bavaria — and his wife, Hendel, daughter of Tewele Ulma from Pfersee, likewise in Bavaria. Now Bavaria, like the rest of Germany, contained Free Imperial Cities, that is to say, towns which were not subject to Bavarian sovereignty but which owed allegiance directly to the Holy Roman Empire. For such towns, the coat of arms was the double-headed eagle. The first town to occur to one would be the imperial town of Augsburg, — not the city itself, for Jews had been expelled from there for centuries — but rather the neighboring towns, Kriegshaber, Steppach, or Pfersee, where the exiles had taken refuge. In one of these suburbs our curtain may have hung. Its donor may have had some special reason for commemorating and emphasizing his allegiance to the Holy Roman Empire. He may, perhaps, have had commercial relations with the Royal Court in Vienna.[42]

[42] Coats of arms, such as the Polish eagle, are, as matter of fact, by no means rare in Jewish art. These can be found on synagogue lamps, on Chanukkah candelabra and lamps, on Mizrach tablets, on Torah-doors and the like.

The hypothesis naming Augsburg and its vicinity is further strengthened by the circumstance that the seal of the Jewish community, already in the Middle Ages, showed the double eagle, dating from the time when the city had become a Free Imperial City. This seal had been printed in a book about Augsburg, including the Jews of Augsburg, which appeared about the middle of the 18th century,[43] and the publication of which may also have become known to the Jews. Thus the double eagle on our curtain may, at the same time, record a reminiscence of the Jewish community which was the home of the donor's ancestors.

One quality of our two double eagles remains to be mentioned which the Imperial double eagle lacked: on their breasts two fish are visible. That too cannot be meaningless, because in this curtain everyting possesses significance. Two fish in a parallel or in an opposite position signify the Zodiac sign of the Fish, and the zodiac has again and again, since the days of antiquity, figured in Jewish art. Also the title page of the *Maḥzor* which we have reproduced (p. 376) bears this sign, together with the sign of the constellation Crab. According to the Jewish calendar, the month of Adar stands under the sign of the Fish. But what has this month to do with our curtain? Possibly the curtain had been finished in Adar, and had been destined to commemorate Purim, the joyous festival of that month. Another possibility would be that the donor of the curtain had been born in the month of Adar. Consequently he may have owned a signet ring on which were engraved two fish which he desires to see also on the curtain. A third possibility is that since, according to tradition, Moses was born on the 7th of Adar, and died on that same day (Meg. 13b, Sot. 13b), the Toraḥ-shrine was considered the proper place for commemorating the man who put the Torah into writing.[44]

[43] Cf. Paul von Stetten, *Geschichte der Heiligen Roemischen Reichs Freyen Stadt Augspurg*, I, Frankfurt and Leipzig, 1743, p. 70. Also reproduced in *Juedisches Lexikon*, I, col. 5711/12 and in *The Universal Jewish Encyclopedia*, I, p. 613.

[44] Mr. Steven S. Schwarzschild, a student at the Hebrew Union College, apprises me that two fishes, ranged parallel, appear on the coat of arms of the city of Forchheim in Bavaria. However, Forchheim is not a Free Imperial

Finally, a word about the curtain's date. From the point of view of the observer, a biblical verse appears to the right of the lower double eagle: "But Thou Israel, my servant, Jacob whom I have chosen, the seed of Abraham, My friend" (Isa. 41.8). This, of course, is an allusion to the donor whose name was Jakob. Simultaneously the letters זַרְעֲ אַבְרָהָם אֹהֲבִין, surmounted by dots, serve as numerals and yield the date 1772 or 1773. Since the curtains which Gans created for Krumbach and Ichenhausen date from the years 1726/27 and 1730 or 1737, this would give a considerable lapse of time. In order to reduce that interval, Prof. Alexander Marx has offered the hypothesis that the dot over the letter ם may be erroneous.[45] If it were missing, the curtain would have originated 40 years earlier. I have a basic aversion to textual emendations wherever the least possibility exists of an intelligible reading without them. Such a possibility certainly obtains here. The interval between the New York curtain and the earliest one by Gans amounts to 46 or 47 years, a period of time certainly compatible with an individual's period of activity. Assuming that Gans was born around 1700, he could have produced the curtains of Krumbach and Ichenhausen at the climax of his power, and would have been scarcely over 70 when creating the curtain which is now in New York. This view would comport with the assumption that Gans was born later than Naumburg and that he studied and worked in the latter's shop.

As we remarked in connection with the Krumbach curtain, and as we can observe again on the New York curtain, Gans' style, by contrast with the fine and delicate art of Naumburg, is somewhat robust and heavy. Both evince, in their technique, the *horror vacui*. But in Naumburg's works the objects are distinguished more clearly and acquire a somewhat restful effect from the foil on which they stand. In the curtain of Gans, on the other hand, the brocade is patterned, and the objects embroidered upon it tell so much that is difficult to comprehend everything

City. So that leaves the double eagle unexplained. Preferable is the explanation deriving the fish from the Jewish sphere of thought.

[45] In *The Jewish Theological Seminary of America, Register* 1944/45, New York, 1944, p. 108.

in one glance. Nevertheless, the multiplicity of phenomena endows the curtain with a special appeal, for through all of the objects here represented, we gain a deep insight into the world of ideas prevailing among the Jews of the 18th century.

* * * *

The New York curtain, if produced in 1772 to 1773, terminates not only the activities of Gans, but also the period in which all of these curtains of Baroque originated. There arose the foreshadowings of a new style, that of Classicism, a style which is also reflected in art among the Jews. "Noble simplicity and quiet greatness" are the characteristics which Winckelmann revered among the Greeks and prescribed for the art of his day. The Torah-curtains of this style dispense with all pomp, and content themselves with a small number of motifs in clear and simple outlines.

At the same time there dawned, for the Jews, the period of the Emancipation bringing them the opportunity to collaborate in European art as architects, sculptors, and painters and not only as illuminators, medalists, and embroiderers. With this entrance into European society, as advantageous as it may have been from one point of view, Jewish art loses something. As long as the Jews lived in the ghettoes, art revolved, as did the entire life of the Jews, around religion and manifested its highest capacities in the synagogues and their adornment. Since the Emancipation, the art of the Jews becomes predominantly secular and its religious branches wither away.

For this reason, we can close our consideration of old Torah-curtains at this point. A long line of development, begun in the Biblical period and continued through the centuries from the Middle Ages to modern times, has now ended.

SABBATH

THE ORIGIN OF THE RITUAL IMPLEMENTS FOR THE SABBATH

FRANZ LANDSBERGER

Hebrew Union College - Jewish Institute of Religion, Cincinnati

D R. Jacob Z. Lauterbach, an eminent authority on Jewish religious usages, devoted attention, among other things, to the ceremonials connected with the Sabbath. In a lengthy contribution to the *Hebrew Union College Annual,*[1] Dr. Lauterbach treats the practice of savoring aromatic plants and spices as the Sabbath comes to an end; while a study among Lauterbach's writings published posthumously,[2] deals with the kindling of lights as the seventh day begins. In neither of these articles is the question raised concerning the implements or concerning the changes which these implements developed in the course of the centuries. This casts no reflection upon the learned author. His manner of treating the subject was the one common at the time. That tendency was superseded only after the study of Jewish art, the youngest offspring of the Science of Judaism, had acquired some standing. We do not correct, we merely amplify, Lauterbach's researches, if we attempt to answer questions such as these: How did those Sabbath implements look? When did they originate and, with the lapse of the ages, what changes did they undergo? Deriving our examples preferably from the works of art in the Museum of the Hebrew Union College - Jewish Institute of Religion at Cincinnati hardly calls for an apology.

I. ANTIQUITY

The earliest mention of Sabbath implements is to be found in the Roman satirist Persius (34–62 C. E.) who wrote at a time when the last of the Temples at Jerusalem still existed. In his "Fifth Satire," the poet enumerates various instances of moral slavery; moral slavery

---

[1] "The Origin and Development of Two Sabbath Ceremonies," *HUCA*, XV, 1940, pp. 367–424.

[2] Appearing under the title, "The Sabbath," in *Rabbinical Essays* by Jacob Z. Lauterbach, Cincinnati, 1951, pp. 437–472.

Reprinted from *Hebrew Union College Annual,* Vol. XXVII, 1956.

being, with him, worse than physical slavery. He adduces as illustration (verses 179–184):

> . . . . . At cum
> Herodis venere dies unctaque fenestra
> Dispositae pinguem nebulam vomuere lucernae
> Portantes violas, rubrumque amplexa catinum
> Cauda natat thunni, tumet alba fidelia vino,
> Labra moves tacitus recutitaque sabbata palles.

Translated this reads:

> But when Herod's days are come, and the lamps, carrying violets, put in the greasy windows, emit their unctuous clouds of smoke; and when the tail of a tuna fish floats curled round in a red dish, and the white jar is bulging with wine, you move your lips in silence and turn pale at the circumcised Sabbath.

As we perceive from the conclusion of these verses, by "Herod's Day" is meant the Sabbath.[3] The poet jeers at the Sabbath custom of placing lamps in the windows. Today when we speak of Sabbath lights, we think of such as illuminate dwellings on the inside. But it was obviously a more ancient practice to turn the lights toward the street, doubtless to betoken joy, as in the case of the earliest Hanukkah lights which, in like manner, brightened Jewish cities or city quarters.

How many were the lights utilized in any one house? The opinion occurs that the number of such lights was two. This number is based upon the fact that the average domicile contained a living room and a bedroom, and that a light was needed for each.[4] And yet, mention of two lamps or lights occurs nowhere in antiquity. To the contrary, the notion existed that the larger the number of the lights the greater the merit. Such is the point to the account in Sabbath 23b: "When Rab Huna (third century c. e.) passed the door of Rabbi Abin on a Friday evening and noticed the numerous lamps, he prophesied that great scholars would issue from that house."

For us, the main question is: What was the appearance of those Friday evening lamps? Persius reports that these lamps stood at the windows and that they carried violets.[5] This description tallies

---

[3] I do not understand how Hermann Vogelstein and Paul Riegner get to apply these verses to the Day of the Temple Dedication in their *Geschichte der Juden in Rom*, I, Berlin, 1951, p. 8.

[4] Thus Abraham E. Millgram, *Sabbath, the Day of Delight*, Philadelphia, 1944, p. 15. He is followed by Stephen S. Kayser in the Introduction to Kayser-Schoenberger, Jewish Ceremonial Art, Philadelphia, 1955, p. 14.

[5] E. R. Goodenough, in *Jewish Symbols in the Greco-Roman Period*, I, New York, 1952, p. 36, translates "unctaque fenestra . . . . lucernae portantes violas" with

with the fact that lamps of clay were, at that time, the vogue in the entire Mediterranean area and that such lamps were suited to the window because of their smallness. Such lamps, covered on top, except for a round opening through which to pour the oil, were also adapted to having upon them violets. Incidentally there has been found in Africa a lamp which answers Persius' description (see our illustration).

a) ANTIQUE JEWISH LAMP, UNEARTHED NEAR CARTHAGE, AFRICA. Clay. Taken from Erwin R. Goodenough, *Jewish Symbols in the Greco-Roman Period*, III, fig. 956.

On this lamp, violet petals in relief were substituted for actual violets, not always obtainable. An additional feature distinguishes this lamp as an implement of religion: the cover holds a representation of the seven-branched candelabrum. The Sabbath light accordingly brought to mind the sacred lights which once glowed in the Tent of Meeting and in the Temple, and thus expresses the hope, particularly vital on the Sabbath, that the Messiah might appear and revive the ancient shrines.

We perceive further, from the verses of Persius, that the fish, especially favored as a Sabbath viand, was served in a red dish. This refers to the unbaked red clay of the vessels which the entire populace, and not merely the Jewish populace, used for holding food.[6] The satirist also mentions the white jar bulging with wine. This also could have been a clay vessel, glazed and curving outward.

In the Roman catacombs there have been found gold-glasses, so-called because the bottom designs were of gold leaf. Surely these

---

"the lamps, put in the greasy windows, along with violets." But that fails to give the precise meaning.

[6] Compare the article "Kochkunst" in Pauly-Wissowa, *Realencyclopaedie der classischen Altertumswissenschaft*, col. 981.

objects were intended not only for the dead. An inscription, for example, as "Drink, live happily," bespeaks someone's use of the object during his lifetime. One of the designs represents a bowl of fish. This has been correctly understood as an allusion to the Sabbath meal. Another glass-bottom, here illustrated, pictures the Temple,

b) BOTTOM OF AN ANTIQUE GOLD-
GLASS. Rome, Vatican.

again a Messianic symbol, with the inscription, as reconstructed: "Take the eulogy with all who are thine." This indicates a wine-filled cup which, after the blessing was pronounced, passed from mouth to mouth.[7] We may therefore reckon these "gold-glasses" among the ancient implements for Sabbath beautification.

A clay jar (New York Jewish Museum) with the inscription ΕΥΛΟΓΙΑ has been regarded by Goodenough as a jar in which the Sabbath wine was brought to the table,[8] but the jar is, in my opinion, too small for having served this purpose.

II. MIDDLE AGES

In the Middle Ages gold-glasses were no longer in style. What was the material of the Sabbath winecups and what were their shapes? In Spain, where the Jews had attained great wealth, it is likely that

---

[7] Cf. Hans Lietzmann, *Messe und Herrenmahl*, Bonn, 1926, p. 209; H. Lietzmann and W. Bayer, *Die juedische Katakombe der Villa Torlonia in Rom*, Berlin and Leipzig, 1930, p. 22 f; E. R. Goodenough, *Jewish Symbols* etc., II, 1953, pp. 108 ff. A colored illustration is provided by Rachel Wischnitzer-Bernstein, *Symbole und Gestalten der juedischen Kunst*, Berlin-Schoeneberg, 1935, plate V.

[8] Cf. E. R. Goodenough, *op. cit.* II, 1953, p. 116 and III, 1953, fig. 979.

such cups were of gold. We perceive such cups in representations of the *Seder*-meal contained in fourteenth century *Haggadahs* (London, British Museum, Or. 2884 and Add 14761).[9] In these cups we detect no particular design. The same applies, no doubt, to the cups of Middle and Eastern Europe. The importance of the day is emphasized by the fact that the cups are of precious metal, while their Jewish significance is indicated by a Hebrew inscription as, for instance, "Remember the Sabbath day, to keep it holy."

It is similar with the jars for the wine of the *Kiddush*. In the aforementioned representations of the *Seder*-meal we discern golden flasks which might also have been for Sabbath use. These differ from other jars only in the preciousness of their material.

This makes especially interesting a Sabbath jar of dark red glass kept in the Museum of the Hebrew Union College - Jewish Institute of Religion at Cincinnati, a jar whose identification with the Sabbath is brought out most distinctly (illustrated on p. 392). This jar comes from an Islamic community, from Asia Minor or North Africa, as shown by the Arabic letters at the jar's neck.[10] The rest of the surface is entirely covered with Hebrew letters cut into the thick glass and swathed in ornamentation. We make out the words recited on Friday evenings, the words, "And the heaven and the earth were finished." Such an able palaeographist as Prof. Isaiah Sonne assured me that the inscription cannot date from a period earlier than the seventeenth or eighteenth century. And yet, when we consider the conservatism of the Orient, we can surmise that similar flasks may have existed even in the Middle Ages.

We return now to the Sabbath lamps. What structure did these assume in medieval times? From the illustration on page 389 we perceive what their structure was in antiquity. We need only add that, in the same period, there also existed lamps with more than one wick, and that these may have likewise been for Sabbath use. We can distinguish two types. One type had the wick-nozzles standing in a straight row. From this type developed the Hanukkah lamp with the rigid back, needed for fastening to the doorpost. In the other type the nozzles encircled an open flat center filled with oil. Later these lamps were supplied with a lid to keep the oil from spilling. It was, however, the open type, shown to exist already in Iron Age I (see

---

[9] To be noticed in this connection is the colored reproduction in the *Encyclopaedia Judaica*, VII, frontispiece.

[10] A similar piece is to be found in the collection of Charles Feinberg of Detroit.

c) ORIENTAL JAR FOR THE SABBATH WINE. Glass.

Museum of the Hebrew Union College - Jewish Institute of Religion.

our illustration), that developed into a lamp for the Sabbath. The

d) Clay Lamp from
Iron Age I.

only thing needed was to make such lamps not of clay but of metal
and to put a shaft in the middle or sometimes to fasten chains around
the edges. The result was a hanging lamp which, when lighted, was
suggestive of a star, thus generating a religious mood.

Of course, such a lamp could not be placed at the window to shine
into the outdoors. It goes without saying that, in the Middle Ages,
when surrounded by hostile neighbors, the Jews had to forego that
display. A lamp had to suffice which illuminated that part of the
dwelling where the family partook of the Friday evening meal.

As an example of such a lamp, we show one which originated in
Italy of the seventeenth or eighteenth century. Here, while the center
bowl is deepened, the structure, on the whole, resembles that of the
ancient lamp pictured above. The accompanying drip-bowl and the
four richly jointed chains converging into a top-piece achieve the
gracious harmony so characteristic of Italian works of art.[11]

From Italy, where such lamps must have existed in early times,
their use spread into Holland[12] and England,[13] only with the difference
that, in these two lands, the Sabbath lamp was equipped not with
chains but with a shaft.

In the Ashkenazic countries it was otherwise. Here also the ancient

[11] An Italian hanging lamp of similar type, belonging to the sixteenth century,
can be seen in the Kayser-Schoenberger publication, *Jewish Ceremonial Art*, Philadelphia, 1955, illust. 68.

[12] Copied in Bernard Picart, *Cérémonies et coutumes religieuses de tous les peuples
du monde*, I, Amsterdam, 1723. A second lamp, also coming from Holland, is pictured
in S. Ph. de Vries, *Joodsche Riten en Symbolen*, I, Zutphen, 1938, facing p. 98.

[13] Cecil Roth furnishes an illustration in "The Art of Abraham Lopes d'Oliveira"
in *Le Judaïsme Sephardi*, N. S. No. 5, London, 1954, p. 203.

e) ITALIAN BRASS SABBATH LAMP. 17th–18th Century.
Museum of the Hebrew Union College - Jewish Institute of Religion.

circular lamp is the starting point, but there is no central bowl. Instead of this, the edges expand into separate oil-holding prongs. This makes the star shape all the more pronounced.

In spite of this structure that meant so much to the Jews, the earliest lamps of this kind appeared among the Christians. The oldest ones known to us, originating as early as the twelfth century, have been preserved in the cathedral at Erfurt, Germany,[14] and in the domains of France. Of the latter, we show here a picture. These

f) CHRISTIAN 12th CENTURY BRONZE LAMP WITH BIBLICAL SCENES.
Formerly in a private collection at Dijon, France.

[14] Illustration in *Reallexikon zur Deutschen Kunstgeschichte*, I, Stuttgart, 1937, col. 653. In "A Silver Lamp from Frankfort-on-the-Main," in *Essays in Honor of*

lamps, made of bronze, surround a cylindrical trunk decked with scenes from the Old Testament. Those scenes led to regarding these lamps as Jewish.[15] But would Jews have tolerated such representations in an age when the biblical prohibition of images was heeded with utmost severity? We must concede that the star-lamp appears first among the Christians. The conclusion is nonetheless valid that it was the Jews who transferred the lamp to the home and vested it with Sabbath sanctity.

We gain a good idea of such a star-lamp from a drawing in a *Maḥzor* of the Vatican Library in Rome (Cod. ebr. 324, fol. 27a).

g) Jewish Sabbath Lamp.
Drawing from a Maḥzor in Rome, Vatican Library, Cod. ebr. 324.
Around 1400.

Georg Swarzenski, Chicago, 1952, p. 196, note 23, Guido Schoenberger doubts the old age of the oil container but not that of the shaft.
[15] Thus Didron in the *Annales Archéologiques*, IV, Paris, 1846, p. 149.

This *Maḥzor* is part of a manuscript compilation which goes back to the end of the fourteenth century.[16] The drawing, when published,[17] was placed upside down. We show it here in its correct position. That clumsy sketch should not lead us astray. What we doubtless have here is a star-lamp with a drip-bowl, the lamp, fastened to a shaft, hanging from the ceiling.

At the time this lamp originated, the Sabbath star must have been a familiar ritual object in Ashkenazic families. Israel Isserlin, the great Talmudic authority of the fifteenth century, in one of his responsa, speaking of round lamps for Sabbath lighting (פמוטות), notes that such are to be found in all the better Jewish homes.[18] To this medieval quotation may be added one from the early eighteenth century: "The lamps are of brass and carry four, six, and even eight nozzles with wicks. It may well be that even the poorest among the Jews have such lamps for the Sabbath."[19]

Meanwhile, brass did not always suffice. When circumstances permitted, the material got to be costly silver. Of such a lamp, fashioned in 1540, we learn from a German goldsmith book of the sixteenth century.[20] The fact that this lamp goes by the name *Judenstern* (Jewish star) proves how such a lamp has become an object of exclusively Jewish usage. At this early date already, non-Jews preferred the hanging lamp with its more brightly burning candles.

No silver lamp of the sixteenth century has come down to us. But a few have been preserved from the seventeenth century,[21] and some years ago the Jewish Museum at Cincinnati was fortunate enough to acquire one (Plate 1). This lamp stresses its star shape by means of no fewer than ten prongs which surround a lion's head on the

---

[16] *Bibliothecae Apostolicae Vaticanae Codicum Manuscriptorum Catalogus*, I, Roma, 1756, p. 308.

[17] Ernst Munkacsi, *Illuminated Manuscripts in Italian Libraries* (Hungarian), Budapest, n. d., ill. 36.

[18] Cf. *Terumath Ha-Deshen*, ed. Venice, 1546, p. 48a. A Sabbath lamp, unearthed near Deutz in the Rhineland and belonging to Mr. Siegfried Strauss of Brooklyn, is regarded by its owner as a product of the fourteenth century. But a similar lamp, attributed to the seventeenth century, is illustrated in H. R. d'Allemagne, *Histoire de luminaire depuis l'époque romaine jusqu'au 19e siècle*, Paris 1891, p. 279.

[19] G. J. Schudt, *Juedische Merckwuerdigkeiten der zu Frankfurt am Mayn wohnenden Juden*, Leipzig, 1714 ff., Book VI, Chap. 34.

[20] This is the so-called *Master Book of the Goldsmiths* at Frankfort-on-the-Main. Cf. Hermann Gundersheimer and Guido Schoenberger in the *Notizblatt der Gesellschaft zur Erforschung juedischer Kunstdenkmaeler*, No. 34, 1937.

[21] Compare the essay of Guido Schoenberger, "A Silver Sabbath Lamp" etc. pp. 189 ff.

lower side (see our illustration). Similar lions' heads are attached to the lower side of the ascending shaft, and this develops into the tower of a fortress with latticed windows, some of them four-cornered and some round, obviously an allusion to II Sam. 22.51, "A tower of

h) BOTTOM VIEW OF A GERMAN 17th CENTURY SILVER SABBATH LAMP.

Museum of the Hebrew Union College - Jewish Institute of Religion.

salvation is He to His king; and showeth mercy to His anointed, to David and his seed for evermore." Since, with David, this utterance associates a tower, the artist — or was it perhaps the patron who engaged the artist? — thinks of a tower of David mentioned in Cant. 4.4, "Thy neck is like the tower of David builded with turrets, whereon there hang a thousand shields." To the tower, some circular shields are accordingly added.

This lamp of ours shows, as craftsman's mark, a V and, in the opening of the V, an S. Those are probably the initials of the gold-smith, Valentin Schueler of Frankfort on-the-Main who, in 1666, entered the employ of Jacob Rapp and who, taking over his employer's workshop upon his employer's death (1670), retained the shop at least until 1681.[22] Because of the lamp's comparative plainness, I am inclined to reckon it among Schueler's earlier products. In the Jewish Museum at New York, two lamps which carry the same marking are more richly embellished; they are adorned with small figures.[23]

Of course only a Jew of means could indulge himself such a lamp. Most people had to content themselves with cheaper material such as brass. But this "popular edition," which has survived to our own day, had the compensatory advantage of being produced by Jewish copper-smiths; and there were a goodly number of such in Eastern Europe. For these less expensive lamps, we can offer a fine sample, also from the Museum of the Hebrew Union College - Jewish Institute of Reli-gion (Plate 2). Judging from its heavy style, it belongs to the begin-ning of the eighteenth century. Over the "star" for the oil, there is attached an upper row of sockets for the candles.[24] Possibly, out of reverence for that ultra-ancient burning material, oil only was used for Friday evening illumination. However, it is also possible that the oil light proved too meager and that candles afforded necessary supplementation.

This brings us to the question: How was it with Sabbath candles in ancient times? Candles are known to have existed in the earliest epochs.[25] But how was it among the Jews? I put this question to my

---

[22] G. Schoenberger, *op. cit.* p. 190, note 7.

[23] A lamp resembling ours, but made of copper, is to be found in the collection of Viktor Klagsbald, Paris. Cf. the catalogue of the exhibit, "Art Religieux Juif," in Musée d'Art Juif, in Paris, Paris 1956, No. 39, with illustration on p. 32. The lamp has eight oil containers and has consequently been regarded as a Hanukkah lamp. In my opinion, it is a Sabbath lamp.

[24] Similar lamps, with oil chambers below and candles above can be seen in Moritz Oppenheim, *Bilder aus dem Altjuedischen Familien-Leben*, Frankfort-on-the-Main, 1866.

[25] Cf. A. S. Harrison, "Fire-Making, Fuel and Lighting," in *A History*

colleague, Prof. Alexander Guttmann. I cull, from Dr. Guttmann's kind reply, that already the Talmud (Sab. 20b) permits wax for the lamp wick, which Rashi interprets to the effect that the wax for the wick refers to a candle. Candles were accordingly permitted. Alfasi, R. Nissin, and Caro similarly permit them. By contrast, the Babylonian authorities like Sherira Gaon and his son, Hai, express themselves as opposed to the use of wax candles on the Sabbath. In other words, there existed a theoretical difference of opinion. So far as practice was concerned, we hear from R. Asher ben Yechiel (1250–1328) that candles were burned in France and in Germany.

This evidences the use of candles in the Middle Ages. But, as regards the manner of their use, we are uninformed until we reach the year 1500. For that period we learn from the illuminated picture here reproduced. This picture comes from the famous prayer book of

i) Sabbath Lamp with Two Candles.

Illumination from the famous Prayer Book of Baron Rothschild.
Italian, around 1500.

of Technology, ed. Ch. Singer, E. J. Holmjard, A. R. Hall, I, Oxford, 1954, pp. 216 ff. and p. 234.

Baron Rothschild which includes the *Haggadah* for Passover. Here is to be seen the *pater familias* sitting at a table on which stands a candlestick with two lights. This pertains to the Seder, the head of the household being in the act of raising the fourth cup. Yet there is little doubt that a similar candlestick was used on Friday evenings.[26] Its structure is, by no means, an invention of the book-illuminator's phantasy. The picture reproduces an actual candlestick. Such a candlestick, made of bronze, is on display, as a piece of fifteenth century German craftsmanship, in the Museum for Arts and Crafts in Frankfort on-the-Main (see our illustration). Obviously some of those pieces reached Italy, and there the Jews put them to religious use.

j) CANDLESTICK FOR PRIVATE USE. Bronze. 15th Century. Germany.

Frankfort-on-the-Main, Museum for Arts and Crafts.
Taken from Walter Dexel, *Deutsches Handwerksgut*, Berlin, 1939.

[26] It is regarded as a Sabbath candlestick also by Rachel Wischnitzer-Bernstein in her essay, "The Sabbath in Art" in the collection, *Sabbath, the Day of Delight*, Philadelphia, 1944, p. 326.

Obviously such candlesticks penetrated also to Eastern Europe where they led to the practice of having combined candle lights on Friday evenings. When the Hungarian Rabbi Isaac Turnau (14th–15th century), says that "on Friday nights one kindles two lights,"[27] he refers either to two single candlesticks or to such a double candleholder. A hanging lamp cannot be meant because, in such lamps, the lights numbered not two but more than two.

The candle combinations occasionally underwent change. For example, among the Jews of Poland, the number of branches on the candlesticks increased to three, four or five. The stretch between the foot and the socket became adorned with lions, the escutcheon figure of Judah or, as in our illustration, with stags in allusion to Ps. 42.2, "As the stag panteth after the water brooks, so panteth my soul after Thee, O God." And the manner in which these animals are interwoven with tendrils answers to a type of artistry associated with the Jews of Eastern Europe. That same artistry appears on Jewish tombstones and on the so-called *Mizrach* placards that indicated the eastward direction, toward Jerusalem, which had to be faced in prayer. This amounted not merely to an adoption of alien elements but also to their transformation both in form and in content. It were superfluous to add that such Sabbath candlesticks issued from Jewish workshops.

III. Modern Times

Our consideration of Sabbath hanging-lamps and Sabbath candles brought us far beyond the Middle Ages. But the first appearance of these objects dates back to the Middle Ages, hence our need of treating them in that connection. It is otherwise with the spice-box used at Sabbath-end. This box is modern. The Talmud (Sab. 33b) relates that, late one Friday afternoon, an aged man was seen hastening with two bunches of myrtle which were to be used in honoring the Sabbath. The myrtle was probably savored while held in the bare hand. And that seems to have remained the usage for centuries. Jacob ben Moses Moelln (Maharil), who lived in Germany about 1400, describes the practice in these words: "He (the head of the family) takes the cup in his right hand and the myrtle in his left."[28] This can only mean that the myrtle was, in a literal sense, held. For earlier times there is

---

[27] *Minhagim Le-Kol Ha-Shanah*, Venice, 1616, fol. 7b. For the reference to this passage as well as to various other sources pertaining to the Sabbath, I am indebted to Dr. Jakob Petuchowski of Cincinnati.

[28] *Sefer Maharil*, ed. Polonoye, 1802, fol. 19d.

k) POLISH BRASS SABBATH CANDELABRA. 18th Century.

Museum of the Hebrew Union College - Jewish Institute of Religion.

mention of a container but not of a closed box. A Rabbi Ephraim, perhaps Rabbi Ephraim ben Jacob of Bonn, who lived in the twelfth century, is said to have regarded a variety of spices as preferable to a single spice and to have preserved his spices in a glass.[29] It was the use of a number of spices in combination that created the need of keeping them together in some kind of holder. There is extant an illustration of such a receptacle in the form of a goblet. The illustration stands in a German-Jewish *Minhagim* book which appeared at Mantua in 1590, and again at Venice in 1593, and once more at Venice in 1601. The illustration of a *Habdalah* service[30] which we give here was, though taken from the third edition, doubtless copied from the previous editions. The picture shows a couple with four children. The *pater familias* holds a wine cup in his left hand, while the boy standing in front of him holds a candle. It follows that another boy, standing behind that first boy, has, in his goblet, some spices which he holds in such wise that these also may receive the benediction. Reference to these spices occurs in the underlying text which speaks of "schmecken" the spices. In Old German, "schmecken" applies not only to pleasant tastes but also to pleasant odors.

Nonetheless the tower-shaped *Besamin* box appeared in Germany somewhat earlier. How much earlier? Madam Wischnitzer-Bernstein believes such a box to be discernible in the *Second Nuremberg Haggadah*, a German-Jewish manuscript of the late fifteenth century.[31] But the airy structure here, within which someone is sitting, resembles a tabernacle rather than a spicebox. In the anti-Semitic, though highly instructive lampoon, "Der Gantz Juedisch Glaub," which dates from 1530, the passage occurs (C. fol. 2b), "They have moreover a silver gem (Kleinot) which contains many good spices." These words speak not about the shape of the object but about its material. Two years later, 1532, a book which we have already mentioned, namely the goldsmith book of Frankfort-on-the-Main, records the item: "meister Steffan Altman, ein hedes[32] Rauchfass, wiget 19 lot." To the word *Rauchfass*, the editors add the word *Besomimturm* (spice-tower). But the word *Rauchfass* (censer) would be evidence against rather than

---

[29] Cf. the '*Or Zaru'a* by Isaac b. Moses of Vienna, ed. Zhitomir, 1862, Vol. II, § 92. Also in the *Tashbaz* by Samson bar Zadok, ed. Warsaw, 1875, § 86.

[30] For this information as well as for the illustration, I am indebted to Dr. Ernst Namenyi, of Paris.

[31] Compare her book, *Gestalten und Symbole der Juedischen Kunst*, Berlin-Schoeneberg, 1935, p. 109.

[32] *Hedes*, or rather *Hadas*, the Hebrew word for myrtle, evidently applies here to other spices as well as to the container in which they were kept.

אין · עם אבר שבתחת לו נלב אז טאעקט אן אך לו דער ווייר ן ·
אונ' בוילט אך רי נעגיל אונ' אלט הבדלה וויא אונטט אץ
שבתות לו נלב :

צו מורגן אזו אזרו חג אן :אט ניט אחנה אך ניט לא מנצמ · אין
עם אם אונטן זט אן אונו וואל אל אך אפים · אונ' אן
עט הען גןן חדש הין תחנה:) לו ווירלאט זעט אן אחנה אך אזרו חג : :
אלי וויאבר זיטן רא אן ניט טאר חלה נעאן בום טאיין רא אן ניט
אין טורן חלה רא בון לו נעאן · אונ' זולט רא אייט פון דען
טיין דער רא אין טורן חלה לו נעאן · רוח אך נך פסח · וון אן איט
בז צו זאונ'מר טאיין רן ידן ברטט אלכ וויא קאן אן חלה רר בון נעאן ·
אין בך רא: בז זאו'מר טאיין ניט חייב חלה לו נעאן · רוח אלן רי ורוזן
וויבר לוויא טאיין · אמין איטרן גו זאו'מר טיג · אונ' רען מנדרן און
זאו'מר טאיין · אונ' טוט זא אל כמיר לו אנגרר · אונ' נעאן חלה כון יעבות
טאיין רא הין זאו'מר טיין רון אין : · זא אין: דער אנרר אך פטור איט רער
זעלב חלה: אונ' דארך אזא ניט זרען ' רא אונ' מיר מולט אין רי הנר קאן בון
רער חלה אין טויק טאיין רא אן ניט טורן אונר חלה רחוכר לו נעאן
עטוילכן אזלכן אין טאיין איט רעם אונ'יר טאיין בום גוי · אונ' נעאן חלה
אזא נרוט אז רער אזו'מר טאיין אין: · אונ' אין וויג אין · מא אין: ניט אין
לו זורערא אץ אץ אן רי הר מילט קאן אזר רי חלה בון רעם אזו'מר טאיין ·
רא וויל עראטווט אין נעאט : אונ' ווען אן זויטט כרט אלכ זא אזל אן
מוארטרן

1) HABDALAH SCENE FROM A MINHAGIM BOOK, PRINTED IN VENICE, 1601.

evidence for the supposition that the object referred to was tower-shaped.

We can be certain of such a tower shape in a sketch dating from 1553 and here illustrated. The outline is by the Frankfort goldsmith

m) SKETCH FOR A SPICE TOWER, by the silversmith
Heinrich Heidelberger in 1553.

Heinrich Heidelberger. The Jewish person who let the order wished a receptacle of the kind that was owned by his father.[33] Accordingly we can somewhat push back the date for the tower-shaped container. We can fix the date as falling within the first half of the sixteenth century.

We proceed now to ask: Why the choice of such a shape as that of a tower? "In medieval times," so runs the answer, "in Western countries spices were very precious and therefore kept in the tower of the city fortification, which makes it understandable that the medieval tower was reproduced for the spice container in the European West."[34] On our silver Sabbath lamp (Plate I) we noticed a fortress tower with its latticed windows. Not more than a glance at the design of our spice-tower is needed to make us realize the great difference between this spice-tower and the fortress tower on the lamp. The spice-box has nothing that suggests a fortress. It is a many-sectioned edifice with many large windows which would sooner attract cannonading than ward it off.

[33] Cf. G. Schoenberger in the essay already mentioned, "A Silver Lamp from Frankfort-on-the-Main," p. 190, note 8.
[34] Cf. Stephen S. Kayser in *Jewish Ceremonial Art*, p. 89.

Other spice-boxes of the sixteenth century, like the one here portrayed (Plate 3), have the structure of a townhall-tower, with its prison cell, its large clock, and its weather vanes, not at all appropriate to the tower of a stronghold.[34a]

Another explanation of the tower shape traces it to Cant. 5.13, "His cheeks are as a bed of spices, as towers (מגדלות) of perfumes."[35] That sounds more persuasive. We must, however, bear in mind that such tower shapes appear for the first time in the art of the Christians, among sculptures and pictures of the Three Kings who, besides offering gold to the child Jesus, also offer incense and myrrh, that is to say, substances yielding pleasant odors. We portray, on page 408, the detail in a German picture of the fifteenth century, a picture which shows two of the three rulers.[36] From such works of art, the Christian goldsmiths may have derived their incentive. Whether the painters and the sculptors may also have had in mind the spice-towers of the Bible, we do not know. When the Jews gave orders for such spice-towers, they assuredly thought of the passage in Canticles.

If the earliest spice-towers followed the style of the Gothic, and those of the later sixteenth century the style of the Renaissance, of which our townhall-tower box is an example, the spice-towers of the seventeenth and the eighteenth centuries acquired the vividness and the splendor of the Baroque. On the twenty-two inch spice-box in the Museum of the Hebrew Union College-Jewish Institute of Religion (Plate 4), the foot of the tower swings vividly. Over this base there rise two stories whose glittering filigree is animated by patches of color for doors and windows. A knob tops the bulb-shaped roof and, over the weather vane, stands the figure of a Jew.

The absence of a maker's mark indicates a Jewish artificer, while the filigree and the form of a caftan wearing Jew points to Polish origin. Though in Germany, for such spice-towers, the Jews resorted to Christian silversmiths, in Eastern Europe — Poland, Moravia, Bohemia — Jews employed silversmiths of their own faith expert at such work.

And these Jewish silversmiths, with their endless phantasy, did

---

[34a] The four bronze arquebusiers on the surrounding balcony are regarded by Rudolf Hallo as a later addition in *Judaica, Juedische Kunst in Hessen und Nassau*, Marburg 1932, text to plate 19a.

[35] See Rachel Wischnitzer-Bernstein, *Symbole und Gestalten der Juedischen Kunst*, Berlin-Schoeneberg, 1935, p. 107.

[36] The illustration comes from the volume by Joseph Gantner, *Konrat Witz*, second edition, Vienna, 1943, Illustration 70. See also Hugo Kehrer, "Die Heiligen Drei Koenige," in *Studien zur Deutschen Kunstgeschichte*, Strassburg, 1901.

n) Two Kings.
Detail from a painting by Konrat Witz
"The Three Magi bringing presents to the Jesus Child."
1444. Geneva, Musée d'Art et d'Histoire.

not limit themselves to towers. They simulated also flowers, fruit, and fish — that favorite edible for the Sabbath — as well as other creatures. Rarely, instead of silver, was use made of wood. The sample here illustrated belongs to the Museum of the Hebrew Union College-

o) WOODEN SPICE BOX, IN SHAPE OF A HUMAN ARM AND HAND. Museum of the Hebrew Union College - Jewish Institute of Religion.

Jewish Institute of Religion. Here one sees an arm with the hand bent so that the fingernails could reflect the Sabbath light.

Once more let us look at the Jew on the pinnacle of our Baroque spice-tower (Plate 4). In his right hand he holds a winecup and, in his left, a candle. The cup, as already stated, does not differ from other cups. But the *Habdalah* candle is unique. This derives from the fact that, in the benediction over the light at the outgoing of the Sabbath, God is praised in the words, "Who createst the lights of the fire." To bring out the plural "lights," the candle was made to consist of several strands of wax and several wicks braided together. Here is a drawing of such a candle which shows striving for beauty even in such a humble object.

p) HABDALAH CANDLE. Drawing. From the Hungarian Periodical *Mult és Jövö*.

Usually this candle was held in the bare hand. But someone hit upon the idea of a lovely candleholder, thus increasing the number of objects for Sabbath-end use. A plate was laid upon a high pedestal, with staves ascending at the four corners. On each of these staves there glided a movable socket. If the candle was fresh, its socket stood far down. As the candle grew smaller, the socket would be raised. In this manner, the candle which would, at any one time, burn but briefly, could be used over and over.

The charm of these candleholders was heightened by substituting, for the foot, a small figure. Such a figure — and not more than a figure — has been preserved, the one in the Museum of the Hebrew Union College - Jewish Institute of Religion (Plate 5). The manikin, holding prayer book and taper, stands on a domed base. His attire is that of seventeenth century Germany, thus differing from that of the Jew on the Polish spice-box who clings to his medieval garb. What makes our fragment of especial interest is the fact that it carries the same maker's mark as the previously mentioned silver hanging lamp. In this way Valentin Schueler is to be recognized as the artist and the middle of the seventeenth century as the time of origin.[37]

About this period there seems to have burgeoned the custom of joining into various combinations the three implements, those for the blessings over the wine, over the spices, and over the lights. Practical reasons may have operated; so that everything could be held in a person's two hands. But a certain playfulness, noticeable in Jewish art works or in art works made for Jews, may likewise have prompted such contrivances.

Thus, for instance, into the candleholder just mentioned, would be slid a spice-box, not anything tower-shaped, only a drawer the size of a matchbox. Of this type also, the Museum of the Hebrew Union College - Jewish Institute of Religion can exhibit a sample, here portrayed, originating with a goldsmith of Bamberg in the early eighteenth century. Or, a socket holding the *Habdalah* candle could be made to rise out of the cover of a goblet. Our sample, on our Plate 6, was fashioned in the eighteenth century by a silver-smith of Nuremberg. A third combination consisted in supplying a winecup with a cover, and that cover served also to hold spices. A superb cup of this type, preserved in a Swedish private collection, is the work of a Breslau silversmith of the seventeenth century. It has the initials "B. I." That the person who ordered this object took a

---

[37] Of a similar candleholder, fully preserved, a picture stands in *Juedisches Lexikon*, II, col. 1461.

q) Combination of a Habdalah Candlestick with Spice Box.
Bamberg, 18th Century. Silver.
Museum of the Hebrew Union College - Jewish Institute of Religion.

1. SILVER SABBATH LAMP. GERMANY. 17th Century.

Fashioned by Valentin Schueler.
Museum of the Hebrew Union College - Jewish Institute of Religion.

2. POLISH SABBATH LAMP FOR OIL AND CANDLES. Brass.

Early 18th Century. Donated by Dr. Eric Werner to the
Museum of the Hebrew Union College - Jewish Institute of Religion.

3. GERMAN SILVER SPICE BOX, MADE AROUND 1550.
Last at Kassel, Germany. Hessisches Landesmuseum.

4. POLISH SILVER SPICE BOX. 17th–18th Century.

Museum of the Hebrew Union College - Jewish Institute of Religion.

5. Manikin with Habdalah Candle and Prayer Book

Foot of a Habdalah Candle Holder. Silver.
Fashioned by Valentin Schueler in the 17th Century.
Museum of the Hebrew Union College - Jewish Institute of Religion.

6. Combination of Kiddush Cup and Habdalah Candle.
Silver. Nuremberg, 18th Century.
Museum of the Hebrew Union College - Jewish Institute of Religion.

7. COMBINATION OF KIDDUSH CUP AND
SPICE BOX. Silver. Breslau. 17th
Century. Owner: Iwan Traugott,
Stockholm, Sweden.

200

8. COVER FOR THE ḤALLOT. Silk. 19th Century.

Museum of the Hebrew Union College - Jewish Institute of Religion.

lively part in its planning is indicated by the scenes hammered into the metal: scenes of Sabbath in the synagogue and Sabbath in the home (Plate 7).

A fourth and our last combination appears to have originated not before the early part of the nineteenth century. This was linked with the custom of pouring a little of the wine into a saucer and extinguishing the candle in the liquid. There would be used, for this purpose, a special saucer of porcelain, majolica, or silver, with some modest inscription and some equally modest ornamentation. But it was hardly before the nineteenth century that anyone arrived at the idea of combining that dish with the spice-box. In such cases the spice-box would take the form of some fruit attached to a stem pushing up out of a concave receptacle (see our illustration).

r) Silver Spice Box with Wine Container for Extinguishing the Habdalah Candle. Germany, Around 1830.

Zalman Yovely Auction at the Parke-Bernet Galleries, Inc., New York 1955.

The juncture of spice-box and *Habdalah* dish enjoyed no great popularity; it vanished after a brief period. The other combinations similarly lost their appeal. Perhaps they impressed people as being too ingenious. People returned to the separate implements.

Nor has our list of Sabbath appurtenances been exhausted. Inasmuch as cooking on Saturday was not allowed, food had to be prepared on Friday and kept warm in an oven, either one's own oven or that of someone else. Here and there the desire arose to impart an attractive appearance to the dishes for such food.

There were also dishes for the Sabbath loaves. These dishes were of silver, but I know of such only from the recent past. *Ḥallot* furnish the theme of their ornamentation.

Over the actual *Ḥallot*, doubtless with the religious urge to conceal and then to reveal, there would be spread a cover. The manner was simple. An English writer of the seventeenth century mentions, in this connection, a napkin.[38] But there are also instances of covers made specially for this purpose. In my *History of Jewish Art*, a picture of such a cover forms the frontispiece, a cover with an especially rich embroidery. Here we offer as our Plate 8 a cloth, again belonging to the museum of the Hebrew Union College - Jewish Institute of Religion. In the middle stands the Star of David surrounded by twelve circles enclosing the symbols of the twelve tribes, all stamped in black upon gold-yellow silk. The charm of the vivid drawing is heightened by that powerful contrast of colors.

Over her head and shoulders, the woman of the house, as she handles the Sabbath lights, sometimes wears a special kind of embroidered kerchief.[39] Also to be noted, as a token of the day, is the table-cloth. While tablecloths were known among well circumstanced Romans,[40] the Jews could indulge themselves that elegance only on special days.[41] But their tablecloths were ornate with weavings and embroideries.

Finally to be mentioned is the special kind of bowl into which the head of the family would dip his hands at the beginning and at the end of the meal. From ancient times, such washing held for the Jews a religious significance.

Let us recall once more the lines from Persius. How few and simple were the objects employed in the private observance of the Sabbath! During the nearly two thousand years that have elapsed since that satire was written, ritual objects for the Sabbath have steadily increased in number and gained in splendor and charm.

We have shown how extensively the shapes chosen were determined by the surrounding world. Those outside influences often went to the point of having Jewish religious objects fashioned by artificers belonging to other religions. This was due not to any Jewish incompetence but to the fact that certain kinds of art had become extinct

[38] Alexander Ross, *A View of the Jewish Religion*, London, 1656, p. 228.

[39] Such a head-dress, gold-embroidered, is in the possession of the Bezalel National Museum in Jerusalem. Cf. the catalogue of the exhibition, "One Nation Out of Many Peoples," 1953, No. 291.

[40] Compare the article, "Kochkunst," in Pauly-Wissowa, *Realencyclopaedie der classischen Altertumswissenschaft*. See also J. Marquardt, *Das Privatleben der Roemer*, Leipzig, 1879, p. 303.

[41] To a tablecloth was probably applied the maxim of R. Eleazar in Sab. 119b: "Though one may need not more than an olive, one should always set one's table properly on Sabbath eve."

among the Jews owing to political and economic pressures. Proof of this is the fact that the Jews of Eastern Europe, living under more favorable conditions, created those works by their own skill.

And who can gauge, in every instance, how intently the non-Jewish artist may have carried out the wishes of the Jewish person whose order he was filling or may, even if unconsciously, have entered into the Jewish spirit? Even where the Jews did not themselves produce their implements, their mode of living merged those implements into a compact unity. The result was Jewish Art,[42] an art which, by reason of its manifold structure and its fine quality, well deserves the consideration which it has here received.

[42] For a more detailed treatment of the question what constitutes Jewish art, one should read the clever article by Stephen S. Kayser, "Defining Jewish Art," in the *Mordecai M. Kaplan Jubilee Volume*, New York, 1953, pp. 457 ff.

THE ORIGIN AND DEVELOPMENT OF
TWO SABBATH CEREMONIES

JACOB Z. LAUTERBACH, Hebrew Union College, Cincinnati, Ohio

JEWISH religious ceremonies have their histories and their fates. They come into being in different ways and have different origins. They may be enacted by divine law; formally introduced by the leaders of the people and decreed by the religious authorities; imported from foreign lands; or borrowed by the people themselves — from non-Jewish neighbors — and then gradually, even if reluctantly, tolerated and accepted by the religious authorities. They may even be born of mere habits which have become fixed, or grow out of mere customs of convenience which gradually acquire some religious significance and thus, in time, become generally accepted. But, no matter what their origin, after they have been recognized as Jewish ceremonies, they all start a certain course of development and begin their history. They change more or less in form and content, flourish and live on, or decay and die.

When, in the course of time, due to the general progress of civilization, new ideas arise among the people and major or minor changes in their beliefs take place, all ceremonies observed by the people in an earlier period, or in a previous cultural stage, meet with difficulties. They are exposed to the dangers either of neglect or of antagonistic criticism which threaten their very existence. In the one case they no longer appeal to the people who now cherish ideas other than those which gave rise to the ceremonies or different from those expressed by these ceremonies. In the other case they may become objectionable to more advanced ways of thinking and be attacked by the cultural leaders. In either case they experience difficulties in maintaining themselves.[1]

---

[1] Comp. Lauterbach, "The Ceremony of Breaking a Glass at Weddings" in *HUCA*, II (1925), 352 f.

Reprinted from *Hebrew Union College Annual*, Vol. XV, 1940.

In this struggle against new hostile ideas and unfavorable conditions, not all ceremonies fare alike. Some ceremonies possess a special aptitude for adjusting themselves to changed conditions and have the capacity of making their peace with advanced ideas and new beliefs. They lend themselves to modifications by which they can retain their appeal to the changed popular fancy; and they readily submit to a process of repeated interpretations by which they assume new meaning and fresh significance in keeping with the newer ideas in vogue among the more thoughtful of the people. They are thus enabled to continue performing some function or serving some purpose, even though it may be a function or a purpose altogether different from the one for which they were originally intended or which they served in a previous period.[2] At any rate, they maintain themselves and remain a part of the cultural or spiritual life of the people.

Other ceremonies are not so successful. By attempts at adaptation to changed conditions and new ideas they too seek to prolong their existence, and they may manage to achieve some passing success. Gradually, however, they lose their adaptability and are unable to withstand the attacks by the hostile forces of a different spiritual climate or a changed cultural environment. Sooner or later they are rejected by the leaders of thought and are neglected even by the people, and thus disappear entirely.

In some instances a ceremony meets obstacles which make it difficult or impossible for it to continue functioning in its totality. It then may break up into parts, each of which forms a separate ceremony that can avoid the difficulties encountered by the parent ceremony as a whole. These new ceremonies, less objectionable than the original ceremony as a whole, pursue their own course of development and are capable of continuing to function as independent religious ceremonies.[3] This method of splitting

---

[2] Even after acquiring a new meaning and being given a new purpose, a ceremony may still retain some of the notions originally associated with it and, in the mind of some people at least, continue to serve the old purpose alongside of the new one. See Lauterbach, *Tashlik*, (Cincinnati 1936) pp. 1–3, and pp. 110–111.

[3] Such an instance is the original ceremony out of which developed *Tashlik*, and *Kapparot*. See Lauterbach *op. cit.*, p. 56 ff., p. 71 f., and p. 131.

itself into parts, however, does not always save the ceremony or any of its parts. In some cases the parts are no more successful in maintaining themselves separately than was the whole. The separate ceremony, formed out of a fragment of the broken up older ceremony, may, for a time at least, show greater adaptability to a changed environment. It may develop a certain capacity for associating itself with new ideas whereby it acquires a new significance and a different character which gives it a fresh appeal to a certain class of people. This does not, however, assure its permanent existence or continuous function. Like the older ceremony of which it was merely a part, it, sooner or later, may face criticism and meet with disapproval; sometimes because the objectionable character of the parent ceremony may still be noticeable in the part, notwithstanding the newer significance and different character given to it, or sometimes the new character itself assumed by the part or the fresh significance assigned to it which at first imparted to it a fresh appeal, provokes new antagonism or meets with objections on the part of some other group of the people. The result is that the ceremony, notwithstanding or even because of its new character, is attacked by hostile forces which cause it to be officially discarded or neglected by the people.

In the following I shall describe the course taken by two Jewish ceremonies observed respectively on Friday evening and Saturday night. Both of these ceremonies grew out of a mere custom or habit and originally were similar in character and form. The one, after being recognized as a religious ceremony, experienced in the course of time, (due probably to some objections raised against it) some reinterpretations. With some modifications, it has been preserved to this day. The other seemingly met with greater obstacles. And even though, or just because, it was given some new mystic significance and assumed a new character, it was not generally favored. It encountered strong objections and was discarded by the great majority of the people, so that it finally fell into utter disuse and became almost completely forgotten.

There seems to have been a custom among the Jews in Palestine in ancient times of providing their table on the Sabbath with fragrant plants or aromatic herbs.[4] The primary and chief purpose of these plants was to enhance the pleasures of the table by affording the participants of the meal the additional enjoyment of the aroma or pleasant fragrance. They were simply a substitute for the incense, or smoke of spices, *mugmar*,[5] which it was customary to provide at the end of every meal.[6] This

[4] We have no explicit reference in the Talmud to such a custom but some indications point to it. Thus the description of a table in the house of a wealthy Jew on a Sabbath mentions that it was laden with all kinds of food and delicacies and aromatic herbs כל מיני מאכל וכל מיני מגדים ובשמים (Sab. 119a), though the Munich Ms. does not have the word ובשמים. See Rabbinovicz דקדוקי סופרים ad loc. Še'eltot I (Wilna 1861) p. 6; 'Or Zaru'a II, p. 10; and Šibbole Ha-leḳeṭ 55 (Wilna 1886) p. 43, when quoting this passage omit the word ובשמים. And Sefer Ha-'ittim (Berlin 1902) p. 241 has פירות instead of בשמים. The Midrash, Lev. Rab. 23.6 speaks of the use of the rose for Sabbaths and Holidays שושנה מתוקנת לשבתות וימים טובים. See also Beẓ 33b מטלטלין עצי בשמים להריח בהם, and Men. 43b בשבתא וביומי טבי טרח וממלי להו באיספרמקי which Rashi s. v. באספרמקי correctly explains as בשמים. Comp. I. Löw, *Aramaeische Pflanzen-Namen* (Leipzig 1881) p. 152. Likewise Persius Flaccus, a Roman satirist of the first century, describing the table in a Jewish home on the Sabbath, says: "The lamps are arranged and adorned with violets" which probably refers especially to the Friday evening ceremonies. Cf. Buechler, "Graeco-Roman Criticism of Some Jewish Observances and Beliefs" in *The Jewish Review*, I (London 1910), 133–134. And last but not least, the story in Sab. 33b to be discussed below, unmistakably points to such an early custom.

[5] מוגמר from גומרא, glowing coal. See Jastrow, *Dictionary* s. v. p. 738.

[6] The Mishna (Ber. 6.6) prescribes that "the one who recites the Grace after the meal over a cup of wine, also says the benediction over the *mugmar*" adding "although they usually serve the *mugmar* only after the meal." והוא אומר על המוגמר אף על פי שאין מביאין את המוגמר אלא לאחר הסעודה. "After the meal" לאחר הסעודה, is understood by the commentators to mean after the meal is over and Grace has been recited. Some commentators add that it only means that it was the usual custom to serve it after the Grace following the meal had been recited but that they would some times also serve it after the eating was finished, before the recitation of the Grace. See Tosefot Yomṭob ad loc. and פירוש בעל ספר חרדים on the Palestinian Talmud to Ber. 6.6 in edition Wilna 1922, p. 96 and p. 98. Whether the *mugmar* had, in the mind of some people, the additional purpose of driving away the evil spirits as the smoke of the incense קטורת was reputed to do (*infra*, note 40), we cannot tell. The statement in the Mishna Beẓ. 2.7 permitting the preparation of the *mugmar* on a holiday מניחין את המוגמר ביום טוב indicates that the Rabbis, at least, understood its purpose to be solely for enjoyment or to help the digestion; hence the work in preparing it like all work for preparing food, אוכל נפש, was permitted on a holiday.

mugmar consisted of some aromatic herbs strewn upon a pan of live coals which thus produced a pleasant aromatic smoke. On week days or even on holidays on which the making and using of fire was allowed, such a pan of live coals could be prepared and, with the aromatic herbs or spices scattered on them, placed upon the table. On the Sabbath, however, when fire could not be made and live coals were neither obtainable nor allowed to be moved or handled, it was impossible to prepare this *mugmar*. Yet the people did not like to do without it on the Sabbath; they did not like to make the Sabbath-day meals less enjoyable than those on the other days of the week. A substitute was, therefore, introduced which did not involve any violation of the Sabbath law. They placed on the table during or at the beginning of the meal[7] fragrant plants, flowers, or perhaps other kinds of aromatic herbs and spices, מיני בשמים which would give out a pleasant fragrance without the necessity of putting them on the fire first. Of course, they recited a separate benediction בא"י אמ"ה בורא עצי בשמים over this substitute, just as they recited the very same benediction over the *mugmar* on week days and just as one had to recite a separate benediction over any kind of extra enjoyment that may have been brought to the table which did not form an integral part of the meal. But the reciting of a benediction over this extra enjoyment did not make the custom of having plants at the table a religious ceremony. Hence, no express reference to such a custom is, to my knowledge, to be found in the *Talmud* or *Midrashim*, nor any discussion of its details. It was just a table custom like the *mugmar*, for which it was substituted, which likewise is nowhere prescribed as a religious ceremony and the details of which are likewise not discussed except in the casual remark in the *Mishnah* (Ber. 6.6), that the one who says the benediction over the wine brought in after the meal also says the benediction over the *mugmar*.

---

[7] See preceding note. In the case of the *mugmar*, they could not place it on the table at the beginning of the meal for the coals might die out during the time of the meal and the aroma would not last till the time after the meal when they really wanted it. But, in the case of flowers, their fragrance is more lasting and would continue till after the meal, even though placed on the table at the beginning of or even before the meal. *Infra*, note 16, and note 25.

This table custom was not limited to one particular meal
of the Sabbath and it was not especially a Friday evening custom, as one might assume from the description by Flaccus.[8] It
was a custom for the whole Sabbath, observed at all of its meals,
since fire for the preparation of the *mugmar* could not be used.[9]

Before the new system of reckoning the day from evening
to evening was introduced, when the Sabbath extended from
Saturday morning to Sunday morning,[10] there were only *two*[11]
meals partaken of on the Sabbath — as on any other day —
one in the morning or forenoon and the other in the evening or
late afternoon.[12] And, of course, at *both* of these meals, flowers
or plants had to be used as a substitute for the *mugmar*. Since
the evening, under that system, belonged to the preceding, not
to the following day, Friday evening was not yet part of the
Sabbath; hence, the meal on Friday evening was not yet a
Sabbath meal: it was simply the second meal of the week day,
Friday. Fire, then, could still be used and live coals could be
obtained, hence there was no need of using plants as a substitute
for the *mugmar* at the Friday evening meal. With the innovation
of reckoning the day from sunset to sunset, which made the
Sabbath extend from Friday evening to Saturday evening, the
character of the Friday evening meal was greatly changed, and
the character of the Saturday late afternoon or evening meal
was likewise greatly affected. Both of these meals were made

---

[8] Flaccus mentions the violets as an adornment of the lamps, which can
have reference only to Friday evening. *Supra*, note 4. This merely means
that, on Friday evening, they arranged the flowers together with the lamps
but it does not mean that, on the Sabbath day, they did not have these violets
or other flowers on the table, even though no lamps were burning.

[9] They have also occasionally enjoyed the fragrance of these flowers even
between meals. See Beẓ. 33b and Men. 43b quoted *supra*, note 4.

[10] This innovation, as I prove elsewhere, was introduced during or near
the end of the Greek period. Comp. J. Morgenstern, "The Sources of the
Creation Story" in *AJSLL* XXXVI (1919–1920), 176, note 1 to p. 179.

[11] The rule for taking three meals on the Sabbath developed much later.
I hope to discuss this (later) development elsewhere. Cf. *infra*, note 19.

[12] There were no fixed hours for all people. Different classes of people hạd
their meals at different hours. But in general it can be said that one meal was
taken in the forenoon and the other in the late afternoon or evening. See
S. Krauss, *Talmudische Archäologie* III (Leipzig 1910), 28–31.

the occasion of emphasizing the new mode of reckoning the day, by declaring, through solemn ceremonies at the table, that Friday night, now belonging to the following day, was part of the Sabbath; and Saturday night, belonging to the following day, Sunday, was no longer part of the Sabbath. This involved some changes in the arrangement of those two meals by introducing these new ceremonies and fitting them in, or adjusting them to, the older habits.

Now, changes in old habits or established customs are not so easily made. It is in the nature of human beings to cling to accustomed ways. And, in their inertia, people yield but slowly and reluctantly to the need of new customs or of changes in old ones if, indeed, they do not, actively or passively, altogether resist their introduction. Even those persons who recognize the need of changes, and even the authorities who advocate new practices and seek to introduce new ceremonies, are very often anxious to retain along with the new practices as much as possible of the older forms. Of course, not all of the older forms can be retained, as not all are compatible with the principles of the advocated changes and newly introduced practices. It then becomes a question of individual judgment or personal preference as to which part of the old is more valuable and should be retained and which should be abandoned. Some people prefer the one feature of the older custom which they claim should be retained even in the new system of practices; others again, emphasize the importance of another feature or principle which they insist should be retained even under the changed conditions. But all of them seek, as much as possible, to minimize the break with the past, and to introduce the new practices without upsetting the older forms and the established order too much. This was also the case when it was necessary to adjust the changed status of Friday evening and Saturday night to the older customs and to combine the new ceremonies necessitated by that new status with the older forms.

In the case of the Friday evening observances, this adjustment of older habits to the new order was not so difficult. Once the innovation of considering Friday night as part of the Sabbath was accepted — and for this there was a good precedent in the law about the Day of Atonement,[13] which was also called a Sabbath — there was no difficulty in arranging the customs or ceremonies at the meal of that evening to suit its new character as a Sabbath evening. All that was necessary was to make the meal a little more festive and to connect with it the Kiddush service, signifying the beginning of the holy day and consecrating it.[14] The fact that the lights had been kindled before sunset or before the starting of the meal did not in any way affect the order and arrangement of the meal.[15] This was left as it had previously been, except that it was considered a Sabbath meal. And instead of the *mugmar* which now could not be provided, since no fire could be used, the substitute for it, the plants, were provided as for the meals on the Sabbath-day.[16]

[13] The law in Lev. 23.32 about the Day of Atonement, a "Sabbath of solemn rest" שבת שבתון, which reads, "From even unto even shall ye keep your Sabbath," was simply taken to apply to all Sabbaths, not only to the Day of Atonement. To be forbidden to work on Friday evening was not a hardship. And this restriction was probably not much noticed by the people, as night work was not common in those ancient times. The only inconvenience to the people resulting from this innovation was the impossibility of making fire or producing light on that evening. This inconvenience, however, was soon remedied. For it was declared that only the labor of producing fire and light was forbidden but, if prepared before the evening, fire and light could be kept in the house. So, all in all, as regards Friday evening, the innovation did not cause an unpleasant break with the former habits of the people and they could well, even by mere inertia, accept the new status given to Friday evening. They probably welcomed the additional joy and the solemnity provided for it by the ceremony of the Kiddush.

[14] There was as yet no other act or rite announcing the arrival of the Sabbath. The תפלת ערבית had not yet been introduced; at any rate, it had not yet been generally accepted. Comp. I. Elbogen, "Eingang und Ausgang des Sabbats" in *Festschrift zu Israel Lewy's 70tem Geburtstag* (Breslau 1911) p. 179 ff.

[15] The הדלקת נר שבת was originally not a positive obligatory ceremony. It was just a permission to have lights on Friday evening, if kindled before dark. It was accordingly merely a preparatory act, performed before the advent of the Sabbath but not one greeting or welcoming the Sabbath. It was only some time later that it came to be regarded as a duty מצוה or even an obligation חובה. Cf. *supra*, note 13.

[16] They could not well prepare the regular *mugmar* before dark, as the aroma might soon dissipate and not last till the end of the meal when they wanted it most. *Supra*, note 7.

Yet no regulation about this is found, nor is it especially' mentioned that or when, in the order of the Kiddush service or the meal, the benediction over these plants, the substitute for the *mugmar*, should be recited. It was taken for granted that like the *mugmar* itself, the substitute for it, the plants, properly belonged at the end of the meal and the benediction over them was to be recited following the recitation of the Grace after the meal. Thus, when the arrangement of the Friday evening meal is discussed, only the new feature or the ceremony added to it after and because it became a Sabbath meal, i. e., the Kiddush service, was considered. This was a new ceremony, and differences of opinion as to which part of it should come first could be entertained. The Shammaites and Hillelites, accordingly, merely discussed the order of the benedictions recited in the Kiddush service, at the Friday evening meal, i. e., whether the benediction over the wine should precede the one declaring the consecration of the day or vice versa (Ber. 8.1). But no mention is made of the benediction over the plants, the substitute for the *mugmar*, which followed the meal. Evidently the feature of having plants instead of the *mugmar* at the Friday evening meal had, as yet, no special significance which might have caused the teachers to consider the question of assigning the benediction over them any special place. Hence there was no need of even mentioning it.

It was different in the case of Saturday night which now, under the new system, was no longer part of the Sabbath. Here the adjustment of the older practice to the new status was more difficult. The meal on that evening, even though it may have been partaken of or, at any rate, finished after dark, was still considered, as it had always been in the past, one of the Sabbath meals. In fact, it was the second meal or the evening meal of the Sabbath-*day*[17] which, however, because the people were free from work, may have begun a little earlier in the afternoon.[18] This meal extended through the twilight until nightfall, when it was followed by the Habdalah rite which declared that the

---

[17] See Elbogen *op. cit.*, p. 183.

[18] See Yer. Ber. 8.1 (11d) שבת מוצאי וחשכה בשבת ואוכל יושב היה, and cf. the commentaries to the Mishnah, Ber. 8.5.

Sabbath was over and that the week day in which work may be done was beginning.[19] A concrete demonstration of this distinction was the lighting of the light, an act which could not be performed during the Sabbath. These were the new features introduced in connection with that meal. But the meal in itself still retained the character of a Sabbath meal. Hence, no *mugmar* was used at this meal but plants were substituted as was done at the other Sabbath meals. The question then arose how the new features, i. e., lighting the light and reciting the Habdalah, should be combined with the older established practices of saying Grace after the meal and serving the substitute for the *mugmar*. All agreed that the meal, being the second meal of the Sabbath *day*, had to be finished and Grace recited after it, before the other ceremonies marking the going out of the Sabbath could be started. They also agreed that the recitation of the Habdalah, declaring that the Sabbath was over, had to be the last feature.[20] Differences arose only in regard to the arrangement of the other ceremonies. In keeping with the tendency, described above, of seeking as far as possible not to disturb the established order of older practices by the addition of new ones, there were three lines of arrangements that could be advocated,

---

[19] In the course of time the connection between the Habdalah ceremony and the last meal of the Sabbath became severed. This last meal of the Sabbath had to be finished before the evening service תפלת ערבית was recited, while the Habdalah ceremony took place after it. This caused great difficulty to some of the commentators who tried to explain talmudic passages, reflecting the older practice, in harmony with the later practice as they knew it. See Tosafot to *Pes.* 102b s. v. מניחו לאחר המזון and 105a s. v. והני מילי. In gaonic times, the distance separating the Habdalah and the last meal of the Sabbath was still further extended, as the time for the latter was set before the afternoon prayer תפלת המנחה. Some Gaonim cite a custom, which they characterize as מנהג אבותינו תורה היא, not to have any meal on the Sabbath between the מנחה prayer and the ערבית prayer. See *Šibbole Ha-leḳeṭ* 127 (p. 50) and cf. Tosafot to Pes. 105a s. v. והני מילי. More of this in the discussion of the development of the custom of having three meals on the Sabbath, referred to *supra*, note 11. Cf. also Elbogen *op. cit.*, pp. 183–184.

[20] Ber. 52a. א'ר יהודה לא נחלקו ב'ש וב'ה על המזון שבתחלה ועל הבדלה שהיא בסוף Of course המזון here means ברכת המזון, the grace after the meal. In Yer. Ber. 8.1 (12a), the saying of R. Judah reads: לא נחלקו ב'ש וב'ה על ברכת המזון שהיא בתחלה ולא על הבדלה שהיא בסוף: *Infra*, note 24.

and actually were followed, by different groups of people. As already pointed out, all agreed that the new ceremony, i. e., the recitation of the Habdalah benediction should be at the very last, when the Sabbath was actually over. They also agreed that the Habdalah, like the Kiddush, should be recited over a cup of wine. In fact, as R. Johanan puts it, its very origin was in connection with a cup, שעיקרה בכוס, i. e., from the very start it was ordained that the Habdalah declaration be made over a cup of wine.[21] But as to the arrangement of the other acts,

---

[21] There can be no doubt that the practice of reciting the Habdalah over a cup of wine was the original practice and older than the one of mentioning it in the prayer. For it was even older than the whole institution of the evening prayer תפלת ערבית. The very statement אנשי כנסת הגדולה תקנו להם לישראל ברכות ותפלות קדושות והבדלות (Ber. 33a) implies that the recitation of the Habdalah was something separate from and independent of, not merely embodied in, the prayers. But the Palestinian Talmud expressly tells us that this was so. To the question, how could the teachers in the Mishna (Ber. 5.2) disagree about the place of the Habdalah in the Saturday evening prayer if there had been an older traditional practice דבר שהוא נוהג ובא חכמים חולקין עליו?, R. Johanan gives the answer: על ידי שעיקרה בכוס שכחוה בתפלה. Because originally they recited it over a cup of wine, the teachers did not remember — more correctly, did not know — which place it should be assigned in the prayer. And the Gemara, there, adds expressly that this statement of R. Johanan declares that the original institution of the Habdalah was to recite it over a cup מילתיה אמרה שעיקרה בכוס (Yer. Ber. 5.2 (9b)). In the Babylonian Talmud (Ber. 33a), the answer of R. Johanan is reported in a different form which does not make very good sense. There it reads as follows: בתחלה קבעוה בתפלה העשירו קבעוה על הכוס חזרו והענו קבעוה בתפלה והם אמרו המבדיל בתפלה צריך שיבדיל על הכוס. "At first, presumably because people could not afford wine, the teachers instituted it to be recited in the prayer. When the people became rich and could afford wine, they instituted its recitation over a cup of wine. But when they again became poor, they instituted its recitation in the prayer. However, at the same time, they declared that even if one had recited it in the prayer, he must recite it again over a cup of wine." One cannot see how the poor people who could not afford wine were helped by the institution that it should be recited in the prayer if, at the same time, it was insisted that, even after having recited it in the prayer, one must still recite it over a cup of wine. It seems that the Babylonians sought to harmonise the report about the original institution of reciting it over the cup with their later practice — after the תפלת ערבית had been accepted as obligatory — of reciting it in the prayer and repeating its recitation over a cup of wine. It should be noticed that there is no discussion of the question whether, after having recited the sanctification of the day, the Kiddush, in the prayer, one should recite it again

marking the going out of the Sabbath, and in what order the benedictions over these acts were to be recited, there were differences of opinion. Some authorities argued that the older order should not be disturbed at all: that the Sabbath meal, begun late in the afternoon, be completely finished, and Grace after it be recited over a cup of wine and then followed by the *mugmar* substitute, aromatic herbs or some fragrant plants, as had always been and still was the order at the other Sabbath meals. And only after all this was finished, there should follow the new features, marking the end of the Sabbath, i. e., lighting the lights which in a concrete manner marks the end of the Sabbath. and the recitation of the Habdalah which declares the distinc-

over the cup of wine, as there is in the case of the Habdalah recitation (Ber. 33a; Pes. 107a). For even after the תפלת ערבית had been introduced and considered obligatory and the sanctification of the day קדושת היום had been inserted in it, it did not affect the older custom of reciting the Kiddush over the wine, as there was no conflict between the two. At most it was a repetition and, after all, one might repeatedly mention the holiness of the day as long as the day lasts. It was different in the case of the Habdalah which speaks of the separation between the holy and the profane, implying that the Sabbath is just over and that the week day has begun. Such a declaration should be recited at the moment of the separation or at the dividing moment between the holy and the profane. It therefore seemed incongruous or contradictory to declare this separation between the holy and the profane over the cup of wine, at a time when it was already profane time, as it had previously, by the recitation of the prayer service, been declared that weekday time had begun. Hence the question arose whether המבדיל בתפלה צריך שיבדיל על הכוס. To obviate this difficulty or to remove this incongruity, it was suggested that the distinction, not the separation, of the holy from the profane etc. is emphasized in the Habdalah and, of course, the distinction is between the whole Sabbath day and all the week days. And of this distinction — not of the one between light and darkness — one can speak even on Thursday (cf. Yer. Ber. 5.2 (9c)) אם לא הבדיל במוצאי שבת מבדיל אפילו בחמישי הדא דאת אמר במבדיל בין קדש לחול אבל בורא מאורי האש אומרה מיד. And just as one can mention the holiness of the Sabbath throughout all the Sabbath day, so one can mention the distinction between the holy and the profane all week, mentioning that the weekdays are different from the Sabbath מי שלא הבדיל במוצאי שבת מבדיל והולך כל השבת (=שבוע) כולו. מי שלא קידש בערב שבת מקדש והולך כל היום כולו (Pes. 105a). According to this conception, the repetition of the Habdalah over the cup after it had been recited in the prayer is not more incongruous than the recitation of the sanctification of the day over the cup of wine after it had been recited in the prayer. Both are merely harmless repetitions.

tion between the Sabbath day and the six work days of the week
This order was advocated by the school of Hillel, according to
the report of R. Judah b. Ilai, and was later followed in practice
by the people.[22] This order caused little or no disturbance whatever in the older habits of the people. It merely introduced at
the end of their older practices two new features which were
deemed important to emphasize the change in the status of the
night following the Sabbath *day*, signifying that it was no
longer part of the Sabbath. Other people represented, according
to the report in our Mishna, by both the Shammaites and the
Hillelites, seem to have considered it of great importance that
the first ceremony or feature of ushering out the Sabbath should
be the lighting of the light with the benediction recited over it,
which in a concrete manner marks the end of the Sabbath,
since no fire or light could be kindled on the Sabbath day.
Accordingly, they advocated that, as soon as it gets dark, even
before finishing the late afternoon meal, the light should be
kindled and the benediction over it recited.[23] But while the

[22] נהגו העם כבית הלל אליבא דרבי יהודה (Ber. 52a and Pes. 103a). It should be
noticed that it was a popular decision. For the phrase "the people practice,"
נהגו העם, means that the teachers merely do not object to the people's doing
so but, if consulted by the people, they do not tell them to do so נהגו אורויי לא
מורינן ואי עביד עביד ולא מהדרי ליה (Ta'an. 26b). This popular decision is still the
practice to this day, except that now the Habdalah is completely separated
from the meal and *only* the cup of wine, formerly used for the recitation of
the grace after meal, is left.

[23] The reason why they insisted that the light and the benediction over
it should come immediately as soon as it gets dark, we can only guess. It
probably was to emphasize the idea that, with nightfall, the Sabbath is over
and light could and should be produced. To allow them to continue to sit in
darkness or even to finish their meal in darkness might have lent support to
the opinion of some heretics who maintained that the Sabbath extended
through the following night. We know of such heretics in later times, see
מסעות ר' בנימין ed. Grünhut part I (Frankfort a.M. 1904) p. 23; cf. also S. A.
Posnanski in his introduction to Eliezer of Beaugency's *Commentary to Ezekiel
and the Twelve* (Warsaw 1913) p. 43. But such opinions must have been held
by some people even in earlier talmudic times, since such a position was
merely the logical adherence to the older system of reckoning the day from
morning to morning. The idea that Saturday night was still part of the Sabbath was not completely eradicated from the mind of the people. See Yer.
Pes. 5.1 (30cd) about the persistent practice of the women to refrain from

Shammaites and Hillelites agreed, according to our Mishna, that the light with the benediction over it should be the first in the group of ceremonies performed on Saturday night, they differed in their opinions as to the order in which the other ceremonies should follow it. The conservative Shammaites, wishing to retain as much as possible of the old order of things, seem to have argued that if, for some good reason, the light and the benediction over it had to be put first, even if the meal had to be interrupted thereby, there was no reason why the older order of established practice should be more upset. Hence they argued that, after the light had been kindled, the meal be finished or, if at the kindling of the light it had already been finished, Grace after it over a cup of wine be recited, then there should follow the benediction over the aromatic herbs, בשמים, the *mugmar*-substitute; this was in keeping with the older established practice that the *mugmar* — or the substitute for it — was to come after the meal had been finished and Grace recited (Ber. 6.6). And after the *mugmar*-substitute, there should, in their opinion, follow the recitation of the Habdalah benediction. The order according to the Shammaites, therefore, was: נר מזון בשמים הבדלה (Ber. 8.5). The Hillelites, however, according to our Mishna, advocated a change in the usual order. They argued that, on Saturday night, the benediction over the aromatic herbs should not follow the Grace after the meal as the *mugmar*, for which they were a substitute, always did but that it should come before the Grace, following immediately the benediction over the light. Their order is: נר בשמים מזון הבדלה[24] (*ibid. l. c.*).

In this discussion of the Shammaites and the Hillelites in our

doing any work on Saturday night, which the teachers declared not to be a good custom לאו מנהגא. But, in spite of the objections of the teachers, this practice has persisted among pious Jewish women to this day. In the Middle Ages, pious men would imitate the women in this. See תש׳׳ב׳ץ 88 (Warsaw 1875) in הנהות where it says נהגו העולם שלא לעשות מלאכה כל מוצאי שבת. Though נהגו העולם may simply mean נהגו הנשים as given in Abudarham (Lemberg 1857) p. 65. See also לקט יושר ed. Freiman (Berlin 1903) p. 58. Cf. also שערי תשובה to *Šulḥan 'Aruk, 'Oraḥ Ḥayyim*, 300, quoting the disciples of Luria.

[24] Of course מזון means ברכת המזון, the grace after the meal. See especially Alfasi to Ber. *ad loc.* (Wilna ed. 1907) 39a: דהא מזון דקתני במתניתין ברכת המזון היא and cf. *supra*, note 20.

Mishna about the arrangement or the order of the ceremonies at the going out of the Sabbath, there is implicitly attached to the use of aromatic herbs some significance greater than a substitute for the *mugmar*, a merely voluntary act of enjoyment, would justify. It is implied that this act is required for a purpose of its own and is not merely a substitute for the *mugmar*. In fact, since it comes after the light had been kindled, that is, after the Sabbath was practically over and fire could already be made, it would seem rather incongruous to use a substitute for the *mugmar* when the real thing could be prepared, unless it be assumed that there was some special reason for using this substitute for a purpose of its own.[25] Especially is this idea suggested in the arrangement of the Hillelites. For this arrangement emphasizes the independent significance of the ceremony of using these aromatic herbs, in that it removed it from the place which the *mugmar* regularly occupied in relation to the meal and thus changed its character from a mere substitute for the *mugmar*, which customarily came after the recitation of Grace after the meal, to a separate and independent feature, seemingly of some importance, and in a class with the ceremony of kindling the light to which it is put in close proximity. Thus a custom, or mere habit, the original purpose of which was merely to afford some additional enjoyment and enhance the pleasures of the table, was imperceptibly changed and transformed into an independent religious ceremony. How this change was effected we cannot ascertain with accuracy. We can only guess at the process that led to the emergence of this new religious ceremony. And the following suggests itself as most likely to have taken place in the popular mind. There seem to have been current among the people certain superstititious beliefs or mythological notions

---

[25] Why did they not prepare the real *mugmar* instead of בשמים, since the light had already been kindled and fire could be made? It may be because the *mugmar* substitute, the plants, were brought in during or even before dark, when it was still Sabbath. Probably they used the same plants which had been used at the forenoon meal. Most likely, however, some people assigned to the use of the plants on Saturday night a secondary purpose which the real *mugmar* could not serve; hence they preferred the use of the substitute, i. e., the plants, to the real *mugmar*.

in connection with some of the plants used as substitutes for the *mugmar*, ascribing to them inherent mystic powers and a capability for peculiar functions. This, at any rate, was the case with the myrtle which must have been prominently, if not preponderantly used as a *mugmar*-substitute. And, judging from some manifestations in the later developments of the ceremony to be considered below, it seems plausible to assume that, even while used merely as a substitute for the *mugmar* the myrtle had, in the popular mind at least, a secondary purpose based on or resulting from the mystic powers believed to be inherent in it. And some people, more mystic or more superstitious, attached greater importance to this secondary purpose than to its primary purpose of serving as a substitute for the *mugmar*. This secondary significance of the use of the myrtle may have caused the people to retain it as a substitute for the *mugmar* on Saturday night even after dark, though the real *mugmar* could already be prepared. For, this secondary function, based upon the mystic notion connected with the myrtle, gave the use of it a value of its own, not dependent on its suitability as a *mugmar* substitute.

At any rate, it finally became an established religious ceremony, even recognized by all of the teachers, to use in connection with the Habdalah rite on Saturday night aromatic herbs, especially the myrtle,[26] for a function and a purpose of its own,

---

[26] In one passage of the Palestinian Talmud, Yer. Ber. 5.2 (9c) quoted by Rabiah to Pes. ed. Aptowitzer II, (Jerusalem 1935), 141, it is said הדס של גדילתו כדרך ניטל הבדלה. This sentence was omitted in our texts, perhaps merely, by the fault of the copyist. (See Aptowitzer note 18.) This is the only instance where the Talmud speaks explicitly of the myrtle in connection with the Habdalah ceremony. Otherwise the Talmud speaks only of aromatic herbs, בשמים, in connection with the Habdalah, without specifying that it was the myrtle. Perhaps this was done consciously in order thus to ignore or oppose the superstitions connected with the use of the myrtle. But there can be no doubt that, when used with reference to the Habdalah ceremony, בשמים means primarily the myrtle. This is evident from the fact that the use of the myrtle persisted throughout the ages; and though some authorities objected to it, it was nevertheless considered an established religious custom as a מנהג אבותינו תורה. Thus in *Sefer Ḥasidim*, ed. Wistenetzki 553 (Frankfort a.M. 1924) p. 154, it is declared that the myrtle is absolutely necessary for the Habdalah ceremony, and it is hinted that the purpose of its use is something

besides the one of merely affording the enjoyment of the fragrance. What this special purpose of the ceremony really was,

besides the enjoyment of its fragrance. For it says that even if the myrtle is dry and without any scent, so that it is necessary to use other aromatics or smelling spices for the enjoyment of the smell, the myrtle should nevertheless be used in combination with those other spices. The passage in the original reads as follows: יעלה הדס והיה לה' לשם לאות עולם לא יכרת (ישעיה נ"ה י"ג) שמרו (ג' י') משפט ועשו צדקה (שם נ"ו א') שומר שבת מחללו (שם שם ב') ושמרו את שבתותי (שם שם ד') סמכם לומר לך ששבת צריך להדס כל שומר שבת מחללו מחול צריך הדס כשמבדיל ואם יש לו הדס שהוא יבש ואינו מריח יעטפנו דברים שמריח מהם ועליהם יברך ברכתם. See also Isserles in Š. 'Ar. 'O.Ḥ. 297, 4. I should add that the justification of the use of the myrtle on the basis of the interpretation of the verses in Isaiah, which is also quoted in Ẓedah la-Derek and in Ṭur 'O.Ḥ. 297, seems to have been taken from an old Midrash lost to us.

Likewise in תיקוני הזהר, while it is admitted that some people may use, for the Habdalah, other aromatic herbs, it is emphasized that the mystically inclined prefer the myrtle and for reasons other than its fragrance. It says: ואנן דעבדינן בהדס בגין דאית ביה תלת עלין דאיתקריא תלת הדסים רמיזין לתלת אבהן (ספר תיקוני הזהר, תיקונא שתיתאה (Wilna 1867) p. 329 (=קס"ה). Cf. also Zohar Bereshit 17b. ועל דא הדס במוצאי וישראל עבדי עובדא בהדס וביין ואמרי הבדלה and Šemot 20a: שבת. From the question of R. Judah b. Kolonymos addressed to R. Ephraim: למה מברכים על הדס יותר מבשמים אחרים, quoted in 'Or Zaru'a II, 92 (Zitomir 1862) p. 48, also תשב"ץ 86 (Warsaw 1875) p. 14, it also appears that myrtle was used preponderantly, if not exclusively. R. Ephraim, though, objects to the preference for myrtle and declares that he used a little glass container in which he kept many kinds of spices. But, the majority of the people seemingly still preferred the myrtle. Thus R. Menaham Ibn Zaraḥ (died 1385) in his צידה לדרך (Warsaw 1880) p. פח =175 says: על עצי ישראל לברך על הדס ורגילין רוב הדס. In Ṭur 'O.Ḥ. 297 it is also stated that the established custom is to use the myrtle, and two reasons are given for this preference. The one is the same as given in Sefer Ḥasidim based upon the interpretation of the verses in Isaiah. The other is because the myrtle was used also in another religious ceremony, i. e., in connection with the lulab and etrog on Sukkoth. This would indicate that they would use throughout the year the same myrtle sprigs which had been used on Sukkoth. Cf. Epstein, in לוחות הברית קיצור שני (Lemberg 1863), p. 66. This, at least, suggests that the function of the myrtle in both of these ceremonies is the same (infra, note 58). And though mentioning that R. Ephraim objected to the use of the myrtle and preferred other spices kept in a little glass container, the Ṭur concludes that the use of the myrtle is an established custom followed in all communities: ומיהו נהגו בכל המקומות לברך על ההדס ומנהג אבותינו תורה. See also Joseph Caro in his commentary בית יוסף ad loc. who adds the significant remark that the Cabbalists say that there is a mystic reason for using the myrtle ובעלי הקבלה אומרים שיש סוד בהדס לברך עליו. This mystic reason or what function the popular mind assigned to it, we may discover in our following investigation, but nowhere in rabbinic literature is it clearly indicated. There must have been some hesitancy, to say the least, on the part of the rabbinic authorities to acknowledge the mystic notions on which this special function was based. And when accepting the ceremony and admitting that it has a function of its own, the teachers preferred to interpret it in what to them seemed a more rational manner, and to give it a meaning compatible with their own more advanced thinking. However, our investigation will show that the meaning and purpose of the ceremony as explained by the rabbinic authorities was not the original meaning of the ceremony or, at any rate, not its only meaning. But these very explanations of the post-talmudic teachers,[27] though mere guesses or at best rationalizations, helped the ceremony to maintain itself throughout the generations and, with some slight modifications, to persist to the present day.

will be revealed to us in the course of our discussion in this essay. Isaac Luria, as one of the mystics, also insisted upon the use of the myrtle for the Habdalah ceremony, and his emphasis was not on the fragrance of the myrtle but on the number of the sprigs used, namely, *three*. See נגיד ומצוה (Lublin 1881) p. 51. So much was the use of the myrtle identified with the Habdalah ceremony that, up to this day, the spice box used at the ceremony, although it contains other spices and not myrtle, is still designated by the name *Hadas*, הדס, the Hebrew for myrtle because, in former times, only or preferably myrtle alone was used. *Infra*, note 99 end.

[27] While the Talmud seeks to explain why a blessing over the light is recited at the Habdalah ceremony (Pes. 54a), no explanation whatever is given in the Talmud why a benediction over aromatic herbs is recited at that ceremony. Evidently no explanation was necessary. Since, as we have seen, this ceremony emerged out of the every-day practice of serving *mugmar*, over which people also recited a benediction, there was no need of a special reason why the benediction should be recited over the *mugmar* substitute served on Saturday night. And, although some mystically inclined people may have, already in talmudic times, attached some special significance or assigned a secondary purpose to this ceremony and although the popular mind connected with it some superstitious notions, the talmudic authorities ignored them and preferred to regard the ceremony as what it really or originally was, merely a substitute for the *mugmar* which required no special explanation. After the practice had, for a long time, been accepted and come to be regarded as an established feature of the Habdalah ceremony, separate from

The change in the character of the custom of using aromatic
herbs or the myrtle as a substitute for the *mugmar* at the Saturday evening meal had its effect upon the similar custom or

and independent of the last meal of the Sabbath, its original nature as a
substitute for the *mugmar* was almost forgotten. It was only then that the
post-talmudic rabbinic authorities could begin to ask questions about its
purpose and, in answer to such questions, seek to offer some reason why it
was introduced. One explanation given by R. Jacob b. Yakar, one of the
teachers of Rashi, was that, at the end of the Sabbath, the fire in Hell, which
was put out during the Sabbath, is started again, issuing a stench. To neutral-
ize this bad odor, the smelling of herbs was introduced for that particular
moment of the going out of the Sabbath. This is quoted in *Vitry* p. 117 and
p. 328 as follows: רבינו שלמה בר' יצחק אומר בשם ר' יעקב בר' יקר דטעם בשמים במוצאי
שבתות דכל יום השבת שבת אור של גיהנם ולא הסריח כלום ולאלתר כשיוצא שבת חוזר ושורף
ומסריח לכך מריח בבשמים להפיג ריח רע. See also סדור רש"י 532 (Berlin 1920) p. 266;
and *Sefer Ha-Pardes* ed. Ehrenreich (Budapest 1924) p. 29; and *Šibbole
Ha-leḳeṭ* 130 (Wilna 1886) p. 104. This explanation, which may be a reflection of some mystic notion about the connection of this ceremony with the
return of the wicked ghosts to Hell on Saturday night (see *Tanḥuma, Ki
Tissa* 33), was not very satisfactory even to the rabbinic authorities. Cf. *'Or
Zaru'a* II, 92 (Zitomir 1862) p. 48, who dismisses it with the remark: ואין זה
אלא דוגמא להראות כבודו של שבת. Probably Tosafot to Pes. 102b s. v. רב had this
explanation in mind when they said that there were some wrong explanations,
ויש טעמים לא נכונים.

Another explanation quoted by the disciples of Rashi connects the ceremony with the belief (*infra*, note 56) that an additional soul comes to every
Israelite on Friday evening and leaves him again on Saturday night. At the
loss of this additional soul, the Israelite is sad and depressed on Saturday
night and the fragrance of the aromatic herbs is to refresh him and to help
him get over his grief. Cf. also Zohar *Vayakhel* (Lublin 1872) p. 416 and
Ẓaw p. 70. This explanation, which somehow connects the fragrant plants
with the additional soul — an idea assumed by the mystics, as we shall see
below (note 69), was in itself not so very satisfactory to the rationalistic
rabbinic authorities. Hence, they rationalize both about the additional soul
and about the refreshing and encouraging effect of the fragrant plants, making
the latter merely a part of the strengthening effect exerted by the prayers
recited on the occasion. I am quoting here the rabbinic statements, because
we can read between their lines that they hesitate to express boldly the crude
notion that an additional soul, as an actual spiritual entity, enters the person
with the entrance of the Sabbath and departs from him on Saturday night.
Thus Vitry p. 117 says שניטלה נשמה יתירה באדם ותהנה הנותרת מן הבשמים ותרווה
ותתחזק בצירוף הברכות. The same words are also used in סדור רש"י 542 (p. 262).
Even more apparent in its effort at rationalization is the rather verbose state-

practice of using the same substitute for the *mugmar* at the Friday evening meal. The thought must have suggested itself, to some people at least, that just as on Saturday night the use of the fragrant plants, especially the myrtle, was not merely a table custom, substituting for the *mugmar*, but rather an important feature of the Habdalah rite and a separate ceremony serving some purpose of its own and suggesting some religious ideas, so also the use of these plants on Friday evening should not be regarded simply as a substitute for the *mugmar*, but as a separate ceremony of some religious significance, in a class with and like the other ceremonies of the evening, the Kiddush and the Sabbath lights.

Accordingly, in imitation of the transformation of the Saturday evening practice, the practice of having fragrant plants on Friday evening was also transformed, and in the minds of some people, at least, was invested with a purpose of its own and gradually emerged as a religious ceremony. This new character, however, was not given to the older practice as a whole, i. e., to the use of all kinds of fragrant plants or aromatic herbs which may have occasionally been used as a substitute for the *mugmar*. It was limited to one part of the older practice, that is, to the use of one special plant, the myrtle, which, as already indicated, figured prominently in the older practice, and which, no doubt, was believed to possess some special quality, and to the use of which the popular mind could assign some special religious or mystic significance.

---

ment in *Sefer Ha-Pardes* (ed. Ehrenreich) p. 26 which reads as follows: מה טעם אנו מברכין על הבשמים בברכת ההבדלה מפני שבשבת ניתנה נשמה יתירה באדם והוא שמח מתוך שאכל נתענג ונח ושקט וכשהיה מבדיל בטלו כל אלו ממנו וניטלה ממנו נשמה יתירה והנה הוא במחשבה מעתה ובטורח ובעסק ונפשו אינה שמחה כאשר בתחלה ותיקנו הראשונים בשעת המבדיל להריח בבשמים ותהנה הנותרת ותשמח ותריח בריח טוב ובכך הוא מפיג צערו ולא יתעצב אל לבו בזוכרו ששת ימי המעשה. וכל זה תיקנו כדי שיהא זכרון שבת בלבו ויהא שמח אף בצאתו. See also R. Solomon b. Adret, quoted in '*En Jacob* to Ta'an. 27b, (ed. Wilna 1883) pp. 75–76. R. Menahem Ibn Zaraḥ in his צידה לדרך p. 174 merely says: בשמים להשיב ולנחם הנפש שכואבת ומתעצבת בצאת השבת, without in any way connecting the ceremony with the נשמה יתירה. All these explanations and rationalizations are disproved or refuted by the fact that the same ceremony was also observed on Friday evening, the very moment when the additional soul was supposed to come to the Israelite. *Infra*, note 62 and note 77.

Thus, out of the general practice of having fragrant plants at the table on Friday evening there emerged a special religious ceremony performed on Friday evening with twigs of myrtle. This new ceremony seems to have been limited to Palestine and, even there, was observed only among mystic groups or by people with mystic inclinations. It was assigned a peculiar function and associated with some mystic ideas about the Sabbath although, as is usually the case when ceremonies or customs are reinterpreted and given new meanings, the original simple meaning of the practice was not entirely forgotten and the feature of enjoying the fragrance of the myrtle was not abandoned.[28] It was merely pushed into the background or, as we shall see, combined with the newer mystic interpretation of the significance of the ceremony.

The only allusion in the Talmud to such a ceremony is found in Sab. 33b in the story about R. Simeon b. Yoḥai and his son R. Eleazar, who are said to have spent thirteen years in a life of contemplative study and prayer in a cave while hiding from the threatened persecution by the Roman government. When they finally came out of the cave, they were, to put it mildly, upset and, especially Eleazar, provoked when they noticed the people busying themselves with the things of this world rather than with the things eternal. Then, late on a Friday afternoon, so the Talmud reports, they encountered a "certain old man" who was running home carrying two bunches of myrtle. They asked the old man, "What are these for?" and he replied, "To honor the Sabbath." They said to him, "Then one should be enough," to which the old man replied: "One is to correspond to the commandment 'Remember' (Ex. 20.8) and the other is to correspond to the commandment 'Observe' (Deut. 5.12)." Then R. Simeon said to his son, "How precious are the commandments to Israel!" and their minds were set at ease.[29] It is evident from this story that, even though some people may have used the myrtle, among other fragrant plants,

---

[28] *Infra*, note 62.

[29] בהדי פניא דמעלי שבתא חזו ההוא סבא דהוה נקיט תרי מדאני אסא ורהיט בין השמשות אמרו ליה הני למה לך אמר להו לכבוד שבת ותיסגי לך בחד חד כנגד זכור וחד כנגד שמור א'ל לבריה חזי כמה חביבין מצות על ישראל יתיב דעתייהו (Sab. 33b).

as a substitute for the *mugmar* on the Sabbath, it was not the general custom to have *only* myrtle for such a use, or to have a special ceremony performed with the myrtle on Friday evening. For, in that case, there would have been nothing unusual in the sight of a man carrying home bunches of myrtle on a Friday afternoon. And there certainly would have been no cause for R. Simeon and Rabbi Eleazar to stop such a man and ask him for what purpose the myrtle bunches were intended. Furthermore, if this had been a generally observed custom, we would find a reference, or at least a casual allusion, to it somewhere else in the talmudic literature. There is no doubt that these myrtle sprigs were not meant by the old man to be merely for the purpose of enjoying their fragrance, as a substitute for the *mugmar*. These myrtle sprigs must have been intended for a special ceremony having some religious significance, since it elicited such a highly appreciative remark on the part of R. Simeon b. Yoḥai. Such a ceremony must have been observed only by some particular people or a certain mystically inclined group to which "that old man" belonged.[30] Hence, the old man carrying these myrtle bunches attracted the attention of R. Simeon b. Yoḥai who, being himself mystically inclined, to say the least, was interested in the purpose for which the old man carried home these myrtle bunches. And being told of its purpose, viz. that it was for a special ceremony, he appreciated it as of great religious value. Of course, we are not told any details of this special ceremony and in what its religious or mystic significance

---

[30] Some authorities are inclined to believe that, wherever ההוא סבא "that old man" is mentioned in the Talmud, the reference is to the prophet Elijah. See Tosafot to Ḥul. 6a, s. v. אשכחיה ההוא סבא. However, as Tosafot themselves there declare, the "old man" in our story could not have been Elijah. See also B. M. Levin, *'Oẓar Ha-Ge'onim*, IX, (Jerusalem 1939), 22. He certainly was not a Samaritan either, as Dobsewitz assumes in regard to many instances where ההוא סבא is mentioned in the Talmud. See A. B. Dobsewitz ספר המצרף (Odessa 1870) pp. 34–57. But this old man seems to have been a member of a special group, particular in observing the commandments. And since his practice was so highly approved of by R. Simeon b. Yoḥai, I rather believe that he belonged to a mystically inclined group. It is perhaps not accidental that R. Samuel b. Isaac, who also performed a certain ceremony with myrtle sprigs, is likewise described as סבא "the old man." Ket. 17a cf. *infra*, note 39.

consisted. All that we are told in this talmudic report is that the old man said that the myrtle bunches were intended for the honor of the Sabbath and that he also gave an explanation, if explanation it may be called, of why he needed two bunches. But it does not explain how and in what way the myrtle was especially suitable for honoring the Sabbath and for pointing to or reminding one of the two forms of the commandment about the Sabbath. "Remember" and "Observe."

This talmudic report certainly does not give full information about this ceremony. We may suspect that some information about this seemingly strange ceremony was consciously withheld or perhaps suppressed in the Talmud, a suspicion which will find its justification in the following discussion. For, not only is the information about this ceremony in this talmudic report very meagre and rather vague but there is, to my knowledge, nowhere else in the talmudic-midrashic literature any reference or even allusion to such a ceremony. And even in post-talmudic rabbinic literature, with the exception of the passage in the Zohar to be considered below, there is no mention of such a ceremony. And up to the sixteenth century, we do not hear of it or find the least indication of its existence. Such a persistent silence on the part of the rabbis of the Talmud and of the post-talmudic rabbinic authorities throughout so many centuries could not have been merely accidental, and certainly cannot be interpreted as approval. It rather suggests hostility to the ceremony and a tendency to suppress it by ignoring it. There must have been some objections to this ceremony on the part of the rabbinic authorities, for which reason they would not even mention it, far less recommend its practice. We can judge and understand these objections only after we know what ideas or superstitious beliefs were associated with the ceremony. This we can learn from a fuller description of the ceremony as it appears in the sixteenth century in the mystic circle of Isaac Luria. For, I believe, we are justified in regarding the ceremony, strongly recommended and fully described by the Lurianic school, as a continuation of the ceremony so highly appreciated by R. Simeon b. Yohai. We are also justified in assuming that, with perhaps slight modifications in some details, Luria performed the ceremony in the same manner, and for the same purpose, as it had been performed by certain mystically inclined people ever since the time of R. Simeon b. Yoḥai,[31] though we have no record of it in the talmudic and post-talmudic halakic literature. For there was a transmission through mystic channels from generation to generation of ideas and practices utterly ignored or even consciously suppressed in the authoritative rabbinic literature.[32] And the information about our ceremony could well have passed through such channels from the time of Simeon b. Yoḥai to the time of Luria. There may even have been some mystic records about this ceremony available to Luria. In fact, one such mystic record, though also incomplete and not very explicit, which Luria no doubt consulted or followed, has been preserved to us in the Zohar, *Ẓaw* (Lublin 1872) pp. 69–70, which reads as follows: "As they (R. Eleazar and his company) were going along, they came across a man with three myrtle branches in his hand. They approached him and asked: 'What are these for?' He replied: 'For the comfort (or enlargement?) of the wandering (soul?).'[33] Said R. Eleazar: 'That is a good answer. But why

[31] For a parallel to such a phenomenon, namely a ceremony alluded to or mentioned in the Talmud which, after being suppressed or passed over in silence for many centuries, eventually turned up again, see Lauterbach, "The Ceremony of Breaking a Glass at Weddings," in *HUCA* II, (1925), especially pp. 361–366.

[32] See Lauterbach, *Tashlik* (Cincinnati 1936) p. 30, note 37. In the case of our ceremony as well as in the case of the custom of staying up the whole night preceding the Shabuot festival, the Zohar alone mentions the usages in question, while the halakic rabbinic literature maintains a complete and persistent silence. This justifies the assumption that the mystics had their secret channels through which they transmitted their information from generation to generation, either unknown to and hidden from or perhaps unheeded by the official rabbinic authorities.

[33] The phrase לרווחא אובדא can have different meanings: it may mean, "for the comfort of the languishing soul," referring either to the permanent soul or to the additional soul to whom the myrtle, as part of her native environment in heaven, brings comfort and refreshment. It may also mean, "for the *enlargement* of the languishing soul," referring to the permanent soul to whom the myrtle, as a vehicle for spirits, brings the additional soul, thus enlarging her. We shall see below which of these two ideas is expressed in this passage from the Zohar. Possibly both ideas are hinted at, as they are not contradictory to one another.

three?' To this the man replied: 'One for Abraham, one for
Isaac, and one for Jacob; and I bind them together and smell
them, as it is written (Cant. 1.3): 'Thine ointments have a goodly
fragrance; thy name is as ointment poured forth.' Because by
this smelling the weak soul is kept up, and by this faithful act
it is sustained, and thus blessings are drawn down from above.'
Said R. Eleazar: 'Happy is the lot of Israel in this world and
in the world to come.' ''[34]

This story which, in a way, may be regarded as a parallel
to the talmudic story is, nevertheless, in very important points
different from the latter. In the first place, it does not explicitly
assign the ceremony to Friday evening, as it does not fix the
time when or on what day the encounter of R. Eleazar with the
man took place. But we may take it for granted that it was
on a Friday and that the ceremony discussed by them was a
Friday evening ceremony. Secondly, we notice that instead of
two bunches of myrtle, supposed to correspond to the two versions of the Sabbath commandment as the Talmud reports, the
man used for the ceremony three sprigs of myrtle, each one of
which he declares to be for one of the patriarchs. It does not,
however, explain in what manner these myrtle sprigs served or
represented the patriarchs, whether they were intended as offerings to the spirits of the patriarchs or were a means of welcoming
them. Nor does it explain how and why these myrtles functioned
as special media for welcoming the patriarchs or why they were
considered as suitable representatives of or especially acceptable
gifts to their souls. It also says that by the smell of these myrtles
or, more correctly, by the act of smelling[35] them, the weak soul

---

[34] The passage in the Zohar, *Ẓaw*, (Lublin 1872) pp. 69–70, reads as
follows: עד דהוו אזלו אשכחו חד גברא דהוה אתי וג' ענפי הדס בידיה. קריבו נביה אמרי ליה
למה לך האי אמר לרווחא אובדא. אמר רבי אלעזר שפיר קאמרת. אבל ג' אלין למה. א"ל חד
לאברהם חד ליצחק וחד ליעקב וקשירנא להו כחדא וארחנא בהו בנין דכתיב (שיר א) לריח
שמניך טובים שמן תורק שמך. בנין דבהאי ריחא אתקיים חולשא דנפשא ובהימנותא דא אתקיימא
ואתגנידו ברכאן מעילא ותתא. אמר רבי אלעזר זכאה חולקהון דישראל בעלמא דין ובעלמא
דאתי. As to the meaning or significance of the phrase דא ובהימנותא "by this
faithful act," see following note.

[35] I. e., the feature of bringing the myrtle near to the nostrils, which
resembles the act one performs when smelling. But in this case it was not
done in order to smell the myrtle, but for the purpose of bringing the vehicle

is sustained and kept up, gets comfort and enlargement. But it does not tell us how this is accomplished, whether the fragrance of the myrtle as such does it or whether the souls of the patriarchs bring with them something of comfort and enlargement for the weak soul or by their mere company comfort it. Thus we see that both of these stories, in the Talmud and in the Zohar, give us neither the full information about this ceremony nor a clear explanation of it.[36] Both, however, unmistakably emphasize that these myrtles were not merely for the enjoyment of their fragrance. For, although the Zohar still speaks of the act of smelling, it is evident that this act was not just for the mere pleasure of enjoyment, but rather to give strength and comfort or enlargement to the weak soul. The main function of these myrtle sprigs was either to remind one of the two versions of the Sabbath-commandment, or to welcome and greet the patriarchs — in either case a rather mystic function.

We therefore have to look for some more specific information to be able to understand fully the purpose of this ceremony. There must have been, in the popular mind at least, certain qualities or characteristics associated with the myrtle, making it suitable for the achievement of the purpose aimed at by our ceremony. In order to find out these popular notions about the myrtle, its qualities and capabilities, we must first ascertain what functions, if any, were implicitly ascribed to the myrtle in its use in other ceremonies and at other occasions.

The oldest use of myrtle in any ceremony that we can find in talmudic literature is the one for making a crown or wreath for the bridegroom עטרות חתנים. This must have been considered very protective and useful. For even after the decree against

carrying the additional soul, with the accompanying spirits of the patriarchs, near to the nostrils, the aperture through which souls or spirits can enter the human body, cf. Gen. 2.7.

[36] Perhaps there is an allusion to our ceremony in the phrase שהשבת צריך להדס "the Sabbath needs the myrtle," in the passage from *Sefer Ḥasidim* quoted *supra*, note 26, which implies that, not only for the Habdalah ceremony at the going out of the Sabbath, but for the whole Sabbath, the myrtle was necessary. *Infra*, note 69.

the crowning or adorning of the bridegroom (Soṭ. 9.14), it was still permitted to adorn him with crowns of myrtle.[37] The purpose of such a decoration must have been, just as in the use of crowns made of salt, to keep the demons away and prevent them from doing any harm to the bridal couple. No doubt they adorned the bride also with such a protective crown.[38] We also

[37] See Tosefta Sot. 15.8 (Zuckermandel p. 322) אבל של וורד ושל הדס התירו להן. Also the saying of Rab in Soṭ. 49b: אבל של הדס ושל ורד מותר, though, according to the opinion of Samuel (ibid. l. c.), even crowns of myrtle were forbidden.

[38] See Lauterbach, "The Ceremony of Breaking a Glass at Weddings," op. cit., p. 357, especially note 3. Conveying the bride to the home of the bridegroom — out of fear that the demons might try to kidnap her — they would carry her in a round covered vehicle made of myrtle branches (see Ket. 17b and Rashi ad loc. s. v. תנורא דאסא and cf. 'Oẓar Ha-Ge'onim VIII, part 2, p. 15. Cf. also Sab. 110a אסא וגידמי לבי הלולא). In one of the מעשיות (Jellinek, Bet Ha-Midrasch V, 153), also in מעיל צדקה by Elijah Cohen (1859) p. 21a, it is told that, before the bridegroom went out to invite the guests to his wedding, his father placed in his hands myrtle leaves. This probably was done to afford him protection from evil spirits that might assail him on his way. To protect a new born baby boy who, before his circumcision, is especially exposed to danger from demons, it was the custom in Palestine to provide, on the day before the circumcision, myrtle twigs and to keep them overnight and then to recite a benediction over them the next morning when the ceremony of circumcision took place. This custom is reported by R. Hirsch b. Azriel of Wilna in his בית לחם יהודה to Yore De'ah 265, (Fuerth 1747) p. 95. He says: ונהגו בארץ ישראל לברך על הבשמים בעת המילה ולוקח ההדס ביום קודם המילה ובליל המילה נהגו לרקד ולשמח. Perhaps an additional reason for securing the myrtle on the day before the circumcision was to provide a resting place for the spirit of a departed ancestor or saint [similar to the practice of providing an extra chair for Elijah כסא של אליהו at the ceremony of circumcision. See Pirke d. R. Eliezer 29, (Warsaw 1852) p. 66b and Zohar Lek Leka (Lublin 1872) p. 93] who is to come on the day before and to rejoice with the parents and to watch with them over the child, throughout the night preceding the circumcision. Probably the custom, introduced by the Gaonim (see Ṭur Yore De'ah 305 and Kolbo 94 (Lemberg 1860) p. 60c) of using a myrtle and reciting over it the benediction בורא עצי בשמים at the ceremony of the redemption of the first born פדיון הבן also had the purpose of helping to fight off the evil spirits. For, according to the Zohar (Preface p. 14 פקודא תליסר), the effect of the redemption is also that the evil spirit or the angel of death should have no power over the child, וההוא סטרא בישא שבק ליה ולא אחיד ביה. This custom, however, is no longer observed.

read about R. Judah b. Ilai that at weddings he would take up a sprig of myrtle and dance with it, waving it before the bride. And R. Samuel b. Isaac would perform a similar dance before the bride with *three* sprigs of myrtle.[39] No doubt this use of the myrtle sprig while dancing before the bride was also for the purpose of driving away the demons. We thus find that one of the properties believed to be inherent in the myrtle was the power to drive away the demons, either by its fragrance, as incense[40] was believed to do, or in any other way. Since the

[39] Ket. 17a. The passage reads as follows: אמרו עליו על רבי יהודה בר אילעאי שהיה נוטל בד של הדס ומרקד לפני הכלה ואומר כלה נאה וחסודה רב שמואל בר רב יצחק מרקד אתלת א'ר זירא קא מכסיף לן סבא כי נח נפשיה איפסיק עמודא דנורא בין דידיה לכולי עלמא וגמירי דלא איפסיק עמודא דנורא אלא אי לחד בדרא אי לתרי בדרא אמר רבי זירא אהניי' ליה שוטיתיה לסבא ואמרי לה שטותי' לסבא ואמרי לה שיטתי' לסבא. Cf. Tosafot *ibid., l. c.* s. v. שיטתיה which quotes the Midrash, Gen. Rab. to the effect that the pillar of fire came down in the shape of a myrtle. The significant passage in Gen. Rab. (ch. 59, not 61 as given in *Tosafot*) reads as follows: ונחתה שבשבה דנור ואיתעבידת כמו שבשבה דהדס ואפסיקת בין ערסא לציבורא. This story about R. Samuel b. Isaac is also told in Yer. Pe'ah I (15d). However, the word דהדס is omitted there, and it merely reads: ואיתעבידת כמין שבשא דנור בין ערסא לציבורא. והוון ברייתא אמרין חיוי דדין סבא דקמת ליה שבישתיה.... Cf. Bacher, *Die Agada d. Palästinensischen Amoräer* III. (Strassburg 1899), 36, note 6. Perhaps the angels were coming down in the shape of myrtle.

[40] About the power of incense to drive away the demons, see Lauterbach, "A Significant Controversy between the Sadducees and the Pharisees," in *HUCA* IV (1927), 196, note 21. It seems, however, that the smoke and not the aroma of the incense had that power. About the smoke as a means of driving away demons, see also Dr. C. Snouk Hurgronge, *Mekka* II (Hague 1889), 122 ff., and I. Scheftelowitz, *Alt-Palästinensischer Bauernglaube* (Hannover 1925) pp. 82–84. The practice of midwives, to hold the baby over smoke prepared by them from some ingredients, mentioned and condemned by Maimonides in his *More Nebukim* III. ch. 37, no doubt was for the same purpose. Cf. also Gaster, the *Sefer Assufoth*, in *Report of the Judith Montefiore College*, Ramsgate (London 1893) pp. 60–61, where it is said that the smoke drives away the spirit that seeks to hinder the delivery of a child. As a cure against magic spells and as a means of driving away the evil spirits from a sick person, smoke prepared from some ingredients is still used among superstitious East European Jews. See Judah Rosenberg ספר רזיאל המלאך (Pietrkow 1911) p. 48 and 49. A rather unusual practice of using smoke to conjure up a spirit is mentioned by R. David Pardo in his ספרי דבי רב (Saloniki 1799) p. 245b to Deut. 18, 10–11. Of course R. David Pardo condemns the practice. *Infra*, note 48.

Sabbath is the bride[41] and Israel the bridegroom,[42] who thus celebrate their wedding on every Friday evening, the suggestion offers itself that the two bunches of myrtle were thus brought to the bride and bridegroom, Sabbath and Israel, for the same purpose, i. e., of keeping away the evil spirits, as it was used for any other bride and bridegroom on their wedding day.[43] This may be suggested in the statement "one corresponding to 'Remember'." For, according to the Midrash,[44] the "Remember" was especially addressed to Israel to impress upon him that he was the bridegroom of the Sabbath. And the statement that the other bunch of myrtle was "corresponding to 'Observe' " (שמור), may suggest that it was to remind one of the protection, שמירה, afforded by the myrtle on Friday evening when, according to the belief of some people, the danger from demons was great.[45]

[41] The Sabbath is called the queen מלכה and also the bride כלה. See Sab. 119a and Zohar 'Eḳeb p. 544.

[42] See Gen. Rab. XI, 9 תני רשב"י אמרה שבת לפני הקב"ה רבש"ע. לכולן יש בן זוג ולי אין בן זוג א"ל הקב"ה כנסת ישראל היא בן זוגך. וכיון שעמדו ישראל לפני הר סיני אמר להם הקב"ה זכרו הדבר שאמרתי לשבת. כנסת ישראל היא בן זוגך היינו דבור (שמות כ) זכור את יום השבת לקדשו.

[43] Isaac Luria in his song for the Friday evening meal (see סדור אוצר התפלות, Wilna 1923, p. 630), says that "the myrtle sprigs are for the groom and the bride that the weak ones may be strengthened" ומדאני אסא לארוס וארוסה להתקפא חלשין which may refer to Israel and the Sabbath or it may refer to the husband and wife in the smallest family. The phrase "that the weak ones may be strengthened" may allude to the power believed to be inherent in the myrtle of increasing sensuality or strengthening the sexual powers. *Infra*, note 46.

[44] Gen. Rab. *l. c.*

[45] On the question whether the Jew need be afraid of demons on the Sabbath, especially on Friday night, there were different opinions. In talmudic times, there prevailed the belief that, on Friday night, the danger of harm by the demons was very great. A *baraita* in Pes. 112b says that on Friday night Agrat, the daughter of Maḥalat, is abroad with a host of one hundred and eighty thousand destructive agents מלאכי חבלה, each one of them having permission and power to do as much harm as he likes or possibly can. See also the statement *ibid.*, 111b בלילי שבת שרו מזיקין עליה and 112a מאי סכנה רוח רעה; also Sab. 24b בשבת משום סכנה which Rashi *ad loc.*, correctly explains to mean סכנת מזיקין. This belief persisted in rabbinic circles even in post-talmudic times and the statement: דשכיחי מזיקין בלילי שבת טפי מבחול or בשבת דשכיחי מזיקין is repeated in *Seder Rab Amram* (Warsaw 1865) p. 25; *Siddur Rashi* (Buber,

There must, however, have been objections to this use of the myrtle on the part of those people who believed that on the Sabbath the demons could not harm the Jews and, hence, there

Berlin 1910) p. 240; *Sefer Ha-Pardes*, ed. Ehrenreich (Budapest 1924) pp. 307–8; *Vitry* p. 81; and others. On the other hand, there arose the idea in gaonic times that, on the Sabbath, there was no danger from demons, as they had no power on that day. This idea is expressed in a responsum by R. Hai Gaon, *Responsa* שערי תשובה No. 80 (Leipzig 1858) p. 8, who quotes, in support of this idea, a midrashic saying which probably originated in some mystic work (see S. Hurwitz in *Vitry l. c.*, note 7). Indeed, the same idea quoted by Hai from a saying of Raba in the name of Zera is repeatedly expressed in the *Zohar*. See Zohar *Vayakhel* (Lublin 1872) p. 409, p. 413, and p. 415. Also Zohar *'Eḳ b* p. 545 ואין מזיק שליט ביומא דשבתא. See also Ibn Yarḥi in המנהיג (Berlin 1855) p. 24 the statement דכתיב מזמור שיר ליום השבת ליום ששובתין מזיקין בעולם which sounds like a quotation from a midrashic work. As a sort of compromise between these two conflicting beliefs, it was suggested that, even though the demons may rove about on the Sabbath and even though they may have רשות להזיק "the power and the permission to harm people," the Jews need not fear them, being protected by their very observance of the Sabbath (*Vitry l. c.*; *Sefer Ha-Pardes l. c.*; and Zohar *Vayakhel* p. 409). This idea gradually came to be more and more accepted, as it was expressed in the Friday evening liturgy where the closing of the second benediction after the *Šema* reads .... הפורס סוכת שלום instead of שומר עמו ישראל לעד (see Zohar *Berešit* 48a and cf. אוצר התפלות p. סדור *š* = 599). There was, however, still the fear of a special class of demons, a fear resulting from other mystic notions. One of these was that Hell is closed on the Sabbath and that its wicked inmates are given a rest and are free to leave the place for the day (see *Tanḥuma Ki Tissa* כי תשא 33; Zohar *Wa'era* p. 31b, *Terumah* 150b–151a and *Jethro* 88b). According to another mystic belief, some demons are the souls of the departed wicked (Zohar, *Aḥare* p. 70a), a belief which is very ancient and which is found already in Philo and Josephus (see L. Ginzberg, Legends of the Jews vol. V, Philadelphia 1926 p. 109). Now, it was feared that those demons, which are the souls of the wicked, might wish to visit their folks on a Friday evening when released from Hell. For, as the demons in general imitate the angels (*infra*, note 95), so also the demons that are but souls of the wicked might like to imitate the souls of the departed patriarchs and saints. And the latter do visit their folks on holidays or on Friday evening, as the spirit of Judah Ha-Nasi did. (*Infra*, note 58.) But the folks here on earth, while they welcome the visits of the spirits of their saintly relatives, are afraid of and dread the visit of the demons, the spirits of their wicked relatives. Gradually, however, this fear was also allayed, and it was declared that the merit of observing the Sabbath protects the Jew against all kinds of demons, even of those that are souls of the departed wicked. See preface to the *Zohar* p. 14b.

was no need of employing such protective measures as the myrtle could afford.

It is also possible that the use of the myrtle for bridal wreaths had something to do with the belief that the myrtle was considered to be the tree of love and to possess the power to stimulate sensuality, for which reason it "was viewed askant by the pious of the ancient world."[46] Hence, it may be that the same function of the myrtle was aimed at by its use on Friday evening when some people considered it desirable to encourage erotic feelings or sensuality.[47] Of course, just for this reason

[46] See Charles M. Skinner, *Myths and Legends of Flowers, Trees, Fruits and Plants* (Philadelphia and London 1911) pp. 190–191. Among the ancient Greeks and Romans, the myrtle was believed sacred to Aphrodite and was regarded as a symbol of or a magic charm for increasing fertility. See Pauly-Wissowa *Real-Encyclopaedie* s. v. Myrtos p. 1182. It was forbidden to bring a myrtle into the sanctuary of the Bona Dea (*ibid.*, s. v. Bona Dea p. 687) probably because it was believed to have the power of increasing sensuality and of strengthening the sexual powers. All of these ideas associated with the myrtle in the ancient world could not have been entirely unknown in Palestine. That they were known and even not objected to among Jews in later times is evident from the description given by Leone Ebreo in his work וכוח על האהבה (Lyck 1871) p. 29b or in the English translation of his work: *The Philosophy of Love* (London 1937) p. 149 "... The myrtle ...." Hence, it may be assumed that at least some people among the ancient Jews cherished these superstitions and associated them with the use of the myrtle at weddings. Of course, many pious but rationalistic people objected to these superstitions and hence did not favor the myrtle in connection with some religious ceremonies.

[47] The idea that on Friday night increased sensuality is desirable and a strengthening of the sexual powers even commendable is very old. The Mishnah, Ned. 3.10 assumes that it was an old, characteristically Jewish custom to eat garlic, supposed to have aphrodisiac effects, on Friday evening. This is supposed to have been one of the institutions of Ezra ואוכלין שום בערב שבת (B. Ḳ. 82a). Comp. I. Loew, *Die Flora der Juden* II (Wien 1924) p. 144. The reason given for this custom is that sexual intercourse on Friday night is especially recommended (B. Ḳ. *l. c.* See also Ket. 62b; also Zohar, Preface 14ab; *Bereshit* p. 50, and *Tazria* p. 98).

It is interesting to note that the garlic is also used to keep the demons away so that, although unlike the myrtle in its smell, it is like it in its supposed effectiveness both as an aphrodisiac and as a protective charm in connection with birth, marriage and death. See I. Scheftelowitz, *Das Stellvertretende Huhnopfer* (Giessen 1904) p. 32, especially note 4. Also idem *Alt-Palästin-*

some rationalistic pious people among the ancient Jews, may have objected to such a use of the myrtle.

There is still another function ascribed to the myrtle which, though apparently the opposite of the function above described, namely, that of driving away the evil spirits, may nevertheless have also been in the minds of those who used it for the Friday evening ceremony. For superstitions are not consistent and often combine opposites or extremes. We find that the myrtle was also considered as a possible vehicle for conveying good spirits, souls and angels, or as a resting place for them. And, perhaps,

ensicher Bauernglaube (Hannover 1925) p. 82. It is a custom among East European Jews to carry with them garlic when, on the fast of the ninth of Ab, they go to visit the graves, and to scatter the garlic on the cemetery. The reason for it, is that, according to Luria, the demons seek to attach themselves to a person going to the cemetery. Cf. also Ḥag. 3b and Rashi *ibid.*, s. v. שתשרה עליו רוח טומאה. Hence the garlic is used as a charm to drive them away, for it is a popular belief that the smell of the garlic drives away the demons וסגולה היא ומרגלא בפומי דאנשי שהשום דהיינו ריח השום הוא גם כן מבריח החיצונים. See שער המלך by R. Mordecai b. R. Samuel, part II, 4, chapter 10 end (Dyhernfurt 1797) p. 38d. Cf. also I. Loew, *op. cit.*, p. 147. For the same reason, one of the great Hassidic Rabbis was in the habit of carrying with him garlic whenever he went to visit a sick person (ספר טעמי המנהגים by א"ש שו"ב part III [Lemberg 1911] p. 171) in order to drive away the demons who according to Ber. 54b (see below note 59) seek to harm the sick. Hirsch Bodek in הלבנון IV (Paris 1867), pp. 228–229 would explain that the custom of throwing garlic when visiting the cemetery was for the purpose of removing the evil odor that comes up from the dead bodies כדי להסב הריח רע מהמתים. But there is no evil odor on the cemetery except the very one brought there by the visitors with the garlic. Joshua Levensohn in an article ישן מפני חדש in הלבנון (*ibid.*, p. 325) argues against Bodek and, in a rationalizing manner, explains the reason for the custom to be that, since garlic is an aphrodisiac we, so to speak, throw it away when at the cemetery, as if to say: Why use these means to make us have more children when the end of man is death? מטעם כי שום מרבה זרע. . .ובבית הקברות כמו רומזים למה לנו להרבות זרע לקיום המין אם סוף אדם למות. Levensohn (*ibid.*) also explains the custom of placing myrtle on or carrying it before the bier to be merely a way of indicating that the dead person was a righteous man הדס קודם המטה. . ,הוא לרמז כי איש צדיק היה. All of these are rationalizations, ingenious, but not true. As a means of driving away the demons, the garlic is still used among East European Jews. And it is recommended to hang white onions and garlic on all of the windows and doors and on each of the four walls of every room in the house in times of epidemic, thus to keep out the evil spirits. See Judah Rosenberg ספר רפאל המלאך p. 52.

these two functions, the bringing of good spirits and the driving away of evil ones, do not actually conflict with one another; for the good spirit or angel, conjured up by or resting on the myrtle, might have the precise function of helping to drive away the evil spirits.[48]

Already in the Bible, in the passage: "The angel of the Lord that stood among the myrtle trees" (Zech. 1.11), it is suggested that the myrtle was an abode or resting place for angels or God Himself. This is especially indicated in Lev. Rab. 30.9. Commenting on the symbolic significance of the myrtle and the willow of the brook, the Midrash says זה (הדס) [49] וענף עץ עבות הקב"ה דכתיב בו והוא עומד בין ההדסים וערבי נחל זה הקב"ה דכתיב ביה סולו לרוכב בערבות ביה שמו. Here the הדסים, the myrtle trees, are taken to be a sort of heavenly abode for the Divine Presence, similar to 'Arabot, the name of the seventh heaven where, according to the Talmud (Hag. 12b), are found the spirits as well as all the souls destined to be born and the angels and the throne of glory with the exalted God on it. Although the Talmud (Meg. 13a and Sanh. 93a), in a rationalizing manner, seeks to

---

[48] The good spirit needs the help of human beings in fighting against the evil spirit, just as he helps the people to fight off or keep away from them the evil spirit. See Lauterbach, *Tashlik*, p. 245, reference to the story of Abba Jose in Lev. Rab. 24.3. Another instance of the belief in the power of the myrtle to conjure up a good and friendly spirit is perhaps to be found in Maimonides' description of the practice of the magician בעל אוב, which information Maimonides, no doubt, derived from an ancient source. The description reads as follows: "He stands there offering some incense, while holding in his hand a sprig of myrtle and waving it etc." כיצד הוא מעשה האוב. זה שהוא עומד ומקטיר קטרת ידועה ואוחז שרביט של הדס בידו ומניפו והוא מדבר בלאט בדברים ידועים אצלם עד שישמע השואל כאלו אחד מדבר עמו ומשיבו על מה שהוא שואל בדברים מתחת הארץ בקול נמוך עד מאד (*Yad, 'Abodat Kokabim* VI, 1). Apparently the incense was intended to ward off any evil spirit, while the myrtle served to attract and bring up the friendly spirit for consultation.

[49] עץ עבות עץ in Lev. 23.4 was understood to mean the myrtle. Onkelos and Jonathan translate it by הדסין, myrtle; and a Baraitha in Suk. 32b says ענף עץ עבות הוי אומר זהו הדס . . . Comp., however, Lev. Rab. 30.15 where this identification of עץ עבות with הדס seems to be questioned, for it is said: ענף עץ עבות מי יאמר שהוא הדס? הרי הוא אומר במקום אחר (נחמיה ח' ט"ו) צאו ההר והביאו עלי זית ועלי עץ שמן ועלי הדס ועלי תמרים ועלי עץ עבות חדושי See R. David Luria in הרד"ל *ad loc.*

interpret the "myrtle trees" among which God stood, to mean only the righteous ones, אין הדסים אלא צדיקים and to refer specifically to some living righteous men; yet some people, already in talmudic times no doubt, took "the righteous ones designated by the myrtle trees" to mean not the living righteous men, but the souls of the righteous that rest under the throne of glory, כסא הכבוד (Sab. 152b) in the seventh heaven ערבות (Ḥag. *l. c.*). And, indeed, in mystic literature the paradise where the souls of the righteous dwell is a paradise of myrtle trees גן עדן של הדס.[50] And in the Zohar it is said: "The holy place whence the souls come is the myrtle."[51] Likewise in the סדר גן עדן[52] it is said that, when the righteous man comes up to the entrance of paradise, the angels provide him with eight sprigs of myrtle and bring him to a place of brooks of water surrounded by eight rose bushes and myrtle trees. From all of these sayings one may safely conclude that the mystics had the notion that not only the place in heaven whence the souls came and whither they returned was full of myrtle trees, but also that a single twig of myrtle by itself might be a resting place for angels and souls, and hence also a vehicle for conveying them to wherever they may want to go. Such an instance in which the myrtle, according to the popular belief, served as a vehicle used by good spirits or souls to move from place to place is recorded in the Talmud (Nid. 36b–37a). Here we are told that two rabbis who had had some differences died on the same day, and their funerals took place at the same time. The people noticed on that occasion that sprigs of myrtle were flying from one bier to the other. Upon seeing this the people remarked that the two rabbis must have settled their differences and become reconciled.[53] This clearly shows that, according to popular conceptions, the myrtle,

---

[50] See מדרש אותיות דרבי עקיבא ed. Wertheimer (Jerusalem 1914) p. 79. In answer to the question where do the righteous who merit the life of the future world dwell, God says: in the Paradise of myrtle היכן דרים כשזוכין לחיי העולם הבא. אמר ליה (הקב"ה) בגן עדן של הדס.

[51] See *Zohar Vayakhel* p. 416: קיומא דאתר קדישא דנשמתין מניה הדס איהו.

[52] In Jellinek's *Bet Ha-Midrasch* II, 52; also in *Yalḳuṭ Šim'oni* to Gen. §20, and in מדרש תלפיות by R. Elijah Cohen (Lublin 1907) p. 194.

[53] חזו דפרח אסא מהאי פוריא להאי פוריא אמרו שמע מינה עבדו רכנן פייסא.

customarily placed on the bier,[54] was in this case, used by the
spirits of the occupants of the coffins as a vehicle by which they
could go visiting one another.

The custom of placing myrtle upon the coffin was intended
for a double purpose. First, it was to drive away the demons
who might try to snatch away the departed soul. Secondly, it
was to provide a vehicle for the soul by which it could fly up
to heaven. Possibly, it was also intended to provide seats or
resting places for the angels who come to welcome the righteous
man when he departs this world (Ket. 104a). It also might have
been to anticipate the act of the angels who, at the entrance of
paradise, meet the righteous man and provide him with sprigs
of myrtle, when they assign him to his place in paradise.[55] It is
therefore evident that, already in talmudic times, mystically
inclined people believed in some intimate connection between
the myrtle and souls, and assumed that spirits, souls or angels,
could and did use the myrtle both as vehicles to move from
place to place and as resting places wherever they wished to
stay or dwell.

Another rather mystic belief, which was current in talmudic
times, was that there comes to every Jew on Friday evening an

[54] See Rashi to Nid. 37a s. v. דקא פרח where he says: רגילין היו להניח הדס
עַל המטה. In Beẓ. 6a it is mentioned as one of the preparations for the funeral
to cut sprigs of myrtle למינו ליה אסא. An interesting variation of the custom
of putting myrtle on the bier is reported by Luria in דרך אמת to Zohar *Vayakhel*
l. c., which consisted of putting the myrtle between the legs of the dead
person: ומכאן טעם שנמצא בשם ר"י דלא'ריידה שצוה להשים הדסים בין ברכיו לאחר פטירתו
וכן צוה לו אביו. This, no doubt, was to provide him with a vehicle on which
he could ride up to heaven. Among the ancient Greeks the myrtle was also
used at funerals and placed on the graves. See Pauly-Wissowa *Real-Encyclopaedie* s. v. Myrtos p. 1182. Among the Bohemians it is still the custom to
use the myrtle at funerals. See Charles M. Skinner *op. cit.*, p. 191. And among
Hungarian Jews, there is still observed the custom of placing myrtle on the
graves when visiting the cemetery. Dr. Abraham Cronbach calls my attention to the prayer in the Concluding Service for Atonement Day (Union
Prayer Book II p. 365) where the phrase: "That from our grave may sprout
not the barren thistle but the fragrant myrtle," may perhaps likewise echo
the age old belief in some connection between the souls of the dead and the
myrtle.

[55] See סדר גן עדן quoted *supra*, note 52.

additional soul, נשמה יתירה, which abides with him throughout the entire Sabbath day, leaving him on Saturday night[56] (Beẓ. 16a). A corollary idea, developed by some mystics, was that when the additional soul comes out from its place in heaven to go down to earth on Friday evening to enter the body of an Israelitish person, there also come out with it certain angels. These angels remove from the Israelites all sadness and trouble, all bitterness and vexation.[57]

Now, if the place where the souls dwell in heaven or under the throne of glory is a place of myrtle, the additional soul that is ordered to descend and come to every Israelite on Friday evening with the entrance of the Sabbath, likewise must come from the same source, the place of myrtle. And just as the soul, when ascending to heaven uses the myrtle for its vehicle, so also, it may be assumed, when descending from heaven to sojourn in man for the Sabbath day, it also uses the myrtle as its vehicle. Likewise, it may be assumed that, when angels or the spirits of the departed saints come down to visit their relatives, they come riding on a piece of myrtle.[58] At any rate man,

---

[56] נשמה יתירה נותן הקב״ה באדם בערב שבת ולמוצאי שבת נוטלין אותה הימנו. See also Ta‘an. 27b. The author of this saying is R. Simeon b. Laḳish, a Palestinian Amora of the second generation (third century). The mystics took the phrase "additional soul" literally, not as a figurative expression for increased spirituality or ease and comfort, as some rationalizing Rabbis understood it. See Moses of Przemysl in his מטה משה part IV (Warsaw 1876) p. 122; also Isaac Lampronti in פחד יצחק s. v. נשמה (Lyck 1864) p. 98, and cf. also R. Solomon b. Adret's remark referred to above note 27.

[57] See Zohar, Piḳḳude (Lublin 1872) p. 511. The passage in the original reads as follows: כד נשמתא אתוספת מערב שבת לערב שבת ואיהי נפקת כד איהי נפקת נפקין אילין עמה ומעברי מישראל כל עציבו וכל יניעו וכל מרירו דנפשא וכל רוגזא דעלמא. Even if one believes the Zohar to be a literary product of the thirteenth century, one cannot deny that it contains older material and embodies ideas which go back to early talmudic times. In this passage, the angels accompanying the extra soul are mentioned by special names. In later mystic literature it is merely stated to which group, מחנה גבריאל etc. these angels belong, but they are not mentioned by name. Infra, note 69.

[58] The idea that departed saints can and occasionally do come back to visit their folks here on earth finds its expression in the Talmud (Ket. 103a) in the legend that Judah Ha-Nasi, after his death, used to come back to visit his home every Friday evening. When, however, one Friday evening, he

to be hospitable to his heavenly visitors, whether it be an additional soul, the spirit of a departed saint, or an angel, should supply the vehicle of myrtle by which they may come down and also provide them with a resting place of myrtle somewhat like the one to which they are accustomed in their heavenly abode.

heard the maid telling a neighbor of his presence at home, he discontinued his visits, in order not to cast reflection on the righteous men of former times, as people might say that they were not as worthy as he, Judah Ha-Nasi, to be permitted after death to return to earth and visit their friends. The passage reads, as follows: כל בי שמשי הוה אתי לביתיה ההוא בי שמשא אתאי שבבתא קא קריה אבבא אמרה אמתיה שתיקו דרבי יתיב כיון דשמע שוב לא אתא שלא להוציא לעז על צדיקים הראשונים. In the Zohar, 'Emor p. 206–207 this idea is expressed in the belief that the Patriarchs, Abraham, Isaac, and Jacob in the company of Joseph, Moses, Aaron and David, come down to visit their people in the sukkah during the seven days of the Sukkoth festival. And in the liturgy for the sukkah there is provided a special prayer based on this passage in the Zohar, by which the Israelite, every time he enters the sukkah, invites and makes welcome these heavenly visitors: סדר האושפיזין (see סדור אוצר התפלות Wilna 1923, pp. 1163–65). But why do these visitors come only on the Sukkoth festival and not on any other festival? Because in their heavenly abode in Paradise, they are accustomed to an environment of myrtle (see above notes 50, 51), and the sukkah was made with myrtle. See Neh. 9.15 and Suk. 12a. Even Isserles in Š. 'Ar. 'O.Ḥ. (638 end) still speaks of instances in which myrtle formed the covering of the sukkah. And in Safed they made the covering of the sukkah of myrtle branches even in the nineteenth century, see Moses b. Menaḥem Mendel Reischer in his ספר שערי ירושלים (Warsaw 1872) p. 39. The sukkah, accordingly, was a suitable environment for these heavenly visitors. Furthermore, the myrtle which is used in the ceremony of waving the lulab and the etrog attracted them and furnished them with the vehicle by means of which they descended. Perhaps the custom of keeping the myrtle sprigs, used for that ceremony, in the home from one year to another — mentioned by R. Joseph Colon in his Responsa, שאלות ותשובות מהרי"ק 41 (Zadilkow 1834) p. 17c — was not, as Colon assumes, for the purpose of making sure that they would have the right kind of myrtle next year, but rather for the purpose of making permanent, as it were, the presence of the good spirits in the home for the entire year. The people may have believed that they might secure thereby protection from evil spirits throughout the year. One is reminded of the Catholic custom of taking home the palms used in the procession of Palm Sunday and preserving them in the home as a sacramental which is believed to have the effect of driving away evil spirits. See *Catholic Encyclopedia* vol. XI p. 433 s. v. Palm Sunday; also *ibid.*, vol. XIII p. 293. s. v. Sacramental.

Now, the idea suggests itself with great plausibility that
perhaps the purpose of our ceremony had, in the minds of the
mystics, something to do with these beliefs. In other words, it
may be assumed that the function of the myrtle in our ceremony was the same as the function of the myrtle on other
occasions, and that it combined all these functions. (For a ceremony may, at the same time, serve many purposes if they are
not incompatible.) It offered protection against demons[59] and
furnished a vehicle by which the additional soul, perhaps with
angels or other spirits of departed saints accompanying it,[60]
would come down; and it also provided a resting place for these
spirits during their visit here on earth.

An examination of the ceremony and all its details as prescribed and explained by Luria and his disciples will confirm
this theory and prove that those ideas actually were in the
minds of the later mystics who observed this ceremony. And,
as already remarked above, they were probably in the main the
same ideas which were entertained by the earlier mystics in
talmudic times; for the later mystics did not altogether invent
these ideas; they received them from earlier generations, though
they may have slightly modified them. This may also help to
explain to us the objections to this ceremony on the part of the
more rationalistic rabbinic authorities who ignored the ceremony
or sought to suppress it.

Now let us see how the ceremony was observed by Luria
and how his disciples explained its significance. The ceremony
as prescribed by Luria was as follows: "A man must be very
careful to place on the table (on Friday evening) two bunches

[59] Perhaps the saying מטלטלין עצי בשמים להריח בהם ולהניף בהן לחולה (Beẓ. 33b)
also means, not merely waving them in order to refresh the sick person,
which function would have been included in the phrase להריח בהם, nor for
the sake of cooling the air or of driving away flies which need not be done
especially with fragrant plants, but in order to drive away the demons, since
a sick person is one of the three categories of people especially threatened
by the demons (Ber. 54b). And עצי בשמים in our passage means myrtle. This
would be another function in which both myrtle and garlic were believed to
be equally effective. Supra, note 47.

[60] And the function of bringing good spirits and driving away evil ones
are not incompatible. See supra, note 48.

of myrtle, and each bunch must consist of three sprigs . . . Then march silently around the table towards the right. Then take the two bunches of myrtle into your hands, hold them close together with both hands, recite the benediction over them and smell them. Then march silently around the table with them a second time and say: ' "Remember" and "Observe" were said in one utterance.' "[61] It is also added that this ceremony, performed before the recitation of the Kiddush, is to be repeated after the meal has been finished and Grace has been recited. It says: "After reciting Grace after the meal you should again smell the bunches of the myrtle, but do not smell them without reciting the benediction over them, and after doing so, say: ' "Remember" and "Observe" were said in one utterance.' "[62] This order for the ceremony is also given by R. Jacob Ḥayyim Ẓemaḥ.[63] It is to be noticed that Luria follows both the report of the Talmud and the one of the Zohar. He combines the different features of each and harmonizes them, by prescribing that there must be two bunches, one corresponding to "Remember" and one cor-

---

[61] See שולחן ערוך של רבינו יצחק לוריא (Wilna 1880) p. כ'ט. The Hebrew text relating to this ceremony reads as follows: צריך האדם להיות זהיר לשום בשולחן שתי אגודות של הדס וצריך להיות כל אגודה משלשה בדי הדס . . . ואח'כ תקיף השולחן דרך ימין בשתיקה ואח'כ קח בידך השתי אגודות של הדס ותחברם בשתי ידך ותברך עליהם ותריח בהם ואח'כ תקיף עמהם השולחן פעם ב' דרך ימין בשתיקה ואח'כ תאמר זכור ושמור בדבור א' נאמרו.

[62] אחר בהמ'ז של שבת תחזור ותברך על אגודות של הדס ותריח בהם ואל תריח בלתי ברכה ואח'כ תאמר זכור ושמור בדבור א' נאמרו. We notice that it is insisted upon not to smell without reciting the benediction over spices ולא תריח בלא ברכה which insistence would seem superfluous if the smelling were for enjoyment. See חמדת ימים I. Ch. 8 (Zolkiew 1756) p. 44 where he seeks to give some explanation why it was necessary to mention that the benediction be recited. The real explanation, however, is that since the act was not for the purpose of enjoying the fragrance, but merely to bring the myrtle close to the nostrils, so as to affect a direct transfer of the extra soul (*supra*, note 35), one might think that it is like the case of one who takes something as a medicine לרפואה and that therefore no benediction is necessary, cf. Ber. 38a. Hence the insistence upon the reciting of the benediction. For, after all, he enjoys the fragrance, even though this is not his real purpose; and therefore, according to the conclusion of the Gemara Ber. *l. c.*, he must recite a benediction כיון דאית ליה הנאה מינה בעי ברוכי.

[63] In his נגיד ומצוה (Lublin 1881) pp. 44, 46, 48. Zemaḥ fled from Portugal in the year 1619. See JE VII, p. 656.

responding to "Observe" as in the Talmud but requiring that each bunch must consist of three sprigs, as in the Zohar. He does not, however, expressly say, as does the Zohar, that the three sprigs are for the three patriarchs. But that this idea of the Zohar was retained in the school of Luria, even if slightly modified, can be seen from an examination of the descriptions of this ceremony given by two exponents of the teachings of Luria; and we shall also learn from them that the function of the myrtle in relation to the patriarchs, hinted at in the Zohar, was similar to the function of the myrtle on other occasions. Thus in the work חמדת ימים, the author[64] of which was an exponent of Luria's ideas about ceremonies and ritual, this ceremony is highly recommended and described as follows: "It is a good custom for those who wish to walk in perfection, to place upon the table on the evening of the Sabbath two bunches of myrtle, each consisting of three sprigs. These two bunches correspond to 'Remember' and 'Observe,' Jacob and Rachel. One must, however, be careful that this myrtle should be the right kind like the 'Abot prescribed in the Torah[65] . . . And my teacher used to say, 'on the eve of the Sabbath there comes to a man three angels from the world of formation מעולם היצירה, one of the company of Michael representing the "mercy of Abraham". . . and one of the company of Gabriel representing the "fear of Isaac". . . and one of the company of Uriel representing the "glory of Jacob."[66] . . . And, therefore, every man of Israel should arrange to have on the eve of the Sabbath, at least three sprigs of myrtle to serve as a chair or throne for the above mentioned three angels who accompany the additional soul. And, when the additional soul notices that the three angels

---

[64] Supposed to have been Nathan Ghazzati (1644–1680) the follower of Sabbetai Zevi (see JE V, p. 651). Cf., however, David Fraenkel in 'Alim, Blaetter fuer Bibliographie und Geschichte des Judenthums heft II (September 1934) p. 54, note 1.

[65] Supra, note 49.

[66] In ספר ציוני to 'Emor (Cremona 1560) p. 80b in a note הגה"ה it is also said that the three sprigs of the myrtle, used in the ceremony of waving the lulab on Sukkoth, point to or indicate the three patriarchs ג' הדסים רמז לנ' אבות, חס"ד, פח"ד, תפאר"ת.

accompanying it have found a place on which to rest until the going out of the Sabbath, then it is glad and joyful. And when, on the night of the going out of the Sabbath, the person recites the benediction (in the Habdalah ceremony) over these three sprigs of myrtle,[67] then the additional soul leaves that person in this very act of smelling and immediately the three angels who have been resting on the myrtle go with it to its (original) place. And therefore one must sniff at these sprigs of myrtle three times (during the ceremony) on Saturday night.[68] And the additional soul, at the moment of its leaving, blesses the person, its host, for the pleasure which it had received. And if one has not prepared these three sprigs of the right kind of myrtle on the eve of the Sabbath, then, when the three angels come and find no place to rest, they move on and go away. And the soul then remains alone, sad of spirit. And when one recites the benediction (at the Habdalah ceremony) over the wrong kind of or 'fool' myrtle הדס שוטה, then an angel from the Other Side, i. e., from the Left Side, attaches himself to the soul (there being no good angels on proper myrtle sprigs to hinder him . . .) and the soul curses the person, its host, who has not troubled himself in its behalf to prepare at least three sprigs of myrtle (as a resting place) for the three angels that were with it.' So far are his (the teacher's) words. Go and learn how doubly beneficial it is for the Israelite to prepare two bunches of the right kind (כשר) of myrtle, so that the beautiful soul may be glad and rejoice with its angels. On the other hand, it is the opposite with one who could have done this thing but neglected it. Such a person causes great harm to himself. Also, if one does

---

[67] He speaks here only of "these three sprigs of myrtle," since he said above that one must have "at least three sprigs of myrtle," that is, actually only one bunch. He thus ignores the requirement of two bunches, corresponding to "Remember" and "Observe." This is also done by Azulai. *Infra*, note 71.

[68] Zemaḥ in נגיד ומצוה p. 51 also says that at the Habdalah ceremony Luria used only one bunch of myrtle: מורי זלה"ה היה מריח על אגודה אחת של הדס דליל שבת כנו' שם והיה נזהר שיהיו בה ג' בדי הדס קשורים בקשר א' ג' הדסים הם סוד נר'ן החול ותכוין בהם כדי להשאיר מקדושת שבת לימי החול. So he also alludes to the significance of the three sprigs, as corresponding to נפש, רוח, נשמה as explained by Azulai. See below note 72.

not have the proper myrtle, he should not recite the benediction over the wild myrtle, lest there come upon him a curse and not a blessing. The same is also true with regard to the ceremony on Saturday night."[69]

Abraham ben Mordecai Azulai (1570–1643) in his work חסד לאברהם[70] gives a description of the ceremony practically identical with the one given in חמדת ימים, with one significant variation. He does not mention the feature of two bunches. The idea suggested in the Talmud that this ceremony somehow had the purpose of reminding one of the different versions of the commandment about the Sabbath is entirely dropped; hence, the feature of requiring two bunches of myrtle, supposed to correspond to "Remember" and "Observe," is not even mentioned.[71]

---

[69] The Hebrew text in חמדת ימים I, ch. 4 (Zolkiew 1756) p. 24d reads as follows:

ומנהג טוב להולכים בתמים לתת על השלחן בע"ש ב' אגודות הדס כשר כל אגודה מג' בדים והמה נגד זכור ושמור יעקב ורחל וצריך להזהר שיהא הדס כשר כעבות האמור בתורה שיהיו ג' עלין בגבעול ... ומורי נר"ו היה אומר כי בע"ש באים עם האדם ג' מלאכים מעולם היצירה אחד ממחנה מיכאל שהוא נגד מדת חסד לאברהם ואחד ממחנה גבדיאל שהוא נגד מדת פחד יצחק ואחד ממחנה אוריאל נגד ת"ת ישראל ולפיכך יש לערוך כל איש ישראל כל ע"ש ג' בדי הדס לפחות שיהיו עבות להיות כסא לג' המלאכים הנזכרים הבאים ללוות את הנפש יתירה ובראות הנפש יתירה שג' מלאכים הנלוים אותה מצאו מקום לנוח עליו עד מוצאי שבת אז היא צהלה ושמחה ובאור מוצאי שבת מברכו על ג' בדי הדס אלו אז הנפש היתירה יוצאת באותו הריח ומיד הג' המלאכים השורים על ההדס הולכים איתה עד מקומה ולכן יש להריח בם ג' פעמים במוצאי שבת; והנפש היתירה בעת הליכתה מברכת לבע"הב בעבור הנחת שקיבלה ומי שלא זימן ג' בדי הדס כשרות מע"ש כשבאים הג' מלאכים אינם מוצאים מקום למנוחתם ויסעו וילכו והנפש לבדה נשארה עצובת רוח וכשמברכים על ההדס השוטה מלאך מסטרא אחרא מסטרא דשמאלא מתלוה עם הנפש והנפש מקללת ח"ו לבע"הב על כי לא טרח בשבילה להכין ג' בדי הדס לג' המלאכים אשר איתה אלו דבריו: צא ולמד כמה טובה כפולה לאיש הישראלי בהכין ב' אגודות הדס הכשר והנפש היפה צהלה ושמחה במלאכים שלה וכן בהפכו אשר נמצא אתו והוא מתרשל בדבר גורם רעה לעצמו ח"ו ואשר לא נמצא אתו הדס לא יברך על השוטה פן יבא עליו קללה ולא ברכה וכן במוצאי שבת ...

[70] עין הקורא נהר מ"ט (Amsterdam 1685) p. 21b.

[71] While the author of חמדת ימים, although also emphasizing more the importance of the number three of the sprigs, at least mentions and even recommends the requirements of two bunches. *Supra*, note 69 but see also note 67. It seems that, for some mystics, the feature of two bunches lost its significance altogether. It was no longer important to refer to "Remember" and "Observe" and even the significance of referring to the "bride and the groom" or husband and wife, as expressed in Luria's song (*supra*, note 43), was disregarded. It seemed no longer important to emphasize the feature of

The main significance of the ceremony, according to this account, lies in the feature of "the three sprigs" which, while reminding us of or representing the three patriarchs, really are meant for the three angels who come down accompanying the extra soul. צריך לבקש ערב שבת אחר ג' בדי הדס שהם רומזים לג' אבות והכוונה לג' בדי הדס לג' מלאכים הנזכרים הבאים ללוות את הנפש היתירה. And though the idea expressed in the Zohar and modified in the Lurianic school, as represented by the author of חמדת ימים, (that these three angels stand for the three patriarchs) is retained, it is added that there is still another reason for expecting three angels to accompany each extra soul, that other reason being that the extra soul that comes to every Israelite on a Friday night may consist of three parts נפש רוח נשמה.[72] And each of these parts of the extra soul is accompanied by a special angel. Hence, three angels may be needed. It may also suggest that the three sprigs were vehicles for the three parts of the soul themselves. Each one of the accompanying angels may manage to come along with the respective part of the soul on each one of the sprigs, which might accommodate both of them. After the three parts of the soul enter the body through the nostrils, each sprig is left with but one occupant, the accompanying spirit, who abides on it through the whole Sabbath day. On Saturday night when the parts of the soul leave the person through the nostrils, ready to return to the heavenly abode, then, each of the waiting attendant spirits makes room on his respective sprig for one of the respective parts, and thus conveys it back to heaven.

We must notice that both the author of חמדת ימים[73] and Azulai leave out the feature of marching around the table with the

protection of husband and wife against demons, as at weddings, since this would only apply to the smallest family where there is only a husband and his wife. *Infra*, note 86.

[72] See *Zohar A ḥare* p. 140 ג' דרגין אינון ואתדבקו כחד נפש, רוח, נשמה. The idea expressed by Azulai *ibid.*, *l. c.*, that the additional soul that comes to a person on Friday night is of the same kind as the soul which that person possesses, is also found in the Zohar *Phinehas*, p. 484, where it says: לכל חד מישראל הכי נחית ליה נפש יתירה כפום דרגא דיליה.

[73] Though the author of חמדת ימים somehow still retains this feature in the discussion of the ceremony at the third meal of the Sabbath (ch. 17, p. 72d) where he says: ויקיף כמו בשאר סעודות, implying that the ceremony

myrtle, prescribed by Ẓemaḥ and by the *Shulḥan 'Aruk* of Luria. This encirclement, הקפה, which no doubt, was to serve as a magic circle keeping away the evil spirits,[74] was not considered so important by these two representatives of the Lurianic school. Not that they did not believe in the presence of the evil spirits, or in the efficacy of the myrtle to keep them away but, for some reasons, they did not feel the need of emphasizing this feature which is the negative function of the myrtle. They merely emphasized the positive function of bringing the good spirits.

In these descriptions of the ceremony by the representatives of Lurianic mysticism, the main function and purpose of the ceremony is clearly stated, though the different descriptions present slight differences in some details. And it is unmistakably plain that this function assumed by the Lurianic mystics is based upon ancient mystic notions about the Sabbath and upon some superstitious beliefs about the inherent powers of the myrtle. Some of these ancient beliefs and superstitions we found indicated in the Talmud. Others we found expressed only in the mystic literature but their origin, no doubt, goes back to talmudic times. The ʾystics of the Lurianic school, or their immediate predecessors, preserved and combined all these mystic notions. They may have modified some of them slightly, but out of them they wove the mystic texture of their explanation of the ceremony. We need not be surprised if we find, in the different presentations, a little confusion and occasionally con-

including the marching around the table is to be performed at every Sabbath meal, not only on Friday night.

[74] Marching around in a circle, הקפות, has the purpose of keeping away the demons and is performed when and wherever there is a special fear of demons. Thus, at funerals, it is customary to make such circles either on the way to the cemetery or at the cemetery, and the purpose thereof is explained to be the driving away of the evil spirits להבריח מעליו רוחות רעות (Aaron Berachyah Modena in his מעבר יבק, chapter 17 of שפתי רננות [Wilna 1922] p. 216): Likewise at weddings, when the fear of the demons is especially great, it is customary to march with the bride seven times, or at least three times, in a circle around the bridegroom under the canopy. See טעמי המנהגים by א"ש שו"ב (Lemberg 1911) part I, p. 112 and part IV, p. 15. See also I. Scheftelowitz, *Das Stellvertretende Huhnopfer* (Giessen 1914) pp. 22–30, and Joshua Trachtenberg, *Jewish Magic and Superstition* (New York 1939) p. 121.

tradictory ideas or slight variations in some details. For, after all, consistent thinking and systematic presentation is not the forte of mystic writers. In the main, however, they all agree as to the chief purpose and function of the ceremony. Their descriptions, notwithstanding the little differences and the occasional omissions of some feature or detail, enable us to trace the development of this ceremony and may also help us to discover the reason why this ceremony was not popular with rabbinic authorities, and the cause of its ultimate falling into disuse.

As our records do not give the exact dates when an idea arose or when it was modified, and as a hint to an idea or notion found in a later source may sometimes actually have reference to earlier times, we shall not be able to document the various stages of this development in their chronological order, but in the main we can trace the course of this development. On the basis of this examination of the various descriptions of this ceremony and the scattered indications of the various notions that entered into the texture of the ceremony or affected its interpretation, I venture to give the following broad outline of the course of its development:

In ancient times, when the myrtle was still used merely as a substitute for the *mugmar*, some people ascribed to it an additional function, based upon the popular beliefs in certain qualities of the myrtle. It was believed to have the effect of exciting or increasing sensuality. This was desirable on Friday nights.[75] It was also believed to have the power of driving away the evil spirits who, according to some people's belief, are especially dangerous on Friday nights.[76] The function of the myrtle then in the ceremony on Friday night was, in both these respects, identical with the functions ascribed to it when used at weddings or for bridal wreaths. The popular superstitions, underlying this conception of the ceremony, of course, were not favored by the Rabbis; but, on the whole, they did not so strongly object to the ceremony. For they could regard the notion that the myrtle on Friday evening had the same purpose as the one used at weddings, merely as a poetic expression and

[75] *Supra*, note 47.   [76] *Supra*, note 45.

and exaggerated presentation of the intimate union between Israel and the Sabbath, picturing it as a wedding in which Israel is the bridegroom and the Sabbath is the bride.

And when the idea that on Friday night every Israelite was given an additional soul that abides with him the whole Sabbath day and leaves him on Saturday night arose and became well-known, the popular mind discovered another possible function for the myrtle used on Friday evening. Remembering the other popular notion that the myrtle was a suitable vehicle or resting place for souls and spirits, some people thought that the use of the myrtle on Friday evening might also serve the purpose of helping to bring down and to make welcome the additional soul. This explanation suited the popular fancy very much, since it was in harmony with the function of the myrtle used in the ceremony on Saturday night when it served the somewhat similar purpose of giving a farewell to the departing additional soul and furnishing it with a vehicle by which it could be transported to its heavenly abode. The people never would countenance the idea that the same means employed on Friday night as a vehicle for or a form of welcome to the extra soul should be used on Saturday night to console or refresh the person grieving over the loss of the extra soul, as some rationalizing people conceived it.[77]

Again, the thought also occurred to some people that the extra soul, living in the delightful abode in Paradise among gardens of myrtle, might be reluctant to leave that abode and go down to earth, even if only for a week-end. According to mystic notions, even the regular soul when, at the time of conception or birth it is ordered to enter the human body, pleads with God to let it remain in heaven and not to send it down to earth. It has to be coaxed and forced to enter the human

---

[77] *Supra*, note 27. From what we have discussed above, it is clear that the purpose of the ceremony was to help the extra soul depart as, on Friday evening, the ceremony helped it arrive. It was not to comfort the remaining soul in its grief over the departure of the extra soul. For, in that case, it would have been entirely out of place on Friday evening when this soul was joyfully anticipating the pleasure of its visitor from heaven.

body.[78] The extra soul, then, presumably no less disinclined to leave its heavenly abode, certainly could not be trusted to proceed to earth by itself. An angel from on high had to be assigned the task of taking it down to earth for the week-end and bringing it back when its visit there was over. Accordingly, the mystics felt, this angelic escort also had to be provided with means of transportation and accomodation for rest. Hence, two bunches of myrtle were required, one for the soul and one for its attendant angel. For originally the people were not so niggardly with their arrangement as to assign but a single sprig for a soul or an angel. They would provide a whole bunch of myrtle in the midst of which, between the single sprigs, the soul or the angel could stand or rest. This was more in keeping with the notion familiar to the people from Zech. 1.9, where the angel "stood among," not on one of, "the myrtle trees."

Some mystics also developed the idea that perhaps it need not be an angel of the regular heavenly hosts who brings down the extra soul. Some spirit of an ancestor or of a departed relative who might wish to return for a week-end visit with his family on earth, as e. g., Judah ha-Nasi used to do for quite a time after his death (Ket. 103a),[79] might take charge of the extra soul and escort it to the place of its assigned destination. In this case, the second bunch of myrtle would serve for the departed spirit in the same capacity as it would serve a regular angel. These superstitious notions connected with the ceremony of using myrtle on Friday evening were even more objectionable to the enlightened teachers. They would never repeat them and would not admit that the ceremony was for such a purpose. Nevertheless, for a time at least, they continued to tolerate, though by no means to recommend, the ceremony and were inclined to consider it as an additional Sabbath pleasure עונג שבת, or a special form of honoring the Sabbath כבוד שבת. And when confronted with an exceptional case of a good and pious man whose intellectual and spiritual attainments could not be

---

[78] See Tanḥuma, *Pikkude* 3; also סדר יצירת הולד in Jellinek's *Bet Ha-Midrash* I, p. 153 ff.

[79] *Supra*, note 58.

doubted, but who was mystically inclined and hence laid special stress upon using two bunches of myrtle for this ceremony on Friday evening, they would, in true rabbinic fashion, judge him on the scale of merit and not impugn to him an indulgence in these foolish objectionable superstitions. They charitably explained that he probably used *two* bunches of myrtle for this ceremony as a symbolic reminder of the two aspects, positive and negative, of the Sabbath laws or, as they put it, corresponding to the forms of the commandment, "Remember" and "Observe." But they would not extend this tolerant attitude, shown in the case of an exceptionally pious person, to the people at large. They could not credit all the people with such ideas of using the myrtle merely as a symbolic reminder. And realizing the impossibility of eradicating from the people's mind the superstitions which were popularly attached to the ceremony, they finally discouraged the ceremony altogether and, in general, were opposed to the use of the myrtle on Friday evening; though they did not object to having other flowers or spices on the table merely for the pleasure of enjoying their fragrance or aroma.[80] Thus, beginning with the later talmudic times, this ceremony came to be suppressed by the rabbinic authorities and no mention of it is ever found in halakic literature.

But the Halakists could not control the private practices of the mystic circles who secretly cultivated their ideas or superstitions and handed them down from generation to generation. Among these mystic circles the ceremony continued to be observed and, in the course of time, some details of it were slightly modified and differently explained. Its main significance was considered to lie in its function of facilitating the coming of the extra soul. This, however, did not preclude the other function

[80] *Supra*, note 4. As a form of כבוד שבת or עונג שבת, the custom of having flowers or plants in the home may have continued in some places and in some Jewish homes. In fact, in Palestine today, it is customary to buy flowers for the Sabbath. What the significance of the custom of spreading the aroma of spices in the Synagogue at the entrance of the Sabbath, introduced in German communities about the beginning of the seventeenth century, may have been, I cannot tell. It is interesting to notice, however, that Joseph Juspa Hahn (1570–1637) in his יוסף אומץ 598 (Frankfurt a.M. 1928) p. 127 objected to it.

ascribed to the myrtle, namely of strengthening[81] the bride and
the groom on their wedding day or the husband and the wife of
the family, by increasing their sensuality and protecting them
from harm by driving away the evil spirits. For ceremonies, in
the popular fancy, can accomplish more than one purpose and
perform different functions at one and the same time.

One change was made in the ceremony which affected the
number of the myrtle vehicles required. Instead of two, the
mystics required three; but at the same time the extravagance
of providing a whole bunch for each spirit was curtailed. It was
felt that a single sprig by itself was sufficient as a vehicle or
resting place for a spirit. And, instead of two bunches, they
required only three single sprigs. The requirement of three sprigs
may have come about in the following way: It occurred to some
people that two angels or spirits were required for the soul to
keep watch over it and to see to it that it stays in the body till
the time of its departure, on Saturday night, arrived. For even
the regular soul, forced to enter into the body of the child is,
while in the womb, watched over by two angels to prevent its
getting out from its imprisonment in the womb.[82] Accordingly,
three sprigs were required; one for the soul itself and two for
the guardian spirits.

Again, some mystics conceived the notion that these guardian
spirits were the spirits of the three patriarchs, Abraham, Isaac,
and Jacob. And it was felt that these spirits could carry the
soul with them on their vehicles, so that there was no need of
providing a separate vehicle for the soul itself. All that was
necessary, then, was to provide three sprigs for the three patriarchs.[83] Why three guardian spirits were required for each soul
was explained by some on the basis of the theory that each
extra soul might possibly be a trinity consisting of three parts
נפש, רוח, נשמה. The function of these spirits was to bring the additional soul near to the door of its temporary abode for the

[81] *Supra*, notes 43, 46, and 47.

[82] See Tanḥuma, *Piḳḳude 3*, referred to above, note 78.

[83] As suggested in the Zohar passage quoted in note 35 above. Cf. also
supra, note 67.

Sabbath, i. e., to the nostrils where, by inhaling the fragrance of the myrtle, the extra soul is drawn in and thus enters the body. Hence, the smelling or sniffing at the myrtle, originally merely an act for the enjoyment of the fragrance, was still considered necessary. It was still insisted upon that the benediction usually recited over the enjoyment of fine scents be recited; though in this case it was really not an act of enjoying the fragrance but of drawing in the extra soul.[84] As each of the three sprigs, serving as a vehicle for one of the patriarchs, carries one part of the three-fold soul, they must all be brought near the nostrils at the same time, so that the whole trinity may enter the body at the same time. Hence the requirement of tying them together[85] before bringing them near the nostrils for what seemed to be an act of smelling, a requirement which would not be necessary if the apparent act of smelling were merely for the enjoyment of the fragrance. Some of the mystics, respecting the talmudic explanations, wished to retain the number *two*, corresponding to "Remember" and "Observe." They therefore combined it with their own interpretation of the ceremony by requiring *two* bunches, corresponding to the two versions of the commandment, but at the same time insisted that each bunch must consist of three sprigs for the three spirits of the Patriarchs carrying the three parts of the additional soul. While retaining, out of respect for the Talmud, the idea about the meaning of two bunches, some added another significance to the number *two*, namely, Jacob and his wife Rachel, or for "the bridegroom and the bride, that the weak ones may be strengthened."[86] In

---

[84] *Supra*, note 62.

[85] See the expression וקשירנא להון כחדא in the Zohar passage quoted *supra*, note 34.

[86] *Supra*, note 43. Some mystics may have retained the feature of having two bunches, explaining that these bunches, each consisting of three sprigs for the three spirits carrying the three parts of the additional soul, were one for the husband and one for the wife in the smallest family. But since, in a larger family they would require more than two bunches, they dropped this feature entirely, relying upon the three angels on the three sprigs to be able to manage to carry as many additional souls as might be required for any family large or small. Cf. *supra*, note 71.

this manner, they revived or retained the idea that the function of the myrtle on Friday evening was the same as its function at weddings.

Again, others ignored this idea that the myrtle was to function as at any other wedding, or be intended for the husband and wife, the smallest family, since such an idea would not hold good in the case of a larger family. They, accordingly, dropped entirely the feature of requiring two bunches. They just required three sprigs.[87]

How the extra souls came down to the other members of the family is not explained, but it must have been thought that souls do not take up much space and many of them could be accommodated on one sprig; or still better, the three spirits who carry down the extra soul to the head of the house can, at the same time with no extra effort, carry along and bring to each household all the extra souls for all the members of the family.

Another change that was made in the interpretation of the ceremony was the reversion to the idea that real angels of the heavenly host, and not the spirits of the patriarchs, had charge of the task. This was necessary, since it could not be conceived that the spirits of the patriarchs could manage to be present at one and the same time in the different localities of the numerous Jewish homes all over the world. However, these regular angels were made, in a manner, representatives of the patriarchs.[88] The soul, it was imagined, would feel better if it knew itself to be in charge of a representative of the fathers, than if it thought it were escorted merely by a heavenly officer.

Some mystics seemed also to have retained or revived the older idea that the myrtle was to drive away the demons. To emphasize this function, they required a procession around the table with the myrtle.[89] This feature of the הקפות or encirclement which, as we have seen, had the purpose of forming a magic circle to keep out the demons[90] was later on dropped

---

[87] Just as, at the Habdalah ceremony, only one bunch consisting of three sprigs was used. *Supra*, note 68.

[88] See the passage in חמדת ימים quoted *supra*, note 69, where the patriarchs are expressly identified with certain groups of angels.

[89] *Supra*, note 61.   [90] *Supra*, note 74.

because they no longer wished to emphasize the fear of the demons. Probably because the idea prevailed and came to be emphasized, even in the Friday evening liturgy, that on the Sabbath the demons could not harm the Israelites, there was no need of any special protection by the myrtle.[91] This was a sort of concession to the rabbinic law. But all these modifications and reinterpretations did not weaken the silent opposition of the halakists to this ceremony. The ceremony continued to be persistently ignored by the halakic rabbinic authorities, and no work on the ritual and ceremonies of the Sabbath by any rabbinic author mentions the ceremony.

There is, to my knowledge, but one exception. And this is Isaiah Horowitz (1565–1630), a great halakic authority, but also a prominent mystic who was greatly influenced by Luria's teachings. In his work, Šene Luḥot Ha-berit, section Sabbath (Fuerth 1764) p. 133, Horowitz mentions this ceremony in a rather simple form without in any way referring to any superstitious beliefs and mystic notions connected with it. He says: "It is proper that there should be (on the table) at every meal (of the Sabbath, not only on Friday evening) two bunches of myrtle for the purpose of enjoying their fragrance."[92] He does not connect it at all with the "additional soul," and does not specify the number of sprigs which each bunch should contain; nor does he mention the feature of marching with them around the table. He completely ignores all of the mystic explanations or justifications of this ceremony, which he certainly must have known, and limits himself merely to mentioning what is said about it in the Talmud, to which, of course, there could be no objection. He cites the passage from the Talmud (Sab. 33b) justifying the requirement of two bunches, as corresponding to the different expressions 'Remember' and 'Observe' used in the Sabbath commandment, even though apparently this does not seem to him to be a completely satisfactory justification.

---

[91] *Supra*, note 45. Those who still retained the feature may have justified it on the ground that the table was like the altar around which they would march with the myrtle on the Sukkoth festival.

[92] (Fuerth 1764) p. 133. של"ה. ראוי לכל סעודה להיות תרי מדאני אסא להריח בהם.

He adds: "Although this purpose of referring to or reminding one of the different expressions, "Remember" and "Observe" is already accomplished by lighting two candles,[93] yet a God-fearing person should also observe this custom of having two myrtle bunches." And, as an additional justification, he further says that he had actually seen, no doubt when on his visits in Safed, that "particularly pious people" observe this custom with the two bunches of myrtle because it is mentioned in the Talmud.[94] This closing remark sounds like an apology for mentioning or recommending such a ceremony. It clearly indicates that the ceremony was not at all popular and that only particularly pious people would observe it; and even they would justify their observing it on the ground that it is mentioned in the Talmud. This only proves that the strong objections on the part of rabbinic authorities to the mystic notions and superstitious beliefs associated with this ceremony, continued even to the time when mystic lore in general had gained favor in rabbinic circles and when its study was encouraged and even cultivated by many authorities of the Halakah. The tendency among rabbinic authorities to discourage this ceremony and to seek to suppress its practice remained unabated; with the result that the ceremony could not maintain itself. But what greatly contributed to the complete abandonment of this ceremony, even among more or less mystic circles, was not so much the opposition of the halakists as, strangely enough, another mystic notion which developed as a corrolary to the main idea underlying the mystic interpretation of the ceremony, viz. that the myrtle was the favored vehicle or resting place for angels and spirits. For, in the realm of the spirits there is division, rivalry and competition. Alongside of and opposed to the right party, סטרא דימינא, consisting of the good spirits and angels, there is the party of the left, סטרא דשמאלא, consisting of the evil spirits and demons. These members of the left party are very much like the members of the right

---

[93] Horowitz takes it for granted that the two Sabbath lights are to correspond to "Remember" and "Observe." Rabiah to Sabbath ed. Aptowitzer I (Berlin 1913) p. 265, merely offers it as a suggestion. He says: יש לומר חד כנגד זכור וחד כנגד שמור.

[94] של"ה l. c. וכן ראיתי המדקדקין נוהגין כן בתרי מדאני אסא מאחר שמוזכר בגמרא.

party and imitate many of their habits.[95] Now the notion developed among the mystics that like the angels and good spirits, the demons and evil spirits being, after all, also spirits by nature, might likewise favor the use of the myrtle for vehicles or resting places. This notion engendered great fear of handling the myrtle. For one could never be absolutely certain about the nature of its invisible occupant, whether it be an angel or a demon. Of course, it was assumed that the right kind of myrtle was very particular and would serve only the good spirits and angels, but refuse to let itself be used by the evil spirits. But there is the other kind of myrtle, the wild or "fool" myrtle, הדס שוטה that looks very much like the right kind, but which is not so particular and may readily lend itself to be used by the evil spirits. And we have seen that the author of חמדת ימים as well as Azulai warn against the danger of great harm that could result from the use of the wrong kind of myrtle. They urge great care and precaution in selecting the right kind of myrtle for the ceremony lest, instead of a good angel, an evil spirit, one from the "Other Side" or left party, may come riding on it or be resting on it, much to the harm of the person performing the ceremony. But not every one is expert enough to distinguish between the two kinds of myrtle which look very much alike. Besides, some consider even the right kind of myrtle, after it has become dried up, as being in a class with the "fool" myrtle.[96] Such a myrtle, it was feared, might also be used by the evil spirit. The result was that very few people, even among the mystics, would care or dare to perform this ceremony with the

[95] A *baraita* in Ḥag. 16a mentions three things in which the demons are like the angels and the habit of riding on myrtle is not one of them. But this *baraita* may be תנא ושייר and does not mean to exhaust the similarities of demons to angels. See Tosafot *ad loc.*, s. v. כבני אדם who remark that the list of the things in which demons resemble human beings, as given in the same *baraita*, is not complete either.

[96] See commentary בית חדש to *Ṭur 'O.Ḥ.* 297 where it is explained that R. Ephraim, who objected to the use of the myrtle at the Habdalah ceremony, considered a dried up myrtle to be "fool myrtle" or הדס שוטה. Whether this was the real reason for R. Ephraim's objection is rather doubtful. It seems that he objected to the use of the myrtle altogether even if it were fresh, for he only used some spices kept in a glass container.

myrtle. And even those who performed it were emphatic in their declaration that they did it merely as a symbolic reminder of "Remember" and "Observe," and because it is mentioned in the Talmud.

In Safed, the place of Luria's activity, the ceremony seems to have lingered on even to the nineteenth century; but even there, its observers, like the מדקדקין referred to by Horowitz, seem not to have emphasized the mystic explanation of it. They merely say that they perform the ceremony because it is an ancient custom mentioned in the Talmud. A report of this ceremony as being still observed in a simple form in Safed in the middle of the nineteenth century is found in the work ספר שערי ירושלים by Moses b. Menaḥem Mendel Reischer, (Warsaw 1872) p. 39, and reads as follows: "It is the custom in Safed to hire a man to bring in sprigs of green myrtle from the fields every Friday and to distribute them in all the synagogues. And on Friday night after the evening service, each person takes home with him two sprigs, one corresponding to the commandment "Remember" and the other corresponding to the commandment "Observe," as is stated in the Talmud; for this is a very ancient custom; and before saying the Kiddush they recite, over these myrtle sprigs, the benediction."[97]

This, to my knowledge, is the last or latest reference to the observance of this ceremony. It is significant that this was in Safed where the myrtle grows plentifully (Reischer *ibid. l. c.*), and where the traditions and memories of Luria were still cherished. But, even there, the ceremony was observed in its simple form without any reference to the mystic interpretations of it. Outside of Safed the ceremony seems either never to have been observed or completely forgotten if ever it had been practiced.[98] For we find no reference[98a] to its being observed outside

[97] The passage reads as follows: מנהג בצפת ששוכרים את א' להביא כל ע״ש הדסים ירוקים מן השדה לחלק בכל בתי כנסיות ובבתי מדרשות ובליל שבת אחר התפלה יקח כל א' שנים א' כנגד זכור וא' כנגד שמור כדאיתא בגמרא כי הוא מנהג קדמון וקודם קידוש מברכין עליהם בורא עצי בשמים ...

[98] H. J. D. Azulai who lived outside of Safed mentions the ceremony in his מדבר קדמות (Lemberg 1864) אות י״נ quoting the elder Azulai. But whether he himself also observed it or merely quotes it, we cannot tell.

[98a] Dr. I. Sonne called my attention to a MS. work in his possession

of Palestine or even in Palestine in any other place except Safed.[99]

מזמור שיר ליום השבת by Hananiah Eliakim Rieti (b. about 1560 — died before 1623. J. E. s. v.) where, on p. 220, Rieti expresses surprise that the rabbinic authorities who discuss the הדס for Saturday night never mention that such a ceremony was also observed on Friday night, as is indicated in the story of the Talmud, Sab. 33b. He also cites R. Nathan Shapira who, in his commentary to the פיוט מהרש"ל, [see ר' פירוש עם פירוש למהרש"ל לשבת עם זמירות המזון ברכת נתן שפירא (Venice 1603) p. 25a] says: לפנים זאת בישראל שהיו משמחין בערב שבת בין השמשות בשני הדסים. Evidently neither Shapira nor Rieti knew that the ceremony was still observed in the Lurianic circle.

[99] We can now sum up and review briefly the development of the ceremony on Saturday night and, comparing it with the development of the one on Friday night, see why and how it succeeded in maintaining itself, even though in a somewhat modified form, to this day, while the Friday night ceremony failed to maintain itself and disappeared entirely.

True, both ceremonies originally served the same purpose and the same superstitions came to be associated with both of them, so that the same objections, on the part of the more enlightened people, could be and were raised against both of them. But certain conditions favored the Saturday night ceremony, helping it to meet the objections better than the Friday night one could. In the first place, as we have seen, the ceremony on Saturday night was the older and was rooted in the habit of the people of serving a *mugmar* substitute even before any superstitious secondary purpose was ascribed to it. Hence, it had a longer time to become firmly established in the practices of the people and to acquire a stronger power of resistance so that, even after some people attached to it certain superstitions, it could withstand any attacks that might have been made against it. The Friday evening ceremony, being the younger one and a mere imitation of the older, did not have such a long time to develop the power of resistance, since the superstitions were attached to it almost at its very emergence as a ceremony. Secondly, as we have seen, the objections to both of these ceremonies were primarily to the superstitions associated with the one kind of fragrant plant, the myrtle, used for these ceremonies, but not to the practice as such. If other fragrant plants, to which no such superstitions were attached, were used, these objections were easily met. And it is significant that in all the talmudic discussion about the ceremony on Saturday night, with the exception of the one reference cited above (note 26) only בשמים, "aromatic herbs" are mentioned and no express reference to the myrtle is found. This would indicate that when the Rabbis acknowledged the well established custom as a religious ceremony, they ignored the one feature or special case of using the myrtle, a usage which entailed objectionable superstitions, and talked only of the use of other fragrant plants, בשמים, in general. And probably they encouraged only the use of the other plants in connection with this ceremony. This, however, did not eliminate the use of the myrtle in the ceremony. The people, as we have seen, continued to use the myrtle and the Rabbis could tolerate the ceremony even with the use of the myrtle among other plants, as long as no special emphasis was laid upon the use of the myrtle in particular. Even after the popular superstition connected it with the belief in the additional soul that comes to a person for the Sabbath and leaves him on Saturday night, the Rabbis could still continue to tolerate the ceremony by reinterpreting it and by giving it a rather harmless and unobjectionable meaning. For the rationalistic people explained this extra soul to mean additional peace of mind and increased spirituality that comes to the Jew on the Sabbath. When, with the going out of the Sabbath, the Jew loses this additional spirituality and faces the worries of the coming week-days, his spirit is rather depressed and needs a little refreshing (supra, note 27). And there was no harm in letting him get this refreshment from the smell of spices or even from the fragrant myrtle, as long as it was fresh and fragrant and its use could be explained to be merely for the purpose of refreshing the spirit, and not for any other superstitious functions. For, after all, the myrtle was also a fragrant plant like any other kind of בשמים and could not be discriminated against, as long as its use was interpreted to be for the same purpose for which other plants could be, and were, used. This reinterpretation of the use of the myrtle as being not a vehicle for the departing extra soul, but merely a means of refreshing the languishing soul facing the troubles of the week, saved the ceremony and caused the Rabbinic authorities to tolerate it. Of course, some of them recommended or preferred the use of spices other than the myrtle, but there could not be or there was not so much objection even to the myrtle. The mystics, as we have seen, preferred the use of the myrtle (supra, note 26) and insisted upon the mystic reason for its use. But gradually the use of other spices became more and more wide spread and the use of the myrtle was not so popular. The fear that the myrtle used might not be of the right kind and, according to the mystic beliefs, that it entailed some danger, as it might have the harmful effect of attracting evil spirits, also discouraged the use of the myrtle, even among mystically inclined people. The mystics could and did find other means of achieving all the purposes, which the myrtle was expected to serve, in other features of the Habdalah ceremony. The feature of pouring out part of the liquor used for the Habdalah ceremony, as an offering to the evil spirits, a sort of bribe, (see מטה משה IV, 504, Warsaw 1876, p. 121 and cf. Lauterbach, "The Ceremony of Breaking a Glass at Weddings" in HUCA II, 374, note 35) secured protection which might have been sought against the demons by the use of the myrtle. The feature of burning the part of the liquor which had been poured out and which thus produced a little ascending flame furnished, in the minds of some mystics, a vehicle transporting the angels to heaven (see Judg. 13.20) — another function expected of the myrtle. The third function ascribed to the myrtle, viz., the stimulation of sexual longing, was not considered desirable on Saturday night. Consequently, even from the point of view of the mystics, there was no urgent need for using the myrtle as the favorite aromatic herb in connection with the Habdalah ceremony. The spice box took its place and also its Hebrew name. For the spice box used on Saturday night with the Habdalah ceremony is called by the special designation *ḥadas*, Hebrew for myrtle.

THE CUSTOM OF LOOKING AT THE FINGERNAILS AT THE OUTGOING OF THE SABBATH*

SOL FINESINGER, Hebrew Union College, Cincinnati, Ohio

IT HAS long been a custom among Jews for people to look at the reflection of the habdalah[1] light in their nails when they say the blessing over the light at the outgoing of the Sabbath.[2] Though the practice is generally assumed to be implied in the Mishnah,[3] no reference to it is to be found in the Talmud.[4]

* Dedicated to my friend and colleague, Dr. Jacob Z. Lauterbach.

[1] Habdalah, unless more rigidly defined, means the whole complex of ceremonies and customs which serve to indicate the separating of the Sabbath from the secular part of the week.

[2] See Šulḥan 'Aruk, Oraḥ Ḥayyim 298, 3; Seder 'Abodat Yisrael ed. S. Baer (Rödelheim 1868) p. 312.

[3] Ber. VIII, 6 אין מברכין על הנר עד שיאותו לאורו. See below pp. 351 and 355.

[4] Abraham ben Nathan (ibn Yarḥi, c. 1150) in his Hamanhig (Berlin 1855) p. 34b, section 68 traces the custom to the Palestinian Talmud: ירושלמי פרק כיצד מברכין מאמתי מברכין על האור משיכיר בין צפורן לבשר וזהו בשיטת מן הגוף. פרקי ר' אליעזר ומסתכל בצפורניו שהן לבנות מן הגוף. The passage cannot be found in our Yerushalmi, neither in chapter VI, where ibn Yarḥi puts it, nor in chapter VIII, where one would normally expect it. See Ratner אהבת ציון וירושלים vol. I (Vilna 1901) p. 189; ירושלים ed. Lunz, vol. VII (1906), pp. 160, 238–239. It is of course not unusual for statements which never were in the Palestinian Talmud to be headed ירושלמי. The word is often used for מדרש and quite appropriately because most of the Midrashim originated in Palestine. See Lunz, op. cit., pp. 149–150. What is strange about Hamanhig's statement, however, is that it actually refers to chapter VI of Berakot פרק כיצד מברכין. My notion of what has happened is this: In chapter XX of Pirḳe de Rabbi Eli'ezer, where nails are for the first time referred to, the first words of Mani's statement are כיצד חייב אדם לברך. This could easily have been taken for כיצד מברכין, or there may even have been a reading כיצד מברכין. And since it came from the Midrash Pirḳe de Rabbi Eli'ezer it was referred to as ירושלמי. Later on, when ירושלמי was taken to mean the Palestinian Talmud, the word פרק could very naturally have been inserted. This is a very tenuous theory, but we must remember that here it is necessary to explain not only how it is that ירושלמי is used when no reference to the Palestinian Talmud was intended — which is simple — but also how פרק כיצד מברכין arose — which is not so simple.

Reprinted from *Hebrew Union College Annual*, Vol. XII-XIII, 1937-1938.

The earliest recorded reference to the custom is found in Pirḳe de Rabbi Eli'ezer[5] and is ascribed to Rabbi Mani,[6] a Palestinian teacher of the fourth century.[7] His statement runs :[8]

כיצד חייב אדם לברך על כוס של יין לאור האש ואומר ברוך מאורי האש
וכשמחזיר ידיו מן האש אומר המבדיל בין קדש לחול. ואם אין לו יין פושט
את ידיו לאור האש ומסתכל בצפרניו שהן לבנות מן הגוף ואומר ברוך מאורי
האש וכיון שמרחיק ידו מן האש אומר ברוך המבדיל בין קדש לחול. ואם אין
לו אש פושט ידו לאור הכוכבים שהן של אש ומסתכל בצפורניו שהם לבנות
מן הגוף ואומר ברוך מאורי האש. ואם נתקדרו שמים תולש אבן מן הארץ ומבדיל
ואומר ברוך המבדיל בין קדש לחול. "How must a man say the habdalah blessing? Over a cup of wine at the light of a fire. And he says: 'Blessed art Thou who createst the lights of fire.' When he removes his hands from the fire he says: 'who dividest the holy from the profane.'

"If he has no wine he stretches his hands towards the light of a fire and looks at his nails which are whiter than his body and says: 'Blessed art Thou who createst the lights of fire.' And when he removes his hand from the fire he says: 'Blessed art Thou who dividest the holy from the profane.'

"If he has no fire he stretches his hands towards the light

---

[5] Zunz, *Gottesdienstliche Vorträge* (second edition with additions by Brüll, Frankfurt a. M. 1892, p. 289 and note a) believes that the book was written no earlier than at the beginning of the eighth century (or according to Brüll's insertion in note a the last third of the seventh century). Brüll also believes that it was done no later than the second half of the eighth century. Zunz believes (p. 290 and note b) that the book is first mentioned by R. Nissim (c. 1030). But it is already mentioned by Naṭronai (died c. 857) quoted in Seder R. Amram (died c. 875). See below p. 350. Friedlander in his translation of Pirḳe de Rabbi Eli'ezer (London, 1916) puts its final redaction in the second or third decade of the ninth century (p. liii). But see the references he gives on p. liv and lv.

[6] The name also occurs as מונא, מנא. It is an abbreviation of מנחם. See Bacher, *Die Agada der Palästinenischen Amoräer* vol. III (Strassburg 1899), p. 443, note 4.

[7] See Bacher *op. cit.* p. 457.

[8] We quote from the Warsaw edition of 1852, with notes by David Luria. The best manuscript seems to be the one on which Friedlander based his translation (see Friedlander, *op. cit.*, p. xiv) but it has not been published. We refer to Luria's text because it is as good as any of the prints and also because it has elaborate and penetrating notes.

of the stars, which are of fire, and looks at his nails which are
whiter than his body and says: 'Blessed art Thou who createst
the lights of fire.'

"If the sky is dark he tears a stone from the ground and
performs the habdalah ceremony that way and says:'Blessed art
Thou who dividest the holy from the profane.' "

The most essential element in the ceremony as it is here
described is light. The cup of wine too is important, for when
one has it one need not look at the nails at all.[9] But the cup of
wine is not indispensable.[10] And the importance of looking at
the nails can be gauged if we notice that it is sufficient merely
to look at the reflection of light in them, no matter if the light
is as pale as starlight.[11] It is only when there is no light at all
that the use of the nails is omitted. But we are given no idea of
the motive for their being used.[12]

The next[13] reference to the custom is found in Midrash
Tehillim on Psalm 35.[14] It reads simply: הצפרנים בהם להסתכל
אור להבדלה "the nails: in them to look at light for habdalah."[15]

---

[9] This differs from the later practice in which one uses both wine and
the nails.

[10] In the later practice it is indispensable.

[11] In the later practice one must use light or omit the habdalah.

[12] Some authorities take the phrase שהן לבנות מן הגוף to be the reason for
using the nails and paraphrase it by לפי שהן לבנות מן הגוף. See p. 358. But this
is hardly so; the phrase here seems to be no more than descriptive.

[13] Putting the quotation from Midrash Tehillim after the one from Pirke
de Rabbi Eli'ezer is arbitrary, for the two books cannot be dated with any
exactness. Still it is possible to date Mani, the author of the statement in
Pirke de Rabbi Eli'ezer, with some assurance, while the statement in Midrash
Tehillim is given anonymously and can not be dated. For the date of Midrash
Tehillim see Zunz, op. cit., p. 279. He puts its composition in the last centuries
of the Gaonic period, though much of its material is much older. See also
Zunz, op. cit., 361, 375.

[14] Buber's edition of Midrash Tehillim (Vilna 1891), p. 248.

[15] The translation is clumsy but the Hebrew also is poor; it does not
seem to hang together. In Yalkut to Psalms (vol. II, Vilna 1908 p. 908a,
section 723 the comment on the nails reads צפרנים לעשות בהם פריעה או מליקת
העוף או שניהם יחד ובוהן להסתכל אור להבדלה. This passage has the added difficulty
of the phrase או שניהם יחד. The reading בוהן, thumb, is usually corrected to
בהן, with them. See Lewin, Ozar Hageonim, vol. I (Haifa 1928), p. 124 note ד.
That does not make the reading any smoother. I get the impression that this

Naṭronai Gaon (died c. 857) is quoted as follows in the Seder of R. Amram (died c. 875):[16] והכי אמר רב נטרונאי ראש ישיבה
במוצאי שבת בבורא מאורי האש כך עושין בשתי ישיבות שמביטין בכפות ידם וכך ראינו רבותינו ז״ל שהיו [עושין] ואומרין [נביט] בידינו כדי שנהנה מן האור כדרך ששנינו אין מברכין על האור עד שיאותו לאורו וכך מנהג. וראינו ששנה בפרקי ר׳ אליעזר בן הורקנוס שמצוה להסתכל בצפרניו מיהו אין רגילין חכמים בכך. "And thus did R. Naṭronai head of the academy[17] say: At the outgoing of the Sabbath in the blessing 'who createst the lights of fire' they do as follows in the two academies[18] — they look at the palms of their hands. And thus have we seen our masters of blessed memory do and say: 'Let us look at our hands in order to benefit from the light, in accordance with the Mishnah passage[19] "one doesn't say a blessing over the light[20] until one has benefited from its light." ' And that is the custom.

"And we have seen that it is taught in Pirḳe de Rabbi Eli'ezer ben Horkenos that it is a duty to look at one's nails. But scholars[21] are not in the habit of doing that."

Even a superficial consideration of this passage shows that the attitude towards the use of the palms is different from the attitude towards the use of the nails. Indeed there is a sharp contrast between them. Here we cannot say that those who are not in the habit of using the nails do not know of the practice.

reading of the Yalḳuṭ means to assign one set of functions to the nails and another function to the thumb, and that the reading בהן is correct. The thumb may have played some role in the habdalah (see below p. 364 and the references there). The editio princeps of the Yalḳuṭ (Salonica 1521–1527) vol. III, page 21c reads: צפרנים לעשות בהם ובהן להסתכל אור להבדלה. This makes no sense at all, for the object of לעשות has fallen out. But that בהם could be followed by בהן may show that the two are not the same thing and that the second one must have meant thumb.

[16] *Seder Rab Amram*, ed. Coronel (Warsaw 1865), p. 32a. *Seder Amram Hašalem*, ed. Frumkin (Jerusalem 1912) vol. II, p. 59a. See Lewin, *op. cit.*, vol. I, p. 124 and the references there.

[17] At Sura.

[18] Sura and Pumbedita.

[19] Ber. VIII, 6. See b. Ber. 53b top, and p. Ber. VIII, 6 (12c top).

[20] However it makes better sense to read the first as אוּר, fire. That makes it an exact parallel to the original Mishnah passage which has נר.

[21] The more enlightened people.

Not only do they know of it, but it is even held that Pirke de Rabbi Eli'ezer regarded it as a *miẓwah*, a religious duty. Actually Mani's statement says nothing that strong.[22] Now if those who do not follow the custom still feel that it is a *miẓwah*, it must have played a considerable role with the people. Further, since it is the *ḥakamim* who do not make a habit of using the nails, we may deduce that it is the popular custom to do so, while it is the more enlightened who reject it. What can be the motive for this? Offhand one can see no good reason why it should be more objectionable to use the nails than to use the palm. The reason certainly cannot be that Mishnah Berakot VIII, 6 implies the latter, as is suggested by Naṭronai, and not the former. For the latter also is not mentioned or suggested in the Mishnah, and the Talmudim commenting on the Mishnah mention neither.[23] In so far as the Talmudic material does suggest anything that is not patent it suggests the use of the nails rather than of the palm.[24] There must be some good reason why one is preferable to the other. And to say that Naṭronai is describing what was prevalent only in Sura and Pumbedita still does not explain the prevalence.

From the statement of Simeon Ḳayyara (c. 825), the reputed author of the Halakot Gedolot, who probably lived at Sura[25] and was a contemporary of Naṭronai we get the impression that it really was the custom not to look at the nails in Sura. For he does not even mention them. Halakot Gedolot has the following:[26] אמר רב יהודה אמר רב אין מחזירין על האור כדרך שמחזירין על המצות ואין מברכין על האור עד שיאותו לאורו ומשום הכי פשטינן ידים בהבדלה מיחזי אי איכא נהורא אי לא דכיון דלאו בורא האש קא מברכינן אלא בורא מאורי האש אי איכא נהורא אין ואי לא לא ואי חזי במידי אחרינא או בחבריה שפיר דאמי. "Said R. Jehudah said Rab: 'One does not go around looking for fire as one does in order to fulfill the other commandments.' And one does not say the blessing over fire

---

[22] See p. 348.
[23] Ber. 53b top; p. Ber VIII, 6 (12c top).
[24] See below p. 355.
[25] Schloesinger in *Jewish Encyclopedia*, VII, p. 461a.
[26] The edition of Hildesheimer (Berlin 1888) p. 47. With a few minor variations, p. 14a of the Vienna (1810) edition.

unless one has benefited by its light.[27] And for this reason do we stretch out the hands at the habdalah, to see if there is light or not. For since the blessing that we say is not 'who createst fire,' but 'who createst the lights of fire,' if there is light one says the blessing, and if there is not one does not. However if one sees something else or someone else it is all right."[28]

For the Talmudic material on the Mishnah statement, in Ber. 53b, which Ḳayyara had available, he substitutes the material on stretching out the hands. And in addition he links the practice up directly with the prescription of the Mishnah. Further Ḳayyara himself does not consider the practice indispensable for he concludes by stating that if one sees something other than his hand or another person that is sufficient and it is not necessary to look at the hand. It must then have been a common custom in his time. But it is different with the nails. Since Naṭronai mentions them and since Ḳayyara was his contemporary and probably lived at the same place, it is unlikely that Ḳayyara did not know of the practice. It looks as though his failure to mention nails is not accidental. And we can feel justified in concluding that though he does not at all consider looking at the hand objectionable — even though it is not indispensable — he certainly is not in favor of the use of the nails.

Saadia (892–942)[29] who was a rationalist can hardly be expected to have taken much stock in looking at the nails. Although we have no complete statement of his, we find:[30] ואמר מר רב סעדיה ופושט המברך וכל היושבין ידיהם ונאותין לאור הנר שבירך עליה. "And said Mar Rab Saadia: 'the one who says the blessing and those who are sitting stretch out their hands and benefit from the light of the lamp over which he has made the blessing.' "

[27] Ber. 53b; but there the order of the statements is reversed.

[28] It is all right to say the blessing without looking at one's hands.

[29] 892 is the standard date for his birth. See Malter, *Saadia Gaon, His Life and Works* (Philadelphia 1921) p. 25. Mann, on the basis of a Genizah fragment, dates his birth between the 30th of March and the 8th of April 882 (*JQR.*, NS. XI [1920–21]), pp. 423–4. But contrast Malter, *l. c.*, p. 422.

[30] Quoted in Isaac ibn Gayyat (11th century) שערי שמחה, מאה שערים, Fuerth (1861–62), Hilkot Habdalah, p. 16.

Hai Gaon (939–1038) deals at some length with the habdalah. In a responsum attributed to him we read:[31] לרב האי. ששאלתם על ברכת האור. ברכת האור חובה היא על כל מי שמכיר בין שני דברים שאינן ניכרין. ונהגו הראשונים להביט בשרטוטי ידים עד שיכיר ביניהם מפני שהן מצויות בכל עת ואין ניכרין בלילה אלא על ידי האור. הלכך אין צריך לבקש דבר לידע אם יאותו לאורו שכיון שהביט בשרטוטי כפיו כבר נאות. ושמענו מהזקנים שאומרים שיש בשרטוטי פסת היד סימן ידוע להתברך בו. ועוד מנהגנו להביט בצפרנים ואומרים מפני שהן פרות ורבות לעולם הלכך מי שרוצה לצאת ידי חובת ברכה זו צריך שיאות לאור הנר כמו שנהגו הראשונים כדי שיתחייב בברכה וגם שליח צבור הנאות לאור מוציא י"ח. "Of Rab Hai: As to your question regarding the blessing over the light. The blessing over the light is obligatory upon any one who is enabled to tell the difference between two things which cannot otherwise be told apart. The early teachers had the custom of looking at the lines of the hand until they could tell them apart — for the lines are always around and can be told apart at night only by light. Therefore it is not necessary to look for anything else to know whether 'one benefits by the light.'[32] For once one has looked at the lines in his palms he has already benefited.[33]

"And we have heard from the elders that there is in the line of the palm of the hand a well-known sign through which one can be blessed.

"Further it is our custom to look at the nails. They say it is because they increase and grow constantly.[34]

"Therefore he who wishes to discharge the obligation of this blessing must benefit from the light as the early teachers were in the habit of doing and thus make himself obligated to pro-

[31] Quoted from Isaac ibn Gayyat, *l. c.* His version makes the best sense. See also תשובת הגאונים (Lyk 1864), p. 20 f.; שערי תשובה (Leipzig 1858) section 103; Lewin, *l. c.*, p. 126 and notes 25 and 26.

[32] Put in quotes because it is verbatim from Mishnah Ber. VIII, 6.

[33] Lewin, *l. c.*, p. 127 and note 1, regards the material from here to the end as an addition of Isaac ibn Gayyat. Even if Lewin is right it just means that ibn Gayyat himself had the attitude towards nails that we are ascribing to Hai. But I doubt that it is by Gayyat; at least the section from הלכך on can hardly be an addition by him. For why should ibn Gayyat, who is not opposed to the use of the nails, of himself add the latter part which, to put it mildly, gives preference to the use of the palm.

[34] These two sentences may be a continuation of the previous one and all three thus would be asigned to the elders by Hai.

nounce the blessing. Also, the deputy of the congregation who benefits from the light fulfills the obligation for the congregation."

The historical relation and relative importance of the Rišonim and the Zeḳenim who use the palm and of those who use the nails is not clear. But we can be reasonably sure that Hai is dealing with two well established practices. It is true that even though he states definitely that it is proper to follow the Rišonim and look at the lines of the hand he does not state that he is opposed to looking at the nails.[35] But his preference certainly is clear. And he has this preference in spite of his knowing that there is a very specific superstition connected with the use of the palms, that of looking for a favorable omen in the lines of the hand. If, in spite of this, he still prefers it to the use of the nails, we may gather that the superstition connected with the nails is worse than that connected with the palm. And that superstition can hardly be involved in the notion that the nails "increase and grow constantly," for if anything that notion is less objectionable than that of looking for omens in the palm. So in spite of Hai's fullness, what the superstition about the nails really is and why it is so objectionable do not appear.

But the motive and the objection do appear very bluntly and without equivocation in a responsum which seems to have originated between 1064 and 1082:[36] מצאתי בתשובות קדמונים שחקקתם

[35] As the other teachers of Sura — Ḳayyara, Naṭronai, Saadia — are or appear to be. It need not strike us as strange that Hai may here be possibly going counter to what was the common practice at Sura. He often does, but just why we do not know. See Marmorstein, *RÉJ.*, LXXIII (1921), p. 100.

[36] Quoted from *Sefer Rabia* (ed. Aptowitzer) part II (Jerusalem 1935) pp. 245–6. See Lewin, *l. c.*, p. 125 f., and consult his notes for the variants. I quote only as much of the responsum as Lewin gives, for the other matters in it have nothing to do with habdalah. Lewin regards the *tešubah* as part of a collection that was sent by R. Elijah Hakohen the head of the yeshibah in Jerusalem and his Ab Bet Din Ebyatar to R. Mosheh ben Meshullam of Mayence between 1062 and 1084. See the references he gives (p. 125) and add Schechter *JQR.*, old series XIV (1902), pp. 450–452. Lewin surmises, and rightly so, that extraneous material got into the responsum through someone who either did not know the difference between looking at the palm and at the nails, or did not wish to distinguish between the two. Since Lewin is not

שאנו נחשי נחישות במה שאנו רגילים . . . ושאנו מסתכלין בצפרנים בבורא
מאורי האש ומטילין מים על כוס של הבדלה ורוחצים פנינו.
נשיב לכם על ראשון ראשון ועל אחרון אחרון. הנה זה הנחוש טוב הוא
ורובו מן יסוד המקרא והאגדות . . .
ומה שאנו מסתכלים בצפורנים זה הדבר שנוי בתל' בבלי ובירוש' אין
מברכין על הנר עד שיאותו לאורו ופי' עד שמרגיש בוהק האור של נר הבדלה.
ומאחר שכן שנינו אין זה כי אם ניחוש של מצוה. "I have found in the
responsa of the early teachers: As for your asking[37] about our
practising[38] divination by being in the habit of looking at our
nails when we make the blessing 'who createst the lights of fire'
and of pouring water in the habdalah cup and washing our faces
with it. We will reply in the order you have asked. Behold this
divination is good and is for the greater part based on Scripture[39]
and Aggadot . . ."[40]

interested in maintaining any theory about habdalah he can be relied on in
deciding how much of the responsum is genuine and how much spurious.
Halberstamm in Kobak's *Ginze Nistarot* III (1872), p. 5, note 2, assigns the
responsum to Joseph Tob Elem (middle of 11th century) in accordance with
what he finds in Maḥzor Vitry (see p. 116–117 of the edition of S. Hurwitz,
Nürnberg, 1923) and Siddur Rashi. Aptowitzer, *op. cit.*, p. 245, note 4, assigns
it to Ẓemaḥ (c. 890) partly because of the occurrence of the strange expression
שחקתם which also occurs in a responsum of Ẓemaḥ's. This is, to say the least,
doubtful. See note 37. I follow Lewin partly because it seems, in spite of
Hai's attitude (see p. 353), that to look at the nails was not customary in
Babylonia and was rather a Palestinian custom (see Lewin's discussion
p. 125).

[37] Although I translate שחקתם "as for your asking," the meaning of the
word is not at all clear, in spite of the fact that Aptowitzer and Halberstamm
(see note 36) prefer it. See Lewin for the other variants. שחקתם is hardly
the word to refer to questioners. To me the reading given by Halberstamm
(*Ginze Nistarot* III [1872], pp. 4–5) ששחקתם ואמרתם "as to your laughing and
saying that we practice divination" is to be preferred. See Lauterbach
"Tashlik," *HUCA*, vol. XI (1936), p. 268 and note 79. ששחקתם could easily
have been corrupted to a vague שחקתם, especially at a later time when
the customs mentioned in the responsum became so much a part of the life
of the people that it no longer seemed possible for any one ever to have
ridiculed them.

[38] Here follow several customs which have nothing to do with habdalah.

[39] What biblical or aggadic passages he is referring to is not evident.
Can he mean Ezek. 21.26 and p. Ber. VIII, 7, 12c? See *Sefer Rabia* ed.
Aptowitzer (Berlin 1913), p. 130 and note 13.

[40] Here follows a discussion of some of the other customs. Mordecai ben

"As for our looking at the nails, this is taught in the Mishnah in the Babylonian and Palestinian Talmud, 'one does not say a blessing over the lamp until one enjoys its light,' which means until one feels the shining light[41] of the habdalah lamp.[42] And since we have learned so in the Mishnah, this is nothing more than divination connected with a religious act."

Not only are contradictory statements found in this responsum, but contradictory terms as well. It is strange that when the author — or authors — has a perfectly rational reason for using the nails — to feel the light on them — he must tie it up with divination. He begins by admitting that there is divination involved in the use of the nails but maintains that it is a good sort of divination since it has a scriptural and aggadic basis. Having admitted this he goes on to point out that there is a good reason for looking at the nails — and this reason could certainly commend itself to anyone. But he again lapses into the superstitious frame of mind when he makes the statement, one half of which contradicts the other, that, since we have a Mishnaic warrant for the custom, the divination is acceptable because it is a ניחוש של מצוה, divination of *mizwah*. Hardly any phrase could so outspokenly blend two contradictory words, ניחוש the lower, the superstitious and מצוה the higher, the rational. And that the phrase is coined by one person shows how easy it is for one person consciously to carry out an act and be aware of the operation of a higher and a lower motive. That he gives the reply he does when he knows a good reason for the custom — regardless of whether that is the true reason or not — shows how deeply rooted the habit is in the lives of the people who practice it. Even though others may have laughed at it they still practice it.

Now we can see more clearly why many of those who use

Hillel (d. 1298) in his comment at the beginning of Yoma adds ואף כי זוכרים על צפרניו של אדם הראשון. For the legends about Adam see Ber. 52b; Pes. 53b; Gen. r. XII, 6; Pirke de Rabbi Eli'ezer ch. 20.

[41] See Ben Jehudah's *Thesaurus* I, 475a.

[42] In the version given in *Ginze Nistarot, l. c.*, the latter part of the responsum, from ומאחר to מצוה, is omitted. Apparently for one editor or copyist the contradiction here was too glaring.

the palm do not use the nails. The former merely involves looking for a favorable omen; the latter involves divination. And for some reason, which is far from clear, the latter was to them more objectionable than the former.[43]

Although the compilations Sefer Hapardes, Sefer Ha'orah, and Siddur Rashi are not by Rashi himself (d. 1105) but by his disciples or school, we can get an idea of his attitude or at least of that of some of his disciples from these compilations. The responsum of Naṭronai appears in one place in the Pardes with a few changes.[44] Naṭronai and the two yeshibas are not mentioned. That is not out of the way for at this late date the responsum probably had a more universal application than it did originally. But in Pardes the quotation does not end as it did originally: מיהו אין רגילין בכך. but מיהו אין רגילין חכמים בכך. This shows that the person who altered the text must have wanted to give the impression that it was common not to use the nails — not just the practice of the ḥakamim not to do so, as appears from the original.

The responsum is again quoted in Pardes[45] and this time Naṭronai is mentioned. But there are several significant additions and changes. וכך מנהג of the original has been changed to וכך מנהגי and with good reason. For in the original no procedure for using the palm was described and וכך מנהג referred to the preceding. But here וכך מנהגי shows that the author is giving his own procedure and the phrase refers to the following: תחלה כופף אצבעותיו לתוך כפו ומחשיך תחתיהן ואח"כ פושטן והנה אור במקום חשך ומברך שכבר נאות מן האור. "At first one bends his fingers into

---

[43] The Rabbis seem to have had less objection to reading omens than to practising divination. See Ḥul. 95b: אף על פי שאין נחש יש סימן. Dr. Lauterbach suggests that this is because reading omens is merely interpreting signs which may be given by God, while in practising divination one attempts to get information — from God or other powers — which involves a belief in or a recognition of the other powers.

[44] Sefer Hapardes, ed. Ehrenreich (Budapest, 1924), p. 30; ed. of Warsaw (1870), p. 49a; Likkuṭe Hapardes (Amsterdam 1715), p. 11b–12a.

[45] Ed. Ehrenreich, p. 26; ed. Warsaw, p. 24a; Siddur Rashi (ed. Buber and Freimann, Berlin 1911), p. 262 f.; Maḥzor Vitry (ed. Hurwitz, Berlin, 1889), p. 117 gives as the reason להבחין בינם לבשר. Cf. Šibbole Haleḳeṭ (ed. Buber, Vilna 1886), p. 104.

his palm and makes it dark under them. And then he stretches them out — and behold it is light where it was dark — and makes the blessing, for he has already benefited from the light." To Naṭronai's quotation from or reference to Pirḳe de Rabbi Eli'ezer there is added לפי שהן לבנים ובהם נהנה האור בראותם which appears to be the author's own reason for the practice found in Pirḳe de Rabbi Eli'ezer. But what is more significant is that for the original conclusion מיהו אין רגילין חכמים בכך, which gives the impression that people other than the ḥakamim did look at their nails, he substitutes the quotation ומשום הכי . . . שפיר דמי from Halakot Gedolot, which does not mention nails at all (see p. 351). Thus he as much as says that, though Pirḳe de Rabbi Eli'ezer thought that the proper way to enjoy the light is to look at the nails, he thinks that the proper way is to stretch out the hand or to look at something. Now the reason for the insertion of תחלה . . . מן האור seems clearer. It is to show that the proper procedure is to darken the palm and then let the light shine there — not to look at the nails.[46]

On the other hand Abraham ibn Yarḥi (c. 1150) in his *Hamanhig*[47] treats the same responsum of Naṭronai differently. He, too, changes the last phrase מיהו אין רגילין חכמים בכך but he changes it to אך רגילין ככך וכך. This shows that, in his day and place, both practices, that of looking at the palm and at the nails, were in vogue. It is true that he does not say definitely whether he favors the use of the nails or not. But, whereas the original מיהו אין רגילין חכמים בכך does contradict the statement of Pirḳe de Rabbi Eli'ezer, Yarḥi's phrase אך רגילין ככך וכך does not.[48] So it becomes clear that ibn Yarḥi substituted for the

---

[46] But in *Sefer Ha'orah* (ed. Buber, Lemberg 1905), p. 57 f. we find: ומשום הכי פשטינן ידים לאור הנר למיחזי אי איכא נהורא שמצוה להסתכל בצפרנים להשכים ולהבחין בין צפורן לבשר והאורה נראית בהם קודם ומברך. This is quite different in spirit from what we have been led to believe about the attitude of Rashi and his disciples. Still it is most likely that the former material gives the truer picture. It is likely that to look at the nails is a Palestinian practice, while not to is Babylonian. Rashi most naturally would follow the latter. Cf. his comment to Ta'an. 10a bot., on תתאי לא בעו מים end: שכל מנהגינו אחר בני בבל.

[47] Ed. Goldberg (Berlin 1855), p. 34 top.

[48] Of course he may just be saying that in spite of the insistence of Pirḳe de Rabbi Eli'ezer on the use of the nails it still is a good custom to use the palm.

original phrase, which was opposed to the practice, his own phrase which is not. We may therefore gather that he is in favor of the practice.

Quite different in spirit from the previous explanations is the one of Meir of Rothenburg (c. 1215–1293) who says:[49] מה שפושטין האצבעות בברכת מאורי האש כלומר כשהוא כופה אצבעותיו על פס ידו אז אין האור שולט בכף ידו וכשהוא פושטן אז האור שלט בכפו ונאות. טעם אחר בתחילה כופה אצבעותיו כלומר עד עתה הייתי כאילו ידיי אסורות שהייתי אסור בעשיית מלאכה ואחרי כן פושטן כלומר מעתה ידיי מותרות במלאכה. "The reason one spreads his fingers out at the blessing over the lights of the fire is this: When he bends his fingers over the palm of his hand the light has no effect over them. When he stretches them out it does and thus he benefits. Another reason: At first he bends his fingers as though to say 'Up to now it was as though my hands were bound for I was restrained from doing work.' And after that he stretches them out as though to say 'from now on my hands are permitted to work'."[50]

The first explanation for stretching out the fingers is practically what we found in Pardes.[51] But the second is a highly rationalized and enlightened one and is far removed from the original crass explanation which took it to be for the purpose of looking for a favorable omen. And it is no wonder that with such an enlightened attitude there is no reference at all to the use of the nails, which is considered the worse of the two superstitions.[52]

Isaac of Vienna (c. 1200–1270) makes the following statement in his 'Or Zarua':[53] הלכה למעשה שאין מברכין על האור עד שיהנה מאורו ולכך נוהגים להסתכל בצפרנים לאחר שבירך על הבשמים כופף אצבעותיו לתוך פיסת ידו ומסתכל על הצפרנים עד שיבחין בין שחור שבצפורן ובין לבן שבו ומברך בורא מאורי האש. "The procedure to be carried out is not to say the blessing over the light until one has benefited

---

[49] שאלות ותשובות מהר״ם, Prag 1608, section תקל״ח. Reprinted with but a few slight verbal changes, Budapest 1895.

[50] The pun on אסר literally "to tie, bind," then "forbid" and התיר "to stretch out, untie, release," then "permit," cannot be rendered in English.

[51] See p. 357.

[52] See p. 357, note 43.

[53] Edition of Zhitomir (1862) II, p. 48b.

from it and for this reason is it the custom to look at the nails. After one has made the blessing over the spices he bends his fingers into the hollow of his hand and looks at the nails until he can distinguish between the black in the nail and the white in it and he then says the blessing 'who createst the lights of fire'. "

With Isaac, looking at the nails in order to benefit from the light has replaced looking at the palm which first appeared in Naṭronai's responsum.[54] Apparently the odium attached to the nails has disappeared with him. The second part of his statement is much in the manner of that of Pardes,[55] but with this important difference. Pardes seems to avoid saying that one bends the fingers in order to look at the nails — which is, of course, a most convenient method. Isaac states that one bends the fingers, not, as Pardes takes it, in order to produce a shadow which is then lighted up, but in order to tell the difference between the black and the white of the nail.[56] It seems that to him the superstition of looking for a favorable omen in the lines of the palm is worse than what might possibly be connected with the nails, particularly since he has a rational reason for looking at the nails. Further, in his procedure, since he does not mention stretching the fingers, the lines of the palm are covered and no light gets at them so that they could be used for any sort of augury.

Asher ben Jeḥiel (c. 1250–1328) unlike his teacher Meir of Rothenburg does mention the nails. Discussing Ulla's comment on Mishnah Berakot VIII, 6,[57] which runs כדי שיכיר בין מלוזמא של טבריא ומלוזמא של צפורי "light enough to tell the difference between a meluzma[58] of Tiberias and a meluzma of Sepphoris"

[54] See p. 350.

[55] See p. 357.

[56] Just what he means by the black on the nail is not clear. He may mean the dirty parts of the nail, or he may be trying to differentiate between the white spots on the nails and the parts that are not white.

[57] Berakot 53b.

[58] מלוזמא seems to mean coin. See Kraus, *Griechische und Lateinische Lehnwörter* etc. (Berlin 1898–1899), vol. II, p. 339b. He compares it with νόμισμα and translates it "Gepräge, Münze [?]." See note 60.

he says the following:[59] לכך נהגו להסתכל בצפרנים בשעה שמברכין
על הנר להראות שיוכל ליהנות ממנו ולהכיר בין מטבע למטבע כמו שמכיר
בין צפורן לבשר. "For this reason do people observe the custom of
looking at the nails at the time they make the blessing over
the light: to show that one could benefit from the light and
could tell the difference between one coin and another just
as one tells the difference between nail and flesh."

Apparently what is at the bottom of Asher's statement is
the belief that looking at the light in the nails replaces the
practice of looking to tell the difference between two coins.[60]

Asher's son Jacob (died before 1340) has little to add to
what his predecessors had to say. His material was obtained
from Pirḳe de Rabbi Eli'ezer, Naṭronai, Hai, and his father.
But he accepts looking at the nails as the common custom for
he says simply ונהגין להסתכל בצפרנים.[61]

It seems to have remained for David Abudarham (middle of
14th century), who may have been a pupil of Asher's son Jacob,
to give an explanation which combines the use of nails and the
palm. In commenting on Ber. 53b, as did Asher, he says:[62]
פירוש בין מטבע של טבריא שהיה מפותח ובין מטבע של צפורי שהי' חלק
בלא פתוח ולכך נהגו להסתכל בצפרנים ואח"כ בכף בשעה שמברכין על האור
להראות שיוכל ליהנות ממנו ולהכיר בין צפורניו שהן כנגד המטבע החלק
ובין כפו שהוא כנגד המטבע שיש בו פתוח. "This means between a coin
of Tiberias which was engraved and between a coin of Sepphoris
which was smooth without any engraving. And for this reason
do they have the custom of looking at the nails and afterwards
at the palm at the time they say the blessing over the light: To
show that one could benefit from it and tell the difference
between his nails which correspond to the smooth coin and

---

[59] Page 70b of the commentaries printed in the back of the Vilna editions
of Babli.

[60] The parallel to Ulla's statement in p. Ber. VIII, 7, 12c reads: אמר רב
חיננא כדי שיהא יודע להבחין בין מטבע למטבע. It seems to me that the one common
element in looking at coins and in looking at the nails is that one is using
shining objects. The practice recommended by Ulla and Ḥinena may go back
to some method of divination in which shining objects are used. See p. 364.

[61] Tur, 'Oraḥ Ḥayyim, 298.

[62] Ed. Warsaw (1877), p. 102.

between his palm which corresponds to the coin that has the engraving on it."

Caro (1488–1575) in his Šulḥan 'Aruk[63] incorporates the use of both the nails and the palm and merely says: נוהגים להסתכל בכפות הידים ובצפרנים. And finally Isserles (c. 1520–1572) in his gloss to Caro's statement adds: ויש לראות בצפרני יד ימין ולאחוז הכוס ביד שמאל ויש לכפוף האצבעות לתוך היד שאז רואה בצפרני' עם הכפות בבת אחת ולא יראה פני האצבעות שבפנים.[63] "One should look at the nails of the right hand and hold the cup in the left. One should curve the fingers into the palm of the hand for then he can see the nails and the palm at one glance. One should not look at the inside of the finger tips."[64] This looks like a compromise in which both the nails and the palm are seen at the same time, while the line in the palm to which there is some objection is covered up.[65]

CONCLUSION

We have traced the history of the custom of looking at one's nails during the habdalah ceremony at the outgoing of the Sabbath through a period lasting many centuries. We have found that the attitudes towards the custom vary all along the scale from opposition to acceptance. From some of our evidence it seems that the more enlightened the teachers were the more opposed they were to it. After the varying attitudes expressed themselves during a long period the custom finally found its way into the Šulḥan 'Aruk and became a fixed part of the habdalah.[66]

We have also found a variety of explanations for the custom — some more enlightened, some less enlightened, some highly rationalized, some starkly crude. It is impossible to decide which

---

[63] 'Oraḥ Ḥayyim 298, 3.

[64] He refers to Zohar (Amsterdam 1805), Berešit vol. I, 20b–21a and Vayakhel, vol. II, 208a–b.

[65] See *Magen Abraham* (Abraham ben Ḥayyim Halevi Gumbiner, 1635–1683) to Šulḥan 'Aruk *ad loc.*

[66] See Kurrein, *Monatsschrift für Geschichte und Wissenschaft des Judentums*, vol. LXX (1926), pp. 46–47.

of the explanations is the more fundamental. But the only one that satisfactorily explains the varying attitudes and the various rationalizations is the one which regards looking at the nails as a means of divination. We know that it has always been common to practice divination by looking at bright and shiny objects.[67] Further we know that the time at the outgoing of the Sabbath has been and still is considered an appropriate time to ask for a favorable and lucky week.[68] It is therefore not at all out of place for people to practice some form of divination at the outgoing of the Sabbath.

Who were the objects of this divination? What power or powers was it aimed to effect?

We have very few clues, but what little evidence[69] there is points to only one answer.

A Baraita found in Sanhedrin 101a reads: שרי שמן ושרי ביצים מותרין לשאול בהן אלא מפני שמכזבין. "One may consult spirits[70] of oil and eggs because they are unreliable."[71] Rashi commenting on שרי שמן says שרי שמן וקרי להן שרי שמן על ידי ששואלין שדים מעשה יש

---

[67] See Ezek. 21.26: כי עמד מלך בבל אל אם הדרך בראש שני הדרכים לקסם קסם קלקל בחצים שאל בתרפים ראה בכבד. See the modern commentaries ad loc. One should note that it is the king of Babylon who is represented here as resorting to divination. See p. 351 and notes 36 and 46.

[68] See, for example, סדור שפה ברורה (Rödelheim 1835), 150b–151a; סדר תפלות לכל השנה (Amsterdam 1852), 135a–137a; סדר תפלות ישראל (Krotoschin 1853), 248–250; סדר עבודת ישראל ed. S. Baer (Rödelheim 1868), 103b ff.

[69] This material is all given by Daiches in his very stimulating and interesting monograph *Babylonian Oil Magic in the Talmud and in the later Jewish Literature* (Jews' College Publications, No. 5, London 1913), pp. 7, 9, 14, 28–31, 35. He thinks that nail magic may be at the bottom of the custom of looking at the nails (p. 31, note 1).

[70] The correct reading may be שידי demons. See Rabbinowitz, *Dikduke Soferim* to Sanhedrin, p. 306.

[71] The translation does not represent the text quoted. אלא מפני שמכזבין cannot be translated and must be a conflate reading arising from מפני שמכזבין and אלא שמכזבין; so Rabbinowitz, *l. c.*, note 9. The first reading implies that there is no harm in consulting these spirits because they do not tell the truth anyhow. Hence the author of such a reading is more enlightened and does not take divination seriously. The second reading implies that it is not wrong to practice divination but that one should be careful because of the possibility of being misled. Hence its author takes divination more seriously. Contrast Daiches, *op. cit.*

והיינו שרי בוהן. "There is a practice involving demons in which they are consulted through oil, and they are called spirits of oil — that is, spirits of the thumb."[72] Rashi again mentions the spirits of the thumb in a comment on a statement of Abaye in Sanhedrin 67b: דקפיד אמנא שד "he who is particular about the instrument he uses is a demon:" שאינו יכול לעשות דבר בלא כלי הראוי לאותו דבר כגון שרי בוהן שצריכין סכין שקתו שחור ושרי כוס שצריכין כוס של זכוכית "he who cannot do anything without the instrument needed for that thing — for example spirits of the thumb who require a knife with a black handle, and spirits of the cup who require a glass cup."

David Ḳimḥi (1160—c. 1235) commenting on Ezek. 21.26 where divination is described has the following: וכל זה ממעשה הקסם ופירוש קלקל כמו והוא לא פנים קלקל והוא שמחדדין וממלטשין פני ברזל החץ עד שיהיה בהיר מאד וְרואין בו בעלי הקסם כמו שרואים בבוהן היד בצפורן לבהירות הציפורן וכן רואים בסיף וכן במראה וכן רואים בכבד שיש לו בהירות. "All this is part of the work of divination — kilkel here meaning the same as it does in Eccl. 10.10 'and he does not sharpen the edge' — and what they do is to sharpen and polish the iron surface of the tip of the arrow until it gets very bright. Diviners look into it just as they look at the thumb of the hand for the sake of the nail, because of the nail's brightness. They also look the same way at a sword, a mirror, and the liver too because it has a shining surface."

One of the late medieval texts published by Daiches is intended for the שרי בהן. In this text the instructions for the diviner are ויסתכל הנער הטב בצפורנו "let the lad look well at his nail." The formula the lad recites is משביע אני עליכם שרי צפורן "I adjure you, spirits of the nail." And these spirits are instructed שתביאו המלך ממון בצפורן זה "You bring your king Mimon in this nail."[73]

---

[72] See p. 349, note 15.

[73] Daiches also gives several texts addressed to שרי כף spirits of the palm (pp. 16, 18, 19, 22) and one addressed to שרי כוס, spirits of the cup. This suggests to me that divination originally was the chief object of most of the methods of performing the habdalah ceremonies as they are first listed in Pirḳe de Rabbi Eli'ezer (see p. 348): One used the palm or hand in order to divine by the spirits of the palm and hand; the cup in order to divine by the

In all this evidence the nails are connected with other bright and shiny objects and the spirits of nails are connected with the spirits of other shiny objects.

Is it then unwarranted to assume that the divination practiced at the outgoing of the Sabbath by looking at one's nails was intended for the spirits of the nails?

spirits of the cup, and nails in order to divine by the spirits of the nails. It is even possible that the wine which is used served to enable one to get a reflection of the light in it and divine that way. Perhaps the wine replaced oil which was more original but also more objectionable because of its widespread use in Babylonia. See Daiches, passim. These are of course only suggestions which need much more investigation.

There are a few passages in the Talmuds which make it appear that the people and authorities had some notions about the looking at shining objects at the outgoing of the Sabbath for the purpose of divination. Those referring to the use of coins (see p. 361) may suggest this. So does Johanan's statement כדי שיהא עינו רואה מה בכוס ומה בקערה (p. Ber. VIII, 7, 12c).

Furthermore it looks as though the observance of the custom of looking at the nails was more in vogue in Palestine than in Babylonia (see p. 348). But that may indicate that the custom was really indigenous to Babylonia (see Daiches, p. 31) and was more widespread there and for that reason had to be opposed all the harder by the teachers. While in Palestine, where it was not indigenous, such opposition was not necessary.

HANUKKAH

OLD HANUKKAH LAMPS

A *Propos* a New Acquisition of the Jewish Museum in Cincinnati

FRANZ LANDSBERGER

Hebrew Union College-Jewish Institute of Religion, Cincinnati

IN THE spring of 1953 our Jewish Museum acquired a silver candelabrum of the kind used for Hanukkah (Illust. 1). By reason of its charm and uniqueness, this candelabrum invites special study.[1]

Two bowls, joined to one another within a latticed framework, rest upon eight lion-bodies — tiny ones. Between these bowls there ascends a hill, alive with creatures of many kinds — two hares, a mother dog with her pups, a roebuck, a diminutive squirrel, a worm, a caterpillar. Some of these creatures are fully formed, and some stand in relief. These animals exhibit varying scales of size; the hare, for example, shows bigger than the roebuck. Out of the hill there rises an oak. Up the trunk of this oak there climbs a bear lured by a honey-comb in front of which buzzes a bee (Illust. 2). Before the bear grasps the luscious honey, he will probably fall victim to a hunter who, kneeling behind the tree, already points his gun from his shoulder (Illust. 3).

At a certain height, boughs project from the tree to the right

---

[1] The candelabrum, acquired through the firm of S. S. Rosenberg, New York, is 23 inches high and 26 ¾ inches wide. It was obtained from the estate of the well known art collector, the late Dr. Fritz Mannheimer, in Amsterdam. When I examined the object, it was my privilege to consult a silver expert no less eminent than Dr. Guido Schoenberger of the Jewish Museum connected with the Jewish Theological Seminary of New York. For help in translating Hebrew texts, my warm thanks are due to Dr. Abraham Cronbach and to Rabbi Jacob Petuchowski. I was aided also by Rabbi Theodore Wiener of the staff of the Hebrew Union College Library. Last but not least, for his efforts in promoting the acquisition of this candelabrum, I am indebted to President Nelson Glueck of the Hebrew Union College-Jewish Institute of Religion.

Reprinted from *Hebrew Union College Annual*, Vol. XXV, 1954.

and to the left — not with any strict symmetry but with nature's own irregularity. These boughs, in their farthest branchings, form leaf-shaped holders of tapers. The trunk, continuing upward beyond the branches, carries at its top the "servant-light" which, according to ancient usage, must occupy a place more elevated than that of the other lights.[2] And, in the foliage near the apex of the trunk, one sees a clambering boy (Illust. 4). The diversity of these animal, plant, and human motifs, in all their distinctiveness, is further enhanced in that the silver, at a number of points, is surfaced with gold which, when the tapers are alight, intensifies the candelabrum's luster.

When and where did our candelabrum originate? The candelabrum carries no master-mark and no hall-mark disclosing the silversmith's name or his place of abode. Still, we detect, at various points, marks of two kinds. One of them, here copied, is a permit — the letters FR stand for "frei" (free) — such as the

Stamp required
by the Austro-
Hungarian-Government
for silver objects
in the years 1809/1810.
Enlarged.

Austro-Hungarian government required for silver-made objects in the year 1809–10.[3] The second mark contains the cipher 12 which is the weightmark of the metal, and the letter D. Both form the assay stamp which, in 1806–7, the city of Lemberg ordained for articles of silver produced or brought within its jurisdiction.[4] Accordingly our candelabrum must have been

[2] Cf., for example, the Isserles commentary to the Shulḥan Aruk, Oraḥ Ḥayyim, 673, 1.

[3] Cf. M. Rosenberg, *Der Goldschmiede Merkzeichen*, third edition, IV, Berlin, 1928, No. 7884.

[4] Rosenberg, *op. cit.*, No. 7989.

extant in Austro-Hungary or, more specifically, in the city of Lemberg at the beginning of the nineteenth century. It follows that the dating of our candelabrum must fall not later than 1806-7.

A more precise dating is indicated by the pattern displayed at the outer extensions of the bowls (Illust. 5). This happens to be rococo — in view of the two marks aforementioned, original rococo and not one of the numerous imitations of rococo that range through the entire nineteenth century. This rococo made its debut in the early part of the eighteenth century and in France. During the subsequent decades, it spread over the entire of Europe until, near the end of the century, it was superseded by the new style, the neo-classic.

As regards the place of its production, the candelabrum could, in view of the numerous mercantile connections of the Jews, have been brought to Lemberg from elsewhere. Such is obviously the opinion of Prof. Otto von Falke, cataloguer of the Mannheimer Collection, who pronounced the candelabrum a piece of workmanship from Germany. The craftsman, in that event, must have been a Christian, because there were at that time in Germany no Jewish goldsmiths of rank.[5] Incompatible with von Falke's assumption is the fact that our candelabrum, as stated above, carries no master-mark and no hall-mark such as would have been imposed by the German guilds for a product of those dimensions.

In Eastern Europe circumstances were different. A number of Jewish goldsmiths lived there in the eighteenth century. These artisans did not sign their productions. Indeed their signing was here and there prohibited — for example, in Moravia and Bohemia under Maria Theresa.[6] The chief center of these gold-smiths in Moravia was Nikolsburg; in Bohemia, Prague. In Poland, their activity appears to have focused in Lemberg where they had founded their own association.[7]

---

[5] Compare my article, "The Jewish Artist Before the Time of Emancipa-tion," *HUCA*, XVI, 1941, p. 398.

[6] Cf. Jacob Bronner, "Die Maehrischen Juden im Goldschmiedehand-werk," *Zeitschrift fuer die Geschichte der Juden in der Tschechoslowakei*, I, 1930-31, pp. 243 ff.

[7] Cf. Albert Wolf, "Etwas ueber Juedische Kunst und Aeltere Juedische

Lemberg held at that time a significant Jewish community of about six thousand persons. Its three synagogues required numerous scrolls which, with their *Rimmonim*, their crowns,[8] their breastplates, and their pointers could keep a number of goldsmiths occupied.

As regards these Torah appurtenances, we have a graphic Hebrew account in the memoirs of Ber of Bolechow (1723–1805), a wealthy, art-loving vintner. Ber narrates:

> In that year — 525 (1765) I ordered from the silversmiths and gold-smiths at Lemberg, who were renowned for their skilful craftsmanship, some sacred ornaments made of pure silver for a Scroll of the Law belonging to R. Ensil Kaz of Tarczal. I ordered a large breastplate for the Scroll made of solid silver, weightmarked 14, beautifully ornamented, well plated with gold and set with precious stones, worth 80 Hungarian gulden; further, two silver rollers [Rimmonim] nicely chased and also plated with gold, valued at 50 ducats; also a silver pointer, very finely worked, worth 12 ducats. Many experts agreed that their like was not to be found throughout all Poland. The aged R. Leibush Malish, a learned and famous Jewish leader, when he saw these ornaments together with the other Elders of the community remarked: "Even in the time of King Solomon, peace be with him, these ornaments would have been fit for the Temple." He was at that time a great expert in all crafts.[9]

The name Ber, borne by the author of those lines, turns up frequently among the Ashkenazic Jews of the eighteenth century. One might surmise that the bear portrayed on our candelabrum alludes to Ber, the name of a patron. Not rarely do Jewish ritual appurtenances as well as Hebrew books of that time carry a representation or a Bible verse intimating the name of the person by whom the object was ordered. So far as the picture of a bear is concerned, we know of another Hanukkah candelabrum, also of silver, dating from the eighteenth century and adorned with a bear and a stag, because the silversmith, who had produced it for his own household, was named Ber and his son Hirsch (stag).

Kuenstler," *Mitteilungen der Gesellschaft fuer Juedische Volkskunde*, Heft IX, 1902, pp. 16 ff. Compare also Mark Vishnitzer's translation of the *Memoirs of Ber of Bolechow*, Oxford, 1922, p. 33.

[8] One of the finest of the 18th century Torah crowns, stamped in Lemberg, is described by Stephen S. Kayser in *HUCA*, XXIII, Part Two, 1950–51, pp. 493 ff.

[9] M. Vishnitzer, *op. cit.*, p. 138.

Albert Wolf, esteemed author of an essay on Jewish art and the older Jewish artists, saw this Ber-Hirsch candelabrum near the end of the nineteenth century,[10] but it has since disappeared. Of course, in this matter, we can hardly get beyond conjecture. Yet sometimes conjectures lead to discoveries.

If we assume the maker of our candelabrum to have been one of the numerous Polish-Jewish goldsmiths, we have to confront this objection: How does the meticulous reproduction of plants, animals, and people comport with the Second Commandment so stringently observed by Poland's orthodox Jewry? And the playfulness of the ornamentation — how does it square with the sternness attending such rigid attachment to the Law? Our reply is that, precisely in Poland and, above all, in Galicia of which Lemberg was the capital, the eighteenth century germinated tendencies toward the enlargement of life beyond the exclusively religious. One hears of a Solomon ben Moses of Chelm (died 1778), later Rabbi in Lemberg, whose studies were not limited to Bible and Talmud; they comprised also philosophy, geometry, and the natural sciences.[11] In the Introduction to his *Merkebet Ha-Mishneh*, begun in 1750, Solomon ben Moses urges the cultivation of those domains on the ground that "the great ones of bygone ages were conversant with those disciplines."[12] We also hear of Israel Zamošč who lived in the eighteenth century (approximately 1700–1772) and was versed in philosophy, mathematics, and astronomy. Moving, in 1742, from Poland to Berlin, Zamošč became the teacher of Moses Mendelssohn. In a letter to Mendelssohn, Lessing praises Zamošč as "one of the first to arouse a love for science in the hearts of Jews."[13] Such an atmosphere would conduce to a more liberal construction of the Second Commandment and, along with that, to greater joy in the world round about.

To this we must add that our candelabrum shows actual

---

[10] Albert Wolf, *op. cit.*, p. 17.

[11] Cf. Jecheskiel Caro, *Geschichte der Juden in Lemberg*, Krakau, 1894, p. 132.

[12] Vol. I, Frankfurt an der Oder, 1750, fol. 3b.

[13] Cf. Jacob S. Raisin, *The Haskalah Movement in Russia*, Philadelphia, 1913, p. 77.

kinship with ceremonial objects produced among the Jews of Poland at that period. The Museum of the Jewish Theological Seminary in New York possesses two *Rimmonim* dating from the middle of the eighteenth century and bearing two Lemberg marks. These were reproduced in the Hebrew Union College Annual of 1950–51 by Stephen S. Kayser. Because of the close resemblance between one of these *Rimmonim* and our candelabrum, I repeat the illustration (Illust. 6). Our candelabrum is suggested so strikingly by the irregular placing of the leaves and the acorns on the silver shaft of the *Rimmon* that I am inclined to ascribe both the *Rimmonim* and the candelabrum to one and the same artist.

Or consider the kinship with our candelabrum displayed by a Polish spicebox (Zagayski collection, New York) though the spicebox carries no mark (Illust. 7). In Germany of the eighteenth century, spiceboxes still retain the tower shape of sixteenth century adoption. The Zagayski spicebox, by contrast, consists of a branch which, emerging from a spirally formed base and bearing numerous leaves placed at irregular intervals, supports a bird whose perforated body constitutes the spice receptacle.[13a]

These examples warrant our saying that, among the Jews of Poland, there arose a trend for embellishing ritual objects with naturalistic forms. Into this trend our newly acquired candelabrum fits. Not only was Lemberg the place of its stamping; but Lemberg or some other Polish city near-by was also, in my opinion, the place of its fashioning, its craftsman having been one of the many Jewish silversmiths probably active in Poland of the eighteenth century.[14]

*

[13a] A similar lamp, formerly in the Jewish Museum of Warsaw, is now preserved in the Bezalel National Museum at Jerusalem.

[14] It should be noted, in this connection, that the above mentioned lions at the base of the candelabrum possess two bodies but one head. In Jewish illuminations, this motif is not without precedent. It appears, for example, in the 13th century German Maḥzor of the Bodleian Library at Oxford. An illustration of the page in question can be found in Rahel Wischnitzer-Bernstein, *Gestalten und Symbole Juedischer Kunst*, Berlin-Schoeneberg, 1935, Illust. 20.

Having thus far elaborated on the progressivism manifest in our candelabrum, let us now, in like manner, show its linkage with the past, a past, as so often in Jewish art, measurable not in centuries but in millenia. A candelabrum shaped like a tree is mentioned in the Bible. Such is the description given for the candelabrum of gold which, in the Tent of Meeting, burnt "from evening to morning before the Lord continually" (Lev. 24.1–3). From a middle shaft, topped by a small lamp, three branches, likewise bearing lamps, bend to the right and three to the left. But this candelabrum of old maintains a rigid symmetry. In keeping with the oriental style of that epoch, its motifs are more conventionalized than the corresponding motifs of our own new acquisition.

Whether any significance attaches to the number seven for those lights, Leviticus does not disclose; yet suppositions on this point started long ago. In his vision of the seven-branched candlestick, Zechariah calls these lamps "the eyes of the Lord, that run to and fro through the whole earth" (4.10). Josephus sees in them the seven planets; and with reference to the seventh among the lamps, he beholds symbolized the majesty of the Sabbath.[15] As regards the almond blossoms in the branches of the candelabrum, a French scholar's explanation seems to me convincing: "L'amandier était le symbole de la vigilance, spécialement de la vigilance divine, par suite d'un jeu de mot sur le nom hébreu shâqêd (Jeremie 1.11, 12), shôqêd (Je veille)."[16] Like the lamps in the temples of the heathen, this candelabrum doubtless served the purpose of protecting the shrine against robbery.

We need not here concern ourselves with the question whether the account of the candelabrum in the Tabernacle reflects anything historical. One thing is certain, namely, that the biblical description exerted a profound influence upon subsequent art. Nor can we determine when that influence began. Important for us right now is the circumstance that, in general outline, the golden candelabrum in the Temple of Herod accords

---

[15] Josephus, *Antiquities of the Jews*, III, 6, 7, and *The Jewish War*, V, 5, 5.
[16] Comte du Mesnil du Buisson, *Les Peintures de la Synagogue de Doura Europos*, Rome, 1939, p. 21.

with the biblical depiction. Direct acquaintance with this candelabrum, we do not, of course, possess. But the arch of Titus in
Rome displays a plastic reproduction. This we show here as it
looks in an old engraving.

RELIEF ON THE ARCH OF TITUS, ROME.
Engraving by Pietro Santo Bartoli (1635–1700).

After the ruin of the Second Temple and the capture of the
candelabrum by the Romans, the Jews clung tenaciously to the
candelabrum's structure. They duplicated it endlessly in lamps,
sarcophagi and the like and later in illuminations and prints.
During the first centuries after the Temple's downfall, seven-
branched candlesticks would be set up in synagogues.[17] But the
Talmud opposed the practice (Rosh Hashanah 24a). To the
Talmud, the Temple and its appurtenances were too sacred for
imitation.

The Jews evidently applied this prohibition not only to the
seven-branched candlestick but to every kind of *Ner Tamid*

[17] Especially well known is the seven-branched candlestick of stone, found
at Hammath near Tiberias and exhibited in 1953 at the exhibition "From the
Land of the Bible" at the Metropolitan Museum, New York. The candelabrum
belongs to the Archaeological Museum of Jerusalem. Its date is taken to be
the third century c. e.

whether it was a small lamp of clay[18] or a lamp hanging from a Holy Ark.[19] In medieval miniatures picturing synagogal interiors, we perceive lamps of various kinds but not one that could be regarded as a perpetual light. Nor do we find mention of such in that era of literature. Not until modern times does the perpetual light again come into use and then, by no means, universally. Thus, in 1683, there is mention of a perpetual light placed before a Torah niche in Italy;[20] but, to this day, the large Jewish community of Baghdad dispenses with the perpetual light in every one of its synagogues.[21]

[18] A pottery lamp, with the inscription נר תמיד was found in Samaria. This has been described by A. Mayer and A. Reifenberg in the *Journal of the Palestine Oriental Society*, XVI, 1936, p. 44 ff. The authors are of the opinion that the inscription is meant as a substitute for a pictorial *Ner Tamid*. It is my belief that, despite its small size, the lamp itself was a *Ner Tamid*.

[19] Such a hanging lamp appears in a panel of the floor mosaic at the synagogue of Beth Alpha (6th century C. E.). The lamp hangs from the top of a chest which has been regarded as a "Holy Ark" (thus recently by E. R. Goodenough in *HUCA*, XXIII, Part Two, 1950–51, p. 453) and also regarded as "The Ark of the Covenant." The latter interpretation, it seems to me, admits of no doubt. The panel is one of numerous representations expressing the hope for a Messiah and for the Messianic restoration of the biblical sanctuaries. An Ark of.the Covenant would be apropos. To a Torah ark there would be no point in a sixth-century synagogue. As the synagogues of that period already possessed such an ark, a pictorial repetition would have been senseless. The birds crouching on top of the chest are the cherubim by which the Ark of the Covenant was surmounted. Already Philo in his *Life of Moses*, III, 8, calls the cherubim πτηνά. This interpretation and none other would render intelligible the two rods — one rod withered, the other flourishing — which made sense neither to Sukenik nor to Goodenough. The withered rod betokens Israel's rebellious clans. The blossoming one is the rod deposited in the Tent of Meeting, the divinely appointed rod of Aaron (Num. 17.1–11). Both of these rods appear frequently in Jewish miniatures of the Middle Ages. If, at Beth Alpha, the Ark of the Covenant resembles a Torah ark, the anachronism is one not unusual in such matters. It is no less anachronistic for the *Ner Tamid* of the Tabernacle to be pictured as a hanging lamp, like those that were, in all likelihood, pendent in synagogues during the first centuries after the destruction of the Temple; until the Talmudic prohibition of the seven-branched candlestick was extended to continuous lights of all kinds. Christianity and Islam, unhampered by this prohibition, introduced the Perpetual Light into their churches and their mosques.

[20] Cf. Giulio Morosini Venetiano, *Via della Fede*, Rome, 1683, p. 245.

[21] Cf. David S. Sassoon, *A History of the Jews in Baghdad*, Letchforth,

A beautiful hanging lamp, originating in Damascus, dated 1694, and preserved in the Jewish Museum of Woburn House, London, though commonly spoken of as a perpetual light, is more likely a lamp such as would shine in any elegant home at the conclusion of the Sabbath. This at least is the import of the words painted in golden letters upon the emerald glass.[22]

Perpetual lights were to be found in Polish synagogues from the sixteenth to the eighteenth centuries. These were placed not in front of the Torah curtain but in a niche of the entrance hall or — if in the auditorium — on a wall.[23] There is obvious reluctance to apply, in the synagogue, the biblical command about placing the *Ner Tamid* "outside the veil of the testimony" (Lev. 24.3); for that command pertains to the Tabernacle.

One can see a hanging lamp embroidered on some curtains from Turkey (Bezalel National Museum, Jerusalem; Smithsonian Institution, Washington, D. C.), substitutes, I presume, for a real *Ner Tamid*. As in the case of the seven-branched candlestick, a picture of the object and nothing more than a picture seems to have been permitted.

*

In Jerusalem, at the time when the seven-branched candlestick disappeared, another sacred light had already gained recognition. This was the lamp of Hanukkah. The precise time of its inception can no longer be fixed. A festival of fire ($\pi\nu\rho\acute{o}s$) is mentioned in II Maccabees 1.18 and a Feast of Lights ($\phi\hat{\omega}\tau a$) in the *Antiquities* of Josephus XII–7–7, but there is no way of inferring whether these expressions refer to lamplight or to flames in the open.

1949, p. 167. The son of the late author apprises me that the conflicting statement on page 101 of this book was due to a mistranslation.

    [22] The verses are: Gen. 27.28, 29; 28.3, 4; 49.25, 26; Deut. 28.12 and 33.29. These are the verses embodied in the concluding portion of the Sabbath prayers. Information was graciously furnished by Mr. Sol Cohen, secretary of the Woburn House Museum in London. An illustration of this lamp, erroneously called *Ner Tamid*, will be found in my *History of Jewish Art*, Cincinnati, 1946, p. 30.

    [23] For more details, see Marvin Lowenthal, *A World Passed By*, New York, 1938, pp. 362, 365, 367.

The Mishnah (Baba Kama VI, 6) mentions, in connection with a case at law, a Hanukkah light placed at the gate of a house. More specific information is vouchsafed by the Talmud (Sabbath 21b) according to which there are three ways in which the Feast of Lights can be celebrated, ways which correspond to ascending grades of piety: 1. One light a day in each household. 2. One light a day for each member of the household. 3. Eight lights for each household or eight lights for each member of the household. The third way involved two possibilities: either, as the School of Hillel teaches, beginning with one light and increasing to eight or, as the School of Shammai teaches, beginning with eight and diminishing to one.

As regards location, this could be the threshold at the house door; or, when the abode was on an upper floor, the lights would stand on a window sill. "But, in times of danger," continues the Talmud, "it is sufficient to place it on the table." It is further noted that all of these lights are holy and may therefore not be used in ordinary illumination. For that purpose, a different light had to be employed.

If we ask how these lamps were shaped, we are again, as so often in Jewish ritual matters, unsupplied with an answer. We must content ourselves with surmises. The supposition is general that, already in antiquity, the Hanukkah lamp contained eight openings and eight wicks.[24] Such lamps in fact existed and, as those lamps were decorated with representations of the Temple or parts of the Temple, they would appear especially suited for a festival commemorating a Temple's purification. But those illustrations also appear on lamps of that epoch even when the openings number four or six or seven (Illust. 8). This inclines me to the view that the lamps with eight orifices, like those with seven or fewer orifices, served a different purpose, namely that of lighting the homes of the living, preferably on Friday evenings, and of accompanying the deceased to their graves. The lamps symbolized the expectation of a Messiah who would rebuild the Temple at Jerusalem and resurrect the dead.

[24] Thus according to Rahel Wischnitzer, "L'Origine de la Lampe de Hanouka," *Revue des Etudes Juives*, LXXXIX, 1930, pp. 135 ff. Also Mordecai Narkiss, *The Hanukkah Lamp* (Hebrew), Jerusalem, 1939.

A lamp with not more than one wick is definitely envisaged by the dictum of the Talmud that, during Hanukkah, a single light day by day suffices for the observance. To increase the number of lights, it was accordingly the practice to set lamp next to lamp or if, following the School of Shammai, eight lamps were used at the beginning, the number would be diminished by the removal of lamp after lamp.

In a later passage (Sabbath 23b), the Talmud speaks of a lamp with two spouts serving two persons. It mentions likewise a dish of oil covered by a vessel, and wicks protruding around and over the brim of the dish. That kind of a lamp could serve a number of persons. Such a lamp represented no augmentation of lights from one to eight. It belonged rather to the provision, already mentioned, of *one* light to be kindled by each member of the household on each of the eight nights of Hanukkah.

With a tenacity characteristic of religious usages, the one-wick lamp persisted for over a thousand years. In a Pentateuch transcribed in Egypt during the year 930 (Leningrad, State Library, MS. II, 17), there is inserted an illustration (reproduced on page 359) upon which M. Narkiss thought he saw a Hanukkah object of metal.[25] He took the bluish streak to be the base of a lamp with eight wicks. The projecting arm he identified with the servant-light. The trefoil at the top was supposedly the loop by which the lamp was hung up.

Looking at these features singly, one feels like concurring. Yet how strange that the beholder perceives none of the eight lights! Our uncertainty increases as we view the total illustration occupying this page. The subjects are the appurtenances of the Tabernacle and the Temple, themes frequent in Jewish art. In such illustrations, the Hanukkah lamp never appears. Usually there is pictured a snuff-shovel by which the seven-branched candlestick was serviced (Ex. 25.38). And that is what we must see in the appurtenance exhibited by the Egyptian Pentateuch. Another page of the same manuscript[26] also contains a representa-

---

[25] In the book just mentioned, *The Hanukkah Lamp*, Plate IV, Figure 14. The whole page, reproduced in colors, can be found in D. Gunzburg and V. Stassoff, *L'Ornement Hébraique*, Berlin, 1905, Plate II.

[26] Gunzburg and Stassoff, *op. cit.*, Plate III.

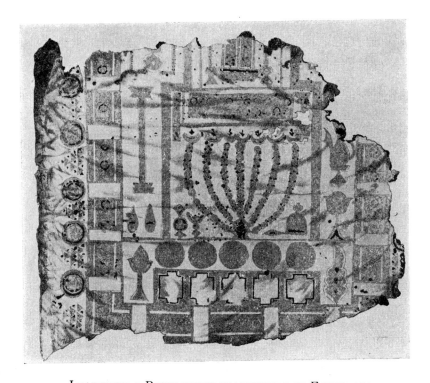

LEAF FROM A PENTATEUCH TRANSCRIBED IN EGYPT, 930,
PRESENT ERA.
State Library II, 17, Leningrad.
Note the small snuff-shovel pictured upside down near the
bottom of the seven-branched candelabrum, toward the right.

tion of sacred implements. And here there can be no mistake.
A lamp is out of the question. The snuff-shovel is too obvious.
Narkiss was evidently misled by the fact that, on the page which
he adduces, the snuff-shovel is pictured upside down, the
draughtsman having placed it thus in order to utilize a maximum
of free space. The arm which Narkiss regarded as the holder of
the servant-light is the snuff-shovel's handle. The blue slit is the
snuff-shovel's opening. The trefoil and the perforations of the
semicircular scoop are, in keeping with the abstract style of that
epoch, nothing but ornamental accessories. The snuff-shovel on
the second of the pages likewise shows perforations. All that is

necessary is to place the two snuff-shovels, as we have done here, alongside of one another. Then we will at once recognize their kinship.

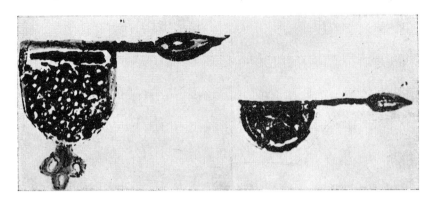

LEFT, THE ABOVE-MENTIONED SNUFF-SHOVEL. RIGHT, THE SNUFF-SHOVEL FROM ANOTHER LEAF OF THE PENTATEUCH IN THE LENINGRAD STATE LIBRARY.

In rejecting the contentions of Narkiss, we also reject the notion that there existed, as early as the tenth century, metallic holders which brought all of the Hanukkah lights together in one appliance. To the contrary, the one-wick lamp of clay continued in use a few hundred years longer. As late as the twelfth century, Maimonides repeats the Talmudic affirmation that, during Hanukkah, it suffices to burn either one light a day in behalf of the entire household or one light a day in behalf of each individual.[27] He repeats also the Talmudic: "A lamp with two wicks will do for two persons." This clearly indicates that the lamp with not more than one wick was still the rule and the lamp with two wicks the exception.

Regarding two important changes in Hanukkah lamps, we can prove that they were instituted not before the thirteenth century. The first change was that of the material. According to Rabbi Jacob ben Asher,[28] Rabbi Meir of Rothenburg (ca. 1220–1293) "would kindle the Hanukkah light not in a lamp of clay

[27] Mishneh Torah, Hilkhot Megillah we-Hanukkah, Chapter IV, §§ 1–4.
[28] Cf. Arba' Ṭurim, Ṭur Oraḥ Ḥayyim, end of § 673.

but in a metallic lamp." The obvious reason was that the lamp of clay was easily damaged; a new lamp, in consequence, being of frequent need.

The second alteration pertained to the structure. People began to assemble all of the lights into one form. Did the ancient lamp of several wicks perhaps serve as a model? The answer, I think, is "Yes." Inasmuch as lamps of several wicks existed far and wide in the Greco-Roman world, such must have been extant in France, in Italy, and in Western Germany, and these are the countries indicated by the oldest lamps of bronze thus far brought to notice. Their style indicates the period from the thirteenth to the fifteenth century. Particularly informative is a lamp (Illust. 9) found in the old ghetto of Lyons and preserved at present in the Musée Cluny of Paris. This lamp must have been finished not later than 1394, that being the year of the Jewish expulsion. This lamp, like the ancient clay lamps of seven openings (Illust. 8) starts with oil containers and wicks. Then come the arches reminiscent of the ancient Temple; but, in the lamp from Lyons, these are cut out from the backpiece. What, in the ancient lamps, were circular holes serving as apertures through which to pour oil, have now become purely decorative rosettes.[29] The handle used of old for placing the lamp at the door has metamorphosed into a punch-hole for hanging up, because the lamp of bronze was hung on the door-post opposite the one with the *Mezuzah*. The backpiece would be put against the jamb so that the flames would not set it afire.

This new type of assembled Hanukkah lamp, with high backpiece, spread through all countries. Without any change of its basic form, it acquired ever varying ornamentation throughout the following centuries down to our own time. To trace these alterations is not our purpose; Narkiss has done this amply. We dwell upon one single lamp which was found in Florence and is now preserved in the Jewish Museum of Cincinnati (Illust. 10). Compared with the lamp unearthed in France, the bench-form lamp from Florence has a broader bottom, indeed so much

[29] In a lamp of the Irving Lehman Collection, next door to Temple Emanu-El, New York (formerly in the Figdor Collection, Vienna), the circle is occupied by a phoenix in relief. The phoenix was a symbol of flame.

broader that the lamp can be plâced on a table. An illumination originally directed to the outdoors tends to be transmuted now into something festive for the indoors. The strikingly tall backpiece of this lamp is covered with a mirror on which symbols, carved out of iron, are set in various colors. The fountain, supported by winged steeds, is genuinely Italian in its style. Needless to say, this represents the Fountain of Life.[29a] The paradisial birds drinking out of the basin are perhaps cherubim; because of the disinclination to picture the supernal, the cherubim are often changed into fowl.[30] The spiral columns refer to the Temple whose reconsecration on this date is the occasion for the feast. Finally, in a semicircle between two vases, there appear the two Tablets of the Law over which two unabashedly naked children hold a crown, the crown of the Torah. The date of this lamp is approximately the same as that of our recent acquisition.[31]

*

The tree-shaped structure of our recent acquisition proves already that the above-mentioned Florentine lamp, benchshaped and with a high backpiece, was not a solitary type. But, before we return to our acquisition, we have to mention another kind of Hanukkah lamp, a kind, to be sure, that is rarely seen.

It pertains to the lamp, above mentioned, in which the lights are arranged not in a straight line but in a circle. Israel Isserlein, a German Talmudic authority of the fifteenth century, raises no objection to using a lamp of that type. Isserlein refers, in that connection, to the Sabbath lamp which was similarly circular and which, he says, could be found in any of the better homes.[32]

[29a] Probably an allusion to Ps. 36.16 "For with Thee is the fountain of life; in Thy light do we see light."

[30] According to the prohibition in the Mekilta of Rabbi Ishmael, Tractate *Baḥodesh*, X. ed. Jacob Z. Lauterbach, II, Philadelphia, 1933, p. 276. In his article, "Die Menorah des Chanukkahfestes," *Beitraege zur Juedischen Kulturgeschichte*, Frankfurt am Main, 1924, Heft 1, p. 10, Erich Toeplitz, mentioning this lamp, regards the birds as dragons. He sees in them a symbolization of the church to whose hostility the Jews of Italy were exposed longer than were the Jews of other lands. The hypothesis is an improbable one.

[31] The oil containers of this lamp are a later addition, the original ones having been lost.

[32] Cf. his Terumath Ha-Deshen, ed. Venice, 1546, fol. 48a.

Judging from ancient samples, that kind of a Hanukkah lamp rested originally on a base or a stand. But it developed into a hanging lamp. And that gave it even more of a resemblance to the Sabbath lamp pendent from the ceiling already in medieval times.

Only of late has a picture of such a hanging lamp been published (Illust. 11). Formerly belonging to a Swedish synagogue, it is now the possession of a collector in England. Eight arms project from a central spindle. The sockets upon these arms are for tapers. There are two indications that this lamp is not a Sabbath lamp: 1. On top, alongside of an oval cage with a bird, it holds a small socket for a servant-light. 2. The counterweight at the lower end of the lamp carries the inscription: "We kindle these lights on account of the miracles, the deliverances and the wonders which Thou didst work with our fathers, by means of Thy holy priests," words spoken immediately after the Hanukkah lights have been kindled.

An approximate date for this lamp ensues from the fact that Jews began to settle in Sweden not before the end of the eighteenth century. Likewise in accord with that period would be the graceful style recalling that of our own acquisition.

That, among the Jews, the Sephardim also resorted to hanging lamps for Hanukkah is evident by the words of Elijahu Guedj who, in his *Zeh Hashulḥan* (1888–1889) reports concerning practices in the city of Algiers: "It is a practice to have hanging in the synagogue a circular Menorah of eight lights. Each evening of Hanukkah, as soon as Psalm 30 is reached in the service, all eight lights are kindled" (Part II, p. 82).

*

This brings us at last to a third type, the type exemplified by our own recently acquired candelabrum. We must observe that, while the Hanukkah light began as a ritual for the home, it did not restrict itself to the home. It also entered the synagogue. When this may have occurred we can no longer determine; at any rate the early part of the 13th century knows the custom. Evidence for this is the statement by Abraham ben Nathan Hajarchi of Lunel: "It seems to me that there exists no obligation to kindle the Hanukkah lights in the synagogue. The obligation pertains only to the home; the dictum being 'The *Mezuzah* at the right side of the doorway, the Hanukkah light at the left.' But, for a synagogue, no *Mezuzah* is required except — as stated in Yoma 11a — when the synagogue contains the dwelling of the overseer. And yet the custom prevails. Since the miracle happened in the Sanctuary Everlasting, Hanukkah lights are kindled in the minor sanctuaries of the Exile so that, in the place where all assemble, the miracle might be proclaimed.''[33]

The place within the synagogue where the Hanukkah light is to stand is specified as follows: "A Hanukkah light, kindled in the synagogue, stands toward the South, thus commemorating the candelabrum of old which had its location toward the South." The passage comes from the *Minhagim* of Isaac Tyrnau (14th and 15th centuries).[34]

That statement makes clear what was intended by displaying the Hanukkah lamp in the house of worship. The lamp was to surrogate for the seven-branched candlestick over the loss of which the Jews ever grieved. While the precise imitation of the seven-branched candlestick was forbidden by the Talmud, nothing in the Talmud forbade making "one with lamps numbering five or six or eight" (Rosh Hashanah 24a). This was virtually an incentive to place in the synagogue a reminder of the seven-branched candlestick, provided there was no copying of that object or no substitute in the form of a *Ner Tamid*. The Hanukkah lamp became the choice for that purpose.

Still, we must not assume the appearance of the multiple holder in the synagogue to have occurred earlier than that of the multiple holder in the home, that is to say, not earlier than the thirteenth century. The synagogal illumination of earlier mention must have consisted, on Hanukkah, in an array of separate lights. As regards the multiple form, I presume that, at the outset, the synagogal lamp resembled the home lamp more closely than it did later when its type became influenced by the description of the seven-branched candelabrum in the Bible and by the relief on the arch of Titus. As proof of this I reproduce a candelabrum

[33] Ed. Goldberg, Berlin, 1855, fol. 106a.
[34] Ed. Lunéville, 1806, fol. 52b.

1. HANUKKAH CANDELABRUM.
Silver, Poland, Eighteenth Century.

New Acquisition of the Jewish Museum
at the Hebrew Union College Campus, Cincinnati.

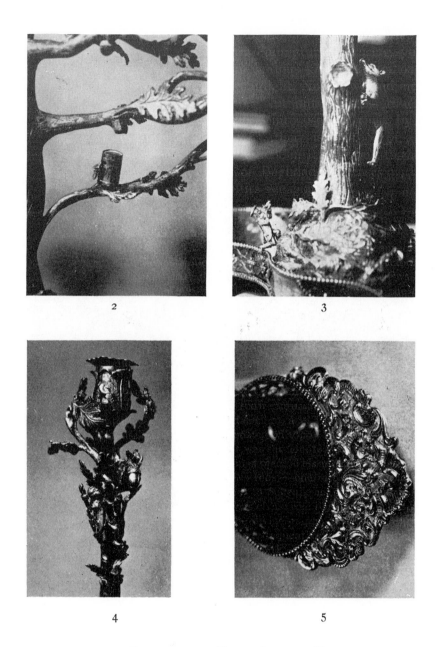

2   3

4   5

2. 3. 4. 5. DETAILS OF THE NEWLY ACQUIRED HANUKKAH
CANDELABRUM.

7. SPICEBOX.
Silver, Poland,
Eighteenth Century.
Zagayski Collection,
New York.

6. *Rimmon.*
Poland, Second Half of the
Eighteenth Century.
Harry G. Friedman Collection,
The Jewish Museum, New York.

9. Hanukkah Lamp.
Found in the Jewish Quarter of Lyons, France.
Bronze, Thirteenth-Fourteenth Century.
Musée Cluny, Paris.

8. Clay Lamp for Seven Wicks.
First Centuries of the Present Era.
The Jewish Museum, New York.

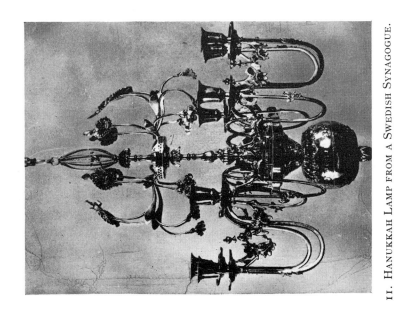

11. HANUKKAH LAMP FROM A SWEDISH SYNAGOGUE.
Silver, Eighteenth Century.
C. Oppenheimer Collection, London.
By Courtesy of the *London Jewish Chronicle*.

10. HANUKKAH LAMP.
Italy, Eighteenth Century.
Jewish Museum, Cincinnati.

12. The Rothschild
Prayer Book,
Folio 35b.
Prayer Relating the
Events of Hanukkah.
Italy, Fifteenth Century.

13. Hanukkah Candelabrum.
Bronze, Italy,
Fifteenth Century.
Synagogue of Padua.

14. Hanukkah Candelabrum.
Bronze, Germany, 1705.
Jewish Museum, Cincinnati.

306

pictured in the *Maḥzor Rothschild*, an Italian manuscript of the fifteenth century (Illust. 12). To be seen here, standing on a strip as in the case of the bench-type lamp, are eight tapers over a high pedestal. But the servant-light is lacking.

Yet the same century, also in Italy, — this time at a synagogue of Padua — brought into vogue the candelabrum (Illust. 13). The servant-light, now present, tops the central shaft. Adorned with delicate tendrils, four arms project to the right and to the left. The middle taper, as was the custom, stands highest and the other tapers descend gradually at the sides.

This type may have made its way from Italy to Germany[35] and thence to Eastern Europe. It is of interest that, placed there in 1689, such a lamp stood in the Nachmanides Synagogue of Lemberg, the city in which our own new acquisition received its stamp. As compared with the model at Padua, the later candelabra follow more closely the Temple counterpart. The servant-light no longer rises above the others; the same height is reached by all nine flames.

German synagogues possessed a number of such large candelabra from the seventeenth and eighteenth centuries down to the time of the Nazi régime when many of them were destroyed. Fortunately, before the onset of those dreadful years, such a lamp, fashioned in bronze, arrived at the Cincinnati Jewish Museum (Illust. 14). According to the inscription, it stood in the synagogue of Aschenburg, more correctly Aschaffenburg, presented to the congregation in 1705, only a few years after 1698 when the edifice was erected.[36] A striking feature of this candelabrum consists in the hands which, emerging from the central shaft, grasp the branches extending at either side. To understand this motif, we must recall that, in ancient days, during the Hanukkah season, people went through the streets bearing

---

[35] A tradition going back to 1458 maintains that there was a Hanukkah lamp of bronze in the synagogue at Hildesheim, Germany. The only information we possess about the structure of this lamp is that its supports were shaped like the feet of a lion. Cf. R. Hallo, *Religioese Kunst aus Hessen und Nassau,* Marburg, 1932, p. 35, on No. 107.

[36] The name of a certain Pessele is given as that of the donor, dedicating the candelabrum to the memory of her husband, Elkanah.

"branches and fair boughs and palms also." Such is the account in II Maccabees 10.7. This would justify the conclusion that the maker of this candelabrum must have been a Christian because, while the Books of the Maccabees had been admitted into the canon of the Protestants, they had not been admitted into the canon of the Jews.[37]

While this particular candelabrum, with its brownish color, its proportions and some of its details betrays some heaviness and massiveness like everything in the baroque style dominant at the time, the structure of such candelabra becomes, in the course of the eighteenth century, more slender and elegant. The new rococo style gets to prevail. We discern this change in a Polish candelabrum produced by the Jewish coppersmith, Baruch, in the city of Pohrebyszcze shortly before 1735.[38] We

HANUKKAH CANDELABRUM
FROM THE SYNAGOGUE AT POHREBYSZCZE
Brass, Poland, First Half of the
Eighteenth Century.

[37] The motif of hands with something in their grasp turns up also in the candelabra of Cleve and Goch, Germany. Illustrations will be found in *Aus der Geschichte der Juden im Rheinland*, Duesseldorf, 1931, pp. 1 and 57.

[38] Cf. Mathias Bersohn, "Einiges ueber die alten Holzsynagogen in Polen," *Mitteilungen fuer Juedische Volkskunde*, VIII, 1901, p. 177.

note the delicate reach upward — here is to be seen already the lattice work which marks our own new acquisition — the tendrils borne by lions, and the taper sockets balanced on the heads of tiny birds (see our illustration).

About 1700, the candelabrum type which had developed in the synagogue was, on occasion, transplanted to the home, naturally in smaller dimensions and, as a consequence, of daintier effect; and this is further augmented by the brighter hue emanating from the silver. Hanging a candelabrum of this type on the doorpost or placing it on the window sill was, of course, inconceivable. Its only place could be the table of the house.

To this type belongs the candelabrum in the Musée Cluny of Paris, crowned with the figure of Judah Maccabee;[39] and, in the New York Jewish Museum, the magnificent candelabrum with the figure of Judith, the work of a silversmith in Frankfurt a. M. at the beginning of the seventeen hundreds.[40] Evidently this type of silver candelabrum for the home journeyed from Germany to Eastern Europe, and that includes Poland where our own recently acquired candelabrum was created.

By means of a minor yet not at all inadvertent detail, the artist who made our candelabrum permits a glimmer of its derivation from the light-tree of the Tabernacle and the Temple to shine through. As with the candlestick of seven branches, not more than six branches emerge from the central shaft. Further branchings are needed that these six might carry the eight tapers completing the number nine. In the riches of these ramifications, in the charm of the sockets which sustain the tapers, and in the playful vivification contributed by the animal and the human figures, our new acquisition ranks as a most fascinating specimen of its type.

[39] Illustrated in the catalogue of the Strauss Collection, Poissy, 1878, on No. 5.

[40] Illustration in my *History of Jewish Art*, Cincinnati, 1946, p. 52.

WEDDING

WEDDING CUSTOMS AND CEREMONIES IN ART

JOSEPH GUTMANN

"The voice of mirth and the voice of gladness, the voice of the bride-groom and the voice of the bride" can still be heard echoing faintly through the pages of the Bible.[1] Unfortunately, however, no visual depictions of wedding ceremonies and festivities have come down to us from the biblical period—nor has archaeology thus far uncovered any bridal gifts, such as the "objects of silver and gold and garments," which Eliezer, Abraham's servant, offered Rebekah.[2] And, though the prophet Isaiah mentions the adornments of the bride, he does not elaborate upon them.[3]

The Talmud, for its part, briefly alludes to bridal processions, dances and other wedding celebrations, which were common in Palestine and Babylonia. It describes the bridal pavilion of "crimson silk embroidered with gold," usually set up in the groom's house. This was the bridal chamber (*huppah*) where, with the marriage consummated in strict privacy, the bride passed from her father's to her husband's authority.[4] It dwells on the elaborate gifts (*sivlonot*)— "vessels of silver, gold and silk garments"—which the groom sent his father-in-law.[5] Yet, for all these details, there are no visual records or objects of the ceremonies extant from this period.

The earliest illustration of a wedding appears in a *mahzor*, dated 1272, from the Rhine region of medieval Christian Germany (fig. 24). It is drawn next to the Hebrew word *itti* (with me)—the opening word of the poetical insertion recited on *Shabbat Haggadol* and taken from the Song of Songs 4.8: "Come with me from Lebanon, my bride." The bride mentioned in the Song of Songs was interpreted by tradition as referring to Israel; and her beloved as referring to God: hence, the depiction of this symbolic union of Israel and God through marriage.[6] To the right, the officiant, wearing the *Judenhut*—the typical "Jew's hat" of the Middle Ages—approaches with a cup of

Reprinted from *The Jewish Marriage Anthology* by Philip and Hanna Goodman, published by The Jewish Publication Society of America, Philadelphia, 1965.

wine to recite the blessings, while, to the left, the veiled bride and the groom, wearing his *Judenhut*, stand under what may be either the prescribed *tallit* (prayer shawl) or the prescribed *sudar* (cloth).[7] By this time, it is clear, the *huppah* (bridal chamber) of the talmudic period had come to be interpreted symbolically as a covering (*tallit* or *sudar*) spread over the bride and groom.[8] This depiction, moreover, may already show the medieval custom of combining the *erusin* (betrothal) and *nissuin* (nuptial) ceremonies, which in talmudic times had been two separate ceremonies held a year apart.[9]

Other miniatures accompanying this poem in German *mahzorim* of the thirteenth to fourteenth centuries do not depict an actual wedding, but rather a symbolic one. In a fourteenth-century *mahzor*, the bride, adorned with a crown,[10] is seated on a bench to the right of the groom, wearing a *Judenhut*—a depiction very similar in conception to the well-known Gothic compositional types for the Coronation of the Virgin used on church tympana and in illuminated Christian manuscripts (fig. 23). The resemblance is not difficult to explain, since Christianity reinterpreted the Jewish allegorization of the Song of Songs by substituting Christ for God, the bridegroom, and the Virgin—symbolic of the Church—for Israel, his bride.[11]

A marginal drawing in the so-called Second Nuremberg Haggadah of fifteenth-century Germany depicts a contemporary wedding in progress to illustrate Moses' marriage to Zipporah. The bridal couple stands under the *huppah* (a cloth), and the officiant approaches with a large cup of wine, while a musician, off to the side, provides music for the festive occasion. The bridegroom is about to recite the betrothal formula and place the ring on the outstretched index finger of the bride's right hand.[12] A plain gold ring had come into use during the Middle Ages as a substitute for the coin (*perutah*, the *kesef kiddushin*) of the talmudic period, which had served as a token to seal symbolically the groom's intention to marry the bride[13] (fig. 22).

Hebrew manuscripts of fifteenth-century Italy give us interesting glimpses into Jewish wedding ceremonies during the Renaissance period. An especially beautiful miniature from the *Arba Turim*, the code of Jewish law of Jacob ben Asher, copied at Mantua in 1436, introduces the section *Even ha-Ezer*, containing laws relating to marriage. It shows, on the right, the bridal couple entering to the accompaniment of music, and, on the left, the groom placing the ring on the right hand of his bride, as the officiant, standing between the couple, looks on.[14] While the luxuriousness and extravagance of costume are typical of the International style, they also reflect the general Renaissance indulgence in lavish dress, to which the rich were given and which synods of Jewish communities, like the one held at Forli in 1418, tried to prohibit by ordinance.[15]

Another Italian manuscript, dated 1452, depicts only the bridal couple, at the moment that the groom places the ring on the left hand of the bride and recites the betrothal formula: "Behold you are betrothed to me with this ring in accordance with the law of Moses and Israel"[16] (fig. 25).

Most of the illustrations in fifteenth-century Hebrew manuscripts from Italy show only the ring ceremony, which does not take place under the *huppah* (*tallit* or *sudar*) and which is not preceded by the betrothal blessings as customarily depicted in manuscripts from Germany. This is in keeping with the *minhag* (custom) practiced in many Italian communities, where the ring ceremony usually preceded the betrothal and nuptial blessings. Whether some of our miniatures depict a separate ring ceremony to be followed at a later time by the wedding ceremony is not too clear from the available evidence. Leon da Modena (1571-1648) writes in his *Riti* that in some places, at the time the contract was written, the groom used to "put the ring upon her finger, and to betroth her"; and that after an interval of two, four, six months or a year the couple would be married.[17]

In Italian communities, the ring was sometimes placed on the right hand of the bride, or, at other times, on the left.[18] Despite various miniatures depicting these rings, no specimens of them have come down to us from this period. Although rings with precious stones are described in the literature,[19] we are at a loss to explain the elaborate gold rings decorated with intricate gold filigree, with enamel decoration, often topped by a building, and carrying the inscription *mazzal tov* (figs. 11, 15). These rings are assigned by many scholars to Italy and are dated from the sixteenth to eighteenth centuries. Some scholars claim they were given to the bridegroom for use during the ceremony, but remained the property of the synagogue. The house on top of the ring has been variously interpreted as symbolizing the new home of the couple, the synagogue, or the Temple of Jerusalem.[20] One scholar even claims that these rings served as bouquet holders.[21]

An interesting manuscript on Jewish customs and ceremonies illuminated in Northern Italy during the late fifteenth century contains miniatures depicting not only the ring ceremony but also the ceremonies that follow. A badly effaced miniature (folio 13r) again brings us the familiar ring ceremony. Above the words *seder hatanim* (wedding service), the groom places the ring on his bride, while the officiant stands in between the couple. Over the words *birkat erusin* (betrothal blessing) in another miniature (folio 17r), we see the bride and groom seated and covered by the *huppah* (a cloth). On the right the officiant approaches with the cup of wine to recite the betrothal (*erusin*) and nuptial (*nissuin*) blessings.[22]

The sixteenth to the eighteenth centuries provide us with an abundance of illustrated material on Jewish wedding ceremonies. Some of these illustrations appeared in the printed editions of the Minhagim books and the books on Jewish customs and ceremonies written by Jewish apostates and Christian theologians.[23] They picture mainly the wedding ceremonies in Ashkenazi Germany and Sephardi Holland. Other depictions appeared on wedding contracts and on the many Torah binders, called *Wimpel*, emanating mainly from Southern Germany and known from the sixteenth century on. These *Wimpel* were usually made from the linen swaddling cloth in which the male child was brought to his circumcision. The cloth was then cut into three or four pieces, stitched together, and presented to the synagogue in a formal ceremony on the child's first visit there (fig. 19). Painted or embroidered on the *Wimpel* was the boy's name, his birthdate and the formula: "May the Lord raise him up to the study of Torah, to the nuptial canopy, and to good deeds." After the word *huppah* (nuptial canopy) an actual marriage ceremony is usually depicted.[24]

From this period, too, ceremonial objects connected with the wedding festivities have survived.

Major innovations were introduced into the wedding ceremony, especially in Medieval Christian Germany. One of these was the *Knas Mahl* (the penalty feast), which is illustrated in the eighteenth-century engravings in the printed editions of Kirchner's *Jüdisches Ceremoniel* and Bodenschatz's *Kirchliche Verfassung*[25] (figs. 31, 37). The *Knas Mahl* was an engagement party at which the conditions (*tenaim*) of the forthcoming match were written out in a formal contract. A monetary penalty (*knas*) was stipulated in case one of the parties later desired to break the engagement. In the engraving in Kirchner, we see the parties agreeing to the terms of the contract and the actual writing of the contract. In the background, the festive meal is in progress and the contract is being read, while, in the foreground, an important aspect of the celebration is seen—a man standing with a pot in his hand about to dash it on the ground to symbolize that just "as this broken pot cannot be made whole so shall this agreement not be hindered."[26]

An important custom observed in Germany since medieval times was the exchange of gifts (*sivlonot*) between the bride and groom, usually on the evening prior to their wedding. These gifts were delivered either by the rabbi or by some official of the congregation. Among the gifts exchanged were special belts. The belt sent to the groom had silver clasps, while the one sent to the bride sometimes had gold clasps,[27] the latter adornment being one which an ordinance in Frankfurt-am-Main tried to prohibit in 1716.[28] Some especially fine belts, long chains, often richly decorated with rosettes, are preserved from seventeenth-century Frankfurt-am-Main[29] (fig. 10). These belts were worn around the waists of the bride and groom during the wedding ceremony, as can be seen in the painting of a wedding by the nineteenth-century German Jewish artist, Moritz Oppenheim[30] (fig. 41).

Another very popular gift of this period, frequently presented to the bride, was a prayer book with a silver binding. Many elegant silver bindings have been preserved from Italy, where they often carried the coats of arms of the patrician families.[31]

It became customary, in many communities, to donate ceremonial objects to the synagogue to commemorate the occasion of a wedding. In Italy, the groom would frequently donate a binder for the Torah,[32] whereas, in Germany, Torah ark curtains carrying Hebrew inscriptions to mark this important event[33] were at times presented to the synagogue.

On the wedding day, both the bride and the groom were led to the synagogue in festive processions. In the engravings in Kirchner, we see first the bridegroom, being escorted, to the accompaniment of music, by a procession of males to the *huppah* set up in the courtyard of the synagogue. There he awaits his bride, who is being escorted by a procession of females, as musicians serenade her[34] (fig. 32).

From the sixteenth century on, it became customary, especially in Germany, to hold the wedding in the open air in the courtyard of the synagogue and to marry the couple under a portable canopy, called *huppah*, as depicted in the engraving in Kirchner[35] (fig. 33). This canopy, as we see, usually consisted of a piece of cloth to which four poles were fastened, one at each corner. Frequently the canopy was held aloft by four boys. The cloth itself often had Hebrew inscriptions; sometimes it was blue and carried depictions of sun, moon and stars, so as to resemble the heavens—as an omen "that their children shall be as the stars of the heaven."[36] The earlier custom of spreading over the bridal couple the *tallit* (previously called *huppah*), which the bride often sent as a gift to her future husband, is still adhered to in our engraving. This continuing practice was explained by reference to the biblical statements: "Spread your garment over your handmaiden" in Ruth 3.9, and "I spread my garment over you" in Ezekiel 16.8.[37] In our engraving in Kirchner, the face of the bride is covered by a veil. Tradition interpreted this custom by linking it to Rebekah who, according to Genesis 24.65, "took her veil and covered herself," when she first encountered Isaac.[38]

We see in the engraving that the officiant stands in front of the couple, a prayer book in one hand and a betrothal ring in the other. Next to the couple stands a man holding a narrow flask filled with wine. Such a flask—with a narrow opening—was used to signify that the bride was a virgin; for a widow, a flask with a wide opening was used.[39] At the conclusion of the wedding service the flask, sometimes filled with wine, was usually thrown against a stone affixed to the north wall of the synagogue building. This stone usually had a carved octagonal or hexagonal star on it and the initial Hebrew letters of Jeremiah 7.34: "the voice of mirth and the voice of gladness, the voice of the bridegroom and the voice of the bride"[40] (figs. 34, 20, 21). The flask was thrown at the stone, often on the north wall of the synagogue, since it was popular belief that demons resided in that region. The wine itself was intended as a bribe for the demons, while it was hoped that the broken pieces of glass would hurt them or that the noise of the shattering glass would at least frighten them. Tradition tried to justify this prevailing custom by saying that it served as a reminder of the destruction of Jerusalem.[41]

Common also was the use of silver double wedding cups, such as the cup from Vienna, 1724. These consisted of two matched cups which fit together to form a coopered barrel. They were usually inscribed with excerpts from the wedding service and were used for the two required benedictions over the wine (fig. 17).

The wedding ceremony among the Sephardim in Holland, as we can glean from an engraving by Picart, shows interesting variations in wedding customs. The huppah, for instance, is not a portable canopy set up in the courtyard of the synagogue, as it was in Germany, but is a curtained canopy affixed to the wall of a room[42] (fig. 35). Similarly, a flask is not thrown against a stone on the synagogue wall, but a glass is broken upon an elaborately decorated silver platter placed on the floor underneath the huppah.[43]

The finest art objects associated with the wedding ceremony are the many illuminated ketubot (marriage contracts), especially those preserved from seventeenth- and eighteenth-century Italy.[44] Though originally intended only as a legal document stipulating the bridegroom's financial and personal obligations to his bride after marriage or in case of death or divorce, the *ketubah* gradually became a work of art. The widespread custom, from the sixteenth century on, of reading the *ketubah* under the *huppah*, usually between the betrothal and nuptial blessings, may have aided this trend.[45] The public display of the *ketubah* undoubtedly invited adornment and led families to vie with one another in commissioning richly illuminated *ketubot*. Witness to this fact are the sumptuary laws enacted by the communal authorities of Ancona in 1766—laws containing a clause forbidding any family under their jurisdiction to pay more than 40 paoli for the illumination of a *ketubah*.[46]

Prior to the seventeenth century, only isolated examples of illuminated *ketubot* are known. One fragmentary ornamented *ketubah* has survived from the Cairo Genizah in Egypt. It is dated from the eleventh century and has the text modestly framed by two intersecting arches which are decorated with interlocking circles.[47] From Krems, Austria, another illuminated contract has been preserved, dated 1392. The text has a broad border decorated with tendrils and the figures of bride and bridegroom facing each other. The bridegroom holds up a large ring at the right, while, in the left margin, we see the bride with a crown on her head.

The most sumptuous *ketubot* in public and private possession today come from various Jewish communities in seventeenth- and eighteenth-century Italy, the true home of this art form. The many contracts emanating from Italy during that period are not only invaluable artistic documents, but serve also as rich sources for reconstructing the social, economic and legal aspects of Jewish life in Italy. Usually large in size, the *ketubot* in some Italian communities had their top edges trimmed in a variety of contours. In Rome, it was customary to trim the bottom edge of the *ketubah*. This shaping gave the contract not only a more attractive appearance, but also made it easier to unroll the parchment scroll.

The text of the *ketubah* was often framed within an architectural portal. Within this frame and above the text proper, there often was written, in large Hebrew letters, the day of the week on which the marriage took place. At other times, in place of the day of the week, we find, in large Hebrew letters, statements such as "He who finds a wife finds good" (Proverbs 18.22), or "With a good sign."

Around the borders of the *ketubah* and at the top, it is not uncommon to find figural decorations. A very popular custom was to depict a biblical scene relating to the groom's or the bride's name. In the *ketubah* from Ferrara, 1775 (fig. 2), we see two women standing on plinths and supporting an architrave crested by the prophet Samuel, who is flanked by Moses holding the tablets and Aaron with the censer. Underneath the prophet is the inscription: "And Samuel grew and the Lord was with him" (I Samuel 3.19). Hands giving the priestly benediction are placed in a cartouche next to the two figures, and an undulating band at the feet of Samuel carries the verse: "Moses and Aaron were among His priests, Samuel also among those who called on His name. They cried to the Lord and He answered them" (Psalms 99.6). The figure of the prophet Samuel was chosen, no doubt, because one of the names of the bridegroom was Samuel; the figure of Moses was probably selected because the name of the father of the bridegroom was Moses; the figure of Aaron, the high priest, was undoubtedly incorporated because the family name was Cohen.

Similarly, a contract made for a bridegroom named Joseph, in Corfu in 1781, depicts the biblical story of Joseph greeting his little brother Benjamin. The inscription above the figures comes from Genesis 49.22: "Joseph is a fruitful bough, a fruitful bough by a spring; its branches run over a wall."

Some *ketubot* have representations of the first married couple, usually shown nude, under the tree of knowledge in the garden of Eden.[48] At times we even find depictions of the present bridal couple and of the elaborate wedding festivities, as in the *ketubah* from Vercelli, 1777 (fig. 4).[49]

The decoration of the borders of *ketubot* often include such standard late Renaissance motifs as nude heralds, putti, caryatid female busts and garlands. Included, too, are the twelve constellations of the zodiac, as popular belief held that these controlled human destiny. Such pagan love deities as Venus and Cupid are not excluded either. In a contract from Pisa, dated 1790, a reclining, seminude Venus is seen next to the winged Cupid, arrow in hand (fig. 6).

Though, in general, we have little information about the artists who made these *ketubot*, there are several cases in which Jewish artists—Shalom Italia and Yehudah Frances, for example—are known to us.[50] In style, the *ketubot* range from the Baroque and Rococo to the Neo-Classic. By and large, however, the regional differences in shape, decoration and motifs appearing in these *ketubot* have yet to be studied.

The artistic remains briefly discussed in this essay give evidence of the unique involvement of Judaism with many cultures and societies, over a period of 3000 years, and show how this interaction is refracted not only in the styles and decoration used, but often in the very wedding customs adapted and interpreted for Jewish use. They tell of the rich diversity and complexity of Judaism itself, which admits great variations in Jewish wedding customs and objects connected with them in each Jewish community in every age. They give eloquent testimony to the joys and lavish festivities connected with the Jewish wedding, linking past generations to the present as we repeat at each wedding the ancient benediction: "Praised be Thou, O Lord, who sanctifies Thy people Israel through the ceremonies of *huppah* and *kiddushin*."

NOTES

1. Jeremiah 7.34, 16.9, 25.10.
2. Genesis 24.53.
3. Isaiah 49.18, 61.10.
4. Sotah 49b; S. Krauss; *Talmudische Archäologie* (Leipzig, 1911), II, pp. 43-44. A. Büchler, "The induction of the bride and the bridegroom into the .chuppah in the first and second centuries in Palestine," *Livre d'hommage à la memoire du Samuel Poznański* (Warsaw, 1927), pp. 82-132.
5. *Baba Batra* 146a; *Kiddushin* 50a; Krauss, *op. cit.,* II, pp. 42, 465.
6. Cf. S. Salfeld, "Das Hohelied bei den jüdischen Erklärern des Mittelalters," *Magazin für die Wissenschaft des Judentums,* V (1878), 110 ff. and VI (1879), 20 ff.
7. E. Róth, "Das Wormser Machsor," *Festschrift zur Wiedereinweihung der Alten Synagoge zu Worms,* ed. E. Róth (Frankfurt am Main, 1961), pp. 221-222. (The manuscript is now in the Hebrew University Library in Jerusalem, Hebr. 4°781, Vol. I, fol. 72v). Cf. also R. Wischnitzer-Bernstein, *Symbole und Gestalten der jüdischen Kunst* (Berlin-Schöneberg, 1935), pp. 50-51, fig. 29.
8. See sources cited in S. B. Freehof, "The Chuppah," *In the Time of Harvest: Essays in Honor of Abba Hillel Silver on the Occasion of his 70th Birthday* (New York and London, 1963), pp. 186 ff. and J. Z. Lauterbach, "The Ceremony of Breaking a Glass at Weddings," *Hebrew Union College Annual,* II (1925), 356.
9. H. Schauss, *The Lifetime of a Jew Throughout the Ages of Jewish History* (Cincinnati, 1950), pp. 129 ff. S. B. Freehof, *Reform Jewish Practice and its Rabbinic Background* (Cincinnati, 1944), I, pp. 85 ff. and 95 ff.
10. Whether the Jewish bride wore a crown, such as is depicted in our miniatures, is difficult to say from available sources. See J. Gutmann, *Jüdische Zeremonialkunst* (Frankfurt am Main, 1963), p. 34, fig. 62 and S. Marcus, "Marriage and its Customs among the Muslims," *Mahanayyim,* No. 83 (1963), 96 (Hebrew).
11. Leipzig, Karl-Marx Universitätsbibliothek, Cod. V 1102/I, fol. 64v. Wischnitzer-Bernstein, *op. cit.,* p. 52, fig. 30. See O. Gillen, "Braut-Bräutigam," *Reallexikon zur Deutschen Kunstgeschichte* (Stuttgart, 1948), II, pp. 1110-1124. Cf. the very interesting, but enigmatic, illustration in a fourteenth-century *mahzor* in the Hamburg Staats- und Universitätsbibliothek, Cod. Levy 37, fol. 170v. The bride is crowned and wears a blindfold like the familiar face of Synagoga in medieval Christian depictions. E. Róth, "Der 'grosse' Schabbat," *Allgemeine Wochenzeitung der Juden in Deutschland,* XVIII, No. 1 (April 5, 1963), 5 and *Monumenta Judaica,* catalog of exhibition held at Kölnisches Stadtmuseum, Oct., 1963-March, 1964, D 28, fig. 18. Cf. also the unpublished miniature in the thirteenth-century *mahzor*

in the Bodleian Library, Oxford, Laud. Or. 321, fol. 61v, where a bride is seated to the right of the word *itti* and faces the groom wearing a Jew's hat, seated on a bench, to the left of the word.

12. The manuscript is now in the Schocken Library, Jerusalem, fol. 12v. Cf. F. Landsberger, *A History of Jewish Art* (Cincinnati, 1946), pp. 212 and 214, fig. 132. Cf. also the related scene in the Yahuda Haggadah in the Bezalel National Museum, Jerusalem, fol. 11v. J. Gutmann, "The Haggadic Motif in Jewish Iconography," *Eretz Israel*, VI (1960), p. 20 and plate XLII, fig. 3. Here the officiant holds the rolled up *ketubah*.

13. Freehof, Jewish Practice, *op. cit.*, pp. 91 ff.

14. Landsberger, *op. cit.*, pp. 211-213, fig. 131 (Vatican Library, Cod. Ross. 555, fol. 220v).

15. L. Finkelstein, *Jewish Self Government in the Middle Ages* (New York, 1924), pp. 292-293.

16. Jews' College Library, London, Ms. 249, fol. 11v. See C. Roth, *The Jewish Museum* (reprinted from *The Conoisseur*, Sept.-Oct., 1933). London, n.d., p. 7 and illustration no. V. H. Hirschfeld, *Descriptive Catalogue of the Hebrew Mss. of the Montefiore Library* (London, 1904), pp. 81-82. Cf. also the miniature in a manuscript from Padua, dated 1477 in the Hamburg Staats- und Universitätsbibliothek, C. H. 337 (Scrin. 132), fol. 75v. The bridal couple in this miniature stands in an open landscape and the groom seems to be placing a ring on the left hand of the bride. See illustration in Monumenta, *op. cit.*, Q 77, fig. 19. In an unpublished miniature in Ms. 163 (3596) of the Biblioteca Palatina, Parma, an officiant joins the hands of the bridal couple, while the groom places the ring on the fourth finger from the thumb of the bride's right hand. Cf. Rothschild Ms. 24, fol. 140v in the Bezalel National Museum, Jerusalem, North Italy, late fifteenth century, where the officiant similarly joins the hands of the bridal couple, as the groom places the ring on the right hand of the bride. K. Katz, *Rothschild Ms. 24*. American Israeli Paper Mills, Ltd., 1959, for a description and illustration of this miniature. An unpublished miniature in a *mahzor* from Pesaro, 1481 in the Oriental Library of the Hungarian Academy of Sciences, Budapest, Ms. 380/II, fol. 230r, also shows the officiant joining the hands of the bridal couple, as the groom places the ring on the index finger of the bride's right hand. The ceremony takes place in front of a building, with the two required witnesses present. M. Weisz, *Katalog der Hebräischen Handschriften und Bücher in der Bibliothek Professors Dr. David Kaufmann* (Frankfurt am Main), 1906, pp. 121-123.

17. Leon Modena, *The History of the Rites, Customes and Manner of Life of the Present Jews throughout the World*, tr. by E. Chilmead (London, 1650), pp. 174-175. Cf. *Mahzor Rome*. Soncino-Casalmaggiore, 1485-1488, II, Sig. 19, leaf 2 and *Siddur*, Benedictions, Italian Rite (Ferrara, 1693), pp. 126 ff. Cf. *Kolbo, Hilkhot Ishut* (New York, 1946), p. 43b.

18. See *supra*, n. 16. *Pahad Yitzhok, Safek Kiddushin* (Lyck, 1866), p. 89a, where the ring is placed on the fourth finger from the thumb of the left hand and *ibid., Kiddushin* (Lyck, 1874), p. 78a, where it is placed on the fourth finger from the thumb of the right hand.

19. Freehof, Jewish Practice, *op. cit.*, pp. 91 ff.

20. C. Roth, "Ritual Art," *Jewish Art*, ed. by C. Roth (New York, Toronto, London, 1961), p. 344 and K. Schwarz, *Die Juden in der Kunst* (Wien and Jerusalem, 1936), p. 97; Landsberger, *op. cit.*, p. 76; S. S. Kayser, *Jewish Ceremonial Art* (Philadelphia, 1959), p. 152; Schwarz, *op. cit.*, p. 97; Roth, *op. cit.*, p. 345.

21. I. Abrahams, *Jewish Life in the Middle Ages*, pp. 181-182. See illustrations in Monumenta, *op. cit.*, E 155-73, figs. 46-51, and *Synagoga*, catalog of

exhibition held at Historisches Museum, Frankfurt am Main, May-July, 1961, Kultgeräte, nos. 416-427, fig. 166. J. J. Schudt, *Jüdische Merckwürdig-keiten* (Frankfurt and Leipzig, 1714), Book VI, Chap. 25, pp. 3-4 mentions betrothal rings with the words *mazzal tov* engraved on them. Cf. M. Narkiss, "An Italian Niello Casket of the Fifteenth Century," *Journal of the Warburg and Courtauld Institutes*, XXI, Nos. 3-4 (1958), 290, n. 17.

22. Princeton University Library, Garrett, Ms. No. 26. J. Bloch, *The People and The Book* (New York, 1954), pp. 42-44, and E. Panofsky, "Giotto and Maimonides in Avignon," *The Journal of the Walters Art Gallery*, IV (1941), 30-31 for a description of all the miniatures relating to the wedding ceremony.

23. See A. Rubens, *A Jewish Iconography* (London, 1954), pp. 5 ff. for a description of these editions.

24. Cf. D. Davidovitz, "Torah Binders—An Extinct Custom and Artistic Tradition," *Museum Haaretz Bulletin*, No. 4 (1962), 25-32. Gutmann, *op. cit.*, p. 18, fig. 12; Syngoga, *op. cit.*, Nos. 256-266, figs. 105-106; Monumenta, *op. cit.*, E 315-328, figs. 102, 104; Kayser, *op. cit.*, pp. 35-37. An early reference to these *Wimpel* appears in the 1530 edition of the apostate's A. Margaritha, *Der gantze jüdische Glaube* (Leipzig, 1705 edition), pp. 273-274.

25. Kirchner, *op. cit.*, pp. 172 ff., fig. 20. Cf. also Johann C. G. Bodenschatz, *Kirchliche Verfassung der heutigen Juden* (Erlang, 1748), IV, pp. 121-122, fig. IX.

26. Kirchner, *op. cit.*, p. 173. See Schauss, *op. cit.*, pp. 165 ff. and 182 ff; Berliner, *op. cit.*, pp. 177 ff.

27. Kirchner, *op. cit.*, pp. 175-176. Bodenschatz, *op. cit.*, p. 122.

28. Johann J. Schudt, *Neue Franckfurter jüdische Kleider-Ordnung* (Berlin, 1912), p. 32.

29. Gutmann, *op. cit.*, p. 34, fig. 61. Synagoga, *op. cit.*, nos. 428-431 and Monumenta, *op. cit.*, E 174-179 and fig. 55. Cf. A. Freimann, "Gürtel jüdischer Bräute in Frankfurt a. M.," *Einzelforschungen über Kunst- und Altertumsgegenstände zu Frankfurt a. M.*, I (1908), 143-144.

30. The griseille painting by Oppenheim differs in many respects from the earlier oil painting, dated 1861, now in the Bezalel National Museum, Jerusalem. See reproduction of this painting in Monumenta, *op. cit.*, C 16, fig. E 44.

31. Silvio G. Cusin, *Art in the Jewish Tradition* (Milan, 1963), pp. 68-81; Roth, *op. cit.*, p. 350; Narkiss, *op. cit.*, p. 290, n. 17. For bridal prayer books from Germany, see M. Grunwald, "Sitte and Brauch," *Mitteilungen der Gesellschaft für jüdische Volkskunde*, I (1898), 37 and *Notizblatt der Gesellschaft zur Erforschung jüdischer Kunstdenkmäler*, No. 22 (1928), 8-9, nos. 147, 155.

32. Such a Torah binder from 1602 is in the Bezalel National Museum, Jerusalem. See I. Shachar, *Jewish Textiles*. Catalog of exhibition at the Bezalel National Museum, Jerusalem (1960), p. 6, no. 12. Cf. *Tashbez* by R. Simon b. Zadok, who died in 1312 (Warsaw, 1924), no. 464 for mention of this custom.

33. I. Posen, "Die Mainzer Thorahschrein Vorhänge," *Notizblatt der Gesellschaft zur Erforschung jüdischer Kunstdenkmäler*, No. 29 (1932), 7-8.

34. Kirchner, *op. cit.*, pp. 177 ff. and fig. 21. Cf. also the related scenes and their description in Bodenschatz, *op. cit.*, pp. 122 ff. and figs. 10-12.

35. Freehof, Jewish Practice, *op. cit.*, pp. 85-86, Schauss, *op. cit.*, p. 164. Freehof, Chuppah, *op. cit.*, pp. 187 ff. and Margaritha, *op. cit.*, p. 98, who mentions this custom in 1530.

36. Kirchner, *op. cit.*, p. 181, fig. 22. Isserles, *Shulhan Arukh, Even ha-Ezer* 61.1. For depictions of various portable *huppot*, see H. Frauberger, "Ueber alte Kultusgegenstände in Synagoge und Haus," *Mitteilungen der Gesell-*

schaft zur Erforschung jüdischer Kunstdenkmäler zu Frankfurt am Main (1903), III/IV, pp. 159-161; Monumenta, op. cit., E. 153, fig. 45. Cf. T. Gaster, The Holy and the Profane (New York, 1955), pp. 111-113, and J. Sauer, Symbolik des Kirchengebäudes und seine Ausstattung in der Auffassung des Mittelalters (Freiburg, 1924), p. 210 for the use of the portable baldachin with four poles in church ritual.

37. Kirchner, op. cit., p. 176; Bodenschatz, op. cit., p. 174 and Gaster, op. cit., pp. 85 ff.
38. Bodenschatz, op. cit., pp. 122-123 and Gaster, op. cit., pp. 102 ff. for similar practices among non-Jews.
39. Kirchner, op. cit., p. 184; Bodenschatz, op. cit., p. 125; M. Güdemann, Geschichte des Erziehungswesens und der Cultur der Juden in Deutschland während des XIV. und XV. Jahrhunderts (Vienna, 1888), pp. 122-123. Cf. Sefer Maharil, Nissuin, 64b and R. Moses Halevi Minz, Responsa no. 109, who mention this custom.
40. Kirchner, op. cit., p. 184 states that they were called Sigillum Salomonis (Seal of Solomon) or Scutum Davidis (Shield of David). Later they were known as huppah stones or stars. Landsberger, op. cit., p. 79. Cf. Bodenschatz, op. cit., II, pp. 35-36; Schudt, op. cit., Book VI, Chap. 25, pp. 4-5. For a huppah stone from Bingen, 1700, see illustration in Monumenta, op. cit., E 154, fig. 56. Cf. also A. Grotte, Deutsche, böhmische und polnische Synagogentypen vom XI. bis Anfang des XIX. Jahrhunderts (Berlin, 1915), pp. 97-99; Jüdische Gotteshäuser und Friedhöfe in Württemberg (Frankfurt am Main, 1932), pp. 54, 75, 90, 109, 113.
41. See the relevant sources and the discussion of the origin and variations of this practice in Lauterbach, op. cit., pp. 364 ff. Cf. Gaster, op. cit., pp. 119-121.
42. Cf. the similar huppah on a Sephardi wedding contract from Hamburg, 1690. E. M. Namenyi, "The Illumination of Hebrew Manuscripts after the Invention of Printing," Jewish Art, ed. C. Roth (New York, Toronto, London, 1961), pp. 428-430, fig. 214.
43. B. Picart, The Ceremonies and Religious Customs of the Various Nations of the Known World (London, 1733), p. 238. Modena, op. cit., pp. 176-177.
44. F. Landsberger, "Illuminated Marriage Contracts, With Special Reference to the Cincinnati Ketubahs," Hebrew Union College Annual, XXVI (1955), 503-542. To the bibliography cited on p. 504, n. 2, the following should be added: I. Joel, "Italian Marriage Contracts in the Library," Kirjath Sepher, XXII (1946), 266-304 (Hebrew) and E. Namenyi, "La miniature juive au XVIe et au XVIIIe siècle," Revue des études juives, CXVI (1957), 31-36.
45. See Isserles, Shulhan Arukh, Even ha-Ezer 66.1 and 62.9; Margaritha, op. cit., p. 99 and Modena, op. cit., p. 177.
46. Landsberger, op. cit., p. 514.
47. Ibid., p. 505 f. For ketubot in Oriental communities, cf. L. A. Mayer, "Jewish Art in the Muslim World," Jewish Art, ed. C. Roth (New York, Toronto, London, 1961), pp. 370-374; K. Katz, "A Yemenite Marriage Contract of 1795," Eretz Israel, VI (1960), 176-178 (Hebrew).
48. Landsberger, op. cit., pp. 507 ff.
49. Cf. the beautiful ketubah showing the wedding ceremony of members of the Sephardi families Teixeira and de Mattos in Hamburg, 1690. Namenyi, Illumination, op. cit., pp. 428-430. Cf. the responsum of Abraham de Boton (Lehem Rav, no. 15) from sixteenth-century Salonica, who objected to the practice of drawing pictures of the bridegroom and bride in ketubot. Landsberger, op. cit., p. 510 f.
50. Ibid., pp. 535 and 539.

Ketubah. Parchment. Ferrara, Italy. 1775. As one of the names
of the bridegroom is Samuel, the prophet Samuel is featured in
the center of the upper border. On either side of him is Aaron
the High Priest, and Moses the Law-giver.

326

Ketubah for Mordecai Treves and Eleonora Segre. Parchment. Painted.
Vercelli, Italy. 1777. The elaborate border depicts the wedding
ceremony with the musicians. The Jewish Museum, New York.

Oriental bridal crown. Silver
decorated with semi-precious stones.
Persia. Eighteenth century. The
pendant chains of the headdress serve
as a veil to cover the face of the
bride. The Jewish Museum, Cincinnati.

Bridal belt. Silver. Frankfurt am Main,
Germany. Probably late seventeenth century.
The Jewish Museum, Cincinnati.

Double wedding cup. Silver. Vienna. 1724. A double cup for the benedictions over wine of the wedding ceremony, with Hebrew iptions of parts of the service. The Jewish Museum, New York.

329

Wedding cup. By Ilya Schor (1904-1961). 1958.
Mr. and Mrs. Nathaniel Hess, Sands Point, L.I.

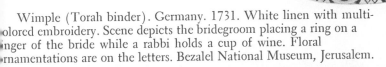

Wimple (Torah binder). Germany. 1731. White linen with multi-olored embroidery. Scene depicts the bridegroom placing a ring on a inger of the bride while a rabbi holds a cup of wine. Floral rnamentations are on the letters. Bezalel National Museum, Jerusalem.

Wedding stone with star in the center. Originally set in the outside south wall of the synagogue in Bingen am Rhein, Germany, built in 1700. Against this stone the groom would shatter a glass. Between the lines of the star are the Hebrew initials of "voice of gladness, voice of joy, voice of bridegroom, voice of bride." Bezalel National Museum, Jerusalem.

Wedding stone with star of David. Originally set in floor of the synagogue in Edelfingen, Germany. In addition to the Hebrew initials of "voice of gladness, voice of joy, voice of bridegroom, voice of bride," the center of the star contains the initials of *Mazzal Tov*.

The marriage of Moses and Zipporah. "Second Nuremberg Haggadah,"
Germany. Late fifteenth century. The Schocken Library, Jerusalem.

332

תיא כגרח בגא החדשיב· אשי תעכגב אשר על גבי חורש
אהכ בזה תחדש מעזרשיב· יר חדשוהגא מזרדשיב
הנגה שפהיי כשזרי· ארבעה חרשיב
חדשיב כבמיחזה· ביארתה זה מזה לחוזה
באשר שמעני ט עד נחזה

Symbolic betrothal of
Israel to God. *Mahzor.*
Germany. Fourteenth
century. Karl-Marx
Universitatsbibliothek, Leipzig.

מילבנין מלה מדאש אמנה השירי· בטוהר עד
לובש התבהני וההפאר· כושב ריקחה הרבשעי מזה
ולבנה התקטרי כי בא עה יהגיע שעה אשר לבילך
תשירי· כין שרי ילין אשכיל הכסף מינעצפה
ותואבית מלה באימרי שפר בני מכון וסילי ריחשיב

Symbolic betrothal of Israel to God. *Mahzor.* Germany.
1272. National and University Library, Jerusalem.

מלבנזן בלה מראש אמנה תשורי· בטוהר שריי לובש ההב
התפמזב והתהפארי· בושב ריקוהת הבשמי מור ולבנה התקטרי
כי בא עת יהגיע שעה אשר לבילך תשורי·
שרי· לין אשבל הכוסף· צפצפת נואמת בלה כאמרי
שפר· כצו ממו זבולו רוחתשיב בלי חפר· וק כר ורשתה
נעריץ ונספר במעלה יתקרש ובמיטה יבתלכל תמיד·

Betrothal ceremony. Prayerbook. Italy. 1452. Montefiore Library Collection, London.

Betrothal scene in Nuremberg: (a) agreement on the dowry, (b) writing of the document, (c) breaking the vessel, (d) reading the conditions, (e) mutual exchange of presents. From *Juedisches Ceremoniel*, by Paul C. Kirchner, Nuremberg, 1726.

Procession of the men (A): (a) the bridegroom, (b left) the rabbi, (b right) the bride sends the bridegroom a *tallit*.
Procession of the women (B): (a) the veiled bride. From *Juedisches Ceremoniel*, by Paul C. Kirchner, Nuremberg, 1726.

The wedding ceremony in Nuremberg: the bridegroom and the bride
and under a canopy with their heads covered with a *tallit*.
rom *Juedisches Ceremoniel*, by Paul C. Kirchner, Nuremberg, 1726.

After the wedding ceremony: (a) the bridegroom throws (b) a
glass at (c) the wedding stone built into the outside wall
of the synagogue while (d) the bride proceeds home. From
Juedisches Ceremoniel, by Paul C. Kirchner, Nuremberg, 1726.

Nuptial ceremony of the Portuguese Jews. From *The Ceremonial and Religious Customs of the Various Nations*, by Bernard Picart, London, 1733.

Nuptial ceremony of the German Jews. From *The Ceremonial and Religious Customs of the Various Nations*, by Bernard Picart, London, 1733.

Betrothal ceremony of German Jews. From *Kirchliche Verfassung
der heutigen Juden*, by Johann C.G. Bodenschatz, Erlang, 1748.

A Wedding. By Moritz Oppenheim (1800-1882). Bezalel National Museum, Jerusalem.

THE CEREMONY OF BREAKING A GLASS AT WEDDINGS[1]

By JACOB Z. LAUTERBACH, Hebrew Union College, Cincinnati, O.

JEWISH CEREMONIES HAVE BEEN unduly neglected in modern times, both in study and in practice. The effects of this double neglect are reciprocally cumulative. With the decline in the practical observance of the ceremonies, the scholarly interest in them is also waning, so that very few students devote themselves to the study of the origins, and the development of the religious ceremonies. On the other hand, the failure on the part of scholars to choose religious ceremonies as subjects for scholarly research ultimately results in a general ignorance of the actual meaning and significance of the ceremonies. This ignorance of the meaning of the ceremonies naturally causes more neglect of the practical observance of them. For ceremonies are merely a means to an end. They are vessels used to carry ethical ideas, to convey religious lessons. Without a knowledge of the ideas they contain and the lessons which they are to teach they appear empty vessels, meaningless forms, which do not appeal to the people and consequently are ignored and neglected by them.

Yet it cannot be denied that the religious life, as well as the science of religion and folklore lose very much by this double neglect of the religious ceremonies.

[1] It is not my intention in this essay to give a study in comparative folklore. I merely wish to treat the development of a Jewish ceremony. For this reason I consider only Jewish practices and quote only references from Jewish sources as to the ideas underlying these practices, though numerous parallels to these ideas and practices could be cited from the customs and folklore of other people. Only in a few cases where non-Jewish influence is likely to be assumed or where direct borrowing may have taken place, reference to the non-Jewish origin or parallel custom will be given.

Reprinted from *Hebrew Union College Annual*, Vol. II, 1925.

The religious life is deprived of a most powerful auxiliary, for ceremonies are not only a great aid in religious instruction by providing the best means of elucidating the lessons and impressing upon the minds of the people the truths of religion, but they are also of great help in training the people in the habit of putting theories into practice and translating beliefs into actions and thus live their religion.

The science of religion and folklore are deprived of a very valuable source of information about the development of religious ideas and popular beliefs, furnished by the religious ceremonies. For religious ceremonies change in their aspects and in their meaning with the change of beliefs and with the broadening of ideas experienced by those who observe them. The interpretation given to the significance of a ceremony does not merely preserve and reflect the beliefs of those who first introduced or instituted it, but it represents also the ideas of the people who retain the ceremony and who have reinterpreted it so as to meet their own religious standards or advanced theological views.

Such a reinterpretation of the meaning of religious ceremonies has been taking place in Judaism throughout its entire history. Its ceremonies have been constantly developed, more or less changed and modified and reinterpreted from generation to generation and from age to age so as to meet the religious requirements of that age and adequately express, or at least be compatible with, the theological views of that generation. True, it was not always possible to preserve all ceremonies even by means of this process of reinterpretation and continuous adaptation. It happened occasionally that all efforts at reinterpretation of a certain ceremony failed, so that the ceremony could no longer be made to convey any religious idea or be brought into harmony with the prevailing beliefs of the people, and consequently had to be entirely abandoned. But even the record of a discarded ceremony has an interesting story to tell. For it gives us valuable information about the spiritual forces that opposed and combatted it and the strength of the advanced ideas that finally brought about its elimination from Jewish religious practice.

This process of constant reinterpretation and adaptation of the Jewish religious ceremonies with the occasional abolishing or discarding of some ceremonies entirely, has been greatly stimulated and furthered by the continuous struggle which has always been going on in Judaism between the teachers and the masses of the people. The higher ethical principles and pure religious beliefs as formulated and taught by the teachers of Judaism were in constant conflict with some of the popular beliefs and superstitious ideas which lingered on in the mind of the people at large, who besides being disposed to preserve and retain older superstitions of their own, were always easily subject to the influence of environment and prone to borrow superstitions from their non-Jewish neighbours.

The Rabbis have always, directly or indirectly, opposed heathen practices and superstitions but did not always succeed in uprooting them.

The process of the development of a ceremony with its interpretations and modifications frequently takes the following course. The people will sometimes accept and retain a ceremony even if its origin be in an older heathen practice or in a foreign superstition, simply because the masses of the people are not always above these superstitions. The Rabbis will oppose such a ceremony and seek to prohibit its observance. In some cases, they succeed in their efforts and the ceremony is discarded. Sometimes, however, especially in the case of a generally accepted practice, its observance is so widespread that all the objections and protests of the Rabbis can not prevail against it. The people simply persist in observing it, and the Rabbis have to tolerate it. And if the ceremony does not violate an ethical principle and does not interfere with another religious duty, the Rabbis gradually relax their opposition. They acquiesce in its practice, considering it a popular custom, a *minhag*, which has its recognized place in Jewish religious life. All that the Rabbis then try to do is to effect slight changes in the ceremony, to modify it a little so as to remove from it some of its most objectionable features or the elements of crude superstition.

When this is impossible the Rabbis do the next best thing, that is, they ignore the superstitious element altogether. They retain the ceremony as such without giving its meaning or explaining its significance. They never call attention to its origin and do not refer to the superstitious belief on which it is based. The real meaning of the ceremony, being thus suppressed, is gradually forgotten by the people. The next generation, receiving the ceremony without any explanation no longer realizes its original meaning. The teachers of this generation, believing it to be a Jewish ceremony since they received it from their fathers together with other Jewish practices, seek to read into it a meaning which would make it expressive of some Jewish religious idea or at least prove it to be compatible with Jewish teachings. They usually succeed in finding in the ceremony some suggestion of an idea to which they could subscribe and they imagine that this actually was the idea underlying the ceremony. They offer this as a possible interpretation of the meaning of the ceremony. They merely guess at it but the following generation accepts this guess as a certainty and believes that this was the actual significance of the ceremony and the original meaning is almost entirely forgotten. In this manner an ancient superstitious practice may in the course of time be transformed into a Jewish ceremony which is reinterpreted from generation to generation so that even the Rabbis, entirely unaware of its heathen source and oblivious of its original superstitious significance, are likely to acknowledge it as a Jewish custom or even to recommend it as a ceremony with some Jewish religious significance.

The evolution of quite a number of Jewish ceremonies could be cited in illustration of this process. In this essay I shall deal with the ceremony of breaking a glass at weddings. I select this particular ceremony because in the history of its development, with the many changes effected in its details, in the veiled objections raised against it by Rabbis at different times and in the many reinterpretations which it received in the course of time by the teachers of various generations, the process above outlined can be well illustrated and its various stages clearly traced. This ceremony goes back to very ancient times and has its origin in a heathen superstition. It belongs to a group of wedding ceremonies which are based upon a common superstitious belief and have the same significance and purpose. For this reason, while limiting myself to a study of this one ceremony in particular it will occasionally be necessary in the course of the discussion, to refer also to other ceremonies of the group.

The idea underlying this group of wedding ceremonies is an ancient heathen superstition, survivals of which are still found, in one form or another, in Jewish life and practice. It is the belief that the evil spirits or demons are jealous of human happiness and therefore seek to spoil it or to harm the happy individual. The bride and the groom about to be married are, accordingly, the objects of the envy of the demons and liable to be harmed by them. It was believed that the bridegroom was especially exposed to such danger. For the evil spirits, like the arch demons or the fallen angels of old, notice the beautiful daughters of men and desire them.[2] Accordingly, they would seek to kill the bridegroom or otherwise hurt him and prevent him from joining his bride, in order that they might keep the bride for themselves. The story in the book of Tobit about the demon who killed the husbands of Sarah is the classic expression of this belief among the Jewish people in ancient times, and the saying of the Talmud that the bride and groom are among those who need to be carefully watched over and guarded, is generally understood to mean that they need to be guarded and protected from attacks of the jealous demons.[3] During the week of the wedding the bridegroom would, therefore, not dare to go out alone. Friends were especially appointed to guard the groom carefully.[4] Usually the face of the bride would be covered so that the demon should not see her. Sometimes the faces of both the bride and the groom were covered in order to be hidden

---

[2] See my article on Shamḥazai in *Jewish Encyclopedia* XI. p. 228–229.

[3] The saying in the Talmud (b. Berakot 54b) reads: שלשה צריכין שימור חולה חתן וכלה, to which Rashi remarks: שימור מן המזיקין, and he goes on to explain that the bride and the groom need to be guarded against the demons because the latter out of envy and jealousy seek to harm them.

[4] Pirke d. R. Eliezer XVI; TAShBeZ by R. Simon b. Zadok (died 1312), 465 (Warsaw, 1875) p. 80. Among East-European Jews the custom is still observed that the bridegroom does not leave the house to go out alone during, the week of the wedding.

from the demons. The custom for brides to wear a veil and the ceremony of "Bedecken" that is covering the head of the bride or, as it was done in some countries, covering the heads of both the bride and the groom with a black and white cloth[5] or with a Talith,[6] as well as the custom of having the wedding ceremony performed under a canopy, though later reinterpreted to have a certain symbolic significance, were originally simple devices for hiding the bride and the groom and thus protecting them from harm by the demons. But this method of guarding the bride and the groom against the demons merely by having them hide and trying to escape their notice was not completely satisfactory. It did not, in itself, offer perfect security. Since the demons themselves are not visible, the people were never certain whether by these methods of hiding they succeeded in making the bride and the groom unnoticeable and invisible to the demons. The people, therefore, sought other means of protection from harm by the demons. There were, according to the belief of the people, three ways of avoiding the danger of the demons and of effectively warding off any attack by them.

The first was to fight the demons and drive them away. The second was to bribe them by gifts and conciliate them. The third was to deceive them by making them believe that the person whom they envy and seek to harm is not to be envied at all since he is not as happy as they imagine him to be but is rather worried and burdened with grief.

Each one of these methods found its expression in special ceremonies. And the various Jewish wedding ceremonies clearly show that all three methods were used by the people to obtain protection from harm by the demons. The method of fighting the demon was employed by Tobias who upon the advice of Rafael smoked out the demon and drove him away by the smell of the heart and the liver of the fish (Tobit VI, 7.VIII, 2–3). But not all the people have the advice of a Rafael who would give them special means wherewith to drive away the demons.

[5] *Orḥot Ḥayyim* by R. Aaron ha-Kohen, II, (Berlin 1902) P. 67; *Kolbo* Hilkot Ishut (Venice 1547) p. 87a.
[6] R. Eleazar of Worms, (died 1238) in his *Rokeaḥ* 353 (Cremona 1557) p. 64a.

They would, therefore, use other means which in their belief would have the power to drive away the demons. Noises, torches, salt and iron were believed to be effective weapons against the demons.[7] And the custom to make noise and loud music, to carry or throw about torches and light numerous candles at weddings even when they take place in the daytime[8] as well

[7] I shall quote here a few references to Jewish sources where the belief that these means offer protection from the demons or drive them away, is either expressly stated or presupposed. As to noise and shouting see the story in Leviticus r. XXIV, 3 (also in Midrash Tehillim XX, 7 and Tanḥuma, Kedoshim 8 and Tanḥuma Buber ibidem p. 39a) where it is assumed that the noise and the shouting helped in driving away the wicked demon. As to torches and lights see b. Berakot 43b where it is said, where there are two persons the demon might show himself but would not dare hurt them. Where there are three persons the demon would not even dare show himself. And אבוקה כשנים if one person carries a torch with him he is as safe as if he had two other people besides himself, in which case the demon would not even dare show himself. As to salt see Midrash quoted in Tosafot Berakot 40a s. v. הבא מלח and Isserles in Sh. Ar. Oraḥ Ḥayyim 167, 5 and especially Kizzur Shelah (Warsaw 1879) דיני האכילה p. 36 where it is said that salt is put on the table in order to drive away the evil spirits מלח יתן על השלחן לגרש הקליפות. The salt used in the crowns of the bride and the groom (Tosefta Sotah XV, 8, b. Sotah 49b, and p. Sotah IX 34b) also served the same purpose. As to iron see Tosefta Sabbat VI, 13 where the practice of putting iron under one's head (evidently as a protection from the demons) is condemned as a heathen superstition דרכי אמורי. The saying in b. Pesaḥim 112a that when food is put under the bed the evil spirits have access to it even if it be covered with iron vessels, also presupposes that ordinarily iron vessels would protect the food from the evil spirits. In the story in Leviticus r. referred to above, it is also assumed that "beating with iron" מקשיין בפרזלא was used to drive away the demon. In a manuscript work by R. Eleazar of Worms, חידושים באותיות חסרות, there is also found the statement להגן כן השדים מקיפין בברזל וכו', quoted by M. Güdemann, Geschichte des Erziehungswesens und der Cultur der Juden I, (Wien 1880) p. 204. In Maharil (Warsaw 1874), p. 6, it is recomended to put a piece of iron into the water, kept in the house during the vernal equinox תקופה so that the demon should have no access to it לתת ברזל אל המים כל זמן התקופה ואז אין רשות למזיק. Comp. also Sabbathai Cohen in his commentary to Yore Deah 115, 6. As to similar beliefs among other people see E. Samter, Geburt Hochzeit und Tod (Berlin 1911) pp. 51, 58, 60, 72, and 151.

[8] R. Eliezer b. Nathan (RABaN) of Mayence (12th century) in his work Eben ha-Ezer (Prague 1610) p. 128c; Orḥot Ḥayyim l. c.; Tashbez l. c.; and Matteh Mosheh (Warsaw 1876) p. 213. RABaN and Orḥot Ḥayyim say that the candles were used for the purpose of increasing the joy משום שמחה,

as the custom to throw salt[9] over the heads of the bride and the groom or to have the groom carry in his pocket a piece of iron during the ceremony;[10] all these were originally intended to serve the purpose of fighting the demons and driving them away from the bride and the groom.

The method of propitiating the demons by offering them gifts also found expression in certain Jewish wedding ceremonies. The pouring out of wine and oil and the scattering of parched grain and nuts as well as dried fish and meat before the bride and the groom[11] were originally intended as offerings to the

Tashbez and Matteh Moshe on the other hand, explain it to be for the purpose of reminding us of the giving of the Law on Sinai. Both these explanations are but later reinterpretations by the Rabbis who no longer knew or did not like the real original meaning of the ceremony.

[9] Rokeaḥ l. c.; also in הלכות ארוסין ונשואין contained in the Manuscript Siddur of Orleans, see *Zeitschrift f. hebräische Bibliographie* XIII (1909) p. 17. The explanation given by Rokeaḥ that it is to suggest that the marriage covenant between the bride and the groom be permanent and lasting through their entire life, is but a later reinterpretation.

[10] Reported by A. Berliner, *Aus dem Leben der deutschen Juden* (Berlin 1900) p. 100.

[11] Tosefta Sabbat VII, 16 ממשיכין יין ושמן בצינורות לפני חתנים וכלות ולא מדרכי האמורי comp. b. Berakot 50b and in Tractate Semaḥot VII, it is stated more fully: מבובים לפני חתנים ולפני הכלות מחרוזות של דנים וחתיכות של בשר בימות החמה אבל לא בימות הגשמים... ממשיכין לפני חתנים ולפני הכלות צינורות של יין וציגורות של שמן ואין חוששין משום דרכי האמורי. The very fact that it was necessary to add the statement that one need not hesitate to perform these ceremonies on the ground that they are like heathen practices דרכי אמורי proves, to my mind, that these practices were based upon the heathen superstition of offering gifts to the demons. It is also evident that there were some objections to these practices, raised at least by some of the Rabbis. For the Rabbis knew very well of the popular superstition and of the practice of some people to offer food and drink to the demons, for they forbade such practices. The saying in b. Sanhedrin 92a כל המשייר פתיתים על שולחנו כאלו עובד עבודה זרה שנאמר העורכים לגד שולחן ולמני ממסך is a protest against the practice of leaving food on the table for the demons or friendly spirits (see Rashi ad loc. and Sh. Ar. Yoreh Deah 178, 3). The Rabbis also forbade the practice of saying: "drink but leave something" as a heathen practice דרכי אמורי (Tosefta Sabbat VII, 7) because it meant, leave something as a portion for the demons, see below note 35. The Rabbis had still another good reason to object to these practices and this was on the ground that they involved the wasting of valuable food. Why then did the Rabbis tolerate these practices and even declared that one need not object to

demons to bribe them not to harm the bride or the groom. The later forms of this custom which consisted in throwing wheat[12], or wheat and coins,[13] was to serve the same purpose of offering a bribe to the demons, though it has, of course, been reinterpreted and understood in another sense by the rabbinical authorities.

The third method, i. e. the one of fooling the demons by making them believe that the people are sad and mourning and therefore not to be envied, is represented in the ceremonies of putting ashes upon the head of the bridegroom[14] or a piece of

them as being one of the דרכי אמורי? Simply, because these practices were too widespread among the people and the Rabbis were unable to make the people give up these cherished practices. The Rabbis tried at least to modify these practices and limit them to such food as would not become spoiled and wasted by being thrown upon the ground and they prohibited the scattering of food which would get spoiled כל שהוא דבר האבד אין מבזבזין לפניהם (Semaḥot 1. c.; comp. Rashi to b. Berakot 50b s. v. ממשיכין). By these restrictions and modifications they made it less apparent that these foods were intended as gifts to the demons and they could interpret these practices as having another significance either as symbolic acts suggesting plentifulness or as modes of honoring the bride and the groom. Compare also A. Büchler, *Das Ausgiessen von Wein und Öl als Ehrung bei den Juden: Monatsschrift für Geschichte und Wissenschaft des Judentums*, 1905, p. 12–40.

The custom of carrying a hen and a rooster before the bride and the groom at the wedding ceremony, mentioned in b. Gittin 57a, or, as it was done in the middle ages, to let a hen and a rooster fly away over the heads of the bride and the groom (Güdemann op. cit. III, Wien 1888, p. 123) was also intended as a gift to the demons or as a sort of a substitute offering כפרות. See I Scheftelowitz, *Das stellvertretende Huhnopfer* (Giessen 1914) p. 10–11.

[12] RABaN 128c; Vitry p. 589; Tosafot to Berakot 50b s. v. ולא בימות הגשמים Rokeaḥ l. c.; R. Moses Minz (15th century) in his Responsa No. 109 (Lemberg 1851) p. 100; Maharil p. 64. The explanation given by all these authorities that the practice was merely to be a symbolic suggestion that the couple may increase and multiply, as well as the other interpretation given byRokeaḥ that it was to be a symbol of prosperity are but later reinterpretations. The mere fact that different interpretations are given shows that those who offered these interpretations were merely guessing and no longer knew the real significance of the ceremony, see above note 8.

[13] Berliner op. cit. p. 47; comp. also Judah Elset מחיי העם in the Hebrew Weekly העברי, edited by Meyer Berlin, New York, XI, No. 2, p. 8–9.

[14] Talmud b. B. B. 60b; Vitry 1. c.; *Kolbo*, Hilkot Ishut p. 86d; *Tur*, Eben ha-Ezer 65; Maharil 1. c.; Moses Minz op. cit. p. 99d; Matteh Mosheh *l. c.*

black cloth upon the heads of both the bride and the groom, thus making them appear to be mourners.[15] The custom to cry and wail at weddings indicated already in the Talmud[16] but especially prevalent among Jews in Eastern Europe[17] also originated in the belief that the demons might thereby be deceived into believing that the people were grieved and unhappy and desist from harming them. Possibly the custom for the bride and the groom to fast on their wedding day[18] was originally meant to serve the same purpose.

It depended, of course, on the temper of the various groups of people and their personal preferences as to which one of the

[15] *Kolbo*, Hilkot Tisha be-Ab p. 67c.

[16] Berakot 31a see below note 23.

[17] Compare *Taame ha-Minhagim* by איש שו׳ב I (Lemberg 1911) p. 111 No. 955.

[18] Rokeaḥ l. c. and Tashbez l. c. mention only that it is customary for the bridegroom alone to fast and they offer different reasons for his doing this. Rokeaḥ says that he found in an agadic Midrash that the reason why the bridegroom fasts on the wedding day till after the ceremony is to show his appreciation of the religious duty which he is about to perform, just as the pious men of former times used to fast before the performance of every re-ligious duty which they especially liked מה שמתענין החתנים עד לאחר הברכה מצאתי באגדה מפני שמצוה חביבה עליהם כדרך שעושין חסידים הראשונים שהיו מתענין על מצוה החביבה כגון לולב ושאר דבריב. Tashbez gives the reason that the wedding day is like the day of the giving of the Torah on Sinai, when Israel was, so to speak, wedded to God. And just as the Israelites fasted on that day so should the bridegroom fast on the wedding day. According to this interpretation, the bride should rather fast, since Israel was the bride. *Matteh Mosheh*, p. 213, gives two other reasons for this custom. According to the one the custom was simply a drastic measure to keep the bridegroom from feasting and drinking. For in case he should get drunk and enter the marriage covenant while in a state of drunkenness, the marriage would be il-legal. The other reason is that the wedding day is for the bridegroom like a day of Atonement since his sins are forgiven on that day (comp. p. Kilayim III, 3, 65cd). But one may ask if the marriage itself atones for his sins why does he need the fasting as another means of obtaining forgiveness. The same two reasons are also given by Moses Minz l. c. though he says that the custom is that the groom as well as the bride fast, and for the bride's fasting there is no reason offered. Isserles Sh. Ar. Eben ha-Ezer 61, I. also says that both the bride and the groom fast. When so many conflicting explanations are given for one and the same custom, one is certainly justified in assuming that they are all merely guesses.

three methods they would employ. Some people chose to fight, others prefered to ingratiate themselves with the demons and still others would seek to deceive them. It may be that these various ceremonies originated at different times and among different groups of the people, and it was only in the course of time that they came to be observed by most of the people. For the people who observe the ceremonies are not always consistent. They often employ ceremonies expressing contradictory tendencies, or are prompted by different and even conflicting motives in the performance of one and the same ceremony, believing it to work in different directions and to serve different purposes. In the ceremony of breaking a glass with which we are here concerned, we find all the three methods expressed. That is to say, in the manner in which it was performed at different times and in some of its details, we can see that the people, possibly at different times or in different countries, understood the significance of this ceremony differently, so that whatever method of dealing with the demons they preferred, they could use this ceremony. In other words all the three methods are represented in the details and various features of this ceremony.

We shall now trace the development of this ceremony and see how all these methods are expressed in it. We shall find that either by slight changes in one of its features or by special emphasis laid upon one of its details, by the meaning ascribed to it by the people or even by the different interpretations given to it by some rabbinic authorities at one time or another, the ceremony could be, and actually was, employed to serve all the three purposes, of fighting, bribing and fooling the demons.

The first mention of this ceremony is found in the Talmud where the following stories are told: "Mar son of Rabina made the wedding feast for his son. When he noticed that the Rabbis were very gay, he brought a precious cup worth four hundred Zuz, and broke it before them and they immediately became sad. R. Ashi made the wedding feast for his son. When he noticed that the Rabbis were very gay, he brought a cup of white glass and broke it before them and immediately they became sad".[19] Significant enough, no express comment is made

[19] טר בריה דרבינא עבד הלולא לבריה חנהו לרבנן דהוו קבדחי טובא אייתי כסא דמוקרא

in the Talmud about this strange performance on the part of these two Rabbis, and no direct explanation of its significance is given. Judging, however, from what precedes and from what follows these stories in the Talmud it is evident that the Talmud understood that the purpose of this performance was to avoid the danger of provoking the envy of the demons by deceiving them and making them believe that the people were sad and grieved. For, immediately preceding these stories, we are told the following story: "R. Jeremiah was sitting before R. Zera. When R. Zera noticed that R. Jeremiah was too gay and hilarious he reminded him of the saying in Proverbs (XIV, 23) which he took to mean that there is advantage in sadness. R. Jeremiah, however, answers saying 'I have the phylacteries on'"[20] The meaning of this conversation between R. Zera and R. Jeremiah, I believe, is this; R. Zera was afraid that the hilarity of R. Jeremiah might provoke the envy of the demons who are not too friendly to the students and are usually jealous of them.[21] He, therefore, advises R. Jeremiah that it would be to his own advantage to appear sad. R. Jeremiah, however, answers that he is not afraid of the demons, since he has on the phylacteries which will protect him.[22]

בת ארבע מאה זוזי ורבר קטייהו ואעציבו. רב אשי עבד הלולא לבריה חזנהו לרבנן דהוו קבדחי טובא אייתי כסא דזוגיתא חיורתא ורבר קטייהו ואעציבו (Berakot 30b–31a).

[20] רב ירמיה הוה יתיב קמיה דר' זירא חזייה דהוה קא בדח טובא אמר ליה בכל עצב יהיה מותר כתיב אמר ליה אנא תפילין מנח:א.

[21] Comp. b. Berakot 54b and Rashi ad loc.

[22] The popular belief that the Tephillin will protect one from harm by the demons is expressly stated in the Targum to the Song of Songs VIII, 3 where it is said: אמרת כנשתא דישראל אנא בחרתא מכל עממיא די קטרא תפילין ביד שמאלי וברישי וקביעא מזחתא בסטר ימינא דדשי תולתא לקבל תיקי דלית רשו למזיקא לחבלא בי. And in Midrash Thillim XCI, 4 the same idea is expressed in a somewhat modified form. Comp. also b. Menahot 43b where the additional proof, added to the saying of R. Eliezer b. Jacob, ואומר חונה מלאך ד' סביב ליריאו ויחלצם also suggests this idea. In p. Sabbath VI 8b it is declared prohibited to put the phylacteries upon a child that is frightened (by demons?) so that it may sleep. That the phylacteries will drive away the demons is expressly stated in p. Berakot V, i (8a) where R. Simeon b. Johai says that all people, even the spirits and demons, will be afraid of thee when they will see the name of God (meaning the תפלין upon the head, see b. Berakot 6a) upon thee. Compare especially b. Berakot 23ab where it is told of R. Johanan

Again immediately following the story of R. Ashi's breaking the glass, it is related there in the Talmud that when at the wedding of Mar the son of Rabina, the Rabbis asked Hamnuna Zutte to sing for them he began instead, to lament, crying, "Woe unto us for we must die".[23] This clearly shows the tendency to deceive the demons by making them believe that the people were not gay and happy but rather worried about their impending death. It is, therefore, evident from the context that the ceremony of breaking the glass or the precious cup was understood by the later Rabbis of the Talmud, to serve the same purpose of deceiving the demons, by subduing the hilarity of the people and making them appear sad for the moment.

Whether it was also intended as a sort of an offering to the envious evil powers, like "the ring of Polycrates" (Herodotus III, 40ff), as Max Grünbaum, *Gesammelte Aufsätze* (Berlin 1901) p. 111, assumes, or whether it was also believed that the demons can be frightened and driven away by the noise made by the breaking of the glass, is not in any way indicated in the Talmudic report. It certainly was not so understood by the Rabbis who performed this strange ceremony for they would not have done the act with such a heathen motive. It may, however, be safely assumed that the original meaning of the ceremony, at least in the popular belief, was to conciliate the envious evil spirits. For, evidently, this was an old established custom which in the course of time had been reinterpreted by the Rabbis and explained as merely serving the purpose of sobering up the people and causing them to be sad for a moment. Had this not been an old established popular practice at weddings, R.

that when entering the toilet-roon where danger from demons was commonly assumed he would carry with him his Tephillim, saying הואיל ושרונהו רבנן נטרן since the Rabbis permitted to carry the Tephillim even when entering this place, I might as well carry them with me so that they protect me. And Rashi there explains נטרן ישמרוני אכניסם עמי וישטרוני מן המזיקין Rashi's explanation here that R. Jeremiah meant to say, that the Tephillin prove that he had accepted upon himself the Kingdom of God, is not quite satisfactory, for this would not justify his being hilarious while having the Tephillin on.

[23] אמרו ליה רבנן לרב המנונא זוטי בהלולא דמר בריה דרבינא לישרי לן מר אמר להו ווי לן דמיתנן ווי לן דסיתנן.

Ashi and Mar bar Rabina would not have resorted to such an expensive and wasteful method of subduing the excessive hilarity of their guests. The more so since this practice actually constitutes a flagrant violation of the religious law prohibiting waste בל תשחית.[24]

We are, therefore, justified in assuming that we have here a case of the reinterpretation of the meaning of an older ceremony by the Rabbis who could not succeed in abolishing it altogether. In the popular mind the meaning of this ceremony was to offer a gift to the demons.

This of course was objectionable to the Rabbis, as it meant worshipping other beings besides God. However, being forced by the widespread popular usage to retain the ceremony, they tried to suppress the original idea about its significance by giving it another less objectionable meaning. This theory is further supported by the persistent silence which the Geonim and all the rabbinic authorities up to the twelfth century maintain in regard to this ceremony, for we do not find this ceremony mentioned in Rabbinic Literature before the twelfth century. This silence can only be explained on the theory that the Rabbis did not like this ceremony, they merely tolerated it, hence they did not care to discuss it or comment upon it and they even avoided the mere mention of it. But, much as the Rabbis objected to it, the people persisted in observing it and in a manner which preserved its original significance and refuted the interpretation given by the Rabbis. This is evident from the remarks of R. Eliezer b. Nathan of Mayence, RABaN (first half of the twelfth century) who discusses this ceremony in his work *Eben ha-Ezer* (Prague 1610) § 177, p. 44d. Commenting upon the stories in the Talmud (Berakot 30b–31a), RABaN recognizes the identity of the acts of R. Ashi and Mar b. Rabina with the ceremony of breaking a glass at weddings prevalent in his time.[25]

[24] The Rabbis understood the prohibition לא תשחית (Deut. XX, 19 to apply to all wasteful destruction of food or property, see Midrash Agadah edition Buber (Wien 1894) II, p. 199a and comp. b. B. K. 91b and Maimonides Yad, Melakim VI, 10.

[25] Vitry l. c. and Tosafot Berakot 31a s. v. אייתי כסא and Rokeaḥ l. c. also acknowledge the identity of the later ceremony with the practice recorded in the Talmud.

But he questions very much whether the reason clearly implied
in the Talmud for the acts of R. Ashi and Mar b. Rabina would
justify the later ceremony. He also expresses some doubts
as to the character of the ceremony itself. His remarks are, as
follows: ותימא לי אם על דבר זה הנהיגו הראשונים לשבר בנשואין כלי זכוכית
כי מה עצבון יש בזה שאינו שוה אלא פרוטה ועוד יש לי תימה שנהגו להבזות
כוס של ברכה ולשופכו הכל לאיבוד "I wonder whether it was really
for this reason, that is, to make the people sad, that the former
teachers instituted the custom of breaking a glass at weddings,
for what sadness is there in this breaking of a glass which is
not worth more than a penny. Furthermore I am surprised
that they instituted such a custom of desecrating the cup over
which the benedictions had been recited and pouring out its
contents all to waste."

We learn from these remarks a few interesting things. In
the first place, we may conclude from RABaN's words that the
ceremony had been observed as an established custom from the
time of R. Ashi up to the time of RABaN, so that the latter
could well believe it to have been a Jewish custom instituted by
the earlier rabbinic authorities. Secondly, it is apparent that
the real significance of the ceremony, having been ignored and
suppressed by the earlier teachers, was not known to the later
teachers, for RABaN cannot find any other meaning of the
ceremony but the one suggested by the context of the Talmudic
reports. And although he finds it unsatisfactory he nevertheless accepts it as the only explanation for the ceremony and
cannot think of any other interpretation of its significance.
This illustrates the theory stated above regarding the effects
which the reinterpretations of a ceremony have upon the course
of its development. When the Rabbis object to a ceremony
and are nevertheless compelled to retain it they give it an interpretation which would at least make it less objectionable.
This interpretation is then accepted by subsequent authorities
who no longer know the original significance of the ceremony.
It is also evident that RABaN does not quite approve of the
ceremony. He certainly does not recommend it. When he
describes the ritual of the wedding with all the ceremonies to
be observed at it (p. 128abc) he does not mention this ceremony.

It is only in connection with his discussion of the passage in the Talmud that he refers to it here, and from his questioning both the correctness of the interpretation and the propriety of the ceremony it is evident that he does not favor it.[26] Finally we learn from RABaN's remarks another important feature of the ceremony, as it was observed by the people. It did not consist of the mere breaking of a glass, it consisted of the breaking of the glass containing the wine over which the benedictions had been recited, so that with the breaking of the glass went also the spilling of the wine. The spilling of the wine in this ceremony must have had the same significance as the ceremony of pouring out wine and oil and the strewing of wheat, mentioned in the Tosefta quoted above, which was to serve the purpose of bribing the demons. It is evident, therefore, that in the popular belief the purpose of our ceremony was, not to make the people appear sad, but to offer a gift to the demons. If the glass was cheap its contents added to its value as an appropriate offering. No wonder RABaN could not see in the motive implied in the Talmud, that is, to make the people sad, a justification for this ceremony, for in the form in which it was performed in his time the ceremony failed to achieve this purpose. And to the pouring out of the wine RABaN rightly objects. Since he would not countenance the idea of its being an offering to the demons he could regard it only as an unlawful waste and a desecration of the cup over which the benedictions had been recited.

This indirect disapproval of the ceremony by RABaN, which other rabbinical authorities no doubt shared, did not have any effect on the popularity of the ceremony. It continued to be observed by the people and was even endorsed by some of the Rabbis of the time. But such objections as were voiced by RABaN had some effect on the development of the ceremony. For the slight changes and modifications made in it, as we shall note, the emphasis laid on one new feature in it, as well as the altogether new interpretation given to it by later rabbinical

---

[26] R. Joseph Saul Nathanson also understood that RABaN objects to the ceremony, for in his notes שי למורה to Sh. Ar. Eben ha-Ezer 65, he remarks וראב'ן מפקפק על זה.

authorities were in all likelihood due to a desire to meet these objections and thus render the ceremony less objectionable.

This is clearly shown by the other early reference to this ceremony which is found in *Maḥzor Vitry* (pp.. 589 and 593) where the ceremony, with a very significant additional feature, is prescribed in the following words: וימזוג בו עוד ויברך עליו שבע ברכות וישתה וישקה וישפוך ומטיח הכוס של זכוכית בכותל ושוברו "He should refill the glass with wine, recite over it the seven benedictions, drink from it and give the bride and the groom to drink and pour out (the rest) and then hurl the glass against the wall and break it".[27] We notice here that the objection to the ceremony had been overcome by some of the rabbinic authorities at least, for the ceremony is recommended and even prescribed. Secondly, we notice an altogether new feature which introduces a new element into the ceremony, or at least suggests a new motive for its performance. Here it is expressly prescribed that the wine be poured out. This, no doubt, was a relic of the older practice of offering wine and food to the demons. Then after the wine has thus been spilled, the other part of the ceremony takes place. The empty glass is thrown against the wall and broken. Formerly, it would seem, the glass with the wine were both intended as an offering and the breaking of the glass may have been considered as merely incidental. The main purpose was the offering of the glass and the wine. This could be achieved only by throwing the glass with its contents, the wine, at the demons, which act incidentally resulted in the glass being broken. In the form as prescribed in Vitry the ceremony is divided into two. The offering, which is done by pouring out the wine, is separate from the throwing and breaking of the glass. There must have been a special reason for this dividing of the original ceremony. I believe that this new feature of throwing the empty glass was prompted by a motive entirely different from the one which produced the original form of the ceremony. It represents the third method of dealing with the demons, viz. by fighting them or frightening

---

[27] In an addition, תוספות, on p. 593, it is expressly stated that the bridegroom should throw the glass against the wall and break it.

them away. This change in the ceremony may have been made to meet the objections raised against it by the Rabbis. And it was due to this modification that the ceremony could be retained after objections, such as those voiced by RABaN, had been made to it. For, this new feature helped the people to overcome the hesitancy and the scruples which they must have felt in performing the ceremony in its original form when both the wine and the glass were offered to the demons. For offering a gift to the demons is almost like worshipping them to which the religious conscience objected. But fighting the demons is theologically less objectionable. The inconsistency presented by the spilling of the wine which is a form of making an offering and the throwing of the glass which is a form of fighting was probably not realized by the people. The mere fact that the wine was poured out on the ground and not thrown together with the glass in the direction of the demons was sufficient to make it appear that the wine was not intended as an offering to the demons.[28] That the smashing of the empty glass was intended as a method of fighting the demons is further evident from the fact that it was flung at the wall. This plainly indicates that the missile was aimed at the demons. For the demons were believed to lurk under the spouts of the roof close to the wall. (comp. Ḥulin 105b). Of course, Vitry ignores this implied significance. He explains the meaning of the ceremony by merely referring to the Talmudic interpretation of the saying in Proverbs XIV, 23 that there is an advantage in appearing sad.[28] But this interpretation can hardly explain why the wine

[28] It may also be that the pouring out of the wine was considered by some of the people to be, not an offering to the demons, but a means of driving them away. Just as the Christians in those days believed that the blessed water had the power of driving away the demons, the Jews could also believe that the wine of the כוס של ברכה would have the same effect. This would explain the special feature of this practice, mentioned in Tashbez l. c. namely to scatter the wine, when pouring it out, over the entire house על פני כל הבית. Tashbez himself, however, explains this feature to have merely a symbolic significance, suggesting that God will bless the house with plenty of good things, comp. b. Erubin 65a.

[29] The same interpretation is also given by Rokeaḥ l. c.

should be poured out and why the empty glass must be broken
in this particular manner.

That this throwing the glass in a specific direction was
intended to fight or frighten away the demons is also clearly
shown by the description of the ceremony as observed by R.
Jacob Moellin (died 1427), reported in *Sefer Maharil* (Warsaw
1874) p. 64b–65a, in the following words: כשגמר הברכה נתן
לחתן לשתות ואחר כך להכלה והרב החזיק הכוס בידו ואחר כך נתן את הכוס
ביד החתן והפך החתן את פניו לאחוריו ועמד נגד צפון חרק את הכוס אל הכותל
לישבר ומיד ממהרין עם החתן דרך שמחה להכניסו לבית חתונה קודם הכלה
"After he (R. Jacob Moellin) had finished the benediction he
gave to the bridegroom to drink and afterwards to the bride,
still holding the cup in his hand. Then he gave the cup into
the hand of the bridegroom. The latter then turned around and
facing the northside threw the cup against the wall so that it
got broke. Immediately thereupon they hasten to run away
with the bridegroom, in a joyous manner, in order to bring
him into the wedding chamber before the bride gets there."
The express requirement that the bridegroom turn around and
throw the glass against the northern wall is significant. It
certainly was done with a definite purpose. And we can readily
understand what that purpose was when we remember that it
was believed that the demons came from the northside and hence
were to be found in their usual haunt along the wall of the northside. This belief that the demons come from the north originated
with the ancient Persians[30] but found its way also into Jewish
Literature. It is frequently mentioned in many of the younger
Midrashim[31] and thus may have become a popular Jewish belief.
It is for this reason that the bridegroom, when ready to fight
the demons, had to turn northward in the direction where the

[30] Comp. I. Scheftelowitz, *Die altpersische Religion und das Judentum*
(Giessen 1920) p. 59.

[31] Pirke d. R. Eliezer III: ושם (ברוח צפון) מדור למזיקין ולזועות ולרוחות ולשדים
לברקים ולרעמים ומשם רעה יוצאת (ילקוט איוב רמז תתקי"ג: ומשם יוצאין) שנאמר מצפון תפתח
הרעה. comp. also Pesikta Rabbati (Friedmann p. 188) and Midrash Numbers
r. II, 10 and III, 12; and Midrash Konen in Jellinek's *Beth ha-Midrash*
II, p. 30 where it is said ושם כת סמא'ל; and מדרש אבכיר by A. Marmorstein in
דביר I. (Berlin 1923) p. 121.

demons were believed to be, to throw the glass at them, thus either hurting them with the broken pieces of glass or frightening them by the noise which the shattering of the glass makes. The significance of the other feature, mentioned in Maharil, namely, that immediately after the throwing of the glass they hurry away with the bridegroom, also becomes clear to us. Maharil's explanation of this running away of the bridegroom, as being a joyous manner דרך שמחה is hardly correct, for one fails to see what special joy there can be in thus running away. In the popular belief this running away was for the simple purpose of escaping danger. Before the demons have time to recover from their fright and rush upon the bridegroom to attack him the people hasten to get away with him. They were especially anxious to get him into the wedding chamber before the bride is there for the demons might endeavour to prevent him from joining his bride.

It further appears from the description in Maharil that at that time, that is at the beginning of the 15th century and in Germany at least, the ceremony was again performed in its original form, namely, that the glass with its contents, the wine, were thrown at the demons and not in the form in which it is described in Vitry, namely, that the wine was first poured out and then the empty glass thrown against the wall.[32] Thus we see how in the various features of this one ceremony all three methods of dealing with the demons found expression. The people who observed this ceremony believed that by one or the other of its features it can serve the purpose of effectively warding off the danger of the demons. Whether they preferred to deceive the demons by appearing sad and unhappy or to bribe them by offering them the wine as a gift or to fight them by throwing the glass at them and hurting them, they could well use this ceremony to achieve their aim.

Of course all these ideas about the efficacy of this ceremony were entertained only in popular belief. The Rabbis, with the exception of the few among them who were strongly inclined to mysticism, did not share in these crude superstitions of fight-

[32] See below reference of R. Pinehas Horowitz to the form in which the ceremony was observed as late as the 18th century

ing the demons and certainly not in the theologically objectionable idea of offering them gifts, which is a form of worship. For
this reason Vitry gives only the one explanation of the meaning
of the ceremony that it is to remind us not to be too gay. And
from the fact that Maharil, though describing the ceremony
in detail, does not give any explanation of its meaning and even
seeks to explain the feature of running away, which clearly
points to the superstition of fighting the demons, as being merely
a "form of joyousness" it is also evident that he did not share
in the popular superstitions and sought to ignore them. This
illustrates our theory, stated above, about the attitude of the
Rabbis towards popular superstitious practices. When unable
to abolish an objectionable ceremony simply because the people
in their superstition cling to it, they at least try to ignore the
real meaning of the ceremony and seek to suppress or explain
away the crude superstition on which the ceremony is based.
We may safely assume that the majority of the Rabbis did not
care much for this ceremony, considering that but very few
authorities mention it. Possibly the ceremony would have
been more strongly opposed and eventually even entirely
abolished by the Rabbis had it not been for an altogether new
interpretation given to it, an interpretation which freed it entirely from all the objectionable superstitious beliefs with which
it had been intimately connected.

This new interpretation is found in *Kolbo* הלכות תשעה באב
(Venice 1547) p. 67, where speaking of the various reminders
of the duty to mourn for the destruction of Jerusalem, the author
also mentions our ceremony in the following words: ועל
זה פשט המנהג לשבור הכוס אחר שבע ברכות "For this reason also the
custom became prevalent to break the cup after the recitation
of the seven benedictions at weddings". This is an altogether
new interpretation and is probably original with the author of
the Kolbo (14th century).[33] For, as we have seen, RABaN

---

[33] Though R. Moses Minz l. c. quotes this interpretation in the name of
the "Zuricher", meaning R. Moses of Zurich, the author of the "Zuricher
Semak". See about him Dr. Ch. Lauer in *Jahrbuch der Jüdisch-Literarischen
Gesellschaft* XII (Frankfurt am Main 1918) p. 1–36.

Güdemann, op. cit. III (Wien 1888) 122 cites another opinion about

could not think of any other meaning of the ceremony than the one suggested in the Talmud. And Vitry also knows only of one reason for the ceremony, namely the advantage and safety that may come to one from appearing sad, and that even in joy one should tremble. But it did not occur to RABaN or Vitry to connect this ceremony with the duty of mourning for Jerusalem. Evidently, the author of the Kolbo, or whoever first gave this interpretation, objected to the superstition underlying the meaning of the ceremony as suggested in the Talmud, namely that the demons seek to harm the happy people and that by appearing sad the wedding guests may deceive the demons and ward off their attacks. He, therefore, accepted only part of the suggestion of the Talmud, namely, that the ceremony was intended to cause the people to be sad, but he interpreted the purpose of being sad differently from that suggested by the context in the Talmud. He took it not as a means of deceiving the demons, but as a reminder of the destruction of Jerusalem and of our duty to mourn for it on all joyous occasions when we are likely to forget it. It was this interpretation that saved the ceremony and made it acceptable to the majority of the Rabbis. For this interpretation removed from the ceremony the element of crude superstition, so that even enlightened pious people could well observe it.

It took some time before this altogether new interpretation was accepted by the majority of the teachers, but it gradually came to be recognized as the most acceptable interpretation of the ceremony. It is significant that the leading rabbinical authorities of the 16th century who mention this ceremony as Joseph Caro in Bet *Joseph Oraḥ Ḥayyim* 560, Moses Isserles in *Darke Moshe* and *Shulḥan Aruk Oraḥ Ḥayyim* 560, 2 and *Eben ha-Ezer* 65, 3, and Mordecai Jaffe in *Lebush*, Hilkot Tisha be-Ab 560, 2[34] do not give any details as to how the cere-

the significance of this ceremony, namely, that it was merely a symbolic act, declaring the marriage as legally contracted and valid. This opinion, whose author Güdemann does not mention by name, hardly deserves any consideration.

[34] In Lebush, however, there is still preserved a trace of the original significance of the ceremony, namely, to drive away the demons,. He says:

mony is to be performed, such as are given by Vitry, Maharil and Moses Muenz. They do not even quote these authorities and they also ignore the connection between the ceremony and the story in Talmud Berakot. They only mention the ceremony with the interpretation given to it by *Kolbo*, viz. that it is to serve as זכר להורבן a reminder of the destruction of Jerusalem. Evidently this was the only interpretation of the ceremony acceptable to them and they did not care to point out the details of the ceremony which clearly indicate that the ceremony originally served another purpose. This other purpose, or the original significance, of the ceremony, however, was not entirely forgotten by the people even though the majority of the teachers accepted only the new interpretation. The people, and some of the teachers more inclined to mysticism, continued to take the ceremony in its original meaning and to perform it for the purpose of warding off the danger of the demons. For, as it frequently happens, no matter what the advanced teachings of the enlightened authorities may be the people retain their cherished superstitions and some of the less advanced teachers will encourage them in their superstitious beliefs. Thus we find R. Isaiah Horowitz in his *Shne Luḥot ha-Brit* (Fuerth 1764), section שופטים, p. 378a, quoting Recanate, gives the following explanation of the significance of the ceremony: ועל כן תקנו לשבור את הכוס בשעת חופה פירוש כדי לתת למדת הדין חלקו ועל ידי כן ועולתה תקפץ פיה "Therefore have they instituted the custom of breaking the glass at the wedding, in order to give to the accuser his due portion whereby iniquity will close her mouth." Here it is expressly stated that the purpose of the ceremony is to offer a bribe to Satan or the demons, for THE ACCUSER and INIQUITY are but circumlocutions for Satan and the demons.

ומטעם זה נוהגין לשבור הכוס תחת החופה להבהיל ולמעט השמחה. The word להבהיל "to terrify" or "dismay" can only mean to terrify the demons and frighten them away, for whom else would they wish, or believe, to frighten at the wedding. Possibly, the words ולמעט השמחה may have the same significance which is implied in the Talmud and in Vitry and Rokeaḥ, namely not to appear too happy. The author of the Lebush may have repeated this interpretation from another source in which the ceremony was understood in its original significance, though Lebush himself, no doubt, understood the ceremony as being a זכר לחורבן for he mentions it in Hilkot Tisha be-Ab.

This plain statement about the purpose of the ceremony made by Recanate in the fourteenth century and endorsed by R. Isaiah Horowitz in the beginning of the seveteenth century, is very interesting. It shows that in the fourteenth century, at about the same time when Kolbo gave his new interpretation to the ceremony, the people and some authorities still held on to the older meaning of the ceremony as being a means of warding off the danger of the demons. It also shows that in the sixteenth or the beginning of the seventeenth century after all the leading rabbinic authorities had accepted Kolbo's interpretation, there were still some great teachers, like Horowitz, who, because strongly inclined to mysticism, accepted and endorsed the older explanation of the significance of the ceremony.[35] This clearly proves the correctness of the statement made above that even after the official authorities reinterpret a ceremony to harmonize with their theological views the original meaning of the ceremony with its underlying superstititions does not entirely disappear from the mind of the people and even of some of the teachers. This observation will also help us to understand some of the changes and modifications subsequently made in our ceremony.

The new interpretation of the ceremony as serving the purpose of reminding us of the destruction of Jerusalem, though accepted by the majority of the rabbinical authorities, did not preclude further developments of the ceremony. On the contrary, quite a few significant changes and modifications were made in the performance of this ceremony after the new interpretation had been accepted by the majority of the Rabbis. In the first place we notice that in the 16th century the ceremony was observed not only at weddings but also at engagement parties. This extension of its observaece was compatible with

---

[35] According to Shelah, the ceremony was performed in the older form, i. e. to smash the glass with the wine in it, thus spilling the wine as an offering to the demons. For the breaking of an empty glass could not be considered as offering to the demons their due portion. The idea of bribing the demons by giving them their due portion is clearly stated in *Matteh Mosheh*, 306 and 504, where the pouring out of part of the wine at the Habdalah ceremony is explained to be such an offering to the demons.

the new interpretation. For, if the purpose of the ceremony was to remind us on all joyous occasions of the destruction of Jerusalem, then it should by right be observed also on the joyous occasion when we celebrate the engagement. And so the custom of breaking pots and dishes at engagement parties came into use.[36]

Another significant change made in the ceremony was that instead of breaking the cup over which the seven benedictions, or ברכות נשואין had been recited, as prescribed by Vitry and Maharil, they would break the cup over which the benediction over the bretrothal, or ברכות אירוסין had been recited. What caused this change was a superstitious fear of another danger that might threaten the bride and the groom besides the danger from the jealousy of the demons. Superstition is not consistent. Superstition which originally considered the ceremony of breaking the glass as a sort of protective measure, believing it to have the effect of warding off the danger of harm by the jealous demons, now sees in this very ceremony a new danger. It considers the breaking of the cup over which the marriage benedictions had been recited a bad omen since it might augur a possible breaking of the marriage bond, suggesting a dissolution of the

---

[36] The earliest direct reference to this custom that I could find, is R. Yomtob Lippmann Heller (died 1654) in his *Malbushe Yomtob*, quoted by R. Elias Spira in *Elijahu Rabbah*. Commenting on the passage in Shulḥan Aruk Oraḥ Ḥayyim (or Lebush?) 560, 7, R. Elias Spira quotes from Heller's work the following remark: ונראה לי שזהו הטעם שמשברין הקדירה בכתיבת התנאים "It seems to me that this (i. e. to remind us of the destruction of Jerusalem) is also the reason why they break pots at the time of the writing of the engagement pact." He does not explain, however, why just pots be broken at the engagement party and not a glass as at weddings. The fact is that this interpretation of the custom of breaking earthen vessels at engagement parties is not correct. Its real purpose was to drive away the demons for which broken pottery was considered more effective. Just as the Germans would break pots on the evening before the wedding, Polterabend, in order to drive away the demons that threaten the bride and the groom, see Samter, *op. cit.* p. 60. That this was also the purpose of the Jewish custom is evident from the fact that just at the moment when the pots are broken the people present make noise and shout מזל טוב "good luck". For, certainly there would be no reason for making noise and shouting Mazel Tob at the moment when one is to be reminded of the destruction of Jerusalem and of the duty to mourn for it.

marriage just now contracted. That this was the reason for substituting the cup of the ברכת אירוסין for the cup of the ברכות נשואין is plainly stated by R. Moses Muenz (*Responsa* No. 109, Lemberg 1851 p. 100a) when he says וראיתי רבותי נהגו ליקח הכוס הראשון לזרוק ולשבר ולא זכיתי לשאל מהן טעמא מאי למה דוקא כוס ראשון ונראה קצת טעמא כיון דיש עתה שני כוסות טוב ליקח ולשבר כוס של אירוסין כי כוס של נישואין אתי לגמר הזיווג ומברכין והתקין לו ממנו בנין עדי עד לכן אין סברא לשבר כוס של נישואין שמורה חס ושלום על שבירת העניין כי אמרינן סימנא מילתא And Isserles (*Darke Moshe Orah Hayyim* 560 and *Sh. Ar. Eben ha-Ezer* 65, 3) likewise says that the custom in his city was that the bridegroom would break the cup over which the ברכת אירוסין had been recited. Isserles also tells us of another change in the ceremony as it was observed in the city of Cracow where he lived, and this was to recite the ברכת אירוסין over an earthen cup, and this was done because of the fact that they would break this cup and not the cup of the ברכות נשואין. He says: ובעירנו נוהגין שהחתן שהחתן משבר הכוס שמברכין עליו ברכת אירוסין ולכן נהגו לברך ברכת אירוסין על כוס של חרס, He does not explain how the use of an earthen cup for the ברכת אירוסין was the necessary consequence of the custom of breaking this cup instead of the one over which the marriage benedictions had been recited. He must have had in mind the custom of breaking pottery at the engagement ceremony. Since the betrothal אירוסין is more of an engagement than a wedding hence when the ceremony of breaking the cup is performed at that part of the wedding ceremony which represents the betrothal the cup to be broken should be of the same kind as the vessels broken at engagement parties.[37] This custom of using an earthen cup for the ברכת אירוסין seems to have been merely a local custom in Cracow and was not accepted in other places. From all the references to this ceremony that I could find it appears that the distinction between breaking dishes at engagement parties and breaking the cup at weddings was strictly maintained. For the former they required earthen pots or dishes while for the latter they insisted upon a glass. Various explanations are offered for this dis-

[37] Compare R. Joseph Teomim (1727–1793) in his משבצות זהב to Orah Hayyim 560,4 who gives a fuller discussion of Isserles' statement.

tinction and reasons given why specifically pottery should be broken at engagements and a cup of glass should be broken at the wedding.[38]

The custom, however, of breaking the cup of the ברכת אירוסין instead of the one of the ברכות נשואין was almost universally accepted. And to my knowledge there is but one reference to the custom in some place of breaking both the cup of the ברכת אירוסין as well as the one of the ברכות נשואין.[39] Besides the reason given by R. Moses Muenz as quoted above there are other explanations offered by some authorities why the cup of the ברכות נשואין should not be broken. These other explanations give the entire ceremony an additional symbolic aspect suggesting the relation between God and Israel. Thus R. Joseph Trani, the younger (1573–1644) in his *Zofnat Paaneah* to section Matot (Venice 1653 or 1648), p. 196c, states that the custom is to break the cup of the ברכת אירוסין and that it must be of glass. And the reason why it must be of glass only is because then the ceremony not only reminds us of the destruction of Jerusalem but at the same time also suggests the hope that the breach in the relation between God and Israel caused by

---

[38] R. Joseph Teomim l. c. makes the following remark: ויראה לשבור תחת החופה כוס שלם ואין משום בל תשחית כיון שעושים לרמו מוסר למען יתנו לב מה שאין כן בתנאים שעושין להבהיל ולמעט השמחה ראוי ליקח קדירה שבורה חרס מחרסי האדמה לשבור והבן זאת. He does not say whom the broken pottery is to terrify, להבהיל, and by adding the words, והבן, he apparently hints at something which he does not care to express. He must have had in mind the popular belief about the purpose of this ceremony. See above note 36 and comp. Elset in Haibri X, No. 39, p. 10–11. For another suggestion why glass should be broken at weddings, see R. Samuel Edels in his Novellae to Berakot 31a. R. Elija Gaon of Wilna is reported to have said that the reason why just pottery must be broken at engagements is in order to suggest that just as the broken earthen vessels cannot be repaired so engagements should never be broken: אמר בשם הגאון זצ"ל שמזה הטעם שוברין בעת התנאים כלים של חרס שכיון שנשברו אין להם תקנה כן אסור לבטל התנאים ובחופה שוברין כלי זכוכית שיש לו תקנה להדבק כן יש תקנה להפרד בנט (quoted in סדר שערי רחמים p. 10 also in ספר תוספת מעשה רב Jerusalem 1896 in שאלתות p. 19 No. 134. The same interpretation is ascribed by others to R. Israel Baal Shem (Besht), see *Taame ha-Minhagim* I. p. 113a.

[39] See R. Ḥayyim b. Israel Benveniste (1603–1673) in his כנסת הגדולה to Eben ha-Ezer 65.

the destruction of Jerusalem will yet be repaired just as a broken vessel of glass can be repaired (comp. b. Ḥagigah 15a). This hope, he goes on to say, is further emphasized by taking another cup, a whole one, and reciting over it the marriage-benedictions, suggesting thereby that God will again be glad to do good to His people and betroth them unto Him in faithfulness forever.[40]

While Trani explains the practice to keep the cup of the marriage-benedictions unbroken as a symbolic sign that in future the relation or the bond between God and Israel will be ever-lasting, there is no doubt that in the popular belief the keeping of the cup of the marriage-benedictions intact was to suggest a good omen that the marriage bond of the couple whose wedding had just been celebrated will remain unbroken. Compare also R. Joseph Teomim (1727–1793) in his משבצות זהב to Oraḥ Ḥayyim 560, 4.

While these Rabbinical authorities thus explained the cere-mony as reminding of the destruction of Jerusalem and as sug-gesting the hope of a renewal of God's relation with Israel as of old, the people, in some countries at least, continued to per-form the ceremony in its original form and for the original pur-pose of giving the demons a bribe. This is evident from a statement of R. Pinehas Horowitz (died 1805) in the קונטרס אחרון of his ספר המקנה (Offenbach 1786) p. 256. Horowitz like R. Joseph Teomim (op. cit.) explains away the objection that might be raised to the ceremony of breaking the glass on the ground that it involves a violation of the law of בל תשחית. But he strongly objects to the manner in which the ceremony was per-formed in his time in Germany, that is, the breaking of the cup while it is full of wine מה שנהגו באשכנז לשבור הכוס מלא יין. This he thinks is wrong since the spilling of the wine is an act of ביזוי אוכלין a slighting of food and thus despising God's gifts. We see from this that even as late as the second half of the 18th century the custom in Germany, or at least in certain parts of Germany, was to throw the cup of wine to the ground, thus smashing the glass and spilling the wine. Evidently then

---

[40] He says as follows: עכשיו נהגו לשבר הכוס של זכוכית של ברכת אירוסין משום
ענבת נפש זכר לחורבן ורומזים בתקוה שכשם שזכוכית שנשברה יש לה תקנה ונוטלין כוס שלם ומברכין
ברכות נישואין לומר שעתיד הקב"ה לשוב לשיש עלינו לטוב כמה שנאמר וארשתיך לי באמונה וכו

it was intended as a gift to the demons.[41]   This is clearly stated
by a contemporary of Horowitz, R. Uri Feivel b.Aaron in His
אור החכמה. Part II (Laszczow 1815) p. 6b.   He describes this
throwing of the glass with the wine as the portion due to the
"Other Side" which is always desirous of bringing about destruction and separation והוא חלק לסטרא אחרא שרוצה תמיד בחרבן ופירוד
The "Other Side" is a designation for Satan and the evil spirits.
They are desirous of doing harm and bringing about separation,
hence we give them a bribe to desist from harming the marrying
couple or trying to separate them.   Thus we see that all the interpretations of the Rabbis and their efforts to make this ceremony
merely of a symbolic character were not sufficient to uproot from
the mind of the people the old superstition that the ceremony is
intended as a bribe for the demons to make them more friendly
to the marrying couple.   It was left to another superstition
to defeat this old supersition, and remove it from the mind of
the people at least in connection with this ceremony.

It seems that the people began to be afraid of breaking even
the cup over which the benedictions of the betrothal were recited.   Since both the ברכת אירוסין and ברכות נשואין are at present
parts of the ritual by which the marriage is solemnized, the people
entertained the fear that the breaking of the cup over which
either one of these benedictions had been recited might augur
a breach in the marriage bond.   The custom was, therefore,
introduced of breaking another glass altogether, i. e., one which
has not been used in connection with the performance of the
marriage ceremony at all.   They usually have in readiness
another glass especially for the purpose of being broken.   This
is now the general practice as far as I know and the earliest
reference that I can find is one by R. Joseph Teomim in his משבצות
זהב l. c. where he says: "But I have seen the custom that
they take a glass cup for the benedictions of the betrothal.
It seems however that they do not break this cup after the marriage benedictions but it is another glass that they break after
the recital of the seven benedictions." אבל ראיתי המנהג שלוקחין
כוס זכוכית לאירוסין ומכל מקום נראה שאין שוברין אותו אחר נישואין כי
אם כוס אחר שוברין אחר שבע ברכות

---

[41] See above notes 32 and 35.

This latest form of the ceremony has also revived and developed some other superstitions. The idea of fighting the demons seems to have been revived and the successful smashing of the glass by the bridegroom is taken as a good omen, auguring that he will subdue and smash all his enemies.[42] If however the bridegroom should fail to crush the glass with the first stamping of his foot, as would happen if the glass slips away from under his foot, then it augurs ill for him. It might suggest that his enemies will escape from him or that he will fail to defeat them. To avoid the occurrence of such a bad omen it is customary to wrap the glass in a handkerchief so that it will not slip away when he steps on it and thus he will be sure to crush it with the first stamping of his foot.

[42] There is a suggestion of this popular belief in the mystic saying ולאחר החופה שוברין כוס שהוא בסוד הפח נשבר שהוא שבירת הקליפות quoted in Taame ha-Minhagim I. p. 111 No. 955. The Palestinian Jews also wrap the glass in a handkerchief and while it is being broken the assembled guests recite also the verse from Ps. 124, 7: "The snare is broken and we are escaped". The wrapping of the glass in a handkerchief also serves the purpose of preventing any of the broken pieces from getting lost. It is a popular belief among the Palestinians Jews that if one familiar with witchcraft got hold of the broken pieces he could by means of it bewitch the groom, making him sick and preventing him from joining the bride. Hence they are very careful to gather up all the pieces of the broken glass and bury them. See A. M. Luncz, *Jerusalem* I (Wien 1882) Hebrew section p. 7-8.

ILLUMINATED MARRIAGE CONTRACTS

With Special Reference to the Cincinnati Ketubahs

FRANZ LANDSBERGER

Hebrew Union College - Jewish Institute of Religion, Cincinnati

THE Jewish marriage contract, of interest from not a few angles, makes, by reason of its rich ornamentation, an especial appeal to connoisseurs of art. The value of these illuminated Ketubahs mounts as we realize that we have here a form of art in which the Jews are unique. Marriage contracts appear from earliest times and among widely diverse peoples. But it occurred only to the Jews to adorn these contracts with sumptuous embellishment. There is to be found in the City Archives of Siena, Italy, not a marriage contract but a marriage certificate of the fifteenth century. Pictured on this certificate is the marriage ceremony of Roberto Sanseverino and Lucrezia Malvolti.[1] But this appears to be an exception. Inquiries which I sent to Florence and to Venice brought the reply that no ornamented marriage contracts had been preserved at those places. This assuredly indicates that such documents were not produced.

Considering the uniqueness of the ornamented Jewish marriage contract, we are not surprised that these have been sought after by museums, libraries, and private collectors. The Hebrew Union College Museum can pride itself on the possession of a large — perhaps the largest extant — set of these documents; one hundred and eleven, to be precise. This makes it all the more astounding that research has accorded that subject but scant attention. Moses Gaster's book[2] stresses the importance of the

---

[1] A picture in the illustrated Phaidon Edition of Jacob Burckhardt, *The Civilization of the Renaissance in Italy*, Illust. 380.

[2] The *Ketubah*, Berlin-London, 1923. For other literature I mention David Kaufmann, "Zur Geschichte der juedischen Handschriften-Illustration im Mittelalter," in his *Gesammelte Schriften*, III, 1915, pp. 195–199; Isidore Epstein, "The Ketubah Collection at the Jewish Museum" (London) in *The Jewish Chronicle*, September 15, 1933; Karl Schwarz, Introduction to the Catalogue of the Ketubah Exhibit in the Museum of Tel-Aviv, 1954 (Hebrew).

Reprinted from *The Jewish Marriage Anthology*, edited by Philip and Hanna Goodman, Jewish Publication Society of America, Philadelphia, 1965.

Ketubah for Jewish living. It carries a few good illustrations. But it concerns itself not at all with those questions of art history to which contracts of that kind would give rise. It behooves us therefore to approach the topic from that angle and to ask: Why and when did the ornamental Ketubah originate? What was its course of development? What forms did the ornamentation assume? And, finally, who were the persons that produced this type of Jewish art?

I. Origin and Development of the Ornamental Marriage Contract

As regards the ornamental Ketubah's "place in life," I would call the reader's attention to the illustration here given of a Jewish marriage ceremony pictured on an English Torah-binder

a) DETAIL OF A TORAH BINDER, LONDON, 1733.
London, Jewish Museum.

of the eighteenth century. We perceive some men holding a beautiful canopy beneath which a bridegroom places a gold ring on the finger of his betrothed. The bride is charmingly robed. In earlier times a crown would have rested on her head. At the bride's left is to be seen another splendidly dressed woman — in all likelihood the bride's mother. At the bridegroom's right stands the officiant holding, in his right hand, a beautifully formed goblet and, in his left, a piece of writing, doubtless the Ketubah. Whether this particular Ketubah was ornamented, I can not tell. The Torah-binder belonged to the Ashkenazic Hambro Synagogue in London, while ornamental Ketubahs prevailed, as a rule, among the Sephardim. What I would suppose is that a contract, publicly displayed in such a radiant setting and afterward preserved by the bride or by her father, must surely have invited adornment. What was intended as a purely legal document, specifying the groom's obligations toward his wife-to-be, became a lovely gift along with the bride's other gifts, such as a silver girdle, an elegantly bound prayer book, and similar objects.

Our next question is: When did the Jews begin the practice of such ornamentation? Our earliest sample goes back to ca. the eleventh century. It consists of a fragment of a vellum Ketubah found near Fostat, a suburb of Cairo, and today preserved in the Bodleian Library at Oxford, England[3] (see illust. on p. 506). The modest decoration consists of two intersecting arches marked with circular patches. Judging from its style, this ornament could have originated centuries — perhaps a millennium — earlier. The adorning of marriage contracts may have begun when the Jews still partook of the Hellenistic predilection for the beautiful; that is to say, in the last pre-Christian or in the first Christian centuries. That was when the practice began of decorating scrolls with gilded letters, especially Torah-scrolls;[4] perhaps even of embellishing biblical codices with ornamental pages and with

---

[3] Cf. Ad. Neubauer and A. E. Cowley, *Catalogue of Hebrew Manuscripts in the Bodleian Library*, II, Oxford, 1906, col. 223, No. 2807, 20.

[4] The Jews sent King Ptolemy II (Philadelphus, 308–246 B. C.) a Pentateuch in a number of scrolls. The lettering was of gold and inscribed on parchment, cf. Letter of Aristeas, §176.

b) FRAGMENT OF A MARRIAGE CONTRACT FROM FOSTAT, EGYPT.
About 11th century.
Bodleian Library, Oxford, England.

pictures, a practice later copied from the Jews by the Christians. It happens that all Jewish samples of such ornamentation date from a later period.[5] Similarly the oldest of the marriage contracts may have been destroyed, none but that of ca. the eleventh century surviving.

For four centuries the one from Fostat remains a solitary example. The next of the ornamented Ketubahs known to us dates from a time not earlier than the end of the fourteenth century (see our illustration). This Ketubah, likewise written on

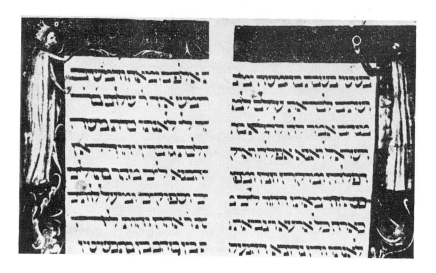

c) MARRIAGE CONTRACT FROM KREMS, AUSTRIA, 1392. Detail.
Vienna, State Library.

vellum, was produced in the year 1392 at Krems in Austria.[6] At present it is preserved in the State Library at Vienna. The script is rimmed by a border crowded with tendrils. Only at the

[5] Of earliest date are the gold-tinged ornamental pages and the illustrations of the Pentateuch of 930 in the State Library at Leningrad. Illustrated in D. Guenzburg and H. V. Stassoff, *L'Ornement Hébreu*, Berlin, 1903.

[6] Cf. Arthur Zacharias Schwarz, "Eine illuminierte Kremser Ketubah aus dem Jahre 1392," in *Archiv fuer juedische Familienforschung*, II, Vienna, 1913, Nos. 4–6; also, by the same author, *Die hebraeischen Handschriften der Nationalbibliothek in Wien*, Leipzig, 1925, p. 23, No. 202.

border's upper end is there an illustration, that of a bridegroom standing at the right and holding high a ring, while the bride, with a crown on her head, appears at the left. This document, prepared for Ashkenazic Jews, is apparently without duplicate. We know not of any other sample, contemporary or subsequent, stemming from the Ashkenazic milieu.

Is it possible that the marriage contracts of the Sephardim may have induced imitation? In Sephardic regions, during the Middle Ages, Ketubahs would, in that event, have gone further than mere ornament. Decoration of a more abstract character predominated, of course, in countries where the Sephardim were influenced by the art of Islam. An example would be a Ketubah dating from 1551 and preserved in the Temple museum at Cleveland, Ohio (see illustration). This Ketubah originated in Cairo, that is, in the same city as the fragment from Fostat and is, like the Fostat fragment, in a poor state of preservation. Here are to be seen triangles and squares. The borders likewise contain shapes other than those of natural objects.

In Europe, development followed other lines. Yet, before we consider these, we must pause over a Ketubah written in Modena and bearing the date: Seventh of Heshvan 5318 (1557). If the date were correct, this Ketubah would rank with the earliest preserved; among the Italian Ketubahs it would be our oldest. But, as I examined the document in the British Museum where it has lain since 1906,[7] I sensed at once that there was something wrong about that date. Those slender columns on high pedestals, this gable with a lambrequin as middle-piece, indicated not the sixteenth century but the eighteenth century (Illust. 1). To become clear about this I had the page photographed and submitted to my colleague, Dr. Isaiah Sonne, who is an outstanding expert on Hebrew manuscripts. Dr. Sonne expressed the following opinion:

Your suspicion against the early date: בששי בשבת שבעת ימים לחדש
חשון שנת חמשת אלפים ו ש ל ש מ א ו ת ושמנה עשרה... (Friday, Heshvan 7, 5318, corresponding to October 12, 1557) of the Ketubah in the British Museum (Margoliouth, 9270/1) was more than justified. A careful

[7] Cf. G. Margoliouth, *Catalogue of the Hebrew and Samaritan Manuscripts*, III, Section VIII–IX, London, 1915, p. 583, No. 1158.

d) MARRIAGE CONTRACT, CAIRO, 1551.
Cleveland, Ohio, Temple Museum.

examination of the Hebrew script leads to the same result. Indeed, the capital, square letters on the top of the Ketubah: בסימנא טבא ובמזלא מעליא have all the characteristics of the middle of the eighteenth century as we know them from many Megilloth in the Kirschstein collection, now HUCL.

However, the decisive proof of the forgery of the date is to be found in the first signature: . . . . מנשה יהושע בכמוהר'ר יהודה מצליח פאדווה "Menashe Joshua ben Jehudah Mazliah Padova." He is a well known scholar, rabbi of Modena, in the middle of the eighteenth century whose approbations (*Hascamoth*) appear quite frequently on Hebrew books printed in Italy between 1740–1756 (cf. for instance, Bassan, Isaiah, *Todath Shelamim*, Venice 1741; Levi Aaron, *Orhoth Hayyim*, Firenze 1750). Some of his responsa are published in Isaac Lampronti's rabbinic encyclopedia *Pahad Yizhak*. In a collection of letters of recommendation in my possession, I find his signature dated 1749, 1751, 1752 (cf. also M. Mortara, *Indice . . . dei Rabbini . . . in Italia*, Padova 1886, p. 47).

Once the identity of the signature has been established, it is not difficult to restore the original date of the Ketubah. As a matter of fact, on closer examination of the word ו ש ל ש it becomes quite clear that the two middle letters were tampered with, and traces of erasures are still visible. Now, the only date which consists of the same number of letters, the last letter being a "Shin," is ו ח מ ש. The original date read therefore: בששי . . . חמשת אלפים ו ח מ ש מ א ו ת . . . Friday, Heshvan the seventh, 5518," corresponding to Nov. 1, 1757.

The calendar favored the forger because, in both dates, 1557 as well as 1757, the seventh of Heshvan fell on a Friday. The forgery could therefore not be detected by checking the day of the week. Luckily, the forger did not think that the signature could betray him; otherwise he might have tried to obliterate the signature, or at least to make it illegible.

Finally, we may add that the two families, Fano and Sanguini, mentioned in this Ketubah, were among the wealthy and influential ones in Modena in the eighteenth century. The Fano family had its private synagogue where, in the second half of the eighteenth century, the Sefardic rite was used."

These findings exclude the London Ketubah from our consideration. Meanwhile a responsum, in which ornamented marriage contracts are the subject of discussion, gives us aid. The author of the responsum is Abraham Ḥiyya di Boton of Salonica who lived from 1560 to 1603, and this approximately fixes the responsum's date. Abraham Ḥiyya's opinion starts thus: "I have been asked concerning the case of a Ketubah in which the scribe drew the picture of the bridegroom and the bride and similarly a picture of the sun and the moon. Is it proper to do so?"[8] The answer runs that a Ketubah, thus ornamented, need not be destroyed once it is in existence, but that basically the making of such a Ketubah is forbidden. This supplies us with proof, from the Sephardic side, that Ketubah ornamentation went beyond mere ornamentation and that it incorporated shapes of sun and of moon and even of human beings.

The representation of a bridal pair reminds us of the Ketubah produced in Krems in 1392. We surmised that the Krems Ketubah may have followed Sephardic models. This surmise is strengthened by the responsum above quoted. Abraham Ḥiyya was the scion of a Spanish family which, together with many others, had made their way to Salonica. It is not unlikely that these refugees brought from their home the practice of embellishing Ketubahs not only with ornaments but also with illustrations which pictured natural objects.

Medieval illuminated manuscripts originating in the Iberian Peninsula show, among the Jews, two divergent tendencies. One is a tendency toward abstraction, following the art of Islam, of which an example would be the so-called Farhi Bible in London. The other is a naturalistic tendency emanating from France and from Italy, of which an example would be the Haggadah of Sarajevo.[9] It could readily be that, to this second tendency, Ketubah ornamentation owes its naturalistic features.

At the time when Abraham Ḥiyya issued his prohibition, still other Jewish multitudes were leaving the Iberian Peninsula. These were the pseudo-Christians who maintained their Judaism in secret and whose lives were, as a consequence, in peril of the Inquisition. Some of these went to Amsterdam where they formed a community whose first Rabbi was Joseph Pardo. Pardo likewise belonged to an old Sephardic family. His forebears also had fled to Salonica, and that is where Pardo was born. Pardo came to

[8] Printed as Responsum No. 15 in his book, *Leḥem Rab*, issued in 1660. For this accurate translation I am indebted to Dr. Jacob Petuchowski who aided me also at the sifting of the Ketubah material in Cincinnati.

[9] The reader will see an illustration of the Farhi Bible in my *History of Jewish Art*, Cincinnati 1946, p. 205. A sample from the Haggadah of Sarajevo will be found there on page 210.

Venice in 1598 and finally to Amsterdam where he remained until his death in 1619.[10] All of which warrants the assumption that Pardo was conversant with Ketubah ornamentation and disposed to transplant that ornamentation to his new home.

A Ketubah transcribed during Pardo's rabbinate (Illust. 2) was extant until World War II.[11] Today it can no longer be found. Its text is framed by a kind of window surmounted by two naked angels, waving flags. Two slender columns rise, one to the right and one to the left. Two cornucopias are to be seen on the lower margin, spilling over with plants and fruits. All of which looks decidedly Italian.[12] Italian Ketubahs doubtless served as models.

This brings us at last to ask regarding Italian Ketubahs: What was their origin? Did they exist already in the Middle Ages? Or were they first introduced by those Jews from the Iberian Peninsula who, after their expulsion, chose Italy as their new home?

About any ornamented Ketubah prepared in medieval Italy, I am uninformed.[13] In the London Jewish Museum there is to be found a manuscript containing a marriage service dated 1452. The picture of a bridal pair adorns the first page. This permits us to conjecture that, in those days already, that is, during the early Renaissance, the Ketubah had ornamentation and that the ornaments probably included representations of objects. But surmise is as far as we can go.

The sixteenth century offers nothing of this kind that has been

[10] Cf. Jacob Swarts, *De eerste rabbijnen en synagogen van Amsterdam*, Amsterdam, 1929, pp. 86 ff.

[11] According to information graciously supplied by the Portugees-Israelitische Gemeente in Amsterdam. My illustration comes from the book by S. Ph. de Vries, *Joodsche Riten en Symbolen*, II, Zutphen, 1932, facing page 144.

[12] Also on book titles of that region will be found those columns entwined with tendrils and those cornucopias. Compare, for example, ספר השרשים printed 1547 in Venice. Illustrated in Mitchell M. Kaplan, *Panorama of Ancient Letters*, New York, 1942, p. 36.

[13] A Ketubah in the Hebrew Union College Museum carries the date 5096 (1336). The ornamentation, however, shows the style of the eighteenth century. The copyist may have erred or he may have omitted the indication of the centuries which, if properly supplied, may have given the year 1736.

preserved. A precise date can be derived from a sample preserved
in the museum of the Hebrew Union College (see our illust. e).

e) Marriage Contract, Ostiano, Italy, 1612.
Hebrew Union College Museum.

This was prepared, 1612, in Ostiano, province of Cremona, in
Upper Italy.

Northern Italy becomes now preeminently the area in which
most Italian Ketubahs receive ornamentation. From Lower Italy

the Jews had been expelled as early as the sixteenth century. Among the Papal States, Rome and Ancona were the only places of residence allowed them; in Toscana, none but the city of Pisa. Meanwhile, in Upper Italy, they were at liberty to reside in a number of choice places. Barring occasional incidents, the Jews here possessed such stability and well-being that they could afford to signalize their nuptials with ornate documents. The wealthy mercantile city of Venice held a particularly large and prosperous Jewish population. Here it is accordingly that marriage contracts display artistic design of extraordinary richness.

But to come back to the Ketubah of Ostiano. Of this, only a fragment remains. Its adornment is sparse, consisting only of a tendril-filled border. In the middle of the upper margin there is a medallion and, in the middle of the lower margin, another medallion. A Levitical pitcher and bowl are represented on the upper one and, on the lower one, the benedictory hands of the Kohanim. In each of the two upper corners, the lower ones having been clipped away, a two-headed eagle betokens the Austrian monarchy which, at that time, held sway over large parts of Upper Italy.[14]

As regards the further development of the ornamented marriage document, the format, relatively small in the Ketubah of Ostiano, becomes, during the seventeenth and eighteenth centuries, larger and larger. A Ketubah prepared in Ancona in 1690 (Illust. 5) is 33 ¾ inches long and 26 ½ wide. The cost of such a document swelled accordingly. The need at length arose to set a limit. The communal authorities of this very place, Ancona, ordain, although not before the year 1766, that the amount to be paid for a Ketubah should not exceed forty Paoli.[15]

As regards the technique of the ornamentation, there developed here and there a certain nicety. This consisted in cutting

---

[14] A double-headed eagle shows also on the title page of ספר כריתות by Samson ben Isaac of Chinon. The book appeared 1558 in Cremona. Illustrated in Mitchell M. Kaplan, *op. cit.*, p. 46.

[15] *Pragmatica ... degli Ebrei*, Ancona, 1766, § XXIX. Cf. Cecil Roth, "New Notes on Pre-Emancipation Jewish Artists," *HUCA* XVII, 1942, p. 503. A Paolo is a half a shilling.

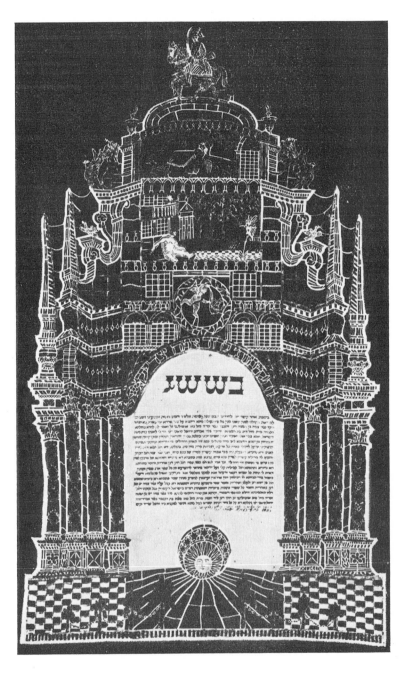

f) Marriage Contract, Firenzuola, Italy, 1832.
Hebrew Union College Museum.

out some of the ornamental designs and inserting a colored underpiece beneath the excision. For an example of this technique, let us look once more at the Ketubah in the British Museum, the one falsely dated sixteenth century although belonging to the eighteenth century (Illust. 1). Here the borders have been treated in this way and a red foil placed beneath. The Jewish Museum in New York has a Ketubah, produced in Modena in 1756, which handles, in this manner, not only the borders but all of the ornamental areas. The same characterizes the Ketubah prepared in 1832 and now preserved at the Hebrew Union College (see preceding page). The script is surrounded by ornate shapes of palace architecture stitched, like a lattice, on a dark brown foil.

At length the fad for ornamental marriage contracts, despite insufficiency of means, generated the wish to procure such pieces ready-made, lacking only the insertions. Technical means for this was provided by the art of engraving which had, by that time, entered Jewish art generally. In Amsterdam such an engraving was made by Shalom Italia who had fled to Holland after the expulsion of the Jews from Mantua in 1630. This engraving rims the text with figures of flowers and of biblical love-mates.[16] There is also a Ketubah attributable to the year 1659 and used during the rabbinate of Isaac da Fonseca Aboab (see our illustration g).[17] A married couple is pictured here at the upper right — a motif which we have found existed earlier. Pictured at the left is a hint of the future — a woman with two children. Beneath these two groups run vertical streaks of flowers sprouting from two large vases. Each vase is flanked by two small pots of tulips which, it is well known, are that country's favorite flower. For decades after Fonseca's death, this engraving was still in demand. An added

[16] A sample of that engraving, dated 1648, is to be found in the Bezalel National Museum at Jerusalem. Illustrated in the catalogue of the Ketubah exhibit held 1954 at Tel-Aviv.

[17] The copy dated 1659 is illustrated in *The Jewish Encyclopedia*, VII, p. 476. The owner is given as the jeweller, Albert Wolf, of Dresden who bequeathed his collection to the Jewish community of Berlin. Since the looting of the Berlin Jewish Museum by the Nazis, the copy has vanished.

g) Marriage Contract, Engraving, Amsterdam, 1706.
Hebrew Union College Museum.

inscription mentioned the Rabbi's name and the date of his death, the twenty-seventh of Adar Sheni 5453 (1693).[18]

[18] Compare the Hebrew article by M. Narkiss, "H. Y. Aboab no Copper Engraver," in the periodical, *Kirjath Sepher*, XV, 1938–39, p. 489.

The engraving got to be used for Ketubah decoration likewise in Italy, and once in a uniquely Italian way (see our illustration h). The delight of the Italians in the nude human form comes to expression in a picture of the first couple reclining under the Tree

h) MARRIAGE CONTRACT, ENGRAVING, MANTOVA, ITALY, 1689.
New York, Jewish Theological Seminary.

of Knowledge. The broad margins contain nude forms of winged cherubs alternating with scenes from the Bible. The style war-

i) MARRIAGE CONTRACT, VERONA, ITALY, 1681.
Hebrew Union College Museum.

rants attributing the cut to the sixteenth century; Eve suggests the Venetian figures of Venus at the height of the Renaissance. Still, the only samples known to me are the one fashioned at Mantua in 1689 and one fashioned at Citadella in 1693.[19] This indicates, for the engravings, a time nearer the end of the seventeenth century. Upper Italy was presumably their place of origin; first, because of the cities just mentioned and further, because of their display of Austria's two-headed eagle.

As in Holland so also in Italy a second engraving for Ketubahs came into vogue. Of this I know a single poorly preserved sample, dated Verona 1681 and housed in the museum of the Hebrew Union College (see preceding page). This sample must likewise have originated toward the end of the seventeenth century and its place of origin, we guess, was also Northern Italy.

Thus both in Holland and in Italy the engraving served as the basic device for marriage contracts. The only difference was that, in Holland, the engraving so dominated the market that the hand-fashioned Ketubah disappeared.[20] In Italy, by contrast, the colorless engraving was regarded as lacking in beauty. The Ketubah was preferred which glowed with color.[21] There was also the desire to have, if obtainable, a Ketubah of which there was no other copy, such being more consonant with the individuality of the person letting the order. Italy is therefore the country which, from the seventeenth century to the middle of the nineteenth century, cultivated and brought to perfection the Ketubah embellished by hand.[22]

[19] The Mantua copy belongs to the Jewish Theological Seminary in New York. The Citadella copy has been in the possession of the Jewish Museum in Berlin.

[20] Still less demanding was England which accepted the engraved Ketubah from Holland but seems never to have taken the trouble to produce a Ketubah made by hand. The same can be said about the Sephardic Jews who settled in the United States.

[21] Only in rare instances did the lack of color in the engraved Ketubahs influence the Ketubahs made by hand, keeping these likewise without color.

[22] In the Hebrew Union College Museum, which is especially well supplied with Ketubahs from Italy, there are a few also from Carpentras and from Bordeaux. But these French Ketubahs, small in format, limit their adornment to a few clumsily drawn flowers. A Ketubah issued at Bayonne in 1705 takes over the Dutch Aboab Ketubah and adds coloration.

II. Means by Which the Marriage Contract Was Beautified

The increasing size of the marriage contract made it desirable to contrive a more attractive appearance for the shape of the page. To this end, one of the shorter sides was shortened still further. In other words, it was run into a point having a contour sometimes simple, sometimes more elaborate. This point, which rendered it easier to open the Ketubah scroll, was placed at the upper end; although sometimes, especially in Rome, it was placed at the lower end.

Ordinarily, as regards the script, the Hebrew square character, pithy and full of charm, was preferred. That the text might show symmetry and solidity, the last line would be as long as the lines preceding. This was achieved either by broadening the letters or by inserting a number of symbols after the last word (see illust. on pp. 519, 524).

From the illuminated manuscripts of the Middle Ages the usage was copied of making the first word stand out by means of enlargement or of coloration or by hoisting it above the text. Traditionally the first word named the day of the week on which the people had their wedding. In the above mentioned Dutch engraving Ketubah (Illust., p. 517) the word ברביעי is part of the printed formula because Wednesday was the day customary for the weddings of maidens.[23]

Sometimes, instead of naming the day of the week, the heading would read; בסימן טוב, sometimes with the addition of ובמזלא מעליא.[24] Also favored as preambles were biblical sentences like: "Whoso findeth a wife findeth a great good" (Prov. 18.22), or "The voice of mirth and the voice of gladness, the voice of the bridegroom and the voice of the bride" (Jer. 25.10), with other biblical texts scattered among the ornaments. As in Jewish art generally, no distinction was drawn between viewing an object and reading a text.

---

[23] Ketubot I, 1.

[24] The preamble מזל טוב is Ashkenazic and appears in Italian marriage contracts only when the bridegroom is not a Sephardi.

Out of regard for tradition, there asserts itself, now and then, a hesitancy about picturing aught "that is in heaven above, or that is in the earth beneath, or that is in the water under the earth"; while in deference to the art of Islam, there arose a tendency to employ shapes woven out of intricate threads, completely alien to anything in nature (see p. 530). An especial fondness is manifest for framing the entire text in a portal. Such portals were familiar from the title pages of printed books. On the marriage contracts they could signify a parallel between beginning a new book and beginning a new phase of life.

With the ordinary Ketubah, a single arch resting on pillars or columns would suffice. But, if special stipulations were added, the portal would, in all likelihood, have a middle support (see illustration, p. 527). The first column in Hebrew, the one to the right, would contain the usual text. In the left column would stand the addenda. Sometimes the columns would twist into spirals (Illust. 1). This spiral motif, appearing first on the title pages of books, had migrated to Torah curtains, Torah covers, and Torah breastplates. These columns were intended as reminders of the columns in the Solomonic Temple. It was erroneously believed that some of these columns had been preserved in St. Peter's at Rome.[25]

To these architectural themes belongs also the replica of Jerusalem with reference to the words of Ps. 137.6: "If I set not Jerusalem above my chiefest joy." Consonant with that verse the Holy City would, as a rule, stand pictured at the peak of the page. From this picture, of course, the Temple could not be lacking. But the Temple is here not oblong, as reported by the Bible and by Josephus. It is shown rather as a central structure resembling the Mosque of Omar erected on the Temple site. Pictures of that mosque may have been brought by pilgrims from Palestine to the West.[26]

Let us now turn to objects of nature. Here also we trace a

[25] See my article, "Old Time Torah Curtains," in *HUCA* XIX, 1946, pp. 373 ff.

[26] Christian painters likewise preferred to give the Temple at Jerusalem the appearance of a central structure, for example, Perugino and Raphael in their pictures of the "Marriage of the Holy Virgin."

gradation from that which was deemed harmless to that which was slightly dubious and thence to that which was forbidden even from the liberal point of view. There was no objection to flowers. Inasmuch as flowers must have graced the weddings, flowers were well suited for the ornamentation of marriage contracts. Painted separately or woven into wreaths or garlands, flowers proclaimed the Jewish pleasure in the things of nature. Particularly lifelike are the flowers in a Ketubah of 1723 — tigerlilies, convolvuli, roses, carnations, tulips, and the like. In our uncolored illustration, these are most imperfectly reproduced.

Hovering around the flowers are insects and birds. The animal world also provokes no objection. Our page 524 exhibits robins, woodpeckers, swallows, and a butterfly showing no less realistically than the flowers.

It is probable that these plants and animals embody symbolism. Ps. 128.3 reads: "Thy wife shall be like a fruitful vine, in the innermost parts of thy house." That is perhaps the significance of the grapevine within a palace, as illustrated on page 515. The verse continues: "Thy children like olive plants, round about thy table"; the olive twigs entwining the columns on a handwritten Ketubah from Holland may be thus interpreted (Illust. 2). Symbolic likewise may be the frequently appearing pomegranates. The plenitude of seeds in the pomegranate bespeaks the hope for a plenitude of offspring.

The purport of animals was similar. The Hebrew Union College collection includes a Ketubah the margin of which is filled with an alternation of branches and of doves. The dove could be a tribute to the beloved maiden, often likened to a dove in the Song of Songs. Of course, we are not altogether certain. Plants and animals can serve a purely decorative purpose. For art, when naively pursued, mingles the weighty and the playful without any sharp distinction. A beautiful Ketubah prepared in Venice in 1645 (Cecil Roth Collection, Oxford, England)[27] shows four peacocks, two with drooping tails and two with spreading plumage. At times peacocks figure as symbols of immortality, but here apparently they serve no other object than that of height-

---

[27] Illustrated in *The Jewish Encyclopedia*, IX, 1932, col. 1183–84.

j) MARRIAGE CONTRACT, ANCONA, ITALY, 1723.
Hebrew Union College Museum.

ening the decorativeness of the page. Among art works of the
Italian Renaissance, peacocks appear on Crivelli's "Annuncia-

tion" in London, and on Mantegna's ceiling of the Camera degli Sposi in Mantua. With these paintings also, symbolic implications seem to have vanished.

So far as the human form is concerned, the days were long past when, to keep within Talmudic restrictions, a human being had to wear the head of an animal or to undergo any other disfigurations. The human form is now utilized without scruple. Loving couples are pictured despite Abraham Ḥiyya's interdict. These are, to be sure, lovers from the Bible like Abraham and Sarah, Isaac and Rebekah, Jacob and Rachel, Ruth and Boaz. The craftsman who made the large Italian engraved Ketubah placed Adam and Eve at the top of his page, and those same figures stand forth in still other marriage contracts. Inspiration for this may have issued from the benediction pronounced at the marriage ceremony: "O make these loved companions greatly to rejoice, even as of old Thou didst gladden Thy creature in the garden of Eden."

Further opportunity for biblical representation was furnished by searching the Pentateuchal portion and the *Haftarah* of the Sabbath which followed the wedding, and picturing, on the Ketubah, some biblical figure there mentioned. Presently we shall become acquainted with a sample.

Still more often the name of the bridegroom occasioned dwelling upon the biblical forerunner with that name. Thus, on one of our marriage contracts the conspicuous figure is that of the prophet Samuel because one of the bridegroom's names was Samuel (Illust. 3). On a Ketubah which mentions as bridegroom a certain Joseph, we perceive the biblical Joseph, in Egyptian attire, joyfully greeting his little brother Benjamin (Illust. 4). Astonishing in this connection is the contract already mentioned, prepared in Fiorenzuola in 1832 (see illustration, p. 515). Here the bridegroom has the name Zemah (sprout) in allusion to Jer. 23.5, "I will raise unto David a righteous sprout." In this context we would expect a representation of the Messiah but, instead, one sees King David as he watches, from the balcony of his palace, the wife of Uriah in the act of bathing.

Ordinarily the biblical theme is determined by the man. Since it is he who orders the Ketubah, he regards himself as entitled to do the choosing. But sometimes the man is gallant enough to order also a biblical construction based on the name of his bride, such as Esther, Ruth, and the like.

On the above mentioned Ketubah with the figure of the prophet Samuel, one recognizes Moses and Aaron sitting at either side of Samuel, and the inscription, "Moses and Aaron among His priests, and Samuel among them that call upon His name, did call upon the Lord, and He answered them" (Ps. 99.6).[28] A Ketubah written in Ancona in 1690 (Illust. 5) shows, near the top, the two tables of the Law while two similarly shaped figures, one on either side of the tables, point at the tables with uplifted arms. Are both figures Moses, or did the artist, for the sake of convenience, picture Moses and Aaron as identical? The connection between the marriage contract and Moses lies in its formula, "Be thou my wife according to the Law of Moses and Israel." Amplifying this was the ancient conception that Israel's relation to God and the Torah transmitted by Moses resembles that of a bride to the groom. It was in this way that the Song of Songs, originally something secular, became vested with religious import.

It is of interest that some of the Ketubahs written in Italy and adorned with figures of Moses and Aaron are dedicated not to any mortal pair but to the relationship between Israel and God. Such a Ketubah, emanating from Italy of the seventeenth century, was procured not long ago by the Jewish Museum in New York.[29]

Representations of God are avoided. There is eschewed even the substitute of a hand outstretched from the clouds such as was permitted in late Antiquity at Dura Europos and at Beth Alpha and such as was permitted in the Middle Ages. Heaven is shown in the Ketubah of the second Dutch engraving (see illust.,

[28] Of a Ketubah dated 1780 and showing similar personages — except that King David takes the place of Samuel — an illustration is given in the *Juedisches Lexikon*, III, col. 675, without, however, indicating the place of preservation. The Ketubah is to be found in the Budapest Academy of Sciences. The master with whom it originated is identical, no doubt, with the one who made our Hebrew Union College Ketubah (Ferrara, 1775).

[29] Cf. Stephen S. Kayser, "Shabuot in Jewish Art," in the periodical, *Women's Week Outlook*, Vol. 23, 1953, No. 4, p. 16.

p. 517), but the visibility of God is shut out by a curtain. Two angels hold up the curtain. Those angels demonstrate that the medieval hesitancy about representing angels had ceased. In

k) Marriage Contract, Venice, Italy, 1649.
Hebrew Union College Museum.

Italian marriage contracts, angels are pictured as small naked boys corresponding to the *putti* of Italian art, or as large girls with huge wings. On the Ketubah just mentioned, with the two-fold figuration of Moses, such angels bear the two tables of the Law; for, according to the ancient conception, angels accompanied God or took the place of God when the Law was promulgated at Mt. Sinai.[30]

Moreover, not every winged shape is to be regarded as an angel. On a Ketubah produced at Venice in 1649 (see p. 527), a winged personage blows a trumpet, but the Hebrew inscription reads: "A good name is better than precious oil" (Eccl. 7.1). According to this, the wife is the Fama who trumpets forth the bridegroom's good repute. The counterpart of Fama is a picture of a husbandman with implements of farming, illustrative of the verse, Eccl. 11.6, "In the morning sow thy seed, and in the evening withhold not thy hand."

Already the Mishnah announces a prohibition against picturing sun and moon.[31] With special reference to marriage contracts, this prohibition was repeated by Abraham Ḥiyya. The prohibition was generally observed. The sun is nonetheless displayed on the Fiorenzuola contract of which we have already made frequent mention (Illust., p. 515). Adjoining the sun is the sickle of the moon accompanied by stars. On Italian marriage contracts stars function prominently as the twelve constellations which were supposed to control human destiny. This ancient oriental belief had penetrated to the Jews in early times. The *Mazzal Tob* spoken at weddings means literally "favorable star" and voices the wish that a favorable star might inaugurate that important stage of life.[31a] Jewish art had long before appropriated this theme. Constellations appear on mosaic floors of late Antiquity (Na'aran, Beth Alpha) as well as in book miniatures of the Middle Ages. In Italy, Jewish belief in the stars was strength-

---

[30] Cf. Louis Ginzberg, *The Legends of the Jews*, Philadelphia, 1911, III, 94; also Jehoshua Guttmann, "Engel in der apokryphen Literatur," in *Encyclopedia Judaica*, VI, col. 635.

[31] Abodah Zarah, III, 3.

[31a] On the Torah-binder, of which the picture is given on page 504, a star is therefore placed between the words מזל and טוב.

ened by the intense addiction to that belief on the part of the non-Jews.[32] The pictures of the constellations added to the marriage contract were accordingly also an aspect of assimilation to the surroundings. The difference lay in that Christian art made the sequence run clockwise, from left to right; while Jewish art followed the opposite course. To this should be added that, in Jewish art, the stars are sometimes pictured in purely formal groupings contrary to normal (Illust. 6).[33] Leo is placed opposite Aries, Capricorn opposite Taurus, these being mammals. Scorpio is placed opposite Cancer, both being crustaceans. Aquarius is placed opposite Sagittarius, Virgo opposite Gemini, that is, person opposite person. Of Libra, with its two scale-pans, the opposite is Pisces, always painted as a double.

Already in Jewish Antiquity, the constellations were associated with the four seasons and, in Italian marriage contracts, the linkage persists. Spring is embodied in a woman who picks roses; summer in a woman who reaps grain; autumn is a woman who gathers grapes, and winter is an aged man warming his hands at an open fire.

These groupings once arrived at were augmented by further groupings. There were the four elements among which fire was represented by the giving of the Law at Mt. Sinai; earth, by a sower; water, by a fountain; and air, by a ship with sails distended by the wind. There were also portrayals of the four senses — four, not five, because at that time touch was not yet reckoned as one of the senses.[34] Sight was a woman looking into a mirror; smell, a woman scenting a flower. Taste was a couple eating fruit. A man performing on a lute represented hearing.

Such groupings embraced likewise the sacred appurtenances of the Temple. On the Ketubah illustrated, p. 530, one perceives

[32] In his *Civilization of the Renaissance*, English Phaidon Edition, p. 268, Jacob Burckhardt says: "From the relations of the planets among themselves and to the signs of the Zodiac, whole lives were inferred, and the most weighty decisions were taken in consequence."

[33] This deviation was noted already by I. Sonne in his article, "Postscript to 'The Zodiak' " in the publication of the Hebrew Union College Library, *Studies in Bibliography and Booklore*, I, 82.

[34] Cf. David Kaufman, *Die Sinne. Beitraege zur Geschichte der Physiologie und Psychologie im Mittelalter*, Leipzig 1884, pp. 188 ff.

1) MARRIAGE CONTRACT, SPILIMBERGO, ITALY, 1752.
Hebrew Union College Museum.

in the corners, beginning at the upper right, the laver and its base, the seven-branched candelabrum, the table with the shewbread, and the Ark of the Covenant.

On the large Italian engraved Ketubah (Illust., p. 518) we descry above and below, an empty cartridge. This was reserved for picturings of a lesser kind, such as the bridegroom's or the bride's coat of arms or such as symbols of religious rank. Kohanim are recognizable by their hands uplifted in benediction, and Levites by their bowl and pitcher.

Only once does there occur the figure of a horseman. This is on the Ketubah of Fiorenzuola (see p. 515). At first I took this to be a representation of the Messiah in allusion to the bridegroom's name, Zemah. The Messiah, however, rides not on a horse but on an ass (Zech. 9.9).[35] Also inappropriate would be the three-cornered hat. The picture suggests Napoleon I who, conquering Upper Italy in 1792, liberated the Jews from their ghettos. After Napoleon's downfall, this emancipation was reversed. A Jew suffering under that disability would naturally acclaim Napoleon as a hero.[36]

We notice the large number of motifs which enter into Ketubah decoration, above all into the Ketubahs fashioned in Italy. All of which reflects an alertness of mind which cannot but command our admiration.

The forms likewise in which these motifs appear are manifold and vary from time to time. In the slenderly rising Tuscan columns, in the blithe little angels, and in the cornucopias at the lower margin, the hand-painted Dutch Ketubah of the early seventeenth century (Illust. 2) exhibits every hallmark of the Renaissance.

The Baroque style, following the Renaissance, inclines toward the heavy, the solemn, and the sumptuous, and this appears in some of our contracts. A marriage contract of 1690 (Illust. 5)

---

[35] Usually regarded as the Messiah, the rider on a white horse in a Haggadah of the State and University Library at Munich (Cod. Hebr. 200), is really Elijah. Illustration in the *Universal Jewish Encyclopedia*, Vol. 7, p. 502.

[36] The bend of the sword has no connection with the Turkish sword. The sword was kept as close as possible to the rider in order to prevent its tearing off.

strikes the eye not only by its exceptional size but also by the
heroic poses of the figures in the side margins, by the scope of the
two shells, by the ponderous gable split for the tables of the Law,

m) MARRIAGE CONTRACT, RIVA, ITALY, 1709.
Hebrew Union College Museum.

and by the angels with their billowing robes. On the marriage contract of 1709, here illustrated, a contract also betraying the Baroque, one sees strong green pillars pushed together and winding upward in spirals. These pillars are entwined with bands of red and crowned with golden capitals. Here the gable is split to make room for the family's coat of arms.

In the eighteenth century, art eventually lost this heaviness and acquired the charming lightness called Rococo. For the double column, a Ketubah of 1723 (see illustration on p. 524) substitutes simple pillars flanked by flowers, birds, and a vase, the vase still showing some Baroque exuberance. Even finer and more delicate is the Ketubah in the British Museum (Illust. 1) which was our reason for assigning it to the middle of the eighteenth century. From lofty pedestals, slender columns ascend, bearing the airy structure which terminates in a lambrequin. The Ketubah dated 1781 (Illust. 4), with the scene of Joseph and Benjamin, exhibits in the loose flowers, the tendrils and the shell-like curves, all the striving after ease and spread by which Rococo is marked. A Ketubah here illustrated, on p. 534, avoids every pictorial representation except the coat of arms. This document contents itself with tendrils ever swaying as they dance around the text.

Then occurs a further change of style. Playfulness and lightness become tiring. The desire emerges for more repose and earnestness. Because some classic motifs are thereupon resumed, the word for this tendency is Neo-Classicism. The movement extends from the later eighteenth century to the early part of the nineteenth century. A Ketubah of 1818 (Illust. 7) shows stately female figures in Empire costume. One of them, inscribed La Bontà (Goodness) is in the act of restoring young birdlets to the nest whence they have fallen. Supplementing La Bontà, La Costanza (Steadfastness) leans against a firm pillar. Thus are depicted the virtues of the married.

In this style of art, religious motifs recede. Ketubahs of this period go so far as to let scenes from heathenism supersede the sacred. In a marriage contract of 1790, belonging once to the Jewish Museum of Berlin but of late transferred to the Hebrew Union College Museum in Cincinnati, the love which joins the

n) Marriage Contract, Verona, Italy, 1764.
Hebrew Union College Museum.

bridal pair is typified by the heathen love deities, Venus and Cupid (Illust. 8).[37]

In the further course of the nineteenth century there asserts itself a certain historicism. The old styles linger in memory, with the result that now one style is followed and now another. The Jewish Theological Seminary in New York preserves a Ketubah from Verona. The graceful tendrils in this Ketubah exhibit a quality resembling Rococo. It is, however, not the Rococo of the eighteenth century but a nineteenth century imitation of Rococo. The date of this Ketubah is as recent as 1849.

We may similarly view the Ketubah of Fiorenzuola, mentioned by us several times and pictured on page 515. The ponderousness of its palace architecture would induce us to class this Ketubah as Baroque and to place it in the seventeenth or the early eighteenth century. As matter of fact, its date is 1832, the artist having simply revived a pattern of the past.

With the middle of the nineteenth century we can, at least so far as Europe is concerned, terminate our study of the ornamented Ketubah. From that time on, ornamented Ketubahs become fewer and fewer, and their quality so deteriorates that they are no longer worth considering. Only in the Orient do people cling tenaciously to Ketubah ornamentation, but here it is something purely decorative, and this does not necessitate further inquiry.

III. By Whom Were Illuminated Marriage Contracts Made?

Let us begin our inquiry with a Ketubah, here pictured, on page 536, to be found in the Hebrew Union College. This Ketubah contains the signature "N.D.M. fecit Lib. (Leghorn) 1782." Beneath this Latin, stand the Italian words: "Serbin felicità si dolci patti," ("May these sweet pacts serve happiness"). If the Latin signature and the Italian adage lead us to suspect a non-Jewish artist, the structure of the work displays nothing opposed

---

[37] The small oval pictures in the vertical borders refer to two of the virtues. The woman with the snake represents prudence. The woman whose finger points heavenward represents faith.

o) Marriage Contract, Livorno, Italy, 1782.
Hebrew Union College Museum.

to that conclusion. Jewish themes are lacking; while the coloration, rather subdued, differs from the vivid color scheme usual in such documents.

There are reasons for conjecturing that a non-Jew also decorated the marriage contract which is in the British Museum (Illust. 1). Judging from the superscriptions of the tiny scenes placed between the pedestals of the columns, these refer to the Sabbath following the day of marriage (Heshvan 7). The Pentateuchal portion of that day yields the scene in which Abraham, Sarah, and Lot, obedient to God's command, leave their native land (Gen. 12.1–4). From the *Haftarah* comes the figure of Jacob, deep in thought (Isa. 40.27). But, in Jewish art, as we noted when treating the constellations, the sequence of the scenes moves from right to left. In the Ketubah of the British Museum this is reversed. The earlier scenes stand toward the left, the later ones toward the right.

Dr. Sonne, who counseled me regarding the date of this Ketubah, expresses this opinion concerning the artist: "The fact that the order of scenes taken from the Parashah and the Haftarah respectively is from left to right, may suggest that they were executed by a non-Jewish artist. Otherwise we would expect the scene with the superscription from the Parashah at the right side, followed by the Haftarah-scene at the left." I should like to add that also the zodiac which adorns the border proceeds clockwise while, in other instances, following the mode of Hebrew script, it proceeds in the contrary direction.

That Christian artists were employed by Jews is nothing to occasion surprise. Without more ado, we can take it for granted that the decorator of this, that, or the other marriage contract may have been non-Jewish.

There is, at the same time, abundant evidence that marriage contracts have been embellished by Jews. The above-mentioned sequence of the zodiac from left to right we have just characterized as Christian by very reason of the fact that it was exceptional. A Jewish artist is therefore to be surmised wherever there is a counterclockwise succession of the scenes. In the Italian engraving which shows the recumbent figures of Adam and Eve (Illustration on p. 518), the unabashed representation of nude human beings comports with Italian art in general. But, on this very page, the small-sized scenes, beginning with the creation of Eve, run from right to left, which indicates the Jewish artist.

p) MARRIAGE CONTRACT, MODENA, ITALY, 1657.
Hebrew Union College Museum.

We have already noticed how, on some marriage contracts, the adornment is inseparably merged with certain Hebrew words and verses. Such peculiarities would also have to be ascribed to Jewish craftsmanship.

Finally, as regards Jewish designers of marriage contracts, we have some definite information. We have this information, of course, only in rare instances because, as a rule, a Ketubah does not carry the artist's signature. The maker of the early Dutch engraved Ketubah signs himself: Shalom Italia. This is the name of a well-known Jewish engraver who immigrated to Holland after the expulsion of the Jews from Mantua in 1630. Of the hand-painted marriage contracts in the Hebrew Union College Museum, only one shows a Jewish signature. This is discernible, in the reproduction, at the bottom (see our illust. at left). It reads "the work of Yehudah Frances." That Frances is a Jew is demonstrated not only by the Hebrew but also by the fact that Frances is the name of a well-known Jewish-Italian family, and a highly talented family. Besides our artist there were two brothers, Emanuel and Jacob Frances, who were distinguished poets.

We turn once more to the responsum of Abraham Ḥiyya of Salonica. The responsum begins: "I have been asked concerning the case of a Ketubah in which the scribe drew the picture of the bridegroom and the bride" etc. Here it is taken for granted that the one who penned the text of the Ketubah is identical with the one who did the adorning. This dual function of scribe and illuminator is nothing new. It adheres to the old tradition, going back to the Middle Ages, when each book was copied separately and when the scribe, if he had the ability, would add initials and illustrations.

With the invention of printing in the fifteenth century, the activity of the Jewish scribe sharply declined. He did nonetheless retain a few of his prerogatives. He could continue to transcribe Torah-scrolls, Esther-scrolls, *Mezuzot*, phylacteries, marriage contracts, and bills of divorce. The trouble was that, for most of such writings, ornamentation was not permitted. Small wonder that a copyist, with artistic inclinations, looked around for other outlets.

During the Middle Ages, in all likelihood, the Esther-scroll was unadorned.[38] The copy used by the synagogal reader continued unadorned, but for private use, the decorated Esther-scroll became accepted. While, in the sixteenth century, scrolls of that kind appear sparingly;[39] in the seventeenth and eighteenth centuries, that is, at the height of the era of ornamental marriage contracts, the adorned Esther-scroll became increasingly popular, and this not only among the Sephardim but also among the Ashkenazim.

The Italian Esther-scroll shows kinship with the Italian contract of marriage. Like the marriage contract, the scroll begins with a tip to promote elegance and to facilitate handling. There was, as with the marriage contract, a fondness for embellishing the tip with a coat of arms indicating the rank of the person who let the order. The margins of such scrolls are, like those of the marriage contract, filled sometimes with verdant tendrils. Pomegranates, such as we noticed in our marriage contracts, show

q) Esther Scroll, Italy, 17th Century.

[38] A forgery, in my judgment, is the hand-painted scroll of Esther in the possession of Mr. Felix Guggenheim of Los Angeles; formerly ascribed to fifteenth century Germany on the basis of an opinion by Adolph Goldschmidt.

[39] The earliest illuminated scroll of Esther known to me is the one transcribed at Castelnuovo, Italy in 1567. Cf. Georg Swarzenski and Rosy Schilling, *Die illustrierten Handschriften und Einzelminiaturen des Mittelalters und der Renaissance in Frankfurter Besitz*, Frankfurt a. M., 1929, p. 263.

also in our illustration of an Esther-scroll.[40] It is therefore safe to assume that the decorators of the Italian Esther-scrolls were also the decorators of the Italian marriage contracts.

We said above that, beginning with the fifteenth century, the printed book crowded out the handwritten book. We must qualify this by observing that the handwritten book did not completely disappear. There was in fact, during the eighteenth century, an artistic revival of the handwritten and handpainted book whose advantage over the printed book lay in its being a one and only copy and in its colorfulness. The chief incentive for the handpainted book of the eighteenth century came from communities of the Ashkenazim.[41] But this liking was shared by the Sephardim and actually by the entire Jewish population of Italy. Isaiah Sonne has called attention to an Italian Haggadah transcribed and ornamented in the year 1743 by a Jacob Ḥay ben Joseph Conegliano.[42] This Haggadah is now in the Hebrew Union College Library at Cincinnati (No. 450). A broad border, occupied by figures of the twelve constellations, encircles the title. In these shapes, which have no bearing whatsoever on the Haggadah's contents, Dr. Sonne correctly perceives the influence of the Italian contracts of marriage. I would go further and assert that the fashioner of this Haggadah was himself a copyist and a painter of such contracts. Habituated to the zodiac, he transplanted, to the Haggadah, that familiar design. Indeed, if one fingers through the Haggadah of 1743, one will find represented there, both in bud and in full bloom, roses completely resembling those in one of the Ketubahs of the Hebrew Union College Museum. Regrettably, since the text of this Ketubah has been effaced, the date is indiscernible. But the surmise is warranted that this marriage contract was produced at the same time and by the same artist as the Haggadah of 1743.

[40] Taken from the auction catalogue, *Jewish Ritual Silver and Other Hebraica, Property of Mrs. Rebecca Davidovitz*, Parke-Bennet Galleries Inc., New York, 1954, p. 6.

[41] Compare with this my article, "The Second Cincinnati Haggadah," *HUCA*, XXIII, Part Two, 1950–51, pp. 503 ff.

[42] Cf. the article "Postscript to 'The Zodiak' " in *Studies in Bibliography and Booklore*, I, 82, with one illustration.

All of this strengthens the supposition that the artist, in the case of most marriage contracts, was a Jew. He was one of those talented copyists who did not limit themselves to transcribing the text but who expanded their endeavors to the utmost of their powers — achieving, at the same time, a position of economic security amid the Jewish life of their age.

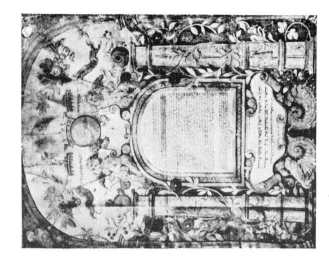

MARRIAGE CONTRACT,
AMSTERDAM, EARLY 17TH CENTURY.
Taken from S. Ph. de Vries,
Joodsche Riten en Symbolen II,

MARRIAGE CONTRACT,
MODENA, ITALY, 1757.
London, British Museum, Or. 6706.

MARRIAGE CONTRACT,
Corfu, 1781.
Hebrew Union College Museum.

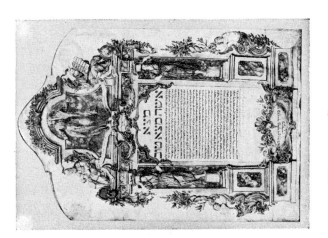

MARRIAGE CONTRACT,
FERRARA, ITALY, 1775.
Hebrew Union College Museum.

MARRIAGE CONTRACT,
BUSSETO, ITALY, 1677.
Hebrew Union College Museum.

MARRIAGE CONTRACT,
ANCONA, ITALY, 1690.
Hebrew Union College Museum.

412

MARRIAGE CONTRACT,
PISA, ITALY, 1790.
Hebrew Union College Museum.

MARRIAGE CONTRACT,
ROME, ITALY, 1818.
Hebrew Union College Museum.

CUSTOMS AND CEREMONIES

HOW TRADITIONAL ARE OUR TRADITIONS?

JOSEPH GUTMANN

Even the most radical of Reform congregations would never think of eliminating from its sanctuary the Eternal Light overhanging the Ark, or the Tablets of the Ten Commandments, or the seven-branched Menorah. Inevitably, one major concern in any new synagogue construction project is what form these beloved symbols are to take and where within the sanctuary they are to be placed. No congregation can do without them, for are they not, after all, hallowed by centuries of tradition? Yet, truth being so often stranger than fiction, it may surprise many to learn that these—among other—holy objects now accepted as ancient and traditional find absolutely no sanction either in the Talmud or in the Shulhan Aruh. As a matter of fact, we peruse rabbinic literature in vain for any mention of most of these synagogue objects prior to the seventeenth century.[1]

The earliest mention of the Eternal Light comes from seventeenth-century Italy—in Giulio Morosini's *Via della fede* (Rome, 1683), p. 245, which speaks of "the lamp *Tamid,* which always burns in front of the *Hechal* [the Sephardi name for the *aron ha-kodesh*]." Although later sources claim that it is customary to light the Ner Tamid in memory of the ancient Sanctuary, the Bible, which uses the words *ner tamid* in connection with the Sanctuary (Exodus 27.20 and Leviticus 24.2), has no special object in mind, but merely refers to the fact that the Israelites were commanded to bring clear olive oil for lighting in order to "maintain lights regularly."

Eternal Lights burned before the tabernacle housing the sacraments in Catholic churches where they symbolized the corporeal presence of Christ, the light of the world, and it is from this source that they probably entered the synagogue in the seventeenth century. In fact, surviving Eternal Lights from eighteenth-century synagogues closely resemble those hung in neighboring churches.[2]

Israel Abrahams was right when he stated that the rabbis "removed the Decalogue from [the] daily liturgy because of the *minim* (*Berakhot* 12a), then possibly introduced the Tablets in imitation of the *minim*."[3]

In no depiction of the Torah Ark in medieval Hebrew manuscripts do we find the Decalogue associated with it as is common practice today, nor do we find any mention of such a practice in the Shulhan Aruh. What we do find in rabbinical literature after the Shulhan Aruh, and persisting until quite recent times, is the strenuous objection of rabbis to the practice of introducing the Decalogue as decoration into the synagogue.[4]

It apparently was common in some European countries during the Protestant Reformation to place the Decalogue on the walls of churches, and it may be from this source that the tablets gradually gained Jewish currency.[5] The Decalogue is first found written out on the inside wings of surviving ark doors in some sixteenth-century Italian synagogues; gradually it became incorporated and universally accepted as decoration above the ark doors of European synagogues from the seventeenth century on.

Similarly, it has become standard practice to place the seven-branched Temple Menorah within the Reform synagogue—this, despite the talmudic injunction that "A man may not make . . . a Menorah after the design of the Menorah [in the Temple]. He may, however, make one with five, six, or eight branches, but he may not make one with seven, even though it be of other metal (*Rosh ha-Shanah* 24b, *Avodah Zarah* 43b, *Menahot* 28b)." Later rabbinic literature, too, strictly forbade the placement of the seven-branched Temple Menorah in the synagogue.[6]

During the Middle Ages, it did become customary to light the Hanukkah candles in the synagogue—even to place a Hanukkah lamp in the center of the synagogue of Sephardi synagogues, and to the south, or right, of the Ark in Ashkenazi synagogues (Exodus 26.35). These lamps, however, as we can see from medieval illuminated Hebrew manuscripts, did not resemble in shape the ancient Temple Menorah. It is only from the 1600's on that we find Hanukkah Menorot in Ashkenazi synagogues appearing in the shape of the ancient Temple Menorah, having of course two additional light arms.[7] Surviving Hanukkah Menorot of this period often resemble the seven-branched candelabra which were prominently featured in medieval Christian churches. The seven-branched Menorah played an important role in the medieval Church, since the Church claimed to be the *New Temple,* the rightful successor to the ancient biblical Sanctuary/Temple. To emphasize this position and to deny the rabbinic claim of a future Messianic Temple, the Church placed in the center of its own sanctuaries representations of sacred Temple implements like the seven-branched Temple Menorah. To the medieval Christian, the Menorah symbolized the image of Christ;

its seven lamps represented the seven gifts of the Holy Ghost. The three lamps on either side of the central stem were also interpreted as symbolizing both the Old and the New Testaments. The stem and central light stood for Christ, who illumined the other six lamps and united them.[8]

Reform Judaism, in placing the seven-branched Temple Menorah in its Temples,[9] probably wanted to emphasize—as Catholics had done centuries before—that there would be no Messianic Temple of the future, despite Orthodox expectations to the contrary, but that every Reform Temple was the rightful heir to that sacred and ancient tradition. The placement of the Temple Menorah in Reform houses of worship, therefore, underscored the belief that the Reform synagogue was the Temple of the present. It was a denial of the Orthodox claim that the synagogue was merely a surrogate for the Temple which would be restored in Messianic times.

Eternal Light, Decalogue, and Menorah are only three of the now common Jewish symbols which raise the question: How traditional are our traditions?

NOTES

[1] Cf. I. Z. Kahana, "Synagogue Art in Halakhic Literature," *Bet ha-Knesset* (Jerusalem, 1955), pp. 268 ff., and the unpublished responsa on these objects by Dr. S. B. Freehof, which the author generously sent me. [See now S. B. Freehof, *Current Reform Responsa* (Cincinnati, 1969), pp. 8-14.]

[2] Cf. F. Landsberger, "Old Hanukkah Lamps," *Hebrew Union College Annual*, XXV (1954), 354-55.

[3] I. Abrahams, "The Decalogue in Art," *Studies in Jewish Literature Issued in Honor of Kaufmann Kohler* (Berlin, 1913), p. 52.

[4] Kahana, *op. cit.,* pp. 272-73.

[5] Abrahams, *op. cit.,* pp. 49-50. Cf. G. B. Sarfatti, "The Tablets of the Covenant as a Symbol of Judaism," *Tarbiz,* XXIX (1960), 370-93. It should be noted that late 15th-century artists, such as Joos van Ghent, already show Moses holding the rounded tablets, with the Commandments in Hebrew, that we are accustomed to in synagogues. *Ibid.,* fig. 16 and p. 382. The Torah Ark from Urbino dates 1551, not 1451, *ibid.,* p. 384.

[6] S. B. Freehof, *Reform Jewish Practice and its Rabbinic Background* (Cincinnati, 1952), II, pp. 24-25.

[7] Landsberger, *op. cit.,* pp. 363-67. The Hanukkah Menorah from Padua, which, according to Landsberger, is from the 15th century, should probably be dated in the 17th century.

[8] P. Bloch, "Siebenarmige Leuchter in Christlichen Kirchen," *Wallraf-Richartz Jahrbuch,* XXIII (1961), 55-190.

[9] The term "temple" was possibly inspired by its use in French Reformed Churches. Cf. R. Wischnitzer, *The Architecture of the European Synagogue* (Philadelphia, 1964), pp. 174-76.

THE JEWISH RITE OF COVERING THE HEAD*

SAMUEL KRAUSS, Cambridge, England

IN my volume on Talmudic Antiquities,[1] when I took occasion to describe costumes and attire, the question arose whether or not the Jews of that time were accustomed to wear a covering for the head. To this question, my reply is in the negative both in the aforementioned work and in the forthcoming third volume of my *Kadmoniyot Hatalmud*[2] where I list the articles in which I defend my view against the dissident views of various scholars. An exceedingly fine *responsum* on the subject is that of J. Z. Lauterbach[3] who, though not quoting from my book, is entirely on my side. Let the following citation from Lauterbach bring out the nature of his problem and his answer:

> QUESTION: Where can one find the rabbinic law prescribing that men should cover their head when participating in Divine worship or when entering a Synagog? If there is no law to this effect will you please tell me where and when did the custom of covering one's head now generally observed in Orthodox Synagogs originate among the Jews?

> ANSWER: There is no law in Bible or Talmud prescribing the covering of the head for men entering a sanctuary, when participating in the religious service or when performing any religious ceremony.

---

* Editorially revised without the participation of the author. Brackets enclose editorial corrections and insertions.

[1] *Talmudische Archaeologie*, I, 189 ff.

[2] The Hebrew work represents an entirely new approach and does not merely translate the German work. In both works will be found lists of articles written on the subject by others as well as by myself.

[3] "Should One Cover the Head When Participating in Divine Worship?" *Year Book, Central Conference of American Rabbis*, XXXVIII, 1928, pp. 589–603. No name heads the article itself, but Lauterbach's authorship can be inferred from prior references to Lauterbach as the chairman of the Committee on Responsa, p. 10 [also pp. 133, 134].

Reprinted from *Hebrew Union College Annual*, Vol. XXVI, 1955.

It will be perceived that the question relates to the so-called rites of the synagogue and to the offering of prayers. But archaeological curiosity, going further, asks: Did our ancestors keep their heads covered ordinarily? And was or was not this practice suspended when the Jews entered the synagogue or engaged in religious devotion? Our investigation should be extended also to include women. This phase deserves special attention in view of the report that the daughters of Israel were, more than the menfolk, obligated even in private to wear a covering on their heads.

Orthodox Jews readily assume that, for the Jew, the covering of the head was a basic command applicable to all situations, literally "when thou sittest in thy house, when thou walkest by the way, when thou liest down, and when thou risest up." Orthodox Jews thus instruct their boys from their tenderest years. There are some who, though otherwise submitting to modern exigencies, would abominate uttering a single Hebrew word while bare-headed; Hebrew the language of the synagogue being sacred on any and all occasions, and every Hebrew word laden with the holiness of the Divine Name. Similar scruple attends the acts of eating and drinking, though not without some justification, in view of the fact that eating and drinking are preceded by a benediction in which the Divine Name actually occurs. What these people fail to recognize is that the sanctity attaches not to the eating or the drinking itself but to the preliminary benediction. Presently we shall recall instances in which Jews partook of their meals in the same manner as the Greeks.

We do not exaggerate when we say that "hat or no hat" has grown to be the huge bone of contention between liberal Jews and conservatives. For the Orthodox, praying in the synagogue bareheaded has become the abomination *ne plus ultra*. And the prejudice is deep rooted. Still a hazy reminiscence persists that a specific injunction on the subject appears neither in the Bible nor in the Talmud. It is maintained that, while the matter possesses only the character of a Jewish custom, that custom is, nonetheless, essential for Jewish life and cannot be ignored. If questioned, the protagonist of covering the head would reply that the practice is a rite descended from long ago

and preserved throughout Israel's wanderings, a feature of
uniqueness which should not be abandoned. A more learned
defender of the practice might concede that covering the head is
an ancient custom common to all oriental peoples. Still others
would contend that this rite was deliberately adopted in opposition to Christianity, the dominant religion, which follows the
contrary practice in its churches. The arguer readily quotes the
words חקת הגוי "Gentile observance," which is, of course, something that every loyal Jew sedulously avoids. The aversion to
praying with uncovered head is thus explained as a protest
against the allurements of non-Jewish life and as imbued with a
momentous psychological import.

Attachment to this Jewish "rite" has thus produced difference
of opinion that is by no means of advantage to Judaism. We
can observe almost any day that, just as the divergent rituals of
Ashkenazim and Sephardim have impaired Jewish unity, so
likewise has this dissention over a point of attire. Yet while
those differences of ritual may possess some justification and
some significance, the same cannot be said concerning the sur-
reptitiously developed squabble over the covering of the head.
One may well feel nonplussed by the vivid and witty description
of a recent Jewish deputation: "There appeared Ashkenazi
Rabbis with their black caps, Sephardi Ḥahams with their
tarbushes and turbans, modern Jews without any head cover."[4]
A Hassidic Rabbi invariably wears, as part of his apparel for
the Sabbath, a *Striml* or a *Yarmulka* which is as distinctive of
him as his earlocks.[5] How burdensome to have to prove that for
Judaism these things are non-essential and neither worth retaining nor defending!

It is hoped that the following citations directly from the
sources will prove conclusively that head covering is not obligatory upon the Jew in his religious life private or public. We
shall begin with biblical times and shall instance corresponding
usages among non-Israelitish peoples. This ranges beyond my

---

[4] David Yellin in *Bizzaron*, II, 210.

[5] See my article "Kleidung," in the *Encyclopedia Judaica*, X, the latest
volume to be issued of this useful work.

previous study as well as beyond the more recent article by Lauterbach. Though the Bible shall be our point of beginning, we shall, inasmuch as the Judaism of today calls itself "Rabbinic," dwell chiefly on the period of the Talmud. In the midst of the controversy on this subject, a certain author[6] terminates his remarks with the observation that the *Minhag* of wearing a head cover during prayer is manifestly at variance with the *Halakah*. I should rather say that it goes beyond the *Halakah*. Moreover, I should separate the question as it pertains to men from the question as it pertains to women, the respective cases involving entirely different considerations. I shall not, however, be of myself able to adduce statements from the vast literature of *Responsa* but shall, for this phase, have to draw upon the work of others.

Finally, it must be noted that our subject has a vital bearing on Christian theology and on usages followed by numerous Christian individuals and churches. The well known admonition of Paul, in II Cor. 3.7–18, can be understood only in the light of contemporary rabbinic opinions.

I. The General Orient and Hebrews in Biblical Times

In attempting to ascertain whether or not headgear was worn by the Hebrews of old, we look first at those two groups of nations whose civilization influenced all neighboring peoples, Israel included. Regarding the Egyptians, we learn from Erman[7] that headgear figures only in connection with members of the royal family; which means that people of the common run went with their heads bare. Only the gods, so far as we know, wore head-dresses in Sumir and Akkad.[8] King (p. 51) furnishes illustrations showing divine head-dresses of earlier forms and later forms. "Again," he says, "the garments of the gods in the earliest period have little in common with the Semitic plaid, and are

---

[6] I. Kahn in *Revue des Études Juives*, LXXXIV, 176–178.

[7] A. Erman, *Aegypten und Aegyptisches Leben im Altertum*, Tuebingen, p. 313 ff. [In 1923 Edit., p. 255.]

[8] Leonard W. King, *A History of Sumer and Akkad*, London, 1910, p. 51.

nearer akin to the plainer form of garment worn by contemporary Sumerians." The divine head-dress differs also from the later mode in which single horns, encircling what may be a symbol of a date palm, give way to a plain conical head-dress with several pairs of horns as decoration.[9] Page 75 presents a stamped terra cotta figure of a bearded god wearing a horned head-dress to which are attached the ears of a bull (Period of Gudea). On p. 112, figure 43 shows an Early Sumerian figure of a woman with Sumerian dress and coiffure. Under the caption "Dress," this book contains nothing on the head-dress of ordinary folk, thus signifying that people in general wore no head-dress at all.

With regard to the Semites, it must be said that, while head-dress existed, the wearing of it was not obligatory. According to the *Encyclopedia Britannica*,[10] "a special covering for the head was not indispensable. The Semites often bound their bushy locks with a fillet,[11] which varies from a single band (so often, e. g., Palestinian captives, 10th century) to a fourfold one, from a plain band to highly decorated diadems.[12] But the ordinary Semitic head-covering was a cloth (as opposed to the feathered ornament of Tirhaka's army, 7th century), which sometimes appears with the two ends tied in front, the third falling behind."

---

[9] Horns suggest a relationship with powerful animals. In Hebrew, the word "horn" has various implications for which one may consult the lexica. Nowhere — unless I Ki. 22.11 be taken as such — does the horn figure as an element of dress. In the prayer book, the word is used with various significations.

[10] Edition of 1910–1911, p. 229b, Article, "Costume."

[11] Such a fillet was also worn by Jews and especially by Jewesses, as this article will presently show. Of some bearing upon this matter may be the following passage from Charles M. Doughty's *Travels in Arabia Deserta* (reprinted Oct. 1930), p. 17: "The Wady Aly of Annezy: The women are not veiled. They mark their faces with some blue lines and spots which I have not seen in Arabia proper, and bind their doubled locks, combed upon their foreheads, with a fillet."

[12] The authorities cited are: W. M. Mueller, *Asien und Europa Nach Altaegyptischen Denkmaelern*, Leipzig, 1893, and E. Meyer, "Sumerier und Semiten in Babylonien" in the *Abhandlungen* of the University of Berlin, 1906.

Well known is the hat of the ancient Persians called in Greek, *karbasia* and resembling the comb of a cock.[13] The talmudic-midrashic designation for this type of hat is כרבלתא which means cockscomb.[14] But even more; in a phantastic account of a soul's reception in heaven,[15] we read: "A righteous soul, to reach its place on high, flies heavenward not in a wordly sense but in a spiritual sense, attired in good spiritual deeds, wearing crown and coronet, a turban-sash and a fourfold fillet-pendant, an adorned robe and other proper apparel." This description is taken from a sacred Pahlavi text, and the Rabbis of the Talmud come near to speaking in like manner.[16] The static orient revels in such flowers of rhetoric.

This brings us to the Israelites. A well known archaeologist,[17] writing in the *Jewish Encyclopedia*,[18] apprises us: "Neither the monuments nor the written documents of Biblical times give any information of value concerning head-gear. On the marble relief of Sennacherib the Israelites appear uncovered; and while on the Shalmeneser stele Jehu's ambassadors have head-coverings, these are evidently patterned after the Assyrian fashion. Only one passage of the older literature (I Ki. 20.31) makes mention of "ḥabalim" (חבלים) that are wound around the head;

---

[13] Such may be, in Ber. 20a, the כרבלתא worn by women among the Cutheans. The *'Aruk* of R. Nathan takes the word to mean "a red cloth." The word, however, implies some form of headwear resembling the comb of a cock. J. Bergmann in the *Monatschrift*, LXXXII, 373, calls it a "helmet."

[14] See *Talmudische Archaeologie*, I, 549 and 606. This is to be distinguished from *כרבלא in Dan. 3.21. See San. 92b.

[15] *The Bible of the World* by Robert O. Ballou and others, London, 1940, p. 624.

[16] צדיקים יושבים ועטרותיהם בראשיהם ונהנים מזיו השכינה is given in Ber. 17a as a pearl from the mouth of Rab who was surely versed in Parsi theology which had, in his time, become the vogue. The dictum, which played such a role in the philosophical polemics of Maimonides, deserves to be quoted in full: "In the world to come, there is neither eating nor drinking nor procreation nor commerce nor envy nor hatred nor contention but" — and here follows what is quoted above in Hebrew. See Abot de R. Nathan, Version I, Chap. I, p. 3a and also *Talmudische Archaeologie*, III, 261.

[17] W. Nowack in *Hebraeische Archaeologie*.

[18] Vol. IV, p. 294.

these recall the Syrians on Egyptian monuments,[19] who appear with a rope coiled around their long, flowing hair, as is still the custom here and there in Arabia. This custom, probably a very ancient one, did not obtain for long, since it afforded no protection against the sun.[20] It may be assumed, therefore, that even the ancient Hebrews had a type of head-covering still used by the Bedouin-Kaffiyah. The use of similar head coverings among the Hebrews seems to be indicated by the noun "*zanif*" (צניף) . . . as well as by the verb "*ḥabash*" (חבש) . . . Since the ancient Hebrews evidently knew nothing of the strict separation of men and women customary among the Moselms,[21] the women wore veils[22] only on certain occasions (Gen. 24.65; 38.14). Later on veils and gauze garments adopted from other nations apparently came into more general use (. . . Is. 3.16 ss.)." Approximately identical are the observations of Benziger at which we need not marvel.[23] From the meager information which the Bible offers on this subject, further details can hardly be expected.

In the Old Assyrian Law Code quoted by A. Jeremias, it is ordained that married women and widows, when appearing in public places, are required to veil their heads.[24] On the other hand, the harlot, ranking like a female slave is, under severe penalty, required to go "exposed." If a man wishes to make a "concealed" woman his lawful wife, he must perform the act

---

[19] These figures have frequently been reproduced. See the works already quoted. See also, in the *Jewish Encyclopedia*, the section "In Post-Biblical Times" written by Joseph Jacobs for the article "Costume." This article contains a beautifully colored plate of illustrations in which all of the men are shown with covered heads. The same plate, without colors, is reproduced by Allen H. Godbey in *The Lost Tribes, a Myth*, Durham, 1930. From those representations, Godbey, of course, derives inferences of his own.

[20] The small son of the Shunemite woman in II Ki. 4.9 was probably a victim of sunstroke. Cf. Isa. 49.10, and also the regret of the maiden in Cant. 1.6.

[21] In modern times, there has been some relaxation of that "strictness."

[22] On the subject of veils, one may consult: A. Jeremias, "Der Schleier von Sumer bis Heute," an exhaustive article which appeared in *Altes Orient* XXXI (1931); also R. P. R. de Vaux, "Sur le Voile des Femmes dans l'Orient Ancien" in *Revue Biblique*, New Series, XLIV (1935).

[23] *Hebraeische Archaeologie*, 3d. edit., p. 86 ff.

[24] Compare the case already cited, that of Tamar in Gen. 38.14.

of veiling her anew. This reminds us of a well known feature in
the life of the Romans, for which, in a footnote, we quote in full
the article "Nuptias" from Festus.[25] We shall find, in the course
of our investigation, that a similar requirement rested upon
the wife among the Jews. The custom, however, which is but a
rite symbolizing the woman's new status, has no bearing upon
modes cf attire in general.

It is likewise exceptional when a distinctive head covering
is worn by the soldier. On this point also, the Bible provides
but meager hints. The Psalmist sings: "O God the Lord, the
strength of my salvation, who hast screened my head in the
day of battle" (Ps. 140.8). God shields the head of His anointed
against the deadly blow. Both parts of the verse allude to the
helmet, otherwise called מעוז, "the defense of my head" (Ps.
60.9).[26] Though poetical phrases, these expressions are undoubtedly based on actual usage. But, even so, the passages refer only
to the king, "the anointed one." Nothing obliges us to infer that
such a "helmet of salvation" was worn by any others, even by
warriors. In view of מראש פרעות אויב in Deut. 32.42 and of בפרע
פרעות in Judg. 5.2 which reputable scholars have interpreted to
mean that warriors, when bound by a vow, would let their hair
grow in time of war,[27] it seems probable that, as a rule, Israelites
went into battle bareheaded. We can, in no event, draw any
inferences about customs in general. Concerning the Greeks,
we know that, while they wore helmets in battle, they were
distinguished otherwise for the beautiful dressing of their hair.
Curiously, foreigners recognized Greeks by this characteristic
just as Polish Jews are recognized by their *Pe'ot*. (The opposite
trait appears in the group of nations mentioned in Jer. 9.25.) In

[25] Nuptias dictas esse — Aelius et Cincius, quia flammeo caput nubentis
"obvolvatur," quod antiqui "obnuere" vocarint; ob quam causam legem
quoque Praenestinam jubere caput ejus "obnubere," qui parentem necavisset,
quod est "obvolvere." — Sextus Pompeius Festus, "E libris de verborum sig-
nificatu," apud Bruns, *Fontes Juris Romani*, 7th edit. Tuebingen, 1909, p. 18.
Also, among the Jews, the accused and the cursed had to be "covered." See
below.

[26] Cf. "Helmet of salvation" in Isa. 59.17, כובע ישועה.

[27] Robertson Smith, Wellhausen, and Schwalle, as quoted by Gesenius,
sub verbo.

the inscription on the mausoleum of Darius I, the Greeks are called *Yauna takabara*.[28] This is probably meant by the *blurit* (בלורית) frequently mentioned in the Talmud and the Midrash as a type of hair arrangement to which the Jew is forbidden to resort.[29] Such would preclude the likelihood that a covering for the head was customary.

At this point, we must mention an interesting incident, if not precisely of biblical times, yet of Maccabean times. One of the innovations forced upon the Jews by Antiochus Epiphanes was the requirement that young men "wear a hat."[30] This aroused the strenuous opposition of the pious who pronounced the custom contrary to Jewish law and practice. "Wear a hat" is the rendering of the authorized version, although Charles translates, "wear the petasus," that is, a broad brimmed felt hat which, as a sign of Hermes, may have proved unusually offensive.[31] Such accounts are worth collecting as indications of the way in which the staunch Jew was averse to everything which he regarded as an approach to idolatry. Today, as already noted, a similar attitude signifies resistance to Christianity.

The Epistle of Jeremy contains the notice:[32] "And in their temples the priests sit on seats, having their clothes rent, and their heads and beards shaven, and nothing upon their heads." Charles permits us to infer an original ובבתיהם הכהנים יבכו קרועי כתנתם ומגלחי ראש וזקן וראשם פרוע. We have here again the Hebrew

---

[28] That is, Ionians with crowns of hair (κρωβύλοι). Justi, "Geschichte Irans" in *Grundriss der Iranischen Philologie*, II, 455.

[29] More is said on this subject in *Talmudische Archaeologie*, I, 193, 197, with notes on same. See also my *Additamenta ad Aruch Completum*, p. 93.

[30] II Macc. 4.12. Edit. Sweete: καὶ τοὺς κρατίστους τῶν ἐφ᾽ ἡμῶν ὑποτάσσων ἀπὸ πέτασον ἤγαγεν. The critical apparatus indicates a reading: ἐφήβων. In the *Stephani Thesaurus* where, surprisingly, II Macc. is not quoted, our word has been explained as ἐφήβων φόρημα, "the attire of youngsters." The parallel passage is in I Macc. 1, 11–15. Cf. A. T. Helmstead, "Wearing the Hat" in *The American Journal of Theology*, Jan. 1914, p. 94 ff.

[31] A deep-seated aversion to מרקוליס, Mercury, and his cult is noticeable in the Mishna. The passages are listed in my *Loehnwoerter*, II, 353. On San. VII, 6, see my *Sanhedrin-Makkot*, Giessen, 1933, pp. 226, 227.

[32] Charles, *The Apocrypha and Pseudepigrapha of the Old Testament*, Oxford, 1913, I, 604.

root פרע whose form פרוע can mean "unbound" (i. e., with un-
wound turban), which was forbidden to priests among the Hebrews (Lev. 21.10, Ezek. 44.20).

In all of these inquiries, we must keep in view rituals practiced outside of the Hebrew domain. Among the Romans, priests,
while offering sacrifices, would have the neck and the back of
the head covered with a toga (*velato capite*).[33] On the other hand,
priests among the Greeks would function *aperto capite*.[34]

In biblical times, Hebrew priests were required to wear special
garments including headgear (Ex. 28.4, 40). The intent of this,
as Lauterbach rightly observes, may have been that of distinguishing the priests of the Temple in Jerusalem from those of
some heathen deity. This hardly warrants the inference that the
head has to be covered in all of our religious ceremonies. The
priests of old functioned in the Temple and at the altar barefoot. Yet who has ever drawn the inference that one is today
obliged to perform religious ceremonies barefoot? Lauterbach's
view, while undoubtedly valid, needs one small correction. Certain rulings in the Mishna (Meg. IV, 8) can be understood only
on the assumption that persons officiating in the synagogue
would seek to imitate the *Kohen* of old in various particulars,
among them, that of refusing to officiate in sandals or in colored
clothes. The Mishna reproves such idiosyncracies.[35] Striking evidence that priests might tarry in the Temple bareheaded is
furnished by a Baraitha in Yoma 25a which describes the daily
allotment of functions in the Temple. The priests would assemble
in "The Chamber of Hewn Stone" (לשכת הגזית) which was

---

[33] Arnobius, III, 43. Roughly, the *Ṭallit* of the Jews corresponds to the
toga of the Romans. Hence the numerous ritual acts in which the *Ṭallit* was
worn. The *Ṭallit* was placed over the head.

[34] Hastings, *Encyclopedia of Religion and Ethics*, VI, 539. Additional
evidence is supplied by Leopold Loew in his *Gesammelte Schriften*, Szegedin,
1890, II, 313. The word *Flamines*, the name for Roman priests, is said to be
derived from *filamines* or *pilamines*, forms of cloth with which the priests would
be covered. Cf. *A flammeo capitis tegumento* and the citation from Festus in
note 25 above. The Persian priests would similarly, when performing sacrificial
rites, cover the head with a kind of tiara.

[35] See my *Synagogale Altertuemer*, p. 170. My view is quoted by Rabbinowitz in his edition of *Mishna Megillah* (London).

a kind of basilica and, standing in a circular arrangement, would await their "lot." Thereupon the supervisor would enter and remove, from the head of one of them, the turban (מצנפת). This indicates that the priest in question stood bareheaded, perhaps not in the Temple itself but in a prominent annex of the Temple, and that is the essential point. Proponents of mandatory head covering would, of course, contend that the priest, deprived of his turban, still retained his "cap," as if a priest of old resembled a Polish Jew of today. Under such presuppositions, argument becomes futile.

From our literary sources, one thing seems evident, namely, that covering the head, thereby concealing the face, is expected of the mourner (אבל). Many scriptural passages vouch for this "rite."[36] With covered head and with bare feet, David flees from his son, Absalom.[37] The biblical expression reminds us of the poignant Jewish lament over the destruction of Jerusalem, in the נחם for the Ninth of Ab, taken from the Talmud: "In mourning for that she is childless, laid waste as to her dwellings, despised in the downfall of her glory, and desolate through the loss of her inhabitants; she sitteth with her head covered like a barren woman who has not borne."[38] The same apparently occurs in the story of Tamar (II Sam. 13.19): "And Tamar put ashes אפר on her head, and rent her garment . . . and she laid her hand on her head, and went her way, crying aloud as she went." With certain variations of phrase, the same rite is indicated in Josh. 7.6, I Sam. 4.12, and in Lam. 2.10. There may also be references to the custom in Amos 2.7.[39]

In Esth. 7.8, "They covered Haman's face," allusion has been found to the Persian mode of covering the head or the face at the imposing of the sentence of death.[40] But either a different

---

[36] See dictionaries and concordances *sub verbo*, חפה.

[37] II Sam. 15.30. Cf. Jer. 14.3 and Esth. 6.12.

[38] Singer's *Prayer Book*, London, 1935, p. 49.

[39] See Driver *ad loc.* However, see also Marti's *Festschrift*, p. 278.

[40] See *The Oxford Hebrew Lexicon*, also V. Ryssel in Kautzsch's Old Testament, as quoted in Hastings, *Dictionary of the Bible*, II, 316, *sub verbo*, "Head." All of these authors were unaware that, as quoted in Mandelkern's *Concordance*, *sub verbo* חפה, already Abraham ibn Ezra had proposed this explanation.

text[41] or a different interpretation is indicated by the Septuagint.[42] Hasting's Dictionary[43] reports Siegfried-Stade[44] as translating *Hamans Gesicht verschleierte verduesterte sich*. The objection is raised that nowhere is חפה used of covering the face. It is always used of the head.[45] In connection with the face, the verbs used are כִּסָּה[46] (Job 9.24, 23.17) or הסתיר (Ex. 3.6, Job 13.24).[47] Therefore, according to Hastings, Esth. 7.8 must be emended to read הפרו. Now it happens that this emendation is fairly old. Mandelkern, in his *Concordance*, takes it from Jacob Reifmann. The word itself appears in Ps. 34.6. I propose that we decide the issue simply by reading, in Esth. 7.8 ופני המן חפו[י], as in Esth. 6.12, פנים, "face" being here in the singular and meaning "head."[48] That would make the terminal words of the sentence similar to II Sam. 15.30. The tiny י may have fallen out by homoioteleuton (see beginning of the next verse). It would accordingly follow that covering the head included covering the face, and that is entirely natural.

Whether or not modern languages, when they adopt biblical phraseology, extend the sense of covering the head to include covering the face, I am uninformed. In German we say: *Weinend* (or *klagend*) *das Haupt verhuellen;*" and nothing further. The brothers Grimm,[49] in their usual manner, quote a verse from a poem by Uhland (*Gedichte*, 287):

[41] Ἀμαν δὲ ἀκούσας διετράπη τῷ προσώπῳ. On διετράπη see the *Stephani Thesaurus* where the explanation is offered: "pudore injecto deterreo" or "confundo." Different is the rendering in Josephus, *Antiquities*, XI. 6. 11 which, of course, throws no light on the question of covering the head. An exact parallel to the text in Esther is the saying of R. Phineas ben Ya'ir: "Since the Temple has been destroyed, the free born and the scholarly have had to cover their heads (וחפו ראשם) in shame" [Soṭ. IX, 15].

[42] The Vulgate reads: "*Operuerunt faciem ejus.*"

[43] See note 40 *supra*.

[44] *Hebraeisches Woerterbuch*, Leipzig, 1893.

[45] Cf. Esth. 6.12, II Sam. 15.30, Jer. 14.3.

[46] Job 9.24, 23.17, and the like.

[47] Ex. 3.6, Job 13.24. סתר פנים in Job 24.15 is of different import and has no bearing in this connection.

[48] Sometimes the subject is in the plural and the predicate in the singular as in Prov. 3.18b.

[49] Jacob and Wilhelm Grimm, *Deutsches Woerterbuch*, Leipzig, 1877, Vol. IV, Part II, p. 600.

> doch den heitern Pilgern folgen/andre barfuss and bestaubt/,
> angetan mit härenen Hemden/Asche tragend auf dem Haupt

It cannot be overlooked that this poem appropriates the biblical mourning rites *in toto*. Similar usages are still practiced by the Jews of today, with the exception of casting ashes upon the head and wearing hair shirts or sackcloth. Logically our conservatives should adhere to those latter usages likewise. We shall presently notice that putting ashes on the head was still the vogue in the period of the Talmud.[50] Should not our conservatives, to be consistent, follow that practice today? Mourning rites, despite a tenacity like that of marriage rites, do not forever retain their vigor. Eventually they survive only in the records of the past. Consider the biblical vestments of widowhood (Gen. 20, Gen. 18.14, 19; Cf. Ruth 3.3.) Could such attire be made compulsory for any Jewish widow of today? What obtains today is but a voluntary following of convention. And this shall be our ultimate standpoint also with regard to the question we are now treating.

We return now to the subject of headwear in general. The matter came to involve points of social status. The brothers Grimm (ibid. p. 601) report the expectation that an inferior should bare his head and bow, while freemen and rulers kept their heads covered as befitted their rank. The Germans undoubtedly imported this custom from the Orient. O. Schrader apprises us that, with some exceptions, both North Europeans and South Europeans went bareheaded until they copied the oriental usage;[51] the terminology employed both in Northern Europe and in Southern Europe shows strong oriental influence. "All in all we get the impression that the custom of wearing headgear, before spreading throughout Europe, originated in the East. Like the reaction among primitives of today, when coming into contact with European civilization, covering the head was

[50] The Hebrew term is אפר מקלה, ashes from vegetable substances such as wood used in roasting. Ashes on the head are part of the ritual for fast days. See Ta'an. II, 1 and its commentaries. Occasions of public distress, private mourning, banishment, or appearance before a court of law have, as regards clothing and various other rites, certain common characteristics.

[51] O. Schrader, *Reallexikon der Indogermanischen Altertumskunde*, 1917–1923. *Sub verbo* "Kopfbedeckung" (I, 623).

probably first adopted by the privileged, by priests (especially for the deities), by kings, and by nobles; later expanding, little by little, among wider circles of the population." I think that this disposes of theories which allege a fundamental disparity between Gentile bareheadedness and Jewish head covering. On the contrary, the two are parts of the same process. This *Minhag* first adopted by priests, kings, nobles and, as we have seen, by warriors, descended slowly into other social strata. The average individual is eager to put himself on a level with the high and mighty. A good example within Judaism is the popular wearing of the *Tallit* (fringed, of course, with *Ziẓit*) and the donning of *Tefillin*, both of which practices were originally limited to the Scribes, Pharisees, or Rabbis. Partly as a result of the striving to rise in the social scale, and partly under steady prompting by the Rabbis, the *'Amme' Ha-areẓ*, the ignorant, at first loath to follow those rituals, became at length acquainted with them, fond of them, and zealous for them. The same process is observable in the world of letters and learning; the advance of peasants and craftsmen into "culture" is too familiar to need mention. Something analogous happened in the case of headwear. Originally a token of rank, eventually it became the attire of the multitude.

We have seen how, in later times, the mourners' rite of putting dust on the head grew obsolete. Nor is this surprising, because even in Judaism of the most rigid kind, rites do not remain unaltered. *Tempora mutantur et nos mutamur in illis.* Many of the mourning rituals mentioned in my *Talmudische Archaeologie*[52] have disappeared, among them the custom of overturning beds and other furniture in the room in which the person had died (כפיית המטה). For this practice, vivid testimony has been preserved in the apocryphal IV Ezra.[53] The ancient

---

[52] *Talmudische Archaeologie*, II, 70 ff. See also II, 63 on the rite of חולצין כתף.

[53] *Die Griechisch-Christlichen Schriftsteller der Ersten Drei Jahrhunderte*, herausgegeben von der Kirchenvaeterkomission der Preusischen Akademie der Wissenschaften, Leipzig, 1924: *Die Apokalypsen des Esra und des Baruch in Deutscher Gestalt*. In Esra, vision IV, 3, v. 2 [II Esdras 9.37], pp. 132–134, there appears a mourning woman whose "clothes were rent" and who "had

rite of uncovering the arm by pulling the cloth from the shoulder[54] was discontinued centuries ago. Various ceremonies once prevailed in connection with and by the aid of חבר עיר, the Council of the Town. Since such a magistracy no longer exists, those ceremonies have been abandoned.[55] Peculiar was the marriage custom of putting ashes on the head of the bridegroom (B. B. 60b)[56] or a piece of black cloth upon the heads of the groom and the bride, as if they were mourners.[57] In modern Jewish life, no trace of this remains.

We shall now consider the affinity between marriage ceremonies and mourning ceremonies, both of which entail the covering of the head.

II. Head Covering of Men in the Talmudic Period

Let us first take note of a significant remark attributed to the Apostle Paul, a remark which seems to have determined, for all time, the practice which was to prevail in the churches and which, according to some Jewish scholars, influenced Jewish custom *in contrariam partem*.

In II Cor. 3.15, 16, the Apostle, using a kind of Midrash

---

ashes upon her head" (read σποδός not κόνις). The account continues, 4 v. 7 [II Esdras 10.2] "Then we all overthrew the lights." The editor of *Die Apokalypsen des Esra und des Baruch* takes the Hebrew original to have been דחה and מנורות. This is not impossible, but the expression in Rabbinic Hebrew would have been כפה. An exact parallel to this rite is the situation in Revelation, 2.5, whose Greek text it would be well to consult and of which the English reads: "Or else I come to thee, and will move thy candlestick, out of its place." *Toratan shel Rish'onim*, I, 33, still enumerates among the rites of mourning: פריעת הראש (1), קריעה (2), כפיית המטה (3) (the opposite of זקיפת המטה). For (1), see Gen. Rab. C, Theodor-Albeck edit. p. 1291.

⁵⁴ Yer. Ber. IX, 13a top. Cf. Isa. 52.10. On all of this, see A. Buechler in *Wiener Zeitschrift fuer die Kunde des Morgenlandes*, XVIII, 97 ff.

⁵⁵ See my חבר עיר "Ein Kapitel aus Altjuedischer Kommunalverfassung" reprinted from the *Jahrbuch der Juedischen Literarischen Gesellschaft*, Frankfurt am Main, 1926. See especially p. 43 ff.

⁵⁶ Again it is Lauterbach to whom we are indebted for a thorough treatment of this subject. See *HUCA*, II, 359, note 14, where additional references are supplied.

⁵⁷ Kolbo, Hilkot Tish'ah Be'Ab, p. 67c.

concerning the veil with which Moses would cover his face (Ex. 34.33), exhorts the new believers to act differently. "But even unto this day, whensoever Moses is read, a veil lieth upon their heart. But whensoever it shall turn unto the Lord, the veil is taken away." May we infer from this that the Jews, in the time of Paul, wore veils upon their faces "whensoever Moses is read," that is, in the synagogue? The answer is "No." In the passage quoted, "veil" is used figuratively. Moreover, a veil does not cover the head. An English commentary[58] to the passage in Exodus reads:

> An interesting reminiscence of this is said to be seen in the Jewish synagogue, where the priest, in pronouncing the Aaronic benediction (Num. 6.24–26) veils his face with his tallith (see on Num. 15.37–41) lest the utterance of the words should bring up the glory that shone in the face of Moses and strike the people dead.[59] St. Paul refers to this incident, II Cor. 3.7–18, and evidently understands that Moses wore the veil in order to hide the *fading* of the glory in his face. (Cf. vv. 7, 13).[60]

To indicate the correct interpretation of Paul's remark lies beyond my sphere. I venture nonetheless to say that the passage in Exodus does not at all refer to any fading of the glory in the face of Moses. To the contrary, the rays emanating from the countenance of Moses impressed the people as so awe-inspiring, so frightening as to make them recoil, their experience being somewhat akin to that of Moses himself at the Sinaic theophany.

> Every man praying or prophesying, having his head covered, dishonoreth his head. But every woman that prayeth or prophesieth with her head uncovered dishonoureth her head; for it is one and the same thing as if she were shaven. For if a woman is not veiled, let her also

[58] *A Commentary on the Holy Bible*, by various writers, edited by J. R. Dumelow, London, 1926.

[59] That sentence certainly looks like a quotation but I could not determine its source. Perhaps the writer is thinking of Ḥag. 16a which cautions that, if one looks into the face of a functioning Aaronide, one will become afflicted with sore eyes. For more on this subject, see Gaguine, *Keter Shem Ṭob* (London), 1934, p. 229.

[60] In English versions of the Bible, "vail" is the old fashioned spelling and "veil" the newer one. On the entire question see Julian Morgenstern, "Moses With the Shining Face," *HUCA*, II, 1925, pp. 1–27.

be shorn: but if it is a shame to a woman to be shorn or shaven, let her be veiled. For a man indeed ought not to have his head veiled, forasmuch as he is the image and glory of God: but the woman is the glory of the man.

We ignore the trend of mind revealed in this command and look only for the underlying facts. What was it that Paul saw in the synagogue, and what was it that he wished to have altered? I agree entirely with Lauterbach who says (p. 592): "He merely stated the Palestinian Jewish practice of his time and did not express any new or un-Jewish doctrine." "It is a mistake," Lauterbach goes on to say — "and one that involves a reasoning in a circle — to interpret this passage in the Epistle as aiming to sever the Christian worshippers from thé synagog by distinguishing their appearance at worship from that of Jewish worshippers, and then to assume that it was Paul's insistence upon his followers worshipping without a hat that, in turn, caused the Jews to attach great importance to the covering of the head during religious service[61] . . . . Paul could not have meant by his saying to put himself and his followers in opposition to Jewish custom or traditional practice, since what he recommends actually was the Jewish practice of his days."[62] Indeed, attaching any other significance to Paul's words is unwarranted. And this puts us on firm ground: bareheadedness for men, head-covering for women; both, however, in connection with the synagogue or some other sacred activity such as that of "prophesying." But this leaves us uninformed regarding activities which were private or other than sacred, regarding

[61] Lauterbach, at this point, corrects some of the flaws of writers who preceded him. He quotes W. Rosenau, *Jewish Ceremonial Institutions and Customs* (Baltimore, 1912). He points out the errors of M. Gaster in his article on the subject in *The Jewish Chronicle* of March 17, 1893, p. 17, replying, I think, to the query of D. Rabbinovicz (of London): "Warum beten die Juden mit bedecktem Haupte" in Rahmer's *Juedisches Literaturblatt*, XXII, 1893, 158. Further literature is listed in my *Ḳadmoniyot Ha-Talmud*, II, 2, 267 ff.

[62] Differing from Jonathan Altar in his *Antwort auf das Sendschreiben eines Afrikanischen Rabbi* (Prague, 1826, p. 30 ab), the pamphlet directed against the well known Hungarian reformist, Aaron Chorin. For a full account of the matter see "Aaron Chorin" in the *Gesammelte Schriften* of Leopold Loew (Szegedin, 1890), a dissertation of which this article makes abundant use.

which the assertions in the rabbinical sources — admirably collected in Strack-Billerbeck[63] — are equivocal and far from unanimous.

As already noted, a wrapping (עטיפה) was required for the performance of any significant act, and such covering was achieved by the familiar *Tallit* extended over the entire body. In Moed Ḳaṭon 24a, Samuel (died 254 C. E.) remarks: "A wrapping (עטיפה) which is not in the manner of the Ishmaelites (=Arabs) is no wrapping." There follows an example and the explanation that the concealment must include נובי דדיקנא.[64] The point involved here is the rite of mourning in connection with which a "wrapping" was imperative. But while this requirement applies to everyone, that which follows pertains only to persons of high standing. We must observe that a wrapping was inseparable from every weighty act i. e. every act imbued with sacredness and solemnity and, according to the Jewish social structure of those days, the principals in such acts were Rabbis and scholars and, indeed, only the most prominent among them.

A wrapping was prescribed for the judge (דיין) at the opening of a trial,[65] for the participants at the nullification of certain vows, הפרת נדרים (Ned. 77b), for one who recited grace in a company at a meal,[66] for one who visited the sick,[67] for one offering prayer (meaning perhaps the one who led in prayer),[68] and for persons in similar situations. The sense and the spirit of these prescriptions can be gauged from the striking act of R.

[63] *Kommentar zum Neuen Testament aus Talmud und Midrasch*, Vol. III, Munich, 1826, pp. 423–434.

[64] [The chin? The dimples of the chin?] See Rashi.

[65] Sab. 10a. This wrap worn by a judge is presupposed in Sifre Deut. No. 13, on the words וידעים לשבטיכם in Deut. 1.13.

[66] "One who reclines while eating shall, before reciting grace, enwrap himself. Thereby he comes to resemble the ministrant angels as described in Isa. 6.2" (Yer. Ber. VII end). Later we shall notice that the one who leads at grace places, upon his head, a *Sudar*.

[67] Sab. 43b. Presumably because the visitor would quote and interpret various consoling passages from Scripture. The word יושב implies a scholar. [The reference should be Ned. 40a.]

[68] In accordance with the statement in R. H. 17b: "This verse (Ex. 34.6) shows that God wraps Himself up like one who leads the congregation at devotion." On the offering of prayer, Sab. 10a.

Johanan ben Zakkai who, while on a journey, was asked to discourse on "matters of 'the Chariot.' "[69] R. Johanan alighted from his ass, wrapped himself up, sat down, under an olive tree, upon a stone, and then startled an inquiring disciple with the remark: "Should I ride upon an ass when, the discussion pertaining to 'Matters of the Chariot,' the Divine Presence (שכינה) is with us and ministering angels attend us?" The belief is here evidenced that such actions were hallowed by the Divine Presence before Whom one is filled with awe and reverence requiring that one be suitably dressed. It is reported of R. Judah ben Ilai (about 150 C. E.) that he would prepare for the Sabbath by washing his face, hands, and feet in hot water and wrapping himself in linen garments, fringed with Ẓiẓit, until he looked like an angel ministrant (Sab. 25b). Similarly would R. Ḥanina (about 225 C. E.) enwrap himself while awaiting "Queen Sabbath" (ibid. 119a).

Nothing like this is reported of ordinary people. Always it refers to Rabbis and scholars. In one instance the type of persons is specified. These are, namely, the Ḥaberim, members of a special order[70] devoted to a particularly rigid observance of the Law, especially to the levitical laws and the laws of tithing the crops. In times of drought when, despite public prayers and fasting, rain would fail to descend, those colleagues would, in token of mourning, suspend their greetings of one another. Ḥaberim would sit wrapped up as if they were bereaved or banished, and would deport themselves like the rebuked of the Lord until Heaven would vouchsafe its pity (Ta'an. 14b). Plainly this precludes such behavior on the part of ordinary people. Between the Ḥaberim, on the one hand, and the 'Ammey Ha-'arez (people of low status), on the other, there are actually features of contrast.

---

[69] In Hebrew מעשה מרכבה. Such was the appelative for mysteries so profound as to be communicable only to persons of "wisdom and spontaneous grasp" (Ḥag. II, 1).

[70] It would take us too far afield were we to dwell at length upon this feature of Jewish life during the Second Commonwealth and the subsequent period. Suffice it to refer to L. Finkelstein, *The Pharisees*, Philadelphia, 1938, I, 76.

Someone has inferred that, where no *Tallit* was available, people would, as a sign of submission to the Deity, cover at least their heads.[71] Even so, the custom must have been limited to the learned and must have taken considerable time to develop. Something indeed of significance can be found in a Midrash whose author may have been R. Isaac (about 300 C. E.). Starting with Micah 6.3, "O My People, what have I done unto thee? And wherein have I wearied thee? Testify against Me," the Aggadist offers this parable: "A king sends a proclamation (*prostagma* in Greek) to a province. How do the inhabitants respond? They receive the announcement standing, with uncovered heads (פורעין ראשיהם). They read it with fear and trembling, with terror and trepidation. But God says: 'My children, my proclamation is the *Shema'*. I will put you to no trouble. I do not ask that you read this bareheaded and standing but "when thou sittest in thy house, and when thou walkest by the way, and when thou liest down, and when thou risest up" ' (Deut. 6.7).[72] Such would seem to indicate that reciting the *Shema'* with covered head was the custom prevalent at the time. But we must not be deceived by appearances. All that the passage implies is the absence of compulsion. One may recite the *Shema'* just as one happens to be attired at the time, with head covered or uncovered, sitting in the house, walking by the way, and the like.[73]

Further support for a negative conclusion comes from the fact that it is deemed abhorrent to recite any prayer while naked. Should one happen to be standing naked in a field (a pos-

---

[71] Strack-Billerbeck, *ibid.*, p. 425.

[72] Pesikta, 77a; Tanḥuma 'Emor, 10 (13 in Buber's Tanḥuma). On the word πρόσταγμα, see *Lehnwoerter*, II, 483. On the political implications of the passage, see I. Ziegler, *Die Koenigsgleichnisse des Midrasch*, Breslau, 1903, p. 131. In Lev. Rab. XXVII, 7, the Greek word has been replaced by כתבין. Strack-Billerbeck, *ibid.*, p. 426, infer from the text that the covered head at the reciting of the *Shema'* was matter of course. I cannot agree with this. To the contrary, the text indicates that, in the reciting of the *Shema'*, the Jews exercized utmost freedom. The *Shema'* could be recited with head covered or uncovered, just as one pleased.

[73] Any restriction would be out of accord with Micah 6.3, the passage with which the discussion opened.

sibility in the Palestinian climate) or should one perform any work, while naked, it is required that one resort to a covering of straw or chaff or anything else available.[74] The continuation of the passage makes clear that there has to be concealment of the *pudenda*, whether any other part of the body, especially the head, be covered or not. This renders somewhat ridiculous the scruples of today's conservative Jew who would omit reciting the *Shema'* or any other piece of liturgy or would convulsively cover his head with his hands sooner than pronounce the sacred words while bareheaded. The Mishna (Ber. III, 5) prescribes that should someone, while bathing, find it needful to hurry in order to get the *Shema'* recited before sunrise, the thing to do is, if possible, to leave the bath, to cover oneself (יתכסה, by all means to cover the *pudenda*), and to recite those paragraphs. If time be insufficient, one should do the reciting while immersed in water. This certainly precludes covering the head.

Among the acts to be performed when one rises in the morning, Ber. 60b ordains:[75] "When putting the *Sudar* on the head, one is to say, 'Blessed be . . . . Who adorns (or crowns) Israel with glory.' " This would seem to imply that a "cap" was part of every man's apparel. Even so, the passage would, at most, give evidence of a custom prevailing in Babylonia: the passage, as can be seen from context and content, is of Babylonian origin. But the fact is that this custom relates likewise only to Rabbis and scholars because, generally speaking, the Talmud and cognate literature deals mainly with the ways and manners of those circles. The very passage before us intimates this because,

---

[74] Tos. Ber. II, 15 (Zuckermandel, p. 4); Ber. 24b.

[75] On the entire benedictory system, there exists a vast literature. To mention but a fragment of it: L. Loew, *Gesammelte Schriften*, IV, 61: A. Berliner, *Randbemerkungen zum Taeglichen Gebetbuch*, Vol. I, Berlin, 1909, p. 15: M. Liber in *Revue des Études Juives*, LXII, 285 ff.: D. Kaufmann, in *Monatschrift fuer die Geschichte und Wissenschaft des Judentums*, XXXVII, 14 ff. On Men. 43b, see Taylor, *Sayings*, Second edit., pp. 15, 26, 139. The paragraph (עוטר) עוטה does not appear in Amram or Abudarham (See the Ehrenreich edition, Cluj, 5683, p. 117; also the editor's remarks on p. 166 and Baer's *Siddur* עבודת ישראל (*ad loc.*). Recently I myself contributed some critical notes on this point in J. Porton, *Bible Studies and Jewish Ideals*, Leeds, 1941, p. 159.

in the first place, the *'Ammey Ha-'Areẓ* were presumed to be incapable of reciting those benedictions and, in the second place, all that follpws applies to scholars exclusively, such as "tying on the shoes," and putting on *Ẕiẕit* and *Tefillin*, all of them insignia of the scholarly class. As regards the *Sudar*, proofs abound which show conclusively that the *Sudar* was worn by scholars only. The word סודר is explained as a *Notariḳon* of סוד ה' ליראיו (Sab. 77b), "The counsel of the Lord is with them that fear Him," (Ps. 25.14). Pes. 111b contains the sentence: "Your *Sudar*, Sir, looks like that of a scholar," on which Rashi comments that scholars only were wearers of the *Sudar*.[76] A passage in Ḳid. 8a observes: "R. Kahana, being a man of importance, a *Sudar* is something that he needs."[77] A similar object was worn by R. Assi (Ber. 51a) and by R. Joseph (Moed Katan 24a) — always Rabbis and always in Babylonia. For those countries, the *Sudar* which can be regarded as a species of turban (concerning which we shall speak later), was a natural form of headwear. Another mode of attire, the *Kumtha*, כומתא, is mentioned only once, and that, in connection with a scholar, a scholar sitting at home, indoors (Sab. 147a). Once, *Kumtha* and *Sudar* are mentioned together ('Er. 84b), again with reference to Babylonia. Either the one was worn or the other; never the two of them together[78] and when, in summer, the weather grew hot, people would remove those coverings from their heads (see Rashi).

In our sources, the *Sudar* (Latin, *sudarium*)[79] is used extensively and applied to various objects. To make the word mean "turban," we would look for the specification סודר של ראש "*Sudar*

---

[76] For details regarding the *Sudar*, see my *Ḳadmoniyot Ha-Talmud*, II, 2, 269, where, however, instead of Pes. 101b, the reference should be Pes. 111b. [Rashi's remark is on Sab. 77b.]

[77] R. Kahana is reported to have placed a *Sudar* on his head at the ceremony of redeemıng the first-born. See the marginal notes to the passage in Ḳid. 8a. The *Pidyon Ha-Ben* must therefore be added to the solemn occasions for which one had to don a wrapping.

[78] As against the view of A. S. Herschberg. See *Ḳadmoniyot loc. cit.*

[79] See my *Lehnwoerter*, II, 373 on importations from the Greek, the Syriac, and the Arabic.

worn on the head," just as we hear of a *Sudar* worn on the neck
or a *Sudar* worn on the arms.[80] Unfortunately, this specification
is nowhere to be found, unless we depend upon the reading of a
famous mediaeval authority who quotes from Sifre,[81] where the
point to a halakic passage is that "the *Sudar* for the head" does
not constitute a coat to which it is necessary to attach *Ẓiẓit*.
It would be exceedingly odd to have *Ẓiẓit* four in number,
dangling from one's skull.

We are brought somewhat closer to a solution by a statement
in Ned. 30b which reports that, while men have their heads
sometimes uncovered and sometimes covered, women's heads
are covered always and children's heads are never covered.[82]
This would seem to be conclusive though, even taken literally,
the passage merely indicates the custom prevalent in Babylonia,
that of Palestine, as already emphasized, being different. The
statement quoted appears in the Babylonian Gemara by way
of an interpretation of the Mishna, Ned. III, 8. But the interpretation is erroneous. ·Lauterbach (p. 591) is not warranted in
saying: "The Mishnah . . . takes it for granted that men go
bareheaded and only women and children cover their head,"
when he continues by saying: "The remark in the Gemara . . . .
וקטנים לעולם מגלו cannot be harmonized with the plain meaning of
the Mishnah, unless it refers only to infants or reflects a different
Babylonian custom." What Lauterbach takes for granted is not
identical with that which the Mishna takes for granted. The
point of the Mishna is not whether the head is covered or uncovered. The force of the Mishna is that when anyone, making
a vow, uses the words שחורי הראש "black-headed," his self-
imposed restriction includes men, all kinds of men, bald-headed
men and gray-headed men but does not include women and

[80] For sources, see *Lehnwoerter, loc. cit.*

[81] Sifre Deut. Chap. 234, p. 117a in Friedmann, p. 267 in Finkelstein,
quoted in Kaftor Uferaḥ Chap. 60 — in the Luncz edition, under the running
head פרט לסודר של ראש.

[82] We discard the commentaries of Rashi, Asheri, and R. Nissim because
their interpretations altogether follow the halakic manner. When Rashi asserts
that the head covering of women is always white, he makes a statement for
which there is even no halakic need or warrant.

children.[83] The words שחורי הראש refer only to men, "black-headed ones" being a current phrase equivalent to "adult males." What the *Halakah* means is that current usage is decisive. *Usus est tyrannus.*

We must recognize that שחורי הראש is used not literally but conventionally; it is a stock phrase of the Mishna. תשחורת is, in fact, an old Babylonian term.[84] As reported by Leonard A. King, "The phrase the black-headed ones, which is of frequent occurrence in the later texts, clearly originated as a description of the Semites, in contradistinction to the Sumerians with their shaven heads."[85] If therefore anything can be inferred from that Mishna in Ned. III, 8, it is that the Semites, including the Jews, were known as "the blackheaded," which does not astonish us. The Gemara retains a lingering surmise that "the blackheaded" were adult males who must also have been bareheaded, while the brunet complexion of the children was not so pronounced.

A piece of evidence apparently on the side of those who deem head covering traditional is furnished by a story which ends with the words ש״מ גילוי הראש עזות תקיפא היא "which shows that bareheadedness is extreme impudence." These words come from Kallah Rabbati.[86] The story, as recounted in this text, relates that, once upon a time, two youngsters passed by in the presence of some scholars, one of the youngsters with head bare and the other with head covered. The former elicited the severe censure just quoted. Something similar which is related in the Toledot Jeshu, the apocryphal "Life of Jesus," has attained considerable popularity and note.[87] Lauterbach bestows upon the passage

---

[83] An exact translation of the prefix ב to words following the terms אסור and מותר is not easy. [In English it can be rendered "as regards."] The halakic rule about current usage reads: בנדרים הלך אחר לשון בני אדם.

[84] F. Perles in the *Schwarz Jubelschrift*, p. 309. Also noted in *Additamenta ad Librum Aruch Completum*, p. 394, where also will be found further remarks on the root שחר.

[85] *A History of Sumer and Akkad*, London, 1910, p. 40. This is the work quoted *supra*, p. 124.

[86] Wilna edition of the Talmud, 52a. The passage was formerly accessible in *Kallah* edited in חמש קונטרסים by N. Coronel, Vienna, 1864, p. 3b.

[87] Krauss, *Leben Jesu nach Juedischen Quellen*, Berlin, 1902, *passim* but especially p. 262, note 6.

only brief and casual attention, remarking that it "is to be understood that it is marked impudence on the part of a young boy to go bareheaded and not, as R. Isaac Aboab (Menorat ha-Maor ch. 337, ed. Warsaw 1890, p. 325) seems to have understood it, that even on the part of adults it would be impudent to walk with uncovered head. For, according to the Mishnah,[88] it was the usual thing for grown men to go bareheaded."

H. L. Strack, in his work devoted entirely to rabbinic texts that treat of Jesus,[89] offers a very sensible comment on the passage in Kallah Rabbati. Strack writes: "Among the Israelites of old, males were not in the habit of going about with covered heads. It is true that head covering was worn by officiating priests but otherwise the head was covered only in war or in mourning. Therefore the incident related in Kallah 41b — even granting that R. Akiba would do anything so improper — need not be regarded as historical. In any event, at the time the story was fabricated, it must have been the custom to keep the head covered in the presence of persons of consequence."[90] Leaving it undecided whether or not Jesus was at all involved in the story, Strack goes on to say: "What Toledot Jeshu indicates is that Kallah 41b was later supposed to refer to Jesus."[91] The definition of impudence proffered by the three scholars is exceedingly old.[92]

The Toledot Jeshu exists in many differing texts and recensions. The incident does not appear in any fixed form but the essential features remain constant. In the Vienna Manuscript edited by me, the text reads somewhat curiously: "When passing in the presence of the sages, their well behaved disciples would go bowed and prostrate and with covered faces. But that bastard, Joshua (sic), when passing before R. Simeon [ben Shetah] and the other sages, would maintain an erect posture, base and

---

[88] The Mishna passage to which Lauterbach refers is Ned. III. 8.

[89] Jesus, die Haeretiker und die Christen, Leipzig, 1910, Hebrew p. 7.

[90] Strack refers to Loew, Gesammelte Schriften, II, 311–328, the well known essay on Aaron Chorin (supra note 62).

[91] Here is where Strack quotes from my Leben Jesu above mentioned in note 87.

[92] See Maḥzor Vitry, Berlin, 1893, p. 552.

worthless fellow that he was."[93] This is not the same as that to which we have been accustomed by the other texts. What matters is not the covering of the head but the covering of the face; as already noted, the former includes the latter. Is not this the same as "wrapping oneself" in the Divine Presence? We go a step further. The Rabbis were held in such inordinate esteem, especially by their pupils, that they were believed to be attended by the *Shekinah*. Not seldom is it said of certain teachers that, when they taught, darts of flame (זיקוקי אש) would issue from their mouths.[94] This obviously indicates an affinity between the presence of scholars and the presence of God. In both cases, the same motive would operate to prompt covering the face and covering the head. We are dealing, of course, with a usage characterizing the *milieu* of scholars and not with one diffused among the people in general.

We emphasize this distinction because the story about the youngster too impudent to cover his head would otherwise conflict with our previous notice that boys went bareheaded normally. The pupils to which Kallah Rabbati refers were adults not yet arrived at mastership. And adults — even among the

---

[93] Chap. III, p. 66. See *ibid.*, p. 277, note 17. The Hebrew reads as follows:
ומנהג תלמידי חכמים כשרים כשהיו עוברים לפניהם (= לפני חכמים) התלמידים היו כורעים ומשתחוים לפניהם ומכסים פניהם מפני כבוד רבם, וזה יהושע הממזר עבר לפני ר' שמעון ולפני החכמים בקומה זקופה כאיש נבל בליעל.

[94] Ḥul. 137b contains an interesting report of the way in which, during halakic discussions, darts of fire would proceed from the mouths of Rabbi and of Rab and pass from the one to the other. See the aggadic interpretation of Num. 21.28 in B, B. 78b and in Targum Pseudo-Jonathan *ad loc*. The notion is widespread. The beams (in Hebrew, "horns," Ex. 34.29) emanating from the face of Moses have been explained as due to sparks issuing from the mouth of God (ניצוצות יצאו מפי השכינה) Tanḥuma Tissa end: Exod. Rab. XLVII, 6; Cf. Jellinek's *Beth Hamidrash*, VI, 151). In IV Ezra, 13.10, a similar emanation is attributed to the King Messiah, *de labiis ejus spiritus flammae*. It is thus understandable why this capacity should have been imputed to Bar Kokba (See my article in the *Jewish Encyclopedia*, also Graetz IV, 138, 4th edit.). This has been found comparable with the fire-spitting attributed to Eunus, leader of the slaves' revolt which broke out in Sicily, 143 A. D. (Florus III, 19). See Stark's *Gaza*, p. 480, note 3 and Pliny's *Historia Naturalis*, II, III; also Jerome's *Adversus Rufinum* II, 559. All of this is ultimately nothing but metaphor for words spoken with burning zeal.

scholarly — were, if unmarried, by no means free of restrictions
as to headwear. Putting on a *Sudar* before one was married was
viewed as presumptuous.[95] Again, where a certain account rebukes for his insolence one who, with uncovered head, passed by
a Rabbi (ibid. 33a), the record continues that the offender may
have been from Mata Meḥaśya, a town in Babylonia, where
arrogance toward Rabbis was the vogue (see Rashi, ibid.).
If, now, the Rabbis were powerless to compel that token of
respect, its omission could hardly have been contrary to religious law. The Babylonian Rabbis themselves deemed it
commendable to keep their heads covered as a sign of humility
before the Divine. R. Huna, the son of R. Joshua, would not,
with uncovered head (בגילוי הראש), walk as much as four cubits.
He gave as his reason: "The Shekinah is just above me" שכינה
למעלה מראשי (ibid? 31a). Such a claim fits not any ordinary
person but only a man of exceptional learning and piety, firm
and habituated in his communion with God. A belief in the
presence of the Deity is presupposed in all of the cases which
involve "wrapping oneself." Something similar still survives
in the rituals connected with the *'Amidah*.[96] A parallel passage
(Sab. 118b) reads: "Said R. Huna, the son of R. Joshua: 'May
Divine recompense reach me[97] for my forbearing to go, with
uncovered head, as much as four cubits.'" The Hebrew expression גילוי הראש has become separated from its Aramaic contexts in both passages and, thus detached, has grown current
among Jews down to the present day.

From these indications, what now may we infer? A close
scrutiny of the quoted passages reveals a host of related customs
having, as their common feature, certain extreme but optional
forms of piety. Thus Ḳid. 31a declares: "It is forbidden to walk,
with haughty mien (בקומה זקופה), as much as four cubits." —
literally, with erect stature, the opposite of which is the bowed

---

[95] Cf. the case of R. Hamnuna, Ḳid. 29b. The question has received thoroughgoing treatment in Maharil (Warsaw, 5634, p. 25) under הלכות נישואין.

[96] For the latest stage of this development, see Shulḥan 'Aruk, 'Oraḥ
Ḥayyim, 123–124. Further details in Shem Tob Gaguine, *Keter Shem Tob*,
5694, p. 63.

[97] תיתי לי, an expletive of confirmation.

stature signalized, it seems, by covering the head. Could this have been generally observed? Of course not. Conclusive proof that such was an act of unusual piety (חסידות) is afforded by the example of the noted teacher, Rab (about 250). In late sources,[98] Rab is reported to have possessed ten portions of *Ḥasidut*, exceptional devoutness, one of which portions consisted in the fact that never, for as much as four cubits, did he walk haughtily and never, for as much as four cubits, did he walk with head uncovered, בגילוי הראש.[99] Does this not imply unmistakably that similar compunction was expected of no one else? Indeed, one seeking to imitate Rab might justly be accused of יוהרא, the above mentioned impudence. A woman demanding such of her son would be classed as a bigot. It is related (Sab. 156b) that the mother of R. Naḥman b. Isaac, having been told by an astrologer that her son was destined to become a thief, never permitted her son to go bareheaded, obviously believing that the evil destiny would thereby be averted. She commanded: "Cover thy head that the fear of Heaven be upon thee."

"One is justified," says Lauterbach, quoting Hastings (*Ency-clopedia of Religion and Ethics*, VI, p. 539) "in surmising that there were some elements of primitive superstition connected with this practice."[100] The action of that worried mother lies

---

[98] Assembled in האורה 'ס Edit. Buber, p. 1 which provides numerous references; also in Rashi's manuscript Pardes (A. Epstein in *Monatschrift*, LII, 716); and finally in *'Oẓar Ha-Ge'onim*, edit. B. Lewin, "Sabbath," p. 110.

[99] As already stated (*supra*, p. 147), this is a later expression. In Talmudic times, the phrase was ראש פרוע or ראש מגולה which came to signify sinful or insolent behavior. Cf. the statement that Nadab and Abihu uncovered their heads and gazed upon the splendor of the Shekinah ('Oshaya in Exod. Rab. III, 1; also 'En Jacob to Ber. 7a — in the Koeningsberg edit. paragraph 31). In the corresponding passages of other texts, the expression פרע or גלה is missing. See Pesiḳta de Rab Kahana, p. 173b and Tanḥuma, 'Aḥare Mot, Chap. 6 (in Buber, Chap. 7); Num. Rab. II, 23 and also XV, 34 which, however, uses the significant words הקלו ראשם. Cf. Lev. Rab. XX, 9 and Bacher, *Aggada der Palestinensischen Amoraeer*, III, 472, note 7.

[100] Cf. A. T. Olmstead, "Wearing the Hat," *Amer. Journ. of Theology*, Jan. 1920, p. 94 ff.; also the chapter, "Costumes and Ideologies" in the *Bibliography of Costume*, compiled by Hilaire and Meyer Hiler, edited by Helen Grant Cushing with the collaboration of Adah V. Morris (The H. W. Wilson Co., New York).

along those lines. Compliant with Amos 4.12, "Prepare to meet thy God, O Israel," various types of preparation for prayer were deemed appropriate. One worshipper puts on beautiful stockings — otherwise, presumably, being barefooted. Another would, as a sign of humility, remove his fine coat (See Rashi) and would clasp his hands, standing before God as a slave before his master. Such is reputed to have been, in time of stress, the practice of R. Kahana who, at other times, would attire himself tastefully and would pray "covered" and "enwrapped" (Sab. 10a). This latter mode seems to indicate apparel of three kinds: robes, head-covering, and *Tallit*, while in other instances, the head-covering is implied by the "enwrapping" itself.[101] All of these "preparations" refer to Rabbis in Babylonia, and not to synagogal prayer but to private prayer.

Apropos this point, Palestinian sources recount an incident which is reported to have caused not a little commotion. Talmud Yerushalmi,[102] after asserting that R. Johanan ben Zakkai would remove his phylacteries neither in summer nor in winter and that he was followed in this by his disciple, R. Eliezer [ben Hyrcanus] proceeds thereupon to impute to R. Johanan something different. The passage continues that, being subject to summer headaches and obliged to take precautions against catching cold, R. Johanan, that outstanding *Amora*, bearer of the Palestinian *Halakah*, would place the phylacteries on his arm and on his head only in winter when he was immune to headaches but would, in summer, wear the phylactery only on his arm.[103] While admitting that there are other and differing explanations, let me suggest that which seems to me the most

[101] In our section dealing with the attire of women, we shall scrutinize more closely the connection between veil and head covering. But, with men also, wrapping in the *Tallit* involves, at least in part, a covering of the face.

[102] Ber. II, 3 folio 4c. A parallel text in *Pesiḳ. Rabbati*, Chap. 22, Friedmann edit. p. 112a.

[103] See the short commentary in the Krotoschin edit. of Yerushalmi. A lengthier explication is furnished by R. Manahem Lonsano in the Wilna edit., 1922, 14a–15a. See also the discussion in the Bet Joseph to Tur 'Oraḥ Ḥayyim, No. 27. An explanation is also given by M. Friedmann, the editor of the somewhat better text in Pesiḳ. Rabbati Chap. 22, p. 112a. See also Strack-Billerbeck, *op. cit.* III, 424.

acceptable interpretation of this passage. It seems probable that, in summer, R. Johanan wore no head covering at all. The most illustrious man in Palestinian Jewry of that day would yield to the exigencies of health and of climate.[104]

A close parallel to the passage just cited can be found in Lev. Rab. XIX, 4, where we find the foreign word "rheumatic." Commenting on Eccl. 10.18, "By slothfulness the rafters sink in," the Midrash observes: "A man will become rheumatic if he is too slothful to cover his head properly .... but Rabbi Abahu interprets the words to refer to women, because a woman is too slothful properly to cover herself. And that is why Lev. 20.18 says: 'If he shall uncover her nakedness, he hath made naked her fountain, and she hath uncovered the fountain of her blood.' " Obviously, being decently clothed is far more urgent for women than for men.

In addition to the term *Gilluy Rosh* already mentioned, there is another term, ריש גלי, which consists of the former words reversed and which, it would appear, occurs only in Aramaic. We find this term in the Targum to יד רמה of Ex. 14.8 and Num. 33.3, describing the manner of the Exodus, and again in Mekilta to Ex. 14.8 with the Aramaic in a Hebrew context.[105] Similar is the implication in Exod. Rab. XVIII, 8 where, however, the Aramaic is replaced by the Hebrew בראש גלוי. "Said God to Pharaoh: 'Wouldst thou let my children go forth at night? Thou shalt let my children go forth not by night but at midday and with uncovered heads.' " For the only additional occurrence of ריש גלי, we must go to Targum Jonathan on Judg. 5.9: "Deborah spake in the spirit of prophecy: 'I have been sent to

---

[104] No sooner was the above statement made than it created bewilderment. "Would not R. Johanan have been too scantily clad (ערוה) in summer to permit the donning of phylacteries at all?" The commentators try to meet the difficulty by maintaining that R. Johanan would divest himself only of his belt or that he wore at least a shirt (on אפיקרסין see *Lehnwoerter*, II, 113) or that the expression *mibifnim* instead of "on his skin" or "on his body" implies that the shirt was worn beneath a *Tallit*. What the commentators blink is the fact that a man sensitive to *Tefillin*, an object immeasurably lighter than a shirt, would have found insufferable a garment of any kind.

[105] Well explained by Levy, *Chaldaeisches Woerterbuch ueber die Targumim*, I, 141. Cf. בגלי in Targum to Isa. 41.2, in the sense of "publicly."

acclaim Israel's scribes who, in times of stress, ceased not to expound the Torah. They are well entitled to sit in the synagogues (houses of assembly), with their heads uncovered, instructing the people in matters of the Torah and blessing and praising God.' "

Now it has been assumed that ריש גלי signifies freedom as opposed to slavery.[106] This does indeed fit the situation of the Exodus but hardly that of the remark attributed to Deborah; because, in the days of Deborah, no transition from slavery to freedom happened to the scribes. Even in the more explicit wording of Exodus Rabbah, the contrast is drawn not between freedom and slavery but between day and night, between light and darkness, between proceeding openly and proceeding furtively. Therefore I do not agree with Lauterbach, Strack-Billerbeck, and others who find in that expression some evidence that the Israelites were accustomed to go bareheaded. On the contrary, it seems that ריש גלי was only a formal expression similar to יד רמה which it paraphrases, similar also to זרוע נטויה, יד חזקה, יד חזקה, קומה זקופה, קוממיות and analogous turns of speech exhibited in various languages. It may be that originally יד רמה and ריש גלי denoted exactly what they say. But, in the course of time, such words come to be used figuratively.[107] They acquired the sense of "walking erect" like קוממיות in Lev. 26.13 or like the rabbinic קומה זקופה "erect stature" as opposed to the "bowed stature" already mentioned, phrases which apply respectively to holding the head high or holding it low.

Our next citation brings our entire inquiry to a focus. Tractate Soferim which, though not exactly a part of the Talmud, nonetheless abounds in valuable material reflecting Palestinian customs, contains the provision that, with uncovered head, one may recite the *Shema'*.[108] The passage reads: "A *Poḥeaḥ*

---

[106] Thus, Strack-Billerbeck, *op. cit.*, III, 424. Jastrow's rendering of "openly" in his *Dictionary*, p. 248, is exceedingly apt.

[107] Like "bold front" in English, "offene Stirne" in German. These phrases suggest the biblical מצח. Cf. especially, Ezek. 3.8. Jer. 3.3 has yielded expressions employed even in Modern Hebrew, such as עזות פנים = עזות מצח ....

[108] Chap. XIV, 15, pp. 198, 199 edit. J. Mueller. See also edit. Higger. For the latest surmises on פורס על שמע, see my *Additamenta ad Librum Aruch Completum*, p. 341.

(פוחח[109] that is, one whose legs are visible or whose garments are
otherwise torn) or one whose head is bare (מגולה) is permitted to
recite the *Shema'*.[110] Some say that one whose legs are visible or
garments otherwise torn[111] may do so but not one whose head
is bare, for such a one may not pronounce the Tetragrammaton.
In either case [whether a *Poḥeaḥ* or bare-headed — Editor]
one may render the Targum (the translation).[112] But a *Poḥeaḥ*
may not do the public reading of the Pentateuch or officiate
before the ark[113] or lift his hands in priestly benediction." There
can be no question of authenticity here because the entire passage
is an expansion of the *Halakah* in Meg. IV, 6 and its Tosefta.
We are accustomed to view those statements as dissenting
opinions such as develop amid the innumerable Rabbinic controversies. But this is incorrect, and Lauterbach's surmise (p.
595) that "this latter opinion reflects the Babylonian custom"
is unacceptable. It is true, there exists on this point a difference
between Babylonian custom and Palestinian custom but the
difference is not what Lauterbach takes it to be. Chapter XVIII,
near the end, alludes to three different usages pertaining to the
same rite, each reference being introduced by יש "some say"
(See also XX, 7). Elsewhere, as in XII, 9, when such variations
are discussed, it is stated explicitly that "they of the East" do
so and so while "they of the West" do so and so. Again, as quoted
by Lauterbach, the Ḥilluf Minhagim[114] indicates such variation
in the following words: "*Kohanim*, with disarranged hair are,
among the Babylonians, forbidden to bless the Israelites, but
in Palestine, *Kohanim* with disarranged hair, do bless the Israelites." It is not clear why the text employs the somewhat antiquated biblical word פרוע. But the word occurs frequently and

---

[109] The word is, in reality, Aramaic. See commentaries and dictionaries.
פוחח is approximately a *sans culotte*.

[110] Leading the congregation in the recital of the *Shema'* is a function
inferior to that of "going before the chest," that is, leading in the main prayer,
the '*Amidah*. See Tosafot Yom Ṭob to Meg. *loc. cit.* [IV, 6].

[111] In the Mishna, this specification is missing.

[112] Also a minor function.

[113] See my *Synagogale Altertuemer*, pp. 132, 171, 372.

[114] Edit. J. Mueller in *Hashacher*, VII, or its reprint. I regret that I am
without access to a certain more recent work on this subject.

is well suited to the passage with its reference to the ancient
biblical rite of *Birkat Kohanim*. Lauterbach's conclusion is valid:
"This, by the way, also implies that even in Babylon it was not
absolutely forbidden to enter the synagog and participate in the
religious service with uncovered head. Had this been the case,
the special mention of a law prohibiting the priests from pronouncing their blessings bareheaded would have been gratuitous."

Previously the same tractate (Soferim XIV, 14) describes
the ritual of returning the scroll to the ark and uses words לכסות
ראשי הקוראים apparently related to our subject. However the
text is plainly incorrect.[115] It should, according to R. Elijah Wilna,
read thus: "For dressing the scroll, the aforementioned person
hands it to him who was the first to function among those invited
to participate (לראש הקרואים); it would dishonor the *Torah* to
leave it unattended."

We proceed now to the most striking passage of all. There
comes a moment in the burial ceremony when the mourner
proceeds with uncovered head. The text, Semaḥot X, in its
corrupt form, we quote in the notes.[116] Here we translate the
better text furnished by N. Bruell in his *Jahrbuecher*, I, 54:
"Not until the stone closing the grave has been set in place,[117]
do the people line up (in two rows) to pronounce, in the mourner's
behalf, the benediction for the bereaved. Once the stone has been
set in place, the people do line up and speak the words of consola-
tion, and then they depart. Moreover, as soon as the stone has
been set in place, the mourner covers his head but, out of respect
for the people who stand in line, he keeps his head bare as he
passes them. Once beyond the rows of people, he again covers
his head. After he returns to his home, people call to voice
condolence; then he bares his head as the callers take leave."
What a curious ceremony![118] We have already referred to burial

---

[115] The conjectures offered by J. Mueller as well as those which he quotes
are inacceptable.

[116] ר' נסים באלפס: [ובא לעמוד בשורה מגלה את ראשו ופוטרן, יצא חוץ לשורה מכסה].

[117] See Jastrow, p. 222 *sub verbo* גולל and my *Talmudische Archaeologie* II,
77.

[118] The usage is comparable with the demeanor prescribed for a high
priest attending the funeral of a near relative. Notice הן נכסין והוא נגלה וכו' in
San. II, 1. See also my *Sanhedrin-Makkot*, p. 95.

rites. This one is remarkable. Considering the tenacity of burial customs, this particular rite must be exceedingly old, going back, perhaps, to biblical times.

Nowhere is it enjoined that there be a head covering upon the corpse lying in the casket. Our modern practice constitutes an innovation. Not even the "cap" which, in later times, figures as part of the burial garb, is mentioned in the sources. A famous and fanciful saying imputed, in Ket. 111b to R. Ḥiyya ben Joseph, presumes that, at the resurrection, the pious will rise in their תכריכין their burial shroud.[119] But the word תכריכין means the robe; "cap" is excluded. Thus it is evident that men were not required to wear any head covering, either in the synagog or in similar situations.

III. The Head Covering of Women in the Talmudic Period

We must distinguish clearly between that which was expected of men and that which morality and decency, emphasized by religion, imposed upon women. Here again, as in a previous connection, we note what is said upon this subject in extra-Jewish circles, that is, outside of that Rabbinic literature which constitutes our main source of information. Christian theology is obliged to deal with the question because of the passage already quoted from I Cor. 11.5, "For if the woman be not covered,[120] let her also be shorn;[121] but if it be a shame for a woman to be shorn or shaven, let her be covered."

[119] See Tosafot, also Pirke de R. Eliezer, XXXIII; Eisenmenger, *Entdecktes Judentum*, p. 934. Contrast Saadia, Emunot we-De'ot, VII.

[120] A few words may be quoted here from a modern commentary: "St. Paul first lays down the principle of subordination. He then speaks of the unseemliness of the practice in question, and of its converse, namely, men covering their heads; and shows how this matter comes under the above principle, while women are not degraded by this subordination. He next uses corroboratory arguments from nature, and finally appeals to the practice of all other Churches." (*A Commentary on the Holy Bible*, edited by J. R. Dummelow, London, 1926, p. 909.)

[121] For an honorable woman, shearing of the hair was a great indignity. See A. Buechler, "Das Schneiden des Haares als Strafe der Ehebrecher bei den Semiten," in *Wiener Zeitschrift fuer die Kunde des Morgenlandes*, XVIII,

The word κάλυμμα and its derivatives have a double meaning. They mean "veil;"[122] they also mean "head covering," and the distinction is not easily drawn as regards the attire of women. The chaste Susanna appears before her judges veiled.[123] According to Philo,[124] ἐπίκρανον, the headband, betokens shamefacedness and innocence. To this, we have a clue in the ordeal of the *Soṭah*, the woman suspected of adultery, as described in Num. 5, 12–31 which directs the priest to "let the hair of the woman's head go loose" ופרע את ראש האשה[125]— a point to which we shall soon revert. Philo apparently construes the biblical words to mean that the priest shall remove the covering of the woman's head. But this interpretation, as noted already by Ritter and Heinemann,[126] does not accord with that of the Rabbis (Soṭ. 9a). Philo who states (III, 60) that the woman has to proceed in the ordeal bare-headed, must have known the Jewish wife as one who ordinarily went about with head covered. This is reported specifically by the famous church father, Tertullian, who wrote about the year 200 C. E. Says Tertullian: "*Apud Judaeos tam sollemne est feminis eorum velamen capitis, ut inde noscantur.*" "So sacred, among the Jews, is the head covering of the women that by this they are recognizable."[127] Though Tertullian, residing in North Africa,

---

91–138; also my *Talmud. Arch.* I, 190 ff. On the other hand, much care was bestowed upon depilation, a subject treated at length in my article, "The Archaeological Background of Some Passages in the Song of Songs," *J.Q.R.*, New Series, XXXII (1942).

[122] In accordance with what has already been noted (*supra* pp. 145, 146) to the effect that covering the head can mean, at the same time, covering the face. The view is supported by Gerhard Kittel, *Theologisches Woerterbuch Zum Neuen Testament, sub verbo* κάλυμμα, *Kopfhuelle, Schleier.*

[123] κατακεκαλυμμένη, The History of Susannah, verse 32, Theodotion.

[124] De Specialis Legibus, III, 56.

[125] We discussed the root פרע above, pp. 128, 130, 140.

[126] B. Ritter, *Philo und die Halacha*, Leipzig, 1879, p. 81 ff., and I. Heinemann in *Die Werke Philos von Alexandria*, II, 200. A totally different significance was attached to in later ages. Cf. Maharil, Warsaw, 5634, pl 25 already quoted, and also the ritual codes: מה שהכלות הבתולות פרועות (צ"ל פורעות) ראשן וסותרין קליעת שערן מפני שצריכין (צ"ל -ות) טבילה וחפיפה הראש... והמנהג שנם שאר הבתולות פורעות ראשן וסותרות קליעתן כדי לחפות עליה לצניעות שאין לגלות שטיוחדת היא לטבילה.

[127] *De Corona*, edit. F. Oehler, I, 1853, p. 424. This is the correct rendering. Other translations are erroneous.

may have in view only the usages of that region, a broader application need not be excluded. Ginzberg, in *Legends of the Jews*, V, p. 90, quoting from Tertullian's *De Habitu Muliebri* (1), *Adversus Marcionem* (5, 8), and *De Oratione* (22)[128] says: "The statement made by Tertullian, in the last-named passage, that the unmarried Jewish women cover their heads, contradicts the assertions of the Jewish sources, according to which married women only covered their heads; comp. e.g. Ketubot 2,1; Yebamot 114b. See, however, Nedarim 3,8; Sifre N., 11, Berakot 24a." But these texts contain nothing decisive for our question. The only telling evidence is that contained in the Mishna, Ket. II, 1, as will be explained later.

The Rabbis, punctiliously devoted to the Law, pivot their views on the biblical word פרע. Everything revolves on what they understood by that word. When the word is used with regard to the wedding of a maiden (Ket. II, 1), the import is that, on such occasions, the bride wore her hair loose. Rashi and Bertinoro explain: "Her hair would fall over her shoulders. Thus would the maiden be conducted from her father's house to the place of her nuptials." Compare the phrases: "She shows her face," "She makes herself known."[129] At her wedding, the bride shows herself for the last time as a girl. Having the hair loose and dropping low is, among several nations, the token of the unmarried state, hence of virginity and chastity.[130] Therefore the married woman who walks abroad with her hair loose (יוצאה וראשה פרוע) violates "Jewish custom."[131] Such is the manner of

[128] This reference figures also in Kittel's *Woerterbuch* with the edition mark, CCSEL, 20, 193, but I could find there nothing a propos.

[129] Exod. Rab. XLI, 6. See also Cant. Rab. and Yalḳuṭ to Cant. 4.11. The expression is מפרסמת עצמה. Cf. Soṭ. 9a, פירסמה בגלוי to divulge, to publish.

[130] Among various peoples, as among conservative Jews, cutting off the bride's hair is part of the marriage ceremony. The reverse of this is the covering worn on the married woman's head. Cf. Mueller-Mothes, *Archaeologisches Woerterbuch*, Leipzig and Berlin, 1877, p. 588, sub verbo *Kopfbedeckung*, French *cover-chef*, English *coverchief*, Latin (or rather Greek) *calyptra*. See the definition of *kerchief* in H. C. Wyld, *The Universal Dictionary of the English Language*: "Square piece of cloth, lace, or other material worn as a covering for the head by women."

[131] Ket. VII, 6. Tos. *ibid.* (p. 269 in Zuckermandel), Giṭ. 90ab. The Mishna, at this point, distinguishes between "Mosaic Law" and "Jewish Law." The

women among pagans (Num. Rab. IX, 16). In all of these texts, the word employed is פרוע derived from Num. 5.18 and aptly translated even by such a conservative as Hertz: "He shall let the hair of the woman's head go loose," with the appropriate comment: "In token of her shame, as it was a sign of lack of morality for a woman to appear publicly with her hair unloosed." The point is the loosening of the hair and not, by any means, the uncovering of the head. The very word ראש in Hebrew often means "hair."[132]

To show that, by the Rabbis of the Talmud, the word פרע was taken literally, let us note one of many instances. Lev. 13.45 requires that the leper rend his clothes and loosen his hair. The Mishna, in Soṭ. III,8, using the biblical words but reversing the order, appends that a man loosens his hair and rends his clothes but that this is not done by a woman.[133] As in the case of a man, so also in the case of a woman, פרע relates, accordingly, to the hair and not to any headwear.

In view of this, it is astonishing that our oldest, so-called "traditional" texts confuse פרע with גלה or with its opposite כסה, applying it not to the hair but to the head. As regards the frequently quoted passage ופרע את ראש האשה, a *Baraitha* in Ket. 72a reports that the school of R. Ishmael grounded upon this the אזהרה, the admonition, that the daughters of Israel[134] should not go outdoors with loosened hair (פרוע). Sifre uses, in this connection, the phrase ראשיהן מכוסין, "that they may *cover* their heads,"[135] implying a head covering — which perhaps the school

woman's head covering is subsumed under the latter classification. The comments of the Tosafot Yom Ṭob, excerpted from older authorities, are under the influence of later conceptions and fail to convey the true implications of the Mishna. These comments read: "As to the meaning of פרוע, so far as the Torah ordains, it suffices that the woman's head be covered by a kerchief even when she appears in public places, but Jewish Law (דת) requires that, for such occasions, she wear, on her head, a veil (רדיד?)."

[132] See commentaries, dictionaries, and concordances.

[133] Out of considerations of decency. For similar compunctions at public executions, see San. VI, 3.

[134] A fond appellative for Jewish women and of frequent use in the Bible and the Talmud.

[135] Chap. XI, edit. Friedmann, p. 5a. Cf. Num. Rab. IX, 33.

of R. Ishmael did not mean. In any case, אזהרה is a mild expression. It hardly looks like a prescription or a command.

The authentic interpretation of the verb פרע in the ordeal of the *Soṭah* was, in the precise language of the Mishna (Soṭ. I, 5) וסותר את שערה, "the priest deranges her hair." The word סתר can best be rendered by the French *déranger*: to put out of order, to loosen. The word alludes to the artistic head dress[136] of the stylish lady, Jewish or non-Jewish.[137] In connection with the *Soṭah*, a *Baraitha* in Soṭ. 9a[138], as well as Tos. Soṭ. III, 3, furnishes an interesting description of a Jewish courtesan: "She plaited her hair to please her paramour, therefore the priest loosens her hair."[139] Both passages describe a further action performed by the priest: "She had placed a sheet[140] [on the bed for her paramour], therefore the priest pulls her cap (כפה) from her head and tramples it beneath his feet." The "cap," however, is not a headcovering but, as archaeologists have shown, a requisite of a lady's coiffure.[141] It is then stated, in the same connection, that the priest, in addition to "deranging" (סתר) the head, does something further which is likewise included in the term פרע: he uncovers the woman's "heart," that is, her breast. At this point, the Mishna (I, 5) observes, in the name of R. Judah: "If her breast was beautiful, he would not expose it; if her hair was beautiful, he would not derange it." The verb, in the first case, is מגלה, in the second case, סותר, wherefore it is incorrect to assume that, in this context, the Rabbinical interpreters understood פרע to mean "uncover."[142] It is true that the Rabbis extended the מצות פריעה, "the sacred act of loosening," to include

[136] This is called בנה. See the midrashic explanation of ויבן in Gen. 2.22.
[137] See *Talmud. Arch.* I, 197.   [138] Cf. Num. Rab. IX.
[139] In Tos. Soṭ. III, 3, p. 295 in Zuckermandel, the significant words appear only in a note taken from old editions and manuscripts.
[140] The word in the Tosefta is סדין, entirely appropriate in this context. In the Talmud, however, the corresponding passage (Soṭ. 8b bottom) reads: "For his sake she placed, upon her head, a beautiful *sudarin*, therefore the priest removes the cap from her head." A close kinship between *sudarin* and *kippah* is obvious. The variant צעיפה for the latter in the Tosefta is distinctly erroneous.
[141] See the discussion in Strack-Billerbeck, *loc. cit.*
[142] *Ibid.*

the woman's bosom,[143] which is hardly contained in the words of the Law itself. Apparently the Mishna is either uninformed about this feature or is inclined to ignore it, for the text reads: "The priest seizes her by the garments,[144] heedless whether they be rent or torn, until he exposes her breast." There is mention here of two procedures: pulling off her "cap" as he deranges her hair and grasping her garments as he bares her bosom. In vain did the old *Tanna*, R. Baroḳba, protest: "You must not dishonor (מנוולים) the daughters of Israel beyond what is prescribed in the Torah." Baroḳa went so far as to maintain that a curtain had to hang between the priest and the public.[145] But, quoting Ezek. 23, 48, the scholars were preponderantly of the opinion that such a woman deserves no consideration.[146]

An aggadic passage alludes to the procedure in the sanctuary as follows: "Like a high priest to whose lot it fell to administer the bitter waters and to whom the woman had been brought. He had already loosened her hair and exposed her breast and was about to take the cup from which she was to drink, when he noticed that it was his mother."[147]

Having observed the extent to which the Jewish lady of Talmudic times would cultivate a sumptuous head dress, I reached this conclusion:[148] "The extraordinary care bestowed upon hair dressing reveals that Jewish women did not go about with covered heads. This is substantiated by information from various sources,[149] and there exists no conclusive evidence to the contrary. The numerous indications that women, like men, would wrap (עטף) the head for mourning show that, with women,

---

[143] Sifre, N. V. 8, Chap. XI, p. 5a.   [144] As a token of scorn.

[145] Soṭ. I, 6 states explicitly that onlookers were permitted to be present, excepting the woman's menservants or maidservants.

[146] Soṭ. 8b, Tos. Soṭ. III, 2, p. 295 in Zuckermandel.

[147] Pesikta Rabbati, Chap. XXVI, p. 129b in edit. Friedmann, Vienna, 1880. The text is uncertain. See Friedmann *ad loc.* In all events, the word used is פרסס.

[148] *Talmud. Arch.* I, 196 ff.

[149] My favorite reference is Sab. VI, 1 which presupposes that a woman took considerable pains in dressing her hair. Cf. the severe punishment favored by R. Akiba for anyone who, to humiliate a woman, would stop in the street and dishevel a woman's head-dress (B. K. VIII, 6).

bareheadedness was the rule. Concealing the head in time of be-
reavement signified the same as cutting or shaving the hair on
like occasions. Whether in mourning, in punishment, or in en-
slavement, such rites carry the same import."[150]

Strack and Billerbeck (ibid. III, 427), obliged to treat I Cor.
11.5, and having collected a vast amount of material — derived
in part from my *Talmudische Archaeologie* — on the subject of
head dress, have arrived at the same conclusion: "Our sources
do not specify in what way or by what means the head and the
face would be covered ... This silence forces us to conclude
that no particular means were employed for covering the head
and veiling the face but that both obtained, as matter of course,
whenever a woman would appear in the hair dress customary
at that time." These same authors observe apropos the ordeal
of the *Soṭah* (ibid., p. 429): "According to the Jewish view, the
covering of the woman's head consists in a well arranged hair
dress, and her veiling is achieved by means of the bands, the
bows, and the כפה, dangling over her face."

A writer in the above quoted *Theologisches Woerterbuch zum
Neuen Testament* of Gerhard Kittel says in a note: "Benziger
(*Hebraische Archaeologie*, 3d. ed., 1927, p. 85) and S. Krauss ...
emphasize that, in Israel, veiling was not always customary
and was, as late as New Testament times, unenforced. But this
tells us little about the actual conditions." The author has in
mind here the passage from Tertullian which we have already
quoted (*supra*, p. 155).

We have seen that Philo, differing from the Rabbis, finds
in the *Soṭah* procedure an actual uncovering of the woman's
head and this is also the view of some of the Rabbinic statements
cited above. We turn now to a series of passages in which the
woman's going about with covered head is treated as a matter
of course. We do not, to be sure, refer to such cases as that of
Ḳimḥit[151] who exemplifies piety of an extreme kind and is so regarded in the source. But there is a passage which presupposes

---

[150] The resemblance between marriage rites and mourning customs has
already been noted, *supra*, p. 135. We shall soon revert to this point.

[151] Yer. Meg. I, 72a. The parallel texts are supplied in the marginal notes
of the Krotoschin edition.

that women appear with covered heads ordinarily. An Aggadist remarks that ten curses were imposed upon Eve,[152] the eighth of which involves her going about עטופה כאבל "enwrapped as a mourner."[153] A parallel is the statement that ten decrees were issued against Eve, the ninth of which requires that her head be covered (מכוסה) like that of a mourner whenever she leaves the house.[154] Or, more explicitly, "Why does the woman cover the head while the man does not? The case is like that of a woman who has done wrong and who consequently feels shame in the presence of others. Similarly Eve, having done wrong, has caused her daughters to wear concealment."[155] Since no scriptural text is quoted in support of this reference, the remark appears to rest on actual observation. And this would seem good evidence. But the passage involves no command, no institution. It entails nothing but some masculine raillery at feminine addiction to stylishness. The passage does not even refer to any actual covering. The woman's own hair forms the covering or wrapping.[156]

The observation follows the line of subtle jesting that marks the entire context (Gen. Rab. XVII, 13), for instance, "Why does the woman need perfume when the man does not?" In like spirit are the questions asked of Hillel in Sab. 31a, for example, "Why are the Babylonians round headed?"[157] Similar pleasantries enter into discussions about animals, for instance, "The camel, having presumed to ask for horns, was deprived even of his ears" (San. 106a bottom). The diminution of the moon is attributed to a quarrel between the moon and the sun.[158] The

---

[152] By "Eve," is meant, of course, women in general, Eve's daughters.

[153] 'Er. 100b. The text continues: "Like one imprisoned and isolated from all mankind." Another bit of sarcasm is the remark, in the same context, "She lets her hair grow like Lilith," that is, like a witch or sorceress.

[154] 'Ab. R. Naṭhan, Version II, Chap. 42, Edit, Schechter, p. 117.

[155] *Ibid.*, I, Chap. 9, p. 25. Cf. Gen. Rab. XVII, 13 and Yalḳuṭ to Gen. 23.

[156] Of the daughter of Nicodemus ben Gorion, Ket. 66b says that, when about to face Rabban Johannan ben Zakkai, she wrapped herself in her hair. For parallel texts, see my article, "*Talmudische Nachrichten Ueber Arabien,*" in *Z. d. M. G.*, LXX, 326.

[157] Among the anecdotes illustrating Hillel's extreme patience.

[158] Consult the vast literature listed in Ginzberg's *Legends*, V, 34 ff.; also V. Aptowitzer, "Arabisch-Juedische Schoepfungstheories," in *HUCA*,

legends of all nations abound in such popular musings, usually in connection with stories of creation. In German, there is *Natursagen* by Daenhardt and *Weltentstehung in Sage und Wissenschaft* (1925) by Ziegler and Oppenheim; in English *The Golden Bough* and *Folklore in the Old Testament* by Frazer; in French, *La Mythologie Primitive* (Paris, 1935) by Lucien Levy-Bruhl.

Recurrent, throughout rabbinic literature, is the expectation that the Jewish woman should not only keep rigidly within the limits of chastity but that she should abstain from everything that might impair her looks. An example closely related to our subject is the law of the *Nezirah*, the female among those devoted to the Nazirite rules in Num. Chap. 6, a type not yet obsolete in the time of the Mishna. While men are nowhere reproved for engaging in such practices; while, to the contrary, the *Nazir* is highly esteemed, it was otherwise with the *Nezirah*. Concerning her, the bitter words are put into the mouth of her husband: "I do not want a wife who is disfigured. I want no wife with shaven head."[159] Among the ancient Rabbis, a similar debate is precipitated by the law in Deut. 21.12[160]

In Hebrew, נלה is easily confused with גלח. "Uncovered" means, accordingly, that the head is hairless, wherefore "covered, the opposite, must mean a head with hair.

What Jewish husband today would ever, in the slightest, restrain his wife from engaging in trade? But a well known Tannaitic text, in Pes. 50b, rebukes the man who depends upon his wife's earnings. "Whoso looks to the earnings of his wife will never in his life see blessing." And what is the type of occupation thus branded? The answer given has been מתקולתא, "weight" which means, according to Rashi, going into the streets and offering the use of scales for remuneration. Such puny traffic is humiliating. The *Aruch Completum* of Kohut (VII, 33) offers two interpretations of this drawback. According to one, the income from yarn which the woman spins and sells is wretchedly small. According to the other, the woman keeps shop and the

VI, 205–246. Civilized people no longer subscribe to such fancies. Why should Judaism be burdened with those infantile notions?

[159] Naz. IV, 5. Cf. Tos. Naz. III, 14, p. 287 in Zuckermandel.

[160] See Yeb. 48a, and Sifre to Deut., Chap. 212, p. 112b.

act of weighing obliges her to lift her arms and expose her elbows, which constitutes פריצות "licentiousness." If such rigidities are antiquated today, why should punctiliousness about headwear be any the less antiquated?

IV. MIDDLE AGES AND MODERN TIMES

In the matter of head covering, Mediaeval times show considerable variety. In one country, covering of the head would be mandatory, at least in prayer. In another country, various synagogal solemnities as, for instance, the public reading of the Scroll would be performed bare-headed. The vast Rabbinic literature of those times informs us what was considered, in this regard, proper or praiseworthy or obligatory, but opinions differ and even conflict. As to the nature of these differences, there is disagreement between Leopold Loew and J. Z. Lauterbach, the two scholars who serve us as guides. Loew maintains that, among the Arabs in the Orient and in Spain, the Jews would wear head-covering, while they would not do so in mediaeval France.[161] Lauterbach holds that, in Spain, the Jews followed the usages of Babylon while, in France and Germany, they followed the ways of Palestine.[162] But, while these conjectures may serve to explain the differences between Sephardim and Ashkenazim, they will not suffice for our present problem. In the first place, the question of head covering was, in Babylonia, undecided and, in the second place, many parts of the Islamic Orient, such as Syria, Egypt, and North Africa followed religious customs which were not of Babylonian derivation. Agreeing with Loew, I should say that, among the Moslems, the Jews became accustomed to the covering of the head and naturally carried that custom into prayer and into the synagogue while, in Christian countries, that inducement did not exist. On the contrary, the older custom of bareheadedness survived until there came a time of reaction

---

[161] *Gesammelte Schriften*, II, 317. Elbogen, in *Der Juedische Gottesdienst²*, p. 500, maintains that the practice of mandatory head covering originated in the wearing of the *Ṭallit* and that it made its earliest appearance in Moslem Spain.

[162] *Year Book of the C. C. A. R.*, 1928, p. 598.

against Christianity and of orientation toward the Arabs as a more kindred people.[163]

An account of the Moslem turban will now be in place.[164] The turban, the head dress of the male in the Moslem East, consisted of a cap around which had been wound a length of cloth. "Turban" is usually traced to the Persian *dulband*, from which also is supposed to come the word "tulip," although this view has been disputed. Turbans are said to have been worn by the pre-Mohammedan Beduins of Arabia. The high cap is believed to be of Persian origin and the cloth wound about it is regarded as the element truly Arabian.[165] There are, in the *Hadith*,[166] many details about the turban of the Prophet. Numerous are the *Hadiths* which construe the turban as a badge to distinguish Moslems from unbelievers.[167] The turban is especially recommended for the *Ṣalat*[168] and for visits to tombs and mosques. Other forms of headwear are the *Tarbush* and the *Turtur*. Jewish authors of the Arabic period were familiar with these "Turkish" head coverings and were inclined to identify them

---

[163] The article "Headgear" in the *Encyclopedia Britannica*, 1910–1911, adequately describes the situation as it existed among the mediaeval Jews; especially the scruple about avoiding articles of apparel characteristic of other people, particularly when associated with religious practice; and, at the same time, the concern to eschew clothing too much at variance with that of unsympathetic surroundings. Conservatism, of course, plays its role, and mediaeval Jews are always depicted in a characteristic costume. The beautiful plate which the *Jewish Encyclopedia* IV, 294 provides to illustrate Jewish attire has already been mentioned (*supra*, p. 127). All of the men are shown here with coverings on their heads. (See my article, "Kleidung," in the German *Encyclopedia Judaica*.) However, the reverse also can be found, as for instance, in the picture on the title page of a Sephardic *Siddur* (מאה ברכות, 1687), where a servant and a physician (or a Rabbi), participating in a circumcision ceremony, are shown with heads bare. (See my article, "*Merkwuerdige Siddurim*," in *Studies in Jewish Bibliography in Memory of A. S. Freidus*, New York, 1929, p. 132.) It is well known that the peculiar costume of the Jews was, in part, forced upon them by the secular authorities.

[164] W. Bjoerkman in *The Encyclopedia of Islam*, sub verbo "Turban."

[165] Jacob, *Altarabisches Beduinenleben*, pp. 44, 237.

[166] [*Hadith* means: authoritative Moslem tradition.]

[167] The Jewish counterpart of this was considered *supra*, p. 130.

[168] [*Ṣalat* means "prayer."]

with various head coverings of ancient times.[169] Many celebrities of Arabic times, such as Maimonides, Alfasi, Shabbethai Ẓebi and others are pictured in these forms of headwear.

We are now in a position to understand the viewpoint of the mediaeval Jewish writers. Alfasi, in his Compendium, alludes to the above mentioned incident of R. Huna ben Joshua (*supra*, p. 147), and Maimonides, in Hilkot De'ot V, 6, regards it as morally incumbent upon scholars to avoid any uncovering of the head or of the body. And yet the juxtaposition of "head" and "body," as well as the remainder of the passage allow no indication of anything like today's *yarmulke* as a requisite of prayer for anyone except a scholar. Maimonides, in Hilkot Tefillah, V, 5, goes so far as to declare that one should forbear to recite prayers bareheaded or barefooted, but the latter requirement is limited to localities where having the feet clothed when standing before persons of higher rank is customary. The remark of Israel Abrahams is correct: "The oriental code of manners showed respect by covering the head and uncovering the feet, in exact contradiction to the prevailing custom of Europe."[170] The Zohar, originating in Spain, also has a word in favor of the covered head during prayer.[171] When R. Abraham ibn Yarḥi of France pleads for the covering of the head not only at prayer but also in general life, he does not neglect to state that, among the Jews of Spain, such was the custom.[172] In the age of Ibn Yarḥi (13th century) and in his country, a kind of *Minhag* had already become established. He says, on p. 37, that according to the *Minhag* prevalent in France, the leader at grace after meals, "enwraps" himself in a cloth or

---

[169] In Liḳḳuṭim min Sefer Meliẓah by Solomon ben Samuel of Ġurgang (See Bacher, *Ein Hebraeisch Persisches Woerterbuch aus dem 14ten Jahrhundert*, Strassburg, 1900), No. 970 reads קלקין כולאה נמדין טרטורא לנעו. No. 506 sub verbo טרטין has אלשוכל "a cap with a tail, like that worn by the Turks and called 'Tartur.'"

[170] *Jewish Life in the Middle Ages*, London, 1896, p. 278. Regarding the Jews of Yemen, the report of Ibn Saphir (I, 57a) states that they remove their shoes but retain their caps.

[171] Zohar Wa-etḥanan, Lublin, 1872, p. 520, quoted by Lauterbach *op. cit.*, p. 599.

[172] Tefillah, Chap. 43, Berlin, 1855, p. 15.

puts upon his head a "cap" (כובע).[173] This shows, first, that the diners ate bareheaded at the meal itself, and second that grace was said by bareheaded participants. In his *Responsa*, Zikron Jehudah,[174] the author, whose father, Asheri, had come to Toledo from Germany, writes: "Anyone who can endure it, should avoid sitting at study bareheaded because, with covered head, he would feel greater reverence. However, sometimes the heat would make such unendurable." This liberal attitude has provoked indignation among more recent halakists.[175] Inasmuch as the codes could not go beyond the limits set by the Talmud, there is hesitancy on this point in the final codification begun by another son of Asheri, R. Jacob (Ṭur Oraḥ Ḥayyim, 2) and continued in the Shulḥan 'Aruk (91, 3) by Rabbi Joseph Karo.[176]

In France and Germany, as already stated, the practice of covering the head shows but a slow growth. Some of the facts are astonishing. R. Isaac ben Moses of Vienna (1200–1270) who, in his youth, studied in France, reports that a *Minhag* of pronouncing a benediction bareheaded prevailed among "our Rabbis" in that country.[177] This certainly refers to the benedictions connected with the reading from the Scroll. R. Isaac himself does not approve of this *Minhag*. In the Maḥzor Vitry (p. 104), a work originating in the school of Rashi, there is an interesting item to the effect that *Kohanim* are permitted to keep on their caps at the *Dukan* if they do so because of the cold but not if they do so for ostentation (כבוד). We get the impression that some who attended synagogue were given to displaying their caps vaingloriously. And does not this violate the sanctity of the place? This calls to mind the display of hats by women at our synagogal service today. Another departure from the good old custom can

---

[173] In meals for company attended by at least three adult males, one is chosen to lead at grace (מזומן).

[174] Berlin, 1846, No. 20, p. 4a.

[175] See Loew and Lauterbach; also A. Freimann in *Jahrbuch der Jued. Lit. Gesellschaft*, XIII, 1920, p. 230, note 3.

[176] To them, mandatory head covering at prayer would certainly have appeared as an innovation. How different from the conservative Jews of today!

[177] שמברכין בראש מגולה וכו'.

be·seen in the decision of a prominent Rabbinical authority that
"to a burial, the mourner is not required to go bareheaded."[178]

We pass over the utterances of noted Rabbis who, in their
day, wielded great influence. We refer the reader to Loew and
to Lauterbach. Let us merely note some incidents reflecting the
impact of the matter upon Christians. Rabbi Isserlein, a noted
Rabbi at the beginning of the 15th century, was asked in an
inquiry from Breslau what Jews must do if compelled by the
authorities to swear bareheaded.[179] Isserlein frankly replied:
"I find, on this matter, no explicit prohibition," even though,
in an oath, one has to pronounce the Divine Name. Eventually
the authorities came to deal with the Jews according to their
own "Law." The Jew had to swear with head covered if his oath
was to be valid. Zunz's famous dissertation written in 1850 on
the oath *more judaico* quotes a paragraph from a Hanover law
of April 25, 1850 which prescribes that "he who swears must
swear with covered head."[180] An incident, hard to comprehend,
occurred in the district of Bodensee where some Jews, condemned to death, made it their final request that their caps be
nailed (?) to their heads and that they be provided with *Ẓiẓit*.[181]

The further question arose whether a king or a prince, graciously visiting a synagogue, should be persuaded, contrary to
his custom, to keep his head covered. Loew (p. 325) reports such
cases and their disposal. In Austria, during the long reign of
Emperor Francis Joseph, there frequently occurred receptions
of Rabbis and other representatives of the Jewish community
who were allowed to pronounce the required *Berakah* with
covered heads. Such scenes, always duly recounted in the news-
papers, are also extant in pictures.

---

[178] Toratan shel Rish'onim, II, 8, line 29, quoted by Loew in the Supplement to his *Gesammelte Schriften*, V, 53. Thus has a practice of former times
been abolished.

[179] See my work, *Die Wiener Gezerah vom Jahre 1421*, Vienna and Leipzig,
1920, p. 4 and *passim*.

[180] *Gesammelte Schriften*, II, 241–264. Cf. L. Geiger, *Geschichte der Juden
in Berlin*, II, 267.

[181] L. Loewenstein, *Geschichte der Juden am Bodensee und Umgebung*
(1879), I, 146.

The peace of many a community has been disturbed by the issue whether Jewish boys are or are not permitted to attend religious classes bareheaded.[182] The entire question is not worth the time it consumes. Everyone should follow his own wishes. Lauterbach aptly summarizes: "The custom of praying bareheaded or with covered head is not at all a question of law. It is merely a matter of social propriety and decorum."[183]

---

[182] I have observed this personally in Hungary, Germany, Austria, Bohemia, Poland, England, and Palestine.

[183] In behalf of this much needed synagogal decorum, I should like to add that, in the house of worship, tattered and soiled *Yarmulkas* are out of place. Improper if worn in public, why should they be any more proper at a synagogal service which is also a public event? . . . . This article may fittingly conclude with the observation of a Polish Rabbi who lived long ago, renowned for his scholarship and acumen. I refer to R. Solomon Luria (Responsa of Maharshal, Fuerth, No. 72). "Today we see the reverse. They walk haughtily (בקומה זקופה) and with stretched-forth necks (Isa. 3.16) but their heads are not bare (נילוי הראש). They are prompted, of course, not by piety (חסידות) but by . . . ."

THE ORIGIN OF THE DECORATED MEZUZAH

FRANZ LANDSBERGER

Hebrew Union College - Jewish Institute of Religion, Cincinnati

DURING the time I was in charge of the Jewish Museum in Cincinnati, I acquired a number of beautiful Mezuzot. This led me to investigate when these tiny ritual implements developed into their present shape and, furthermore, when and how they came to be objects of art.

It is well known that the use of the Mezuzah rests upon the twice expressed command (Deut. 6.4–9; 11.13–21) that the essentials of the Jewish faith be written upon the doorposts of the house and upon the gates. That command might have been taken figuratively[1] like the admonition to the young man who is told, regarding the parental commandments which he is to obey:

> Bind them continually upon thy heart,
> Tie them about thy neck (Prov. 6.21).

Those commands of Deuteronomy, however, were — we know not when — construed literally, perhaps because of a related Hebrew phenomenon which they suggested. The first Temple had, on each side of its portal, a bronze pillar which obviously carried an inscription. One of these pillars was named Boaz; the other, Jachin (I Kings 7.21). The significance of these names has been debated.[2] Yet there can be no doubt that they were names of exalted religious import; at the entrance of the Temple, all comers were to be impressed with the omnipotence of God. That which stood at the entrance of the Temple was extended to the private dwelling in the form of the Mezuzah.

Still, it is not entirely clear how the Deuteronomic command was to be understood in detail. "Doorposts," in the plural, could apply only to the two posts flanking the abode's entrance. Ever intent upon a strict interpretation of their ordinances, the Jews became inclined

---

[1] It was so construed by the Karaites.

[2] The usual translation of Jachin is: "He (God) will establish," and of Boaz: "In Him (God) is strength." However, in his *Archaeology and the Religion of Israel*, Baltimore, 1953, p. 139, W. F. Albright discerns, in those names, the opening words of dynastic oracles. Albright conjectures that the complete formula of Jachin may have read: "Yahveh will establish the throne forever," and that the Boaz formula may have read: "In Yahveh's strength the king shall rejoice."

Reprinted from *Central Conference of American Rabbis Journal*, April, 1968.

to attach a Mezuzah to every door in the house, no matter how many rooms. Meir of Rothenburg had twenty-four Mezuzot in his domicile.[3] Such a large number could hardly have proved conducive to the ornamentation which we shall presently discuss, since the ornamentation of one Mezuzah necessitated the ornamentation of all the others.

"Gates," in ancient times, must have meant the gates of the city. The city, already at an early period, had a surrounding wall, and gates leading through the wall. With advancing urbanization, the Mezuzah may have become attached to other gates, for example, the gates of courthouses such as those mentioned in Yoma 11a. From the obligation to have a Mezuzah, religious edifices were exempt; the edifice itself made those entering aware of the Divine Presence (Ber. 47a). In the Second Temple, only the Nicanor Gate bore a Mezuzah, for the reason that, behind it, lay "the cell of the counsellors" (Yoma 11a).

How the Mezuzah was originally attached to doorposts and gates, we are not entirely clear. Was the inscription written directly on the building, or was it attached separately as in later usage? The ancient Egyptians are reported to have had, at the entrance of the home, the inscription of some sacred adage. It has been surmised that this custom may have been borrowed by the Israelites.[4] In Palmyra, Syria, there has been found a door lintel of the third Christian century with the Jewish creed of Deut. 6.4–9 in Hebrew letters (Illust. 1).[5] The grandeur of that portal suggests a synagogue, but the synagogue, as we have heard, did not require a Mezuzah. That portal may have belonged to some large secular edifice, possibly one of the above-mentioned courthouses. All this warrants the surmise that the text of the Mezuzah, perhaps in an abbreviated form, stood inscribed directly on the door or on the gate. Owing to the complications of the procedure, as well as to the subsequent expansion of the text, the requisite words would stand on a piece of parchment.

Such a strip of parchment would come rolled up in such a way that

---

[3] Cf. Joshua Trachtenberg, *Jewish Magic and Superstition; A Study in Folk Religion*, New York, 1939, p. 146.

[4] This is the opinion of J. G. Wilkinson, *The Manners and Customs of the Ancien Egyptians*, New Edition in three volumes, Vol. I, Boston, 1883, p. 361. Moreover, there still prevails, in modern Egypt, the custom of having on the doors of houses, the inscriptions of certain sayings, such as, for example, "He (God) is the great Creator, the Everlasting." Cf. E. W. Lane, *An Account of the Manners and Customs of the Modern Egyptians*, Vol. I, 1871, p. 73.

[5] Cf. Samuel Landauer, "Ueber die von Euting in Palmyra gefundene Synagogen-inschrift," in *Sitzungsberichte der koeniglich-preussischen Akademie der Wissenschaften zu Berlin*, Vol. XXXIX, 1884, pp. 933 ff. Further, E. Mittwoch, *Hebraeische Inschriften aus Palmyra, Beitraege zur Assyriologie*, IV, 1902, pp. 203 ff. And, finally, Erwin R. Goodenough, *Jewish Symbols in the Greco-Roman Period*, Vol. II, 1953, p. 84.

470

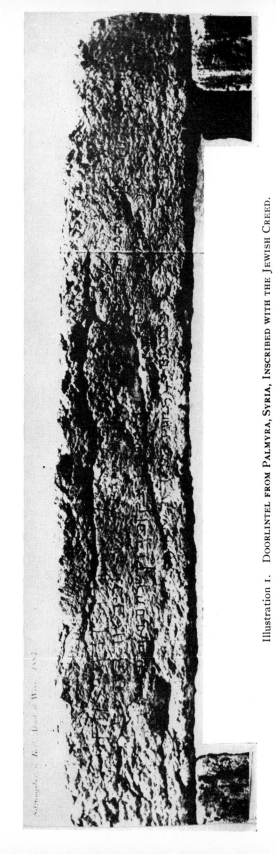

Illustration I. Doorlintel from Palmyra, Syria, Inscribed with the Jewish Creed.

the inscription was on the inside, the empty side lying outward. Thus was the inscription protected. The writings of the non-Jews were on scrolls likewise. The difference was that the Jews have, down to the present, clung to scrolls for such of their sacred literature as were read aloud in the synagogue, while the non-Jews have, since the second century of the present era, substituted the codex, the type of book in common use today.

We now raise the question how the roll was attached. Originally the method seems to have been to place the roll in a cavity scooped in the doorpost. This procedure is mentioned in the little tractate Mezuzah (II, 10). Maimonides (1135–1204) still regards this as permissible.[6] To us, such a thing seems strange — boring a hole in a post as a place for storing. But we have a visible demonstration of this usage. About ten years ago, E. L. Sukenik published an account of a stone (Illust. 2) which was once part of a synagogue in Palestinian Caesarea.[7]

Illustration 2. STONE WITH CIRCULAR CONCAVITY FROM THE SYNAGOGUE IN PALESTINIAN CAESAREA.

[6] Cf. Yad Haḥazakah, Hilkhot Tefillin u-Mezuzah we-Sefer Torah, V, 6. For directing my attention to this and to some other passages, I am indebted to the kindness of Prof. Jakob J. Petuchowski.

[7] Cf. Bulletin II of the Museum of Jewish Antiquities of the Hebrew University, Jerusalem, 1951, plate XVI.

Engraved on this stone are the Greek words: "O God help! The donation of the people in the time of Marutha." (Marutha was probably the head of the synagogue.) The stone shows a perfectly circular concavity in which, according to Sukenik, there was kept "a candelabrum or something similar." My surmise is that there was kept not "a candelabrum or something similar," but rather the Books of Moses on a number of scrolls, or perhaps one scroll containing the entire Pentateuch. At the time when the synagogue was not yet equipped with a fixed cabinet for the Torah, the Torah would, after the service, be carried outside the synagogue and, as in our case, placed in that concavity. Similarly, a small niche in the doorpost of the home may have admitted the Mezuzah.

The tractate Mezuzah (II, 10) also mentions the practice of enclosing the Mezuzah in a "hull" (שפופרת). There is nothing unusual about this custom. The scroll of the Torah was likewise protected either with a mantle or, as in the Orient, by enclosure in a chest of wood or metal. That the incasement of the Mezuzah was, in the Talmudic period, an innovation is indicated by the fact that it was a matter of debate. Rabbi Meir (second century of the present era) favored it; Rabbi Judah (third century) objected. That was, nevertheless, the usage which came to prevail. The result was the tendency to give the container artistic embellishment. Originally, however, the container was completely plain — a botanical reed[8] or a closed receptacle of wood or metal.

The ordinance of the Mezuzah was regarded as a constant admonition to be mindful of God and His laws. But, as early as Talmudic times,[9] there came to be associated with the Mezuzah, the apotropaic intent of safeguarding the inhabitants of the house by barring the entrance against evil spirits.[10] During the Middle Ages, with their mystic tendencies, this conception came to be held with growing intensity.[11] The increasing perils of Jewish life and hostile surroundings likewise generated a deepening concern for protection. What could be more likely than making the Mezuzah an expression of this solicitude? This was achieved by placing on the hitherto blank side of the roll the word שדי, the Almighty, a word often inscribed on amulets. This was

---

[8] Leone da Modena (1571–1648) in his *Riti Ebraici* (II, 2), still mentions a reed as suited for holding a Mezuzah roll.

[9] 'Aboda Zara 11a; Menaḥot 33b; J. Peah I,1 (15a).

[10] For the belief that the threshold must be guarded against the entrance of evil spirits and for the extension of that belief among other peoples, see J. G. Frazer, *Folk-Lore in the Old Testament*, III, London, 1918, pp. 1 ff. "The Keepers of the Threshold."

[11] Cf. Joshua Trachtenberg, *op. cit.*, pp. 146 ff.

further accomplished by adding certain touches to the text written on the inner side. For example, to various lines of the text were added the names of certain angels; in the Bible already there is imputed to the angels the role "to keep thee in all thy ways" (Ps. 91.11). Five-pointed or six-pointed figures would stand sketched in the Mezuzah's margins; the six-pointed star was deemed especially potent.[12]

A protagonist of this usage was Eliezer b. Samuel of Metz, an Ashkenazic Rabbi of the twelfth century, in his Sefer Yere'im, Amud Ha-yir'ah, No. 18 (ed. Wilna, 1881, 18b): "To enhance the security of a dwelling, it is customary to supply, in the Mezuzah, at the ends of lines, certain seals and the names of certain angels. This is neither forbidden nor commanded. Its purpose is merely that of greater security." By contrast, there was, among the Sefardim, outspoken protest against that innovation. According to Maimonides,[13] "Those fools are not satisfied to make nothing of a commandment. They go so far as to take the great command pertaining to the unity of God, the love and the worship of God, and to treat it as an amulet for their personal advantage." Maimonides sanctions nothing more than the word שדי on the side that is otherwise blank. This has remained, while the addenda on the text side have completely disappeared.

As a result of this development, what happened to the container? While, in its oldest form, the container has no opening, the newer form is supplied with a round or rectangular orifice through which peers the word Shaddai (Illust. 3).

New conflicts were generated by that exposure of the Divine Name. The Name was regarded not as a mere piece of writing; it happens often in religion that a word gets supposed to be imbued with a divine potency. A word can be honored; but, were it to look upon something unseemly, that word would be desecrated. Moses of Coucy, a French Rabbi of the thirteenth century, points the way out of this difficulty: "If the Mezuzah is intended for a room occupied by small children, I cover the opening of the Mezuzah with a little wax."[14] The Shulḥan Arukh[15] lays down the rule: "In a place where there is filth, it is well to keep the Mezuzah covered." In the Ture Zahab, a commentary on the Shulḥan Arukh, David b. Samuel Halevy (ca. 1586–1667), discussing

---

[12] Compare V. Aptowitzer, "Les noms de Dieu et des anges dans la Mezouza" in *Revue des Études Juives*, Vol. 60, 1910, pp. 38 ff. Further, Gershom Scholem, "The Curious History of the Six-Pointed Star," in *Commentary Magazine*, VIII, 1949, pp. 243 ff.

[13] Yad Haḥazakah, Hilkhot Tefillin u-Mezuzah we-Sefer Torah, V, 4.

[14] Sefer Mizwot Ha-Gadol, Positive Command, No. 23.

[15] Yore De'ah, Hilkhot Mezuzah, par. 286, No. 5.

that passage, observes that the covering of the Divine Name applies, by extension, to the bedchamber of the wedded. A singular procedure! But we must recall that, in Eastern Europe, the sacred pictures of the Christian house-altar receive a covering when something unseemly is to take place in their presence.[16]

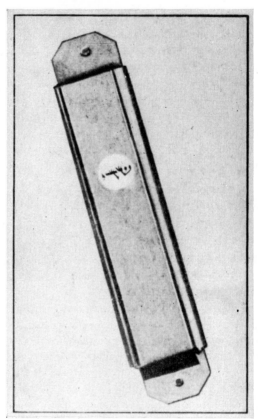

Illustration 3.   MEZUZAH WITH A ROUND ORIFICE
THROUGH WHICH THE WORD *Shaddai* APPEARS.

Instead of covering with wax — hardly an ideal solution — there sometimes came into use the device of placing, over the orifice through which the Divine Name appears, a kind of doorlet the wings of which could, as occasion demanded, be closed or opened. The beautiful Mezuzah originating in 1800 or a little later is an example (Illust. 4).[17]

[16] Ludwig Feuerbach, *Vorlesungen ueber das Wesen der Religion*, Leipzig, 1851, p. 233.

[17] A related Mezuzah is to be found in the Jewish Museum of New York.

Illustration 4.   SILVER MEZUZAH WITH SHUTTERS.   AROUND 1800.
Museum of the Hebrew Union College - Jewish Institute of Religion.

Let it finally be noted that originally the container of the Mezuzah stood on the doorpost in a vertical position as recommended in the Shulḥan Arukh, Yore De'ah 289, 6. Others preferred it horizontal. Isserlein, in his commentary on the passage, urges the sloping position as a compromise between the two.

So much for the development of the Mezuzah into its present form. What about its beautification? Concerning phylacteries, based upon the same Biblical verses as the Mezuzah, we hear about case overlays of gold. This is reported in the Mishnah, a source dating from the third century of our era.[18] About further adornment, nothing is reported for almost a millennium and a half. From the seventeenth century, not any earlier, there have been preserved silver and golden receptacles in which phylacteries were kept when not in use.[19]

Was it likewise with the Mezuzah? As regards the inscribed parchment, artistic attempts are discernible from an early date. The Talmud (Men. 31b) quotes a remark of R. Joḥanan bar Nappaḥa (died 279): "A Mezuzah is permitted if it is written with two or three or even one word [to the line], provided the writing does not form a tent (קובה) or a tail (זנב)." This obviously refers to an ornamental style of writing familiar already to the Romans who would write out poems in such a way that the lines, by their varying lengths, formed the shape of some object such as an altar, a double-axe, a shepherd's flute, or a Cupid's wing. Poems thus shaped were called *carmina figurata*.[20] This practice, like many another Roman practice, evoked Jewish imitation. The Jews would, here and there, write out the text of the Mezuzah in like manner. Why the form of an animal's tail is to be avoided needs no explanation. As for the tent, the word *Kubbah*, while it means a vaulted tent, also means a place of prostitution. On a Mezuzah, this would, as a matter of course, not be allowed. The practice of fashioning various figures out of letters persisted in Jewish writings for a long time. For example, in Biblical codices, such was done with the marginal Masorah when its words were no longer commonly understood.

When this playful kind of writing disappeared from the Mezuzah, we do not know. That selfsame passage, Men. 31b, mentions writing in a column, in the manner of the Torah. It needs no telling that such writing had to be done with utmost care. One's Mezuzah was not to be written by one's self. One purchased it from a professional scribe who

---

[18] Megillah IV, 8.

[19] Such a one, chased with flower patterns, was on display at the Anglo-Jewish Historical Exhibition in London, 1887. Catalogue No. 1851.

[20] Cf. Theodor Birt, *Die Buchrolle in der Kunst*, Leipzig, 1907, p. 286.

saw to it that the inscription was not something printed but that it was handwritten on parchment, and that every Mezuzah had twenty-two lines, and every corresponding line the same number of words, thus making a regularized structure (Illust. 5). The Mishnah (Men. III, 7) asserts that the lack or the malformation of a single letter would

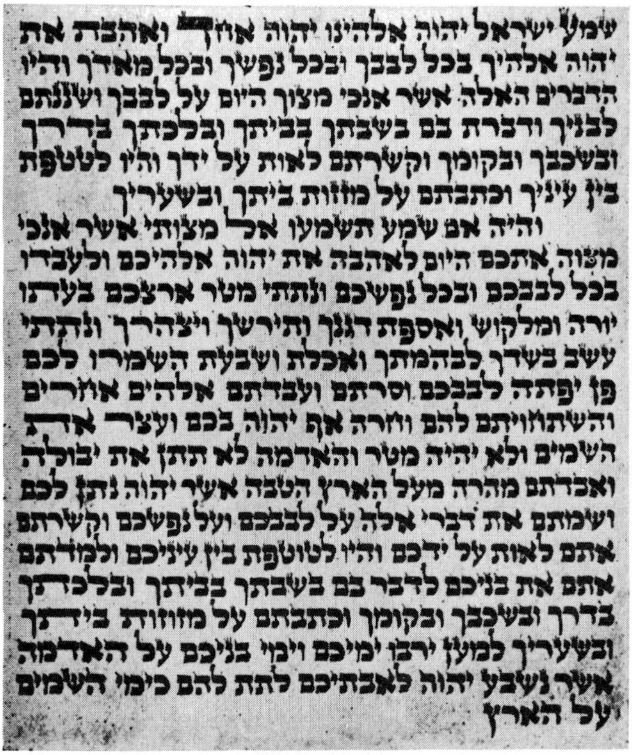
שמע ישראל יהוה אלהינו יהוה אחד ואהבת את
יהוה אלהיך בכל לבבך ובכל נפשך ובכל מאדך והיו
הדברים האלה אשר אנכי מצוך היום על לבבך ושננתם
לבניך ודברת בם בשבתך בביתך ובלכתך בדרך
ובשכבך ובקומך וקשרתם לאות על ידך והיו לטטפת
בין עיניך וכתבתם על מזזות ביתך ובשעריך
והיה אם שמע תשמעו אל מצותי אשר אנכי
מצוה אתכם היום לאהבה את יהוה אלהיכם ולעבדו
בכל לבבכם ובכל נפשכם ונתתי מטר ארצכם בעתו
יורה ומלקוש ואספת דגנך ותירשך ויצהרך ונתתי
עשב בשדך לבהמתך ואכלת ושבעת השמרו לכם
פן יפתה לבבכם וסרתם ועבדתם אלהים אחרים
והשתחויתם להם וחרה אף יהוה בכם ועצר את
השמים ולא יהיה מטר והאדמה לא תתן את יבולה
ואבדתם מהרה מעל הארץ הטבה אשר יהוה נתן לכם
ושמתם את דברי אלה על לבבכם ועל נפשכם וקשרתם
אתם לאות על ידכם והיו לטוטפת בין עיניכם ולמדתם
אתם את בניכם לדבר בם בשבתך בביתך ובלכתך
בדרך ובשכבך ובקומך וכתבתם על מזוזות ביתך
ובשעריך למען ירבו ימיכם וימי בניכם על האדמה
אשר נשבע יהוה לאבתיכם לתת להם כימי השמים
על הארץ

Illustration 5. MEZUZAH TEXT, WRITTEN ON PARCHMENT.

render the Mezuzah unusable. The manifestation of religious zeal through punctilious penmanship is a Jewish characteristic.

We come now to the adornment of the container. Before elucidating this, we must consider an object which has been regarded as a Mezuzah, but erroneously so. In the Hungarian Museum of Fine Arts in Budapest, there is a four-cornered terracotta which has been described by Rabbi Alexander Scheiber (Illust. 6).[21] Scheiber has interpreted its Greek inscriptions to read: "God is one," "Holy," "the Helper." This,

[21] In *The Jewish Quarterly Review*, Vol. 48, 1957, pp. 6 ff.

beyond question, indicates religious utilization. But why must the object be a Mezuzah? Two of the perforations in the terracotta are alleged to have served for fastening the object to a doorpost. But, through those perforations, a cord might as readily have been drawn for fastening around the neck. No, the object is not a Mezuzah. It is an amulet worn during life, and hung around the neck of the dead.

Illustration 6.   AMULET, ERRONEOUSLY CALLED
A MEZUZAH.
Budapest, Museum of Fine Arts.

Indicative of this is the palm branch. Psalm 92 says that "the righteous shall flourish like the palm-tree." That is why Hellenistic Jewish grave inscriptions often show a palm branch in their embellishment.[22]

Something must be said about yet another object, this time really

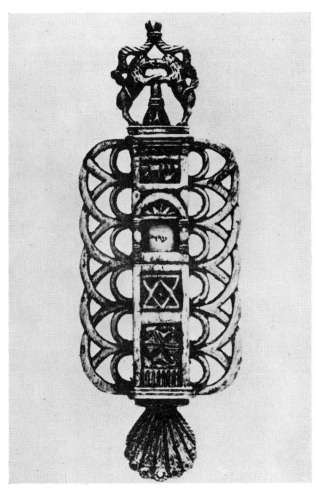

Illustration 7. IVORY MEZUZAH.
London, Jewish Museum.

a Mezuzah which, if correctly dated, might be regarded as the oldest ornamental Mezuzah extant. This one is to be found in the Jewish Museum of London (Illust. 7). It has been explained as a product of the

---

[22] Cf. Erwin R. Goodenough, *Jewish Symbols in the Greco-Roman Period*, Vol. VIII, 1958, pp. 121 ff.

late fifteenth or the early sixteenth century.[23] But that dating is incorrect. Beginning with the palmetto at the lower end, and ascending to the garlands spreading over the two lions, everything shows the neo-classical taste dominating the latter part of the eighteenth century.

In a previous essay[24] I have shown how recent was the ornamentation of some Jewish cult objects, such as the breastplate and the pointer. Barring the golden phylactery cases of antiquity, our oldest ornamented phylactery cases are known to date from the seventeenth century. Could it have been similarly with the ornamented Mezuzot, namely that, in the fifteenth century or the early sixteenth century, they were not yet in existence? In some quarters there was hesitancy

Illustration 8.   DUTCH MEZUZAH.
Illustration from Bernard Pickart, *Cérémonies et Coutumes religieuses de tous les Peuples du Monde,*
1723–29.

on this score as late as the seventeen hundreds. In his *Cérémonies et Coutumes religieuses de tous les Peuples du Monde* which appeared in 1723–29, Bernard Pickart supplies the picture of a Mezuzah in Holland (Illust. 8). The container has the form of a staff with a number of bulgings. There is no other ornamentation. The container lacks even the little window exposing the Divine Name; owing to the scruple,

---

[23] Cecil Roth in his article on the Jewish Museum in London in the periodical, *The Connoisseur*, September-October 1933; also in his book, *The Jews in the Renaissance*, Philadelphia, 1959.

[24] Compare my article, "The Origin of European Torah Decorations," *Hebrew Union College Annual*, XXIV, 1952–53, pp. 133 ff.

Illustration 9. WOODEN MEZUZAH WITH MOSES
HOLDING THE TABLETS OF THE LAW. RUSSIA.

no doubt, to avoid everything that might give the Mezuzah the
character of an amulet. The same happened in England, to which the
Jews, after a long period of expulsion, were in the seventeenth century
readmitted. In his *Hebrew Ritual . . . of the Jewish Community in
England,* London 1819, Levy Alexander furnishes the illustration of a
Mezuzah which is totally plain. France, except for certain areas,
excluded the Jews until the end of the eighteenth century. I can say
nothing about the Mezuzah in seventeenth and eighteenth century
Germany. From here, only the purely functional Mezuzah has come
to my attention. From Italy has emanated the richly ornamented
Mezuzah which rests in the Jewish Museum of London (Illust. 7). But

this, as I have stated, is obviously the product of the late eighteenth century, and was, even at that time, a solitary instance.

The actual home of Mezuzah decoration appears to have been Eastern Europe — countries such as Poland, Russia, or Bohemia, though there is no evidence that even here such existed prior to the seventeenth century. In the woody Carpathians, the woodcarving of the Mezuzah became popular as a specimen of a folk art continuing to this day. Though generally avoided, the human figure is sometimes employed, especially when expressing a religious thought. The illustration (Illust. 9) here given shows Moses with the Tablets of the Law, the Law on which the Mezuzah is founded. From a realistic standpoint one might criticize the figure of Moses as being anatomically too short. But now that we have learned how to cherish primitive art, we can appreciate the power compressed in that diminutive figure.

In other areas of Russia, the Mezuzah is beautified by means of silver. Let it be recalled that, in the artistic use of silver, the Jews of Eastern Europe, unlike those of Western Europe, showed skill. It is especially to be noted that the artistic adornment of the Mezuzah was the work of the Jews themselves. I know of one Mezuzah only which was produced by a non-Jew. It is a Mezuzah of the early nineteenth century with the trademark of the Breslau goldsmith Gottlieb Freitag. This Mezuzah is preserved in the New York Jewish Museum.[25]

The piece here illustrated (Illust. 10), which I acquired in 1957, betrays its origin through its Russian double-eagle. As happens so frequently in Jewish art, there is an announcement of the sovereignty under which the work was performed. All of the other adornment is derived from the world of plants, but the tendrils and the grapes are symbolic; they signify Israel.[26]

Another Mezuzah, recently acquired (Illust. 11) shows a crown — the *Kether Torah* — and, beneath it, the Tablets of the Law. Then follows the tiny window with the shutter which, to our surprise, carries the inscription שדי, thus displaying what, in other instances, is concealed. Beneath this is a long-necked bird of which I do not know the significance. The origin of this Mezuzah is divulged by an identical piece in the Jewish Museum of Prague. We are, therefore, justified in assuming that our Mezuzah originated in Bohemia. It dates, in all likelihood, from the early eighteenth century.[27]

---

[25] Illustration in the catalogue of this collection, *Jewish Ceremonial Art*, Philadelphia 1959, No. 172.

[26] Over the portal of the Herodian Temple in Jerusalem, there hung a golden cluster of grapes.

[27] The Prague piece is pictured in the catalogue of this collection, the catalogue

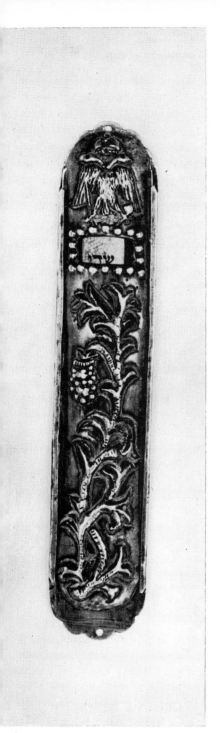

Illustration 10. SILVER MEZUZAH
FROM RUSSIA.
Museum of the Hebrew Union College -
Jewish Institute of Religion.

Illustration 11. SILVER MEZUZAH.
PROBABLY FROM BOHEMIA.
Museum of the Hebrew Union College
Jewish Institute of Religion.

483

Illustration 12. WOODEN
MEZUZAH. GALICIA, CA. 1850.
New York. The Jewish Museum.

Illustration 13. SILVER MEZUZAH,
FASHIONED BY YEHUDA WOLPERT.
Museum of the Hebrew Union College -
Jewish Institute of Religion.

By way of adornment for the Mezuzah, the nineteenth century
added nothing. Deferring to historical sentiment, it assembled traditional motifs — as shown in the illustration (Illust. 12), motifs piled
up in heaps.

In the twentieth century it was otherwise. In accordance with the

which appeared in 1948. The bird is interpreted as a pelican, a symbol of mourning
over Zion. The dating, conjectured as about 1800 is, in my opinion, too late.

general tendencies of the age, there is now sought for the cult-object something new. As a sample, we present here a Mezuzah of Ludwig (now Yehudah) Wolpert (Illust. 13). While Wolpert resided in Germany he adhered to the simple functionary style customary at the time. When, in 1933, he became a refugee to Israel, he added, to his art, fresh decorative elements, particularly by means of the Hebrew script. The *Shaddai* has become shortened into an initial, but the ש has the festive shape of a candlestick, beneath which are six parallel lines with the motto: "Blessed shalt thou be when thou comest in, and blessed shalt thou be when thou goest out" (Deut. 28.6).

The Mezuzah began its development as a mere inscription. In our last item, an inscription now stands even on the outside of the container, and it is an inscription in the phantasy-rich Hebrew lettering which characterizes the Israeli art of today.

CEREMONIAL CREATIVITY AMONG
THE ASHKENAZIM

By Solomon B. Freehof, Pittsburgh

THE UNIQUE IMPORTANCE OF THE NOTES of Moses Isserles to
the *Shulchan Aruch* has long been discussed by students of
the law. His glosses to the *Shulchan Aruch* started the hundred
year process which made this Sephardic code usable by all
Jews. Thus he may be considered responsible for having
achieved a large degree of unity in legal matters among all
Jews for the first time since the Talmud and the Gaonim.
Theoretically, the same achievement could have been accomplished by a Sephardic scholar under the reverse circumstances.
If, for example, Mordecai Jaffe's *Levush* had spread early to
Sephardic lands, and could have commanded serious consideration as a possible code guiding all Jews everywhere, then we
might imagine that some Sephardic scholar, a sort of an
"opposite number" to Isserles, would have written glosses
to the *Levush*, and thus started a process of its acceptance
as a world-wide Jewish code. But it did not happen that
way. It was Isserles who amplified a Sephardic work and
helped achieve an all-Jewish code.

Besides giving variant opinions from Ashkenazic and
Sephardic scholars to the decisions of Caro, Isserles also
records hundreds of variants of another type which are not
the opinions of scholars, but which he describes as, "This is
our custom," [1] or, "The custom of these lands is . . ." These
hundreds of customs constitute a treasury of observances
which are not the thought-out product of the scholars, but
the anonymous creations of average Jewish communities.
Of course,there were earlier collections of customs in existence
for a century or two before the time of Isserles, but these

[1] וכן נהגו וכן נוהגים בעירנו

Reprinted from *The Seventy-Fifth Anniversary Volume of the Jewish
Quarterly Review*, edited by Abraham Neuman and Solomon Zeitlin,
Dropsie University, Philadelphia, Pa., 1967.

were collections of local customs or district customs. By the time of Isserles, a long process of sifting and diffusion had taken place. Some of these local customs had dropped out and were forgotten; but others spread and were widely adopted. Isserles records, therefore, those customs which had enough meaningfulness and the appeal to spread from the original locality. It is these original customs which should throw a light on a unique characteristic of Jewry. For it must seem surprising in a religion governed by strict, logical interpretation of the Divine Law, that there should be room for so much creativity in popular custom.

Scholars might well turn their attention to the large number of customs which Isserles records, and study them from a point of view entirely different from that of the Halachist. The Halachist would be concerned with whether these customs can be harmonized with existing law; the historian would be concerned with how did such customs arise and why did they spread. The Halachist would be concerned with validity; the historian would be concerned with originality.

The purpose of this paper, therefore, is to provide a few notes on this ceremonial creativity, its sources and its achievement, in the hope that other students will study more systematically the vast treasury of ceremonies recorded in Isserles, and will consider them from the point of view, not of their legality, but as an outstanding example of folk-creativity.

Let us consider those which are the most beloved and, therefore, the most generally observed Jewish ceremonials today: There is the Kaddish by the orphan for the first eleven months, the Yahrzeit, the breaking of the glass at weddings, the Bar Mitzvah ceremony. They are universally Jewish and have an unflagging appeal, even today.

Mourner's Kaddish and Yahrzeit

There is certainly no Jewish ceremonial with a universal appeal equal to that of the mourner's Kaddish. One would, therefore, expect that the legal codes would be rich in their

descriptions and precise as to the definitions involved in it.
They are so, indeed, but in a curious way: In the *Shulchan
Aruch*, in *Yore Deah* 376, § 4, Joseph Caro, speaking of the
burial rituals, merely mentions the graveside Kaddish. But
then follows the note by the Ashkenazi, Moses Isserles, which
is one of his longest notes in the Shulchan Aruch. He discusses
the graveside Kaddish (in fuller detail than Caro) and then
goes into an elaborate description of the mourner's Kaddish
throughout the year of mourning, and also on the Yahrzeit
at anniversaries of the death. He than also speaks of the
various "rights" to say Kaddish, when there is a dispute in
the synagogue between local people and visitors, etc. Since
Joseph Caro has merely a brief statement and Isserles a long
and detailed discussion of scores of observances, it is obvious
on the face of it that the mourner's Kaddish must be of
Ashkenazic origin.

Of course, Joseph Caro, in his larger commentary, Bes
Josef to the *Tur*, *Yore*§ *Deah* 403,[2] where he gives the opinions
of all traditions, has a discussion of virtually the same material. He mentions the various rules, much the same material
that is discussed by Isserles, but it is noticeable that every
authority whom he quotes is an Ashkenazi. He cites the
Tashbetz (Samuel b. Zadok) the pupil of Meir of Rothenburg;
he quotes Isserlein, Trumas ha-Deshen; and then, finally,
he quotes the North Italian Rabbi Joseph Colon (§ 31) who is
under Ashkenazic influence, and then ends up with a quotation
from a Franco-German, Jochanan ben Mattathias of Troyes
(Rabbi in France, 14th-15th Century).

The Talmud has references which formed the basis of the
Kaddish, when it speaks a number of times of the benefit of
making the response, "Ye-hey Shemay Rabba," etc., after a
scholarly discourse (b. Sota 49a, Shabb. 119 b.) but it is not
even hinted at in the Talmud that this is for the benefit of

---

the dead. The first notion that the Kaddish can be recited for the benefit of the dead is in the oft-quoted Midrash, a form of *Taana D'be Eliahu*, with the well known story of Akiba meeting the ghost of a tortured man, whom Akiba then saves from the tortures of Gehinom by teaching the child to participate in the service. From the discussion by Ginzberg in *Ginze Shechter*, I, p. 29 (where he gives a form of the Midrash found in the Geniza) what the child recited in the service was the *Borochu*, and the people responded. The original response to *Borochu* by the people was not as today, *Boruch Adonoi*, etc., but *Ye-hey Shemay Rabba*. Because that original participation of the child acting as cantor and reciting the *Borochu* and evoking the response of the people raised doubts as to a minor acting as cantor, gradually the child's participation was transferred to the saying of the Kaddish by the orphan, evoking that response at the close of the service. Dr. Ginzberg believes that many of the older texts were changed because of the confusion of the response to the *Borochu*. Machzor Vitry, by the pupil of Rashi (11th-12th Century) on page 112-113, when it gives the story of the Midrash, speaks of the orphan saying *Borochu*. Then he adds: Therefore it is the custom on Saturday night to have a man who has no parents to conduct the service and say Borochu or Kaddish.[3] Here this early source still speaks of "Borochu *or* Kaddish," and not yet of the duty of every orphan to recite the Kaddish. The clearest reference to the Kaddish by orphans is by Isaac of Vienna (13th Century) in his *Or Zorua*, Vol. II, 22b, in which he quotes his teacher, Elazar of Worms, who also cites the Midrash, and then says that the boy, for the benefit of his father's soul, should say Yiskadal. So by the time of Elazar of Worms (d. 1238) the custom became fairly established for every orphan boy (no matter how young) to say Kaddish. The custom spread to the Sephardic lands and by the time of Joseph Caro, it was a well established all-Jewish custom;

---

[3] ועל כן נחגו לעבור לפני התובה במוצאי שבת אדם שאין לו אב או אם לומר ברכו או קדיש.

but as we have seen, when Caro discusses the custom in his Bes Josef, he has only Ashkenazic authorities to quote.

This is true, also, of the extension of saying the orphan's Kaddish from the first year to the anniversary every year, namely, the Yahrzeit. The Talmud, of course, refers to fasting on the anniversary of a parent's death (b. Nedarim 12a) but makes no reference to special prayers to be recited on that occasion. Rashi (to Yebamos 122a top) says that it was the custom in ancient times, at the anniversary of a teacher's death, for students to gather at his grave and study. Evidently they recited Kaddish after their study.

The pupil of Meir of Rothenburg, Samuel b. Zadok (Tashbetz) (13th-14th Century, § 427) says that his teacher fasted every year on the anniversary of his parents' death. Since this passage proceeds to talk about saying Kaddish for a parent, we may assume that Meir of Rothenburg said Kaddish on these anniversaries. But even so, it is recorded only as an act of special piety by a great teacher. But by the time of Jacob Moellin (d. 1427) the reciting of Kaddish on the anniversary of a parent's death was a regular custom for every orphan, and, indeed, was so well established that a man could claim the right to recite it. (Cf. also his Responsa § 36.) Nevertheless, the "Mourner's Kaddish" was not so firmly rooted that *only* a mourner could recite it. If there was no mourner present, the reader could recite it, unless his parents objected to his doing so (his Responsa § 64). Moses Minz of Bamberg (15th Century) in his Responsa § 80 discusses the various "rights" to recite the Kaddish and uses the word "Yahrzeit" (p. 91, col c). Perhaps this is the earliest record of the use of the term. So Isaac Tyrnau, Moellin's schoolmate (*Dine Kaddish Yathom*) mentions the anniversary Kaddish as a matter of course, and also uses the word "Yahrzeit."

The whole concept of the living helping the dead would have been strange 'to the philosophic minded Sephardim, or certainly to their intellectual leaders. Abraham b. Chiya (Barcelona, 12th Century) may have heard of this Ashkenazic custom. At all events, in his *Hegion ha-Nefesh*, p. 32, he said, "So any one who believes that after his death he can be benifited by the actions of his sons and their prayers for him, is harboring false ideas (i.e., self-delusion); for we do not find in the Torah any citation from which we can derive that any action of the living in this world can benefit the dead."

As late as the seventeenth century, the Sephardic Jews resisted this custom. Since the mourner's Kaddish was not to be recited longer than eleven months, "so as not to proclaim the deceased a wicked man," etc., the Sephardim felt that to *need* to say Kaddish year after year would imply that the deceased father was wicked indeed. Menassah ben Israel of Amsterdam, in the seventeenth century, mentions that the Sephardim of Amsterdam have taken over the custom of annual Yahrzeit and that the sages of Jerusalem (i.e., the Sephardic rabbis) mocked the idea, using the argument above; but he defends the custom (*Nishmas Chayim* II, 27). Since then it has become virtually world-wide, even though some oriental authorities have a hard time explaining the German word "Yahrzeit."

Breaking the Wedding Glass

With regard to the mourner's Kaddish, we have seen that Joseph Caro says nothing about it in the *Shulchan Aruch*, but there is full detailed description in the note of Isserles. This by itself would indicate, as was mentioned above, that the origin of the ceremony is entirely Ashkenazic. The situation is precisely the same with regard to breaking the glass at the wedding. Joseph Caro knew about the custom because he mentions it in his "Bes Yosef" to the *Tur* (*Orah Hayyim* 560) in the laws of Tish b'Av. But in the *Shulchan Aruch*, in the laws of Tish b'Av, he does not mention the custom of breaking the glass at all, nor does he in the laws of the wedding ceremony in Even Hoezer, 65. But in both places, Isserles gives a clear description of the ceremony. That, again, is in itself a strong indication that the ceremony was well known, and indeed arose, among the Ashkenazi.

Of course, as is the case of many medieval ceremonies, there is a foundation or a hint in the Talmud. The well known passage in Berachoth 30b-31a tells that Mar, son of Rabbina, and also Reb Ashi, at the wedding of their children, when the guests were hilarious, broke an expensive glass article. There is no indication that these were more than two isolated incidents. It is not mentioned as a custom in the whole of the Talmud, in the whole Gaonic literature, nor among the earlier Poskim before the twelfth century. But the Tosfos ad loc says, "This is the source of our custom to break a glass at weddings."

J. Z. Lauterbach, in his pioneer article on the breaking of the glass, in *Hebrew Union College Annual*, Volume II, believes that the two talmudic incidents were really motivated by the fear of demons, that the ceremony may well have been widely observed, but that the rabbis consciously ignored it, since it was superstitious. At all events, whatever the explanation of the silence may be, the fact remains there is no mention of such a ceremony as an observed ceremony up to the twelfth century; and all the early mentions of it for centuries thereafter are Ashkenazic. Eliezer ben Nathan (12th century) in his "Even Hoezer," paragraph 177, says that the former teachers instituted the custom to break the glass. Perhaps this a what led Dr. Lauterbach to the conviction that it was a continuous custom from ancient times. The Machzor Vitry (p. 589, 593) tells of the custom, that the cup used for the wine of the wedding blessing is thrown against the wall and broken. Jacob Moellin (Maharil) in his *Minhagim* on the laws of marriage, says that the bridegroom throws it at the north wall.

A new interpretation of the custom is given by the *Kol Bo* in the laws of the Ninth of Av, namely, that because of our sorrow for the destruction of Jerusalem, the glass is broken at weddings.[4] The *Tur* does not speak of the breaking of the

4. וכתב הכלבו ... ועל זה פשט חמנהג לשבר הכוס אחר שבע ברכות

glass, although he does speak (both in the laws of Tish B'Av and in the marriage laws) of a correlative ceremony, namely, putting ashes as a symbol of mourning on the head of the groom. While Caro quotes the Kol Bo in his commentary to the Tur on the laws of the Ninth of Av, he does not include it, as we have mentioned, in the Shulchan Aruch.

However, by the time of Chayim Benvenisti (died 1673) the custom was well established among the Sephardim. In fact, Benvenisti (*Keneseth Ha-Gadolah* to *Even Hoezer* 65) has a long discussion as to which glass should be broken, the glass of the first blessing or of the second, or both, and he tells of the varying customs of glass breaking in the different cities of Turkey, and quotes the fact that his teachers observed the ceremony.

Thus the Ashkenazic custom became a regular Sephardic custom, although it might be noted that the Sephardim varied it somewhat from the Ashkenazim. They usually have it (according to Ben Zion Uziel, the late Chief Sephardic Rabbi of Israel) between the two sets of blessings and not at the end of the whole ceremony. He expresses his regret that the Sephardim in Palestine have now adopted the Ashkenazic habit of breaking the glass at the end of the ceremony, for, since it is the end of the ceremony, the shouts of *Mazel Tov*, etc., destroy the dignity of the service. He says, rather ruefully, that he wishes he could abolish this ceremony (*Mishp'te Uziel*, part II, *Even Hoezer* p. 431).

Bar Mitzvah

Nowadays the most enthusiastically observed Jewish ritual is the Bar Mitzvah. In fact, one might well say it is the one Jewish ritual whose observance has grown greater and more elaborate than ever before. Yet it is certain that the observance was unknown to the Talmud and to the early Poskim. Since Leopold Loew first called attention to this fact (Lebensalter, 210 ff.) scholars have been searching the literature for earlier traces of Bar Mitzvah. There is, of course, the statement

in Abot (V, 21) that thirteen is the age for religious responsibility; and there is also the Midrash (Genesis R 63: 10) which
limits the father's responsibility for the son's education to
the age of thirteen, and mentions the words "Blessed be He,
Who has rid me of this responsibility." There is also the
statement in Soferim 18: 7 (ed. Higger) that it was the custom
in Jerusalem to bring the lad at his maturity to the priest to
be blessed. The passage refers to the age of twelve.

But none of these references are descriptive of the actual
ceremony as we have it, namely, that at the age of thirteen
and a day, the lad is called up to the Torah; often he is blessed
by the rabbi; there is a party given at home; the lad delivers
a discourse, either at the synagogue or at the home celebration. The ceremony seems so natural that one wonders why
it did not develop in Talmudic (or even Mishnaic) times,
when so much effort *was* expended on child education and
some sort of graduation or maturity ceremony would have
been expected.

But there were two difficulties in the law which had to be
disposed of before the ceremony as it is at present could have
evolved. First, there was the question of when a boy should
be considered mature. Was it when he showed signs of puberty
or when he had reached the age of thirteen (whether physically
maturing or not)? The other difficulty was the fact that the
Talmud says that even younger boys may be called up to the
Torah on the Sabbath (m. Megilla IV, 6, and b. Megilla 23a).
If a boy of eight or nine is called up to the Torah, what special
significance would there be in calling up a boy at his Bar
Mitzvah? But gradually it was decided (arbitrarily) that
physically mature or not, the age of thirteen would be considered the age of maturity (Asher ben Jehiel, Responsa 16: 1).

Yet this question was not settled for all of Israel. Many
Oriental Jewries let a boy put on Tefillin at twelve, and even
Solomon Luria (16th century) expresses some doubts because
many of the thirteen year olds have not yet shown signs of
puberty (Yom Shel Sheloma, B.K., Ch. VII, 37). As for the

Torah reading by very young boys, this was gradually discouraged and restricted (Cf. Felder: *Yesode Yeshurun* IV, 403). But among the Yemenites, young boys are still regularly called up to the Torah (quoted from E. Brauer, Ethnologie d. Jemeniten, by Rifkind in *L'os u-l'Zikaron*). But as these difficulties were overcome (or by-passed) among the Ashkenazic communities, the present ceremony of Bar Mitzvah developed among them.

Rifkind (*L'os u-l-Zikaron*) is anxious to prove an early date for Bar Mitzvah, and reports one incident which would show that Gaon Jehuda observed some such ceremony. The citation is from *Orchoth Chayim I* (ed. Florence, Hil. Berachot § 58, p. 89a) by Aaron Ha-Cohen of Lunel. Aaron Ha-Cohen who lived in the early fourteenth century was well acquainted with the ceremony. He says that when a man's son reaches thirteen years, he must say the blessing, "Who has divested me of the responsibility," etc. Then he continues: "The Gaon Jehuda rose to his feet in the synagogue and recited the blessing the first time his son was called to the Torah." But this report does not say that the boy was thirteen. They called them earlier than that to the Torah in the East. But at all events, this was a single incident and does not prove the existence of an established institution.

Jacob b. Asher, in the Tur (which was written in Spain) does not mention Bar Mitzvah at all. But Moses Isserles, in his commentary to the Tur (Darche Moshe) finds a place where he can mention it. In *Tur*, Orah Hayyim 225, where various miscellaneous blessings are referred to, Isserles adds: "Maharil has written in the name of the Mordecai that when a man's son is Bar Mitzvah, he must pronounce the blessing, 'Praised be Thou, Who hast rid me of the responsibility,' " etc.

So also in the *Shulchan Aruch*, Joseph Caro makes no mention of such a ceremony, but Isserles again makes mention of this parental blessing at the Bar Mitzvah. In *Shulchan Aruch*, Orah Hayyim 53, Caro discusses what is the minimum age for a cantor, and on § 55, he speaks of the minimum age for being counted in the Minyan. In neither place does he mention Bar Mitzvah. But Isserles to Orah Hayyim 55, 10, speaks of when "he is made Bar Mitzvah." [5]

Maharil (14-15th century) (or his disciple) mentions the Bar Mitzvah ceremony twice. In the section of his Minhagim, dealing with the Torah reading for Passover, we are told that Maharil would bless the congregation and the cantor. Then, we are told, "Thus, too, he would also bless every boy who was Bar Mitzvah." The other reference is the one to which Moses Isserles referred. It is the section dealing with the Sabbath Torah reading. When Maharil's son was Bar Mitzvah and read the Torah, Maharil recited the blessing, "Praised be Thou Who has rid me," etc. "Thus it is in the Larger Mordecai."

If the author of Mordecai (13th century) considered the ceremony sufficiently valid to permit the recitation of the blessing (using God's Name "B'shem u'Malchus") then clearly it was fairly well established by then. Nevertheless, two elements of the ceremony were still considered debatable as late as the sixteenth century. Isserles (Orah Hayyim 225, 2.) doubted the validity of the father's benediction, and his contemporary (and kinsman) Solomon Luria doubts whether the home party can be considered a *Seudah Shell Mitzvah*. In referring to the home party he speaks of it as the "Bar Mitzvah party which the Ashkenazim have." He suggests that the boy gives a Halachic discourse that would make it truly a Seudah Shell Mitzvah (*Yam Shel Shelomo* l.c.).[6]

It is clear that the earliest definite references to the cere-

[5] הנה ובמקומות שלא נהג כן אין לקטן לעבור לפני התיבה אפילו בתפלת ערבית אפילו הגיע לכלל י"ג שנים ביום השבת אין להתפלל ערבית של שבת דהרי עדיין אין לו י"ג
הגה יש אומרים מי שנעשה בנו בר מצוה יברך בא"י אלהנו מלך העולם שפטרני מענשו של זה.
[6] וסעודת בר מצוה שעושים האשכנזים לכאורה אין לך סעודת מצוה גדולה מזו ושמה מוכיה עליה ועושים שמחה ונותנים למקום שבח והודיה שזכה הנער להיות בר מצוה...והאב זכה שנדלו עד עתה להכניסו בברית התורה בכללה (ים של שלמה ב"ק פ"ז)

mony date from the thirteenth, fourteenth centuries (Maharil)
or possibly a century earlier from Mordecai b. Hillel). All the
discussions are Ashkenazic. There are no early Sephardic
references. Rifkind (in L'os u-l'Zikaron) quotes Isaiah Sonne
who says that the observance of the Bar Mitzvah ceremony
in Italy spread southward from Northern Italy, from the
communities of Ashkenazic origin.

These four greatly beloved ceremonies are all of German or
Franco-German origin. There are, of course, hints for some of
them in the Talmud, a phrase or some incident upon which
the ceremony was based, but the ceremony itself, as an entity,
and as a widespread regular observance was an original
creation.

What is equally remarkable about these particular observances is that they spread from the land of their origin
and were gradually accepted by all the major Jewries. The
Orphan's Kaddish, the Yahrzeit, the breaking of the glass
at weddings, and Bar Mitzvah at thirteen and with Torah
reading, became all-Jewish ceremonies. The reverse direction
of ceremonial diffusion did not occur at all. One cannot think
of any ceremony relating to family religious life such as
marriage or mourning which, originating in the Sephardic
lands, spread to the Ashkenazic lands and, like Yahrzeit,
became all-Jewish. Clearly these Ashkenazic ceremonies
came to be considered so appropriate that they overcame the
normal Sephardic pride and were accepted.

We see, therefore, that the Ashkenazim had developed a
unique ability in ceremonial creativity. It was a power of
visualizing. It can be called an artistic ability, enabling them
to mold religious laws and doctrines into outward and enduring
physical form. The Sephardim had other special abilities
equally vital to the development of world-Judaism. Their
talent was in the direction of system and order in observances,
in law and in doctrine. As to observances (such as Hanukka
lights, Succah, Havdala, etc.) their tendency was to remove
them from the home and reorganize them as public observan-

ces conducted in orderly unision in the synagogue. (Cf. "Home Rituals and the Spanish Synagogue" by Solomon B. Freehof, in the *Abraham Neuman Festschrift*, 1962, pp. 215 ff.) All the effective systemization of Jewish law came from the Sephardim. Without them, there would be no Yad Hachazaka and no Shulchan Aruch, nor any philosophic clarification of Jewish thought in the Middle Ages. If one might make a further use of artistic terms, the Sephardim were architectural and the Ashkenazim picturesque; the Sephardim turned to the classical and the Ashkenazim to folk-genre.

This Ashkenazic ceremonial imaginativeness was not the product of a few talented men but a genuine folk-product. The ceremonies were not invented and ordained by authorities. They simply emerged and were later officially accepted. Only in the case of one of them does any early reference say: "Therefore the older teachers *ordained*," but even that statement could simply mean that the teachers confirmed what was already observed by the people (Eliezer b. Nathan, cited above, as to the breaking of the glass).

It might be permissible to speculate as to why the Ashkenazim developed in this special direction. Life in the Ashkenazic lands was less centrally organized than in Spain. The cities they lived in were virtually independent city-states. Each Jewish community in such an environment was more isolated from each other than in Spain. It, therefore, could more easily develop its own customs and communal habits. Besides this localism, there were more civil disorders, expulsions, etc., than in Spain, or certainly shorter periods of peace and order. In periods of order and security, the rabbinical authorities could scrutinize any new popular observance, and if it seemed to them to be contrary to law or to the spirit of tradition, they would discourage it, as they did with many customs. But in long periods of loosened authority, popular customs had time to root themselves, and in a generation or two, if they were not too flagrantly absurd or superstitious, the rabbinate would accept them and say: "They must have some good basis"

(Yesh lo-hem al mah l'hishoyen), and soon they would be embodied in books of Minhagim and eventually into the codes. It is noteworthy that many of these popular ceremonies emerged from anonymity and entered into rabbinic literature at the time of first recovery from the disorders of the Crusades in the twelfth century and after the recovery, from the disturbance during the Black Death in the fifteenth.

Besides the possibility that the frequent periods of communal disorder which gave popular customs a chance to take root, the general mood of the Ashkenazic scholars themselves was sympathetic to new ceremonial imaginativeness. They themselves ornamented their own lives with additional personal observances in order to voice their love for the Mitzvos. (Cf. Zimmels "Ashkenazim and Sephardim," especially "Hibbub Mizvah," p. 259 ff.) Often these additional observances of the honored teachers, their special way of life, was lovingly recorded by some disciple. So the observances of Jacob Moellin of Mainz were written down by Zalman of St. Goar (Minhage Maharil); Meir of Rothenberg's special observances by Samuel ben Zadok (Tashbetz); and Israel Isserlein's by Joseph b. Moses (Leket Yosher). There are no such biographical ceremonial-diaries in Sephardic Jewish literature. Either the Sephardic rabbis did not feel the need of developing an extra ceremonial piety (until later under Kabbalistic influences in Safed, led by Isaac Ashkenazi) or if they did, no disciple (before the Safed period) felt that they were of general importance and needed to be recorded.

The Ashkenazim did feel that these ceremonial creations were vital. They not only recorded those which were observed by their teachers, but even the "anonymous" ones were carefully preserved as beloved local Minhagim. Only later in the sixteenth century in Safed, when the disciples of Isaac Ashkenazi began to record his personal ceremonial acts of mystic piety, did an influence from Sephardic lands begin to affect Ashkenazic Jewry. But this was only in the common public worship, not in events of family life.

The large number of Minhagim preserved in Isserles' glosses
to the Shulchan Aruch and in his "Darche Moshe" to the
Tur, were only a small part of a vast mass of Ashkenazic
Minhagim. Those which he records were the ones which have
survived of the innumerable local Minhagim, and particularly
those which had spread beyond the community of their
origin. He cites those Minhagim which became all-Ashkenazic
and some of them, as we have seen, have become all-Jewish.
This material deserves to be studied as a whole, since it
provides an opportunity to look deeply into a spiritual folk
art, the unique ceremonial imaginativeness of North-European
Jewry, most of which has now, alas, moved out of life into
history.

HOME RITUALS AND THE SPANISH SYNAGOGUE

By Solomon B. Freehof

Rodef Shalom Temple, Pittsburgh

In honor of the seventieth birthday of Abraham A. Neuman, whose monumental history of the Jews of Spain will long be greatly valued, the author dedicates the following article on some aspects of the religio-cultural life of the Jews of Spain.

The well-known statement of Moses of Coucy concerning the observance of the mizwoth among Spanish Jews, has considerable religio-cultural implications. He says that in the year 4996 (1235) he was in Spain to "reprove the people" and that God gave him strength, so that as a result of his preaching "thousands and tens of thousands took upon themselves to observe the commandments of *tefillin, mezuzoth* and *zizith.*" (*Semag,* Positive Commandments, end of § 3)

If, then, because of his preachments tens of thousands resolved henceforth to observe the commandments mentioned, then there were vast numbers of Jews in Spain who hitherto had not observed these commandments; and "tens of thousands" of those who did not hear him preach remained, for a time at least, non-observant.

Moses of Coucy is not the only witness to a widespread neglect of ritual observance in Spain. Jonah Gerondi, the Spanish moralist, was a contemporary of Moses of Coucy. He died in Toledo in 1263. In his books, *Shaare teshuba* and *Sefer ha-yirah,* he rebukes the people for the neglect of the commandments. While due to his moralistic purposes he may be somewhat overstressing the neglect, nevertheless he is frequently quite specific as to the commandments which are neglected. In *Shaare teshuba,* Chapter 3, §8 (all references are to the Mesivta edition, New York City, 1943) he says,

Reprinted from *Studies and Essays in Honor of Abraham A. Neuman,*
edited by Meir Ben-Horin, Bernard D. Weinryb and
Solomon Zeitlin, Leiden, 1962.

"You will see men mocking the commandment of washing the hands, and sit down to eat without blessing before the meal or after the meal." Chapter 3, §27: "There are many kinds of Sabbath works which some of the people are not careful about because they know nothing about them." Chapter 3, §76: "Some are not careful with making meat kosher by salting." In his *Sefer ha-yirah*, p. 8, he warns the people not to eat without a blessing and he adds: "If one is not able to recite the blessing, let him go to someone who knows in order to learn."

Joseph b. Todros Halevi, in his letters published in Kobak's *Jeshurun* (vol. viii, p. 37) attacks those who "treat holy things as profane and consider themselves free of prayer and *tefillin*." Isaac bar Sheshes (Responsa § 447) speaks of many who mock the rabbinical laws of *terefah*.

This neglect of commandments was not restricted to Spain. Moses of Coucy (*loc. cit.*) says, "And so it was in other lands." Meir of Rothenburg, in his Responsa (ed. Cermona §108) discusses with his correspondent the question of rebuking people who do not observe the commandment of *mezuzah* because they believe that only the man who actually owns a house is commanded to affix the *mezuzah*, but not one who merely rents a house or rooms. In the course of his responsum he cites a statement of Rabbenu Tam, "For the last ten years there has not been a *mezuzah* in the entire kingdom." Rabbenu Tam adds that this complete neglect should not be considered as constituting a valid *minhag*, but that people should be told that they *should* affix a *mezuzah*.

Also in his responsa (ed. Prague, Budapest, § 649) Meir speaks of those who do not put on *tefillin*, and he again quotes Rabbenu Tam who refers to those who mock the commandment of *tefillin* and ask scornfully:- "What do these straps avail?" In his responsa (ed. Lemberg, §223), Meir of Rothenburg quotes Judah b. Barzilai who refers to the neglect of *tefillin* in these words: "Even in the time of prayer most people (*ruba de-alma*) sin against this commandment."

Posnanski in his Preface (p. lxix) to the commentary of Eliezer of Beaugency on Ezekiel and the Minor Prophets, quotes Joseph Bechor Shor who denounces those Jews who say that to wear *tefillin* and to affix *mezuzoth* or to cover the blood after *shehitah*, are not actually commandments, but are only symbolic statements, as in the Song of Songs:- "Place me as a seal upon thy heart."

The fact that the neglect of these commandments was rife in France and Germany, as well as in Spain, indicates that this was not primarily due to philosophizing and allegorizing of the commandments. The neglect was present in lands where philosophizing hardly penetrated and is noticed as early as the time of the Tosafists. If the observance of the commandments had been well rooted in the lives of the people, it is hardly likely that the allegorizing of a few sophisticates would have effected so vast a neglect as the sources indicate.

As a matter of fact, the neglect of some of these commandments goes back at least to the time of the Geonim. The Gaon Joseph (*Ozar ha-Geonim* to Berakot, p. 41 §90) is asked whether a man who is not a great man (*gavra Rabba*) should be permitted to put on tefillin "since if he does put on *tefillin* it will appear to be false pride (*yohara*) inasmuch as the entire community does not put on *tefillin*." The Gaon answers, of course, that everybody should put on *tefillin*.

So too Sherira Gaon (*Ozar ha-Geonim*, Rosh Hashana, p. 28) is asked a similar question:- "Why do the majority of people scorn (*mezalzli*) the commandment?" He explains also that in Palestine, due to the many persecutions, the people have forgotten all about this commandment.

Michael Guttmann dealt with the questions of the neglect of the commandments in his pamphlet *Behinnat kiyyum ha-mizwoth* (Breslau, 1931), but he confines himself to the Greek (Alexandrian) period. Clearly there is need for a full study of this question going back to the *am ha-arez* of tannaitic times. Perhaps we have misjudged the significance of this widespread non-observance. Except later in philosophizing-allegorizing circles, it was not at all a *relapse* into neglect of commandments which once had been fully observed; rather, the fact was that full observance came later and was the result of slow and persistent effort. The double connotation of the word am *ha-arez* is significant. The word which at first meant careless non-observance, "yokel," came to mean an ignoramus. This surely hints that the growth in learning and of observance went hand in hand; that just as the knowledge of rabbinic law slowly spread among wider and wider circles, so did the observance of the commandments. The latter was as great an achievement as the former. There has been considerable investigation and writing of the ever-widening circle of the learned, but almost none in the gradual spread of the commandments.

This essay has for its purpose to gather some evidence of the process of the spread of observance in Spain. There were certain observances in Spain which were not found in the rest of Europe. Some of these were learned from the Babylonian Gaonim and some seem to have originated in Spain. These special observances seem to the writer to have been motivated by the purpose of training the Jews of Spain to observe commandments hitherto not widely observed. Other methods of training were developed in other lands.

Morning Blessings

The Talmud in b. Berakoth 60b gives a series of short blessings which are to be recited during the process of getting up in the morning. When a man opens his eyes, he should say, "Praised be Thou," etc. "Who openeth the eyes of the blind." When he throws off the bedclothes, he says, "Praised be Thou... "Who freest the bound." When he puts on his garments, he says, "Praised be Thou...Who clothest the naked," etc. These blessings are unmistakably provided to be home ritual, to be recited at each successive stage of the process of getting up in the morning by each individual.

These home blessings are now part of the regular prayerbook in the *birkoth ha-shahar*. How did they come into the public prayerbook when they properly belong at home? We have a clear statement as to how that happened in the great liturgical responsum of the Gaon Amram. Early in his responsum he says that Gaon Natronai answered a question from the city of Lucena, Spain. He mentions that these various blessings are incumbent upon each individual as he rises from bed, but that it is the custom of all of Israel in Spain that the Reader in the synagogue recites them in behalf of those who do not know how to recite them. The report is given more fully in *Ha-manhig* of Ibn Yarchi, p. 7, section a. "Thus wrote Rav Amram that it is the custom of all the land of Spain in order to allow those who are not skilled to fulfill their duty, the cantor begins all the blessings with loud voice and they answer 'Amen' to each blessing." Clearly, then, the widespread custom to have these home personal blessing part of the public ritual originated in Spain, or, at least, we have no earlier reference to it with regard to any other country.

It may seem strange to us that the average Jew in Spain was not skilled enough in Hebrew to recite these simple blessings. This may well have been so; but it also must have been a fact that whatever the reason was, the rabbis were aware that these blessings which each man was obligated to recite at home were almost universally neglected and therefore to train the people into the habit of reciting them, the rabbinical authorities in Spain moved the blessings over to the synagogue and made them part of public worship. Thence it spread to other lands, and the original custom so clearly defined in the Talmud of reciting the blessings one by one at each stage of the process of getting up was never restored.

Kiddush in the Synagogue

The law (b. Pesahim 101a) is that *kiddush* should be made only in the place where the meal is eaten. However, the custom

is now widespread that the *kiddush* is also recited by the
cantor in synagogue. This is clearly a violation of the law
of the Talmud. Rab Amram (see *Seder* of Amram, *ad. loc.*)
says that *kiddush* is made in the synagogue for the sake of
wayfarers who eat there. But Natronai says that we do so
even though there are no wayfarers who eat there. He then
explains how it can be that the wine is tasted by the congregation (which they should not do since *kiddush* should be
at each man's home). He explains that the congregation is
given some of the wine to place on their eyelids for the sake
of healing. This is based upon the Talmud in Berakoth 43b
where it is said that he who takes a haughty step loses a
fraction of his eyesight; but one can restore it by means of
the Friday night *kiddush*. The same responsum is given in
Ozar ha-Geonim, Berakoth, p. 97, in the name of Natronai,
and the Gaon Hai adds that they certainly *drank* the wine
in the synagogue. Clearly this custom began or spread in
Spain. Asher ben Yehiel (to Pesahim 101a at end), explaining
how it happens that *kiddush* was instituted in the synagogue,
uses virtually the same phrase which was used in explaining
the Spanish custom of transferring the home morning blessings to the synagogue. He says, "Since there are people who
do not know how to make *kiddush*, they establish the custom
to make *kiddush* in the synagogue in order that they fulfill
the duty of *kiddush* prescribed by the Torah." His son, Jacob
ben Asher, in the *Tur, Orah hayyim* 269, says at the beginning
of the section, "I wonder that this custom has spread," and
ends the section by saying, "If I had the influence I would
abolish it." Since the custom is justified by Natronai and is
mentioned in the *Seder* of Amram, and since Jacob ben Asher
wonders at it and would like to abolish it, it seems clear that
the transference of the home ceremony of the *kiddush* on
Friday night as a synagogue observance everywhere in
Europe, had spread from Spain.

Unison Prayers

Asher ben Yehiel, having come from the Rhineland to Spain, frequently comments on Spanish customs, especially those of which he does not approve. In his responsa, section 4, §19, he objects to the custom of people joining with the cantor and singing the services in unison. Since it is the cantor's duty to fulfill the obligation of prayer for those members of the congregation who are not skilled in reading, it becomes the duty of the congregation, then, to listen intently to the cantor and say "Amen" after the blessings. If, however, they join in the singing with the cantor, there will not be a *minyan* of intent listeners. He ends up by saying that "those who sing along with the cantor seem to me to be acting in a light-minded way."

At all events, Asher ben Yehiel here refers to a custom which became established early in Spain, that the congregation joined in with the cantor in singing the services. This custom was referred to with admiration by Ashkenazic authorities in more recent times. Both Jacob Ettlinger and Jacob Emden, who were in Hamburg in the eighteenth to nineteenth centuries where they had opportunities to observe this Sephardi custom, refer to it approvingly. Jacob Emden in his *Siddur*, discussing the complicated customs of the Ashkenazim with regard to the selection of who shall be given the privilege of saying *Kaddish*, praises the custom of the Sephardim in that they all say it in unison and thus all disputes are removed. Jacob Ettlinger, in his responsa *Binyan Zion* (§122) refers to the custom of the Sephardim to recite in unison the entire service. He says, "For all the service of the Sephardim is in unison with equal voice without lagging behind or hurrying ahead. Therefore since they are accustomed to this unison recitation, they manage to be heard individually even though they are in harmony. Since we are not skilled, as they are in unison reading, it becomes ludicrous when we try it." He mentions this as a reason why we Ashkenazim should *not* institute the Sephardi custom. At all events, this congregational singing and recitation of both the *Kaddish* and the prayers is in consonance with the general Sephardi tradition of emphasizing the communal worship.

Cantor on the Bimah

The Sephardi custom is for the cantor to stand on the *tebah* (*bimah*) in the center of the synagogue to conduct the service. It is the Ashkenazic custom that only the Torah is recited from the central *bimah*, and the rest of the service recited by the cantor at the foot of the platform on which the Ark stands, thus fulfilling the implication of the verse, "Out of the depths I call unto the Lord." Abraham ibn Yarchi, in *Ha-manhig*, p. 19, refers to this difference of custom and explains it as follows: "It is a good custom in Spain that the cantor stands on the *tebah* (the *bimah*) in order that the entire congregation may hear the prayers, and thus he can fulfill the duty of prayer for those who are not skilled. If he did not do so, the majority of the congregation gathered there would not hear the prayers." Then Ibn Yarchi justifies this Spanish custom from the description in the Talmud (b. Sukkah 51b) of the synagogue in Alexandria where the leader stood on a platform in the center. At all events, it is clear that this custom too was derived from the fact that the public synagogue service itself was used as the prime method of training the people in worship.

Mourner Attending Synagogue

The Spanish emphasis upon the synagogue reflects itself even in the case of the mourner and his worship during *shibah*. Here, as in many of the other customs, there is some basis in Gaonic customs for a rather unusual observance in Spain. It is generally held that a mourner during *shibah* stays home during the whole week except on the Sabbath when he goes to the synagogue. Ibn Gayyat (*Shaarey Simhah*, vol.

ii, 51) quotes the Gaon Paltai to the effect that the mourner goes to the synagogue every day of the *shibah* if he does not or cannot have a *minyan* at home. Hai Gaon adds: "In Babylon everybody goes to the synagogue (everyday) except that in large cities most of them stay in their homes." Nachmanides reads this responsum more specifically to the effect that in Babylon *in the villages* they go to the synagogue every day; that is to say, in the villages where they cannot have *minyan* at home, mourners go daily to the synagogue during *shibah*.

This Babylonian village custom was carried over as a more general practice in Spain, and Ibn Gayyat says: "It is our custom from our ancient teachers to go to the synagogue (during *shibah*) and pray." So also Nachmanides in *Torath ha-Adam* (ed. Warsaw, 1840, p. 45a) quotes Ibn Gayyat as deciding that a mourner should go to the synagogue every day of *shibah*. These responsa and more are collected in *Ozar ha-Geonim*, Mashkin, p. 36. §94 ff., where there is also a quotation from *Shaareh Zedek* to the effect that in Babylon the mourners went to the synagogue every day but that are Palestine they did not do so. The law and its variations are discussed fully in *Tur, Yoreh Deah*, 393. Isaac bar Sheshes, in his responsa §158, says, that the custom varies in Spain; in Catalonia the mourners go to the synagogue only on the Sabbath, but in Saragossa they go every day to the synagogue; and, he adds, "Their custom should not be abolished."

Hanukkah Lights in the Synagogue

Abrahm ibn Yarchi, who was born and raised in the Provence, but who settled in Toledo in 1204, frequently notices the difference between his native customs and those which he met in Spain. In the *Ha-manhig*, p. 105, §148, he speaks of the duty of lighting the Hanukkah light in each house, so that the *mezuzah* should be at a man's right hand as he enters and the Hanukkah light (which they used to light at the door) should be at his left. Then he continues, "It seems to me that there is no duty to light the Hanukkah lights *except* at home where the man lives, and that the synagogue, being free from a *mezuzah*, is also free from the Hanukkah light unless, of course, the cantor lives there. "Nevertheless," he says, "the custom arose to have it in the synagogue since the original miracle occurred in the Temple, and also since the entire congregation gathers there." Abudraham, describing the customs of Spain (the new edition [Jerusalem 1959], p. 199) says that it is the duty of each individual to light Hanukkah lights at the door of his house, with the *mezuzah* on his right as he enters, and the Hanukkah light on his left. Then he adds (p. 201) that the custom has been established to have a Hanukkah light in the middle of the synagogue and to light between *minha* and *maarib*, etc. Thus, although all admit that the lights should be kindled at home, it is clear that the custom of lighting the Hanukkah lights in the synagogue arose in Spain.

Kapparoth

Apparently the slaughtering of a fowl as an atonement for each member of the household was more a German custom than a Spanish one. This can be seen from the responsum of Solomon ben Aderet (volume i §395). He says that when he found the custom had spread in his city (Barcelona), he abolished it. "Nevertheless," he adds, "I heard from worthy men from Germany who are with us in the school that all the rabbis of their country follow the practice before the Day of Atonement." Gaon Rab Sheshna is asked about the custom (see *Ozar ha-Geonim*, Yoma, p. 62) and he says he does not know the reason for the custom and then speculates as to possible reasons for it. Then, giving the procedure, says that the *shaliah* seizes the hen and places his hand upon its head, etc., saying, "This one in place of this one." Jacob ben Asher, who saw the procedure in Spain, makes the phrase *shaliah* clearer and says the *shaliah zibbur* places his hand upon the fowl and says, etc.

The Franco-German custom was that each householder performed this ceremony at home (*see*, for example, *Mahzor Vitry*, p. 373, at the beginning of the section on Yom Kippur). But the custom, when carried over into Spain, was moved over to the synagogue. Thus Abudraham, after saying that on the eve of the Day of Atonement "in some places it is the custom to slaughter the fowl for atonement," then quotes the same responsa of the Geonim and says also, "Thus it is the custom here; the cantor seizes the fowl and places his hand upon him and makes atonement and says, 'This one instead of this one, etc.'"

Congregational Sukkah

The Geonim Natronai and Hai (*Ozar ha-Geonim*, Sukkah, 33 ff.) say clearly that to fulfill the duty of *sukkah*, each must have a *sukkah* in his house; but that nevertheless it would be permissible to have a *sukkah* on the synagogue premises for the benefit of travellers (just as *kiddush* should be recited at home where the meal is eaten, yet is recited in the synagogue for the benefit of travellers). Therefore, if a *native* of the city makes use of a synagogue *sukkah*, it would not be a fulfillment of his duty. Then Hai Gaon says that there was a congregational *sukkah* in Bagdad.

Ibn Yarchi repeats most of these responsa in *Ha-manhig*, p. 64, and then adds, "Thus we learn from the responsum of Hai that the Spanish custom of a *sukkah* in the courtyard of the synagogue into which the members of the community come and sit, is not a proper fulfillment of the duty of the *sukkah*." In the recently published *Sefer ha-Miktam* by David bar Levi of Narbonne (ed. by Moses Blau [New York City 1959], on page 148) this Provençal scholar refers to the communal *sukkah* in Spain and mocks it as based upon an erroneous understanding of the law and, of course, as illegal. He refers to the statement in the Talmud, b. Sukkah 27b, according to which a man may fulfill his duty by borrowing another man's *sukkah*. Then the Talmud (based upon Leviticus

23: 42) says: "All Israel is able to sit in one *sukkah*." David
bar Levi says, "This statement of the Talmud is misunderstood. In some places in Aragon they make a *sukkah* in the
court of the synagogue and the entire congregation makes
kiddush there and then they leave and go home and eat. This
is surely," he continues, "an error of theirs." Thus again
with regard to the *sukkah*, the tendency in Spain was to
emphasize public communal observance, even though the
law is clear that this should be a household ritual.

Congregational Seder

The twelfth-century Rhineland scholar, Eliezer ben Joel
Ha-Levi (*Rabiah*, volume i, p. 179) reports that the custom
in Spain and in Babylon was to have the *seder* in the synagogue.
He says: "And in responsa I saw that even these days it is
the custom in Spain and in Babylon that the cantor on Passover conducts the *seder* in the synagogue for the benefit of
the ignorant who are unskilled in reciting the *hagadah*." Yet
it is the consensus of opinion of the authorities that there
should not even be *kiddush* in the synagogue on Passover
evening because thus it would make five cups on Passover
eve and there should be only four. There is no other reference
to this statement of the *Rabiah* except a modern one in which
Shemtob Gagin in *Keter Shemtob*, vol. iii, p. 106, praises this
ancient custom and wishes that it still continued. There is
no reason to doubt this reference of the Rhineland authority
even though there is no parallel to it. It fits into the general
mood of Spanish custom.

From these various indications it becomes fairly clear how
the leaders of Spanish Jewry coped with the problem of
building in the life of the people the habit of the fulfillment
of the *mizwoth*. They used the public worship as a pedagogic
instrument. Everywhere in Jewry it was chiefly the Torah
reading in the synagogue which was the instrument of public
instruction. Therefore it had to be read from the central

bimah that all might hear, and emphasis was put upon close attention. But in Spain, not only the Torah reading but the entire service was read from the central *bimah* because the entire worship was used for the same pedagogic purpose. Hence also many rituals which should be fulfilled by the individual and in the home were carried over into the synagogue where they could be taught to the people until the custom of individual worship might become established. So it was with the simple blessings to be recited at home on arising, so it was with the *kiddush,* so it was with the joint recitation of the service, and so with the *sukkah,* with the *seder,* and so it was even in the case of mourners worshipping in the synagogue during *shibah.*

This method of using the public worship pedagogically was evidently not the one followed in the Rhineland. There the habit of the fulfillment of the commandments was inculcated not publicly but one might say privately and individually. Honored rabbis adopted strict observances in their own lives and their various observances were recorded by their disciples. Thus people were guided by their admiration of saints and scholars. There are no such books published by Spanish Jewry recording the individual scrupulous observances of famous rabbis as were written in the Rhineland. Generally when references are made to certain debatable customs, if the reference is to a Spanish scholar, it will be "So Rabbi So-and-So said," but if the reference is to an Ashkenazic scholar, it is more likely to be "So Rabbi So-and-So *did.*" In the Rhineland it was the piety in the personal life of the individual saint, in Spain it was the unison worship of the community which trained the people to the observance of the commandments.